Tim Clayton was educated at Cam... specialised in the graphic satire of James Gillray. He is the award-winning and bestselling author of a number of books on naval and military history, including the winner of the 2008 Mountbatten Literary Award, *Tars*, and the critically acclaimed *Trafalgar*. Tim is also an Associate Fellow of the University of Warwick and a Fellow of the Society of Antiquaries. He is currently working at the British Museum as co-curator of the exhibition *Bonaparte and the British*, which will be shown in 2015 to mark the 200th anniversary of the Battle of Waterloo.

'Magnificent and magisterial' *Literary Review*

'The best of the many books commemorating next year's 200th anniversary of Napoleon's final defeat at the Battle of Waterloo' *Evening Standard*

'Authoritative, concise, lucid and thrilling, as well as sobering' *Daily Mail*

'Clayton makes the fog of war central to the narrative; we are pitched into the chaos and din of Waterloo ... We experience it as Wellington or Napoleon or an ordinary soldier would have done' *Daily Telegraph*

'Stirring ... a fabulous story, superbly told' Max Hastings, *Sunday Times*

'Tim Clayton not only gives a masterful account of the battle that changed the face of Europe but also sets it in its proper context ... Clayton manages the difficult trick in military history of providing a blow-by-blow account without losing the flow of the narrative' *Express*

'An incisive analysis of how the battle unravelled and why' *The Times*

'Nuanced, broad, searching and elegant ... the overall integrity of his scholarship is undeniable. This book may well become the most authoritative account of the four-day campaign' *Spectator*

Waterloo

Four Days that Changed
Europe's Destiny

TIM CLAYTON

ABACUS

First published in Great Britain in 2014 by Little, Brown
This paperback edition published in 2015 by Abacus

3 5 7 9 10 8 6 4 2

Maps drawn by John Gilkes

A CIP catalogue record for this book
is available from the British Library.

ISBN 978-0-349-12301-1

Typeset in Caslon by M Rules
Printed and bound in Great Britain by
Clays Ltd, St Ives plc

Papers used by Abacus are from well-managed forests
and other responsible sources.

MIX
Paper from
responsible sources
FSC
www.fsc.org   FSC® C104740

Abacus
An imprint of
Little, Brown Book Group
100 Victoria Embankment
London EC4Y 0DY

An Hachette UK Company
www.hachette.co.uk

www.littlebrown.co.uk

To James and John
in memory of happy
evenings at Worcester

CONTENTS

PART III: The Battle of Waterloo

LIST OF MAPS

PROLOGUE

This Short Campaign of 'Hours'

'Nothing in ancient or modern history equals the effect of the victory of Waterloo,' proclaimed *The Times* a week after the news broke, and it was not long before it became clear that the intense four days of fighting that culminated in the battle of Waterloo had put an end to twenty-two years of warfare.[1] Few battles are so decisive. 'The fate of Europe was at stake,' wrote the Prussian General Gneisenau.[2] Soon people began to be variously confident or fearful that the career of the phenomenal Napoleon Bonaparte was really over, and with it an age on which he had stamped his extraordinary personality; that revolutions were a thing of the past. Aristocracy ruled in Britain, the French king was restored to his palace and other hereditary monarchs could sleep soundly on their thrones once again. These had indeed been momentous days.

As the world realised that Waterloo had been an exceptionally hard-fought battle with exceptional consequences, in which the greatest army in the world had been utterly routed, the prestige of the little British army led by the Duke of Wellington rose to unprecedented heights. On behalf of a grateful nation that had already accumulated a debt of £850 million through its efforts to defeat the French Emperor, Parliament voted the Duke £200,000 for a mansion to add to the £500,000 that he had already been given to support a place in the hereditary aristocracy, and his status as destroyer of Napoleon gave him the last word on all matters military. All those lesser mortals who had survived the bloodbath near Brussels basked in the glory of having been a 'Waterloo Man'. Waterloo, the Poet Laureate Robert Southey soon declared, was the greatest victory in British history, and the battle continues to enjoy that status to this day.

It was true that the army that sustained most of the pressure during the decisive battle of the campaign was led by a British general, and that it had been his British troops who had borne the greatest responsibility within the allied army. However, it had taken the combined efforts of all the allied forces to defeat Napoleon over four days of frantic marching and hard fighting. At the end of it, the only battle fought between Wellington and Napoleon had been, as the Duke himself famously put it, 'a damned nice thing – the nearest run thing you ever saw in your life'.[3] Wellington's improvised army of British, German, Dutch and Belgian troops would have lost if the Prussians had not intervened when Napoleon thought their intervention impossible – but this was always part of their plan. For, as a British engineer admitted, 'This short campaign of "Hours" was a joint operation. The honours must be shared.'[4]

Victory rewarded the dogged determination of Wellington and the Prussians to act in unison, despite Napoleon's best efforts to drive them apart. At the heart of this successful Anglo-Prussian axis were three very different men: Wellington aged forty-six, an austere loner, efficient, socially ambitious; Blücher a hard-living, hard-drinking seventy-two-year-old cavalier, so loved by his troops that it was said they would follow him into the mouth of hell; and Gneisenau, Blücher's brain, who organised, planned and restrained his chief, reputedly republican and ill at ease among the Prussian and British aristocrats. They were facing an old enemy, 'the devil unchained', Napoleon Bonaparte, who had returned from the exile imposed upon him after his defeat in 1814: genius, upstart, moderniser, liberator, tyrant, enigma, the man widely considered to be the best general since Alexander the Great.

This amazing story demanded publication and the Duke of Wellington received the first enquiry from a would-be historian within weeks of the event. 'The object which you propose to yourself is very difficult of attainment, and, if really attained, is not a little invidious,' he replied in August 1815. 'The history of a battle is not unlike the history of a ball. Some individuals may recollect all the little events of which the great result is the battle won or lost; but no individual can recollect the order in which, or the exact moment at which, they occurred, which makes all the difference as to their value and importance.'[5] This simile, curiously evocative of the Duchess of Richmond's ball, danced on the night before the first battles, was remarkably apt. More than most campaigns, Waterloo was a jumble of things done in a desperate hurry, without time for food, sleep or much in the way of official recording, and even so soon after the events it was difficult to recall exactly what had happened when.

Wellington's second objection to a history was that it would inevitably expose those who did not perform well, since 'the faults or the misbehaviour of some gave occasion for the distinction of others, and perhaps were the cause of material losses; and you cannot write a true history of a battle without including the faults and misbehaviour of a part at least of those engaged.' Here, too, he had a point: at that time the honour of regiments and nations was sacred and individuals were forgiven most lapses in the wider interest. Individual participants are now long dead, but regiments and even nations have proved lastingly tender of their honour and insistent on having the story told their way, to the detriment of objective truth.

Despite Wellington's misgivings, at least seven histories were published in 1815 and another nine the following year. The Duke did not think much of them. To a correspondent he replied testily:

> The people of England may be entitled to a detailed and accurate account of the battle of Waterloo, and I have no objection to their having it; but I do object to their being misinformed and misled by these novels called 'Relations,' 'Impartial Accounts,' &c. &c., of that transaction, containing the stories which curious travellers have picked up from peasants, private soldiers, individual officers, &c. &c., and have published to the world as the truth.[6]

To another historian who wondered to what sources, if all 'accounts' were unreliable, he might safely resort, Wellington wrote,

'You now desire that I should point out to you where you could receive information on this event, on the truth of which you could rely. In answer to this desire I can refer you only to my despatches published in the "London Gazette".[7] Later, he amplified this view of the duty of the battle historian, who was

> to seek with diligence for the most authentic details of the subject on which he writes, to peruse with care and attention all that has been published; to prefer that which has been officially recorded and published by public responsible authorities; next, to attend to that which proceeds from Official Authority, although not con-temporaneously published, and to pay least attention to the statements of Private Individuals, whether communicated in writ-ing or verbally, particularly the latter, if at a period distant from the date of the operation itself; and, above all, such statements as relate to the conduct of the Individual himself communicating or making the statement.[8]

Once again this was sound advice and, had his own accounts only been a bit more complete, honest and reliable, historians might have followed it. Unfortunately, Wellington's own dispatch was written in a hurry when he was very tired: it was a fair enough account of the battle that Wellington had seen but there was much that he had not seen. The glory that he bestowed on the Foot Guards and the heavy cavalry put them at the centre of most subsequent British accounts to an extent that was not really justified. Moreover, he said little that was positive about his allied contingents, and although he paid warm tribute to the Prussians, his claim to have won the battle with his final charge before they made their breakthrough succeeded in belit-tling the significance of their contribution in the eyes of the average Briton.

Even at the time, many were dissatisfied with the completeness and impartiality of the Duke's account and wary of his interest in news management. One participant in the campaign waited until he could use the French civilian post system at Paris before sending home his version of events:

for as half the letters from the army do not go, but are probably overhauled by clerks, as the Duke of Wellington is not a little disposed to repress all strictures on his conduct etc, it would not be altogether safe to say all one might think or know. It is impossible to contradict the Gazette statement of the battle for it is strictly true, yet there are many things omitted which would considerably tend to alter the account, but for good reasons they are suppressed. You would not however imagine that on the 17th the charge of the Life Guards was preceded by the complete rout of the 7th & part of the 23rd or that on the 18th the rear of the army was thrown into confusion in consequence of a panic first spread by some German and Belgic cavalry who fled towards Brussels, which if it had been more extensively propagated would most probably have lost the battle. We were all in a state of sleep when Bonaparte first attacked our lines . . .[9]

Assistant surgeon John James's words serve to remind us that official sources can be just as forgetful or mendacious as private individuals, and that from a very early date people conspired to suppress certain episodes and shape the public record.[10]

Moreover, if Wellington was anxious to have the story of the Waterloo campaign told in a way that reflected well on him, he was not alone. The most dramatic intervention in the early historiography of the battle came in a book written by Napoleon's aide Gaspard Gourgaud, recently returned from Saint Helena, who claimed to express the opinions of no less an authority than Napoleon himself. Gourgaud's account shifted the blame for the calamitous outcome of the campaign away from Napoleon onto the treachery or incompetence of others, chiefly Marshals Ney and Grouchy. Ney could not defend himself – though in fact several others did – because he had been executed in December 1815, while Grouchy had fled to the United States.[11] Napoleon made a second contribution with his *Mémoires*, published in the 1820s, and most subsequent French historiography divided over the extent to which Napoleon was the hero or the villain of the piece and whether others should be blamed.

After the battle, through their arrogantly exclusive assumption of the mantle of victory, the British (and in particular the Duke of Wellington, who had a political interest in magnifying Britain's contribution to that victory) succeeded with remarkable speed in upsetting their allies, and much of the historiography on the allied side has revolved ever since around disputes over the respective contributions of the various allied forces. British officers were scathing about the Belgians, while the Prince of Orange, wilful and inexperienced though he may have been, could not possibly have committed all the military crimes of which, behind his back, he was accused by Anglo-German officers within days of the fighting. Grolmann, Gneisenau and the Duke of Wellington disliked each other and, though they suppressed their personal feelings quite effectively in 1815, they gave freer vent to their prejudices afterwards in arguments about who was most responsible for winning or for almost losing the campaign, arguments influenced by the political circumstances at the time they took place.

The battle became difficult to investigate and describe because it mattered so unusually much. First, people lied about what happened in order to excuse their deficiencies and to magnify their triumphs. This applies to everybody from the Emperor Napoleon to the least significant officer interviewed for Captain William Siborne's detailed history of the campaign, published in 1844. Second, people rarely knew much about what was happening outside their own immediate surroundings. This was especially true of the battle of Waterloo itself, where even onlookers like the British supply officers who 'retired a short distance to the rear watching the progress of the action' soon found that 'as it spread from right to left the whole position became enveloped in a dense smoke, and nothing could be perceived'.[12]

As days and then years went by, and tales recounted over port and cigars hardened into fact, or as people made their own memories fit what the historians said had happened, certain picturesque episodes – some based in fact, some entirely mythical – came to dominate the account, while more mundane detail slipped away. By 1842, when he was fifty-four and asked to provide his version of events for William Siborne, Wellington's secretary Fitzroy Somerset found that 'whenever he has to talk over that battle, he finds himself so much deceived in his recollections, that he cannot rely with any confidence upon himself, and cannot conceive the possibility of your being able to attain to accuracy, considering how conflicting are the statements one continually hears from persons, all whose testimonies one considers undeniable.'[13]

Given these difficulties, it is a challenge to discover what really happened during the Waterloo campaign. It does no harm to take the Duke of Wellington's advice and set most value on official records, while recognising how these, even, might be bending the truth in order to please the recipient. There were reports to Wellington from senior officers but no regimental records survive centrally (and in any case the pace of the campaign was too fast for accurate recording). French reports from senior officers are useful until 17 June but, naturally enough, little survives for 18 June, except what was sent to the official newspaper, the *Moniteur*, and subsequent speeches and reports, such as those by Ney and Drouot. Prussian and Hanoverian reports are better and fuller and have recently been made more readily available.

It is not surprising that from an early stage historians sought to supplement the official records with accounts by individuals and these were soon very plentiful. Only on the French side was there a degree of reticence; accounts from Wellington's army were plentiful. This kind of 'oral history' was not to the Duke's taste and the very idea of 'history from the bottom up' would have appalled him, although he identified the pitfalls of such accounts correctly enough: they are unreliable, sometimes ill-informed, sometimes sensational, sometimes deliberately mendacious, often exaggerated and frequently self-glorifying or self-justifying.

These problems with the stories told by participants were compounded by the market for them: the Napoleonic wars turned the war memoir into a saleable literary genre, and as a by-product fictional or semi-fictional biographies and serialised accounts began to appear. It is sometimes difficult to distinguish the factual from the fictional: the narrative of a genuine participant may be dressed up with invented detail, while a fictional narrative may be based on the composite experiences of real participants so well observed as to be as valuable as a genuine memoir.[14]

Given these difficulties, it is only by piecing together as many fragments of evidence as possible, while interrogating each of them in order to discover what impression they might have been seeking to convey, that anything resembling the true pattern of events can be reconstructed. The most extraordinary thing about this extraordinary campaign, given that it came to be studied in such detail, is that so much of what happened still remains unknown. How both sides failed to bring their full force to the battlefield on 16 June has provoked enduring controversy and each phase of the battle on 18 June remains contentious.

In recent years a number of diligent researchers have made readily available for the first time a vast number of new first-hand accounts as well as official reports and statistics from British and European archives. Important among these are the publication of most previously unpublished letters to Siborne and (to date) five volumes of letters, journals and memoirs relating to the Waterloo campaign, by Gareth Glover. This source is supplemented (and sometimes duplicated) by at least 250 accounts published online by 1815 Limited and in volumes devoted to the Netherlands and Hanoverian forces. I wanted to use the fresh insights afforded by this significant body of new material to reconsider the various controversies that bedevil the story of the Waterloo campaign. With many new revelations to take into account, and details that influence interpretation, I have re-examined the early primary and secondary sources, stripping back as far as possible the layers of later legend to try to rediscover the true sequence of events. This task was facilitated by the recent digitisation of many rare and otherwise inaccessible books as well as maps and prints. I have also benefited from the efforts of Pierre de Wit to unravel the details of each army's progress on his website, where he has published most of the surviving orders and reports in their original languages. Many other web-based studies also contributed significantly to research.

I have taken the opportunity to incorporate all the new material into a detailed and authoritative account of the campaign that seeks to bring out all the elements of luck, judgement, planning, accident and weather that combined to decide the outcome.

New accounts affect the interpretation of almost every familiar element in the campaign: the difficulties encountered by Napoleon on 15 and 16 June; Wellington's spies and intelligence; the delayed concentration of his army and his commitment to help the Prussians; the reasons for d'Erlon's failure to contribute to either battle on 16 June; and Wellington's retreat in the rain on 17 June. The impact of new insight is most appreciable wherever German troops were fighting with Wellington's army: a great deal is revealed about the fighting in and around Hougoumont, and especially about the collapse of the centre of Wellington's line at Waterloo. Waterloo itself was a narrow victory but if things had gone only a fraction better for Napoleon on the first and second day of the four, there would have been no battle to give us its name. The battle alone is at most half the story.

I have tried to get into the minds of the commanders as their plans changed on contact or unravelled in the smoke and confusion, or as the pouring rain ruined a rapid forced march. I wanted to explain the significance of each new revelation, each unfortunate blunder, as the generals thought their way through the fog of battle from moment to moment. In conveying a sense of the discomfort, fear, hunger, and hideous wounds suffered by those who took part, and in describing the anxieties and motivations of generals and common soldiers of all the nations involved in the campaign, I hope to give a vivid impression of what it was like to be there. Fresh material has allowed me to describe the previously overlooked participation of Hanoverians, Brunswickers and Nassauers much more fully. I have sought to offer glimpses of the lives and mentalities of participants from all nations and social backgrounds, to provide a flavour of this rich and vibrant period, its dramatic politics and its colourful fashions.

I have sought too to give the view of all sides and to offer a fair account of the part played by all national contingents – although, this book being an English-language publication, most attention is paid to the British. I hope I shall not offend national sensibility by robbing British troops of the superhuman qualities with which some authors have endowed them in the past, by allowing other nations a greater share of credit for the victory than they have sometimes been given and by attempting to account for the love felt by French and even foreign soldiers for Napoleon.

This book was designed to be not only a full and thorough account of the Waterloo campaign, but also to convey a sense of the realities of Napoleonic warfare to the general reader who comes fresh to the subject. My aim is to provide sufficient detail to satisfy those who are already familiar with Napoleonic warfare without straining the patience of those who are not. This is a difficult trick to pull off and I beg indulgence from all sides, but this is why I have avoided naming every officer, unit and place.

The sequence of events that followed Napoleon's sudden and unexpected invasion of Belgium is crucial to an understanding of why the famous battle of Waterloo turned out as it did. Indeed, Napoleon's best chance of beating the allied armies came not on 18 June but on 16 June. Consequently, this book describes in detail the three days of marching and fighting that preceded Waterloo, including the less celebrated but vitally important and bloody encounters at Ligny and Quatre Bras, and gives a much briefer account of the fourth battle, fought simultaneously with Waterloo, a few miles away at Wavre between the Prussian rearguard and a detachment of troops commanded by Marshal Grouchy. I have given only a brief summary of the action that followed Waterloo.

Before describing the four-day campaign, I have tried to lay out some of the historical, military and cultural background to it. For more than twenty years following the French Revolution, Europe had been in a state of near constant warfare. For the last fifteen years world events had been dominated by Napoleon Bonaparte, the Corsican artillery officer who had made himself Emperor of France, forged a reputation as the greatest general of modern times and proceeded to redraw the map of Europe to his own design. In 1814 the combined might of all the other European powers had finally defeated Napoleon. He had been forced to abdicate and accept exile as ruler of the tiny island of Elba off the coast of Italy. Everybody celebrated the general peace. King Louis XVIII had been restored to the French throne, but in France the restoration of the Bourbon

monarchy was not universally popular and many mourned the passing of the Republic or yearned for the return of the Emperor.
Nevertheless the last thing that people expected, least of all the rulers
of the victorious Great Powers, was that suddenly, early the following spring, Napoleon would have the temerity to invade France at
the head of the army of Elba, a force of a thousand men.

1971

PART I

Preparations

I

The Violet Season

The violet was Napoleon's flower. The Empress Josephine wore them at her wedding and Napoleon's second, Austrian wife, Marie Louise, cultivated them too. Before he left for exile as ruler of the island of Elba in April 1814, Napoleon promised his supporters that he would return in the violet season. They displayed their secret allegiance by wearing bouquets of artificial violets instead of the proscribed tri-colour cockade of the Empire. Friends were identified by the question '*Aimez-vous la violette?*'; a Bonapartist answered not '*Oui*' but '*Eh bien?*', to which the response was '*Elle reparaîtra au printemps.*' They drank to the return of Corporal Violet and prints were published in which the silhouettes of Napoleon, his wife and son could be discovered, concealed in a pot of violets.[1]

Nobody expected Napoleon to fulfil his promise the very next spring but on 26 February 1815 he left Elba. Two days later, the horrified British commissioner discovered that Bonaparte's little fleet had sailed away while he had been visiting his Italian mistress on the mainland. He alerted the nearest ports, Livorno and Genoa, expecting the former Emperor to head for Italy, but instead Napoleon landed on the French coast near Cannes, where his soldiers camped on the beach while the mayor, François Poulle, sought out bread, meat, post horses and wagons. Bonaparte's army consisted of 551 grenadiers of his Old Guard, 94 Polish lancers and 301 *voltigeurs Corses* (Corsican light infantry), in a total expeditionary force of 1026.[2]

Napoleon led his band by night into the mountains, along what is still known as the 'Route Napoléon'. Marching at their famous fast pace the Old Guard reached Grasse next morning and then raced for Sisteron, a hundred miles from Cannes, whose citadel, guarding the bridge over the Durance, presented the only serious obstacle to their progress. The governor put up no resistance when their advance guard seized the bridge in the middle of the night, and their march continued another thirty miles to Gap, where the townspeople, in their enthusiasm, raised a liberty tree and sang revolutionary songs.[3]

At 11 a.m. on 5 March the Bourbon court learned of the invasion. Courtiers laughed, confident that Bonaparte's robber band would be rounded up and hanged, but Louis XVIII foresaw a new revolution in the news. He sent for his minister of war, Jean de Dieu Soult, formerly one of Napoleon's marshals, who ordered the regiments quartered in the Alpine foothills to arrest the renegade's progress. It looked simple: Fitzroy Somerset, twenty-six-year-old military secretary to the Duke of Wellington and acting British ambassador to France, reported to his brother the Duke of Beaufort, 'Preparations are making to get rid of the monster and I hope to god they will kill him.'[4]

On 7 March a battalion of the 5th Regiment of the Line barred the road to Grenoble at the village of Laffrey. Followed by generals Antoine Drouot, Henri Bertrand and Pierre Cambronne, his companions in exile, Napoleon walked calmly towards them, then stopped, threw open his familiar grey greatcoat, and shouted, 'Soldiers of the Fifth – you recognise me. If there is one among you who wishes to kill his Emperor, I am here.' Nobody pulled a trigger; instead, with shouts of '*Vive l'Empereur!*' they threw away their white Bourbon cockades and ran forward to embrace the men of the Imperial Guard.

The same day a second regiment joined his cause, led to him this time by its colonel. Charles de la Bédoyère assembled the 7th Regiment to more cries of '*Vive l'Empereur!*' and, after a brief consultation with his officers, marched them south to double Napoleon's force. The Emperor made La Bédoyère an imperial aide-de-camp, his first task to write a proclamation from the 7th Regiment to the army in general, inviting them to join the cause.

Soldiers barely needed such prompting. Napoleon's little army of 3000, now 190 miles from Cannes, halted outside the barred gates of Grenoble, an artillery arsenal defended by 5000 men, only until La Bédoyère strode to the gatehouse and shouted to those within to join Napoleon. They too responded with a resounding chorus of '*Vive l'Empereur!*' When the governor delayed opening the gates, the townsfolk brought up wooden beams to smash them apart; they sang the *Marseillaise* as Napoleon left. The march north-west became a series of triumphal entries and when the king's brother, the comte d'Artois, arrived at Lyons on 9 March to defend the second city of France, he found it in turbulent insurrection against royal rule; he fled north while the garrison marched south to join the Emperor, whose army was now 12,000 strong.

Soult summoned the great hero Marshal Ney to Paris. The son of a cooper, the red-headed Michel Ney was a revolutionary who had become a key supporter of Napoleon, making a reputation as the *brave des braves* (bravest of the brave), the hero of rearguard actions against the Russians in 1812, before he had helped to force him to abdicate. Ney left Paris with Artois' son, the duc de Berry, declaring to the king that he would bring back Napoleon 'dead or alive in an iron cage'.

When Ney reached his troops at Lons-le-Saulnier his call for loyalty to the king was answered by murmurs of discontent. Learning that Lyons and other cities had declared for Bonaparte, Ney reached the conclusion that a new revolution was what the nation wanted and when, on 14 March, the time came to march against Napoleon, he surprised his closest aides by changing sides. Instead of delivering a rousing speech in support of the French king, Ney commenced his harangue, 'The cause of the Bourbons is lost for ever ... Liberty has triumphed finally, and Napoleon, our august Emperor, will consolidate it for ever ... *Vive l'Empereur!*' His regiments joined Napoleon at Auxerre four days later.[5]

'The English who had flock'd to Paris are flocking back again, & say that the Troops at Calais & Boulogne are not to be depended on

& are crying out *Vive l'Empereur*,' wrote Lady Lucas, the blue-stocking granddaughter of a former Lord Chancellor whose cousin and nephew were in government, on 16 March. Half-pay officers were recalled to Paris wondering what would happen, but events moved fast. One such officer, André Ravard, arrived too late to witness the climactic scenes which were described to him, as he wrote to his brother:

> I think I said to you when I left you that I had no idea whether I was on my way to serve the king or the emperor; you will know now that it is the latter. On the 19th of this month the king reviewed the troops that were in Paris to the number of about sixty thousand men. He asked that those who would volunteer to defend him should step forward. About 150 of them stepped forward. At that, the king, seeing himself abandoned by all his soldiers, decided on the night of the 19th to the 20th to leave with his whole household for England ...

In essence, the report was true: the elite regiments had marched off to Fontainebleau to welcome Bonaparte and the National Guard refused to fight for Louis XVIII, who left the Tuileries soon after midnight and fled to Belgium.[6]

By the middle of the next day, a British diplomat remarked, 'The King's pictures, which the day before had ornamented the shops, gave place to pictures of Bonaparte. The white ribbon disappeared, and the red, and in some cases the tricolour, usurped the place of it.' More than five hundred unemployed officers, recalled to Paris by the Bourbons to fight the usurper, now declared for Napoleon and, led by General Exelmans, marched on the Tuileries, taking control after negotiation with the National Guard. A tricolour flag rose over the palace. As the news spread, Bonapartists sporting bouquets of freshly picked violets gathered to celebrate at the Café Montansier in the Palais Royal.[7]

That afternoon Napoleon's sisters-in-law, Julie Clary and Hortense Beauharnais, began to redecorate. They found that in the throne room the blue carpet that used to buzz with Napoleonic bees was now a vast field of fleurs-de-lys, but one of their ladies noticed that a lily had a loose edge. 'She tore it, and soon the bee was revealed. All the ladies set to work, and in less than half an hour, amid shouts of joyous laughter from the whole company, the carpet became an imperial one again.' Meanwhile, gradually, the entrance hall filled with unemployed officers until at nine o'clock a huge shout of '*Vive l'Empereur!*' rang out and Napoleon entered the Tuileries to wild acclamation, 'literally carried in triumph by generals Lobau, Exelmans and others' up the grand staircase. Bonaparte was back.[8]

On the Belgian border *chasseurs-à-cheval*, light cavalrymen formerly of the Imperial Guard, haunted the cafés, waiting impatiently for the next newspaper. 'The first were sarcastic and insolent. They said: *The Corsican Ogre has landed.* The next, *Bonaparte the Usurper is marching on Grenoble.* The third lot: *General Bonaparte has entered Grenoble.* The fourth bunch: *Napoléon Bonaparte has entered Lyon.* The closer he got to the capital, the less colourful their epithets.' For two days no newspapers arrived at the cafés, then, late in the afternoon of 21 March, one came: the impatient chasseurs learned that *The Emperor had left Lyons and was marching on Paris*; finally, next day, *The Emperor Napoleon had made his entry into Paris on 20 March.* 'We hugged each other in the cafés, in the streets, in the squares, we sang, we danced, the whole place went crazy.'

Soldiers from ordinary regiments were equally pleased. Lieutenant Jacques Martin had spent a tedious six months with the 45th Regiment at the northern fortress of Condé, where the troops celebrated wildly. Martin, a volunteer from Geneva aged only twenty but already a veteran of bitter campaigning, was devoted to Napoleon. In 1813 he had swum the swollen Elster to escape capture after the French defeat at Leipzig, and he was keen for a rematch at slightly better odds. Corporal Louis Canler's battalion of the 28th had left Saint-Omer, near Calais, to 'fight the usurper', as their royalist colonel put it. Canler was the son of a soldier: brought up as an *enfant de troupe*, he had joined the 28th in 1811 at the age of fourteen as a drummer, for each company was allowed two children of this age and Canler had already learned to play the drum. Two years later he was a proper soldier; promoted to corporal, he helped to defend

Antwerp against the allies. Now his regiment was marching against their hero, but having reached Béthune they were sent back to Saint-Omer, and in the evening they learned that Napoleon was at Paris. 'All the windows were illuminated spontaneously, as if by enchantment, and a real party began, celebrated to cries of "Vive l'Empereur!"'[9]

Within a month, Napoleon's negligible band of a thousand renegades had conquered France, ejected the Bourbons and reinstated the social changes of the Revolution, to the delight of the common people, including the majority of ordinary soldiers. As a result, the most feared military genius in Europe was back in charge of Europe's most potent army, then some 210,000 strong.[10] Only Napoleon could have pulled off such a feat. This was a man capable of extraordinary achievements, endowed with extraordinary luck. A sardonic caricature, published in April, showed Ney with his head to Napoleon's arse, saying, 'I swear it smells of violets.'[11]

2

The Devil is Unchained

On 7 March 1815 there was to be a stag hunt at Eisenstadt, the palace of Prince Esterhazy near Vienna. The British Ambassador kept a pack of hounds there, and the Duke of Wellington intended to run them now the snow had thawed. The hunt gathered in Esterhazy's English-style landscape garden, where the waterworks were powered by an imported British steam engine, and where 'the turn-out was thoroughly English; the hounds English, and horses English; master, huntsmen, and whippers-in, all decked out in English costume.'

The wealthy British were conspicuous at the Congress of Vienna, where representatives of the allied powers – Austria, Britain, Prussia and Russia being the most important – had met to thrash out the shape of post-Napoleonic Europe, and the Duke of Wellington, Britain's undefeated general, was universally respected. His aide, young William Pitt-Lennox, was vastly fond of hunting and intent on the preparations, until he noted with disappointment that the Duke had not turned up, and gradually realised that everyone was looking very serious. He asked Napoleon's stepson Eugène Beauharnais what the matter was. Eugène, former viceroy of Italy, was attending the conference with his father-in-law, the king of Bavaria, having retired to Munich after Bonaparte's abdication. 'Have you not heard?' replied Eugène, 'Napoleon has escaped from his prison on the Isle of Elba.' Abandoning his cherished hunt,

Pitt-Lennox rode the forty miles back to Vienna, thinking that Wellington might wish to leave instantly.[1]

There were not just diplomats at Vienna; this was a vast social gathering of European aristocracy. Entranced by a constant whirl of waltzes, concerts and plays, spectacular shows at the Imperial Riding School, sledge trips to the palaces outside Vienna, and once the snow had finally melted, hunting with the ambassador's hounds, the courtiers played while diplomats and soldiers wrangled.

Within weeks the wrangling became acrimonious. During his years of prosperity the tyrant that everybody feared had redrawn the map of Europe, throwing out feudal lords at will and creating kingdoms for members of his own family. Having forced Napoleon to abdicate and exiled him to the island of Elba, the other princes of Europe were now gathered to carve up his huge empire, to return the world to how it had been before the revolution, to reward some and punish others. By Christmas the conflicting territorial ambitions of the allied Great Powers had brought them to the brink of war.

Napoleon's biggest change had been the dissolution of the Holy Roman Empire, the archaic structure based in Germany and comprising innumerable small feudal princedoms, free cities and prince-bishoprics. In 1806 Napoleon had forced Francis II of Austria to resign as Holy Roman Emperor and had created a confederation of new states along the Rhine as a buffer between France, Austria and Prussia, Austria's rival power in Germany, but in 1815 the dispossessed princes wanted their lands back. A sense of common nationhood was awakening among the German-speaking peoples, but it clashed with the interests of the princes and, meanwhile, the Great Powers were intent on expansion.

The thorniest issue at the Congress was a Russo-Prussian proposal that Poland should become a Russian possession while Saxony should go to Prussia. The Duchy of Warsaw and Saxony had been Napoleon's most loyal ally and, along with many Rhinelanders, had still been fighting for him at Leipzig, the great battle of the Nations, in 1813. At this enormous four-day battle involving half a million men, Napoleon had finally lost his grip on Germany. Lord Castlereagh supported Austrian and French objections to the proposal, surprising

Prussians who thought he had been on their side. Things came to a head when the Tsar announced to Castlereagh, 'I shall be King of Poland, and the King of Prussia shall be King of Saxony,' and pointed out that the Russians had an army of 480,000 men occupying Poland and Saxony. The Prussians could not believe that Britain could be so deferential to the French and on 1 January Prussia threatened war and began to mobilise its army. Two days later Britain, Austria and France signed the Secret Treaty of Vienna, a covert alliance against Prussia and Russia. The pair eventually backed down, and the allies patched up an agreement whereby Saxony was split, its king ceding roughly half his territory to Prussia. Nevertheless, the Prussian generals at Vienna received an impression of British perfidy in which the Duke of Wellington, who was ambassador to France and had replaced Castlereagh at Vienna when the foreign secretary returned to England, was deeply implicated.[2]

It took the shocking news of Napoleon's escape to reunite the alliance. On 13 March, after learning that he had landed in France, the Congress of Vienna declared him an outlaw. On 17 March Prussia, Russia, Austria and Britain each pledged to raise armies of 150,000 men to oppose Napoleon.

The Great Powers appreciated that their decisions as to which king should rule which region would not always be received with enthusiasm in the regions concerned and they worried now that in these places many might remember Bonaparte more fondly. Such nostalgia was feared most immediately in Belgium. Before the French Revolution, the southern Netherlands, modern Belgium, had belonged to Austria, while the northern Netherlands, modern Holland, had been the Dutch Republic. The southern Netherlands had been annexed to France in 1795, while the Dutch were first the Republic of Batavia, then the Kingdom of Holland ruled by Louis Bonaparte, and finally from 1810 to 1813 part of France. For commercial and strategic reasons Britain was interested in the fate of the Netherlands, especially the important Belgian port of Antwerp, through which a large proportion of British exports to Europe flowed. At the Congress Austria accepted a British plan to install the Orange family, traditional Stadtholders of Holland, as rulers of a new state powerful enough to resist France. The Prince Regent had planned a marriage between his daughter and the young Prince of Orange, but she didn't like him and broke off the engagement, while the allies were still bickering about just what lands the Netherlands should include.

During Bonaparte's march on Paris the Congress agreed to unite Holland, Belgium and Luxembourg and on 16 March Willem I was proclaimed first king of the Netherlands. Willem of Orange had been acting ruler of Belgium since the end of the previous July but Protestant Dutch hegemony was resented. After he decreed that Dutch should replace French as the official language of Belgium, the Dutch national anthem, *Oranje Boven*, was whistled in the theatres. Tom Morris, an articulate Cockney sergeant, realised that Willem needed conspicuous British backing in the form of a British and Hanoverian army of occupation. Morris's 73rd Regiment had been sent to Holland in 1813 to support the Dutch rebellion against Bonaparte but was now in Belgium, he supposed, 'to ensure the tranquillity of the people, until the annexation of Belgium to Holland should be carried into effect'. The proclamation announcing the unification of Belgium and Holland was 'very unpopular; so much so, that where we were, they could not prevail on any of the inhabitants to assist in the reading of it; and that duty had to be performed under a guard of British bayonets'.[3]

The Belgians had flourished under Bonaparte and the Francophone portion had welcomed incorporation into France. A very large number of Belgians had served in the French army and some remained in it, although during 1814 Louis XVIII had ejected most soldiers who were no longer French nationals. A priority case had been 9000 Belgian members of the bloated Imperial Guard, who crossed the border back into Belgium still in uniform. Willem I was prepared to make use of these experienced soldiers for his new army, but his allies were distinctly uneasy when he entrusted the military administration of the southern Netherlands to a general from Napoleon's Imperial Guard. There were acute fears that a lightning strike by Napoleon against the Netherlands would be followed by the immediate defection of Belgium, with its 9000 former Imperial Guards of dubious loyalty.

The new king's twenty-two-year-old son, the Prince of Orange, took command of 14,000 British, 9000 Hanoverian and 10,000 Dutch and Belgian troops. In 1795, when he was two, William and his family had fled from the French and anti-Orange 'Patriots' to England. He was given a military education in Prussia, was sent to the University of Oxford, and then joined Wellington as an aide-de-camp in the Peninsula from 1811 to 1813, rising, without ever commanding troops, to the rank of lieutenant-general. He was coura-geous, vain and excitable: on hearing that Napoleon had reached Lyons he proposed invading France to save Louis XVIII who was at Lille, but was dissuaded by his military secretary Sir John Colborne, one of Wellington's best soldiers, who had been appointed to keep a mature eye on the prince.[4] As one British officer noted:

> it appears that the Prince has made himself unpopular in our army, and that the present situation has a little turned his head, nor have flatterers been wanting to make him believe that he is as great a general as some of the ancient princes of his house; which, judg-ing from the present state of the army under his command, and from the mode in which everything is carried on by him, does not appear to be the case.[5]

Orange was out of his depth, and although Colborne considered him essentially sound, other British officers came to regard him as a liability, and were later to blame him for many things that went wrong on the battlefield.

On 22 March a rumour in Brussels that Napoleon was in northern France with 50,000 men caused the British Guards to head for the frontier and the banks to close. Most of the British civilian popula-tion – an estimated 1500 people – fled to Antwerp; Louis XVIII reached Ostend en route for London, but was persuaded to remain in Belgium. Meanwhile, the Congress of Vienna decided to entrust command of the army in the Netherlands to the Duke of Wellington and on 29 March he left for Brussels.[6] The Prussian army in the Rhineland, reduced over the winter to a strength of only about 30,000, recalled troops that had just been demobilised. Everyone in

Belgium was jumpy. Edmund Wheatley, an English officer serving at Tournai, noted in his journal on 2 April, 'While dressing to go out to a party, the girl came in pale and aghast telling me the cannon was planted "sur la grande place" with lighted matches, and that Boney was at Lille.' The northern French town was just a few miles across the border.[7]

3

Glory, Liberty and Peace

The man the rulers of Europe all feared was a prodigy and an enigma. 'He has indeed no Model but in Antiquity,' wrote the republican Earl of Wycombe in 1797, during the first wave of enthusiasm for the saviour of the Revolution. Two years later a Swiss journalist who had just been exiled for criticising Bonaparte was nevertheless confused what to make of him: 'Never were human valour and contemptibleness, capacity and false-greatness, understanding and shifts of ignorance, insolent immodesty and brilliant qualities, so mixed as in this man.' Fifteen years were to reveal much more of his character, but portrayed so differently by friends and enemies as to baffle interpretation. Even after his fall Bonaparte was still loved and hated, admired and despised in almost equal measure. 'If it be doubtful whether any history (exclusive of such as is avowedly fabulous) ever attributed to its hero such a series of wonderful achievements compressed into so small a space of time, it is certain that to no one were ever assigned so many different characters,' wrote a wry commentator in 1819; but even British enemies admitted that 'he was and will remain the greatest man of his time.'[1]

To British comic artists Napoleon was 'Boney', a conceited, furious, upstart tyrant, a diminutive hero with enormous hat and sword. In reality Napoleon stood five foot six or seven inches tall – average height for the period – but the British public became convinced that he was tiny (in part also because his height had been reported in

France, where the inch was longer, as five foot two). 'Boney' remained a lean figure with a thin, sallow face and aquiline nose, as Bonaparte had been in 1797 when the first portraits of him reached Britain, even though by 1815 the real Emperor was stout and paunchy.

On the continent caricaturists drew him with the darker knowledge of experience. They parodied the characteristic bicorne hat and blue or green uniforms of his own propaganda, and produced a figure to be feared, bombastic but sinister. For many more people in Europe than in Britain Bonaparte represented hope betrayed. Enthusiasm for the young, handsome, brilliant republican hero who had preserved the social changes of the French Revolution turned gradually to fear and hatred. A generation had grown up with constant warfare and Napoleon came to represent universal slaughter and devastation: in his wars about a million Frenchmen had died, together with rather more of their enemies. The most striking of many caricatures issued in Germany at the end of 1813 showed the Emperor with his face composed of corpses. Sometimes he was the Antichrist: by a standard numerological system the letters of his name added up to 666, the Number of the Beast (but only if one spelled his name 'Napolean'). Often he was the Devil.

Inevitably, propaganda oversimplified Napoleon. He was an immensely complex figure, one of the greatest men of any age. Handsome in his youth, Napoleon was charismatic, charming and highly intelligent. People became wary of his eyes, and also of his voice with which he could cast a spell to bend men to his will: the mayor of Brussels believed he had bewitched the young men of the city.[2] Even in Britain he had sympathisers and William Gibney, assistant surgeon to the 15th Hussars, was one. Gibney, an Irishman, qualified as a doctor at Edinburgh and Trinity College Dublin, took the view that the French should be allowed the ruler of their choice:

Why the French, if they preferred Napoleon to a Bourbon, should not be allowed to retain their choice I never could see. Napoleon was cold-blooded, selfish, and ambitious, but he had the glorification and love of France in his heart, and showed by his government and laws that he knew how to rule and not improbably was often driven into war by combinations made against him. Napoleon was a heaven-born general, and knew it; he was, too, a far-seeing and resolute ruler, very much the sort required to govern the French people; and had he been left alone might have acted otherwise than he did. Anyhow, he could have and would have licked all Europe, had we Britons not come to their aid; and with our money and obstinate resolve finally disposed of this clever but somewhat unscrupulous leader.[3]

Nobody denied that Bonaparte was a brilliant general, perhaps the greatest of all time. Through much of Europe he had swept away the *ancien régime* and in Italy, Germany and elsewhere enlightened liberals had flocked to his banner, for he was a man of the meritocratic future, not the feudal past.

Born to an influential family in Corsica, Napoleon had the modern, scientific education of a French artilleryman. During the French Revolution he had joined the Jacobin party, first attracting notice when he commanded the artillery that recaptured the port of Toulon from royalists and the British navy in 1793. After gaining the favourable attention of the Convention in 1795 by dispersing royalist rebels with a 'whiff of grapeshot', Napoleon first commanded an army in Italy in 1796 at the age of twenty-seven. France was in chaos and defeat seemed imminent but Bonaparte reversed the fortunes of war, winning many admirers for freeing Italy. Further campaigns there and in Egypt and Syria brought victories at Arcola, Rivoli and the Pyramids that established a reputation as an invincible commander. In October 1799, after the *coup d'état de Brumaire*, he became one of three consuls ruling France and before long he was First Consul. A victory at Marengo in 1800 made him the hero who brought peace to Europe, after which Napoleon threw himself into a series of legal, educational, social and infrastructural reforms that proved of lasting value to the nation.

Peace did not last long, for the British government didn't trust Bonaparte and Bonaparte didn't trust them. At this stage Napoleon had many admirers in Britain, but the royal family was fundamentally opposed to his republican government. Moreover, Bonaparte represented not just revolution but France: Britain had long been competing with France in what French historians describe as a second Hundred Years War for command of global trade. Napoleon was a thoroughly dangerous leader of the arch-enemy – Louis XIV in a different guise.

From May 1803 he was at war with Britain, with his army, trained to perfection, lining the Channel coast. In 1804 he crowned himself Emperor of France and in 1805 King of Italy. The army created for invasion of Britain was Napoleon's finest, a war machine worthy of the imperial Roman legions. Carrying eagle standards like the Romans they emulated, and renamed the *Grande Armée*, his soldiers marched to destroy the forces of the Third Coalition to be formed against France, this time between Britain, Austria, Russia, Sweden and Naples. In 1805 Napoleon mesmerised the Austrians at Ulm and then crushed them and their Russian allies at Austerlitz. When a Fourth Coalition was formed by Prussia, Russia, Saxony, Sweden and Great Britain, he humiliated the Prussians at Jena and Auerstädt in 1806, invaded Prussia and won the war at Friedland in 1807, converting an admiring Tsar into an ally of France. Directly or indirectly Napoleon now ruled most of continental Europe.

British Whigs again made overtures for peace, but King George III remained as implacably hostile to the new upstart Emperor as he had been to the old Republic. Napoleon sought to break Britain commercially by imposing a continental embargo on trade, but this proved widely unpopular and impossible to enforce. It caused Napoleon to become embroiled in a long war in the Iberian Peninsula that tied down French troops and resources and enabled Britain to develop an efficient, veteran army led by the Duke of Wellington. The embargo irritated Russia and in 1812 Napoleon attacked the Tsar Alexander at a time when Wellington was ready to take the offensive in the Peninsula. The Russian campaign cost Napoleon and his allies half a million men, while his brother's rule in Spain collapsed after Wellington's victory at Vitoria. First Prussia, then Austria and the German states deserted the French alliance and after the great defeat at Leipzig in October 1813 Napoleon lost all territory east of the Rhine. He could still win battles but he was losing the war. In 1814 the allies invaded France. When they reached Paris, Napoleon's marshals deserted him and he finally abdicated. The victorious monarchist powers reinstalled the Bourbon family on the throne of France, in the immensely obese shape of Louis XVIII.

Louis' royalist supporters handled affairs spectacularly badly. The returned *émigrés* seized every opportunity to remind the French of why they had had a revolution in the first place. Their handling of the army – in particular their failure to pay people – alienated the senior officers who had made their return possible and reinforced the nostalgia for Napoleon that was widespread among junior officers and lower ranks. Soldiers began to count, '15, 16, 17, *gros cochon* [fat pig], 19, 20 . . .' Two hundred thousand newly repatriated prisoners of war were convinced that Napoleon could not have been beaten had they been present, and detested the restored Bourbons and the betrayal of the republican principle for which they had suffered cruel incarceration. Meanwhile, the allies were practically at war with each other.[4]

So Napoleon returned. He considered and quickly rejected an instantaneous strike on Belgium. Several veteran officers stressed the low risk and high reward of such a move, but Bonaparte was well aware that he lacked political support for the aggressive schemes of his soldiers. Tempting though it would be to chase out Louis XVIII and the king of the Netherlands and bring Belgium back to the fold, the French people would not forgive him for plunging them straight into a war of conquest. If there was to be a war, it was imperative he didn't start it. However, Napoleon hoped that if he accepted the borders of France as they stood, his resumption of his throne might be accepted by the other rulers of Europe. He had at least to put this notion to the test, so he wrote to all the princes assuring them of his peaceful intentions. Should the allies obstinately reject these peaceful overtures, then he would prepare the country for defence, or at least that is what he said. Those who were ill-disposed towards Napoleon argued that he was merely anxious to convince people that he desired peace when the reality was that with him in charge war was inevitable, and he knew it.[5]

Bonaparte's own propaganda sought to reconcile nostalgia for military might with peace and a renewed commitment to revolutionary liberties. In *Le départ précipité et le retour imprévu*, a print published in April celebrating his return, the sun shines on an eagle bearing an olive branch. Napoleon rides another eagle with a tricolour in its beak bearing the legend 'Gloire, Liberté & Paix'. 'Veni, vidi, vici,' announces Napoleon, striking a fleeing Louis XVIII with his lightning. A more expensive print was titled *Rentrée de Napoleon le Grand dans la Capitale de l'Empire Français, le 20 Mars 1815*. It showed Napoleon in classical costume as a Roman emperor, surrounded by emblems of agriculture, trade and justice, with tributes to his achievements and a flag declaring 'Honneur aux Braves' – the brave soldiers of his army. The writing described how France having experienced some unexpected reverses had been suffering for several months under a foreign yoke. Her hero and liberator had retired to Elba but left on 28 February at the head of a handful of his 'Braves'. He crossed France unopposed in twenty-two days, welcomed everywhere.

Bonaparte had marched to Paris on a wave of popular support from the peasants of eastern France in which the most startling ingredient was renewed revolutionary fervour, with the recrudescence of liberty trees and similar symbols. To a senior administrator he confided, 'Nothing has surprised me more on returning to France, than this hatred of priests and the nobility which I find as universal and as violent as it was at the beginning of the Revolution. The Bourbons have restored their lost force to the ideas of the Revolution.'[6]

In reality he had sought to stir up this revolutionary fervour from his first landing: his proclamation of 1 March had labelled the feudal nobility, *émigrés* and clergy 'enemies of the people'. Once more he presented himself as the Saviour of the Revolution that he had been back in 1800. For this reason decrees of 21 March abolished the nobility and feudal titles, expelled the *émigrés* and sequestered their property and removed nearly all the detested excise duties on alcoholic drinks. A pamphleteer announced 'A general appeal to all the peoples of Europe to join with the French to shake off the yoke of their oppressors, to give themselves a chief of their choice and laws which establish liberty, equality and the rights of all citizens'. The cause was clearly defined: once again, the French were striving to preserve their Revolution, struggling against despots and seeking to make common cause with the oppressed in places such as Belgium.[7]

Popular support for Napoleon was not universal, however, and some cities in the south, west and north, notably Marseilles and Bordeaux, came out in favour of the king. Emmanuel de Grouchy, a cavalry general who, rusticated by Louis XVIII, had rallied to Napoleon, defeated the royalists in Provence, but the Vendée soon rose in revolt. In northern France the Bonapartist Lieutenant Martin found 'townspeople and country folk appeared less happy than us [soldiers]; not, I believe, through some ideal love for the Bourbons, about whom they knew little, but through fear of war.'[8]

The appeal to Revolutionary fervour was double-edged and royalists used it to alarm the bourgeoisie, whose support Napoleon coveted. They were far more sceptical about his prospects, happy to see the back of the Bourbons who had shown too much favour to the émigrés, but worried that Bonaparte's reappearance was certain to entail the renewal of war against the whole of Europe. Was gloire compatible with paix? Even loyal officials struggled to believe in a future for the regime: 'It was impossible for us to reawaken the illusions of the dream which had just ended. Nothing could make us believe in a change of fortune, unheard-of in history. We were certain that it was all over, and yet we had to carry out the orders that we were given.'[9]

Simple republicans bought Bonaparte's renewed revolution, but the sophisticated were sceptical of the man whose version of liberty had so resembled tyranny and whose gloire required perpetual war. Most liberals felt that the concessions that he made towards constitutional reform did not go far enough. He also made gestures towards foreign opinion, banning the French slave trade for the benefit of those English Whigs who were well-disposed towards him.

Despite all his efforts to make his coup appear popular rather than military, he constantly appealed to his army, to notions of gloire and to the high value he set on his 'Braves'. In the army support for the Emperor was strongest among ordinary soldiers, who still worshipped him. The army remained more Jacobin in its sentiments than was typical in France and most soldiers were enthusiastic to fight to defend the Revolution against invading princes, although even they were averse to the idea of foreign conquest, at least of territory beyond Belgium and the Rhine frontier.

Army officers – especially senior officers – were more circumspect. Some were royalists, others felt that they could not break their oath to the King, and yet others had serious reservations about Bonaparte, or about his chances of success. Many senior officers felt that war was inevitable and defeat scarcely less certain. A royalist-sympathising artillery officer recalled a conversation with General Ruty, Napoleon's overall artillery commander, in which Ruty gave his opinion that Bonaparte was doomed to failure. 'I felt sorry for this poor general who, royalist at heart, joined the army against his principles and convinced of the inevitability of defeat.' Duty, employment and legal obligation, rather than political enthusiasm, kept many senior officers in place, and even the many ardent Bonapartists or republicans who were delighted to see the Emperor back in charge, welcomed him with a degree of foreboding.[10]

Napoleon began to inspect his army from very early on. The Imperial Guard were given back their old eagles at the Tuileries on 21 March. Bonapartist half-pay officer André Ravard, freshly arrived from the Charente, saw Napoleon review about ten thousand soldiers on 26 March, watched by a crowd of fifty thousand shouting 'Vive l'Empereur!' with 'joy and approval painted on each face'. These military reviews featured a favourite and characteristic performance from the Emperor. At a review on 28 March Jean-Baptiste Lemonnier-Delafosse saw Napoleon at close quarters for the second time in his life. This comfortably employed staff officer with the 1st Division was not predisposed in the Emperor's favour – Napoleon's sudden reappearance had ruptured a peaceful life for his family at Paris and subjected him once again to the hazards of war – but he was profoundly impressed at close quarters. 'It did not do to approach him, much less to hear him. He exerted a magnetic attraction on everyone who came near him,' he recalled. The presentation of the eagles was a set-piece with a standard formula:

Soldiers, here are your standards; these eagles will always serve you
as a rallying point. They will go wherever your Emperor judges
necessary for the defence of his throne and his people. Do you
swear to sacrifice your life to defend and maintain them constantly, through your courage on the path to honour and victory?
Will you swear to this?

Yet, however formulaic the words might have been, Lemonnier-
Delafosse found Napoleon's performance utterly spellbinding:

The expression that he gave to each short phrase, making them
scan like verse, gave this oath incredible intensity. You were frozen
to the spot, immobile, your skin prickling with goose bumps. His
regard, indescribable, was that of an exterminating Deity. When
he cried, 'Do you swear to defend them? … Will you swear to
this?' it was as if he said, 'Do it, or I shall crush you to dust!'[11]

4

Old Hooky Takes Charge

Before midnight on 4 April the Duke of Wellington arrived in Brussels to take over command of the allied forces from the Prince of Orange. The Duke got down to work immediately, contacting his Prussian ally General Gneisenau to form a new plan. Wellington felt that they should be prepared to resist 'a sudden stroke' that might be delivered in the imminent future, but in his view it was imperative for political reasons to defend Brussels. 'It would be of the greatest importance to Bonaparte to drive us back behind Brussels, to chase away the King of France and to reverse the order of things that the King of the Netherlands has established here. It would have a terrible effect on public opinion.' He said that he could put 23,000 troops in the field, the Dutch could contribute 20,000 men and 60 guns, and recommended to Gneisenau that the Prussians should bring all their forces closer to Brussels and concentrate them on a line from Charleroi, a fortified town thirty miles south of the city, eastward to Namur and Huy, spread over about forty miles and protected from French attack by the rivers Sambre and Meuse.[1]

Having announced his presence to his Prussian allies, Wellington put 20,000 men to work repairing the defences of the ports and border fortresses. He sent off deliberately unrealistic requirements for more and better troops from a home government that he felt needed to shake off its lethargy and realise that his need was urgent. He wrote to Earl Bathurst, Secretary of State for War, requiring 40,000

more good infantry, 18,750 cavalry and 150 guns, together with the
special equipment required for a major campaign:

> I beg you also to send here the waggon train, and all the spring
> waggons for the carriage of sick and wounded; and that you will
> ask Lord Mulgrave to send here, in addition to the ordnance above
> mentioned fully horsed, 200 musket ball cartridge carts at present,
> and as many more hereafter; and an entrenching tool cart for each
> battalion of infantry, and 200 more for the corps of engineers, and
> the whole corps of sappers and miners. It would be also desirable
> that we should have the whole staff corps ... Without these equip-
> ments, military operations are out of the question.[2]

This demand was characteristic of Wellington's precise and somewhat abrasive style. At forty-six, Arthur Wellesley, Duke of
Wellington, was the same age as Napoleon. Born Arthur Wesley, he
was the third son of an Anglo-Irish peer, a passionate musician whose
compositions had brought him a professorship at Trinity College
Dublin; it was Arthur's brother who adopted the more aristocratic
spelling Wellesley in 1798. Educated at Eton and the École Royale
d'Equitation at Angers in France, Arthur was a gifted violinist but
showed little interest in anything else. His relatives bought him a
commission in the 73rd Foot in 1787 and the following year he went
to Ireland as aide to the Viceroy.

By 1792 he was a captain and had fallen for Kitty Pakenham,
daughter of Lord Longford. In 1793 he borrowed from his brother the
money needed to buy the two promotions necessary to make him
lieutenant-colonel of the 33rd Foot. He then asked for her hand, but
Kitty's brother, the head of the family, turned him down.[3] That year
he fought in Belgium, in temporary command of a brigade, under
'the Grand Old Duke of York', an experience which, he said, taught
him 'what one ought not to do'.[4] In 1796 he sailed for India and
spent eight years there, with his remarkable brother Richard as governor general, carving out an empire at the expense of French allies.
He learned to handle difficult terrain and conditions, subtle enemies
and temperamental allies, and won a reputation for steely discipline

and self-control. Although by no means rapacious, he returned a rich man, as well as a national hero.

Richard Wellesley, himself back from India, had been a key supporter of Pitt and in 1806 he brought Arthur into Parliament as Chief Secretary for Ireland in the Duke of Portland's Tory ministry. He was persuaded by mutual friends to write to Kitty Pakenham to ask her to marry him. She was alarmed by the indifferent tone of his letter – 'is there one expression implying that *Yes* would gratify or that *No* would disappoint?' she wrote to a friend – but she eventually accepted. Wellington did not see her before their marriage, and his first sight of her after such a long period produced an unpleasant shock. 'She has grown ugly, by Jove!' he remarked to one of his brothers. Wellington later explained somewhat disingenuously to a friend that 'I married her because they asked me to do it & I did not know myself. I thought I should never care for anybody again, & that I shd. be with my army & in short, I was a fool.'[5] It was not a happy marriage.

In 1808 he was sent to Portugal and won the battle of Vimeiro. He commanded the force that returned in 1809 and in 1810 his defensive lines at Torres Vedras baffled Marshal Masséna. The following year he tied down Marshal Soult's forces in southern Spain and in 1812, with much of Napoleon's army withdrawn from Spain for Russia, took the offensive, capturing Ciudad Rodrigo and Badajoz and winning the battle of Salamanca. In 1813 he won a decisive victory at Vitoria and, after a struggle in the Pyrenees, invaded France, winning a final battle at Toulouse in 1814. On his return to London he was created Duke of Wellington. He had never fought against Napoleon himself but, unbeaten by the French in any pitched battle, he was arguably the Coalition's best champion to oppose him.

Wellington was a complicated personality and even those who observed him closely over many years found it difficult to sum him up. 'His is one of those mixed characters which it is difficult to praise or blame without the risk of doing it more or less than justice,' wrote one such. 'Confident, presumptuous, and dictatorial, but frank, open, and good-humoured', he liked to exercise complete control, which worked in a small army but was to prove a fatal flaw in his later political career.[6] Arrogant, disdainful and aloof, some of his officers knew him as 'the peer'; others referred to him as 'the Lord'. When his own reputation was in peril he could be caustically critical of subordinate officers and soldiers, which they tended to resent. On the other hand, he was extremely professional, efficient, brave, cool and unruffled. He had a fine eye for the military potential of the landscape and was so good at deploying troops that opposing generals became wary of what might be hidden in a wood or behind a ridge. He usually won his battles, extricated his armies from trouble and did his best to keep his troops supplied and as comfortable as possible. He shared their hardships and put his own steely body on the line, taking active control wherever the danger was greatest. He was physically very fit and lean and of slightly above average stature – his height was variously estimated between five foot eight inches and five foot ten.

His troops did not love him in the way that sailors idolised Nelson – indeed they tended not to like him – but they trusted and admired him. They called him 'Old Hooky' after his nose, or 'the Bugger that beats the French'. He gathered around him a staff and field officers in whom he had faith, and he made good choices – his lieutenants were usually talented and highly efficient in their sphere. Even so, he was reluctant to give them free rein: he liked to control in detail, delegated unwillingly and disliked unauthorised initiative. If people showed initiative without orders they were liable to be reprimanded at least. He was somewhat vain and won a reputation as a womaniser: another nickname among officers was 'the Beau'.[7] Although he charmed women and children, men generally found his conversation unimpressive and he spoke 'as if he affected a kind of boyish slang'.[8]

When Bonaparte landed in France, the government in London had its hands full. 'No Corn Bill is chalk'd upon half the Walls in London,' noted Lady Lucas in her journal that day, and from 6 March there were violent riots in which the windows of government ministers were smashed and their houses broken into. The 16th Light Dragoons, quartered at Hounslow and Hampton Court, were 'called up to the neighbourhood of Westminster Bridge for the purpose of being in readiness for the riots occasioned by the passing of the Corn Laws', and several more regiments were also deployed. However, the return of Bonaparte to France, confirmed on 11 March, so focused minds that the rioting ceased and in early April the Dragoons embarked for Ostend.[9]

Britain accepted the need to fight. 'Mr. Whitbread has already said in the H: of C: that we ought not to interfere in the Affairs of France. – But Alas! If we do not Buonaparte will interfere with us,' wrote Lady Lucas. Lord Byron was sickened by the 'barking of the wardogs' but the Whig leaders in Parliament who spoke against war carried very few with them. Assistant surgeon William Gibney recalled:

> The call to arms was universal, and well responded to; but to judge by what was written in the papers and by general conversation, there was little enthusiasm. None cared to begin war again, or have increased taxation for the relief of a nation or nations proving themselves somewhat unthankful for former assistance ... However, all felt that war was inevitable, and that this disturber of Europe must be crushed; for so long as he was free or lived, thus long would there be war. It was necessary therefore to put him down, and with him destroy the power of the French nation to do harm and create revolutions.[10]

The problem for Britain was what to fight with, for Wellington's demands for more and better troops could not easily be met. Many of his experienced Peninsular veterans were still in America, where the war declared against Britain by the United States in 1812 had only recently reached a conclusion, and many troops that were in Britain were needed to discourage insurrections and riots, especially but not exclusively in Ireland.

The most reliable body at Wellington's disposal when he arrived in the Netherlands was the King's German Legion, and even that was seriously under-strength. The Legion had been formed from volunteer refugees from the Electorate of Hanover after the French invasion of 1803. Its core consisted of excellent former Hanoverian regular soldiers, such as Christian von Ompteda who had commanded a battalion of Hanoverian Guards before taking ship for England in 1803. Volunteers from the Guards were incorporated into the 1st line battalion of the Legion, of which Major Ompteda became the second-in-command. The Legion fought throughout the Peninsular campaign, with its light battalions especially often taking the most dangerous assignments. Over time, it accepted all sorts of foreign volunteers, but non-Hanoverian recruits had been discharged in 1814.

Friedrich Lindau had joined in 1809 when he was twenty, having been apprenticed to a shoemaker in Hamelin and run away from home to escape to England. This was an extraordinary adventure that involved going up the river Weser and making contact with Englishmen clandestinely based at the island of Heligoland, from where the British smuggled goods into Germany and picked up recruits. He was marched from Harwich to the depot of the King's German Legion at Bexhill in Sussex where he joined the 2nd Light infantry, then commanded by the Scot Colin Halkett, before being sent to Portugal in 1811. He fought the Peninsular campaign in what was a spearhead unit, his memoir demonstrating greater interest in theft of food than fighting, though his prowess at both became notorious. The Legion had a number of British officers, of whom Edmund Wheatley was one. He had joined the 5th line battalion of the Legion as an ensign in the Pyrenees in 1813 and had fought the last, difficult stages of the campaign in Spain and southern France with a unit that was usually in the vanguard under Christian von Ompteda, who had been promoted to command it. In 1815 the Legion comprised eight small battalions of infantry, five large regiments of fine cavalry and three batteries of artillery.

Wellington considered much of the British army of occupation in the Netherlands fit only for garrison duty, and four regiments that he accepted for the field army were entirely raw, though the 73rd Foot had gained confidence from a campaign with the Hanoverians in north Germany: to the regret of Sergeant Tom Morris, they had narrowly missed taking part in the battle of Leipzig. Only one of the four battalions of Foot Guards had any experience in Spain, and only the 30th Cambridgeshires and 44th East Essex were hardened Peninsular veterans.

The Hanoverians had fought alongside Britain since the Elector of Hanover became King George I in 1714. The Electorate had been overrun by France in 1803, annexed by Prussia in 1805 and ceded to France in 1807, after which it ceased to exist, its territory providing the largest part of Napoleon's new kingdom of Westphalia. But on 12 October 1814 the Congress of Vienna decided that Hanover should be reinstated as a kingdom with George III as king. Field battalions of volunteers had been raised to fight in 1813 and these were being supplemented by freshly conscripted militias or 'Landwehr' with experienced corporals, sergeants and officers from the King's German Legion or the former army of Westphalia. Hanover eventually provided a field force of two light, five line and fifteen Landwehr battalions, 37,576 men, together with a reserve force 9000 strong which was assigned to garrison duty. It also raised 1682 cavalry and two good foot batteries. Wellington trusted the loyalty if not the military readiness of the rapidly forming Hanoverian levies.

The Dutch and Belgian regular units contained soldiers with considerable experience of fighting for Napoleon, chiefly against the British in Spain. Wellington did not want officers who had fought with Bonaparte in charge of important garrisons, while Orange's secretary Colborne reported 'I would not trust the Belgian Troops an inch.'[11] A Dutch officer found the spirit of the 8th Hussars especially worrying: in March at Antwerp a fight had broken out between some 8th Hussar officers and Hanoverians in which sabre blows were exchanged, before the Belgians, whose colonel had formerly commanded the French 16th Chasseurs, disappeared into a crowd from which shouts of '*Vive l'Empereur!*' were heard. Two hundred and sixteen of the 8th Hussars deserted between January and 17 June 1815.[12] The Duke of Wellington shrewdly suspected that the Belgians might change sides given half a chance and a report for the Prussians reached similar conclusions, while the mood of the civilians in the French-speaking Walloon regions of Liège and Hainault ranged between sullen resentment and open hostility to the foreign, monarchist forces billeted upon them.

The Netherlands militia, a combination of volunteers and conscripts raised for the 1814 campaign, armed with British muskets and stiffened by regular NCOs and officers, were considered more reliable in terms of loyalty. Many were young soldiers with a year's experience or less; others had served longer, but usually in the French army. Eventually, including its battalions from Nassau in Germany, the army fielded a total of twelve line, eleven light and fifteen militia battalions, together with seven regiments of cavalry, making 3405 cavalry, 24,305 infantry and 72 guns.

Wellington was anxious to reinforce his army with Germans but there were bitter disputes between Prussia and Britain at Vienna over which force the smaller German states should join. The Prussians wanted all the north German states to fight with them, but Wellington argued that this would leave him impossibly short, so the Prussians conceded Brunswick, Oldenburg, the Hanseatic cities of Hamburg, Bremen and Lübeck and, most unwillingly, Nassau and the 7000 or so Saxons who remained Saxon after the projected partition agreed in Vienna.[13] The wrangling went on so long that most states did not mobilise in time to fight for either army. Although the newly recruited Brunswickers set out from Braunschweig on 15 April, the Hanseatic contingent only turned up to fight for Wellington in July.

In organising this army, Wellington sought to combine good British troops with weaker and less experienced foreign units, as he had done to good effect in the Peninsula. The king of the Netherlands refused, insisting that his men fought in national divisions, but the Hanoverians were split up, much to their disappointment, for they felt that British officers looked down on them and made no attempt to understand their traditions or to socialise with them.[14] Meanwhile, the British government was still dragging its heels. Three weeks after he had demanded 150 guns, Wellington was being offered 72, for which he would have to buy horses. The problem was not horses, he explained, but drivers, of which there were none to be had anywhere. If they couldn't find proper artillerymen he wanted them to send dragoons to do the driving.[15] None of the best of his seasoned troops and trusted assistants had yet arrived and in early May Wellington thought he had 'an infamous army, very weak and ill-equipped, and very inexperienced staff'.[16] His vehemence reflected a deep anxiety: that Napoleon might yet attack him before he was ready.

5

The Prussians

'Boys, clean your rifles', said my old and venerable father, entering my room where I was studying Loder's *Anatomical Tables*; 'he is loose again'. – 'Napoleon?' – 'He has returned from Elba.'

My heart beat high; it was glorious news for a boy of fifteen, who had often heard with silent envy the account of the campaigns of 1813–14 from the lips of his two brothers, both of whom had marched in 1813, in common with most young men of good families, as volunteer riflemen, and returned as wounded officers.

Following his brothers' example, Franz Lieber volunteered immediately to be a rifleman, choosing the Pomeranian Colberg Regiment, named after the fortress that they had defended with glory in 1807 when the rest of Prussia had fallen to the French. There was such a huge throng at the recruiting table in Berlin that he had to queue for three hours to enlist.[1] In Germany it was common for middle-class boys to volunteer to be riflemen. They had the means to provide their own rifle – thus saving the state money – as well as the intelligence to survive a form of infantry combat that demanded initiative.

As Lieber's introduction to the army suggests, the Prussians were animated by fierce patriotism and a burning loathing for Bonaparte and for Frenchmen in general, cordially reciprocated by the French. During their long domination of Prussia the French had exacted heavy taxes and taken whatever they wanted. In 1813 Prussia had led the German rising against their French overlords. Patriotic young men joined Ludwig von Lützow's Freikorps, a unit that attracted artists, students and academics from all over Germany as well as more ordinary folk. Ludwig Nagel, son of a joiner from Schwerin, now a highly educated polylingual theologian, was one such, soon elected a lieutenant by his fellow 'Black Jägers'. They dyed their own clothes black for uniforms and some students swore they would not cut their hair or beards until the French had been driven from Germany.

Napoleon had destroyed the old Prussian army, considered the best in Europe under Frederick the Great, in 1806 in humiliating defeats at Jena and Auerstädt. In the following years Gerhard von Scharnhorst and August von Gneisenau had rebuilt it, imitating the French model, as a citizen army of conscripts and volunteers, organ-ised in self-sufficient corps. Most Prussian men were subject to compulsory military service, but few conscripts ever served with such good will.

In 1815 the army was again in the process of reorganisation. Having contracted to save money in 1814, it was suddenly expanded on Napoleon's return and this meant many regiments had to be brought up to strength with inexperienced troops. A third of the army was made up of Landwehr militia units, and although many of their men had battle experience, the regiments lacked training, cohesion and equipment. Throughout the Prussian army troops were making do with a mixture of British, Russian and French uniforms and weapons.

Large numbers of men in the Prussian army came from parts of old Prussia that had recently been recovered, having been 'Westphalian' since 1807, or from lands recently ceded to Prussia like Napoleon's Duchy of Berg (the area around Düsseldorf). Eight thou-sand new recruits had been raised from newly Prussian territory between the Maas and the Rhine in spring 1815 and another 8000 bilingual Rhinelanders, mostly from Bonn, Cologne and Düsseldorf, were already serving, having recently fought for the Emperor. Their commitment and loyalty were suspect. As the Prussian chief of staff later explained, 'in the course of a few days [men] found themselves belonging to a new country, owing a new allegiance, subject to a new organisation and fresh levies, [and they] had not joined the army above six or eight weeks before hostilities began.'[2] Some joined one of the six Westphalian Landwehr regiments and some reinforced regular units. Of 523 Rhineland conscripts who joined the 24th Regiment on 11 May, 93 had deserted by early June.[3]

Prussian troops theoretically wore blue but there was insufficient stock to supply the troops with new uniforms, for the Prussian state was desperately short of money. Reserve units that had worn grey or black continued to do so, while the regiments from the Duchy of Berg still dressed in the shabby white uniforms they had worn when fighting for France. The British supplied some equipment, but this was a scruffy, under-equipped army of many hues. A British officer who saw them pass through Brussels in 1814 described 'hardy rough-looking men' in ragged clothes, with women who rode astride and 'had as campaigning an aspect as their lords' and pathetically under-sized horses pulling their guns.[4] Throughout continental Europe the long wars had caused a dearth of good horses, and cavalrymen as well as artillery drivers were poorly mounted. Prussian *uhlans* were nominally lancers (they had adopted the Polish name for their lancer units) but some were not – having no lances and no training in their use. Whereas the Dutch, knowing the quality of Belgian roads in bad weather, had issued their troops with three pairs of shoes, the Prussians got one pair and one spare shoe. That these shabby troops were to march and fight with such determination owed a great deal to the personality of their beloved general, Blücher.

Prince Gebhard Leberecht von Blücher was seventy-two and a half years old. Born in Mecklenburg, like Queen Charlotte of Britain, he joined the Swedish army as a hussar at sixteen and, having been captured by the Prussians, switched to their service. His love of gambling, women and drinking was noted; after one drunken frolic Frederick the Great announced that 'Captain von Blücher can go to the Devil' and never employed him again. After Frederick's death Blücher took part in the suppression of the Dutch revolution in 1787 and distinguished himself as a colonel of hussars in the campaigns of 1793 and 1794. He was promoted lieutenant-general in 1801, fought at Auerstädt and, after the main army surrendered, led a rearguard in a fighting retreat until he was trapped against the Danish frontier. The influential patriot and reformer Gerhard von Scharnhorst had served as Blücher's chief of staff in this campaign and fought alongside him again during the war of liberation until he was fatally wounded. After Scharnhorst's death Blücher took Gneisenau as his chief of staff, defeating two French marshals before meeting Napoleon at Leipzig. It was the fourth battle between them and the first that Blücher won, for it was Blücher's army that took the town on the last day of the battle. He was defeated a further three times by Napoleon during the latter's retreat towards France, but crushed the heavily outnumbered Emperor at Laon and then marched on Paris. Afterwards he visited England where the press trumpeted him as a hero.

Inseparable from his pipe, Blücher called his soldiers his children. Having limitless courage, energy and determination, after each setback he would dust himself down and drive onwards: '*Alte Vorwärts*' (Old Forwards) was what his soldiers called him, along with 'Papa Blücher'. They loved him, and he could get troops to do things that few others could. Diplomacy, subtlety and guile were not part of Blücher's character, but he was not stupid and had abundant common sense. He was intensely patriotic and, in common with many other Germans, his enmity to Napoleon had the strength of a personal vendetta. To Blücher Napoleon's return meant unfinished business: he told his soldiers that he was going back to look for the old pipe that he had left behind at Paris.

Politics, logistics and tactical detail were all handled by the field marshal's quartermaster-general and right-hand man. 'If I am to be made a doctor,' Blücher remarked in 1814 of an honour conferred by the University of Oxford, 'they should at least make Gneisenau an apothecary, for we go together.'[5] On another occasion he claimed that he was the only man who could kiss his own head, demonstrating it by kissing Gneisenau's substantial cranium. Blücher freely recognised his own limitations, lacked vanity and welcomed help towards the common cause. This greatly lubricated relations with Wellington, for whom Gneisenau had no great liking.

Born in 1760, August von Gneisenau was nine years older than Napoleon and Wellington. The son of a Saxon artillery lieutenant, he was an outsider among the Prussian aristocrats who dominated the senior military ranks and he gravitated towards Blücher, who was also a foreigner. As a youth he went to fight rebel American colonists in a German unit in British pay, though the war ended soon after he reached America and he merely joined the garrison of Quebec. On his return he applied for Prussian service, fought at Jena in 1806 and defended the fortress of Colberg until the war ended. After that he had helped Scharnhorst remodel the Prussian army, but he resigned in 1809 when the king of Prussia refused to join his planned national rising. He visited Austria, Russia, Sweden and England before returning to Prussia as a leader of the patriotic party. Gneisenau was thought to be republican by inclination and the king of Prussia referred to him and Blücher as 'mad Jacobins', but still chose to put them in charge of his army.[6]

There was political tension between Britain and Prussia and much potential for misunderstanding between the two armies, despite their common cause against Napoleon. Nevertheless, when on 5 April Wellington requested Gneisenau to move Prussian troops closer to Brussels in order to ward off a sudden strike from Napoleon, Gneisenau responded by issuing orders for his two most complete corps to march to Charleroi and Namur. He was not happy, though, suspicious of Wellington's pro-Bourbon politics and worried that the move might compromise his own responsibility to defend Germany. The loss of the Prussian army in a battle for Brussels was too catastrophic for Gneisenau to contemplate. He distrusted the arrogant Wellington, who outranked him both socially and militarily, and disliked being kept in the dark. He had the Prussian liaison officer in Belgium write to the Duke to ask what the plan was, where Wellington intended to give battle, how many Prussians would be involved and what would be the course of action were they to be defeated. Napoleon then further poisoned the suspicious atmosphere in Prussian headquarters by allowing an emissary carrying a copy of the Secret Treaty of Vienna to fall into Gneisenau's hands. The discovery of the combination between Britain, Austria and France against Prussia did not go down well. Wellington responded sensibly and decisively to dispel suspicion and make his position clear. He sent a trusted and charming young staff officer, Henry Hardinge, to give Gneisenau a private explanation of the embarrassing revelation of the secret pact, and then to remain with the Prussian staff as liaison officer, to act as a channel of communication and explanation between the two camps.[7] On 10 April Wellington wrote to Gneisenau with a candid exposition of his thoughts and plans, reassuring him that in the case of a setback the whole army could retreat eastwards to continue to protect Germany.[8]

At this stage the two generals resolved their concerns and anxieties. Both wrote in French, which introduced potential for misunderstanding, but they did their best to be honest with each other. Gneisenau said that he intended to commit his whole army, not just a part of it, but stated plainly that his real worry was that if he marched the Prussian army to Brussels and they suffered a defeat, Wellington would find it necessary to retreat towards the sea leaving the Prussians exposed to annihilation. He was determined to share the fate of Wellington's army, and if Wellington was prepared to retreat towards Germany all difficulties were removed. He then explained his own plans. Wellington replied to the effect that although he might normally retreat towards the sea and look to the defence of Holland, current circumstances dictated that his army should remain in theatre; if he retreated owing to local enemy superiority it would only be in order to combine British and Prussian forces elsewhere. So long as they stuck together they were too strong to be defeated. This clear exchange of views established a vital understanding between the British and Prussians: both were determined to cooperate in close mutual support and this was to prove crucial to the success of the campaign.[9]

One reason for Gneisenau's caution was that, like Wellington, he was worried about untrustworthy troops, having 16,000 Rhinelanders and 14,000 Saxons who had fought with France until 1813 and might change sides at the slightest reverse. The Saxon problem soon came to a head in a way that confirmed all Wellington's suspicions and Gneisenau's fears. The experienced Saxons were in Liège, anxiously awaiting the outcome of discussions in Vienna about the fate of Saxony. Blücher had been doing his best to charm them, but they were understandably averse to the notion that within each regiment some soldiers might soon become Prussian while others remained Saxon. Then Blücher received blunt orders from Vienna to divide the Saxon force into those who remained Saxon and those who became Prussian.

On 1 and 2 May he attempted to implement his instructions. A correspondent reported candidly on 2 May to a London newspaper on the result:

> The Saxon regiments in garrison here were ordered to appear in the square this morning, in order to be incorporated with the Prussians. They did not come to the appointed place until the afternoon, and when the incorporation was announced to them they left their ranks in the greatest disorder, crying, Live the King of Saxony! and the Emperor of the French! Most of the officers followed the example of the soldiers, and the confusion is complete. The Saxons are now running through the streets with their swords drawn in quest of the Prussians. We fear for what may pass at night. The people of Liège are disposed to favour the Saxons.[10]

That night Blücher was chased from his headquarters by a mob of Saxon grenadiers hurling stones through the windows and fighting hand to hand with Prussian officers. The next day, 3 May, the Prussian general had an appointment for a summit meeting with Wellington at Tirlemont, a town situated halfway between their respective headquarters. Intelligence sent by Bathurst, the Secretary of State for War, and confirmed by other sources, had revealed that Napoleon was heading for the northern border with the stated intention of inspecting the frontiers and fortresses. He had just ordered the concentration of four army corps and it was quite possible that the 'sudden stroke' might be imminent. Before Wellington left for the meeting, he advised King Willem to flood the water defences of his border fortresses.[11]

At Tirlemont, both Blücher and the Prince of Orange argued for an immediate attack to take the war to the enemy before he strengthened his borders, but Wellington counselled waiting until their own forces were stronger and the Austrians and Russians were ready to lend support. At this stage the Prussians had two corps of about 66,000 men around Charleroi and Namur, along with the 14,000 Saxons at Liège, while Wellington could field about 70,000 men.[12] They agreed to attack Napoleon together on 12 July if possible.

Little is known about the detail of discussions at this meeting, but the generals probably defined the areas for which they would be responsible, either side of the Brussels to Charleroi highway, and agreed mutual support in the event of a French assault. To speculate from the evidence of what eventually transpired, it seems likely that each command called the tune in its own area, and selected a position in which they would fight were they to be attacked. Wellington's favoured battlefield was at Hal, ten miles south-west of Brussels on the direct route from Paris, whereas the Prussians' chosen position was closer to the frontier.[13] Wellington still wanted more Prussians nearer Brussels. The Prussians had been unwilling to cross the border because they could not afford to pay cash to feed so many of their troops, but Wellington obtained a promise that the king of the Netherlands would supply them with food. Two days later Blücher summoned 60,000 men from Luxembourg and Cologne, moving another army to cover the German border with France.[14]

Blücher also offered Wellington the Saxons, but the Duke turned them down saying that he already had enough mutinous troops on his hands with the Belgians.[15] He had assumed that the Saxons had mutinied in support of Napoleon, rather than for reasons of national pride, and reckoned that troops that had changed sides once, as the Saxons had at Leipzig, might well do so again. He continued, too, to reject requests from the Saxons themselves to join his army, for as he afterwards wrote to Hardinge, 'it is very obvious that they will be of no use to any body during the war; and our object must be to prevent them doing mischief ... the most fatal of all measures will be to have 14,000 men in the field who cannot be trusted.'[16]

Wellington's words probably reduced Blücher's trust in the Saxons, with whom he was already thoroughly angry, and a final incident on his way back from the conference pushed him over the edge. Blücher passed a Saxon light regiment who, to his utter fury, refused to salute him. Having ordered the Prussian commander of II Corps to make sure that the Saxons didn't march off to France, the field marshal disarmed the Saxon Grenadier Guards, ordered them to hand over ten men, had these executed by firing squad, and had the regimental flag, which the Queen of Saxony had embroidered personally, publicly burned. When the corps commander protested he was relieved of his command. The whole Saxon contingent was then sent back to Germany in disgrace.

Once his 60,000 reinforcements arrived, Blücher was more or less at full strength to fight, with four corps amounting to about 126,000 troops, but this was an underfunded, half-trained force and, like Wellington, Blücher was doubtful of the loyalty and attitude of a good number of his men.

6

Honneur aux Braves

By the beginning of May any Frenchman could see that war was inevitable. Napoleon blamed the failure of the letters stating his peaceful intentions on his brother-in-law Joachim Murat, king of Naples, who had attacked the Austrians in Italy. Murat had been Napoleon's best cavalry commander and, since 1795, one of his closest associates. He had deserted the Emperor on an Austro-British promise that he could keep his Neapolitan throne, but it now looked as if they wished to depose him. Napoleon's version of events was that he desired to maintain the existing friendship between France and Austria and was enormously irritated when on 15 March King Joachim declared war on Austria; Murat's that he had declared war on Napoleon's instructions, since Bonaparte fondly expected Italy to rise in his favour.[1] Whoever was to blame, Napoleon did not lift a finger to help his erstwhile lieutenant. Joachim was finally defeated on 2 May, deserted by most of his troops and obliged to flee to France, where Napoleon not only refused to employ him – he refused even to see him.

Napoleon now began pondering his options thoroughly. The first was to fight a defensive campaign, similar to the one that he had undertaken the previous year, but with 200,000 men instead of 90,000 and with Paris fortified and defended by a further 80,000 men under the redoubtable Marshal Davout. He would mass his troops near Paris and Lyons and by the time the allies could reach him – towards the end of July – he would be strong while they would have had to detach troops to protect their lines of supply from the garrisons of his fortresses. Militarily speaking, this was a sound and attractive plan, but politically it was fraught with risk. He would have to cede large parts of France before fighting his battles and the French people would suffer the ravages inflicted by invading armies. They might not stand for it.

The second option was riskier militarily but offered a better prospect of unifying the nation and yielding political dividends. The plan was to make an attack on the enemy armies in Belgium before the Austrians and Russians were ready to fight. The difficulty was to ensure that he fought one army before the other, for the Anglo-Dutch and Prussian armies combined much outnumbered the *Armée du Nord* and the Guard. If he could but win two battles, all the old confidence would surge back into the French soldiers and the people would back him. The Belgians would join him and eject the king of the Netherlands from Brussels and Louis XVIII from Ghent. This would bring down the hostile Tory government in London, the Whigs would make peace, and without British finance the other allies would lose their enthusiasm for war. In any case, his reinforcements would be ready before he had to face the Austrians and Russians. If, on the other hand, he failed to break the allies in Belgium, he could simply retire on his reinforcements at Paris and resort to the defensive plan. There was a lot of wishful thinking in the offensive plan and, at best, it was a desperate gamble. But Napoleon had always been a gambler and he decided that this was the option to take.

In so doing, he was reliant on the army that loved him, on his 'braves'. So Napoleon threw his energy into the task of raising and arming men. He recalled the conscripts of 1814 and from some regions, at least, recruits flocked in to defend France against foreign tyrants. He employed deserters, officers on half pay, men in retirement, the gendarmerie, the National Guard, aiming to have 500,000 men in arms by September. Soon he would recreate the old mighty machine.

There were three types of soldier in Napoleon's armies, as in his rivals': infantry, cavalry and artillery. Infantrymen fought on foot armed with a musket and a bayonet. They were grouped into companies, commanded by captains and lieutenants with the help of sergeants and corporals. A number of companies made a battalion – six in the French army. Battalions were the basic tactical unit, varying greatly in strength, but averaging 500–800 men. In the French army two or three battalions made a regiment and two regiments formed a brigade. Two brigades combined to make a division, led by a general. A division contained between 4000 and 8000 men and had its own artillery. Four infantry divisions, one cavalry division and their artillery, engineers and staff made a corps.

Cavalry fought on horseback in squadrons, of which an average of three made a regiment. Two regiments made a brigade, two brigades a division and two divisions a cavalry corps. One division of cavalry served with each infantry corps but there was also a central reserve of cavalry.

Artillery fought in horse batteries of six cannon or foot batteries of eight. Each gun also had a limber or carriage and an ammunition wagon, and the battery had spare ammunition wagons. Each wagon and gun was pulled by a number of horses, so a battery on the move consisted of some twenty vehicles, pulled by around 200 horses and maintained by about 200 men.

These basic elements were supported by specialist engineering units, transport and staff. The staff was responsible for planning, supply and communication and there were staff officers attached to brigades and divisions, and more at corps and army level.

The final element in Napoleon's army was the Imperial Guard, effectively an elite corps with its own infantry, cavalry and artillery, all of which was the best of its kind. The Imperial Guard had been 112,000 men strong in 1814, but only 7390 soldiers remained on 20 March. By mid-June the Guard was 28,328 strong. The Emperor enlarged the cavalry regiments and recreated the artillery of the Guard, gendarmes (policemen), sailors and sappers (both engineering units). The Old Guard, Napoleon's personal bodyguard of selected veterans, the elite of the elite, traditionally contained two regiments of grenadiers – assault troops chosen from the strongest and largest – and two of chasseurs – marksmen expert in manoeuvre at speed. In

1815 Napoleon added two more regiments of each – the 'Middle Guard' – together with eight regiments of *voltigeurs* and eight of *tirailleurs* – elite light infantry skirmishers – which constituted the Young Guard. The Guard had traditionally recruited on merit and experience and an invitation to join it was a reward for long and distinguished service, but many of those who returned to its ranks in 1815 were short of the standard to which the Guard had once aspired.

There being nothing like enough weapons to equip the new recruits, Napoleon launched a massive effort to get more. French manufacturers had the capacity to make only 20,000 muskets a month, so he bought guns from England (40,000 according to his minister of police),[2] smuggled them from Holland and Germany, repaired old ones and offered rewards for handing guns in. The arsenal at Vincennes made twelve million cartridges in two months. With the need to make bayonets a priority, only grenadier companies were given swords. Cuirasses – breastplates – were made as fast as possible, but at least one regiment of Napoleon's famous heavy cavalry, the cuirassiers, had to take the field without the armour plating that gave them their name. Workshops were created in Paris to make 1250 uniforms a day but, there being insufficient blue cloth, greatcoats were produced in various shades, chiefly grey. Since the cavalry and artillery had only 35,600 horses, of which 5000 had been lent to farmers, Napoleon requisitioned 4250 fine horses from the gendarmerie, and within three months the cavalry had 40,000 horses and the artillery 16,500.

What Napoleon saw during his reviews must generally have pleased him. This new army was his best since 1809. Whereas the armies with which he had fought in 1813 and 1814 were largely comprised of young and inexperienced conscripts, this one was much more experienced. The surviving conscripts of 1813 were now battle-hardened, while the influx of a huge number of prisoners of war provided a backbone of troops with long experience of campaigning, old revolutionary principles and a hatred of the enemy. Like veteran Roman legionaries the army was almost all they knew and their allegiance to the eagles was surpassed only by their loyalty to their emperor, their adored *petit caporal* who went around in a shabby grey

greatcoat and a characteristic black hat, conspicuously drab amidst his
gorgeously plumed entourage.

The British sergeant Tom Morris felt that the French soldier's
devotion to Napoleon was easily explained by the manner in which
he ran his army. While this was a rose-tinted view of how the French
system really worked in practice, it remained preferable to the British
system, which Morris came to regard with disillusioned contempt:

> If we seek a reason for such extraordinary attachment, we shall
> find it in that constant attention of Napoleon, to the wants and
> wishes of his men; his identity with them in all their dangers; his
> prompt, profuse, but impartial distribution of rewards, his throw-
> ing open to the meanest soldier, the road of promotion to the
> highest honours; so that every man had a strong incentive to good
> conduct. When officers were killed or disabled, the vacancies were
> filled up from among the men who had been serving, who could
> sympathise with their comrades, in their dangers and privations;
> and while they had no difficulty in maintaining their authority,
> their conduct towards the men was kind and affectionate. No
> man, however elevated in rank or connexion, had any chance of
> promotion, but by passing through the various grades, commenc-
> ing with the lowest.[3]

A man like Tom Morris might well have earned the advancement
of which he dreamed had he been serving with the enemy. One of the
former prisoners of war released in 1814 was André Ravard, a thirty-
eight-year-old from the Charente. His peasant family welcomed the
Revolution and his brother volunteered in 1793 but André remained
at home until he was conscripted in 1799 as a barely literate private in
the 13th Light Infantry. He campaigned in Italy in 1800 and
Switzerland in 1801, becoming a corporal. Fighting with the *Grande
Armée* his regiment figured bloodily at Auerstädt in 1806 and Eylau
in 1807 and Ravard was promoted to sergeant and enrolled in the
Légion d'honneur. He fought at Wagram in 1809 and became a sous-
lieutenant. Having been wounded at Smolensk and promoted to
lieutenant, he was wounded again at Borodino in 1812, and was dan-

gerously ill in hospital at Moscow and still weak when the retreat
began. He was shot in the head in a rearguard action in November
but survived the winter by eating the flesh of the horses that had
died.[4] Promoted to captain, he fought at Dresden in 1813, and was
wounded and captured at Kulm on 30 August when his regiment
took very heavy casualties. He then spent a year as a prisoner in
Romania. When he returned to France in September 1814 he wrote to
his brother that he reckoned he had covered 9000 miles in the last
two and a half years and it was a miracle that he had survived so
many dangers. He had been hoping to enjoy the sweets of a long
peace in tranquillity but still welcomed Bonaparte back.[5]

Ravard's sixteen-year survival in the army was unusual. Of the
216 conscripts who joined alongside him in 1799, 24 had been killed
in action, 28 had died from illness, 50 had been declared unfit for
service and 84 had disappeared in Russia.[6] He exemplifies the tough-
ness of the veterans. Having started a poor peasant, he had spent
almost his entire adult life in the army and in the process had learned
to write fluent French; as one of only three of his fellow conscripts to
reach officer rank, he now earned 2000 francs a year. Whereas nearly
all officers in Britain bought their commission, three-quarters of
Napoleon's officers had risen through the ranks.

Compared with the Netherlands, Hanoverian and Prussian
armies, which contained high proportions of barely trained militia, all
of the French units were regular and all had considerable experience
of war. On the other hand, many regiments had been reorganised
recently and their men were unfamiliar with their officers, whom
they did not always trust, for even after Bonaparte ejected known
royalists in May 1815, he left behind a good number who deserted
during the campaign in June. Regiments brought to strength with
drafts of fresh recruits, former prisoners of war or remnants of other
shattered units had had little opportunity to train together. In this
respect the cavalry was better than the infantry, 'which could have
done with a few months of manoeuvres in which to develop the
team spirit that binds soldiers to one another and constitutes the
strength of that arm'. There simply wasn't time to instil the high
morale and discipline of the army of 1805.[7]

The army similarly lacked the cohesion acquired by veteran forces after several years and possessed, to some degree, by the British. Officers did not know one another, generals were unfamiliar with their troops and sometimes with their colleagues, people were uncertain of their duties, of all the skills and routines that came with practice. This was especially the case with the general staff and the staffs of the senior officers. Most of all they had to get used to each other and develop working routines: there was no chance for exercises or any kind of practice. The rawness of the army in this respect was to play a large part in its undoing.

Fear of treachery was widespread and nobody was quite sure who could be trusted. On 25 April General d'Erlon wrote to Marshal Davout, having discovered that the magazine at Lille was distributing dud cartridges. He had the director of artillery there put under surveillance and all regiments were ordered to check their cartridges.[8] The soldiers were moreover suspicious of the marshals who had betrayed Napoleon the year before – the kind of treason they referred to as a *ragusade*, after Marshal Marmont, Duke of Ragusa, who in March 1814 had opened the gates of Paris to the allies instead of defending the city.[9]

Whether to employ his old marshals and, if so, how to employ them, was a difficult issue. A number were too old to campaign, others were in disgrace and some were needed to cover Napoleon's back. Although their presence with the field army might have seemed desirable, Napoleon appointed the formidable Marshal Louis Davout to look after affairs in Paris, the superbly efficient Marshal Louis Suchet with VII Corps to command on the Austrian border, where he might need a man with initiative, and the dependable General Jean Rapp with V Corps to defend the north-eastern border, based near Strasbourg.

The Emperor's single most serious handicap was the absence of Marshal Louis Berthier, who had been his chief of staff and closest military colleague since his first Italian campaign in 1796. Berthier had created the Imperial Staff and had organised every war the Emperor had fought. On campaign he travelled with Napoleon, ate with Napoleon and knew Napoleon's mind so intimately that he could translate his intentions into orders and supply any detail that the Emperor had omitted in the celerity of his thought.

The sixty-two-year-old Berthier had followed Louis XVIII to Ghent, had then gone to visit his family in Germany and had not returned. In his place Napoleon initially appointed his experienced and capable deputy, François Gédéon Bailly de Monthion, but then he persuaded himself that he needed a marshal in charge and decided to appoint Marshal Soult as *major-général*, the French title for the chief of staff. Soult's apparent zeal as war minister to the Bourbons had made him odious to many republicans and Bonapartists and that may be why Napoleon did not give him a field command. Napoleon may still have hoped for Berthier's return, but Berthier fell to his death from the window of a castle in Bamberg on 1 June. Whether he was murdered by royalists or by Bonapartists, committed suicide or fell by accident has never been resolved.[10]

Napoleon's other wartime intimate was also unavailable. Louis Bacler d'Albe was a fellow artillerist who had fought with Bonaparte at the siege of Toulon in 1793 and had been by his side ever since, a longer acquaintance even than that with Berthier. Bacler was Napoleon's chief topographer, keeper or maker of his maps. His office at the Tuileries opened onto Napoleon's own room and in the field his tent had always been close to that of the Emperor. They planned campaigns and marches together, employing huge maps spread out on a table with pins with flags stuck into them to mark the current positions of units. Napoleon's private secretary said that on several occasions he had found the pair stretched out on the table in close study of the map as Bacler explained to the Emperor what the terrain would look like. Now in charge of the topographical department in Paris, Bacler had retired from campaigning, exhausted, in 1813. However, his substitute, General Simon Bernard, was himself a very able topographical engineer.

As it once again strove to rid France of Bourbons and drive back invading tyrants, Napoleon's army was encouraged to revive the egalitarian ideas of the Revolution. The negative side of this was the reawakening of a revolutionary mood in which noble officers were not to be trusted and in which priests deserved to be looted. This revival of old revolutionary attitudes seems in part to have underlain the poor disciplinary record of the army which would be revealed during the campaign. Discipline in French armies was usually lax when it came to matters like looting, and in this army it was spectacularly poor.

The positive side was enthusiasm for a cause in which, once again, they were clearly fighting for the freedom of France and a world without kings, feudal rights and rich priests. And to reinforce these ideals, on 1 June Napoleon held the ceremony of the Champ de Mai. A throne was set up against the façade of the Ecole Militaire. A covered room, open at the centre to allow the throne to be seen from the Pont d'Iéna, and equipped with benches for 10,000 people, housed deputations from the regions, the electoral colleges and the representatives of the people. The route from the Tuileries Palace to the Pont d'Iéna and the Champ de Mars was lined with 30,000 Imperial Guards and Parisian National Guards, while 300,000 people stood beyond the human hedge to watch. The sun shone for the great set piece and around 10 a.m. all the officials took their places. The Emperor left the Tuileries at eleven and processed to the throne. The acceptance of the new constitution was announced, a *Te Deum* was sung and a choral mass was celebrated. Then the eagles were blessed and the Emperor took his place on a second, raised throne 200 paces into the Champ de Mars. The colonels of the regiments gathered with the officers of the Imperial and National Guard and they swore their oaths to defend their eagles to the last.

General Claude-Etienne Guyot, commander of the Horse Grenadiers of the Guard and a devoted adherent of the Emperor, was impressed by the good order and calmness in this gathering of innumerable people from every part of France and thought that 'it must prove to our external enemies and might teach our internal ones that they should despair of again changing the form that the Government wishes to adopt and the chief that France has just chosen once more.'[11] The rhetoric of Marshal Soult's order of the day, meanwhile, matched the inspiring grandeur of the spectacle:

What does this new coalition hope for? Does it want to eject France from the ranks of the nations? Does it want to plunge 28 million Frenchmen into servitude? Has it forgotten that the first league to be formed against our independence contributed to our independence and our glory? A hundred striking victories that some temporary setbacks and unfortunate circumstances cannot efface, remind it that a free nation led by a GREAT MAN is invincible. Everyone is a soldier in France when national honour and liberty are at stake.

He promised the army a new career of glory, more striking because the enemy was numerous, but nothing beyond the genius of Napoleon or their strength ... 'Napoleon will guide our steps, we will fight for the independence of our beautiful patrie, we are invincible!'[12]

The Bonapartists were putting a brave face on it. Yet, as he later admitted, even the great man himself was inwardly troubled, his self-confidence dented to the point that he no longer trusted his instinct: 'I no longer had in me the feeling of ultimate success; my early confidence had gone ... I had within me the instinct that things would turn out badly; not that this in any way influenced my decisions or my course of action, to be sure; but I always had that feeling lurking inside me.'[13]

The Emperor said this long afterwards and there is little evidence of such anxiety at the outset of the campaign. As misfortunes began to occur, however, uncertainty would start gnawing into his self-confidence.

7

The Scum of the Earth

One day in late March 1815 the 51st West Riding light infantry were at Portsmouth having breakfast when the bugle-major came in with the post and the newspaper.

> Someone opened it, and glanced his eyes carelessly and coldly over its contents, when suddenly his countenance brightened up, and flinging the newspaper into the air like a madman, he shouted out: 'Glorious news! Nap's landed again in France! Hurrah!' In an instant we were all wild – 'Nap's in France again' spread like wild-fire through the barracks – the men turned out and cheered – nay, that night at mess, the moment the cloth was removed, the President rose and drank success to old Nap with three times three – our joy was unbounded, and few, I believe, went to bed that night sober.

This unexpected news brought back 'all the delights of service, novelty, hopes of promotion, and active service' and flung to the winds 'the frivolous and dissipated life of a peace-soldier, only to be felt by him who has never felt the delights of a war one'. In less than a week the battalion was off to the Netherlands.[1]

Not every officer rejoiced at the prospect of renewed fighting, however, and some had become downright cynical. A lieutenant of the Gordon Highlanders, while admitting that others 'who had friends who could give them an additional hitch up the ladder, or help them to some snug staff situation, were quite delighted on the occasion', recalled that men like himself 'who, during the previous contest, had ascended the ladder of promotion at a pace little swifter than that of the snail, viewed the prospect of another interminable contest with no very agreeable feelings'.[2]

War-weary or keen as mustard, troops were loaded into transports to cross the Channel. The voyage was usually uncomfortable but short. Departure from a relatively distant port like Portsmouth or Cork, combined with adverse winds, could make it much longer and more uncomfortable still, with men hideously seasick for days on end. Assistant surgeon John Haddy James of the Life Guards, a twenty-six-year-old from Exeter, who had qualified as a Member of the Royal College of Surgeons in 1811 in London and then secured an appointment with the Life Guards, 'had not been on board more than three hours when that vile sensation, seasickness, came upon me. Wrapped in my cloak, I lay upon deck, until the spray obliged me to go below.' Another surgeon, William Gibney of the 15th Hussars, whose broad-minded view of Bonaparte was noted earlier, passed his voyage discussing with his senior colleague 'medical subjects and politics; these last leading to an argument for and against the return of Napoleon; my view being that if the French liked to have him as their ruler, they were justified in welcoming his return, and that a Frenchman's view of war and glory altogether differed from ours'.[3]

The troop transports had to be small to get over the sandbar to Ostend. The 16th Light Dragoons embarked, said one eye-witness, in 'small colliers, holding from ten to thirty-five horses each'. Their horses were loose in the hold; others described them as standing on a ballast of beach stones with their backs to the boat's sides and a manger down the centre to which they were tied. The 16th disembarked 'by throwing the horses overboard, and then hauling them ashore by a long rope attached to their head-collars'. Sir George Scovell's groom saw his horses unloaded with swing pulleys, after which the men had to wade out into the water to bring them in. 'Fancy between 20 and 30 ships discharging a similar cargo to the Scipio's, [40 horses] all onto the beach – the luggage thrown in all directions, numbers of horses running loose . . .' But within an hour and a half the sailors had discharged their cargoes and the transports were sailing back for more.[4]

From Ostend the infantry marched a mile to the canal head and embarked in barges for the twelve-mile journey to Bruges, while cavalry rode along the towpath of the canal. Sergeant William Wheeler of the 51st West Riding was a Peninsular veteran who had been with his regiment for six years. Wounded at the end of the campaign, he had recently been promoted to sergeant in an experienced battalion brought to strength with many new faces. Bruges was an attractive city and Wheeler found 'plenty of good grub, gin and tobacco' there, while the Flemish-speaking inhabitants welcomed him and his companions.

On the other side of town they embarked again and more substantial barges took them the twenty-one miles to Ghent, both legs being much longer by land. The large, regular passenger barges were comfortable – 'At either end is a cabin, nicely fitted up. In the middle is a kind of public house; on one side an excellent kitchen, on the other larders and storerooms' – and Wheeler enjoyed his journey: 'On board the boat it more resembled a party of pleasure than soldiers going in search of the enemy, the social glass and song went round 'til midnight, all was mirth and festivity, then sleep put an end to our carousals.'[5]

On the news of Bonaparte's return a British force, resembling as closely as possible Wellington's Peninsular army, gathered in the region of Brussels. In some respects old-fashioned, the British army was organised on significantly different lines from its continental equivalents. British regiments were organised into battalions theoretically containing 1000 men in ten companies of 100 each, but rarely that strong in reality. A regiment had a first battalion supposedly made up of the best soldiers and junior battalions serving at home in support. When sent to serve abroad, senior battalions were brought up to strength by drafts from the second battalion, and junior battalions by drafts from the militia. The core of experienced veterans, like Wheeler, in a battalion quickly knocked the unfamiliar recruits into shape and gave them confidence.

Unlike the conscripted citizen armies of France and Prussia, the British rank and file was composed of men who had volunteered to enlist for a fixed term of years. Whereas for British seamen service in the navy was obligatory in time of war, Britain's small army was a mercenary force of professionals who enlisted for a bounty, a princely sum of up to eighteen guineas paid in advance. This incentive attracted what Wellington called 'the very scum of the earth. People talk of their enlisting from their fine military feeling – all stuff – no such thing. Some of our men enlist from having got bastard children – some for minor offences – many more for drink; but you can hardly conceive such a set brought together, and it is really wonderful that we should have made them the fine set of fellows they are.'[6] There was much truth in the Duke's analysis of his soldiery, but there were also patriotic adventurers of good character in the ranks, and some of these, like Tom Morris, became sergeants – although this was another class of men towards whom Wellington's attitude was ambivalent: 'nothing so intelligent, so valuable as English soldiers of that rank, if you *could get them sober*, which is impossible!'[7]

Indeed, heavy drinking was normal at all levels of the British army. A surgeon wrote with despair of a convalescent patient who had become ill again – and subsequently died – after he 'drank Lord Wellington's health. The extent of this patriotic draught I ascertained to be nearly one pint of brandy and some quarts of strong Brussels beer, swallowed within three hours in an adjacent brothel, where he had passed the night with a most abandoned crew of Belgian prostitutes.' The same surgeon described the typical arrival of a wounded British soldier at hospital: 'They too often come either furious or stupid from intoxication, totally bereft of their necessaries, or with such masses of rags as serve only for fomites of contagion, and often with a female attendant, whose appearance and behaviour are more those of an infuriated bacchanal than a nurse.'[8]

Soldiers were badly paid and subject to a discipline enforced by corporal punishment that made the floggings inflicted in the navy look gentle. Where 24 lashes was theoretically the legal maximum at sea, the maximum on land was 1200 lashes, and 200 lashes was a commonplace punishment for a minor offence. The official defence, maintained by senior army officers for decades, was that 'the British Army is raised by voluntary enlistment for bounty, and its ranks are thus unavoidably filled by men of dissipated habits, requiring great restraint, and the enforcement of a very strict discipline.'[9]

Service in the lower ranks of the armed forces tended, therefore, as Wellington said, to appeal to desperate men from very poor rural areas or those who had a very good reason to disappear from local society. Usually, between 20 and 40 per cent of men in English infantry regiments were Irish and the army also contained a high percentage of Scots.[10] Lifeguardsman Thomas Playford, a big, handsome Yorkshire lad, left his south Yorkshire village to join the army at fifteen after getting his schoolmistress pregnant.[11] Some of these people turned out well in the rough but comradely society in which they found themselves and grew to like the life.

Officers came from a different class and there was a social chasm between them and their men. There was no prospect of promotion to motivate British soldiers: talent might get you as far as sergeant-major, but commissions had to be bought. 'When I joined the army,' wrote Sergeant Tom Morris, 'I was foolish enough to imagine that by steady good conduct, or some daring act of bravery, I should be fortunate enough to gain a commission; but I very soon discovered the fallacy of this expectation. I certainly have known two or three instances in which commissions have been bestowed as the reward of merit; but such cases are "like angel's visits, few and far between".'[12]

Both commissions and the equipment an officer needed after obtaining one were so expensive that a career as an officer was only open to the wealthier classes and influence tended to limit entry to a circumscribed elite. Most officers came from the landed gentry, often again Irish or Scottish, while officers of the Guards were sometimes titled aristocrats. Some officers took their profession very seriously; others did not. The hard experience of a few years of campaigning was usually required to sort the wheat from the chaff, and this made veteran British units a great deal better than raw ones. Not only had they learned to live and fight as soldiers, but they had usually shed those who one way or another did not pull their weight.

*

As the troops came in, so also Wellington's people began to arrive. The two principal staff departments were those of the Adjutant-General, dealing with discipline, arms, ammunition and clothing, and the Quartermaster-General, responsible for movement, quartering, encampment, deployment and equipment. The third department was the commissariat, whose business was to procure and supply food and forage and to provide transport. As Adjutant-General, Wellington got Sir Edward Barnes, who had served on his staff in the Peninsula and had commanded a regiment before that. As Quartermaster-General, he inherited Sir Hudson Lowe, but he quickly made it plain that he wanted his own man.[13] He first demanded Sir George Murray, his right-hand man in the Peninsula, but Murray was in America and had not yet received his orders to sail to Belgium. Meanwhile, therefore, he took Murray's deputy, the newly married Sir William Delancey, who arrived at Brussels in late May and, as it turned out, had little more than a fortnight in which to find his feet.

Nor was Wellington allowed the services of his trusted cavalry commander. Stapleton Cotton, who was reliable rather than brilliant, was not appointed to Wellington's army. Instead, as second-in-command and cavalry leader he was given the forty-seven-year-old Henry Paget, Earl of Uxbridge, who was brilliant rather than reliable. Uxbridge had commanded the cavalry in Spain under Sir John Moore in 1808, but had then run off with the wife of Wellington's brother Henry, making him *persona non grata* with the Wellesley clan, and he had not served with Wellington since. This meant that Uxbridge lacked battlefield experience, but he was highly regarded and new colleagues generally liked working with the flamboyant officer who wore the uniform of his favourite 7th Hussars. Sir Augustus Frazer, the capable and experienced commander of Wellington's horse artillery since 1813, found Uxbridge agreeably 'quiet in business and very decided; this is the true way to do much in a little time'. According to Surgeon Gibney of the 15th Hussars, usually a critical witness, 'it was a universal opinion that his lordship was the first cavalry general in the British army.'[14]

Rowland, Lord Hill, aged forty-two, commanding II Corps, had been one of Wellington's generals throughout the Peninsular campaign and, latterly, his second-in-command. In contrast to the Duke, he was loved by the troops, who called him 'Daddy Hill', reflecting his well-deserved reputation for kindness and generosity to his men. His admiring aide jotted in his journal that when Hill was ennobled in 1814 he 'ought to have taken the title of Lord *Mountain* because he is a *great hill*'.[15]

During May twelve crack battalions of veteran Peninsular infantry arrived. Reaching Brussels on 12 May, the first battalion of the 95th Rifles found the French-speaking inhabitants much less friendly than the Flemings; one of their number recalled 'crowds of natives who were gaping and staring at us. I heard no Vivas, they appeared to treat the whole concern very coolly indeed.'[16] The Highland Brigade united at Ghent in mid-May and marched to Brussels on the 28th.

Two of the three Highland battalions, along with other veterans, should have been on their way to fight the Yankees, but had been delayed by bad weather. The 28th North Gloucesters had embarked at Cork for America in January but adverse winds held them there until mid-March, and when they finally sailed, a storm drove them back to harbour the same night. Learning that the war against the United States was over, they marched to Northern Ireland where they heard of Bonaparte's return and left for Dublin to embark for England. On 10 May they anchored in the Downs, trans-shipped to transports and sailed to Ostend. Having spent a week at Ghent, they arrived at Brussels on 26 May. Had they all sailed for America in January they might never have made it back in time, and Wellington would have been in a sad plight.

By June Wellington had four battalions of Foot Guards, twenty of line infantry, three light and three rifle battalions, and eight of the King's German Legion, including two of riflemen. Of these, only four line battalions were seriously inexperienced, while eighteen of the British battalions and all of the German had seen years of proper campaigning.

Cavalry had also trickled in from early April to reinforce the crack squadrons of the King's German Legion. The German squadrons were large, well disciplined, highly experienced and trusted even by

Wellington: the 1st Hussars was regarded as the best cavalry in the army (although they had been brought to strength with former Westphalian soldiers and forty of these had deserted between March and May).[17] The others were of mixed quality: the Royal Dragoons and four of the five regiments of light dragoons were highly experienced, the four Hussar regiments less so. Dressed in spectacular uniforms and known as the 'Glory boys' or 'Wellington's darlings', the Hussars were a racy lot, favoured by Lord Uxbridge who regarded himself as one of them.[18] The Household Cavalry had seen little active service, while the King's Dragoon Guards, the Scots Greys and the Inniskilling Dragoons were complete novices, the Greys having only one officer who had ever campaigned.

The horse artillery arrived from Britain troop by troop and was gradually re-equipped with more powerful 9-pounder guns. There were new British guns for the Hanoverian troops, too, though the problem there was finding enough men and horses to pull them, as the heavier artillery required eight horses instead of six.[19] By June the horse artillery had five troops with 9-pounders, three with 6-pounders, one specialist howitzer battery and one troop armed with 12-pounder Congreve rockets.

Rockets were a British secret weapon, one they had stolen from Indian enemies. After admiring their use by Hyder Ali and Tipoo Sultan, William Congreve researched the technology. Small numbers had been employed in America and at Leipzig. They were, however, still at an experimental stage and Wellington barely tolerated their presence on the battlefield, considering them as dangerous to friend as to foe. When he told the artillery commander, Sir George Wood, that Captain Whinyates's rocket troop must deploy with 6-pounder guns, Wood replied that this would break Whinyates's heart. 'Damn his heart, sir,' insisted the Duke; 'let my order be obeyed.'[20]

In battle, the horse artillery was under the orders of the cavalry commander, but Wood also controlled ten companies of British and Hanoverian foot artillery with 9-pounders and two with 18-pounders, though in June the latter were still struggling to find enough horses and drivers. Wellington had amassed 132 British and Hanoverian guns, excluding the siege train.

Other promised reinforcements appeared too. It was natural that Friedrich Wilhelm, Duke of Brunswick should fight with the British, since his mother was George III's sister and his own sister Caroline was married (very unhappily) to George III's son the Prince Regent. Friedrich Wilhelm had been a Prussian officer from 1789 until his father was mortally wounded commanding the Prussian army at Jena. He then inherited Brunswick because his eldest brother was dead and the next two were mentally retarded, but the French took his duchy from him and made it part of Westphalia. In 1809 he raised a corps to fight with the Austrians and dressed them in black to signify mourning for his dead father and lost duchy. His Black Legion of Vengeance and Death refused to surrender after the Austrian defeat at Wagram and, joined by Wilhelm von Dörnberg, who had led a failed rising in Westphalia, they marched north, briefly liberating Brunswick before marching to the coast, seizing ships and sailing to British Heligoland. Friedrich took his corps to fight for the British in Portugal and Spain, while many of his other male subjects died fighting for the French in Spain and in Russia. The Duke was popular and highly regarded as a soldier and a freedom fighter.

With the exception of a couple of experienced elite battalions, the corps of 6000 infantry, 1000 cavalry and 16 guns that Brunswick brought to Brussels from 15 May was composed of very young men – mere boys – as various British soldiers noted, although they were animated with fierce patriotism and their dedicated Duke trained them hard. One day in May a touring British officer was alarmed to see riflemen posted and on the alert near his road; he thought the fighting must have started, since he could hear shots in the woods. But a sergeant told him that the troops he could see were Brunswickers and that, being inexperienced, the Duke made them behave as if at war, with sentries and outposts set; the firing 'proceeded from a party practising with their rifles at targets cut in the shape of, and painted to resemble, French soldiers'.[21] Many Brunswick officers had also seen years of campaigning with the Duke, so the new recruits slotted into an established structure.

Last to arrive – they did not reach Brussels until June – were very inexperienced contingents of nearly 3000 young soldiers from the

Wiesbaden area on the Rhine sent by the Duke of Nassau under General August von Kruse, and a second battalion of Orange-Nassauers from Dillenburg. When added to the Nassovian regiments already with the Netherlands army they took the contingent from the mid-Rhineland and Hesse to over 7000 men.

A wet spring turned to a wet early summer, with a bewildering alternation of hot sun and torrential downpours, but despite repeated rumours and alarms Napoleon didn't attack, and day by day Wellington became stronger, more confident and better prepared. By early June his army may not have been 'the most complete machine for its numbers now existing in Europe', as he had dubbed his Peninsular force, but it was no longer the 'infamous' army of early May, however much the Duke might continue to bemoan its inadequacies. The solid British and Hanoverian component at the core of it was very well equipped and for the most part battle-hardened. The other German and Netherlands troops looked fragile, but they were to prove more determined than their sceptical British colleagues expected.

Defensively, Wellington was confident, almost complacent. Between them the allies had nearly 220,000 men and 500 guns, far more than Napoleon could deploy against them, and enough not only to defeat but probably to deter any attack. It was now just a case of waiting for the Austrians and Russians to be ready before launching an invasion of France.

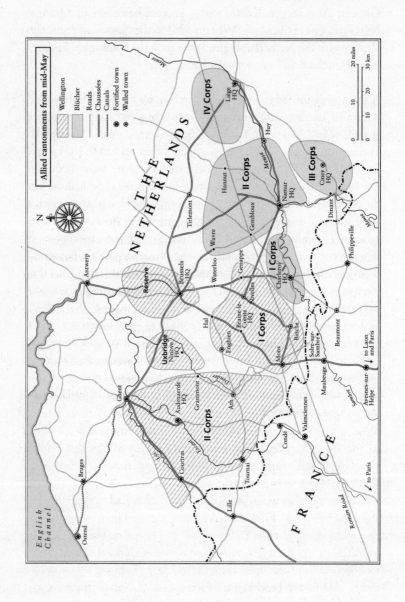

8

Intelligence

In the spring of 1815, acquiring intelligence about the enemy's intentions was not straightforward. Once war had been declared generals would send cavalry patrols into enemy territory to probe defences and seize prisoners for interrogation, but in this case there had been no declaration of war. With France and the Netherlands at peace, visitors to France required a passport and cavalry patrols that strayed over the border were ushered gently home to their lodgings.

Before an army began a campaign its troops were billeted over areas in which they could be fed and housed conveniently. The position of these 'cantonments' was a compromise between strategic and logistical considerations. Cavalry and horse artillery required abundant supplies of fresh grass or hay – forage – for their horses, so Wellington's were scattered around the villages in the lush meadows of the Dender valley about twenty miles west of Brussels. There, they bought their supplies from the local population and lodged with them in their houses and barns.

While the allies waited to attack France they had to guard against the possibility that France would attack them. Their armies had to defend roughly 150 miles of frontier from Ostend on the sea to Liège in the east. Only for a few miles was the border defined by a river barrier; generally it was open but protected by chains of fortresses on either side of the border, until to the east of Namur the hills and forests of the Ardennes prevented fast movement by invading armies.

Wellington's troops were disposed to resist a variety of possible French attacks. The general had to guard against a march aimed at severing his communications with the sea at Ostend and Antwerp, and he was especially anxious about a move from Lille to seize Ghent, forty miles to its north-east, to cut the British supply line to Antwerp and sweep down on Brussels from the rear. Napoleon had pulled off such bold moves in the past and some such sudden swoop might make Wellington look as foolish as the Austrian General Mack had at Ulm in 1805, when an Austrian army subsidised by Britain surrendered without even fighting, mesmerised by the speed of French manoeuvre.

To counter such a strike he posted his trusted lieutenant Rowland Hill behind the fortress city of Tournai, on the border opposite Lille, with II Corps. I Corps under the Prince of Orange was placed with its headquarters at Braine-le-Comte, about twenty miles south-west of the capital, to block the most direct route from Paris via the French fortress towns of Valenciennes or Maubeuge to Brussels through the Belgian fortified city of Mons. The reserve was in Brussels itself, where the officers and staff rented houses or rooms. As a consequence of these combined considerations, Wellington's men were spread over an area fifty miles wide and fifty miles deep.

The Prussians were in a similar situation, guarding a long stretch of border territory to the east of Wellington, with their troops widely distributed to put less pressure on the resources of the local population. The distance from the westernmost Prussian post at the walled town of Binche near Mons to the eastern headquarters at the city of Liège was seventy-four miles. Ludwig Nagel's Lützow Freikorps had been placed in advance of the main defence line fifteen miles south of Namur near Dinant on a picturesque stretch of the Meuse, where Nagel enjoyed walking on the wooded cliffs over the river and dining in a medieval castle perched on an island.

To discover the enemy's intentions both sides relied on travellers, deserters and spies. The Duke of Wellington believed his espionage was good. Henri Clarke, duc de Feltre, who had been Minister of War for Napoleon and then for Louis XVIII, had provided the order of battle for the French army in March as well as a stream of information sent by 'a person of the War Office, upon whom he could depend'. On 16 May Wellington passed on to the Dutch and Prussians an updated account of the strength and disposition of the French army corps as at the beginning of May.[1] Further reports emanated from the French king's brother, the comte d'Artois, who controlled what was thought to be a reliable organisation of royalist agents. Finally, Napoleon's magnificently duplicitous Minister of Police, Joseph Fouché, duc d'Otranto, claimed in his memoirs to have been in contact with the Duke and to have promised Wellington advance warning of any attack by Napoleon, together with his plan of campaign. After their publication doubt was cast on the authenticity of Fouché's memoirs, but current opinion is that they are genuine. Although he was well aware that both Fouché and Napoleon wove webs of trickery and deception, Wellington put great faith in his Parisian sources.

During April and May Wellington even entertained high hopes that Bonaparte would be assassinated by republicans during the Champ de Mai 'and that Bonaparte and his reign would both be put an end to on that day'. Insight into a republican plot might well have come from the old Jacobin Fouché. When nothing happened Wellington laughed it off in public, but the British ambassador said of him that 'I never saw a fellow so cut down in my life than he was in the morning when he first heard the news.'[2]

It was not until 22 April, however, that the outgoing chief of staff, Sir Hudson Lowe, first established an intelligence branch, with Wellington asking a week later for Colquhoun Grant to be 'head of the Intelligence department'. During the Peninsular War, Grant, wearing uniform to avoid being shot as a spy, had gone deep into Spain, penetrating French lines, and had been hugely successful at gathering news of enemy deployments and intentions. Wellington also demanded Sir George Scovell, the cipher specialist who had broken the French codes in the Peninsula, to be 'at the head of the Department of Military Communications'.[3] They did not arrive until the end of May, so neither of these experienced experts had time to find their feet before the campaign opened and there is little evidence of their activities.

It has been said that Grant recruited a man and a woman as spies and sent them into Paris, and that he himself took up station 'in advance of the British outposts', but there is no evidence that Grant really crossed the border into France. He is mentioned only twice in Wellington's papers. First, on a list obtained on 25 May of the troops commanded by Napoleon's general Honoré Reille, is an instruction to 'communicate this to Colonel Grant and let him take an account of the corps in Reille's army, their strength, commanding officers, & c. Wellington', which Wellington was unlikely to have written had Grant been under cover in France; second is an incomplete and fairly inaccurate attempt at a detailed French order of battle, signed by Grant and dated Brussels 7 June, indicating that a week before the campaign opened Grant was at headquarters, which was indeed the proper place for a head of intelligence.[4] In any case, Scovell and Grant's main efforts were presumably directed towards planning the coming invasion of France.

Fortunately, arrangements for intelligence gathering had been made before Wellington arrived and refined after the Prussians moved closer. The allied intelligence centre was at Mons, close to the border, astride the principal route from Paris to Brussels, whence reports were sent to Wellington's secretary Fitzroy Somerset in Brussels, via the Dutch headquarters at Braine-le-Comte, about halfway between Mons and Brussels. Significant messages also passed east and west along a chain of forward headquarters linking Mons with Hans von Ziethen's Prussian I Corps headquarters at Charleroi, twenty-three miles east of Mons and thirty miles south of Brussels. There was a French royalist officer at each military post whose job was to debrief deserters from the French army and interrogate any other Frenchmen crossing to the King.[5]

The man gathering information on enemy activity was Wilhelm von Dörnberg. Dörnberg was fluent in French, English and German and that in itself set him apart, for nobody on Wellington's staff spoke German well enough to read Blücher's letters; this obliged Blücher to write in French, a language in which he was not entirely comfortable.[6] A nobleman from Hesse-Kassel, Dörnberg was a highly experienced soldier and spy, a famous champion of German patriotism, and a tried and trusted friend of Gneisenau, Blücher and Brunswick. An outstanding personality who helped to bond the allies and kept his post after Wellington arrived, he also commanded a brigade of light dragoons, and had orders to leave Mons and join it should Napoleon attack.[7]

Dörnberg established a network of travellers and smugglers who gleaned information for him as they passed through French towns, and he received frequent bulletins from French deserters and other French visitors to Mons. At first his informants told him that there was nothing to fear, but at the end of April trouble seemed to be brewing; there were alarming reports of large troop movements from both east and west producing a huge concentration of troops around the French border fortresses of Maubeuge and Valenciennes, facing Mons and little more than fifty miles south-west of Brussels. The French had closed the border, and Bonaparte's arrival was rumoured to be imminent.[8]

Bonaparte's movements were crucial because it was taken for granted that he would lead any attack in person. So long as he and his Imperial Guard remained at Paris, French deployments were probably defensive. Conversely, any movement of the Guard was to be noted because it was certain that it would take part in any offensive. By 9 May strong French forces appeared to have gathered close to the border either side of Mons.

Wellington was undismayed. 'I am inclined to believe that Blücher and I are so well united, and so strong, that the enemy cannot do us much mischief,' he wrote on 8 May to the ambassador to Vienna. Nevertheless, the following day he admitted to General Rowland Hill, commander of his army's II Corps, that 'matters look a little serious upon the frontier', while the Prince of Orange, commanding I Corps, investigated possible defensive positions covering a French attack to the east of Mons, reporting that the high ground above the town of Nivelles, a few miles east of his headquarters, looked suitable. Wellington warned the Prussians of the danger, and in response Blücher moved his headquarters westward to Namur, while Karl von Müffling joined Wellington's staff as liaison officer.[9] Müffling did a good job of representing the Prussian point of view to Wellington and the British point of view to the Prussians, and Wellington came to value him highly: 'There is no person who, in his situation, has done more to forward the objects of the operations,' he wrote to Blücher in July.[10]

The crisis soon subsided as the British and Prussian staff concluded that the French troops to the east of Maubeuge were engaged in defensive measures. They were breaking down bridges, making roadblocks with trees, cutting trenches and generally obstructing the roads into France from Ziethen's headquarters at Charleroi. According to Felton Hervey, a long-serving aide to Wellington who had lost an arm at the battle of the Douro in 1809, this 'gave rise to the idea that they would never advance in that direction'. In fact the French concentration was probably a rehearsal, covered by a calculated and successful subterfuge, for this was exactly where Napoleon eventually attacked.[11]

Many of the reports Dörnberg received were equally inaccurate. Most derived from confused sources but some were planted by Bonaparte.[12] The most insidious and effective disinformation arrived on 6 June via an agent sent to Paris by the French royalist representative at Mons. The agent had gazed with admiration at the spectacle of the Champ de Mai; he thought the Emperor would leave Paris on 6 June; he had seen a lot of troops and vehicles and had spoken to some people from the military movement section of the *Quartier Général* who had told him that the Emperor would go to Avesnes, a few miles south of Maubeuge, from where he would stage a false attack on the Allies while the real attack was launched from the Lille area, forty miles further west. This news chimed with reports reaching Dörnberg to the effect that 'Buonaparte ... will certainly attack as soon as possible; and he has said himself he would have destroyed the Allies before the Russian army could arrive. It is supposed he would make a false attack on the Prussians and a real one on the English.'[13] These carefully laid false trails help to explain why when Napoleon did attack the Prussians, the British expected the thrust to be a mere decoy and waited for the real attack on them to follow.

Nevertheless, there was no concealing from the outposts a picture of a French army once again gathering on the border opposite Mons.

On 5 June the commander of the cavalry outposts at Tournai, about twenty-five miles west of Mons, told his general, Lord Hill, that the French outpost line opposite them had been abandoned and the troops had marched eastward to Maubeuge. Ziethen, commanding the Prussian front-line forces to the east, sent news that the French IV Corps had marched into his area. A British artillery officer wrote to his wife on 8 June, telling her that the newspapers said that Bonaparte 'intends to be with the army on the 15th'. Over the next few days Dörnberg made frantic attempts to establish whether Napoleon had arrived at the frontier. He had sent a spy south to Laon in France, halfway to Paris, to watch for Napoleon's arrival, although he was afraid that three other spies he had put in place might have been arrested.[14]

The commander of the outposts just to the east of Mons, Jean-Baptiste van Merlen, was one of those Belgian officers with extensive experience in the French army that Wellington so distrusted – he had been colonel of the Red Lancers of the Imperial Guard and his younger brother was in the French army. Merlen believed that Napoleon was already present and expected an attack any day. Ziethen was equally convinced that he was not and that the French were still behaving defensively, since they were still digging up roads. Dörnberg later claimed that on about 8 June a soldier from the office of General Bertrand, the head of Napoleon's *Maison Civile*, brought a warning that the French would launch an offensive in eight to ten days' time and that Napoleon's plan was to attack on a line between the British and Prussian armies, although if Dörnberg passed this information to Wellington his report is no longer in the Wellington papers.[15]

For the French, intelligence was easier to gather because the allied armies were essentially static. A branch of Soult's *Grand Quartier Général* was devoted to intelligence and the Emperor's *Maison Militaire*, his personal staff, also included a *Bureau de Renseignements* (intelligence department) which claimed to have good sources of information within the Belgian army.[16] The English newspapers too provided fairly accurate news from the front, while Napoleon also had spies on the enemy side of the border to tell him where the allied armies were deployed: on 12 May one had been arrested in the cantonments of the British 69th Regiment.

And the Emperor was now considering where to strike. A move from Lille or Condé in the western sector against Louis XVIII in Ghent was appealing as it would cut the British supply lines to Ostend on the coast, while even though the enemy had strengthened the border fortresses, Napoleon could bypass them. The main draw-back of this course was that even if he took Brussels he would thereby roll the Anglo-German-Dutch army eastward onto its Prussian allies. An attack on the Prussians via the valley of the Meuse which led to Namur in the eastern sector was less attractive, since it would simply drive the Prussians into the arms of the British before Napoleon even reached Brussels. The place to strike was where the two armies joined on the line from Charleroi to Brussels. That way Napoleon could roll back the Prussians towards Germany and the British in the opposite direction, towards the sea, while heading straight for the Belgian capital, only thirty miles away.

The results of such an attack would become clear as it developed but it offered a variety of attractive possibilities. Both enemy armies were so spread out that with any luck a sudden attack might not only allow Bonaparte to eliminate first one army and then the other, but even to destroy them corps by corps. He decided to aim at the Prussians, knowing that their army was spaced out along its line of communication with Germany, and that Ziethen's corps was exposed close to the border around Charleroi. He would march eastward from his position opposite the British and attack Charleroi, using the river Sambre to protect his left flank against any possible intervention by Wellington. He hoped to crush Ziethen and send the Prussians rolling back eastward to Liège before they even concentrated their forces. Failing that, if the Prussians succeeded in concentrating an army close enough to Ziethen to support him before he was destroyed, Napoleon hoped to fight a decisive battle against them and then to advance on Brussels.

Napoleon sent Soult north on 7 June with orders to find out all he could about the enemy's deployment, to set up an espionage office at

Lille, and to put together a company of men familiar with the roads in Belgium. At the same time he sent his own aide, Charles de la Bédoyère, into Belgium to make a final check that the British and Prussians were still calmly waiting in their cantonments to launch their invasion of France. La Bédoyère spent the days between 7 and 12 June touring the villages and towns where the Anglo-Dutch army was living. He was in Brussels when Wellington held another magnificent ball on 8 June, and reported to Napoleon at Avesnes that Wellington thought an invasion possible but improbable, especially not immediately. The British and Prussian cantonments remained widespread. They were too extended and it was perfectly possible to cut between the two armies.[17] The Emperor's plan seemed to be falling into place.

9

Waiting for the Invasion of France

Wellington's army was happy enough in its cantonments, sheltered from the torrential rain that pelted down on Belgium that spring. British commissaries bought fresh food and forage locally, paying with Treasury bonds, which could be redeemed after a set delay, or converted immediately into a smaller sum of cash (thus enabling the commissaries to make fortunes). As a semi-literate trooper of the King's Dragoon Guards explained, rations were tolerable but they did not always arrive: 'hour alounse Per Day is One Pound of Beef a Pound and half of Bred half a Pint o Gin But the worst of all we dont get it Regeler and If we dont get it the Day it is due we Luse it wish It is ofton the Case i asure you.' The soldiers spent their pay on tobacco and more gin – the latter, they were delighted to find, cost only 10d. a quart in the Netherlands – while officers bought champagne for only 4s. a bottle. Sergeant William Wheeler of the Yorkshire light infantry was one of many soldiers who handed over their rations to their hosts, who provided generous hospitality in return:

> The people are remarkably kind to us. I with one man are quartered at a tobacconists, so we do not want for that article, we eat and drink with the landlord and family, coffee stands ready for use

all day long, when we get our rations we give it to the Mistress of the house, except our gin, this we takes care of ourselves. We never see a bit of the bread after, if the meat should be good, it is cooked, if not, it is given with the bread to the beggars.[1]

Officers were also generously treated by their hosts. The tall, slim, blond Christian von Ompteda was placed with the Count and Countess van der Burcht at the Château d'Ecaussines, with his old comrades in arms Carl von Alten and Colin Halkett. Alten, aged fifty, a man with chiselled features and piercing eyes, had commanded the German Light Brigade in the Peninsula from 1808 until 1812, when Wellington promoted him to command the British Light Division, an enormous compliment since he was the only foreigner Wellington allowed to command British troops. His brigadiers, Ompteda and Halkett, had both commanded German Legion light regiments. Ompteda was another dedicated German freedom fighter, a personal friend of Gneisenau and Scharnhorst, and a sensitive soul who shared with Goethe's Werther a passionate, requited, but hopeless love for a woman who unfortunately was married to somebody else. Ompteda's aide was utterly charmed by the Countess van der Burcht and remembered his stay there as one of the most agreeable periods of his life.[2]

Inevitably, women were a preoccupation for the young soldiers, who naturally made friendships wherever they were billeted. Wheeler noted that:

There are some very pretty young women here, some of them are got very much attached to our men, and I doubt not when we move there will be an augmentation in the number of women. I must here observe that your humble servant does not intend to get entangled with any of them. It might be all very fine in its way and no doubt there are many sweets in having a pretty lovely young woman for a comrade, but then, I know from observation that there is an infinite number of bitters attending it, a soldier should always be able to say when his cap is on, his family is covered, then he is free as air.

In May Tom Morris was billeted on the miller of a little village and he and a mate spent many hours strolling with the miller's young daughters through the meadows. 'One of the girls was much attached to my comrade, and would not have needed much persuasion to become his wife.'[3]

Morris's fellow sergeant Burton had brought his wife with him. About five or six wives were officially permitted to follow each company, although some regiments allowed more. This meant fifty or sixty to a battalion, so four thousand or so with the army, and more women followed the army unofficially. And they shared most of the hardships of their men; Sergeant David Robertson of the Gordon Highlanders was a Scot from the Duke of Atholl's estates, five foot nine tall, blond and grey-eyed. He was brought up to be a shoemaker but in troubled times he volunteered, transferring to the Gordons in time to fight in Egypt in 1801. He went to Spain in 1808 and fought under Wellington thereafter. Robertson lost his wife in 1814 when, having given birth to a daughter in the snowy pass of Roncesvalles in the Pyrenees in midwinter, she was shot through the heart in a skirmish during their advance into southern France. His journal never explained whether his wife was Scottish or Iberian, nor did it mention the fate of his child, but it dwelt on the moment when, at the regiment's departure for home, it was decided 'that all the women who had followed the army from Portugal and Spain, should return with the troops belonging to the respective countries, whether married or not, as none of them would be allowed to embark for England'.[4]

For those who didn't find a willing local girl, there were

> most excellent pieces to be had at Brussels, Ghent and other large towns at regular licensed bawdy houses, indeed some of the French girls are beautiful and their action surpasses anything I have before met with at Drury Lane or Covent Garden. When you enter one of these houses you are ushered into a room adapted for the purpose and immediately 10 or 12 girls present themselves so that any one that may be a good judge of that species of biped may have an opportunity of selecting a capital goer. All the girls are examined

three or four times a week by a surgeon and before I was allowed
to perform, the girl just examined his worship.[5]

The end of May saw a series of reviews and dinners as formations
reached completion. On 19 May Sir Augustus Frazer, commander of
Wellington's horse artillery – ultimately he had eight troops of British
and two of German gunners – gave a dinner to all the British and
German horse artillery officers under his command. Three days later
a review took place of the Duke of Brunswick's Black Legion of
Vengeance and Death, 'all cloathed in Black, with deaths heads and
Horses tails on their Caps', including 'two squadrons of lancers in the
Polish costume'. It rained hard all day and the corps was sadly
bedraggled by the end of the parade.[6] On 24 May Uxbridge reviewed
the heavy cavalry and the next day the hussars. It continued to rain,
with at least a shower almost every day in the second half of May.
Officers rode around holding umbrellas.

On 27 May the Duke held a ball at his house in the highest and
most fashionable area of town, on the corner of the park and the Rue
Royale, in honour of the visiting Prince Blücher. The guests walked
through illuminated gardens to be greeted by Wellington at the door.
Dancing took place on the ground floor while the apartments on the
first floor were laid out for a magnificent supper. General Hill's aide
remarked that:

> The Duke himself danced, and always with the same person, a Lady
> Caroline [*sic*: Frances] Webster, to whom he paid so much attention
> that scandal, who is become goddess here, began to whisper all sorts
> of stories, but we are not bound to believe all she says; not but that
> the well-known bad private character of His Grace would warrant
> any suspicions whatever. There must have been something essen-
> tially bad in the education of the Wellesley family: on the score of
> gallantry not one of its members, male or female, is *sans reproche*.
> When the Duke of Wellington, after Lord Uxbridge's appointment
> to the command of the British cavalry, was asked whether he would
> not feel it unpleasant to meet with the man who had run off with his
> sister? 'Why?' said he, 'Damn him, he won't run off with me too.'[7]

The Duke spent a great deal of time with the attractive Lady Frances, whose husband had given her ample reason to seek solace elsewhere. On another occasion Basil Jackson of the Staff Corps saw them in the park, disappearing into the bushes together. She had a taste for dangerous celebrities: the poet Lord Byron had 'dallied with' but then 'spared' her in 1813. Lady Frances was pregnant, but that doesn't seem to have impeded her social life or Wellington's affection for her. Wellington's own womanising was notorious, and he had a marked taste for those whose behaviour other women considered scandalous, as Caroline Capel wrote to her mother in June:

> The Duke of W— has not improved the *morality* of our Society, as he has given several things and makes a point of asking all the Ladies of Loose Character. Everyone was surprised at seeing Lady John Campbell at his House, and one of his Staff told me that it had been represented to him her not bein [*sic*] received for that her Character was more than suspicious.
>
> 'Is it, by—,' said he, 'then I will go and ask her Myself. On which he immediately took his Hat and went out for the purpose.[8]

Two days after his ball, the Duke reviewed the British cavalry and horse artillery. The Welshman Thomas Jeremiah was employed filling in holes and levelling hillocks in the meadow by the river Dender in which the review took place. For once, the weather was fine, and his battalion watched as 'about from 10 to 11 o'clock the troops were streaming from every direction until by ½ past 11 the plains seemed literally choked up, by ¼ to 12 the whole of the artillery and cavalry were drawn up in three lines which extended nearly an English mile'. The first line was composed of hussars in flashy uniforms; the second consisted of the two brigades of heavy cavalry, big men on big horses, blacks for the Horse Guards and Life Guards, whites for the Scots Greys. The Greys belonged to the Union Brigade, so called because one of its regiments was Scottish, one Irish and one English. The third line was light dragoons, and together they amounted to about five thousand men. The horse artillery was posted at intervals between the lines.[9]

The men, dismounted, were brushing the last dust off their finery when the Duke and his huge cortège, including Blücher who had arrived the previous night for another summit meeting, came galloping down the hill. Jeremiah remembered how people had been talking and greeting old friends and relations in other regiments when 'all of a sudden we could see a dense column of smoke and dust ... the advanced squadrons of Prince Blucher's Cossacks entered the area followed closely by all the Allied generals and a large concourse of people'.[10]

Jeremiah caught the mood as 'the British trumpet sounded to prepare to mount, in a moment all was silent as the grave, not a word; we could hear a pin fall when in an instant 18 thousand men [*sic*] were in their saddles and steady.' A cavalry officer wrote that 'the Duke was accompanied by the Hereditary Prince of Orange, & his brother; the Duke de Berri, Marshal Blucher, and an immence [*sic*] train of big wigs, & staff people. The heat of the day was very great, not a cloud in the sky, or a breath of air stirring, all of which added to the brilliancy & beauty of the scene though it roasted us all to death.' The 'big wigs' rode along the lines and then the cavalry 'marched past by half squadrons and filed to our quarters where we did not arrive till between 7 & 8 in the evening. It being King Charles's Restoration day all the troops wore a sprig of oak in their caps which had a very good effect as we had no feathers with us.'[11] One of the 'staff people' overheard Blücher compliment Wellington on his horsemen, 'When the English cavalry gets to Paris each soldier must make a child in order to regenerate France.'[12] Afterwards, the cavalry commander Lord Uxbridge invited all his commanding officers to meet his illustrious guests at dinner in the monastery at Ninove.

Meanwhile, more serious business proceeded. Blücher's new representative on Wellington's staff, Karl von Müffling, laid out the Prussian agenda for Blücher's summit meeting with Wellington. The Prussians were almost ready, and eager to start fighting: 'The first four corps of the Prussian Army will be up to full strength in a few days. Indeed, they will be stronger than required by treaty. As the Belgians are causing us so many problems with supplies, it would be desirable to commence the war as soon as possible. Would your

Grace kindly give me his opinion as to when this would be likely?'[13]

Blücher was under pressure to obtain a quick resolution. His government, close to bankruptcy, could not afford a long war, and his militiamen wanted to get back in time for the harvest. In addition, the promised supplies at the expense of the king of the Netherlands had not always been forthcoming and relations between the Prussians and the local population were deteriorating. Gneisenau complained to his friend Dörnberg that the Dutch king's 'hostility to the Prussians causes ill will towards us, not to speak of his minister with his background in administering for the French and his sympathy towards them. Day by day, relations are getting more bitter. The delays in opening hostilities are causing more harm than a defeat.'[14] Wellington tried to mediate, but the king of the Netherlands was equally anxious to start in order to get rid of the Prussians. Wellington himself was still waiting for reinforcements of seasoned troops and personnel under orders to join him from America and did not want to attack until the Austrians were ready. However, when Blücher dined with him on 28 May and reiterated his desire to recover his old pipe from Paris, Wellington agreed, reluctantly, that they could take the offensive on 1 July.

The decision made no difference to army life in Belgium. A few days later, the hussars held a race meeting at Ninove. The racing was halted by yet another downpour, but the Mayor provided 'an excellent cold dinner, liberally lubricated with champagne'. As one of the 18th Hussar officers dimly recalled, they then behaved like true English heroes:

> Two hours sufficed the company to eat and get slaughtered together: I believe I remember that a bad boy from the 10th Hussars, standing on one of the tables, began to use a large stick to break all the crockery, all the bottles and all the glasses; that the remainder of the company took part in this facetious entertainment, and that, throwing themselves onto their horses, they returned to the racecourse, half of them falling off on the way, and many of the horses galloping to the stables without their riders. The most drunk hurtled off in a race to the bell

tower, across the fields, at night, and gave the peasants some idea of the independent-mindedness of the English hussars by shouting through the village streets 'Long live Napoleon!' Finally – and I must not forget to mention the fact, because this thing happened or I was dreaming – they pushed over two carriages and terrified the ladies who were in them into fits of nerves, while charging their husbands and chaperones in the true Cossack manner.

The following day they got the bill: 979 francs for wine, 730 for food and 90 for service, amounting to a charge of 50 francs for each officer of the brigade. A number of complaints had been made to the general, and they expected that they would also face a bill for the damage they had caused; the mayor of Ninove declared that he would never have anything more to do with such a band of English Cossacks. One officer suffered an 'apoplexy' from which he never recovered.[15]

It was not the only jape of its kind. At Grammont, where weekly race meetings were held in May and early June, 'a few of our officers one night in a drunken frolic gave cause for offence' by interfering with the town's Manneken Pis:

a naked boy, apparently about four years old, his left hand rested on his hip, and with his right he held his little c— out of which the water flowed into the bason or more properly the well, for it is some twelve feet deep. One night some of our officers had been indulging themselves rather too much, they sallied out in quest of adventures, they managed to get a rope round the neck of the little urchin and pull him off his pirch. He being made of lead, down he sank to the bottom of the well.

Fortunately, he was restored undamaged to his perch and the incident was forgotten.[16]

As May turned to June Brussels continued to be lively, although the son of staff officer Sir George Scovell's groom recalled that they were now working towards a deadline:

The town was very gay and bustling, all day long soldiers were parading, music playing and the streets continually full of all sorts of uniforms. There were balls every night and plenty of amusement for those who wanted it. It appeared more like troops assembling to be reviewed than to fight, for no one seemed to think of fighting, though towards the 13th or 14th it was said they were going to prepare for hostilities on the 25th and soldiers were to be seen in various parts with their swords taking to be ground, and linen drapers shops were full of them, purchasing cloth to make themselves bandages, but in a general way things were going on as if nothing was the matter.[17]

Wellington's spies had told him that he was safe from attack until 1 July, and according to Napoleon's Minister of Police, Joseph Fouché, the Duke had been convinced by false reports that no French offensive would start before the Anglo-Prussian invasion.[18] Despite the air of normality, however, the allied army was now in the last stages of preparation for a concerted attack on France.

10

The French in Motion

Before dawn on 12 June, a bell summoned Louis Marchand, the Emperor's principal valet, to Napoleon's office. 'I leave at four,' the Emperor announced.

Imperial journeys always began this way: the staff had known for some time that they would move, but nobody knew precisely when until the Emperor told Marchand. Now the palace sprang into action as secretaries packed papers, grooms prepared horses and valets loaded boxes into carriages. Marchand himself packed the Emperor's mahogany and ebony *nécessaire de voyage*. At first light the Emperor climbed into his green carriage followed by the *Grand-Maréchal*, General Bertrand, and his brother Prince Jérôme. Louis-Etienne Saint-Denis, known as Ali, the Emperor's Mameluke, dressed in his exotic oriental costume, took his place on the front box and the vermilion wheels of the deep blue imperial carriage rattled over the cobbles northward out of Paris.

Most of the French army was already in place. The Guard had left unit by unit, beginning on 5 June, the senior regiments remaining until last to escort the Emperor to the opening of the *Corps Législatif*, the new legislative body whose name deliberately harked back to the Revolution.[1] Then they carefully folded their dress uniforms away in their packs, put on the wide blue trousers, blue greatcoats and bearskins that they wore on campaign and at 4 a.m. on 8 June left their barracks to march northward to the hill fortress of Laon at a pace that only the Old Guard could sustain, covering 135 miles in six days.

On 10 June Napoleon had issued an order telling his generals where their troops should be three days later. The following day Marshal Davout wrote to Marshal Ney instructing him to be at Avesnes-sur-Helpe, just short of the border fortress at Maubeuge, by the 14th. Ney set off as soon as he received his summons, posting ahead with his principal aide, while other aides followed with the marshal's horses and equipment.[2]

On the border II Corps was already gathered opposite the British at Mons, the last of General Honoré Reille's troops having marched twenty miles east from the fortress city of Valenciennes on 11 June for the villages behind Maubeuge. Lieutenant Jacques Martin kissed his girlfriend farewell and the 45th Line cheerfully marched seven miles south from the fortress of Condé to Valenciennes, as soon as II Corps had marched out, for reviews on 12 and 13 June by their corps commander General Jean-Baptiste Drouet, comte d'Erlon. Corporal Canler's 28th Regiment reached Valenciennes on 13 June, having lost their royalist colonel en route when he suddenly rode off to join Louis XVIII at Ghent.[3]

The regiments that had been stationed in the north were presented with the eagles received by their colonels from the hand of Napoleon at the Champ de Mai. Jacques Martin was astonished by what he witnessed on the vast plain outside Valenciennes. He had seen larger gatherings of men, but never

anything so striking as these sixteen regiments of infantry of the finest quality, showing admirable precision in their manoeuvres, full of enthusiasm and receiving with emotion those eagles under which they had fought for so long. The plain was entirely covered by men, for apart from the infantry the corps contained 3000 cavalry and artillerymen. At the moment of the presentation of the standards, the silence was shattered by the voices of 20,000 men swearing to conquer or die. ... Never did an army set out with such certainty of victory. What did the number of the enemy matter? We had men in our ranks who had grown up with victory.

Chance had made them prisoners for a few years but this had only made them more fearsome. The desire to avenge their suffering added anger to their natural bravery. These faces, tanned by the sun of Spain or the snows of Russia, lit up at the thought of a battle.[4]

After the review I Corps also marched to Maubeuge, south of the British at Mons.

In the afternoon of 12 June, to the ecstatic pealing of the city's bells, Napoleon's coach rattled up the steep hill into the great French fortress city of Laon. There, more than halfway to the border, his Guard awaited him. Napoleon stopped at the Prefecture where his staff had already installed his 'palace', but was unpleasantly surprised on his arrival to find that Emmanuel de Grouchy's 13,000 cavalry were still in the area, the order to leave having somehow not reached their commander. Now the cavalry had to ride sixty miles north in two days with no time to rest before the fighting began.[5]

Napoleon left Laon before dawn, worked in his coach during the forty-five-mile journey, and was shown into the 'palace' his *maréchal des logis* had prepared in the sub-prefecture within the fortress at Avesnes. Wherever Napoleon spent the night was always the 'palace' even if it was a small farm or a tent, and his staff always went ahead to choose the best accommodation and prepare it for him. Within, Simon Bernard had the operations map ready, spread out on a huge table, with pins marking the present position of all the units they knew about.

The map Napoleon was using was based on a highly detailed survey undertaken between 1771 and 1775 by Joseph, comte de Ferraris, commander of the artillery of the Austrian Netherlands and head of its mathematical school. Published in 1777–8, the survey was engraved on twenty-five sheets at a scale of 1:86,000, to match the great map of France by Cassini, then also in process of publication. Ferraris used the same scale and the same innovative topographical symbols as Cassini, whose map had introduced a new sophistication to mapmaking, distinguishing between eight different sizes of settlement, five different religious buildings, three kinds of mill and nine different types of terrain, and grading six qualities of road.

When the French invaded the Netherlands in 1792–3 they had seized 400 copies of Ferraris' map from a Brussels printseller and in 1794 they confiscated the copper plates and carried them away to France, so that they could print further examples when required for their own military purposes. Having stolen the enemy's map, the French engineer Louis Capitaine made a copy of it, engraved on sixty-nine smaller, more manageable sheets, as well as a small-scale version on six sheets. These maps were commercially available in peacetime and so the Duke of Wellington was armed with one, while the Prussian general staff probably also had one. The French printed copies for their generals in April, marking the present frontier and other updates. When the historian Henry Houssaye saw the Capitaine map used by Napoleon and the Ferraris map belonging to his First Orderly Officer, Gourgaud, he was able to observe that there was little significant difference between the two; although extremely detailed and useful, both were nearly forty years out of date. For instance, they marked none of the coal mines that had since been developed near Charleroi.[6]

These maps were neither cheap nor easily portable and junior officers, who had to provide their own maps, bought single sheets engraved on a much smaller scale. The information contained in the Ferraris survey soon got into the hands of other mapmakers in other nations, and they produced their own versions in a multiplicity of different formats, suitable for every purse and every purpose. An English mapmaker issued a single-sheet version in 1789, while a four-sheet version published in Vienna circulated widely in Europe. The Prussian staff officer Ludwig von Reiche was using the *Nouvelle Carte des Pays-Bas réduite d'après celle de Ferraris*, a sheet of only 20½ × 28 inches (520 × 720mm), recently published at Brussels.[7] Most officers were probably armed with a map based on Ferraris, but on a much reduced scale, so that many names of smaller places were missing and the road network was less than complete.

Napoleon pored over the map while Bernard, using all the information gathered by his topographical office, explained the terrain that lay ahead and the options available. Then Napoleon dictated his orders and messages. Next he drafted an inspiring order of the day and sent it to Soult's nearby *Quartier Général* to have it printed by the topographical department printers on their portable printing press. The Emperor had a long meeting with Jean-Baptiste Drouet d'Erlon, commander of I Corps, at which they discussed plans for the coming campaign and for the provisioning of the border fortresses.[8] Finally in the late afternoon he toured Avesnes and its fortifications, designed by Vauban. The Guard and VI Corps gathered there that day and Napoleon closed the frontier on pain of death. Almost all the army was now close by: only Maurice Gérard's IV Corps was still on the road, a day's march from Philippeville, twenty-five miles to the east, having left Metz, 115 miles away, on 6 June.

Napoleon ordered II Corps to march on 14 June to a bivouac on the border near the Sambre with I Corps behind them, these two forming a left wing alongside the river. The Guard was to spend the night in and around Beaumont, a little town on a hill twelve miles east, dominating the approaches to the Ardennes forest. Dominique Vandamme's III Corps camped three miles ahead with George Mouton's VI Corps behind them.

Napoleon himself worked on state papers with the secretaries of his *maison civile*, then drove on to Beaumont, where, as they arrived, Napoleon's coachman witnessed one of those incidents that so endeared him to the ordinary soldiers of his army, especially the privileged veterans of his Imperial Guard. As his coach passed, an officer of the guard struck a soldier, who presented his bayonet and 'told his superior that if he dared to strike him again he would run him through. The Emperor seeing the whole from his carriage, called the officer toward him, and putting his hand out of the chariot window, tore off his epaulettes, and the cross of the legion of honour, telling him he was not worthy to command those brave men.'[9]

After thus demonstrating that his veterans had to be treated with respect by their officers, Napoleon dismounted at his new 'palace' and there, closeted with Bernard and Soult, he devised the movement orders for the next day's invasion of Belgium.

The troops marched off with considerable gaiety, lively conversation and frequent songs, despite the pouring rain and the heavy going. It rained all day, but they found their allotted positions and trudged dripping into camp to make the best of a short night. Lieutenant Martin's 45th Regiment reached their bivouac about seven in the evening:

> We hardly slept because of the rain which had fallen abundantly and was still falling, but we got to talking about the next day's operations. Everyone had a clear-cut opinion of the general's plan, without understanding much about what was afoot, so each camp-fire became a council of war, while these resourceful people pushed wood on the fire and boiled the stewpot.[10]

In the evening the order of the day that Napoleon had composed at Avesnes was distributed to all units and read out to the troops, who clustered around to hear the Emperor's inspiring words, recalling glorious battles of the past and the spirit of the Revolution: 'Soldiers! Today is the anniversary of Marengo and of Friedland, which twice decided the destiny of Europe ... The princes we allowed to remain on their thrones ... have begun the most unjust aggression: let us march then to meet them; they and we, are we not still the same men?'

He reminded them how they had beaten the Prussians against numerical odds. He invited those who had been prisoners in English hulks (of whom there were a good number in the army) to tell of the suffering that they had endured; he told them that the Saxons, Belgians, Hanoverians and Rhinelanders, who had once been liberated, now fretted at being obliged to bear arms in the cause of princes who were hostile to justice and the rights of man and were even now gobbling up the smaller German states.[11]

They all had orders to be ready to march at first light. The cavalry commander, Emmanuel de Grouchy, had joined Claude Pajol's cavalry corps during the day to ensure that they stopped short of enemy outposts that might raise the alarm. Marshal Grouchy and the cavalry generals Pajol, Exelmans and Subervie all had Belgian aides-de-camp who knew their way about.[12] During the evening, a local inhabitant appeared at headquarters and told them that if they wanted to cross the frontier it was essential first to repair the roads which had been blocked by obstacles in the woods. Nobody had thought to tell Pajol about the recently constructed roadblocks, including the troop of customs officers stationed at the frontier town, who were supposed to serve as their guides, and they spent the night clearing roads.[13]

Napoleon had succeeded in bringing a massed force of 123,000 men to the border with Belgium, having thoroughly confused his enemies as to his intentions.[14] He calculated that the enemy knew that I and II Corps were at Maubeuge, but hoped that his other forces had approached undetected. His plan was that, having allowed Wellington to perceive that his troops were stacked up opposite the British at Mons, they would march off in a completely unexpected direction, along the broken roads through the woods. They would then launch an attack on the Prussians at Charleroi with his Order of the Day's final words of inspiration ringing in their ears:

> Soldiers! We have forced marches to make, battles to fight, dangers to face; but with steadfastness, victory will be ours; we shall recover the rights, the honour and the happiness of our native land.
>
> For every Frenchman with a heart, the moment has come to vanquish or to die.

11

Sang-froid

Although Napoleon thought his army's concentration had been achieved in secret, in fact few of his movements had gone unperceived. A French landowner and the Earl of Uxbridge sent cautious warnings on 12 June that the French army believed it was about to attack. And the same day, a report sent by Dörnberg to Wellington contained what turned out to be very accurate information:

> A French gentleman coming from Maubeuge to join the King, gives the following intelligence. The corps of General Reille is come yesterday to Maubeuge and its vicinity. The headquarters of the Army are transferred from Laon to Avesnes, where a division of the Guards is to arrive today. Buonaparte is expected every minute but nothing certain is known when he had left Paris, where it appears he was still on the 10th. Jérôme Buonaparte is at Solre-le-Château. Soult passed through Maubeuge this morning, coming from Laon, but the gentleman did not know where he was gone to. He estimates the forces between Philippeville, Givet, Mézières, Guise and Maubeuge at more than 100,000 troops of the line. A very considerable corps of cavalry was reviewed at Hirson two days ago by Grouchy. The general opinion in the army is, that they will attack, and that the arrival of Buonaparte at Avesnes, will be the signal for the beginning of hostilities.[1]

Indeed, reports of French activity were far from lacking. The following day Dörnberg reported French troops converging on Maubeuge, d'Erlon having reviewed his corps. One of Ziethen's brigadiers reported that the French had closed the border, and an assistant to Quartermaster-General Grolmann who visited Brussels was assured that Wellington's army could concentrate on its left wing within twenty-two hours of the first cannon shot.[2] Sir Hussey Vivian, the dashing commander of the Hussar brigade, inspecting the 1st Hussars at Tournai, found the French cavalry pickets gone and replaced by customs officers who told him that the French army was concentrating and about to attack. 'We treated this with contempt, supposing he would hardly dare such a thing,' Vivian wrote to his wife. Nevertheless, he reported to Uxbridge and Hill what had been said.[3]

Had Wellington ordered the concentration of his forces on the receipt of this intelligence, the campaign might have been very short. The allied armies were so strong in combination that the only risk they ran was to be attacked and defeated separately, before one could come to the aid of the other. As one of his staff officers pointed out years later with the benefit of hindsight, Blücher should have brought his headquarters to Genappe, twenty-two miles south of Brussels, with his men camped north and south along the road to Charleroi, and Wellington should have placed his men along the road between Brussels and Mons. This course would have drawn the armies inseparably close together along near-parallel lines running roughly north to south. On the most fertile land in Europe, for a short period the difficulty of supplying both armies with food could have been overcome.

Instead, however, Wellington placed total confidence in his spy network, from which he had received no warning but instead assurances that he was safe until July. As Müffling recalled, 'the Duke learned through me that the espionage of Prince Blücher was badly organized, while he believed himself to be very secure on this point, and expected to hear immediately from Paris everything indicating a march against the Netherlands.'[4] The likelihood of receiving ciphered messages from Paris, moreover, explains the desirability of the cipher expert Sir George Scovell's presence as a member of Wellington's staff.

But in Paris something had gone wrong. In his memoirs, Joseph Fouché claimed that he had devised an elaborate deception. As soon as the Emperor left Paris, he had sent a certain 'Mme D' with a ciphered note for Wellington betraying Napoleon's plan of campaign (which had been revealed to Fouché by Marshal Davout), but had then deliberately set up obstacles to delay her on the French side of the border so that Wellington did not receive the promised information until it was too late to be of use.[5] It is possible that while seeking to please Wellington in case Napoleon lost, Fouché was really working for the Emperor. There is a curious similarity between this story of Fouché's and one told by William Napier, a friend of intelligence chief Colquhoun Grant, about an important message sent by Grant's agents. So delayed at the border was this communication (for which Napier blamed Dörnberg) that the document, when seen by Napier, was annotated 'received from Grant, June the 18th, 11 o'clock'. One might speculate that Grant's agents were invented as a cover story for the real agent, who was Fouché, or else that they were the agents chosen to liaise with Fouché.[6]

The story, however, may not have been quite as Fouché told it. Napoleon knew that Fouché was not to be trusted: 'The Duc of Otranto is betraying me,' he told Lazare Carnot, Minister of the Interior, a few days before leaving Paris.[7] It may be that Napoleon intercepted Fouché's message, or forced him to act against Wellington. In July, soon after the battle of Waterloo, the Tory politician Lord Grantham visited the battlefield with intimates of Wellington. He subsequently reported that 'The Duke own'd that he did not expect Buonaparte to have attack'd so soon, & that he had believ'd the Reports of Spies who had never deceiv'd him before. It is said that Buonaparte had discover'd those Spies & made them send false Accounts to the Duke to redeem their Lives.'[8] Whatever the reason, it seems that Wellington's espionage system in Paris was compromised and his faith in it was misplaced.

Thanks to that misplaced faith, however, he continued for the moment to place more reliance on what he was told by Paris than on the rumours reaching him from the frontier. He remained confident that there was no danger and the army continued to behave as if they were on holiday. On 13 June Uxbridge attended a huge race meeting at Grammont where the handsome Lord Hay, aide to General Peregrine Maitland of the Guards, won a sweepstake.[9] The Duke passed the day at a cricket match at Enghien with the sixteen-year-old Lady Jane Lennox; her father was among those playing, along with a number of Guards officers, including Maitland, Sarah Lennox's beau and one of the best cricketers in England. Jane's tutor wrote:

> Though I have given some pretty good reasons for supposing that hostilities will soon commence, yet no one would suppose it, judging by the Duke of Wellington. He appears to be thinking of everything else in the world, gives a ball every week, attends every party, partakes of every amusement that offers. He took Lady Jane Lennox to Enghien for the cricket match, and brought her back at night, apparently having gone for no other object but to amuse her.[10]

Moreover, when the tutor spoke of 'reasons for supposing that hostilities will soon commence' he was referring to the supposition that the allies were about to invade France. He was not expecting Napoleon to commence hostilities, for by this stage neither Wellington nor Blücher believed that they were about to be attacked. As early as 3 June Blücher had written to his wife, 'we could perfectly well stay here for another year because Bonaparte won't attack us', and his view was shared by General Gneisenau who wrote on 12 June that 'the danger of attack has almost disappeared'. From royalist spies Wellington had just received figures confirming that the French army was considerably weaker than the combined Allied armies, and on 13 June he wrote to an old military friend and colleague that, despite reports, Napoleon's departure from Paris was 'not likely to be immediate ... I think we are now too strong for him here'.[11] Instead, Wellington had a different agenda. His sang-froid was no longer connected with fear of a French attack on him. Rather he was intent on concealing from the local population and any other curious onlookers his own preparations for an imminent attack on Napoleon, now only a fortnight away. That was why everything had to appear normal and the British had to behave with studied insouciance.

Both the British and the Prussians therefore had perfectly adequate intelligence of Napoleon's attack, but his timing and disinformation were so good that they simply didn't believe it. However, Karl von Grolmann had become sufficiently alarmed to have sought reassurance from Wellington, and the Prussians gave more credence to the indications from the frontier than the Duke did.

On the night of 13–14 June both the Prussian and Dutch outposts reported the clouds glowing pink with the reflection of numerous campfires around Beaumont and Solre-sur-Sambre. The French had tried to camp in woods and valleys in order to conceal their fires, but they had been betrayed by the reflective cloud banks. Early next morning Jean-Baptiste van Merlen, the commander of the Dutch cavalry outposts that linked Dörnberg's at Mons to those of the Prussians, reported to Ziethen the campfires near Beaumont and added that the French outposts near Mons were weaker, concluding that the French had moved towards the Prussians. On this warning, Ziethen took his own precautions, ordering I Corps' heavy baggage to move back beyond Gembloux, fifteen miles to the north-east, in accordance with a defensive plan that had been devised on 2 May. This proved to be a crucial preparation, for by the time Ziethen had to retreat the roads were clear and his troops unencumbered.[12] Dörnberg reported the same French movement towards Charleroi, and when Sir Harry Clinton, commander of the 2nd Division, rode from his headquarters for news, Dörnberg told him that the French army was concentrating and that Bonaparte was present. Clinton heard him out and said, 'Yes, I believe it now, but the Duke, despite being very well informed, doesn't believe it.'[13]

When French deserters warned Ziethen of an impending attack next day, Gneisenau decided at last to issue an alert. At noon on 14 June he warned Friedrich von Bülow's distant IV Corps to prepare to

concentrate and march westward as an offensive might be imminent; he then wrote to III Corps, requesting the same of Johann von
Thielmann. When they received this warning, each corps would
require about twelve hours to bring together its scattered brigades
and then III Corps had twenty-six miles to march, IV Corps about
fifty from Liège.[14] At 9.30 in the evening Dörnberg wrote direct to
Blücher's headquarters at Namur, with a blunt warning that the
French opinion was that an attack would begin early the following
morning;[15] half an hour later liaison officer Hardinge wrote to
Wellington telling him that the French were in movement with provisions for eight days and that 'the prevalent opinion here seems to be
that Buonaparte intends to commence offensive operations.'[16] At
11.30 p.m., Gneisenau ordered II and III Corps to gather their regiments together and be ready to march; front-line troops went to bed
prepared for immediate action and the 6th Uhlans had been ordered
not to undress.

Finally, at midnight, Gneisenau wrote again to Bülow at Liège,
asking him very politely and respectfully – too politely as it turned
out – to march westward the following day. With Blücher already
asleep, preparing for a long day, the message went unsigned by the
commander in chief:

> I have the honour humbly to request your Excellency to be kind
> enough to concentrate the IV Corps under your command tomor-
> row, the 15th, at Hannut, in close cantonments. Information
> received makes it more and more probable that the French army
> has concentrated against us and that we must expect from it an
> immediate change to the offensive ... Your Excellency had doubt-
> less better make Hannut your headquarters.[17]

Still Wellington did nothing. Though he did not yet know about
Gneisenau's last-minute decision to initiate concentration of his
forces, there was a degree of obstinacy in his continued sang-froid,
and his rejection of intelligence from the frontier. Others sensed it
and told the politician Lord Grantham when he visited Belgium. 'Ld.
Grantham had heard that the Prince of Orange had two days before

sent Information of his own to the Duke of Buonaparte's intended Advance, & perhaps the Duke too much recollected that His Royal Highness had been no more than his own Aid-de-Camp, & did not pay quite sufficient Regard to Information that came through him.' Many, like the staff officer cited here, have suggested that both Wellington and Gneisenau should have concentrated their troops earlier, or that Wellington should at least have reacted when Gneisenau did on receipt of such ominous information from the border. But he simply did not believe that the French would attack. Still relying on his spies in Paris, he was unaware that he had been double-crossed.

PART II

The Invasion of the Netherlands

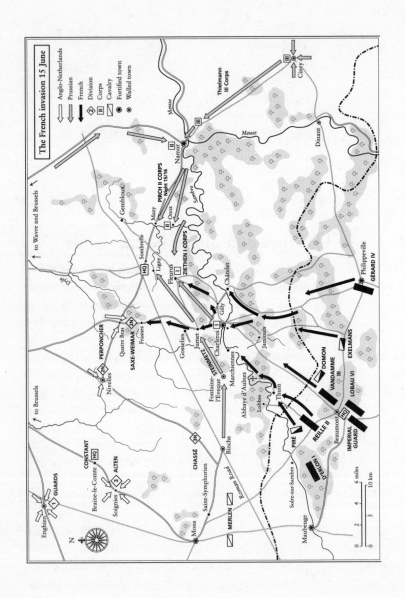

12

The French Cross the Border

15 June, 2.30–7 a.m.

For Napoleon speed and surprise were crucial. The allies knew that an army was massed behind Maubeuge, the French border fortress on the river Sambre, but assumed it was there to defend France, not to attack Belgium. Napoleon realised that the allies were ready for an assault since they had had months to prepare, but he hoped that they did not know that he and his Guard were present, he hoped that they didn't expect him to attack them and especially he hoped that they didn't expect him to attack Charleroi. In order to succeed, he had to catch the enemy forces off balance before they could combine. On 14 June he brought all his troops to the frontier and issued orders for an invasion the following morning.

The marching orders issued by the Emperor covered only the approach to Charleroi and the Sambre crossings about fifteen miles away. This was a sideways move away from the British and towards the Prussians and as the French marched east, the wide river would guard their left flank against possible interference from Wellington's army. In this border country, the terrain was difficult: rivers and streams cut steep valleys into the wooded landscape and the roads were poor, none being cobbled and most mere paths. At Charleroi, where the river was thirty yards wide, there was a large stone bridge. A narrower, older bridge crossed the river about three miles west at

Marchiennes and a third at Châtelet five miles to the east.

Once over the river, Napoleon intended to give new orders to his generals according to circumstances. There was no fixed objective for the day, but the ultimate goal was to seize two strategically important crossroads on the cobbled road linking Namur in the east to Nivelles in the north-west at the inns of Quatre Bras and Point du Jour, thus cutting the main line of communication between Wellington's and Blücher's armies. These crossroads were about thirty miles distant, and Napoleon must have appreciated that to get so far in one day was ambitious. French armies normally marched between ten and twenty-two miles in a day, so on one when he expected fighting and a contested river crossing, a march of thirty miles was an ideal outcome rather than a realistic expectation.

Heavy rain had been falling all day on 14 June on ground that was already sodden from previous downpours. It was a first depressing blow for the Emperor that conditions for marching were so poor. As a British Guards officer wrote on 15 June, 'the weather here is at present very unfavourable for campaigning and indeed for all manner of field sports as it rains at all times of the day and night and has done for the last fortnight and promises fair to do the same for another fortnight. I wonder whether St Swithin has anything to do with the state of the weather in this country as in England.'[1] The riders carrying Soult's movement orders rode down from Beaumont in darkness and were soon drenched. The wet conditions did have compensations, though: if Napoleon's men found progress slow and difficult as they filed along muddy tracks through woodland, it was at least a night to discourage sentries, and even the most zealous and alert could see and hear little in torrential rain that gave way during the night to drizzle and thick mist. The sun rose about a quarter to four but the fog lingered.

The Emperor had ridden out of Beaumont at about half past three with his *petit quartier-général* and his duty squadrons of Guards cavalry, followed by his *service d'expedition* of senior staff in a convoy of fourteen carriages and his *service léger* of thirty green-liveried valets riding mules with portmanteaux strapped to them. Each valet led two more mules each carrying two leather-covered boxes containing silver plates and cutlery, coffee cups, decanters, provisions and bottles of the burgundy – Chambertin – that Napoleon invariably drank, usually diluted with water.

He rode with his Grand Equerry, Albert Fouler, who was responsible for the imperial train and for Napoleon's horses, one of his duties being to provide a constant supply of fresh mounts. Whenever the party came up against any feature capable of concealing danger, Fouler led the way. Close to the Emperor rode a page with his telescope, Mameluke Ali with a flask of brandy, a cloak and a spare coat, three grooms, Napoleon's personal surgeon and Dominique Larrey, the Imperial Guard's surgeon. They were surrounded by a bodyguard of twenty mounted chasseurs, one of whom had charge of a portfolio with maps and writing equipment, and followed by aides and orderlies. Napoleon announced that he would be found riding with the advance guard and wanted his lieutenant-generals to send information and reports to him quickly and frequently. The target was to cross the Sambre before midday.

Jean-Siméon Domon, one of the more brilliant French cavalry commanders, with a thousand green-coated *chasseurs-à-cheval*, the specialist scouts of the army, had led the way at 2.30 a.m., sending parties of fifty horsemen in all directions to investigate the ground ahead and seize or drive in enemy outposts. The job of the light cavalry, especially these 'hunters', was to chase down the enemy – locate, harry and pursue. They were armed with a curved sabre, a pair of pistols and a short musket called a carbine which was generally fired from the saddle, though in emergency they were capable of fighting on foot.

Behind this screen, over which he had authority, rode Claude-Pierre Pajol with six regiments of hussars, lancers and chasseurs – nearly three thousand more light cavalry. Pajol, who had made his name in Napoleon's great victory over the Austrians and Russians at Austerlitz in 1805, was another of the Emperor's most trusted lieutenants, brave and flamboyant, astute and resourceful, and a highly experienced leader of horsemen. The hussars differed little from chasseurs except in their brightly coloured dress, fierce moustaches and traditional élan. The lancers meanwhile were the shock troops of the light cavalry, wearing green uniforms with brass helmets; their front rank were armed with nine-foot spears, while their rear rank usually carried carbines. Each cavalry division had its own battery of horse artillery, in which all the gunners were mounted so that it could keep up and act in close support. These intrepid artillerymen regarded themselves as an elite and came into their own in mobile situations such as this, where they could be called in to blast away obstacles obstructing a rapid advance. French horse batteries had four conventional guns firing 6-pound solid shot, and two howitzers to lob explosive shells at troops under cover. Domon had been ordered to give his artillery to the leading battalion of III Corps' infantry, but Pajol had two batteries with his troops.

The 16,000 infantry and artillery of Dominique Vandamme's III Corps had orders to march on Charleroi at 3 a.m. Each division was to be accompanied by its artillery and field hospital, but the baggage was not to move until all the troops had passed, and any unauthorised vehicles found with the columns were to be burned. Georges Mouton, comte de Lobau's VI Corps, 10,300 strong, was to march an hour behind Vandamme and the 4000 Young Guard an hour behind Lobau, followed by the Old Guard.

The trumpets of the leading division of Grouchy's heavy cavalry sounded the *boute-selle*, the signal to mount up, at 5 a.m. and they walked off, taking by-roads parallel to the main column. The heavy cavalry were big men on big horses for use on the battlefield as shock troops and were not generally employed for scouting and outpost duties. They comprised cuirassiers who wore steel breast- and back-plates as well as helmets over their blue uniforms, carabiniers whose breast-plates were coated with brass and who wore white with red crests over their brass-plated helmets, and dragoons, dressed in green, who did not wear armour and were more versatile, capable of undertaking any cavalry duty and even of fighting on foot. They were armed with long, straight swords, pistols and dragoon muskets, shorter and lighter than the infantry model.

On the right flank, the 16,000 men of Maurice Gérard's IV Corps, 'the army of the Moselle', was a little behind schedule, straggling after the tough last leg of an eight-day march. Its leading division had passed Philippeville, twenty miles east of Maubeuge, but the other three were all short of the town with the rear one trailing by eleven miles. Their orders were to march on Charleroi at 3 a.m., trying to keep pace with Vandamme, but this was conditional on the corps being closed up at Philippeville; since it was not, a delay while Gérard's trailing units caught up was inevitable. To slow him down further he was to march closed up in order of battle in case he might be attacked, with his cavalry scouting ahead and to the east. Jacques Delort's division of cuirassiers was to follow as a rearguard.

On the left flank, on the bank of the Sambre, the drummers of Honoré Reille's II Corps were to beat the *diane* at 2.30 a.m. and his 25,000 men were to march at 3 a.m., aiming to reach Marchiennes-au-Pont, eighteen miles away and just to the west of Charleroi, before 9 a.m. On the way, moreover, they were to secure each crossing of the river and let no one pass over so that no news reached Wellington. They were to make sure they captured the bridges before the enemy could destroy them, especially the bridge at Marchiennes by which they would cross the river. Reille was moreover to interrogate the inhabitants of the towns of Thuin and Marchiennes and the intervening villages about the strength and location of the enemy armies and was to seize and read all letters in the post offices. To advance at three miles an hour over minor, winding roads was therefore a challenge.

Jean-Baptiste Drouet, comte d'Erlon's I Corps, another 20,400 men, was to follow Reille, throwing bridgeheads across the Sambre to secure the bridges at the small town of Thuin and at the ruined Abbaye d'Aulnes. He was to guard the bridges and to send cavalry patrols towards the fortress of Mons and the walled town of Binche to keep an eye out for enemy movement, but they were not to cross the border.

The generals were to keep in touch with each other through chains of cavalry patrols and arrange to arrive simultaneously at Charleroi. Each corps was to have Flemish-speaking officers with forward patrols to gather news without revealing that the whole army was behind them, and sappers were to march just behind the first light infantry to clear any obstacles. Sappers were big engineers armed with axes and trained to build and repair bridges and roads, break into a building or prepare it for defence; light infantry was seen as the dynamic innovation of the last twenty years of warfare, being trained to move quickly and to shoot fast and accurately in dispersed formations or in small squads. Little, agile men, they were taught to think for themselves and fight in pairs. They were trained to set ambushes and conduct raids, taught how to operate in woodland, seize hills and storm buildings. Naturally they led an advance or formed the rearguard in a retreat.

The sappers and sailors of the Guard – the sailors were also specialist engineers, for the navy was excellent at improvising ropes, boats and pulleys to move cannon up mountains or across rivers – with the army's reserve of sappers, were to march just behind the leading element of Vandamme's III Corps. They were to take only two or three wagons of equipment, leaving the bulk to follow the main body of the corps, and deal with any obstacles on the main route, repairing bad areas of road and making bridges across any awkward streams, ditches or floods. A section of engineers with sufficient components for three pontoon bridges over the Sambre was to accompany the engineering wagons following Vandamme's men. The heavy cavalry of the Guard – the Empress's dragoons and the proud Horse Grenadiers – acted as a final rearguard, leaving at 8 a.m.[2]

The baggage of the entire column came last of all under the orders of the *vaguemestre-général*, remaining a long distance behind the army. His thankless role was to direct a vast array of vehicles carrying supplies and equipment. First onto the road was the heavy baggage of the Emperor's household, a huge column of carriages, wagons and horses, followed by the headquarters baggage. After that came the army's field hospital, the baggage of the Guard and of III and VI Corps, while at the same time the *vaguemestre* was to get the heavy cavalry baggage following in the wake of the horsemen. The *intendant*, responsible for paperwork and procurement, was to attach all his administrative staff and their wagons to this column. Each unit was assigned its place and each wagon was numbered and identified.

Every battalion had four authorised women and each squadron two, and they all rode with the baggage. Usually two were *vivandières*, some owning wagons and some riding horses with huge panniers, carrying brandy and items like writing paper, buttons and vinegar to sell to the soldiers; two were *blanchisseuses* who washed the soldiers' shirts and gaiters. Strictly speaking, there was a distinction between *vivandières* and *cantiniers* or *cantinières*, the latter being authorised to bring mobile shops selling a wider range of goods from wagons, but in common usage *cantinières* and *vivandières* were synonyms. In addition to these licensed traders there were wagons carrying rations for men and horses. It took fifty wagons to carry two days' supply of forage for 2500 horses. There were hundreds of wagons carrying rice, dried peas, beans, lentils and salt under the direction of the despised and detested *riz-pain-sels* who supplied the troops with food. There were masons to build bread ovens and bakers to bake bread. Fifty ovens could supply an army such as this of 123,000 men. Fifty gendarmes helped the *vaguemestre* keep each vehicle in this immense column in its allotted place. Behind and beside the vast convoy of vehicles there were herds of cattle and sheep being driven along to supply the troops with fresh meat, and behind all that the unauthorised camp followers.

Unsurprisingly perhaps, things did not go smoothly. While trying, in pouring rain, to find Vandamme, who had changed his headquarters without telling anyone where he had gone, the single messenger carrying his movement orders fell off his horse and broke his leg. Consequently, the first Vandamme knew of his order to move came at least an hour late when first General Joseph Rogniat, commander of the army's engineers, and then Colonel Janin of the staff of VI Corps, tracked him down, complaining that Vandamme's men, who should be on the march, were instead blocking their path. With the rain having given way to fog, Vandamme's troops were unaware that the army was on the move, much of it stacked up behind them. Whatever the main cause of the failure to contact Vandamme may have been, the blame has to lie ultimately with Soult's staff, who should have known Vandamme's location and should have sent more than one messenger. This was a first, crucial example of the poor staff work that was to prove disastrous during the campaign.[3]

Taking on Dominique Vandamme was like confronting Shakespeare's Ajax. Catapulted from private to brigadier-general during the Revolution, Vandamme had led the charge at Austerlitz in the greatest victory of 1805 that regained the Pratzen heights. Napoleon, who rated him for his bravery, brutality and determination, is supposed to have said that were he to launch a campaign against Lucifer in Hell, he would give Vandamme the vanguard, but looting, insubordination and a bad temper made him a difficult colleague. More Jacobin than Bonapartist, he hated Soult for going over to the king and detested Grouchy, the aristocratic cavalry commander, for being made a marshal ahead of him. An officer whose aunt was married to Grouchy reckoned that Vandamme was embittered by the campaign of 1813 and tired of war. He had all the faults of an old *grognard*: truculent, wilful, insubordinate, ill-disciplined and malevolent, he executed orders in his own time and when he felt like it, not even fearing Napoleon. An aide to Grouchy who delivered messages to Vandamme received so much foul-mouthed abuse that he refused to take any more.[4]

Vandamme moved fast once he realised he was holding up the army, but the damage was done. Rogniat set off ahead with his engineers but the main column was three hours late. Napoleon ordered the Guard to make forced marches on a parallel byway to overtake Vandamme; its commander, Marshal Mortier, was struck down by sciatica, gout or disgrace and did not leave Beaumont.[5]

Gérard's IV Corps was also delayed, first by waiting for its straggling rearguard to reach Philippeville and then when shortly after 5 a.m. the commander of its leading division, Louis de Bourmont, deserted to the enemy taking his staff with him. It took some time for the new divisional commander to reassure and pacify his 9th Light Infantry, who led the column, and the division did not advance until 7 a.m., an hour behind Vandamme.

There had been delays, but the huge operation of moving a large army rarely went off without some time-consuming hitch. By the time Gérard's men and the Guard broke camp, however, muffled gunfire could already be heard from somewhere deep in the woods that loomed ahead through the mist and drizzle.

13

The Prussian Outposts Attacked

15 June, early morning on the border near Charleroi

Napoleon's opponent that morning, Hans von Ziethen, the commander of the Prussian I Corps, was intelligent, diligent and energetic, a few months younger than the Emperor. Blücher thought highly of the former hussar who, in the campaigns of 1813 and 1814, had always been ready to execute orders, and had never criticised the high command or complained that too much was being asked of him or his men.[1]

In the event of a French attack through Charleroi the Prussian staff had determined to make a stand above the village of Ligny, in front of the cobbled highway from Namur to Nivelles. They had reconnoitred this potential battlefield, and distributed the resulting survey to senior officers on 22 May.[2] Ziethen's orders were to fall back as slowly as possible to the town of Fleurus, just in front of the pre-selected battlefield, fighting delaying actions during his corps' withdrawal.

Ziethen had issued a contingency plan on 2 May so that each of his units knew what to do if the French attacked, and so when they really did attack no fresh orders were needed.[3] Ziethen had a line of outposts to raise the alarm, situated roughly seven and a half miles in front of his brigades. A Prussian brigade was equivalent in size to a French or British division and Ziethen had four, of which two were in action: Karl von Steinmetz's 1st Brigade, based furthest west at the walled town of Fontaine l'Evêque, adjacent to the Netherlands cavalry outposts, and Otto von Pirch's 2nd Brigade, guarding the bridges at Marchiennes-au-Pont and Charleroi, directly in the French line of march; the 4th Brigade was engaged in watching river crossings further east and Ziethen's 3rd Brigade was in reserve at Fleurus. In total he had 30,000 men.

On the French left flank it was the job of Honoré Reille, commander of II Corps, to drive things forward. The conscientious Reille was a revolutionary volunteer who had started his career as a simple grenadier. He distinguished himself in Bonaparte's early Italian campaigns, commanded a division after Austerlitz and was an aide to Napoleon in 1807 and 1809. In Spain he became one of Marshal Soult's key lieutenants. Reille's men marched along the narrow road following the high ground south of the river Sambre, which flowed through a valley with wooded hills either side. Scouting ahead were 2000 mounted chasseurs and lancers and a six-gun battery of horse artillery, led by the thirty-seven-year-old Breton aristocrat Hippolyte de Rosnyvinen, comte de Piré, a devoted Bonapartist. Piré's family had left France at the Revolution. In 1795 he was wounded at Quiberon during the British-inspired royalist attempt to retake Brittany, before fighting with the royalist *Armée de la Vendée*. When Bonaparte sought reconciliation with the royalists, Piré joined the First Consul's volunteer hussars. After distinguishing himself at Austerlitz, he fought with the *Grande Armée*, rising to become *général de division* in 1813. At Napoleon's return, Piré immediately declared for him and campaigned with Grouchy against the royalists in Provence. In close support of his cavalry was a light infantry spearhead, the four battalions of the 2nd Light, well over 2000 strong and commanded by another trusty Bonapartist, Pierre-François Maigrot.[4] The French were considered to have the best light infantry and Maigrot's men were the best in Napoleon's army.

About two miles into Belgium Maigrot's men encountered six hundred Westphalians defending the bridge over the Sambre at Lobbes and drove them across the river to the north bank, towards the church on its steep hill. The Prussians alerted General Steinmetz, who began to call in his outposts and muster his brigade. Not for nothing was Steinmetz commander of the first brigade of the first corps: he was a fearsome, highly decorated fire-eater, a dynamic leader whose reputation was based on his performance defending the fortress of Colberg in 1807 when, though only a captain, he had been chosen by Gneisenau as second-in-command.

The rain had turned to foggy drizzle, and Piré's dripping cavalry trotted forward until the imposing walled hill town of Thuin loomed out of the mist. After coming under fire Piré called up his horse artillery, and at 4.30 a.m. the first cannon fire boomed out, quickly damaging the church on top of the hill. The defenders were six hundred fusiliers – light infantry – of the 2nd Westphalian Landwehr led by Major von Monsterberg, with orders not to abandon his post prematurely.

Monsterberg's fusiliers were defending a strong position and it took time to dislodge them. Maigrot's better-trained veterans stormed up the narrow paths into the upper town, but it took nearly an hour and some sharp street-fighting to make the Westphalians escape eastwards. They had left too late, for the French had already seized the bridge and the Rhinelanders had to run for the woods on the southern bank. More Westphalian fusiliers concealed among the picturesque ruins of the Abbaye d'Aulnes briefly delayed Maigrot's men, but when Monsterberg emerged from the trees the squadrons of West Prussian dragoons sent to cover his retreat were overwhelmed by Piré's cavalry and Monsterberg's men were ridden down. The French cavalry killed 100 fleeing Germans and captured 260.[5]

Across the river, on the north bank, Steinmetz warned the neighbouring Netherlands light cavalry that he was about to evacuate Binche and Fontaine l'Evêque. He then commenced his pre-planned retreat to Gosselies, a small town about eight miles away and three north of Charleroi.

Further east, in the central French column, Hubert-François Biot, aide-de-camp to Claude Pajol, had joined Domon's *chasseurs-à-cheval*, the most advanced scouts of the army, the advance guard of the light cavalry. In the early morning Domon had driven an outpost of white-coated fusiliers into the woods. Three more companies of the 28th Regiment, stationed further back and ordered to retreat, had already reached the bridge at Châtelet, three miles east of Charleroi, but the outpost company was not so lucky. After a few miles of hide and seek in the mist, the 4th Chasseurs spotted the two hundred men as they emerged from the trees and trapped them in a farm close to the Sambre. They defended themselves bravely until Biot sent for a howitzer, on seeing which they surrendered.[6] Domon and Biot rode westward with their prisoners back to the main road, whereupon they came under fire from Prussian infantry concealed among the houses and hedges of the village of Marcinelle. Since there was little that cavalry could do to dislodge infantry from such a position, they pulled back, idly watching Prussian cavalry squadrons retiring slowly over the hills on the far side of the river valley.

Charleroi had been built in 1666 to guard the river crossing against the French. To the north, the town was vulnerable, the ground sloping gently upwards through woods, but the fortification was designed to prevent approach from the south. Its citadel stood on top of a steep hill dominating the river, lakes commanded by ramparts obstructed any approach from the west or the east and a fortified 'Ville Basse' defended the south side of the river, projecting into swampy water meadows that could be flooded. But the defences of Charleroi had been allowed to decay after the most recent siege in 1794 and, unlike those of the fortresses in Wellington's sector, they had not been repaired in the last few months. The town, which straggled up the hill between the Ville Basse and the citadel, had rather more than 5000 inhabitants and was rapidly growing thanks to coal. There were factories making cloth and glassware, but coal was the region's main industry, large quantities being mined from the surrounding woodland. The town's commerce was aimed towards France and French was the only language spoken there.[7]

From the village of Marcinelle to the south, a causeway led across the flood plain to the decaying ramparts around the Ville Basse; from here a lane led to a central square lined with trees and opening onto a stone bridge, forty yards long and nine wide, with a wooden parapet, which spanned the broad river. General Pajol rode up to join his aide and sent one of his brigadiers to see if he could ford the

Sambre further east and take the bridge from the rear. While Pajol waited, the Prussians pulled out of Marcinelle, anxious that they might be cut off by so many cavalry. When Pajol saw them retreating he launched the 1st Hussars in their distinctive light blue uniforms in a dash across the causeway, but determined volleys from the West Prussian regulars defending the Ville Basse sent the horsemen scurrying back. The brigadier reported (wrongly, in fact) that there was no ford and so Pajol waited for the infantry to catch up. The morning sun was burning off the mist and the day promised to become very hot indeed.

Napoleon was not far behind. He had set up his headquarters at the village of Jamioulx (marked on his map as Jamignou) from where paths led to both Marchiennes and Charleroi, three miles to the north. Grand Marshal Bertrand indicated a halt and the *maître d'hôtel*, two cooks and a boy got to work, warming pre-prepared food, as the extended entourage caught up with the Emperor's party. Eventually, General Rogniat appeared with his sappers and seamen and Napoleon followed them to Marcinelle, the elite engineers being the first infantry to arrive.

On the other side of the river, at his headquarters at the Château Puissant, a mere half mile from the Sambre bridge, General Hans von Ziethen had been struggling to assess the extent of the danger. He was woken at the first sound of gunfire and soon after reported to Blücher, twenty miles away at Namur, that 'since 4.30 there has been cannon fire and now musketry on the right wing; so far we have received no report.' Between 5 and 6 a.m., judging that I Corps probably faced an attack rather than some inconsequential night alarm, Ziethen's chief of staff, Ludwig von Reiche, ordered the firing of the alarm cannon, the signal for their troops to take up prearranged defensive positions around Charleroi.[8] Otto von Pirch was already deploying his brigade with battalions guarding bridges and the rest in reserve behind Charleroi on the road to Fleurus.

After receiving reports from the front, Ziethen sent a second message to Blücher at 6.30 a.m. to inform him that his outposts had been attacked and that the enemy appeared to be aiming to seize the river crossings at Charleroi. It might have been a good idea to alert

Wellington at this point, but he didn't, cautious of embarrassing himself by issuing a false alarm. He still did not know whether he faced a real attack in force, a dummy attack concealing a main thrust elsewhere, or merely a flare-up between outposts.

At 9 a.m. Blücher received Ziethen's first message and ordered him to find out all he could about the strength and direction of the French columns. Blücher's staff were worried that Steinmetz's evacuation of Binche and Fontaine l'Evêque could have allowed the French to cross the river and strike at Brussels from that direction (thus bypassing Mons and Charleroi); alternatively, they might have crossed the river at Thuin in order to get onto the Roman road leading north-east to Gembloux, which would enable them to outflank the Prussian position at Charleroi. Blücher warned Ziethen, therefore, to keep an eye on Binche and the Roman road. Blücher was anxious to discover the nature of this attack, and whether it was the only one.

Ziethen had recognised the danger that the French might have crossed the river at Thuin, and had ordered Otto von Pirch to establish on which side of the river and by which roads the enemy was advancing. At 8.15 he wrote to Blücher again, saying that the enemy had taken Thuin and was advancing along the left, southern, bank of the Sambre, and that Napoleon was present with his Guard, which suggested that the attack was serious. He advised his chief that he was pulling his brigades back to Gosselies, the town on the high road to Brussels three miles north of Charleroi, and to Gilly, a village on the road from Charleroi to Fleurus.[9] He told Blücher that he had informed Wellington of this and had begged Wellington to concentrate near Nivelles.[10]

By 8.30 the sound of musketry was alarmingly close to Charleroi, and since Ziethen was not to know that the French infantry were lagging behind their cavalry, he had every reason to suppose that the lower town and the bridge would soon fall, in which case it was high time to remove his headquarters to a safer place. Staff hurriedly packed up and got on the road to Fleurus, the streets of Charleroi and the roads out of it, black with wet dust from the region's coal wagons, becoming clogged with refugees as many of the five thousand inhabitants sought to leave before the town became a battlefield.

The direct route to Brussels was dangerous, since French cavalry might already have crossed the river, so the messenger sent to Wellington might well have chosen the safer, longer route via Fleurus and Point du Jour, or even Fleurus, Gembloux and Wavre; he must moreover have set out in an atmosphere of confusion. And even if he took the direct route, Ziethen's messenger had thirty-three miles to cover before he could issue the alarm.[11]

14

The Fall of Charleroi

15 June, 5 a.m.–3 p.m.

As Napoleon's army surged along the south bank of the Sambre, aiming to seize the bridges at Charleroi, the Anglo-Dutch army to the north of the river was alert to danger but – as the fog and the wet, heavy atmosphere dulled sound to an unusual degree – unaware that anything dramatic was happening. At about 5 a.m. the Prince of Orange rode the fifteen miles from his headquarters at Le Miroir, an inn in the marketplace of Braine-le-Comte, to Jean-Baptiste van Merlen's headquarters at Saint-Symphorien near Mons. All was quiet around the Dutch outposts, but while the Prince was there he heard some rumour of hostilities – probably a report from the forward vedettes reporting gunfire. As a sensible precaution, given the intelligence predicting a French attack, he ordered Merlen to concentrate his light cavalry division on the road to Mons and General David Chassé to bring together the 6500 infantry of his 3rd Netherlands Division on high ground on the road to Nivelles, dispositions aimed at countering a potential French thrust northward across the river from Thuin. In mid-morning Orange returned to headquarters, informed his chief of staff of his actions, and set off for Brussels where he was engaged to dine with Wellington before attending the Duchess of Richmond's ball, the highlight of the social week.

At about 9.30 Dörnberg added a postscript to an otherwise unremarkable report to the effect that he had just heard that the Prussians had been attacked. He sent it on to Braine, where its forward progress was delayed because Sir George Berkeley, the British liaison officer, unaware that the Prince had already left for Brussels, kept it to show to the Prince.

In the early afternoon the Netherlands chief of staff, Jean Victor Baron de Constant Rebecque, learned that Steinmetz had been attacked at Thuin, had abandoned Binche and was retreating to Gosselies. All was quiet around Mons. With the Prince absent, responsibility for his army corps devolved upon Constant, but it was better that way. Orange's appointment had been political – his father had insisted that he should command a corps – and he was young for such a command; his former tutor in contrast was a very capable officer whose presence mitigated the Prince's inexperience. Constant was a career soldier: son and grandson of Swiss officers in Dutch service, he had escaped from the massacre of the Swiss Guards in Versailles in 1792 and had then fought in the Dutch, Prussian and British armies. About 2 p.m. he forwarded the various messages – including Dörnberg's, which Berkeley had finally brought over – to Orange at Brussels.

Constant then ordered the Prince's corps to concentrate ready for action, instructing Hendrik de Perponcher to assemble his first brigade at Nivelles and his second at Quatre Bras, telling the cavalry commander to join Chassé, and warning Generals George Cooke and Karl von Alten, whose British divisions belonged to Orange's corps, to gather their forces in a state of readiness.[1] A messenger alerted the Guards division at Enghien and although Cooke, both brigadiers and most senior staff had already left for the ball at Brussels, their deputies began to summon the troops from their scattered lodgings. The headquarters of Alten's 3rd Division at Soignies was only four miles away, so messages were quickly relayed to the regiments and Ompteda's 2nd Brigade was ready by 3 p.m. Sergeant Tom Morris of the 73rd recalled that 'some of the officers and men were playing at ball against the gable-end of a house in the village' when an orderly dragoon from General Colin Halkett rode in about 4 p.m. with their marching orders.[2]

*

At Brussels the morning passed quietly. An aide bringing a message from Field Marshal Schwarzenburg, the Austrian commander, had arrived together with a Russian general during the night, and Wellington wrote a long letter to the Tsar about their plans to attack France, since the Russians were now ready to cross the Rhine. At 1 p.m. Wellington, still blissfully insouciant, wrote to General Clinton about the renumbering of the British divisions. He remained confident that the apparent threat to Mons was no more than a bluff, and told the Dutch Secretary of State for Belgium, 'I do not believe that they will attack us, we are very strong' and that he only intended to move when it became clear what, if anything, the French were up to.[3] The Prussian liaison officer at Brussels, Carl von Müffling, sent Dörnberg's report of the massing of French troops around Maubeuge and Beaumont to Blücher, but reassured him that Wellington's corps could concentrate very quickly, having concerted plans with Wellington to counter French attacks on either flank.[4] There was no sense of any urgent threat.

Ziethen's second message, announcing a definite attack towards Charleroi, probably reached Prussian headquarters at Namur shortly before 11 a.m. The Prussians took Napoleon's presence to indicate that this was the main threat. Accordingly, Quartermaster-General Karl von Grolmann ordered Ziethen to hold the French at Fleurus because Blücher intended to concentrate the army to fight in the Ligny position next morning, and told him that headquarters was about to move there. At 11.30 Grolmann ordered Bülow to reach the battlefield area at daybreak tomorrow at the latest, sending the message to Hannut in the belief that Bülow had marched there in accordance with the order sent the previous night. Unfortunately, there had been a serious misunderstanding and IV Corps was still at Liège.

Friedrich von Bülow was a Prussian hero of a stature almost equal to Blücher. He had defended Berlin against Marshal Oudinot, defeated Marshal Ney at the battle of Dennewitz, played a conspicuous part at Leipzig and subsequently visited Britain with the successful allied leaders. At sixty, he was older than the other Prussian corps commanders, and though talented, he was vain and touchy

and tended to implement orders only after close scrutiny and modi-
fication (Prussian military convention allowed officers more initiative
than was countenanced in Britain or France). A pure Prussian aristocrat, he disliked being subordinate to Blücher. Ziethen's chief of
staff, Reiche, thought him 'truculent, passionate and obstructive' and
Gneisenau simply did not know how to handle him: their strained
and prickly relationship was almost to lead to disaster.[5] Bülow was
senior to Gneisenau and considered Blücher's Saxon-born henchman
an upstart; it was his consciousness of this that had caused Gneisenau
to phrase his midnight instruction to march to Hannut so over-
politely. Moreover, since it was not signed by Blücher, Bülow had
taken this second warning of imminent action as advice from a junior
officer and had mistaken or ignored its urgency. His corps was still
thirty miles further east than the Prussian staff thought, and
Grolmann's messenger, thinking Bülow's arrival imminent, compounded the catastrophe by waiting for him at Hannut rather than
going to look for him.

At midday Grolmann wrote to Müffling in Brussels to inform
him that the French had attacked at dawn towards Charleroi, that the
Guard and probably Napoleon were present, that Ziethen was to
retreat no further than Fleurus, and that Blücher was concentrating
the army at Sombreffe, where he would set up his headquarters,
intending to accept battle next day. He asked Müffling to 'inform us
as soon as possible when and where the Duke of Wellington intends
concentrating his forces and what he has decided to do.' An hour
later Blücher wrote to tell his wife: 'At this moment I have received
the report that Bonaparte has engaged my whole outposts. I break up
at once and take the field against the enemy. I will accept battle with
pleasure.'[6]

Unaware that the Prussian army was mustering to oppose him,
Napoleon emerged from the woods and got his first sight of
Charleroi a little before 11 a.m. The sun had broken through the mist
and the day was becoming increasingly hot. When they saw General
Rogniat's engineers together with Napoleon, his staff and his escort
squadrons, the Prussians in the Basse Ville withdrew across the

Sambre, leaving the bridge intact. Rogniat's sappers and seamen quickly dismantled the barricades the Prussians had constructed and General Pajol crossed the river in pursuit of the retreating enemy.[7]

Napoleon was welcomed enthusiastically by citizens who preferred the French to the Prussians, and was invited to eat Ziethen's lunch at the Château Puissant, where his lodgings marshal and palace quartermaster had established his palace. He had reason to be satisfied since, despite unfortunate delays, the Sambre bridges had all been captured intact. Around 1.30 p.m. he rode up to the citadel of Charleroi to check the whereabouts of his other columns, to be told he could get a better view to the west, just outside the Brussels gate at Belle Vue. From the coal pits there the ground cut away steeply to the flood plain, revealing Marchiennes, three miles away, and the Brussels road. Taking a seat outside the miners' canteen, the stout little man in the famous grey greatcoat and black bicorne surveyed the progress of Reille's corps, his page supporting his telescope, surrounded by his staff with their plumed hats and his orderly officers in sky blue and silver. Meanwhile, his Young Guard filed down from Vauban's ramparts and marched past him onto the cobbled main road, throwing up coal dust, cheering loudly. Napoleon snatched some sleep, dozing in the hot sunshine. The first stage had not gone badly, but now there were new decisions to be made. The breakthrough had to be exploited.

At about two Gaspard Gourgaud found Napoleon at Belle Vue and reported a concentration of Prussians defending the town of Gosselies three or four miles up the Brussels road. Napoleon sent him with an order to Reille to hasten his crossing of the Sambre and to attack Gosselies. He sent the light cavalry of the Guard, about 2000 strong, in the same direction, and posted one regiment of the Young Guard in reserve a mile up the Brussels road. Soult ordered d'Erlon's corps to follow Reille's towards Gosselies.

Around this time, Marshal Ney appeared at Belle Vue with his aide, Pierre Heymès. The red-headed Ney had ridden along the columns, marching cheerfully to fifes and drums and bands, to the cheers of soldiers who regarded the appearance of the great hero as a good omen. '*Voilà le rougeaud!* (There's the redhead!)' they cried.[8]

To Ney the Emperor revealed the next stage of his plan. Having crossed the river they were only thirty miles from Brussels with a good cobbled road ahead of them, but there was evidently a substantial force of Prussians to the north and east and they were not yet physically out of the woods that encompassed Charleroi. Napoleon intended to lead the bulk of his army north-eastward in an attempt to roll up and destroy the Prussians, while deploying a substantial force to his left to prevent intervention from Wellington to the north or west. He gave Ney verbal instructions to take command of I and II Corps and press ahead along the highway to Brussels.

Until now, Napoleon had given orders directly to each of his five corps commanders and to Marshal Grouchy, who commanded the cavalry. Now, the Emperor was creating a viceroy in Ney, who was to take control of a detached force destined to prevent British interference in the Emperor's manoeuvres for the destruction of the Prussians.

Ney's first task was to drive out whatever Prussians were holding the town of Gosselies, about four miles north; his next target would have been the crossroads with the old Roman road, another important east–west route, that lay about three miles north of Gosselies.[9] Napoleon gave Ney the light cavalry of the Guard and promised that tomorrow he would receive General François Kellermann's corps of heavy cavalry. Bonaparte kept the bulk of his abundant cavalry with his own force, still hoping, no doubt, to create and exploit opportunities to turn the orderly Prussian retreat into an uncontrolled rout.

To give Ney such a command at such a moment courted danger. On one hand, Napoleon had to put someone in command since this detached force might have to fight on its own if, as was likely enough, Wellington or some large Prussian force chose to deny him an easy march to Brussels. But it placed the popular, talismanic marshal under enormous pressure. Ney knew nothing about the officers or the units under his command and they did not yet know that he was in charge of them. Moreover, he had no staff to advise, organise, aid, and carry messages for him – which was unfortunate, since Ney was not so clever or coolly precise as he was brave. In his great days he had

had a brilliant young Swiss military theorist called Antoine Jomini to advise him, but in 1813 Jomini had fallen out with the Emperor's own chief of staff, Marshal Berthier, and, being Swiss, had joined the Russian army instead. Since his other aides and equipment had not yet caught up with him, but for Heymès Ney was now on his own.

While Ney was still receiving his instructions and having the strategic situation explained to him, a messenger from Grouchy arrived at Belle Vue and reported that there were 20,000 Prussians three miles ahead towards Fleurus, blocking the road on the heights above the little village of Gilly. Napoleon wrote to General Gérard to suggest that his corps cross the river at Châtelet to avoid the congestion at Charleroi. From there they would be in a position to outflank this blocking force, although Napoleon probably realised that they would arrive too late to be useful that day.

When he received this order, Gérard was in the woods just to the east of where Napoleon had stopped for breakfast, trudging very slowly through deep mud in the traffic jam on what passed for a road. He turned off to his right along boggy tracks through the woods, but did not reach Châtelet until the evening. Meanwhile, realising that he needed to assess the situation at the front for himself, the Emperor rode forward to see what was happening at Gilly.

The Skirmishes at Gilly, Gosselies and Frasnes

15 June, 3–10 p.m.

Lieutenant-General Claude Pajol had been riding with nearly 3000 horsemen towards Fleurus when, after two miles, they reached the village of Gilly. Here the road became a bottleneck lined with houses. Anticipating an ambush, Pajol sent the 5th Hussars forward to reconnoitre, but at the far end of the village they rode into Prussian artillery fire and quickly withdrew. Pajol spread his men to scout and sent a message back to Marshal Grouchy, while a company of Guard sappers began to fortify the village.

Grouchy galloped to the front. Studying the position at Gilly, he decided the Prussians were far too strong to attack without infantry, and sent an aide to find Napoleon. Having raced to Charleroi, the Guard infantry was now halted at the far end of the town, which puzzled them, since speed appeared to be of the essence.[1] Napoleon was presumably waiting for news of what was happening up the Brussels road before deciding which way to send them.

At 1.30, from the heights above Gilly, General Ziethen reported to Blücher that Otto von Pirch's brigade was with him, Karl von Steinmetz was retreating towards Gosselies covered by the reserve cavalry, and his other two brigades were at Fleurus. He informed

Blücher that the French general de Bourmont had deserted and had revealed that Napoleon was present with 120,000 men.[2] In fact de Bourmont had surrendered himself to the Prussian outposts before receiving movement orders; he had then been interrogated by Ludwig von Reiche, but according to Reiche had told them little, beyond confirming that they were facing a major attack in which Napoleon and his Guard were participating.[3] Ziethen sent de Bourmont on to Blücher, who disdained to speak to him but allowed him to proceed to Ghent. It is said that when it was pointed out to Blücher that de Bourmont was sporting a white Bourbon cockade, the old man replied, 'A shit stays a shit, whatever colour cockade he wears!'[4]

When Napoleon arrived at Gilly around 4 p.m., he studied the Prussian positions. Estimating their strength to be no more than 10,000, he prescribed a frontal attack by infantry backed up by light cavalry, together with a flanking march by Grouchy's dragoons in order to force them to retreat. Although the Prussians were in a strong position on a wooded hill above a stream, Napoleon judged that what he could see was very thinly spread and so probably not numerous, though it was possible that a larger force was hidden by the trees. The Prussian brigade in fact numbered 7000 at most – far fewer than Grouchy's estimate of 20,000.

Nevertheless, it was a good place to set a trap, and Napoleon had to be cautious in case that was what the Prussians were up to. For that reason, he was reluctant to use the infantry of the Guard to make the initial frontal attack, in case the Prussians suddenly enveloped them with hidden hordes emerging from the woods. To make such a mistake would be disastrous, so – presumably feeling that time was still on his side – he preferred to wait until Vandamme's men came up. He returned to Charleroi to chivvy the infantry along.

The delay proved to be an error, for it took at least another hour for III Corps' leading units to reach Gilly. Moreover, there proved to be no trap and as soon as the French infantry finally advanced, the Prussians began to withdraw. Had he risked his Guard immediately, Napoleon might yet have turned into chaos what was in fact a steady Prussian retreat.

About 6 p.m. Vandamme's men finally advanced. The moment the French waded across the brook that separated the forces, however, Pirch withdrew, with his fusilier battalions acting as rearguard. Furious to see the Prussian infantry escaping towards the woods, Napoleon launched the four duty squadrons of Guard cavalry at them, led by a favourite aide, General Louis-Michel Letort, who caught the two fusilier battalions in open ground and destroyed one,[5] before – to the Emperor's grief and dismay – being shot in the stomach and mortally wounded. The Prussian rearguard then took heavy losses from French infantry fire and was captured by Grouchy's cavalry when it reached the far side of the wood.

The main body of Prussian infantry were nevertheless able to retreat through an advancing screen of Ziethen's reserve cavalry and horse artillery. These then protected the retreat, skirmishing with the pursuing French until the fighting died down about seven or eight o'clock and the two sides made camp for the night.

On the western flank, having heard Gourgaud's report of Prussian troops defending the town of Gosselies, Napoleon had sent Marshal Ney with the light cavalry of the Guard to take control, and ordered General Reille to march there as fast as possible. Gosselies was at the northern edge of the forests surrounding Charleroi, and from there a vast plain of rich agricultural fields dotted with woodland stretched away northward until the Forest of Soignes provided a final barrier before Brussels. From Gosselies the ground rose and fell in a series of slight ridges, essentially flat and easy, and a wide cobbled road, much used by coal wagons, led all the way to the capital, twenty-six miles further north.

The 3000 Prussians discovered by Gourgaud at Gosselies had been ordered to hold the village until Karl von Steinmetz arrived with the 9000 men of his retreating brigade. General Steinmetz arrived around 1.30 to see French cavalry ahead of him and others visibly approaching to his right; realising that his brigade was in danger of being cut off, he prepared to fight his way through. Lacking infantry, however, the French fell back in the face of such numbers, and Steinmetz was able to march into Gosselies unchallenged.

Ney arrived around 4 p.m. and launched an attack with the Guard horse artillery, whereupon Steinmetz pulled out, using his fusiliers and Silesian Hussars as rearguard. During the skirmishing a party of forty hussars was cut off and rode towards Nivelles, where the next morning they joined the Netherlanders. About half an hour later Maigrot's light infantry occupied the abandoned town and took a number of stragglers prisoner, while both sides suffered a few casualties from shooting and half-hearted charges. At this time most of Reille's corps was still marching towards Gosselies in a vast dusty column that stretched from Jumet to Marchiennes.[6] Ney sent Piré's cavalry to shadow and harry Steinmetz's retreating column east towards Fleurus and ordered the Guard light cavalry to explore the main road north towards Brussels with the aim of occupying Quatre Bras if possible. They trotted off towards Frasnes, four and a half miles further north up the Brussels road, followed eventually by Maigrot's light infantry and the rest of General Gilbert Bachelu's division, which was leading Reille's corps. Gilbert Bachelu was the son of a lawyer from Franche-Comté on the German border, and trained as an engineer. A hightly experienced officer, he had been promoted to command a division for his conduct with the rearguard in the retreat from Russia and his defence of Danzig in 1813. His chief of staff was devoted to his energetic, tenacious, frank, loyal and generous commander.

By abandoning Gosselies and retreating towards Fleurus, the Prussians had left the cobbled highway to Brussels open and exposed the nearest elements of Wellington's army to the French attack.

At Frasnes, a battalion of green-coated Nassau light infantry was the most advanced unit of Wellington's army. These Germans from Wiesbaden, who were fighting with the Netherlands army, had been on the alert for some days, gathering on the parade ground during daylight hours before dispersing to their cantonments at night. They were already aware that something was up, for around noon heavily laden peasants seeking refuge, with children driving their cattle before them, had warned them of a French invasion.

In charge were Major Philipp von Normann commanding the

light battalion and Adriaan Bijleveld with a battery of Dutch horse artillery, both with long experience in the French army.[7] Normann was on the drill ground that morning when he was surprised to hear gunfire. Headquarters told him this was a Prussian exercise, but by the time their reply reached him in the afternoon the noise was unmistakably closer. With panicky refugees speaking of invasion, the distant rattle of musketry and no orders, he became agitated. He sent a mounted artilleryman to his regimental headquarters and, without waiting for orders, assembled his men.

At 3.30 the artilleryman found Johann Sattler, who had taken command of the regiment that morning after the colonel had had his shin broken by a kick from a horse.[8] Sattler immediately sent warnings to his divisional commander, Hendrik de Perponcher, four miles further west at Nivelles and to Prince Bernhard of Saxe-Weimar commanding the Orange-Nassau Regiment three miles further north along the road at the town of Genappe. He ordered his own regiment to march the short distance to the prearranged assembly point for the brigade at Quatre Bras, the strategically important crossroads of the Brussels–Charleroi highway with the main road between Nivelles and Namur.

The twenty-three-year-old Prince Bernhard had also been alarmed by the fugitive peasants on the Brussels road and was nervous because he had no orders. Thanks to the Nassau colonel's broken leg, Bernhard had been left as the senior officer in the brigade but without an appointment to command it. Not that he was without experience: born in Weimar, he had fought as a boy for the Prussians at Jena before joining the Saxon army on the French side. As an aide to Marshal Bernadotte he had distinguished himself in 1809 in the victory of Wagram over the Austrians before changing sides again in 1813. Bernhard was immensely tall, a conspicuous figure on the big black arabian stallion that the Tsar of Russia had given him.[9] When the head of the military police of Charleroi arrived at Genappe and told him of the French attack, he too decided to march to Quatre Bras.[10]

Hendrik de Perponcher-Sedlnitzky was an Orangist courtier, like Netherlands chief of staff Constant, and had fought with the British until Napoleon threatened to seize his lands unless he resigned his commission. Soon after sending his aide to investigate Sattler's report of gunfire, he received orders from Constant to assemble his brigades. By then Prince Bernhard had already left for Quatre Bras on his own initiative.

About 6 p.m. a wounded Prussian hussar burst into Frasnes, shouting that the French were close behind. Then the Dutch commissariat convoy of provision wagons from Charleroi came in, having also been ambushed by French lancers who had been driven off by its escort of Prussian lancers. Normann pulled back to the high ground above the village, leaving a token outpost below. When more French lancers appeared and began to slip round his flank, he ordered a retreat towards the woods near Quatre Bras. Saxe-Weimar was already at the crossroads with the other two Nassau battalions, minus three hundred men detached by Sattler to occupy the end of the Bossu wood nearest Frasnes. Hearing cannon shots and musketry coming from Frasnes, Bernhard set light to the alarm beacon at Quatre Bras.[11] The Germans watched French lancers rein in just out of musket shot and then disappear again.

From the allied point of view it was important that they had some troops blocking the road towards Brussels and that through them they had become aware that French troops were moving in that direction.

Marshal Ney has received a great deal of abuse over the years for his failure to seize Quatre Bras. Close examination of the evening's events, however, would seem to suggest that this is unfair. There is no documentary evidence as to what exactly Ney was ordered to do that evening. According to Gaspard Gourgaud's account, written during the Emperor's exile on Saint Helena and claiming to express Napoleon's views, Ney was to attack anything he found on the Brussels road and take position at the hamlet of Quatre Bras about ten miles ahead:

After giving these orders to him, the Emperor added, 'Monsieur le Maréchal, you are familiar with Quatre Bras?'

'Yes, Sire,' replied the Marshal; 'how could I not know it? I fought in this region twenty years ago; that position is the key to everything.'

'Well then,' the Emperor said to him, 'collect your two corps, and if necessary, build some field defences there. Hurry d'Erlon along and have him call in all the detachments that he will have left at the Sambre bridges: everything must be together before midnight.'

Ney replied immediately, 'You can rely on me: in two hours we shall be there unless the whole enemy army is there.'[12]

Ney denied that he was ordered to take Quatre Bras that night and it is likely that he wasn't: Napoleon probably named the strategically important but distant crossroads as an objective, but it is unlikely that he demanded its capture that evening at all costs, since neither of them knew what lay ahead and it was important that the two columns should proceed at a similar pace to maintain mutual support and communication. There is evidence that Charles Lefèbvre-Desnouëttes had been hoping to seize the crossroads, however. An aide to Napoleon at his great victory at Marengo in 1800, Lefèbvre-Desnouëttes had always since then been a loyal follower and a trusted cavalry general, and had commanded Bonaparte's favourite *chasseurs-à-cheval* of the Guard since 1808. He had made his way towards the crossroads but, seeing that there was significant opposition ahead and that the light was fading, he decided to halt for the night at Frasnes. He was reinforced between half past eight and nine o'clock, when a very tired and dusty battalion of the 2nd Light, the vanguard of Reille's column, marched into the village. These men had been up since the early hours if they had ever slept, had covered about twenty-nine miles during the day and had fought in several sharp skirmish actions. They were very tired, ready to eat and sleep.

As it grew dark, Lefèbvre-Desnouëttes wrote a report for Ney who had remained at Gosselies.[13] He said that he had driven Nassauers northward from Frasnes to the woods, had taken fifteen prisoners, caused about forty casualties and suffered about ten. Colbert's lancers had approached within musket shot of Quatre Bras but, under fire from enemy artillery, and finding it occupied by infantry, they had withdrawn. A tired battalion of infantry had arrived at Frasnes as he returned there just before 9 p.m. The Nassauers belonged to Wellington's army but they were stationed locally and had not come from Brussels, so there was no indication that Wellington's army was yet on the move, nor had they taken part in the fighting at Gosselies.

The way in which the report is couched indicates that Lefèbvre-Desnouëttes' objective had been the crossroads at Quatre Bras, but his disappointment at failing to take post there was not acute – it had not mattered that much. There was in any case absolutely no way that he could have seized Quatre Bras with five battalions of infantry defending it, since his guns were still behind two miles south with Bachelu, who had occupied the crossroads of the Roman road with the Brussels highway. Lefèbvre-Desnouëttes expressed the opinion that the forces occupying Quatre Bras would probably retire during the night.

For Ney's part, even if he had pressed Bachelu's infantry to the limit of their endurance it is unlikely that he could have driven out the Nassauers before nightfall. In any case, it mattered little: he was well placed to cut the Namur–Nivelles highway and he commanded the direct east–west route offered by the Roman road.

16

The French and Prussian Camps

Overnight, 15–16 June

Instead of driving his vanguard on to Quatre Bras, Marshal Ney had pursued the more urgent business of establishing a headquarters and making contact with the divisions that were now under his command. He chose for the former purpose the most imposing house in Gosselies, belonging to a nail merchant named Melchior Dumont, and while his wealthy host prepared an extravagant supper and opened numerous bottles of fine burgundy, Ney sent messengers to locate his various generals and discover the strength of their regiments and the names of their colonels.

In this he was only partly successful; he was in contact with the leading divisions that had been close to Gosselies during the afternoon, but he had not apparently located Reille. Colonel Toussaint Trefcon, chief of staff to General Bachelu who commanded the vanguard division, returned to Ney at Gosselies three or four times during the evening, bringing reports and details of the composition and location of his regiments.[1] Before midnight Ney reported to Soult. He claimed 500–600 Prussian prisoners after the engagement at Gosselies, and told the major-general that the lancers and chasseurs of the Guard were at Frasnes, General Bachelu's division was a couple of miles further back, where he controlled the junction with the Roman road – one of his objectives – and General Foy's division was at Gosselies. Piré's light cavalry was tracking Steinmetz's Prussians. 'I do not know where General Reille is,' Ney concluded.

Reille was actually in the same town, but the two generals had not yet discovered each other's whereabouts. In Reille's own, realistic and matter-of-fact report to Soult he stated that one battalion of the 2nd light infantry had reached Frasnes around 9 p.m., while the rest of Bachelu's division and the cavalry were just behind. Two divisions were around his headquarters but Jean-Baptiste Girard's division had followed Napoleon's order to take the road toward Fleurus. The light infantry had suffered about eighty casualties and the 1st Chasseurs around twenty to twenty-five, but they had taken 260 prisoners.

The comte d'Erlon, commander of I Corps, was at Jumet, a mile south of Gosselies. Although he had written several letters on the subject, his order to hold the Sambre crossings had not been rescinded, so his troops were still guarding points along his line of march and one brigade of his cavalry was acting as rearguard all the way back between Solre and Thuin. A brigade of cavalry and three divisions of infantry were camped along the road between Gosselies and Marchiennes, but the fourth, Joachim Quiot's division, was guarding the crossings near Thuin, seventeen miles further behind. In the evening they were belatedly given orders to destroy the bridges across the Sambre from Thuin to Marchiennes and march forward at first light.[2]

This was another example of the sort of detail that Marshal Berthier, had he been present, would have dealt with on the Emperor's behalf. Bad communication with Vandamme had led to one crucial delay; now failure to communicate properly with d'Erlon led to another. In guarding the bridges Napoleon had taken sensible precautions to prevent any flank attack by Wellington's troops, but he had forgotten to issue orders to destroy them once it was clear that he no longer needed them intact. Soult, however, did not spot the problem emerging and did not remind Napoleon of it when he needed reminding. Consequently, next day when d'Erlon's troops were suddenly needed at the front, they were still strung out miles back along the road. Though there had originally been a perfectly good military reason for keeping them in that position, the fact that they were not now further ahead was entirely the Emperor's fault.

These troops stacked up idly behind the front line had been misbehaving and General François-Xavier Donzelot, who had spent the years from 1807 to 1814 in Corfu as a benign governor of the Ionian Islands, wrote a strongly worded warning to the regiments of his division – the hard-bitten André Ravard's 13th Light included – about their conduct. He complained that 'people have smashed open the doors of houses, broken up the interior furniture, pillaged, mistreated the inhabitants, forced priests to hand over their silverware and their consecrated vessels, acts of rape have been committed.' He emphasised that the Belgians were to be treated like the Frenchmen they had been and would shortly become, and ordered that officers were to supervise the gathering of firewood and forage and that any future marauders would face a court martial.[3]

Nor was the marauding confined to Donzelot's division. Lieutenant Jacques Martin's 45th Line was in General Marcognet's division and bivouacked near Marchiennes:

> This night was better than the preceding one. It didn't rain. The soldiers went to find wood and straw and, as was usually the case, while searching the attic for wood, they found some wine in the cellar. It is an inevitable evil: to look for forage, it is necessary to enter houses. Indeed, it is fortunate when nothing more serious happens. Among those given this job, one of our soldiers who had fought in Spain went straight to the village priest and, as he knew the ways of these gentlemen, he went down into the cellar and from it brought us back several bottles of an excellent, well-aged wine, which we drank to the health of the good cleric.[4]

Despite his failure to occupy Quatre Bras, Ney had done much better than the right wing. Having stopped several miles short of the crossroads that had been its ultimate goal, the French right wing camped about two miles short of Fleurus, the town that had probably been their main objective. Marshal Grouchy later claimed that they were obliged to halt because General Vandamme refused to obey his order to support the cavalry in attacking the town, and whether or not this was true they were evidently not getting on well together.[5] In any case, Napoleon must have been fairly satisfied with what his army had achieved. Unless the French had induced a panic rout in the Prussian corps that was contesting their progress, they could never have got beyond Fleurus that day. You could only push troops so far without courting disaster.

Overnight, the Guard camped near Charleroi. By 9 p.m. Napoleon had returned to his headquarters at the Château Puissant, where Hippolyte de Mauduit's battalion, the second of the 1st *Grenadiers-à-pied*, took their turn as headquarters guard, piling their guns and camping in the courtyard. Mauduit was a twenty-year-old Breton who had fought in the campaign of 1813 in Saxony. Awarded promotion for bravery, he had elected to become a sergeant in the Old Guard rather than an officer of the line.

They spent the evening cooking food, both for present consumption and for the next day. They had been on the march for nearly eighteen hours and had had no chance to cook and they expected that the next day might well follow the same pattern.[6] The Emperor slept while he waited for reports to come in.

The vanguard camped at the edge of the woods just south of Fleurus. Grouchy wrote a report full of praise for his intrepid troops, claiming that the 15th Dragoons had broken a square and taken 300 prisoners. The ill-feeling and bickering between the three generals was evident in their reports. Pajol complained about Vandamme's unsoldierlike failure to support his outposts with infantry, while Vandamme wrote a matter-of-fact statement of the location of his troops. Vandamme said that in his opinion the enemy was 12–15,000 strong and in retreat beyond Fleurus, while Grouchy estimated their strength at 30,000. On this occasion Grouchy may have been closer to the truth, but Vandamme was evidently a difficult colleague.

Count Lobau with his VI Corps camped for the night on the south side of the Sambre. Slowed by narrow defiles that forced the men to go through almost one by one, and tired because bad roads churned up by the passage of preceding troops were thick with cloying mud, they had only reached the river at 8 p.m. after marching twelve miles at a snail's pace. The leading division of Gérard's IV

Corps had meanwhile crossed the Sambre in the evening and formed a bridgehead on the north side. Two more divisions were at Châtelet, just east of Charleroi, but the last infantry division and the cavalry were further back. The rear divisions had marched a very creditable distance under the circumstances and camped late and tired, along with the cuirassiers of Jacques Delort's rearguard.

Once again the army's travelling printing press went to work after these reports reached headquarters at Charleroi, producing the first Army Bulletin of the campaign. This claimed that Reille had taken 300 prisoners and Domon 400 during the advance to the Sambre. At Gilly they had caused 4–500 casualties and taken 1500 prisoners by breaking three squares. French losses were ten killed and eighty wounded.

For their part, the Prussians admitted to about 1200 losses in total, while the real losses were probably about 600 French and 2000 Prussians.[7] General Ziethen had reason to be satisfied with the performance of his corps, having retired almost intact to the overnight position at Fleurus that Quartermaster-General Grolmann had ordered him to occupy. At 10 p.m. his cavalry camped behind the town, leaving strong outposts to the south. Otto von Pirch's tired brigade bivouacked at Ligny, a couple of miles north of Fleurus, while Steinmetz's trooped into the neighbouring village of Saint-Amand towards midnight after a harassing fighting retreat. Ziethen's other two brigades guarded Fleurus and Ligny, so that his whole corps was united in the area that the staff had selected for a battle next day.

However, the concentration and movement of the other Prussian corps was not going so well. Blücher had set up his headquarters at the presbytery at Sombreffe during the afternoon, finding the staircase carved with French graffiti from 1794, and there he waited anxiously for news of the rest of his army. Delayed by rain and mud, small elements of Georg von Pirch's II Corps had reached their points of concentration at the villages of Mazy and Onoz, about four miles east of Ligny as the crow flies, by 5 p.m. on 15 June, but most stumbled in between midnight and the early hours of the following morning, for some of his troops had been lodging more than thirty miles north and east of the point where Gneisenau had ordered them to unite. After marching all day to the sound of sporadic gunfire not far to the west, the intellectual patriot Ludwig Nagel's 25th Regiment reached the huge camp at the village of Onoz just before midnight: 'The fires were burning brightly in the wooded valley. Everything was as quiet and peaceful as the blue sky above us from which a friendly moon shone clearly.'[8]

Franz Lieber's regiment was billeted near the town of Wavre, a good fifteen miles north of Mazy. The youth from Berlin whose father had told him to clean his rifle when the news of Napoleon's escape from Elba had reached the Prussian capital, had volunteered as a rifleman with the 9th Colberg. Wilhelm Häring, later a novelist, was another *Freiwilliger Jäger* in this regiment. Their draft of 600 recruits had crossed the Rhine on 16 May and had been reviewed by Blücher on 25 May before joining their various units.

On 2 June the volunteer riflemen had paraded with the regiment and Lieber had his first sight of Friederike Krüger, their famous female sergeant, who wore three medals. Having cut her hair short and put on male clothing, she had joined the army in 1813 aged twenty-three. By the time her sex was discovered she had so impressed her comrades with her bravery and presence of mind that her brigadier allowed her to stay. Promoted to sergeant at the battle of Dennewitz, she had won the Iron Cross and the Russian order of St George for refusing to leave the field after being wounded. She was the only woman officially serving in the Prussian army, although Lieber knew of another in his brigade who had gone in her brother's clothes so that he could help their parents avoid starvation, and there were many more following the troops. They got orders to assemble around midday and set off southward for Mazy in the evening, marching all night.[9]

The 22nd Regiment had been billeted in villages halfway between Namur and Liège and it took until 9 p.m. for the regiment to assemble before they marched through the night to reach Namur at four the following morning. There, a lieutenant noted in his diary: 'Tired out by the night march, we rested for two hours under the beautiful lime and chestnut trees. The entire military road was covered with troops that were marching to the army's assembly point at Sombreffe. The residents of Namur were standing in crowds on the main road, watching the troops march by.'[10] III Corps also concentrated very slowly, but reached Namur before midnight; this was nothing compared to the disaster of miscommunication with regard to Friedrich von Bülow's IV Corps, which remained at Liège.

At 10.30 p.m. Gneisenau ordered Georg von Pirch to get his corps to the battlefield before dawn and Johann von Thielmann to have his troops at Mazy by daybreak, but they were incapable of moving further without rest. Gneisenau had no idea where IV Corps had got to. The chief of staff reluctantly allowed Ziethen to pull back from Fleurus at first light, uneasy because the other corps were badly behind schedule and it was far from certain that there would be enough troops present to hold the position in the morning. Ziethen began to withdraw to the far side of the Ligny brook and onto the right flank. He had hoped to be able to rest his men, but Gneisenau told Reiche that Ziethen's corps must be prepared to hold off the French until the other troops reached the battlefield.[11]

Blücher faced the agonising prospect that Napoleon might attack in the early morning while exhausted Prussian troops were strung out for miles along the highway. At dawn he sent a staff officer to find out what was happening on his right flank at Frasnes, where gunfire had been heard the previous evening, and then waited impatiently outside his headquarters at the presbytery of Sombreffe for II Corps to march in. It was looking as if at least a quarter of the Prussian army would fail to reach the battlefield that day, and he had a decision to make. With so many troops missing, dare he give battle?

17

The Duchess of Richmond's Ball

15–16 June, 3 p.m.–2 a.m.

At Brussels, meanwhile, the first outlines of what was happening only twenty miles south were being sketched in the early afternoon.

The social event of the week was soon to commence. There had been at least one ball a week for a month or two, but today was the first to be held by the Duchess of Richmond and she wished it to be a splendid occasion. When, however, the Prince of Orange arrived at the Duke of Wellington's smart rented mansion on the Rue Royale in time to dine at three o'clock prior to attending the ball, he announced with all drama that there had been fighting around the Prussian outposts that morning. Wellington was surprised: he had received no warning from Paris of an impending French attack, and thought that this was probably merely some minor disturbance on the border. He wanted more information before he would act, and the Prince, somewhat crestfallen, sent a message to Constant to stand down his divisions unless Constant had new information that would cause him to do otherwise.[1]

Dinner was interrupted by news from Constant. Richmond's son, who had ridden at top speed the twenty-two miles from Braine-le-Comte by changing horses, burst in about four o'clock and confirmed the loss of Thuin and Steinmetz's retreat to Gosselies.[2] Ziethen's messenger arrived at Müffling's house around the same time and, after paying a flying visit to the envoy from Württemberg, Müffling came to tell the Duke that Charleroi was being attacked.[3] Müffling recalled that

> The Duke of Wellington, who usually received daily accounts from Paris (from whence till now the diligences went unimpeded to Brussels), had heard nothing from Paris when I communicated to him the news from General von Ziethen; for the diligences had not been allowed to cross the frontier, and his spies had not yet found means of getting to him by cross roads. It seemed improbable to him that the entire French army should advance by Charleroi; he expected, in particular, that one column would show itself on the great chaussée to Brussels by Mons, where his advanced posts stood.[4]

Wellington's trusted aide Felton Hervey confirmed in July that this was the view at headquarters: 'thinking it probable that these attacks were only a feint, and that the real intention of the enemy was to penetrate by Mons ... [Wellington] merely ordered the different divisions of the army to assemble at their several alarm posts, and wait for further orders.'[5]

When a messenger from the Duke arrived at Quartermaster-General Sir William Delancey's house, Magdalene Delancey sent him on to where her husband of six weeks was dining with the Spanish envoy, Miguel Alava. She then saw from her window Sir William tearing past on horseback to the Duke's. On Delancey's arrival Wellington told him to order his troops to concentrate and be ready to march at a moment's notice, and then briefed him on their movement orders. Sir William summoned his staff to his office, where he spent the next few hours writing. Orders to get ready to march were sent off straight away, but the movement orders were to be held back until Wellington learned whether there was any threat to Mons.

Confused by these utterly unexpected reports of hostilities, Wellington acted cautiously, preferring a slow move to a move in the wrong direction; in this he was possibly influenced by the French royalist intelligence of early June predicting that Napoleon's real attack would be preceded by a feint at the Prussians.[6] Grolmann's message – announcing Napoleon's attack and stating that Blücher intended to fight next day – sent at midday to Müffling, had not yet arrived when at 7 p.m. Müffling reported to Blücher that after receiving Ziethen's message the Duke was concentrating his forces and endeavouring to discover the direction of the attack.

Word soon spread. The local naval commander had dined with Wellington; he went straight to Uxbridge's house, where Sir Hussey Vivian and other cavalry officers had been eating, to deliver the shocking news.[7] Rumour was hard on the heels of official information, if not ahead, for the officers of the Royal Scots were at dinner in the Hotel de Tirlemont when they heard a commotion outside. Soon some 'Belgian gentlemen' came in and told them of a clash on the frontier, just over thirty miles away.[8]

After dinner Wellington walked in the park, as was the general custom. An ensign of the Royal Scots recalled that while he himself was walking there he encountered two Prussian ADCs, who had recently arrived with news of the attack, and one of Lord Hill's aides also learned in the park 'that we were going to move immediately, but on enquiry I found that everybody meant to stay out the ball, I therefore determined to do so myself'.[9] Since all the officers who had been invited to the ball were already in Brussels and further clarification of events at the front might reasonably be expected, Wellington probably saw the gathering as an opportunity to brief them in person without losing much time. Naturally, he did not want to disappoint the Duchess, or to create any greater sense of panic than was inevitable.

Nevertheless, the park hummed with rumour and anticipation that evening. Thomas Picton, who had arrived in Brussels to command the 5th Division that very afternoon, found the colonel of the 28th Foot walking with his officers and told them how pleased he was to have them under his command.[10] Wellington's secretary Fitzroy Somerset, who had dined at his own quarters and there learned the news, 'found the Duke in the Park, giving the necessary orders to those around him'. Wellington left the park towards dusk, deep in conversation with Sir Charles Stuart, the British ambassador.[11] He wrote to the duc de Berri, the French royalist general, asking him to concentrate his forces midway between Brussels and Ghent, and then at ten o'clock to the duc de Feltre, to suggest that the King should be ready to leave Ghent if necessary.

At about this point Müffling brought Wellington Quartermaster-General Grolmann's assessment of the situation at midday, confirming that the Imperial Guard was involved, which implied Napoleon's presence, and stating Blücher's intention to fight at Ligny. This removed any lingering doubt: Wellington had to march to support Blücher. The Duke instructed Delancey to issue the 'After Orders', timed at 10 p.m., which directed the troops towards Nivelles as Ziethen had asked, and Müffling reported to Blücher that this was where Wellington would be concentrating his army.

The route of the march to Nivelles protected a broad area to the south of Brussels, in case the attack against Charleroi should prove to be a feint and another attack should develop from the direction of Mons. The troops at Brussels, Wellington's powerful reserve, were told to stop at Mont Saint-Jean at the junction of the roads to Nivelles and Charleroi, for from there they could still move in either direction. Wellington certainly didn't order his troops to race to help Blücher, but while he still had so little information he was most anxious not to make an irreparable blunder.

The Prince noticed that the Dutch cavalry had been forgotten and penned a postscript to Constant, moving them closer to Nivelles, a large walled town dominated by a huge Romanesque abbey. To this town he ordered his headquarters to move. Nobody thought to summon the two brigades of heavy artillery – twelve 18-pounder guns – that were fitting out only six miles north of Brussels. Next day the commander of one of the two batteries wrote to his wife, 'My brigade is not yet ready, principally I believe for want of drivers,' but this does not sound like an insuperable problem. Rather, neither he nor headquarters judged the situation to be sufficiently dangerous to warrant getting this powerful field artillery on the move ahead of the scheduled advance into France. They must have regretted the decision by Sunday, when such firepower would have been invaluable.[12]

*

Meanwhile, at Quatre Bras the German troops settled down to rest. As it grew dark, Prince Bernhard reported to General Perponcher requesting reserves of ammunition, anxious that he knew nothing about what faced him and that he had no cavalry with which to scout and patrol his open flank. He reminded Perponcher that the second Orange-Nassau battalion, which had arrived from Dillenburg in Hesse only three days ago, was armed with French muskets and had only ten rounds of ammunition each, and that the volunteer Jägers, who had arrived with them, had only six rounds.[13]

Perponcher, four and a half miles further west at Nivelles, had a clearer and more terrifying idea of what was afoot than anyone else. Reconnaissance had established the loss of Gosselies, and a French deserter had confirmed the fall of Charleroi and warned that Bonaparte, at the head of 150,000 men, was marching on Brussels.[14] This was serious to say the least. If Brussels really was the target, should he reinforce Quatre Bras or evacuate it to save his troops from annihilation? At dusk he sent his aide ten miles west to Braine to get guidance from Constant, but ordered all the division's baggage northward up the road to Waterloo.

At Braine-le-Comte, meanwhile, Constant had received no new information for some hours. Since he had every reason to keep his troops outdoors, he ignored Orange's instruction to disperse them to their billets. Then Perponcher's aide announced the attack on Frasnes, the appearance of French cavalry at Quatre Bras and the reported threat to Brussels. Constant was astonished that the Prussians had left the road from Charleroi to Brussels open. It was evidently a flaw in the arrangements between the two armies – it was unclear who was supposed to be guarding it, just as Napoleon had hoped. Constant sent Orange's aide Henry Webster to inform Brussels at top speed. His statement that the French had reached Quatre Bras, only twenty miles from Brussels, slightly exaggerated the danger, but Constant probably designed it to jolt his superiors out of their complacency. He sent another aide to Quatre Bras to get a first-hand insight and to advise Perponcher to defend the crossroads, but to fall back westward on Braine if it proved impossible.

Half an hour later, Constant received an order from Wellington to concentrate both his infantry divisions at Nivelles, which meant abandoning Quatre Bras and leaving the Brussels road open. Like the earlier order to stand his men down, he thought this the wrong thing to do, and decided not to obey, considering that if the Duke had known that the French were poised to advance up the Brussels road he would not have told him to evacuate. Consequently, Constant ordered General Chassé to withdraw to Nivelles but did not order Perponcher to leave Quatre Bras. The initiatives taken by Saxe-Weimar and Perponcher and the calculated insubordination of Constant would prove vitally important to the allied cause in the light of what happened next day.

The Duchess of Richmond's ball was held at the Lennox family's rented house in the rue de la Blanchisserie. Wellington playfully called it 'the wash-house', although the *blanchisserie* itself was further along the street.[15] The house belonged to a carriage maker, and his showroom, linked to the main building by a stair and a covered passage, was used as the ballroom. Like a number of other British families, the Richmonds had moved to Brussels in order to economise, the cost of living being lower in Belgium than in London, but in spring 1815 the British colony had suddenly expanded. Families had moved there from Paris after Bonaparte's return, and then the troops had arrived, accompanied by wives and children or people providing services for the army.

The most distinguished British civilians were invited to the ball, alongside foreign diplomats, aristocratic army officers and the cream of Belgian society. Their carriages began to pull up outside about nine in the evening as the first of the two hundred or so guests arrived. Of these only sixty-seven were women and even fewer were young women, but there were enough young ladies to fill a small ballroom while their illustrious elders sat around as spectators. Few of the older guests were elderly – the Duchess herself was forty-six – and most were soldiers dressed in their most splendid uniforms, a dazzling array of elegance and colour.

Dancing commenced about ten, as the musicians turned to the newly fashionable and exciting waltz, 'the indecent whirling-dance of the Germans', controversial for its capacity to inflame the passions through bodily contact. Not until the following year did this 'voluptuous intertwining of the limbs' first make an appearance at the Prince Regent's court. 'So long as this obscene display was confined to prostitutes and adulteresses we did not think it deserving of notice,' *The Times* fulminated in consequence, 'but now that it is attempted to be forced on the respectable classes of society by the evil example of their superiors, we feel it a duty to warn every parent against exposing his daughter to so fatal a contagion.'[16]

Needless to say, young officers and seventeen-year-old ladies loved waltzing, but the Duchess was keen to show her foreign guests the fashionable dances from her native Scotland, for she was a Gordon, daughter of the 4th Duke of Gordon, and 'Lady Charlotte Gordon's Reel' had been composed in her honour. As a *pièce de résistance* the adjutant, pipe-major Alexander Cameron, and four sergeants of the Gordon Highlanders performed a sword dance.[17]

The Duke arrived 'rather late', probably about eleven, while nineteen-year-old Georgiana Lennox was dancing. Soon afterwards an aide began to distribute movement orders to the officers present and, as the dancing progressed, the whispered rumour began to circulate that there had been an action between the French and Prussians. 'About half past eleven it was said that the French army was advancing & I found that orders were immediately going off to Lord Hill to move his corps, I therefore determined to stay no longer, & consequently I went off to Grammont, & reached it on Friday morning', noted one of Hill's aides.[18] At first the civilians didn't believe the rumour, but 'when the General Officers whose corps were in advance, began to move, and when orders were given for persons to repair to their regiments, matters began to be considered in a different light.'

Wellington spent some time sitting with Jane Dalrymple-Hamilton (Admiral Duncan's daughter) while the dancing went on:

> Although the Duke affected great gaiety and cheerfulness, it struck me that I had never seen him have such an expression of care and anxiety on his countenance. I sat next to him on a sopha

a long time, but his mind seemed quite preoccupied; and although he spoke to me in the kindest manner possible, yet frequently in the middle of a sentence he stopped abruptly and called to some officer, giving him directions, in particular to the Duke of Brunswick and the Prince of Orange, who both left the ball before supper. Despatches were constantly coming in to the Duke.[19]

In contrast to Jane Dalrymple-Hamilton, Elizabeth Ord recalled 'Lord Wellington walking about with Lady F Webster on his arm sometimes talking nonsense to her and sometimes reading reports and giving orders but not seeming as if he had more than usual on his mind'.[20]

Almost every senior British officer in the army of the rank of brigadier and above was present, along with their ADCs and most of the officers of the Guards brigade. Wellington briefed these people and sent them off to their units as soon as supper was over, or in some cases sooner. The forty-three-year-old Duke of Brunswick, with a leonine blond beard and piercing blue eyes, cut a fine figure in his jet black uniform with sky blue facings. His sabre was a present from Princess Charlotte, with a lock of her hair adorning the scabbard. He left after receiving instructions from the Duke to muster his men and march to Waterloo. Sir George Scovell sent instructions to have his black stallion saddled at midnight. Uxbridge got his orders just before supper and left at 1 a.m., 'giving a hint for all cavalry officers to repair to their quarters', although one of Sir Hussey Vivian's aides admitted that he did not leave Brussels until 4 a.m. Some officers recalled that the Duchess tried to stop them leaving before supper and spoiling her party.

Between midnight and supper Orange's aide Henry Webster arrived with the news that the French were at Frasnes on the Brussels road.[21] Wellington studied a map with the Duke of Richmond, exclaiming, 'Napoleon has humbugged me, by God, he has gained twenty-four hours march on me.'[22] It is conceivable that he also indicated, as 'witnesses' reported, that if he couldn't hold the French at Quatre Bras, he would have to fight at Mont Saint-Jean, for that position had been chosen and surveyed as a possible battlefield earlier in the year.

Supper was normally served at one o'clock in the morning. Georgiana Lennox claimed that she sat next to Wellington and he gave her a recently painted miniature of himself, although the Marquise d'Assche remarked that he paid 'ardent court' to the pregnant beauty Frances Webster on his other side. At supper the Duke returned thanks to the toast to the allied armies proposed by General Alava.[23] After supper the ballroom became substantially depopulated and although dancing continued for a while, the party, which should have lasted until six in the morning, ended early. As Lady Jane Lennox remarked:

> I know I was in a state of wild delight – the scene itself was so stirring, and the company so brilliant. I recollect, on reaching the ball-room after supper, I was scanning over my tablets, which were filled from top to bottom with the names of partners to whom I was engaged; when, on raising my eyes, I became aware of a great preponderance of ladies in the room. White muslins and tarletans abounded; but the gallant uniforms had sensibly diminished. The enigma was soon solved. Without fuss or parade, or tender adieux, the officers, anxious not to alarm the ladies, had quietly stolen out.[24]

According to Elizabeth Ord, 'The young officers insisted on our dancing but it was with such an effort that of course it did not last long. Little parties with pale cheeks and red eyes were to be seen in many parts of the room.'[25]

The order to be ready to move at the slightest notice had been received in plenty of time for the officers attending the ball to instruct their servants to have everything packed and ready, but not all of them learned in time of the new order to march at 4 a.m. Some stayed late, and a few were to end up fighting in the outfits they had worn to the ball:

> It would appear that the aforesaid 'ball-room votaries', trusting to the directions they had left with their servants, spent more time in making their adieux to the ladies than they otherwise should have

done. They arrived at their billets, intending to doff their ball dress, and proceed forthwith to the place of rendezvous, when 'donner and blitzen', they found their quarters empty, their baggage, servants, horses, all gone ... These unfortunates had no alternative but to set out in the dress they wore at the ball.[26]

The Duke must have left fairly late, for Jane Dalrymple-Hamilton said that when she left at half past two, he was still there. As far as was possible, no doubt, he wished to convey an impression of calm confidence, even if it was rumoured afterwards that it was his attachment to Lady Webster that 'was the cause of his not being at the Battle in time'. Finally, however, he slipped away to bed.[27]

18

Marching Orders

15–16 June, 11 p.m.–10 a.m.

Communication was something that Wellington's armies generally did well, and in this campaign they were to make the French and the Prussians look amateur by comparison. The Duke's system had been tried and tested in Spain: he explained his wishes to his Quartermaster-General, who had orders written out by officers from the Royal Staff Corps and distributed by orderlies of the 3rd Hussars who had been selected for their steadiness. These German Legionaries usually spoke French and English as well as their native German. 'To each was explained the rate at which he was to proceed, and the time when he was to arrive at his destination; he was directed also to bring back the cover of the letter which he carried, having the time of its arrival noted upon it by the officer to whom it was addressed.'[1] This enabled Quartermaster Delancey to track the progress of his units.

In emergency, messages were carried by aides-de-camp, nearly all wealthy young noblemen, trained to ride well, and equipped with several exceptionally fine horses. It was widely believed that English mounts, bred for hunting and racing, were faster and better adapted for cross-country endurance than foreign horses, trained for obedience in manoeuvre; Müffling was impressed that a British aide-de-camp was capable of covering fourteen miles in an hour at top speed. Officers of the Royal Staff Corps carried duplicate dispatches 'to guard against the possibility of mistake'.[2]

However, on this occasion communication was not as slick as had been hoped. The British army did not concentrate on its left wing within twenty-two hours of the first cannon shot, as the Prussians claimed Wellington had promised. Indeed, twenty-two hours after the first shot concentration had barely commenced, and twenty-two hours after that it was far from complete. Müffling reckoned the projected timetable had rashly assumed concentration would happen in daylight, whereas 'In dark nights orderlies cannot ride fast on cross roads; in the various cantonments they find every one sunk in deep slumber; and delay in arriving at the rendezvous is the inevitable consequence of a calculation grounded on the time it will take to execute an order by day, and not by night.' This was a moonlit night but the minor roads in Belgium were so bad as sometimes to be difficult to recognise as roads.

Basil Jackson carried the duplicate order to Colonel Cathcart, Lord Greenock, to assemble the cavalry at Ninove, their headquarters, eleven miles west of Brussels. As he approached the town, Jackson encountered one or two orderly dragoons speeding to outquarters and saw lights flickering in the nearby villages, which indicated that the German hussar who had left ahead of him had already arrived successfully.[3] However, only Cathcart and Major Thornhill were at Ninove to write out orders, for almost all of the cavalry staff was with Lord Uxbridge at the ball. So there was a further delay before the 2nd Life Guards, based only a mile away, 'having just received orders to march at a moment's notice', began to assemble 'in complete marching order, with all forage and baggage, ready to commence its march'. Private Thomas Playford remembered that 'about two or three in the morning of the 16th of June I happened to be awake and heard the notes of an English bugle at a distance.' Sure enough, it was not long before their own bugler sounded the alarm, quickly followed by the notes of 'to horse'.[4]

Surgeon John James of the 1st Life Guards had dined with the officers of the 2nd after a review of the brigade, and 'returned to Ninove replete with my friends' excellent dinner and vintage wines at twelve o'clock on that fine warm night'. He slept through the alarm and was roused by his friend Captain Edward Kelly, who told him 'the trumpet had been sounding "to horse" for an hour or more.' His servant packed his things and he went over to Kelly's for breakfast. 'It was a lovely morning, the sun about to rise and our trumpets sounding "to horse" in every direction, the suddenness of the call being sufficient excuse for the troops being so little prepared and the tremendous air of bustle, clatter, and indeed confusion, that was over all.'

As he strode, excited, to the captain's quarters, he 'met two Hussars, staggering down very drunk and all unconscious of the call to action around them. One said to his companion, "I don't think I shall go to bed now." One of our lads who heard him laughed and called out, "Belike you will be put to bed with a shroud this night, and know nothing about it."'

By four o'clock his own regiment was ready, with its baggage loaded, but they had to wait another four hours for the King's Dragoon Guards to ride in last from their quarters six miles away. Their marching orders arrived shortly after daybreak, but they were ordered merely to march ten miles south to Enghien and there await further instructions; moreover 'it was generally thought that it was only intended to concentrate the Army'.[5]

Frederick Ponsonby, second son of the Earl of Bessborough, the young, sandy-haired commander of the 12th Light Dragoons, had been invited to Brussels to attend the Duchess of Richmond's ball, but had learned of the attack before he got there and decided to ride back to Ninove instead. 'We were on the ground at 6 o'clock in the morning, the rest of the cavalry, having further to come, did not arrive till nine or ten,' he wrote, but Sir John Ormsby Vandeleur, Ponsonby's commander, led his brigade off without waiting for the whole of the cavalry to reach the rendezvous. The hussars of generals Grant and Vivian started from further away, a good ten miles south-west, and left later. Some of the Royal Horse Artillery was also further away to the north and Captain Cavalié Mercer realised when his order to leave for Enghien arrived that his ammunition and supply wagons were scattered all over the place.[6] Mercer was acting commander of G-troop and the voyage to Buenos Aires for an ill-fated campaign in 1807 had been his only active service, so this sudden call to arms was enormously exciting.

Separate instructions were sent to the German hussars on the French border. The 2nd Regiment was ordered to remain on watch around Mons, and the 3rd was told to leave pickets in place on the border further north, so only 500 of their 700 men joined the army, riding direct to Enghien.[7] The 1st left the frontier at midday for Braine-le-Comte. Wilhelm von Dörnberg's regiments north of Brussels, having been delayed getting food and forage, then followed Wellington's reserve southward via the capital.

It took a long while simply to contact the most westerly troops. Sir Charles Colville, forty miles west of Brussels at Audenaerde, got orders for the 4th Division only at 6 a.m. and his troops were marching south-east towards Enghien by ten. Prince Frederick's men assembled around noon, but could not march until the late afternoon, leaving behind 500 militiamen to garrison Audenaerde. Orders did not reach General Henry Clinton, commanding Hill's 2nd Division, based thirty miles south-west of Brussels, until about 7 a.m. He had not been to the ball and was unaware of the emergency; it was not until around ten that his British regiments were gathered. Carl du Plat's German brigade had been on an exercise since 2 a.m. and took the order to march immediately literally, leaving without rations or baggage, although by regulation these veteran legionaries already had iron rations in their packs.

The 5th Division at Brussels had been prepared for a sudden start. Sergeant David Robertson of the 92nd Gordon Highlanders explained that 'the orderly sergeants were desired to take a list of the men's quarters, with the names of the streets, and the numbers of the houses. It was also arranged that every company and regiment should be billeted in the same, or the adjacent streets, to prevent confusion if called out at a moment's warning.' That day 'the sergeants on duty were all in the orderly room till ten o'clock at night; and no orders having been issued, we went home to our quarters. I had newly lain down in bed when the bugle sounded the alarm, the drums beat to arms, bagpipes played, and all was in commotion.' When the alarm sounded, 'sergeants and corporals ran to the quarters of their respective parties to turn them out.' Robertson 'went to the quarter-master for bread, and four days' allowance was given out of the store'. The men also received a pint of gin, four days' ration of beef and 120 rounds of cartridge.[8] Another veteran orderly sergeant, Ned Costello of the Rifles, a short, twenty-six-year-old Leinsterman, commented that of the rations he drew and handed out to his men, 'the chief part of this was left behind, as none but old soldiers knew its value.' Young soldiers gave the heavy rations to their hosts or left them on the pavement.[9]

Although in theory the soldiers' wives and camp followers were supposed to remain in Brussels, there is abundant evidence that this was not so in practice. A visitor who had arrived in Brussels earlier that day watched the scene from her rooms in the Hôtel de Flandre:

> Numbers were taking leave of their wives and children, perhaps for the last time, and many a veteran's rough cheek was wet with the tears of sorrow. One poor fellow, immediately under our windows, turned back again and again, to bid his wife farewell, and take his baby once more in his arms; and I saw him hastily brush away a tear with the sleeve of his coat, as he gave her back the child for the last time, wrung her hand, and ran off to join his company, which was drawn up on the other side of the Place Royale. Many of the soldiers' wives rushed out with their husbands to the field, and I saw one young English lady mounted on horseback, slowly riding out of town along with an officer, who, no doubt, was her husband.[10]

The same visitor was nonetheless amused to see that:

> Into this confusion of soldiery quietly moved a long trail of carts from the country coming in to market as usual, with old Flemish women sitting among piles of cabbages, baskets of peas, early potatoes and strawberries, gaping with wonder at the strange scene around them as they jogged through the Place Royale and through the crowds of soldiers and the confusion of baggage wagons.[11]

Once the companies were equipped, the battalions marched into the park in front of the Royal Palace, where the brigades were inspected.[12] Basil Jackson returned in time to see the whole division gathered in the park and stood by the Hotel Bellevue as the veterans marched off. First came the 95th Rifles in forest green, with black facings and belts, then the 28th North Gloucesters playing 'The British Grenadiers', then the 42nd Highlanders, the Black Watch, 'marching so steadily that the sable plumes of their bonnets scarcely vibrated'. The 79th Cameron and 92nd Gordon Highlanders were also wearing tartan kilts and plumed bonnets covered with black ostrich feathers. Jackson watched, along with many others in the golden dawn, as Picton's veteran division marched south along the broad street to the Porte de Namur.[13]

An ensign of the Brunswick Guards arrived at the Allée Verte on the northern fringe of Brussels to find the Duke of Brunswick lying on the grass under the avenues of trees poring over a huge map, while he waited for his scattered battalions to march in. The commander of his hussars, Major von Cramm, had held a boozy party where they played music, sang songs and shot at a target and his men had hardly lain down to sleep when the alarm sounded, summoning them to the Allée Verte before daybreak. Since the more distant units had only received orders to move an hour after they were due at the rendezvous, the Duke marched off at sunrise with what was present, leaving three battalions, the Uhlans and artillery to follow. The artillery mustered at eight, reaching Waterloo at two in the afternoon; when, an hour further on, one of the Duke's aides summoned them to hurry, they sent an advance guard to clear the way ahead by pushing the wounded and the baggage off the street.[14]

Before dawn Wilhelm von Dörnberg arrived in Brussels from Mons. Having waited for more news from his outposts, then ridden into Binche and found the Prussians gone, he decided the campaign had probably begun and that he should report to headquarters. After getting a taste en route of the alarm at Braine-le-Comte, he was concerned that at Brussels there was still no sense of the real urgency of the situation and believed that it took his arrival to get the Duke of Wellington out of bed.

Refreshed by his brief repose, the Duke sent Colonel Canning to fetch Sir Thomas Picton, who had slept at the Hotel d'Angleterre after his arrival in Brussels the previous evening. Picton abandoned his breakfast to join Wellington, Fitzroy Somerset and the Duke of Richmond in the park, where he found the Duke at his most formal and haughty:

> Picton's manner was always more familiar than the duke liked in his lieutenants, and on this occasion he approached him in a careless sort of way, just as he might have met an equal. The duke bowed coldly to him, and said, 'I am glad you are come, Sir Thomas; the sooner you get on horseback the better: no time is to be lost. You will take the command of the troops in advance. The Prince of Orange knows by this time that you will go to his assistance.' Picton appeared not to like the duke's manner; for when he bowed and left, he muttered a few words, which convinced those who were with him that he was not much pleased with his interview.[15]

Picton nevertheless rode off after his men to reinforce the Prince of Orange.

Meanwhile Constant at Braine-le-Comte had the troops belonging to the Prince's corps assembled significantly earlier than the other elements of Wellington's army. Karl von Alten's 3rd Division had assembled at Soignies in the early evening, many of them crammed into the town's huge church. Told to move in the small hours, they formed up in the marketplace and left immediately, receiving their 'after orders' as they marched, but their route to Nivelles led through thick woodland 'and as it was not known how near the enemy might be, it was necessary to throw out an advanced guard and proceed with caution'. According to Sergeant Tom Morris, 'the progress we made through the wood was so slow, that by eight o'clock in the morning we had not proceeded more than ten miles.'[16]

At Enghien, where the Guards were already concentrated, the drums beat an hour after midnight, and the men stumbled from their quarters. There they waited for their officers to return from the ball and change their clothes, and the column eventually took the road south-east towards Braine-le-Comte around dawn.

Wellington's army was even further behind schedule than Blücher's; if any battle were to begin early in the morning very little of it would be present. But they were now at least on the move.

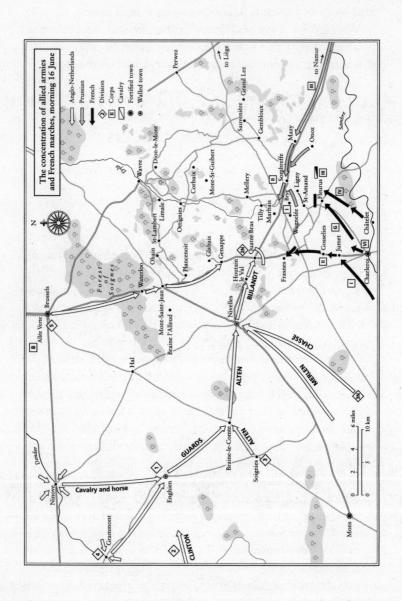

The concentration of allied armies and French marches, morning 16 June

Anglo-Netherlands
Prussian
French
Division
Corps
Cavalry
Fortified town
Walled town

19

The Emperor's Orders

16 June, 4–10 a.m.

Around four o'clock Napoleon got up to study the reports from his generals and issue them with fresh orders. It looked as if the Prussians were behaving as he had wanted them to. They appeared to be retreating eastwards, and they had made no attempt to move north in order to link up with Wellington. He sent an aide to Frasnes to assess Ney's situation, for yesterday's events were bound to provoke a reaction from the enemy, but he hoped that the other army would also retreat. Napoleon later claimed that he had expected the rash Blücher to help Wellington, but did not expect Wellington to hurry to Blücher's aid; he thought that a forceful attack would send them reeling in opposite directions, with each looking after his own national interest. In reality, he had underestimated their determination to help each other.[1]

However, the immediate priority, whatever Wellington and Blücher might be doing, was to destroy the Prussian troops that had eluded him yesterday. To this end Napoleon's first plan was to seize control of the roads leading towards Brussels from the Prussian bases in the east, block them with French troops, and then march on Brussels, defeating Wellington's army or driving it to the sea. As the day's events unfolded, however, he was to change his plans several times. A day intended to start with the completion of yesterday's business against Ziethen's corps and end with a march on Brussels, would evolve quite differently. To understand why things turned out as they did it is important to grasp how Napoleon's appreciation of the opportunities open to him changed. Early that morning he did not anticipate having to fight two bloody battles during the day, and it was because he had to react to the unexpected that staff work and communication were to take on such importance as the day went on.

By 6 a.m. *Major-Général* Soult was writing orders. Jean de Dieu Soult was a clever man who had been a difficult opponent for Wellington in the Peninsula. Cold, hard, ambitious and ruthless, in his role as one of Napoleon's original marshals he had played a key part in Bonaparte's glorious victories long ago. But Soult was a controversial choice for the job. Having served as chief of staff to General Lefebvre during the Fleurus campaign of 1794, he had some experience of the topography and conditions in that part of Belgium, and had been nominal chief of staff to Joseph Bonaparte in Spain, but he had not previously done the job with Napoleon. His deputy, Bailly de Monthion, resented his demotion to assistant, while the staff that Soult had hurriedly gathered had no experience of working together and was distinctly inferior to that of his long-trusted predecessor, Marshal Berthier. Inadequacies had already emerged in conflicting orders to d'Erlon that had resulted in two divisions and a cavalry brigade remaining miles behind the front. Moreover, Soult's apparent enthusiasm for the role as war minister to Louis XVIII he had occupied until he was sacked on 11 March 1815 had made him very unpopular in an army that was largely Bonapartist or republican. He had reintroduced chaplains to regiments that had little love for priests, set up a monument to the *émigrés* who, wearing British uniforms, had been defeated by the French revolutionary government at Quiberon in 1795, and had prosecuted several of his current colleagues who had declared prematurely in favour of Napoleon. General Vandamme refused to shake his hand and would not take orders from him until made to do so by Napoleon.

Napoleon had decided to emphasise Marshal Grouchy's authority by giving him the prime role that morning. Grouchy was to take command of the corps led by Gérard and Vandamme and march, first on Sombreffe to cut the road from Namur to Nivelles, and then on the nearby town of Gembloux to cut the road from Namur to Brussels. He was to carry out extensive reconnaissance, especially towards Namur, to discover as much as possible about the location of Prussian forces.[2]

As Napoleon's most recently appointed marshal, promoted in April after his defeat of the Duc d'Angoulême in Provence, Emmanuel de Grouchy was the senior ranking officer after Ney and Soult and had to be given this command, though it is questionable whether he was up to the task. He came from the liberal aristocracy, his sister being the Girondin intellectual Sophie de Condorcet; Grouchy had shared her principles, and had been ejected from the Royal Guard for supporting reform in 1789. He became a general under the Republic, but quickly accepted Bonaparte's régime, distinguishing himself at Eylau and Friedland and commanding a cavalry corps in Russia. Unemployed under the King, Grouchy rallied to Napoleon and won the swift victory over royalist forces in Provence that caused Napoleon to make him a marshal. The nephew of Grouchy's wife wrote that Grouchy was an extremely distinguished, brave cavalry officer, but had never been in overall command and had no experience of commanding infantry and combining arms. He was little known by the soldiers, little liked by his colleagues, weak, and incapable of taking a decision. Above all, he was fearful of displeasing Napoleon, even to the point of acting against his own instinct. A long habit of passive obedience had robbed him of initiative.[3]

To support Grouchy's aggressive thrust, Antoine Drouot was to march the Guard to Fleurus. Meanwhile the comte de Lobau was to wait at the crossroads outside Charleroi, ensuring that the prisoners and the wounded were sent back to Avesnes, and protecting the artillery park, which contained the reserve ammunition. From there he could reinforce either Grouchy or Marshal Ney, who was on the road towards Brussels.

Soult's orders to Ney assumed that the hostile force at Quatre Bras would have retreated during the night towards either Nivelles or Brussels, as General Lefèbvre-Desnouëttes had anticipated. Ney was to occupy Quatre Bras and then scout ahead along the Nivelles and

Brussels roads. If at all possible, he was to place an advance guard at Genappe, three miles nearer Brussels, and a division at Marbais, a village halfway between Quatre Bras and Sombreffe. Soult instructed Kellermann's corps of cuirassiers to join Ney. The light cavalry of the Guard and the 1st Hussars were also to ride to Marbais, unless they were already engaged in following the enemy.

At this point Napoleon was exploring. He had no idea that the whole Prussian army was attempting to gather close by and no knowledge of what Wellington was doing. His scouts told him that the Prussians had at most 40,000 men opposed to him, hence his plan to thrust north-east and seize first Sombreffe and then Gembloux, thus blocking the two main routes to Brussels from Namur and Prussian bases further east. With the Prussians prevented from interfering, he would strike suddenly at Brussels with the rest of his men.

At the same time as Soult sent movement orders Napoleon sent out his own instructions. His *Maison Militaire* of aides and orderlies had always duplicated the *État Major-Général*, the headquarters staff, and he liked to amplify important orders sent by the *Major-Général*, partly as a safeguard, but also because his own aides, having better horses and more initiative, were likely to reach their destination faster and to be capable of interpreting the Emperor's wishes in the face of the unexpected. Napoleon's senior aides were far more than just messengers: as personal emissaries of the Emperor their word carried extra weight. They all had the rank of *général-de-brigade*, thus outranking mere colonels, and they were often used to conduct reconnaissances, lead attacks or command detached forces. Napoleon's own orders naturally reveal a great deal more of his thinking than do those sent by Soult, and if any doubt remained in the mind of the recipient or if there were any conflict between the orders those sent by the Emperor took precedence. With duplicate orders being dispatched, however, there was always potential for confusion.

To Ney Napoleon sent Charles de Flahaut, supposed love-child of Talleyrand, lover of Josephine's daughter Hortense, and one of the most gifted of his loyal followers. Napoleon's letter told Ney that he was dividing his army into two wings and a reserve. He instructed

Ney to take up position at Quatre Bras. Just what Napoleon would do depended on what happened after Grouchy's attempted advance on Sombreffe, but Ney was to be prepared to march on Brussels later in the day, since Napoleon hoped to be there next morning following a forced march through the night. Napoleon's staff expected the enemy to have evacuated not only Quatre Bras but also Nivelles and assumed Wellington's outposts would fall back as Napoleon advanced.

The Emperor's letter to Ney acknowledged that there might be some flare-up with the English but he expected Ney to have a quiet day gathering his troops in readiness for a march in the evening. He instructed Ney to place a division at Marbais, to cover the open space between the two wings and in order to reinforce either wing if necessary, and he wanted Kellermann's cuirassiers stationed at the intersection of the Brussels high road with the Roman road so that they might also be in a position to support either wing. Ney could order Kellermann to join him if the Emperor did not need him. He told Ney to keep Lefèbvre-Desnouëttes' Guard light cavalry with him because they would probably have to ride to Brussels later, but if there was fighting to be done to use line cavalry instead.

Napoleon sent a similar letter to Marshal Grouchy, placing it in the hands of General de la Bédoyère. Intended to reinforce his authority over Vandamme, this confirmed that Grouchy was now in charge of the right wing, that Vandamme and Gérard were to take his orders, and that they knew that Napoleon himself would only give them orders when he was present in person. Until now Grouchy had commanded the cavalry and had no authority over Vandamme beyond that of a marshal over a lieutenant-general: despite the accounts of some historians, he was only now placed in charge of the right wing. Grouchy was to advance on Sombreffe with 9000 cavalry supported by Vandamme's 17,500 men and Gérard's 15,400, seize the village and then drive on through to Gembloux. Jean-Baptiste Girard's infantry division was close behind but was not to be used unless necessary, because he would later be required to march to Brussels. Napoleon himself would be at Fleurus by 11 a.m. with the Guard, but he did not expect them to have to fight either, since all intelligence indicated that Grouchy already had sufficient strength to beat what was estimated to be at most 40,000 retreating Prussians.[4]

There can be no doubt that at this point in the morning Napoleon was still full of optimism, confident that his original plan was working. He intended to smash Ziethen's corps and possibly a few Prussian reinforcements and then, leaving a blocking rearguard behind him, march on Brussels along a road that was likely to be relatively free of troops. He expected that if the Prussians retreated, the British would retreat too.

Meanwhile, the troops still south of the Sambre spent the early morning eating, reorganising and crossing the river, although Gérard complained that he had been ready to march at 2 a.m. but that movement orders did not reach him until 9.30.[5] Gérard's men would not reach Fleurus until the early afternoon, but it seems that Napoleon had decided that before pressing forward again they needed rest and food, having been marching day and night.

Ney's first job was to bring all his forces to the front. Jean-Baptiste Drouet d'Erlon's corps was on the move in the very early morning, but the cavalry rearguard had over twenty miles to ride and the hindmost infantry seventeen to march to join up with Reille's men, each unit setting off when the one behind it caught up. Meanwhile, Lefèbvre-Desnouëttes had sent out patrols as soon as it was light and had discovered that instead of retreating from Quatre Bras, the enemy had reinforced the troops there. Having reported this to Soult and briefed Reille, Ney rode forward to Frasnes to study the situation at the front, where it appeared that he would have to fight in order to drive away the Netherlanders.

Netherlands troops were spread across about two miles of ground either side of the cobbled road to Brussels, and on the western flank was a large, deep wood, capable of concealing large numbers of men. Lefèbvre-Desnouëttes' patrols had watched Netherlands infantry marching into Quatre Bras from Nivelles, but had ridden into Genappe to the north of Quatre Bras and found it empty. So far, there was nothing approaching from Brussels. About 7 a.m. Guard cavalry made several probing attacks to test the attitude and strength of the Netherlanders.[6] Apart from a single troop of Prussian hussars, there was no allied cavalry to stop Ney learning that the force at Quatre Bras was isolated and locally unsupported. Unless large numbers were hidden in the woods there were not many of them, but they were strong enough to resist the few infantrymen that Ney yet had near Frasnes.

Around 10 a.m. Jean-Baptiste Girard reported to Reille at Gosselies that he could see a column of Prussian troops marching along the main road from Namur to reinforce the Prussians who were near Fleurus. Reille requested Ney's confirmation that he should march to Frasnes, rather than towards this Prussian concentration. Ney received Napoleon's instructions around 10.30 and ordered Reille to Quatre Bras, in accordance with Soult's marching orders. One division of cavalry was ordered to Marbais with one of d'Erlon's divisions, and the others were to march to Frasnes. The other cavalry division was to scout in front and on the flanks of the column. Ney then reported to Soult, telling him that there seemed to be about 3000 enemy infantry and practically no cavalry at Quatre Bras, and that he thought it should not be difficult to execute the Emperor's order to march on Brussels.

Ney's messages still betray muddled uncertainty over just which divisions were where and who they were commanded by. The previous evening he had only known the position of two of Reille's divisions and had the impression that most of d'Erlon's troops were with him at Jumet. Now he believed that Reille was controlling Girard's corps when in fact it had been borrowed by Napoleon, meaning that Ney had 5000 fewer front-line troops than he thought. This was ominous; he was using lancers of the Guard as messengers to supplement his skeletal staff, and all through the day he was to borrow members of Soult's staff on the grounds that he had none of his own.

In response to Ney's early morning situation report Soult ordered him to concentrate his forces and destroy whatever enemy was at Quatre Bras.[7] Kellermann's cavalry corps started from south of the Sambre near Charleroi at a leisurely pace, knowing that it had a night march to Brussels to look forward to, and Kellermann probably then obeyed Napoleon's instruction to halt at the junction of the *chaussée* with the Roman road between Gosselies and Frasnes, from where he was only to move on to join Ney if the Emperor did not need his help at Fleurus. Similarly, Ney was only to employ Lefèbvre-Desnouëttes' men if he had to, keeping their casualties to a minimum and saving them for the evening's march on Brussels. These orders were never modified and were to have the effect of keeping three powerful divisions of cavalry largely inactive for the entire day.

Napoleon arrived at Fleurus about 11 a.m. and his engineers adapted the windmill of Naveau, overlooking the vast plain that stretched towards Sombreffe, as his observation post and headquarters. It was there that he received Girard's report warning that there were Prussian regiments marching in from the east, and so he ordered Soult and Grouchy to inspect the front line and find out what they could about the strength and position of the Prussian troops.[8]

Napoleon later blamed himself for not spending the night on the front line, but he had no reason to sense impending danger. Had he been near Fleurus he would have seen what was happening sooner and might have acted more dynamically, but he would still have been short of troops. It may have been an oversight by the staff that the rearmost troops, such as Gérard's, were not on the march in the small hours, but it may have been judged that they needed rest. Both Ney and Napoleon were proceeding at a methodical pace and Ney was aware that he had to conserve the energy of his men for a gruelling night march later on. Both generals have been accused of lethargy on the morning of 16 June, but with many of their troops a long way from the points at which the enemy was awaiting them and having to be brought up, there was really little that either man could do to make things happen faster.

20

The Prince of Orange at Quatre Bras

16 June, 5–12 a.m.

The hamlet of Quatre Bras was clustered around the crossroads of the Nivelles–Namur highway and the Charleroi–Brussels *chaussée*, twenty-three miles south of Brussels and nine miles north of Charleroi. There was nothing naturally strong about the terrain there and it did not lend itself to defence; it was only strategically important thanks to its location at the junction of the two routes from Nivelles and Brussels that Wellington's army would naturally use to come to Blücher's aide, or by which Blücher would most naturally retreat towards Brussels.

Both roads were wide and cobbled for vehicles, with broad dirt tracks for horses beside the cobbled area, and both were relatively level because they ran through cuttings or on causeways where the surrounding contours changed. Dominating the flat, golden plain towards Frasnes, where the French were based, was the large Bois de Bossu, extending for a mile and a half from the Nivelles–Namur road towards Frasnes and between 500 and 1000 yards wide. The wood was a remnant of an ancient forest of beeches with a few oaks, dense at its fringes but largely clear within, where the mature trees prevented much undergrowth.[1] A sunken lane ran between high banks along its eastern edge and another track ran through it from east to west. To the east of the village of Frasnes was a similar huge wood, the Bois Delhutte, and it was into this wood that French troops were directed as they arrived, so as to remain concealed.

General Perponcher and Prince Bernhard toured the outposts at first light on a misty morning. Perponcher moved a battalion of Nassau light infantry into the Bois de Bossu to support the rifle-armed Nassau Jägers who were guarding it, and deployed the light infantry of the Dutch 27th Jäger battalion as skirmishers in the fields of tall crops between the strongly built farm of Gémioncourt and the hamlet of Piraumont. After grabbing a couple of hours' sleep, the young Prince of Orange arrived and inspected the position, to find that the mist had still not cleared. He ordered the front line to under-take a fighting reconnaissance to get a sense of French strength, and his Netherlands Jägers and Normann's Nassau light infantry pushed forward and seized back all the ground that had been lost the previ-ous evening. The French retreated tamely, their cavalry outposts skirmishing with the troop of Silesian Hussars that Perponcher had persuaded to join them.

Blücher had sent a Prussian staff officer to discover the cause of the gunfire that had been heard by Prussian troops the previous night, and he reported to Blücher at 6.30 that according to the Prince of Orange all the Belgian troops and many of the British would be at Nivelles in three hours. The Prussian sent the displaced troop of Silesian Hussars to Marbais, hoping they might keep the road open.

Orange was still worried, understandably, that while his forces were pinned down defending Quatre Bras, the French might make a thrust at Nivelles. So he sent orders for Chassé's division to take up defensive positions above the town and Alten's 3rd Division to rein-force them as soon as they arrived from the west. Needing cavalry desperately, not least in order to discover what was happening around him, he summoned Merlen's light horsemen to Quatre Bras. A second forward probe by the Nassauers was met by artillery, which suggested that the French had been reinforced. Orange sent a mes-senger to Wellington to report what he had learned and what he had done.

Wellington left Brussels with his staff about 8 a.m., trotting past the reserve column which had halted, as instructed, between

Waterloo and Mont Saint-Jean where the road forked right for
Nivelles or left for Charleroi. The 95th Rifles were in front: 'The
recruits lay down to sleep, while the old soldiers commenced cooking,' wrote Sergeant Ned Costello, who noticed the astonishingly
loud birdsong at the forest edge that beautiful morning.[2] The sun had
broken through the mist and it was one of those days you knew from
the start was going to be hot, so most of the column had stayed in the
shade under the trees.

Waterloo was a small village towards the edge of the Forest of
Soignes. As you marched south the trees remained thick on the left
but thinned out towards open fields on the right. Whitewashed cottages roofed with slate or tiles lined the road on both sides, and
opposite a couple of inns, catering to the carters carrying coal from
Charleroi to Brussels, was an open space around a surprisingly
imposing domed church with an elaborate portico. From the forest
edge the ground rose gently to a long ridge, with the road running
through cuttings where the gradient was at all steep. The trees
stopped just before the windmill of Mont Saint-Jean, where there
was a first straggle of thatched cottages, followed by a second where
the road forked. Higher up the slope towards Charleroi stood the
large enclosed farm of Mont Saint-Jean. Along the top of the ridge
ran a lane, and from there the open fields of grain and clover dipped
gently down and up to another, higher ridge. While Picton's men
rested, waiting to be told which branch of the road to take, Carl von
Rettberg's artillery battery caught up with them, and the Brunswick
Leib-Battalion overtook them, marching rapidly after their Duke
who had ridden ahead with Wellington towards the town of
Genappe on the road to Quatre Bras.

Wellington arrived at Quatre Bras in mid-morning, to see the
tail of two Netherlands militia battalions and a battery of guns march
in from Nivelles. The troops of both sides were cooking. Nothing was
happening and Wellington's cool approach to the crisis seemed
entirely justified. The Netherlanders had identified their opposition
as chasseurs, lancers and horse artillery of the Guard with some
infantry of the line; this led the officers gathered at Quatre Bras to
admit, somewhat sheepishly, that this might be merely a strong

reconnaissance by the French. Possibly it was masking some other attack, perhaps on the Prussians, perhaps on Nivelles.[3]

Wellington discussed the situation with Blücher's emissary and sent the marshal a note containing his assessment of the current location of his forces and their expected time of arrival. The Duke, however, was wildly over-optimistic: in reality, the British troops still covered the roads to Brussels from Tournai at Enghien, from Mons at Braine and from Binche at Nivelles. Although part of it would arrive by nightfall, Wellington told Blücher that Lord Hill's corps was already at Braine-le-Comte when it had actually barely reached its points of concentration and had not yet received the order to march. Similarly, he told Blücher that he expected the cavalry to be at Nivelles by noon.

Some historians have suggested that it was Wellington's deliberate policy to mislead Blücher or to deceive him into basing calculations on false hopes; others speculate that he and his staff knew they had blundered and were too embarrassed to reveal the full extent of the likely delay before their troops appeared. If this was so then it was wrong. However, it seems more likely that a problem was discovered only after the message was sent. Although Wellington had sent orders to proceed onwards to both bodies before he left Brussels, he may have learned only at Quatre Bras that a mishap had occurred for, according to Dörnberg, he there made out a second order for the cavalry to move from Enghien to Quatre Bras. The memoirs of cavalrymen confirm that many regiments were delayed at Enghien for a considerable period awaiting further orders.[4]

At 10.30 Picton received orders to march on the ten miles to Quatre Bras rather than towards Nivelles, while Alten's division entered Nivelles and promptly collided with Chassé's battalions which were marching through it. Fortunately, Constant arrived and got all 15,000 men into position to defend the town, with the British on the east side nearest Quatre Bras. When a convoy of commissariat wagons appeared, the troops were issued three days' allowance of salt beef and ship's biscuit.[5] Ompteda's brigade of legionaries was sent forward to check any French advance from Binche. General Cooke's Guards division had meanwhile reached Braine-le-Comte, fifteen miles west of Quatre Bras, but had found the road through it blocked by baggage wagons. The men, sweating under their weighty packs in the extreme heat as they waited, ceaselessly sang a popular song with the refrain 'All the world's in Paris'.[6] Cooke rode to Le Miroir for orders but discovered that headquarters had departed for Nivelles without leaving him any new instructions, so he decided to make his own reconnaissance while the troops threw their packs down and rested.

To defend Quatre Bras there were now nine battalions of infantry and sixteen guns, a total of 6500 men present despite rather than because of Wellington's orders, and Prince Bernhard felt that he was owed some thanks for having had the initiative to prevent the French from occupying the place the previous evening. However, since it now looked as if the threat had been exaggerated, Wellington ignored him, so the Prince was left sullen and resentful.[7]

After making this brief assessment of the situation at Quatre Bras, where the small French force then present did not seem very threatening, Wellington set out on the seven-mile ride along the cobbled *chaussée* to Sombreffe, with Dörnberg, Müffling, some staff and a small cavalry escort. Just after he left, however, the light troops resumed their skirmishing and cannonading recommenced.

21

The View from Brye

The 'Sombreffe position', 16 June, morning

The Prussians were as keen as Wellington to concert plans for the cooperation of the two armies. So Gneisenau sent Hardinge to find Wellington, bringing with him a deserter from Grouchy's staff. They met on the tree-shaded *chaussée* and returned together, turning off the cobbles into burning sunshine down a track to the village of Brye, which lay on a stream in a slight valley, then climbing up a wooded slope to a farm on high ground five hundred yards south-east of the village.

Nobody noticed the Duke as his party approached, until Ziethen's chief of staff Reiche recognised him from the cavalry review the previous month. Then everyone turned to gaze at 'the famous war hero', as his Prussian admirer called him. Reiche was struck by the modesty of Wellington's dress and even more impressed by his fine chestnut horse and the utilitarian practicality of his equipment. Behind his saddle was a little case in which Wellington kept a change of clothes; and where most officers had pistol holsters in front of their saddle, Wellington strapped a little mule box containing pieces of prepared hide – better than paper because it did not disintegrate when wet – on which he wrote orders in pencil.[1]

Reiche ushered Wellington up the stairs onto the balustrade around the wooden windmill of Bussy from where, through telescopes, the Prussian generals were studying French columns in movement in the hazy distance around Fleurus, nearly two miles south. It was clear that a large French army was converging in front of Blücher; he estimated it at 130,000 men, though this was certainly more than could be seen, and his estimate was probably based on what he had been told by deserters.

Overnight the Prussian staff had been very fearful for their prospects as they realised how late their troops were going to arrive at Sombreffe, and Ziethen's I Corps had been forced into the front line because there were no other troops present. Now Ziethen's men were lined up before and beside the generals in the open fields that sloped gently downhill towards the village of Saint-Amand in the valley below them. Viewing the disposition of Prussian troops from his position in the windmill, Wellington later claimed to have deplored the manner in which Ziethen's corps, on the slope down to the Ligne stream, had been displayed to the enemy, exposed to French artillery. Ziethen's men did indeed suffer in consequence, but much of the Prussian army was concealed from French view behind Wellington on the reverse slope beyond the cobbled road from Namur to Nivelles.[2]

Twelve hundred yards behind the generals, the cobbled road ran along a slight ridge forming a watershed from its intersection with the Roman road to Gembloux at the inn of Les Trois Burettes; it then dipped into a valley at the village of Sombreffe before climbing up to the inn called Le Point du Jour, which stood at the crossroads with the road from Fleurus to Gembloux. The road continued eastward to Mazy and Namur, from where tired Prussian regiments were still marching proudly in.

Below the windmill hill occupied by the generals the ground dropped away either side and in front to the valley of the Ligne, a stream lined with the straggling villages of Wagnelée, nearly a mile to their right, Saint-Amand-la-Haye just over half a mile south-west, Saint-Amand proper reaching south, with its church a mile away and almost in front of them as they faced Fleurus, and Ligny, half a mile south-east on their left. Beyond Ligny, the stream, widening to a small river, meandered to Sombreffe, more than a mile north-east, and to further villages beyond. Karl von Steinmetz's brigade had occupied the high ground above Saint-Amand in front of them, Friedrich von Jagow's was close by around Brye and the windmill, those of Prussian aristocrat Count Wilhelm Henckel von Donnersmarck in and behind Ligny to their left, and Otto von Pirch's in reserve behind them. Friedrich von Röder had covered the withdrawal from Fleurus with his cavalry and then took up a position between Brye and Ligny. He maintained an outpost of Black Lancers near the conspicuous tumulus called the Tombe de Ligny, south-west of the village.[3]

In the early morning Gneisenau had suffered the sickening realisation that the 32,000 men of Bülow's IV Corps could not possibly reach the battlefield before evening, so they would have to fight with a quarter of their army missing. The messenger he had sent to meet Bülow at Hannut reported back in a note timed at 11.30 p.m. that IV Corps had still not arrived and that – somewhat belatedly – he was about to set out for Liège to try to find it. Meanwhile, a message from Bülow announced that he would complete his concentration at Hannut that morning. Gneisenau must have been torn between fury and despair, since the misunderstanding was partly his fault. Bülow's corps left Liège at dawn but stopped for two hours around midday to rest and eat when they reached the old Roman road, still twenty-five miles away. There Bülow received Blücher's order to keep marching along the Roman road to Gembloux.

Despite this setback, time passed with no French assault, the Prussian troops of II and III Corps began to assemble at the edge of the battlefield and the generals gradually became more confident. Meanwhile, the forward skirmishers of Ziethen's division fortified the villages in the valley, made loopholes in walls and barricaded the approaches.[4]

Around nine o'clock, the first regiments of Georg von Pirch's II Corps marched past Prince Blücher, who was standing outside the presbytery at Sombreffe, and cheered him. The field marshal was still there when Ludwig Nagel's regiment arrived, 'his head in his right hand as if deep in thought, watching us march by'. Volunteer rifleman Franz Lieber's Colberg Regiment arrived slightly later, having marched all day and all night. As they approached the battle-field they got a grandstand view of the troops manoeuvring below, drums rolling and richly embroidered white flags with crosses in bright colours drooping in the listless air. The roads to a battlefield were always strewn with litter: soldiers would lighten their packs by throwing away books and old shoes, while the more superstitious threw away playing cards, for there was a widespread belief among these religious men that playing cards attracted musket balls. The same applied to dice and bawdy songbooks which, like packs of cards, had to be thrown over the head without a backward glance in order to free the soldier from their ill effect. Lieber, who was not supersti-tious, picked up a nice-looking pack of cards on the outskirts of Sombreffe.[5]

Having reached a position level with the village of Ligny, the men of the Colberg Regiment turned right and rested on the downward slope north of the cobbled road while their stragglers caught up with the main body. They waited nervously for action. Some swallowed cartridges, thinking that gunpowder prevented infection, or in the belief that they would not be shot if they already had a bullet inside them. Since each man in Lieber's company of volunteer middle-class riflemen had brought his own rifle, they were of different calibres and they had to make their own balls to fit; they had received a supply of lead in order to cast their own ammunition just a week earlier. 'It is one of the most peculiar situations a man of reflecting mind can be in,' wrote Lieber, 'when he casts his balls for battles near at hand.' That night Lieber and two comrades lay in a hayloft feeling home-sick and looking out thoughtfully through a hole in the roof at the stars. One friend said that his father had predicted that he would not come home again. The other, a Jew, said that he also had the feeling he would be killed. Lieber had been confident he would survive with no more than a scratch.[6]

The soldiers checked their muskets and rifles and prepared their cartridges. Cartridges for muskets were distributed in paper packages of twenty, which were only opened just before use. Bandages and lint were distributed to each soldier. Behind Lieber's company stood a cavalry regiment, out of which a near neighbour from Berlin rode up and asked Lieber to write home should he fall, agreeing to do the same if Lieber were killed.

Thielmann's III Corps had left Namur before dawn, following II Corps closely, and its first elements began to deploy on the eastern flank about noon. The Silesian 22nd Regiment from Pirch's corps, travelling from furthest away, was one of the last to arrive, and was still marching when Wellington joined Blücher in his windmill. At 7 a.m. they had set off from Namur after two hours' rest and soon met a wagon full of wounded from the previous day's skirmishing. They were delayed by traffic and when the sun broke through they began to roast:

> There was not a cloud in the sky. The June sun was burning hot, the dust suffocating, and we were all suffering from thirst; the wells in the villages we passed through were already dry. Our men were already falling down with exhaustion, and with every hour the number of stragglers increased. It was past noon when the regiment stopped in a village, partly to wait for the stragglers to catch up, partly to quench its thirst from a pond; the water tasted wonderful, despite the fact that artillery and cavalry horses had drunk there, mixing it up with mud. A despatch rider arrived with the order to hurry up to reach the battlefield, as the honour of the regiment depended on it. We marched off immediately, even though more than half of the stragglers, exhausted by their 24-hour march, had yet to catch up.[7]

With three corps within striking distance, Blücher had something like 83,500 men and 216 guns.[8] The Prussians thought themselves to be at a great numerical disadvantage, and almost all of them had been marching all day and all night. In reality, their army was more than twice as large as Napoleon had bargained for and substantially outnumbered the 65,000 men he was gathering round Fleurus.

A Prussian plan for a battle at Sombreffe had in fact been developed by the staff when they surveyed the position weeks earlier. Its details are not known, but I Corps was to take a position on the right around Brye and Saint-Amand with IV Corps in reserve behind it, while II Corps defended the road from Fleurus to Point du Jour with III Corps in reserve.[9] The idea was to defend the strong position on the left between Sombreffe and Tongrinnes, a mile or so to the east, and to attack on the right from Brye with a hook at the French flank and rear. When the Prussians realised that Bülow would not arrive during daylight on 16 June they had to decide whether to fight or to retreat. Thinking their defensive position strong, they decided to fight. They ordered Bülow to march to a position in the rear of their army on which they could fall back, or from which he could attack next day.

Their revised plan envisaged Thielmann's III Corps defending the eastern flank with von Pirch's II Corps poised behind Ziethen's men, ready to deliver an offensive blow on the right wing. The original plan had not envisaged any British involvement, but now it seemed that the Prussian army might hold the French until Wellington arrived to deal the decisive blow from the west, so discussions began as to how he might intervene. Still under the impression that there was negligible French opposition at Quatre Bras, Wellington believed that the bulk of his army was likely to be available to fight within an hour or two.[10] If, by now, he harboured fears that he might have begun to concentrate his army too late, he did not confess them to the Prussians.

Wellington's idea was to drive any French troops in front of him back along the road towards Charleroi and then turn into Napoleon's rear, but Gneisenau opposed this on the ground that it would take too long. His own proposal was for Wellington simply to turn left along the Namur road and reinforce the Prussian right flank. According to Müffling, Wellington left with the intention of carrying out this manoeuvre, while Fitzroy Somerset wrote that Wellington 'told Blücher that he would give him all the support in his power'. At any rate Gneisenau had the impression that 'the Duke of Wellington had promised to strike the enemy in the rear'. With some such assurance, Blücher decided to accept battle in the present position, signalling his decision by firing a gun.[11]

Blücher accompanied Wellington for a short distance along the road back to Quatre Bras with the loud 'Hurrahs' of Prussian troops ringing in their ears, and then the old man wheeled his horse around. 'What a fine fellow he is!' exclaimed the Duke as he watched him canter back to lead his men into battle.[12]

22

Napoleon Changes his Plan

Ligny, 16 June, 1–2.30 p.m.

Shortly after Wellington climbed down from the windmill at Bussy, Grouchy and Soult returned from their reconnaissance and met Napoleon at their own windmill at Naveau just outside Fleurus. The two mills were in clear view of each other, about two miles apart, and French headquarters was established under Napoleon's with a table and chair at which he could study his maps. When a messenger arrived with Marshal Ney's report that he thought it would be easy to brush aside the estimated 3000 hostile troops at Quatre Bras, Napoleon replied with a brisk note instructing Ney 'to attack with the greatest impetuosity'.[1] The plan was still for Ney to clear the path for a night march and a sudden appearance at Brussels next morning, while Marshal Grouchy sent the Prussians reeling and seized Sombreffe and Gembloux. To that end, Grouchy's horsemen were riding towards Tongrinelle, sweeping the area immediately north-east of Fleurus, General Vandamme's corps was resting in front of the town, while General Gérard's and the Imperial Guard were approaching from the south.

However, the marshals had concluded that during the morning Prussian reinforcements had arrived, and more were still arriving, though for the most part they could not be seen, while Prussian front-line positions were concealed among houses, gardens and orchards. After making their report, Soult and Grouchy followed Napoleon onto the gallery that Napoleon's sappers had built round the windmill to take a further look at the enemy. Colonel Charles de Forbin-Janson of the *État Major-Général* leaned on a rail while the Emperor used his shoulder to support the end of his large and powerful telescope, through which he made a careful, lengthy survey of the terrain occupied by the Prussians.[2]

Napoleon's windmill was close to the road from Charleroi to Gembloux, on the highest ground of an essentially flat plain. Before him was an undulating expanse of wheat, rye and other standing crops, rising to a slight ridge where the main road from Namur to Nivelles ran in the distance. Three miles north-east of his mill the Charleroi road intersected the main road at the crossroads marked by the Point du Jour inn above Tongrinnes, a mile west towards Nivelles was the village of Sombreffe, and more than a mile further west, in front of Napoleon as he looked at the main Prussian position, was the village of Brye. Half a mile behind it to the north-west the highway to Nivelles met the old Roman road to Gembloux at Les Trois Burettes.

The stream that meandered through boggy ground in the populated valley was hidden from their view in a dip, but Napoleon's local guide, a surveyor from Fleurus named François Simon, must have pointed it out to him.[3] A little brook flowed south from Brye to join the main stream, which rose further west and ran through the village of Wagnelée, two miles away. It meandered to the east of Saint-Amand-la-Haye, winding past its castle and to the east of the hedged gardens of Saint-Amand proper. Saint-Amand church, the nearest point of the village, was nearly a mile away. In a marshy area below the church more little brooks flowed in and the more significant river Ligne, widening to five yards, flowed on north-eastward for nearly a mile, past a moated castle, to the edge of Ligny. This larger village was nearly a mile from Saint-Amand church, and a mile and a half from Napoleon's mill. The Ligne then flowed through the centre of Ligny, bending east to Potriaux, and meandering south and east past Tongrinelle, Boignée and Balâtre. Within these villages various châteaux, farms and churches formed significant strongpoints.

'The old fox will not break cover,' said the Emperor. Just what Napoleon saw as he watched the Prussians remains mysterious, but his survey had indicated that there were more of them present than he had initially thought. He may even have picked out Blücher's staff gathered round their own windmill. Below and behind it many of the 30,000 men of Ziethen's corps were standing in full view, with a line of guns on the ridge between Saint-Amand-la-Haye and Ligny that commanded Saint-Amand and the open fields between it and Ligny itself. But more Prussian regiments had been marching in for some hours, partly concealed behind the ridge, while others were still on the road to the battlefield. The Emperor found it difficult to believe that they had mustered an army, but he cancelled Grouchy's attack on Sombreffe and instead sent out scouts, while he and his marshals conducted a reconnaissance closer to the enemy lines.

General Maurice Gérard was trying to find the Emperor, while making his own reconnaissance with a small escort of staff and hussars, when suddenly he was charged by a squadron of black-clad Prussian lancers. Gérard's horse fell as the French galloped away, unseating his rider; his companions turned and threw themselves into a fierce mêlée in which Gérard's aide was shot in the kidneys and his chief of staff stabbed by a lancer. They were saved only by the arrival of a detachment of chasseurs who drove off the Prussians.[4]

Gérard finally located the Emperor at the Naveau mill, to which the Imperial party had by now returned. Meanwhile Grouchy's eastern patrols had identified more troops on the highway marching towards the battlefield, and as Bonaparte came to terms with the reality of ever-increasing numbers of Prussians a new plan formed in his mind. Instead of simply driving the Prussians towards Gembloux by striking at Le Point du Jour, he would set a trap so that they could not again escape him.

The new plan required Vandamme to pin the Prussians down and suck in their reserves, while Gérard attacked their right flank and General Girard's division their left. If these forces proved insufficient then, with the enemy fully committed, Ney would complete their destruction by marching in from the west while the Guard attacked from the east. All Napoleon had to do was to tell Ney that the plan had changed and the new priority was to destroy the Prussians. So he instructed Soult to send another message to Ney, timed at 2 p.m.:

> Marshal, the Emperor instructs me to warn you that the enemy has brought together a body ['*corps*'] of troops between Sombreffe and Bry, and that at 2.30 Marshal Grouchy will attack it with III and IV Corps.
>
> His Majesty's intention is that you should also attack what is in front of you, and after having vigorously pushed it back, you should turn back on us to help us envelop the corps of which we have just told you. If this corps has already been broken, then His Majesty will manoeuvre in your direction to hasten the conclusion of your operations.
>
> Inform the Emperor immediately about your dispositions and about what is happening on your front.[5]

The wording of this message was problematic. Until now, Ney had been reminded repeatedly not to tire troops destined to march on Brussels with 'false marches', so an order to march back to Ligny implied strongly that the Emperor now thought that the 'corps' – or 'body' (the French word is ambiguous) – might in fact amount to an army. But that Soult did not tell Ney that an all-out effort was required at Ligny in order to annihilate the Prussian army indicates continued uncertainty about the real strength and determination of the Prussians in front. Since Soult also said that if they beat the Prussians quickly they would march to Quatre Bras, Ney had no real reason to conclude that his intervention was needed urgently, or that the plan to march on Brussels had been abandoned. Naturally, Napoleon assumed that as Ney only faced a few battalions he could choose his course of action.

Depending on their route, Napoleon's messengers had six to eight miles to ride to Frasnes. Then they had to find Ney, who would be somewhere further forward. It would take them more than an hour to deliver the order: if Ney were to receive it towards 3.30 p.m., he might arrive two or three hours later.

*

Behind Vandamme's corps the French army was still marching forward in snake-like columns. Edouard Milhaud's 3500 cuirassiers halted close to Fleurus. The infantry of the Imperial Guard emerged from the town about 2 p.m. and took position beneath the Naveau mill, with the Young Guard in front, then the chasseurs and grenadiers. The heavy cavalry of the Guard were to the right rear of the grenadiers.[6] Without its light cavalry the Imperial Guard was 18,600 strong. Excluding Lobau's corps, which was still at the crossroads near Charleroi, Napoleon's force totalled about 65,000 men and 232 guns, nearly 20,000 fewer than the actual number of Prussians.[7]

Like the other troops, the Guards were wearing greatcoats and they were sweltering hot. Sergeant Hippolyte de Mauduit of the 1st Grenadiers recalled that as they marched, 'an overwhelming dust enveloped us like a thick cloud, making it difficult to draw breath. The heat became stifling, there was no hint of a breeze to refresh the face, the sun was beating straight down.' They piled their muskets and lay in the rye, hanging cloths to shade them from the glare. Some old grenadiers had fought in the campaign of 1794 and one even got an old map out of his pack, over which the veterans discussed the battle of Fleurus and explained it to youngsters like Mauduit.[8]

The French had formed up beyond effective cannon range of the Prussians. Vandamme's 17,500 men took their positions in front of Fleurus opposite Saint-Amand, with Jean-Baptiste Girard's division, 4600 strong, to their left, facing Saint-Amand-la-Haye. Grouchy's cavalry was already out ahead on the right sweeping two miles of ground to the east of Napoleon's windmill. Antoine Maurin's division were to the west of the village of Boignée, and further right Rémy Exelmans' 3300 dragoons and Claude Pajol's 2400 light cavalry were sending patrols to the east of the village of Balâtre.

The first attack was to be launched by General Etienne-Nicolas Lefol's division, 4700 strong, against Saint-Amand. In preparation for the assault, Lefol, an ardent republican, harangued his men, talking them to a pitch of excitement and enthusiasm. Then they formed up, looking across the ripening rye, baking in the heat, at the steeple of

Saint-Amand church, almost hidden by the willows and orchards that gave the sleepy village the appearance of a wood.

At half past two the church clock chimed in Saint-Amand, the artillery of the Imperial Guard fired three shots – the traditional signal for battle to commence – and the skirmishers of the 15th light infantry trotted forward, fanning out into the corn. Behind them strode the battalion columns of Lefol's three line regiments, sweating beneath grey greatcoats and heavy packs, led by Lefol in person. The 23rd Regiment had a band, as regiments whose colonels were wealthy generally did, with a bandmaster and brightly dressed musicians playing clarinets, flutes, hautboys, bassoons, horns, serpents and cymbals to supplement the drum-major, drummers and fifers of the field music. Some of the musicians might be as young as fourteen, for the *enfants de troupe*, orphans of soldiers and *vivandières* or *blanchisseuses*, could draw pay in the band from that age and might serve unofficially as fifers, although they could not be drummers until they were sixteen and strong enough.[9]

As they led the battalions into battle, the musicians played *Le Chant du Départ*, the old republican song about the defeat of foreign tyrants. '*La Victoire en chantant*', it began, and it rose to an inspiring chorus:

> *The Republic calls us; we must know how to conquer or to die,*
> *a Frenchman must live for her, for her a Frenchman would die.*

23

Ney Attacks the Netherlanders

Quatre Bras, 16 June, 1.15–3.30 p.m.

Napoleon, having assessed the strength of the Prussian force in front of Fleurus, had accordingly changed his plan. Meanwhile Marshal Ney, seven miles to the west at the village of Frasnes, had been impatiently awaiting the arrival of enough of Reille's men from Gosselies to enable him to launch an attack on the battalions that were blocking the road to Brussels at Quatre Bras.

Reille joined Ney on the high ground above Frasnes at 1.15. Hidden behind them to their right in the trees of the vast Bois Delhutte they had only General Bachelu's 5000 infantry, the comte de Piré's 1700 cavalry and fourteen guns, together with the 2000 Guard light cavalry and their twelve guns.[1] Ney obeyed his instructions not to tire the Guard cavalry unnecessarily, but he employed their artillery.[2] While he and Reille waited for the 5300 infantry and eight guns of General Foy's division, they tried to assess what was in front of them.

Ney now feared that his operation would not be the pushover that he had anticipated, for things had changed since he had told Napoleon that he thought it would be easy to brush aside the opposition. Around noon a member of Lobau's staff had spoken to several senior officers and had then questioned deserters; they had estimated enemy strength at up to 20,000 men – a huge increase on the 3000 thought to be there earlier, and many more than the 6500 actually

present at that time. Presumably a deserter had warned that reinforcements were expected or cavalry patrols had watched Picton's
columns approaching. But, recalling from his Peninsular experience
Wellington's habit of concealing his troops, Reille was also anxious
about what might be hidden in the Bois de Bossu.[3]

Looming to the west of the road to Brussels as Ney looked northward, the Bois de Bossu was a large wood capable of concealing
thousands of troops. For more than half a mile, close to Quatre Bras,
the wood was within five hundred yards of the *chaussée*, a nasty
prospect if guns were hidden at its edge. A path from Frasnes ran past
the farm of Grand Pierrepont, which was held by enemy skirmishers,
and then through the wood to the village of Houtain-le-Val on the
main road to Nivelles. To the east of the Brussels highway the ground
ahead was open, rolling slightly, with marshy streams in the low areas.
The fields were planted with wheat, rye and clover. These crops concealed stealthy movement and provided magnificent cover for
skirmishers: The wheat stood five foot high and here, as elsewhere in
Belgium, the rye was astonishingly tall. Recently a British cavalry
officer had written home, amazed that 'we rode through some rye
that was high enough to conceal one on horseback: I brought home
a root of it & found one stalk measure seven feet nine inches and this
was by no means uncommon.' Another had remarked that 'The rye
is now standing 7 feet high, the barley up to my chin.'[4]

About a mile to Ney's right was the village of Piraumont and
beyond it a lake; beyond them was the other cobbled road, running
south-east from Quatre Bras towards Sombreffe and Namur. Behind
the French generals to the east the Bois Delhutte, in which most of
Ney's troops were hidden, extended almost to Piraumont in the north
and for over a mile southward to Villers Perwin; it was more than half
a mile wide and cut off from sight the area in which Napoleon was
operating.

General Maximilien Foy was a hardened fighter, a doughty adver-
sary of the British in Spain, and a staunch republican whose
promotion had been delayed by his principled opposition to
Bonaparte's seizure of individual power. As soon as he arrived with his
division, taking French infantry strength to 10,300, Ney insisted on an

immediate attack, whatever the risk might be. About 2 p.m. Maigrot's light infantry stormed out of the wood towards Piraumont and drove away the skirmishing Jägers from the high ground to the west of the village where Ney placed his artillery. Finding Piraumont empty, the 2nd Light Regiment occupied it to secure the army's right flank.

The Prince of Orange meanwhile now had a complete division united at Quatre Bras, although they were thinly spread, pretending to be stronger than they really were. On the right, Saxe-Weimar's Nassauers lined the Bois de Bossu, with a strong reserve behind the wood towards Houtain-le-Val, supported by two guns. On the left General Bijlandt's brigade of Netherlanders occupied the main road and the farm of Gémioncourt, with a second line in support behind Quatre Bras and the wood. The Dutch Jägers had outposts concealed in the seven-foot rye, observing a broad area to the east. Two 6-pounders and one howitzer were on the Charleroi highway with another gun and another howitzer to their right. The remaining three guns of the battery that Captain Bijleveld had withdrawn from Frasnes the previous evening had been placed on the eastern flank, in an effort to command the road to Namur. Six guns of the newly arrived battery were in reserve at Quatre Bras. When Maigrot's light infantry pushed forward the Jägers fell back to the hedges along the stream that ran past Gémioncourt, with their elite companies in the buildings.[5]

About this time the staff at Quatre Bras received very disturbing news. In the early morning General Pierre Durutte's chief of staff and principal aide had ridden from their camp near Jumet towards Nivelles in order to desert to the enemy. Having surrendered to a Netherlands light cavalry patrol, General Durutte's chief of staff revealed that coming up the Brussels road towards Quatre Bras were eight divisions of infantry and four of cavalry amounting to nearly 50,000 men, commanded by Marshal Ney.[6] While Napoleon might still attack Nivelles, all indications now pointed to an attack up the main road to Brussels, in which case they would soon be overwhelmed. The Prince dispatched all his aides to summon reinforcements to Quatre Bras as fast as possible.

Thousands of heavily laden allied troops were already converging on the crossroads at Quatre Bras. Just after 2 p.m. a messenger summoned Picton's weary division, who were refreshing themselves two and a half miles away. 'The day was oppressively warm, and the road very dusty,' recalled Sergeant Robertson of the Gordon Highlanders. 'We moved on slowly till we reached the village of Geneppe [sic], where the inhabitants had large tubs filled with water standing at the doors, ready for us, of which we stood in great need. They told us that a French patrole had been there that morning.' Picton's men overtook the Brunswickers, who were resting in the shade. The Duke of Brunswick told his men to load their guns and follow: 'Children,' he said, calmly puffing on his pipe, 'let us charge the weapons quickly!'[7]

On the high ground above Nivelles, Alten's Anglo-Hanoverians had recognised small arms fire and their three generals, Alten, Halkett and Kielmansegge, had ridden eastward to investigate when one of the Prince's aides met them and ordered them to hasten to Quatre Bras. Halkett turned back to summon the men who, halted in a clover field, had just started cooking, so they threw their meat away or packed it half-cooked and marched off with artillery leading the column. They left Christian von Ompteda's brigade behind in case the French attacked Nivelles.

General Cooke had marched the British Guards division towards Nivelles on his own initiative, for Orange's earlier messenger had somehow failed to find him. He halted his men just short of the town in burning heat and dust and the companies sent out parties for water, expecting to spend the night there, but at 3 p.m. one of Orange's aides found them and begged Cooke to make an immediate forced march to Quatre Bras. Private Matthew Clay of the 3rd Guards was nineteen; a native of the Nottinghamshire village of Blidworth, he had enlisted in the local militia in 1813 before transferring to the light company of the Scots Guards. He recalled:

> The men whose wives had followed us to our halting ground were permitted to take farewell of them. They were ordered to the rear, and going a short distance away from the throng in the open field were joined by others who delivered to them for security their

watches and various other small articles which they held in esteem. Others whose families were absent desired that their expressions of affection might be communicated to their absent wives and families. The parting embrace, although short, was sincere, affectionate and expressed with deep emotions of grief as their state of widowhood had suddenly come upon them, while the loud thunder of the destructive cannon was sounding in their ears.[8]

Meanwhile, to the south, Jérôme's division of 6600 men with sixteen guns was approaching Frasnes; behind it d'Erlon's corps, nearly 20,000 strong, complete, rested and fed, was marching north from Gosselies to reinforce Marshal Ney.

Ney's attack developed methodically: a brigade of lancers protected the right flank while Bachelu's light infantry pushed forward to the east, one of Foy's brigades marched straight up the cobbled road towards Brussels and the Guard cavalry probed the left flank.[9] Foy's advance was designed to draw fire, in order to reveal the positions of enemy artillery. Orange obliged by calling forward his second battery of guns into the front line.

Excellent artillery was a traditional strength of French armies. They began with counter-battery fire, designed to destroy or drive away the enemy's guns. Thirty-four French guns opposed Orange's sixteen, and the Netherlanders lost the duel. The French gave Bijleveld's battery such a pounding that it limbered up and withdrew half a mile, before shifting the full weight of their fire onto the other battery, disabling two guns and forcing the remaining four back to Bijleveld's new position. When these guns opened fire again the French quickly ranged in on them and their commander was killed by a cannonball. A gun had to be left behind when they fell back hurriedly to Quatre Bras.

The young Prince sent the 5th Militia forward up the *chaussée* with the 7th line battalion to their right, to take position between Gémioncourt and the wood, west of the Jägers, holding the strongest defensive line available. Gémioncourt was a sturdily built dairy farm of which the oldest part was medieval, with hedged gardens and orchards on three sides of it and a stream fifty yards to the north. The edge of the Bossu wood was about 400 yards west of it and the marshy stream rose at the edge of the wood, trickling eastward under a bridge to feed the Etang de Materne, a lake three hundred yards long and one to two hundred wide, close to the Namur road. Orange was unwilling to retreat without a fight, but with the Dutch artillery driven back, the French guns pounded his infantry with impunity. The militiamen were inexperienced – of 454 men raised in Arnhem only 19 had ever seen action before – and they almost cracked under the barrage.[10]

A mile to the east squads of Colonel Maigrot's 2300 light infantry trotted in loose order towards the hamlet of Thyle and the Bois des Censes, to the north of the Namur road, turning the Netherlanders' left flank. At the same time three battalions of the 4th Light Regiment, over a thousand strong, marched up the road to Gémioncourt and stormed the farm. Foy's other brigade drove the Nassauers on the western flank back from the farm of Grand Pierrepont towards the Bossu wood.

The militiamen now gathered in a mass on the *chaussée* under fire from Gémioncourt. They defended themselves against successive squadrons of *chasseurs-à-cheval*, who then veered away towards the 7th line battalion, causing them to run back into the wood. When the cavalry fell back to reorganise, the Prince of Orange ordered a counter-attack, pushing his Jägers forward against Gémioncourt and ordering the 5th Militia back up the main road.

It was at this juncture that the Duke of Wellington returned to Quatre Bras, having had to detour northward from the road for the last mile in order to avoid snipers. He would later claim to have arrived before the fighting started, but it is difficult to see how his party could have ridden sufficiently fast. The scene was utterly different from when he left: a major French attack was in progress and he could see instantly that it threatened to overwhelm the young Netherlanders defending the crossroads, who were on the brink of disaster. Where was his army? Wellington looked anxiously north and was relieved to see that clouds of dust announced the imminent appearance of Sir Thomas Picton and his steady veterans.

24

Probing Attacks on Saint-Amand and Ligny

16 June, 2.30–3.30 p.m.

Seven miles south-east, the light of battle was in Napoleon's eyes and he was enjoying himself. He had launched a first probing attack on the Prussian-held villages beneath the windmill hill at Brye, the first move in what he hoped would be a major engagement and a glorious victory. He now thought that he probably had a Prussian army in front of him, although he was still uncertain of the enemy's real strength and determination: only one corps of about 30,000 Prussians was plainly visible, whereas some 40,000 French infantry and 11,000 cavalry were in motion around Fleurus. But Napoleon knew that more Prussians were hidden further back and more still were arriving. They were evidently not going to attack him, but would they stand and fight? If they did, he would gradually intensify the fighting until they were trapped there and then, with Ney's help, he would wipe them out. After that, with one allied army removed from the board, he would turn on the other.

Prussian brigades normally contained three infantry regiments, one regiment of cavalry and a battery of artillery. Karl von Steinmetz's brigade now stood in full sight of the French on the heights behind Saint-Amand and at Brye, with his Silesian Hussars on the right flank ordered to throw out a chain of patrols to maintain contact with Wellington. On Steinmetz's left, between the head-quarters windmill and Ligny, stood Otto von Pirch's brigade with his cavalry and guns in reserve. Blücher rode among the regiments near the windmill saying, 'Look over there! The enemy is gathering at Fleurus! Get ready, this is the moment, children!'

The brigades of Generals von Jagow and Henckel, which had done less hard work than the rest of I Corps the previous day, were down in the valley in the front line. Three of Jagow's nine battalions marched forward at 11 a.m. to defend Saint-Amand, where they joined a company of green-coated Silesian Jägers and the rifle-armed volunteer Jägers of the 12th Brandenburg Regiment who were already there. In German armies Jägers – hunters – were all armed with rifles. The Silesians were elite Jägers recruited from Polish foresters, specialists in woodcraft and trained from a young age in accuracy with the rifle.

Rifles were much more accurate than the muskets with which most infantrymen were armed. A rifleman wrote that 'the calculation has been made, that only one shot out of two hundred fired from muskets takes effect, while one out of twenty from rifles is the aver-age.'[1] In perfect conditions a skilled forester with a rifle reckoned to hit the head of a man at 200 yards and a man at 300, while it was claimed that volunteer riflemen hit a man at 200 as often as they missed and at 100 yards at least one in five shots would hit the centre of a target.[2] Combat conditions reduced accuracy a great deal, but rifles were the weapon of preference for sniping at officers. For max-imum accuracy riflemen used a ball wrapped in leather that had to be rammed slowly down the barrel, reducing the rate of fire to perhaps one shot per minute, but at short range they used common cartridges to gain a faster rate of fire.

Two musketeer battalions of Jagow's 29th Regiment, wearing the white coats of the Duchy of Berg, occupied the houses which lined both sides of a single lane leading to the church at the south-eastern extremity of the village. The lane ran to the south and parallel to the Ligne stream. Either side of the houses, hedges and orchards pro-vided further cover. A company of Westphalian Landwehr occupied an orchard close to the church and three more companies formed a reserve. The riflemen covered both flanks of the musketeers.

Nearly half a mile to the east two battalions of Jagow's fusiliers took cover in limestone quarries just west of Ligny. Each Prussian regiment had a battalion of fusiliers: these were light infantrymen, armed with a shorter and lighter musket, while their corporals and sergeants carried a rifled sharpshooter musket. Their job was to protect Ziethen's heavy artillery which, including Henckel's cannon, was lined up as a grand battery of forty-six guns, stretching from Ligny to Saint-Amand-la-Haye. Teams of horses dragged twelve 12-pounders, eighteen 6-pounders, and sixteen howitzers into line. Then the horses and limbers retreated some distance behind the guns, while further back still were the ammunition caissons. Ziethen's cavalry moved forward as the battle began, taking positions to protect the gun line and the army's right flank.

Artillery came in two principal types, cannon firing several varieties of solid shot and howitzers that were designed to lob explosives. Prussian cannon fired solid shot weighing six or twelve pounds. Maximum range was about a mile measured to the first 'graze' or bounce, though accuracy dropped beyond their effective range of about half a mile. Balls would whistle through the air, then bounce a few times and finally roll. The best defence against artillery fire was to lie down; anybody in the path of a round shot was likely to be killed outright or to lose a major limb. People might lose their head or be cut in half and a lucky shot along the line of a file might kill several men at once, while even when rolling, roundshot were capable of taking off a foot. Twelve-pounders had a longer range and more power but 6-pounders could be fired faster, simply because the balls were less heavy to load. Their rate of fire might start at two or three rounds a minute, but quickly decreased as the crew tired, and 12-pounders probably only fired one shot a minute at best.

Howitzers could lob explosive shells with a higher trajectory to explode over or among troops. Shells consisted of an iron sphere filled with powder and when they exploded they scattered twenty-five to fifty jagged shards of iron over a radius of twenty yards. These caused savage wounds with compound fractures of the bones

(meaning fractures with bones exposed to the air) and torn flesh.
The shells exploded when a fuse burned down: the art was to set the
fuse correctly since it was possible, if hazardous, to hurl away a shell
with a burning fuse.[3] Howitzer ammunition wagons carried a small
number of special incendiary shells to set fire to buildings or dry
vegetation and flare shells to light up targets at night. Artillery was
the most feared and most potent weapon on the battlefield and usually the one that caused most casualties.

The opening moves were usually made to test the strength and
determination of the enemy at various points on the battlefield.
Napoleon thus began with an attack on Saint-Amand, the village
directly in front of Vandamme's men, in order to find out whether the
Prussians would withdraw, as they had the day before, or whether
they would stand and fight.

The 4700 men led by Etienne Lefol had joined with their musicians to sing the *Chant du Départ* as they marched to assault
Saint-Amand. When the columns came into range of the Prussian
artillery, hidden in the tall rye on the heights above the village
orchards, a new music struck up:

> The music of the cannon ball doesn't vary; it has only two notes.
> When these projectiles arrive in full flight they remain invisible
> and announce their passage only with a short whistle which chills
> the soul. When they ricochet, which is to say, after they first hit the
> ground, they travel on in successive bounds, and then you can see
> them coming through the air like so many black dots when they
> make a sort of moaning noise, a plaintive sound, inexpressible in
> words. They then produce an extraordinary optical illusion: each of
> these points seems to be heading straight for your face. That is
> what makes people duck or bend down to avoid the blow.[4]

A ball killed a file of eight men in one of Lefol's columns but the
others marched on, closing ranks.

Ahead of the battalion columns, the light infantry, all in blue, and
thinned out in skirmish order, were well hidden as they pushed
stealthily forward through the rye and wheat. The white-coated

Rhinelanders defending Saint-Amand did not see them until they were nearby: 'the red, yellow, green plumes and epaulettes of the grenadiers, tirailleurs and voltigeurs looked like poppies and cornflowers growing in those tall crops. Everywhere, the rye came to life with attackers whose sudden appearance was just as frightening as their well-aimed shots.'[5]

The French and Prussians in particular employed large numbers of men as skirmishers. Acting individually, invisibly if possible, often crouching or lying on the ground, skirmishers worked in loose, extended order, using any cover. Whereas 'line' infantry relied on firing close-range volleys at large targets, light infantry skirmishers were taught to aim at individuals, although to have any hope of hitting your target with a flintlock musket – the most common weapon on the battlefield – you had to creep close.

Firing was a laborious process. The musketeer bit open a cartridge, primed the pan with powder, poured the rest down the barrel and spat the ball after it. Inserting a ramrod into the muzzle, he rammed the charge home, pulled back the cock which held the flint (otherwise the gun would go off half cock) and pulled the trigger. The cock flew forward and the flint hit the frizzen, forcing it back and allowing sparks to hit the powder in the pan. This caused a flash that reached the charge through a hole in the side of the barrel. The particles of powder from the flash burned your face, but if you didn't prime with enough powder to ignite the charge you merely produced a flash in the pan, while a proper explosion caused a recoil that bruised the shoulder. It was possible to fire three or four rounds a minute at first, but soldiers quickly tired.

In French light infantry regiments all the men were capable of skirmishing, but in each French line and light regiment one of the six companies consisted of elite *voltigeurs*; these were selected from the best shots in the regiment and the smallest, most agile men, and were distinguished by yellow plumes. Originally conceived as infantry who could be transported by cavalry, the *voltigeurs* – 'vaulters' – were supposed to be able to leap onto the back of a horse, and although the concept proved generally impractical, *voltigeurs* did occasionally hitch a ride behind dragoons. Generally, *voltigeurs* performed on foot, first to advance and last in a retreat. Their sergeants, corporals and officers were armed with rifled carbines which had an excellent sights, were forty inches long, weighed eight pounds and fired a half-ounce ball.[6] The rest carried the French dragoon musket, shorter and lighter, but just as good as the infantry musket. They aimed at officers and sergeants to induce demoralisation, confusion and paralysis. Their job was to do as much damage as possible before the main columns attacked, although their first opponents were usually similarly minded enemy skirmishers, with whom they duelled, darting forward to seize a good position, falling back when pressed, like a swarm of midges on a sultry day.

Sharpshooting at Saint-Amand continued for half an hour with more Prussian rifle detachments running in to reinforce the hard-pressed front line. Meanwhile, French guns were hauled forward and deployed, before bombarding the village with shot and shell while the assault columns prepared their attack. Lefol drove the Rhinelanders back from the church north-west towards La Haye. His men followed them over the lane, past cottages and gardens and into the fields bordering the stream, but there they were showered with canister from the Prussian artillery. Lefol himself had his horse shot under him and was narrowly saved by his nephew from being captured.[7]

At close range – up to about 400 yards – both guns and howitzers fired canister or case shot, which consisted of balls packed with sawdust into a tin. There were two types: light case contained musket balls; heavy case or grapeshot contained fewer, bigger balls. The tin exploded as the gun was fired and the canister spread out in a cone as if from a shotgun. The diameter of the cone was about 32 feet at 100 yards, 64 feet at 200 yards and 96 feet at 300 yards. Canister had a murderous effect on closely packed targets. The maximum range for heavy case was 600 yards, but it was usually only fired at 300; that for light case was only 250 yards.

As Lefol's attack on Saint-Amand began, a new French column emerged into view of Blücher's staff from behind Fleurus. While Etienne Hulot's division marched straight up the Charleroi–Gembloux

road to guard IV Corps' flank against attacks from Sombreffe, Maurice
Gérard's remaining 10,600 men marched along the main road towards
Sombreffe and then turned sharp left opposite Ligny, over a mile from
Saint-Amand, and threw out a skirmish line towards the village.

Count Wilhelm Henckel had about 3000 men in Ligny, a village
built from blueish stone and whose houses, roofed with thatch,
ranged along two lanes, the *rue d'en haut* south of the stream and the
rue d'en bas to the north of it. The main buildings were on the south
side and in the centre was a church within a walled graveyard. Above
and below the churchyard were two strongly walled farms, the Ferme
d'en Haut to the south and the Ferme d'en Bas to the north, linked
by a footbridge. The stream which ran just to the north of the church
was a serious obstacle, three yards wide and hedged on each bank.
There were several wooden bridges over it, but just one stone bridge
at the eastern entrance to the village. To the west and north-east of
the church was an open common.

Henckel's men had prepared the village for defence, making loopholes in houses and walls, barricading tracks, building low earth banks,
and cutting down the crops close to the houses. One battalion of the
19th defended the moated medieval castle at the south-western
extremity, and another the western part of the village, while two
Landwehr battalions from the Münster area of the northern
Rhineland held the eastern part. Henckel kept one battalion of each
regiment in reserve, and his cavalry with eight guns took position
behind the village to the east.[8] Henckel's opponent, Maurice Gérard,
was one of Napoleon's best soldiers, an excellent officer, experienced
but still energetic.[9] He launched a first exploratory attack with just a
brigade of nearly 3000 men in three columns preceded by skirmishers.

Only the centre column, from the 30th Regiment, penetrated into
the village. Two hundred yards from the hedges they deployed and
charged. Captain Charles François, who had been with the army
since volunteering in 1792, jogged with his company and two others
up a hollow way. Hollow ways were earth roads set below the level of
the ground on either side, and enclosed by steep banks usually topped
by hedges. Such roads gave shelter and cover from fire to troops
within them, but were quite difficult to get in and out of laterally.

This one had been blocked with a barricade of felled trees, carts, harrows and ploughs, which the French infantry had to clamber over, under fire from Prussians behind thick hedges. Firing as they jogged along, they passed the Ferme d'en Haut and emerged to their left into an open space in which the church stood:

> On the far side of the church we were stopped by a stream, and the enemy, in houses, behind walls and on the rooftops, inflicted considerable casualties, both through musketry and through canister and cannon shot, which took us from in front and from the flank.
>
> In a moment Major Hervieux, commanding the regiment, and the battalion commanders Richard and Lafolie had been killed; battalion commander Blain was slightly wounded and his horse killed under him; five captains were killed, three wounded; two adjutants killed, nine lieutenants and sub-lieutenants were killed, seven wounded, and almost seven hundred men killed and wounded.

Most observers reckoned that the French Charleville musket was better than the others. It weighed 10 lb, was five feet long and fired a 0.69 inch ball weighing 1/20 lb. The old Prussian model was shorter and heavier, the new model similar to the French, but many Prussians were using either British or French muskets. The nature of the fighting in Ligny meant that much firing took place at unusually short range. At less than 50 yards musket balls could shatter major limb bones and joints, while at 100 balls tended to flatten on impact and inflict large conical wounds, complicated by carrying cloth or other foreign bodies with them. At two hundred yards they had lost velocity; a ball might cause a flesh wound, might merely bruise, or might be deflected by equipment or objects in pockets. Some soldiers hit by spent balls were able to pull them out of their own flesh.[10]

One of Gérard's aides recalled that some of the 30th got across the stream but were pinned down there, leaderless, under intense musketry. He pulled them back to the French side of the main road, but they were driven from there by a Prussian attack and the survivors fled from the village in disorder, to be rallied behind the artillery.[11]

On the western flank, the French made little headway against the Prussians defending the walls and towers of the medieval castle and two hedged orchards in front of it. On the eastern flank, they fled before a charge by Major von Zastrow and his Westphalian fusiliers, but the Prussians pursued the retreating French too rashly into a hail of canister fire, running back to the village with French *voltigeurs* at their heels.[12]

Meanwhile, in Saint-Amand, Lefol's men exchanged fire with the Prussians who had regrouped on their reserves around a fortified farm in Saint-Amand-la-Haye. Then the dynamic General von Steinmetz sent forward the four musketeer battalions of the 12th and 24th Regiments in a fierce counter-attack. The French reserve held onto the churchyard of Saint-Amand, but Steinmetz drove the French out of the rest of the village.[13]

Both exploratory attacks had been repulsed with loss, telling the French staff that this time the Prussians had no intention of making a show before falling back at the first attack, as they had done the day before. Whether or not Napoleon's scouts had yet identified the true strength of Blücher's force, the behaviour of Ziethen's men proved that he had a real battle on his hands. It was a glorious opportunity to crush the Prussians.

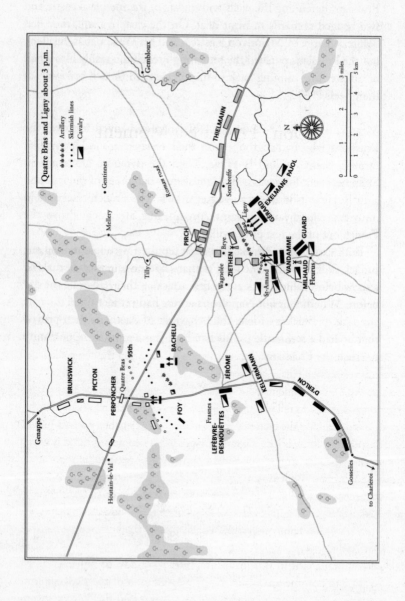

Quatre Bras and Ligny about 3 p.m.

⚜⚜⚜⚜ Artillery
• • • • Skirmish lines
▮ Cavalry

N

0   1   2   3 miles
0   1   2   3   4   5 km

Gembloux

THIELMANN

Sombreffe

PIRCH

Roman road

Mellery

Gentinnes

Tilly

Ligny

GÉRARD EXELMANS PAJOL

VANDAMME   GUARD

Brye

ZIETHEN   MILHAUD

Wagnelée   St-Amand   Fleurus

BRUNSWICK

PICTON

PERPONCHER   Quatre Bras

Genappe

95th

BACHELU

FOY

Frasnes

JÉRÔME

LEFÈBVRE-
DESNOUËTTES

KELLERMANN

D'ERLON

Houtain-le-Val

Gosselies

to Charleroi

25

Don't Hesitate a Moment

Fleurus, 16 June, 3–3.30 p.m.

Having observed the initial phase of the fighting at Saint-Amand and Ligny, *Major-Général* Soult sent a much more urgent demand to Marshal Ney. Timed at 3.15, it instructed him to march east as quickly as possible and fall upon the Prussian flank and rear:

> Marshal, I wrote to you an hour ago to say that at 2.30 the Emperor would attack the enemy in the position they had taken between the villages of St Amand and Brye.
>
> At this moment the engagement is very intense. His Majesty charges me to tell you that you should immediately manoeuvre so as to envelop the enemy's flank and fall with clenched fists on his rear. His army is lost if you act vigorously. The fate of France is in your hands. So don't hesitate a moment before undertaking the movement the Emperor orders and head for the heights of Brye and St Amand so as to contribute to a victory that could be decisive. We've caught the enemy with his trousers down just as he's trying to combine with the English.[1]

It is notable that in this order the 'corps' or 'body' of previous messages had become an 'army'. The determination of the Prussians to resist the attacks on Saint-Amand and Ligny had finally convinced

Napoleon that he was now fighting a battle, not an inconsequential skirmish; moreover the stream of approaching troops had persuaded him that he had surprised Blücher's army on the march. This offered an unexpected opportunity, for with Ney's help, Napoleon was perfectly placed to trap the Prussians and obtain a crushing victory. By contriving to produce an army Blücher had reacted faster than Napoleon had expected, but his impetuosity provided a golden chance to destroy one of the two enemy forces instantly, in isolation from the other.

Very soon after this order had been written, however, a message arrived from Count Lobau, saying that his aide had just returned from Frasnes and reported that there might be up to 20,000 Anglo-Dutch troops at Quatre Bras.[2] This shocking news required another change of plan. If Ney really faced such a large enemy force at Quatre Bras, he might not have already obtained the quick, crushing victory that had been expected in the morning and therefore he might not be in a position to march straight to Brye. However, the Emperor thought, Ney should be able to contain 20,000 Anglo-Dutch troops with Reille's corps alone, in which case d'Erlon's corps could be spared for the attack on Brye. At this juncture, Napoleon sent Ney a pencil note containing a direct order to have d'Erlon march with his corps towards Brye and Saint-Amand and attack the Prussian right flank. Since this message did not reach Ney there has been much debate about whether or not it was ever sent.

This is another highly controversial episode in the history of the battle – the problem being that whereas d'Erlon received this order, Ney did not. Every participant subsequently gave a different version of what happened. A duplicate of the message sent to Ney, for a duplicate later reached him, survived in Ney's archive, whereas the note that d'Erlon claimed to have been shown has not survived; nor, surprisingly, was it entered in Soult's staff register of orders, although some messages that do survive – such as the earlier one to Ney requiring him to attack with the greatest impetuosity – were omitted from the register. If the message was carried by one of Napoleon's aides, it is possible that it was merely verbal.[3] It has even been suggested that Napoleon did not send a message at all, but that the order sending d'Erlon's corps to attack the Prussians was issued by one of his general officer aides on his own initiative.[4] However, Soult's message to Ney the following day and his report to War Minister Davout both mention a movement that the Emperor had ordered d'Erlon to make, which proves that it was Napoleon himself who had ordered d'Erlon to Ligny, so this theory can be discounted.[5] Possibly one messenger carried both messages, with orders to deliver the second order direct to d'Erlon and then to go on to Ney to give him the first order and explain what had been done.[6] At the same time Napoleon ordered Count Lobau to bring his corps to Fleurus, for he now realised that to destroy the Prussians he would need all of his reserves.

Further officers were sent with duplicate orders to make sure that the messages got through. These messages were absolutely crucial, for it was imperative that Ney should appreciate that since the morning the case had altered. Napoleon's plan had now changed completely. Instead of crushing the opposition to open the road through to Brussels, Ney now merely had to perform a holding role while d'Erlon's corps surrounded the Prussians and drove the survivors towards Namur. Guillaume de Baudus, an aide to Soult, claimed to have been ordered to carry one such duplicate message to Ney and said that he was instructed by the Emperor:

> I have sent count d'Erlon the order to march with his entire corps against the right rear of the Prussian army. You will carry the duplicate order to Ney, which should already have been communicated to him. You will tell him that whatever the situation in which he finds himself, it is absolutely necessary that this order must be executed, that I do not attach great importance to what happens today on his flank; that the business is where I am, and that I want to finish off the Prussian army. As far as he is concerned, if he can do no better, he must aim to contain the English army.[7]

Napoleon could not be in two places at once and so he was dependent for the execution of this brilliant idea on messages, written and verbal. This was why he gave important messages to intelligent senior aides who were capable of understanding and explaining his intentions. Moreover, while Napoleon could watch the battle at Ligny unfolding before his eyes, he had little idea of what was going on eight miles away at Quatre Bras, so he tried to choose emissaries who were capable of adapting their instructions, on the hoof, to circumstances that had not been anticipated. In this crucial instance, however, something was to go desperately wrong. During his exile Napoleon complained much about Soult, the poor quality of his staff, and the youth and inexperience of his orderly officers. He expressed perplexity about the fate of some messages: 'It is equally probable that several officers, bearers of dispatches, disappeared.'[8] Messengers could be delayed, get lost, make mistakes, be ambushed by the enemy or even go over to the other side.

But as he dispatched his chosen messengers to Ney, Napoleon had no reason to anticipate that they would miscarry, and at that moment he was confident of a resoundingly successful outcome. When Count Gérard had come for final instructions regarding his attack on Ligny, Napoleon told him, 'In three hours the fate of the war may be decided. If Ney executes his orders properly, not a cannon of the Prussians will escape. They are completely surprised.'[9]

26

Thin Red Line

Quatre Bras, 3.30 p.m.–5.30 p.m.

At the time that Napoleon sent these orders, Marshal Ney was on the brink of success at Quatre Bras as his troops advanced to envelop the Prince of Orange's division and block the route through to the Prussians. However, Wellington had just returned to the battlefield and he had fresh British troops at hand to restore stability: Picton's division was close by, approaching from Genappe, and Wellington's staff galloped over to meet Picton's.

Concerned that the French were cutting the road to Ligny, Wellington first sent for Colonel Barnard, whose 95th Rifles led Picton's column. Fitzroy Somerset instructed the riflemen to thrust east along the cobbled Namur highway and seize the Bois des Censes and the village of Piraumont in order 'to keep the road open for communication with the Prussians'.[1] Having seized the wood to the north of the road, however, they soon recognised that Piraumont was too strongly held for them to retake, so they put two companies into the hamlet of Thyle on the highway north of Piraumont. Barnard's Scottish adjutant, John Kincaid, recalled that in the burning sun one of his overdressed and overburdened men died of heatstroke as they trotted forward. The two companies at Thyle were quiet until the French brought up artillery and counter-attacked: a pretty Belgian girl was giving a glass of water to Ned Costello when a ball went

straight through her house, covering them with dust.[2] The riflemen
pulled out of the houses before they were surrounded and fell back
northward to the wood of Censes, fighting a running battle with
French *voltigeurs*.

Near La Baraque, an alehouse three hundred yards north of the
crossroads, Wellington conferred with Picton and his brigadiers.
There was no more determined man in a tight spot than Picton, the
stocky Welshman who in 1812 had driven through the storming of
Ciudad Rodrigo and Badajoz and had taken on the most dangerous
role in the victory at Vitoria in 1813, obstinately holding a bridgehead
in the face of devastating fire. Picton's 'fighting third' division had
become legendary in the Peninsula, although he now commanded
different battalions and had first met their senior officers in the park
at Brussels the previous evening. But everybody knew Picton by reputation, and the many Peninsular veterans among his men already
admired, respected and feared this 'stern-looking, strong-built man,
about the middle height'. In private Picton was livelier than his austere image suggested: an aide who had just joined his staff expecting
him to be all cold iron had been surprised at Ostend to hear his boss
'in excellent French, get up a flirtation with our very pretty waiting-
maid'. The general was wearing civilian dress because his uniform
had not yet arrived from Britain: 'a blue frock-coat, very tightly but-
toned up to the throat; a very large black silk neckcloth, showing little
or no shirt-collar; dark trousers, boots, and a round hat'.[3] His
brigadiers, the Scot Sir James Kempt and the Irishman Sir Denis
Pack, were both experienced Peninsular veterans.

To the south of the generals, on the highway leading to Charleroi,
the Prince of Orange had launched a desperate counter-attack on the
French troops holding Gémioncourt, nearly a mile straight up the
road. Kempt ordered the next battalion to arrive to support the
Prince, but then cancelled the order when he saw the attack was failing. The rest of the 5000 British infantry turned left onto the road to
Namur, using the ditches and embankments for cover against French
artillery fire. Kempt's Cameron Highlanders marched furthest east,
nearest the skirmishing riflemen, followed by the 32nd Cornish; then
came Pack's division, the Royal Scots, the 44th, the 42nd Black

Watch and the Gordons. Behind them, as they marched in, General Charles Best's brigade of 2500 Hanoverian militia formed a second line and at first the Brunswickers, of whom there were soon about 5000, formed a third.

The 92nd Gordon Highlanders in their dark green and blue kilts hurriedly took up a strong defensive position on the crossroads itself, as Sergeant David Robertson recalled:

> The 92d was now brought to the front of the farmhouse, and formed on the road, with our backs to the walls of the building and garden, our right resting upon the crossroads, and our left extending down the front. We were ordered to prime and load, and sit down with our firelocks in our hands, at the same time keeping in line. The ground we occupied rose with a slight elevation, and was directly in front of the road along which the French were advancing.
>
> Shortly after we had formed here, the Duke of Wellington and his staff came and dismounted in rear of the centre of our regiment, and ordered the grenadier company to wheel back on the left, and the light company on the right; so that the walls of the house and garden in our rear, with the eight companies in front, joined in a square, in case that any of the enemy's cavalry should attack us.[4]

When threatened by cavalry, infantry would form square, to prevent the speedy horsemen from finding an unguarded flank. A square (usually an oblong with two companies each side and three front and back) was formed four ranks deep; the front two ranks knelt with their muskets braced against the ground, bayonets pointing outwards, and the rear two ranks were ready to fire. When many squares formed simultaneously they tried to take up a chequered formation so as to minimise the risk of hitting each other when firing at passing cavalry.

In this case the Gordons faced three ways instead of four. The substantial farmhouse they had their backs to stood in the north-east quadrant of the crossroads with an enclosed courtyard and a huge brick barn behind it. Diagonally opposite them in the south-west corner of the crossroads was an inn with outbuildings, named (confusingly) Les Trois Bras, and not very far beyond was the edge of the beech wood, the Bois de Bossu, from which the sound of musketry could be heard. To their right, opposite the farm and the inn, were a tollbooth and a barn. In front of them the south-east corner of the crossroads was open but, on the left of the road to Charleroi two hundred and fifty yards ahead, was a small farm called La Bergerie, with a garden across the road, at a point where the highway ran close to the Bossu wood.

Two artillery batteries trundled in, adding ten 9-pounder guns and two heavy howitzers to what was left of the Netherlands artillery. Carl von Rettberg's lined up to the east of the Gordon Highlanders behind the Namur road, while Major Thomas Rogers's battery was sent much further to the left, beyond the Cameron Highlanders, opposite some French guns which were behind the Materne lake. As soon as Rogers deployed, the French brought down fire on his guns – he estimated the range at only 5–600 yards – and killed several of his men and horses.[5] Indeed, from the start of this battle the allies were made painfully aware of their shortage of artillery and cavalry. The French had at least thirty-four guns – maybe fifty by now – and as allied batteries deployed on the battlefield, so the French destroyed them, one by one.

And as Picton's men deployed, the Netherlands troops in front of them began to disintegrate. With the Dutch attack on Gémioncourt melting away in the face of strong French fire from the surrounding hedges, Piré's lancers closed in. Dressed in green with brass helmets and imposing nine-foot spears with red and white pennons, the lancers were a frightening prospect for the young Dutch soldiers. Piré's men saw the Jägers wavering, charged, and speared and rode them down as they fled; their colonel had his horse shot under him and his head cut open by a sabre.

In an attempt to save the Jägers, Orange ordered the first cavalry to appear, Merlen's newly arrived 6th Dutch Hussars, to charge before they had even had a chance to form line. Some Jägers who had been captured or were hiding in the corn escaped, but the hussars were soon also in headlong flight, having been counter-charged by

French lancers and chasseurs. The victorious French cavalry caught five guns limbered up to support the hussars and overtook them, hacking through leather traces and slashing at gunners.

Waves of French cavalry now swept across the field through the tall crops. The 5th Militia saw them too late and were ridden down and stabbed as they fled. Seeing this, the morale of the 7th Line broke and they ran for the woods, pursued by lancers who skewered everyone they caught up with. The Prince of Orange himself was surrounded by French horsemen and an aide beside him was wounded and captured, before a few hussars cut a way through to the Prince and they all found refuge within a cluster of men of the 7th Line who had stood firm amid the general disintegration.

Somewhat panicked, the Prince ordered his other newly arrived cavalry regiment to charge, and they launched themselves at the French 6th Chasseurs. By coincidence many of the Belgians had previously served with their French opponents and knew them well; by another, unfortunate coincidence they were wearing near-identical uniforms of green with yellow facings.

The French got the better of the encounter. The Belgian colonel received two pistol balls in the arm, a canister ball in the kidneys, was knocked to the ground by a sabre blow and trapped beneath his dead horse. Amazingly, he survived, for during a fierce mêlée some of his men got him away on a fresh horse, before, defeated, the rest of the Belgians turned and galloped off towards Quatre Bras, nearly half a mile back.[6]

There at the crossroads the Gordon Highlanders fired into the mass of rapidly approaching green-coated cavalry, thinking them to be one hostile body, and brought down horsemen of both sides.[7] The Duke of Wellington made the opposite mistake: recognising the fleeing dragoons as Belgian, he failed to see until the last minute the pursuing French chasseurs intermingled with them and had to leap his horse Copenhagen over a ditch and bank to escape into the ranks of the 92nd.[8]

The arrival of Picton's division and the Black Brunswickers steadied the line just in time. General Pack led forward the Black Watch and the 44th past La Bergerie to occupy the higher ground north of

Gémioncourt, and to their right the Duke of Brunswick's hussars chased away the French chasseurs while the Brunswickers marched into the area between the Charleroi highway and the wood. The Black Watch, like their colleagues, found the going very difficult through the tall crops. 'The stalks of rye, like the reeds that grow on the margin of some swamp, opposed our advance,' recalled a Highlander. 'The tops were up to our bonnets, and we strode and groped our way through as fast as we could.' The 44th had their light company in front as skirmishers, 'but finding that the French had the advantage of seeing us, and picking off many, Colonel Hamerton called them in, and file firing commenced from each company, to clear the rye [as] we advanced'. The kilted and bonneted Black Watch met Foy's 4th Light Infantry advancing from Gémioncourt, having routed the Dutch Jägers, and succeeded in pushing their skirmish line back in the direction it had come:

> By the time we reached a field of clover on the other side, we were very much straggled; however, we united in line as fast as time and our speedy advance would permit. The Belgic skirmishers retired through our ranks, and in an instant we were on their victorious pursuers. Our sudden appearance seemed to paralyze their advance. The singular appearance of our dress, combined no doubt, with our sudden debut, tended to stagger their resolution.[9]

When the Brunswick 2nd Light battalion arrived, the staff sent them to the left wing to reinforce the British riflemen who were holding the Bois des Censes on the extreme eastern flank. As Adjutant Kincaid recalled, however, the young Brunswickers were raw, trigger-happy and so prone to fire at skirmishing riflemen rather than the French that in the end he was sent to order them not to shoot. Nervous infantry would frequently fire off all their ammunition as quickly as possible and then hurry to the rear, thinking they had done their bit, and Kincaid tried to teach these inexperienced officers and men to reserve their fire for the right target at the right range.[10]

Just to the west, Picton's battalions sent their light companies

forward to engage Maigrot's skirmishers, who were holding the
line of the stream that ran eastward from Gémioncourt to the
northern edge of Thyle and exchanging fire with the riflemen in the
wood further east. Picton's skirmishers, though, were outnumbered
and outclassed by the French. An ensign of the Royal Scots reckoned that the lighter weapons the French soldiers used gave them
a considerable edge in this kind of fighting: 'Their fine, long, light
firelocks, with a smaller bore, are far more efficient for skirmishing
than our abominably clumsy machine. The French soldiers whip-
ping in the cartridge, give the butt of the piece a jerk or two on the
ground, which supersedes the use of the ramrod; and thus they fire
two for our one.'[11] The shorter dragoon musket used by French
voltigeurs was lighter still and even better adapted for rapid fire.

Picton's battalions nevertheless advanced behind their skirmishers
onto the higher ground about three hundred yards from the stream –
or closer, near the lake where the Camerons were – and deployed into
their usual two-deep line. Although they advanced and manoeuvred
in columns – having narrower frontage and greater depth, columns
could change direction more easily, even if their greater depth made
them more vulnerable to artillery – infantry usually chose to fight
against infantry in line, two or three deep, making the most of their
firepower.

Behind the duelling skirmishers the other battalions of Bachelu's
division emerged from the Bois Delhutte in assault columns. His battalions marched forward to the stream, where their progress was
obstructed by two thick hedges either side of the water. As the
French approached the lake Major Rogers's battery of guns made first
use of a weapon that was unique to the British. Spherical case shot,
invented in 1784 by Henry Shrapnel, was a shell filled with a mixture
of gunpowder and about a hundred musket balls. It was an airburst
weapon, designed to explode over its target, propelling musket balls
2–300 yards from the point of burst. Shrapnel could be fired by both
howitzers and ordinary guns, giving the British the option of firing
canister at long range – when the weapon worked, for it required skill
and luck to get the shell to explode in the right place (which may
explain why the French did not copy it).

Bachelu's infantry, 3000-strong without Maigrot's skirmishing light infantry, were organised in seven battalions; ahead, out of sight in the rye, were four strong British battalions, the Camerons, Cornish, Royal Scots and the 28th North Gloucesters, totalling around 2700. But Picton's soldiers had been up all night and had marched twenty miles, the last ten in scorching heat, so they were not at their freshest, whereas Bachelu's were well rested after their gruelling march the previous day.

The French passed through their skirmishers, who were lining the first hedge, and then crossed the difficult terrain. But they became disordered in the process: near the lake the hedges had been cut to two to three feet and were low and easy to cross, although there the stream itself was relatively wide; to the west, in front of Philippe Higonet's 108th Regiment, the whitethorn hedges were six to nine feet high and three feet wide and quite impenetrable. Higonet halted his men and called forward his sappers and grenadiers, who used axes and saws to cut a gap the width of a platoon. By the time the 108th had cut their gap and the first battalion had pushed through, they were trailing behind the leading battalions of other regiments.

While the slopes on either side of the stream were covered in very tall rye or wheat, the bottom of the valley was planted for cattle with grass or clover. The British advanced and formed line, their skirmishers running back at the approach of the French columns.

As these came on up the slope, the British suddenly opened fire. The British 'Brown Bess' musket was half a pound heavier and an inch and a half shorter than the French Charleville, and fired a 0.76 inch ball of soft lead weighing 1/14 lb. Its broader bore and shorter length made it fractionally less accurate, but its bigger bullet might do more damage and the British were well drilled in rapid, short-range fire, which they followed with a fierce and confident bayonet charge.

The range here probably varied from fifty yards at the east to a hundred at the west. The French stopped in sheer surprise as men tumbled and screamed. 'As, at first, we couldn't see where this fusillade had come from, there was a slight hesitation in the column,' wrote Bachelu's chief of staff, Toussaint Jean Trefcon. 'The English took the opportunity to charge us at top speed. They yelled a fierce hurrah and for a moment we were completely stunned.'[12]

Infantry attacks such as this usually took the form of a brief duel with muskets followed by a bayonet charge. Charges were rarely followed by hand-to-hand fighting, for one side or the other almost invariably turned and ran before an attack went home. It was rare for two large formations to meet and start stabbing each other: the French surgeon Dominique Larrey studied the wounds inflicted in two mêlées between French and Austrian soldiers and found that whereas there were over a hundred bullet wounds there were only five caused by bayonets. And as a French officer noted:

> ... in these bayonet fights the business is most often decided before anybody crosses iron. The battalion or square that is going to give way shows it visibly with a sort of wavering in its line at the critical moment, and the catastrophe follows immediately. It is as if they are blown away by the breath of the attackers, and it is true enough, because a unit's superior intensity acts like a magnetic current on a less resolute enemy.[13]

On this occasion Picton's men rose out of the rye, lowered their bayonets and ran down the slope, sweeping the 61st and 72nd Regiments away in flight towards the bottom of the valley. However, the British failed to catch up with their adversaries. The Camerons might have stabbed or captured a few Frenchmen as they sought to cross the hedges and stream, but most of the British were too far behind. As a lieutenant of the 32nd Cornwall described:

> we no sooner set up the usual shout and moved on than the cowardly rascals ran in every direction; our poor fellows were so fagged (not having had any sleep the night before, and marching that day 20 miles under a broiling hot sun) that we were not able to get up to them and we were wading up to our middle in corn; however we peppered them pretty well as they were getting through the gaps in the hedges ...[14]

On the left the kilted Camerons chased the French beyond the hedges and up the hill, where Trefcon was almost captured when his horse reared up and refused to move. The Scots were close behind and he was about to jump off and run for it when his horse shot away at a gallop.

When they attacked, infantry bodies would leave behind a strong reserve on which to rally, should they be forced to retreat. This tactic now came to the rescue of the French. The Camerons' charge carried them into a hail of canister from French cannon behind the lake, and left them isolated and vulnerable to the French reserves, as Private Dixon Vallance explained:

> the French seeing our regiment alone and at a considerable dis-
> tance in front of our main body, advanced against us in great
> numbers, and made an attempt to surround us, to make us pris-
> oners, shouting to us, 'Prisoners! Prisoners!' Our commanding
> officer, seeing this, called to us to, 'Run like devils – the French
> shall not make us prisoners.' We soon got clear of the French;
> they were afraid of coming near us, numerous as they were. We
> had to pass through a fence in our retreat from the French, which
> hindered us greatly, as we could only get through it at openings
> and slaps [sic]. The French directed their fire at us as we were
> crowding to get through the hedge and killed and wounded many
> of us in our retreat to our station in a field of rye.[15]

The 32nd stopped and reformed at the first hedge, while their enemies turned about and fired at them from behind the second hedge beyond the stream. The Royal Scots crossed the hedge but ran into fierce fire from the 108th. Higonet had marched his first battalion back through the hedge and it reformed behind the other two battalions who lined the obstacle. After the routed 72nd cleared their front, the 108th engaged the pursuing British and drove them back again. When they recovered the lost ground, Higonet's men were very favourably impressed to discover a wounded corporal of their grenadiers lying, bandaged by the British with food and drink beside him.[16]

Trefcon's men reformed in front of Piraumont. Then it was their turn to produce some sharp musketry, backed up by the cannon which had remained on the ridge above the village, protected by the lake. 'General Piré's cavalry arrived in the nick of time and they charged the English in their turn who had to get back to their own lines. They executed this retreat in a good order that filled us with admiration. Their squares were so remarkably well-formed that our lancers and chasseurs couldn't break into them.' Picton's men fell back in square and harassed by French cavalry, to form a line between La Bergerie and the Bois des Censes, protecting the Namur road.

Ney's first confident attempt to seize the *chaussée* had recoiled from a thin red line of determined British infantry. Prisoners taken by the French during this engagement revealed that they belonged to a force of 15,000 men who had marched from Brussels that morning under the Duke of Wellington. It confirmed to Ney that victory in his battle would be a struggle, since it was likely that the whole British army would soon come to support the Duke.

However, for the present Wellington only had some 20,000 men, and Jérôme's strong division had now arrived with sixteen more guns, accompanied by General Kellermann and a brigade of cuirassiers. Ney had a force of similar strength; what was more, he had fresh troops with which to launch another powerful attack.

27

Clubbed Muskets and Bayonets

Ligny, 3.15–5.30 p.m.

Seven miles south-east of Quatre-Bras, Napoleon was trying to draw as many Prussians as possible into gradually escalating fighting in the chain of villages that straggled along the marshy Ligne stream north of Fleurus. It was his intention that in late afternoon, either Ney's entire wing or the corps commanded by d'Erlon would strike them from the flank and rear, and those of Blücher's men that were not surrounded and killed or captured would be sent reeling back towards the east. Victory had to be achieved economically given his numerical inferiority, so Napoleon would commit as few troops as possible; using his own men sparingly, he would inflict on the enemy as much damage as possible.

Under the supervision of General Antoine Drouot, a French gun line had been established opposite the Prussian one, and Drouot was delighted to see that his was having the greater success. 'The troops destined to protect our batteries, being at a distance, and masked by the sinuosities of the ground, experienced no injury. Those of the Enemy, on the contrary, being placed in masses, in the form of an amphitheatre, behind these batteries, suffered very great losses.'[1] It was Drouot, the son of a baker grown up to be the army's best gunner, who had transformed the Artillery of the Guard into a battle-winning instrument. One of Napoleon's marshals spoke of him as 'the most upright and modest man I have ever known – well educated, brave, devoted, simple in his manner. His character was lofty and of rare probity'.[2] He is sometimes said to have served at the naval battle of Trafalgar in 1805 in the *Indomptable*, but as that vessel went down with all hands in the storm after the battle, it was fortunate for him that he had left the ship a month earlier to rejoin the *Grande Armée*. Drouot became a trusted general officer aide to the Emperor and, in the absence of Marshal Mortier, had been given command of the Guard.

A second French attack drove back some of the Prussians in the western sector of Ligny, but try as they might, the French could not take the castle or the churchyard or establish themselves on the far bank of the Ligne, where the Prussians held the Ferme d'en Bas. The firefight was fierce: General Henckel, in command of the Prussian defence, recalled that Gröben of the Westphalian Landwehr, who was his second-in-command, had two horses shot under him. Gröben was addicted to snuff and when he first fell he took a huge pinch before mounting a second horse. The death of the second horse required another large pinch of snuff, and afterwards Gröben decided he was less conspicuous on foot.[3]

Under the fierce sun it was extremely hot by now. Each time a soldier loaded a musket, he had to bite open the cartridge and hold each greasy, powder-encrusted bullet in his teeth. Saltpetre tasted bitter, left grit in the mouth and quickly dried it out. At the same time, soldiers were working in smoke thick enough to sting the eyes, and it was not long before such conditions induced burning thirst. Nor was it easy to find water in Ligny. Henckel called over a man who was drinking and asked him for some. As Henckel lifted the jug to his lips the soldier, who was holding the general's horse, was shot dead.

Gérard now attacked the eastern side of the village but the French columns broke when their skirmishers fell back on them, pursued by Prussians who briefly captured two guns. For the second time Major von Zastrow led the Westphalian left wing into canister fire from the supporting French guns; this time his arm was shot off and he fell from his horse, to be carried away to the surgeons.

After probing the defences on both sides of the village, Gérard

launched a massive assault, but found the Prussians willing to fight
for every cottage and every hedge. To advance, the French had to
clear each house: there were men in the cellars firing from the holes
into which coal was loaded and men in the attics firing from the
rooftops. At really close quarters – when bursting into a house, for
instance – the walnut stocks of muskets could be wielded as a club,
while fixing a seventeen-inch steel bayonet turned the weapon into a
spear. But it was slow, bloody work: cornered men stabbed and
clubbed each other in their desperation, as a Westphalian described:

> In the streets of the village, we fought with clubbed muskets and
> bayonets. As if overcome by personal hatred, man battled against
> man. It seemed as if every individual had met his deadliest enemy
> and rejoiced at the long-awaited opportunity to give expression to
> this. Quarter was neither asked nor given; the French plunged
> their bayonets into the chests of those already falling from their
> wounds; the Prussians swore loudly at their enemies and killed
> everyone that fell into their hands.[4]

Finally, after a bout of fierce and bloody fighting, the French took
the medieval castle at the western edge of Ligny and the churchyard
in the centre of the southern part of the village. They drove the
Prussians north across the Ligne, and out of every stronghold except
the Ferme d'en Bas, opposite the church on the north bank, in which
the Prussians held out obstinately. Frenchmen described the fighting
in exactly the same terms as their opponents:

> I really know not how to describe the inconceivable fury and exas-
> peration of the soldiers on both sides. It seemed as if every man
> had to avenge himself of some personal injury, and saw in his
> adversary only his implacable enemy. The French refused to give or
> take quarter; the Prussians, it is added, had previously announced
> the intention of massacring all the French who should fall into
> their hands. ... The French themselves regarded all the Prussians
> and other Germans as fugitive slaves, and treacherous malefactors.
> In a word the mutual hatred was inflamed by the memory of past

injuries, and the certainty that whoever should be victors, the victory would be abused by cruelty.[5]

This intensity was vividly illustrated by the rapidity with which the usual codes regarding prisoners broke down. In normal circumstances it was perfectly possible to show a white flag or throw down your arms and expect to survive, but at Ligny 'no quarter' – no prisoners – was a motto from the start. Within a short time tales of opposition atrocities spread and throats were cut, men hanged or bayoneted; few prisoners were taken.

By now Henckel's brigade had lost 2500 men out of 4700 and the remainder were running out of ammunition. Good flints lasted thirty to fifty rounds and then needed changing, while coarse grain powder meant that the barrel required cleaning after every 50–60 rounds. Fifty rounds was what each soldier usually carried in battle, and when they had been fired a new supply had to be fetched from the wagons that travelled with the artillery. These could not reach Henckel's men in Ligny, so while isolated pockets held out in strongholds like the Ferme d'en Bas, the rest were forced to evacuate the village in order to replenish their ammunition and reorganise.

As Henckel's men retreated, General von Jagow led in his reserves, the fresh musketeer battalions of the 7th West Prussian infantry and the 3rd Westphalian Landwehr, along the lane from Brye. With the light companies winkling the French out of the cottages, the first West Prussian battalion pushed eastward along the *rue d'en bas* north of the Ligne, while Jagow himself led the second battalion along the *rue d'en haut* to the south. Jagow's fusilier battalions assaulted the castle and succeeded in recapturing it. Under fierce French artillery bombardment the second battalion of West Prussians reached the church and mounted a furious attack on the graveyard, which they succeeded in capturing.

Just as the Prussians broke into the churchyard, though, they were hit from two directions by French battalions, one slicing into their flank. Captain François took part in this counter-attack, leading about a hundred men from his shattered 30th Regiment. Slipping silently along the sunken lane that led to the Ferme d'en Haut, they almost ran into Prussians in the thick smoke; François shouted 'Fire!' and threw himself to the ground as his men shot over him, while in the mêlée he broke his sword and was trampled underfoot. But a charge from east by the 96th Regiment broke the Prussian defence.[6] The Prussians were so completely routed that they carried their first battalion away with them as they fled. The French recaptured the churchyard, which was full of dead West Prussians and Westphalians, and crossed the stream into the northern half of Ligny.

Once again, Blücher invited four fresh battalions to storm the village, having summoned reserves from Georg von Pirch's II Corps. The battle for Ligny was sucking in more and more Prussians, just as Napoleon hoped it would. Having reorganised, Jagow's men again attacked the west of the village while the new regiments assaulted the east.

For two hours Franz Lieber's company of the Colberg Regiment had been lying down to avoid cannonballs, longing to advance. The volunteer riflemen, distinguished from the blue-coated musketeers by their green jackets and black belts, were very young lads, and their experienced officer, Carl von Bagensky, tried to explain that waiting under fire was the severest test that a soldier could face. Finally, an aide galloped up and told Colonel von Zastrow, 'Your column must throw the enemy out of the left wing of the village.' The colonel rode to Lieber's company and spoke: 'Riflemen, you are young – I am afraid too ardent. Calmness makes the soldier; hold yourselves in order.' Then he turned round. 'March!' The drum rolled. After half a mile's march the two musketeer battalions of the famous Colberg Regiment and two of Elbe Landwehr prepared to attack Ligny, preceded by skirmishers that included the eighty-strong detachment of Colberg volunteer riflemen. A bugle told Franz Lieber's Colbergs to halt before the village.[7]

All of Ligny south of the stream was in French hands except the castle on the western fringe. To the north of the stream the Prussians held the western half including the fortified Ferme d'en Bas, but the French had taken the eastern half. That was the Colbergs' objective. The noise now was deafening. Clouds of smoke obscured the village, punctuated by flashes of musketry, explosions and plumes of debris.

Cannonballs whined overhead. Occasional shells were falling, exploding in plumes of dust and throwing out dirt and jagged shards of metal. Lieber was to walk into that.

Another bugle-call told Captain von Bagensky and his veteran professional sergeant-major to lead the skirmishers forward. Riflemen normally worked in pairs, with a front man and a rear man covering each other. They should have edged forward cautiously, pausing in cover to fire, one reloading while the other fired. Instead, the youngsters ran towards the enemy at top speed without firing, leaving their sergeant-major puffing furiously behind. Lieber saw his Jewish friend pitch forward with blood spurting from his throat where a ball had cut it, but they kept running and at the impetuosity of their advance the French slipped away from the whitethorn hedges at the edge of the village. They reached a street where the Prussian sergeant-major regained control.

The sergeant-major sent Lieber to 'a house around the corner of which he suspected that a number of French lay'. Lieber stepped round the corner 'and a grenadier stood about fifteen paces from me; he aimed at me, I levelled my rifle at him. "Aim well, my boy," said the sergeant-major who saw me. My antagonist's ball grazed my hair on the right side; I shot and he fell; I found I had shot through his face; he was dying. This was my first shot ever fired in a battle.'

Years later Lieber tried to gather scattered recollections of his first combat. He remembered asking whether this was a proper battle and being reassured that it was. He saw a hog and a child, a bird trying to protect its young. Once, feeling thirsty, he stopped to pull water from a well. His company last advanced along a hollow way, piled deep with the bodies of dead and wounded men, and Lieber remembered the sensation of stepping on them. He had to help drag a cannon over the mangled bodies, and recalled the wounded squirming in agony when the wheel rolled over them.[8] They drove the French back across the stream and recaptured the northern part of the village, but were stopped to the south and the bitter, bloody house-to-house fighting continued.

The struggle for possession of the village was now deadlocked. Even though casualties on the French side were much higher than

Napoleon would have wished, General Gérard had succeeded in drawing nineteen Prussian battalions into the fighting – a much larger number of men than he had sent in himself – and by late afternoon the Prussian reserves were committed. But so were most of Gérard's; when Gaspard Gourgaud, Napoleon's chief orderly officer, who had been observing Gérard's progress, returned to headquarters at the Naveau windmill it was to report that despite tremendous efforts Gérard still could not break through. The time was just about ripe in the Ligny sector for Napoleon to make the decisive flank attack that he had envisaged in order to cut the Prussians off. But to complete this manoeuvre to his satisfaction the Emperor required intervention from Marshal Ney's wing of the army. The question was, how were things going over to the west?

Napoleon with his marshals

'I swear it smells of violets':
Marshal Ney deserts King
Louis and joins Napoleon

The rapid departure of
Louis XVIII and the
unexpected return of
Napoleon: March 1815

LE DÉPART PRÉCIPITÉ ET LE RETOUR IMPRÉVU.

Napoleon presents eagles to his soldiers at the Champ de Mai of 1815

The Duke of Wellington, 'the great war hero', riding Copenhagen and dressed as he was at Waterloo

The Prince of Orange, Wellington's former aide, riding Waxy and dressed for battle

Prince Blücher, 'Old Forwards', at the Katzbach in 1813, his first victory over the French

General Gneisenau: 'Blücher's brain'

Hans Ziethen, commander of I Corps

Volunteers of Lützow's Freikorps on outpost duty. *Auf Vorposten* (1815) by Georg Friedrich Kersting, who fought with the Freikorps, shows three of his comrades, the painters Friedrich Friesen and Ferdinand Hartmann and the writer Theodor Körner

Maurice Gérard, who led the assault on Ligny © Bildarchiv Preussicher Kulturbesitz

Franz Lieber, the Prussian volunteer rifleman who became Professor of History and Political Science at Columbia University and drafted the code of conduct for Union troops during the American Civil War
© Library of Congress

Burned-out ruins of Ligny, drawn soon after the battle from close to the quarry

Ligny castle with Blücher's windmill and Brye church in the distance on the left, Sombreffe on the right

Quatre Bras from the west with the farm left, the alehouse centre and naked bodies and La Bergerie right, sketched by Thomas Stoney on 21 June 1815

Quatre Bras from the east; above, the alehouse with the Bois de Bossu behind it; below, the farm and the crossroads

Thomas Picton (left) and the Duke of Brunswick (right), heroes of Quatre Bras

Marshal Grouchy, scapegoat for defeat; Marshal Ney, 'brave des braves' or battle-fatigued and brainless?; below, the Earl of Uxbridge, dashing commander of Wellington's cavalry

28

Ney's Second Assault

Quatre Bras, 16 June, 3.30–5 p.m.

At Quatre Bras, General Picton's arrival had saved the allied force from collapse and prevented the capture of the crossroads, but Ney was still applying tremendous pressure. Picton's easterly battalions, the Camerons and 32nd, were taking severe casualties from the French artillery behind the lake. The gunners aimed at the British flags: when a shell burst next to the regimental colour of the 32nd a captain had his head 'literally blown to atoms' and several men were wounded. The flag's white silk was torn, but the ensign carrying it was only slightly injured.[1] The British troops eventually pulled back to lie down under cover behind the banks in the ditches of the road.

Further west, French chasseurs and lancers had mounted a series of charges against the Royal Scots and 28th Foot, who formed square to repel them. But the cavalry never completed a charge, veering away from contact over the final yards as the veteran infantry remained steady. As one British officer observed, it was extremely rare for cavalry to charge home against an unbroken square:

> The infantry either break before the cavalry come close up, or they drive them back with their fire. It is an awful thing for infantry to see a body of cavalry riding at them full gallop. The men in the square frequently begin to shuffle, and so create some

unsteadiness. This causes them to neglect their fire. The cavalry seeing them waver, have an inducement for riding close up, and in all probability succeed in getting into the square, when all is over. When once broken, the infantry, of course have no chance. If steady, it is almost impossible to succeed against infantry, yet I should always be cautious, if in command of infantry attacked by cavalry, having seen the best of troops more afraid of cavalry than any other force.[2]

His view was confirmed by a French infantry officer:

It is extremely difficult for the best possible cavalry to break soldiers who have formed square and who defend themselves with intrepidity and coolness. When the infantry is in disorder, it is simply a massacre in which the cavalry run practically no risk, however brave and formidable the troops attacked might have been in other circumstances.[3]

In the tall rye, moreover, it was as difficult for the cavalry to judge how far infantry were away and when to accelerate as it was for infantry to see cavalry coming. An officer of the 28th spoke of a lancer riding up and planting his nine-foot lance in the ground to serve as a mark to charge at. Since the square did not waver, a French officer rode right up to the British bayonets to set an example, whereupon a grenadier shot him. The man's lieutenant struck him on the cheek for firing without orders, but as the two discussed this afterwards, General Kempt called out, 'Silence, gentlemen, let the men alone; they know their duty better than you, the men please me, and not a word gentlemen.'[4]

If a square successfully resisted cavalry then it had to be dislodged either by infantry attack or by artillery. It was exceptionally vulnerable to the latter, owing to the concentration of many men in a small area, several ranks deep, and Picton's densely packed men now took heavy casualties from the French artillery and skirmishers. If their own skirmishers left the square they ran the risk of being caught in the open by cavalry, while it was dangerous to deploy into line because the rye so reduced visibility that it was not always possible to see cavalry coming from a distance.

The adjacent British battalions, the 44th East Essex and 42nd Black Watch, had not yet been threatened by cavalry and remained in line. Nicolas Galbois with the 380 men of the 5th Lancers now charged the 42nd. With its men unable to see anything through rye that was above head height, a German orderly dragoon shouted a warning and skirmishers ran in yelling, 'Square, square, French cavalry!' But they failed to close their square in time and outlying troops were speared as they raced for safety.[5] When the square finally closed, lancers were trapped within it. The colonel was killed by a lance thrust through his chin and into his brain and the major and both senior captains were wounded or killed. The 42nd were to lose 288 of their 613 men during the day, most to musketry and artillery, but also some in this near-catastrophe.

The 44th meanwhile were attacked by lancers and chasseurs who had passed the squares of the Royals and 28th and were returning to their own lines from behind the British front line. The officers of the 44th assumed the cavalry was friendly until they began to slaughter the bandsmen and surgeons, and charged the infantry from the rear. It was too late to form square and so Colonel John Hamerton ordered the rear rank to turn about and fire a volley, which proved enough to deflect the charge.

It being regarded as a great dishonour for a unit to lose its colour and a very great honour to capture one, the French made disproportionately intense efforts at capturing British colours. One bunch of lancers made a serious attempt to capture the battalion's colour, and Ensign James Christie was stabbed in the left eye, through his tongue and lower jaw. He fell, pinning his flag beneath him. A lancer tore off a small part and made off but he was shot and bayoneted immediately afterwards. Piré's staff tried to seize a flag but the British formed a compact circle round it and wounded several Frenchmen.[6]

'The loss of the French cavalry at this time, was very great, in proportion to the British infantry,' it was claimed, and most British infantrymen got the impression they were cutting swathes in the French cavalry in firing on them when their charges on squares failed.[7] But the figures do not bear this out, for the 6th Lancers lost only two officers killed and five seriously wounded and less than seventy of their 347 men – about a fifth of their strength – over the entire day. To judge from figures for officer casualties (which are all that we have), the 5th Lancers suffered similarly, while the two stronger regiments of chasseurs lost two officers and one officer respectively. Colonel Galbois was shot in the chest but kept fighting.[8] Despite the sustained efforts and repeated charges of Piré's roaming horsemen, their casualties were low.

As French pressure increased, the allied skirmish line fell back. Some skirmishers of the Verden battalion, to the east of the 42nd, were ambushed by French *tirailleurs* who had hidden in the tall rye; others were sabred or taken prisoner by the French cavalry. The skirmishers of the 44th used up their ammunition and fled, fighting their way past bands of marauding French cavalry to reach the sanctuary of their square.

Meanwhile, Wellington had ordered the Duke of Brunswick to march his contingent to plug the gap left by disintegrating Netherlands militia units to the west of the Charleroi–Brussels highway. Duke Friedrich Wilhelm sent his *Gelernte Jäger* – four hundred elite grey-coated riflemen recruited from foresters – into the Bossu wood, with the two light companies of the Avant-Garde battalion skirmishing on the western fringe of the trees. The German riflemen were highly regarded. Behind this skirmish line the Brunswick Guards and 1st Line advanced two hundred yards from the crossroads to a position between the sheep farm of La Bergerie and the wood. They stood in column, with their hussars in support. Two Brunswick line battalions remained in reserve to the right of the Gordons with the Brunswick lancers behind them.[9]

Around this time in the late afternoon Ney had received Soult's two o'clock order to crush what was in front of him and then march back towards Brye to fall upon Blücher's right wing. Earlier this had looked easy, but not any more. Colonel Charles de Forbin-Janson of the staff, who probably carried this message from Soult, found Ney just behind Gémioncourt where the fire was intense. He had no aides, so Forbin-Janson volunteered to stay. A captured staff officer had confirmed that Wellington was present and Ney concluded that it was only a matter of time before he faced Wellington's entire army.[10] Ney immediately hurled Jérôme's division into the fray in another impetuous attempt to break through.

Pierre Bauduin led an assault on the Bossu wood, which was guarded by Prince Bernhard's Nassauers. Bauduin had first fought with Napoleon at Toulon in 1793, then in his Italian campaigns and all those of the *Grande Armée* except 1805 when he was with Admiral Villeneuve's fleet. It was a very brave veteran who led the way into the wood. A Nassau officer harangued the Frenchmen until a rifleman shot him and carabiniers of the 1st Light Infantry stormed the sunken lane that ran along the edge, a position their leaders had taken for entrenchments. During a fierce firefight among the trees a ball hit Prince Jérôme's sword hilt and bruised his hip, but the French drove the Nassauers out of the wood and an attempt to retake it with the second Nassau battalion, supported by Brunswick Jägers, failed.[11]

Having secured his left flank by clearing most of the Bois de Bossu, Ney prepared to attack just to the east of the wood. First he pounded the Brunswickers with the 12-pounders of the corps reserve, while French skirmishers picked them off from concealed positions in the corn. The young Brunswickers endured this patiently to begin with, but it was an ordeal. A hussar thought theirs 'the worst possible task I can think of, because you stand with your sword in your hand without being able to defend yourself against the missiles and shells, let alone parry them. The Duke smoked happily on his pipe and rode up and down in front of our corps.' Brunswick was doing his level best to set a calm example but the French heavy artillery was murdering his men. A shot took off the leg of the hussars' commander, Major von Cramm, and he bled to death.[12] After an hour's punishment the Duke sent the hussars back to the eastern side of the Brussels road.

To the west of the Bois de Bossu the Nassauers gave ground slowly, but Saxe-Weimar became increasingly worried, having no fresh orders and no idea whether he had any support. An officer sent to obtain guidance had failed to return so, after a nervous wait, the young Prince decided to pull out to the west and ordered a retreat to the village of Houtain-le-Val.[13] The first battalion of the 2nd Nassau were pursued from the wood by French light infantry and retreated hurriedly across the fields towards the village. Private Johann Peter Leonhard was close to panic – 'my comrades fell to the left and right from the enemy balls. The screams and moans of the wounded penetrated to the core and set my teeth on edge' – but when they crossed the crest of a ridge the Nivelles road came into view. 'On the other side of the village on the road from Nivelles, to our relief we could see the fields on the left and right of the road were red with the English. The soldiers cried, "Praise be to God! Our saviours are coming to becalm the storm!"'[14]

Alten's division had arrived from Nivelles. Sir Colin Halkett's British brigade halted behind the wood, while Count Friedrich von Kielmansegge's Hanoverian regulars continued eastward along the Namur road. The men were already very tired, 'having marched about twenty-seven miles, exposed to the burning sun'.[15] Halkett conferred with Sir Thomas Picton and was ordered to go into the Bois de Bossu and, if possible, fall on the French left wing, but then an aide announced that Sir Denis Pack's British brigade needed support, having expended almost all of its ammunition. The French cavalry that was roving at will over the battlefield kept intercepting the ammunition wagons that were sent forward. Meanwhile, the twelve guns attached to Alten's division trundled into position on either side of the Brussels road.

Brunswick begged Wellington for artillery – his own had not yet arrived – and when Captain Lloyd's battery arrived ahead of Alten's troops four guns attempted to silence the French 12-pounders near Gémioncourt, but the French fire seemed to redouble. 'Before we unlimbered some three or four horses of each gun and wagon were killed, some wheels disabled, and literally some of our gunners were cut in two, for we were not more than four to five hundred yards from the enemy's batteries.'[16] Two of Lloyd's 9-pounders were dismounted and had to be left where they were when the battery pulled back to make repairs, one howitzer joining Rettberg's guns further east.[17]

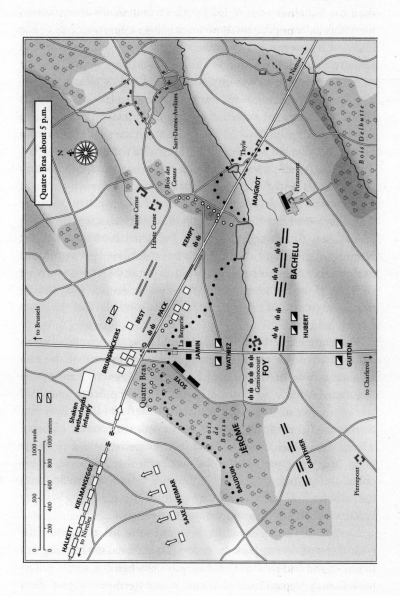

Quatre Bras about 5 p.m.

to Namur

Bois Delhutte

Thyle

MAIGROT

Piraumont

Sart-Dames-Avelines

Bois des Censes

N

Basse Cense

Hutte Cense

KEMPT

BACHELU

to Brussels

BEST

PACK

HUBERT

BRUNSWICKERS

La Bergerie

JAMIN

WATHIEZ

GUITON

Quatre Bras

SOYE

Gemioncourt

FOY

to Charleroi

Bois de Bossu

Shaken
Netherlands
infantry

JÉRÔME

1000 yards

1000 metres

800

BAUDUIN

600

KIELMANSEGGE

SAXE-WEIMAR

GAUTHIER

400

Pierrepont

200

500

HALKETT

0

0

to Nivelles

After an intense bombardment, the 1800 men of what had recently been the King's Regiment, led by Major Jean-Louis Baux, known inevitably as 'le beau', bore down on the shaken Brunswickers.[18] The Duke of Brunswick led his lancers in a charge against the French infantry, but there were too few of them and they were driven off easily. The Brunswick infantry commenced a slow retreat, but the elite French infantry inflicted heavy casualties, and seeing cuirassiers advancing behind the French, the young Brunswickers panicked and began to run in disorder. As the Duke strove to steady his veteran Guard battalion, he was shot off his horse close to the alehouse, Les Trois Bras. A ball passed through his bridle hand and into his liver and he was dead when he reached the surgeon. The French 4th Light Infantry were able to capture La Bergerie, which gave them a stronghold a mere two hundred yards from the crossroads itself.

Carl von Alten's eight battalions had arrived just in time. Just when his right wing had seemed to be crumbling, Wellington had fresh troops and fresh hope. The sight of the British troops arriving encouraged the Brunswickers and they rallied. Despite heavy casualties and the death of the Duke himself, the solid block of the Black Legion held firm.[19]

Wellington ordered the Gordon Highlanders to drive the French light infantry out of La Bergerie, with the support of the two Brunswick line battalions that had been in reserve. Led by the Adjutant-General, Sir Edward Barnes, the kilted Scots scrambled from the cover of their ditch and stormed forward into heavy fire, their grenadier company leading the way up the cobbled highway. Their much-loved leader, Colonel John Cameron, was shot in the groin from an upper window and lost control of his horse, which bolted and then stopped suddenly, throwing Cameron head first onto the cobbles.[20] Cameron was carried from the field by his foster brother but died in a cart on the way to Brussels.

Despite very heavy casualties, his men succeeded in storming the enclosures and driving back the enemy. They cleared the building, but found on the far side that they had only been fighting a strong skirmish line. A formed body of enemy infantry was waiting for them beyond the garden hedge. The Gordons charged and were driven back again – in disorder, according to the adjutant of the Brunswick 2nd Line – whereupon they ran to the shelter of the nearby trees of the Bois de Bossu.[21] Up to the point that they left their ditch they had suffered relatively few casualties, but during the attack on La Bergerie they lost 23 out of 35 officers and roughly half their strength, ending the day with 39 killed and 245 wounded out of a paper total of 699 (far fewer were in the field fighting because many were behind the lines as servants to officers or baggage guards). The many wounded, like Ensign Angus Macdonald, shot through the thigh while carrying a colour, were treated in a makeshift hospital inside the farm at Quatre Bras and evacuated next morning to Brussels and Antwerp, from where Macdonald wrote to his father to tell him of his sorrow 'that the greatest part of the regiment are killed and wounded'.[22]

Donald Finlayson, assistant surgeon to the 33rd, had been sent on hospital business to Nivelles, but had returned and was now search-ing the battlefield for his regiment. When Colonel Cameron was shot a hundred yards away from him, he became acutely aware of the danger he was in. A random shot took away his spur, and then he spotted Lieutenant Arthur Gore, who despite being on the sick list had followed him from Nivelles. Gore was excited to be in a battle and 'said he "would not have missed this for anything"'.[23] Together they turned to the west and found their battalion behind the wood.

Napoleon's trusted aide Charles de Flahaut, who remained with Ney during the day, was subsequently full of praise for Ney's great courage and 'contempt for death' but critical of his direction of the battle. 'Our forces were thrown in piece-meal as they arrived upon the scene' in 'a series of spasmodic attacks delivered without any semblance of a plan'.[24] While this was true, piecemeal reinforcement and improvisation was the nature of the day's fighting: it could also be said of Wellington that he threw his men in as and when they arrived. Circumstances at Quatre Bras changed so frequently that a consistent plan was difficult and crushing numerical advantage was what was needed for success.

Believing he could produce that crushing superiority, Ney was again poised to deliver the death blow. Although Alten's reinforcement took

Wellington's theoretical total strength to 28,000 men and 42 guns, facing Ney's 21,000 and 56 guns, Ney assumed he had d'Erlon's entire corps waiting in reserve, hidden safely behind the Bois Delhutte, together with most of Kellermann's cavalry.

But when he summoned d'Erlon to make the big attack that would crush resistance in front of him, his messenger returned with the news that d'Erlon had marched off towards Ligny. The 20,000 men on whom Ney had counted to bring him crushing victory were no longer there. Ney was stunned, and furious. Ordering him to take the captured British staff officer along as proof, he sent Colonel Forbin-Janson to find the Emperor. Forbin-Janson was to tell Napoleon that Ney was fighting Wellington's entire army, and that without d'Erlon's men he would be crushed.[25]

29

Saint-Amand

Saint-Amand, 3.15–5.30 p.m.

On the eastern battlefield, fighting raged at Saint-Amand as well as at Ligny, and in this straggling cluster of hamlets there was more ebb and flow. In the first attack the French had almost broken through, but a counter-attack had driven them from all but the churchyard of Saint-Amand proper.

To reinforce General Lefol, who was holding out in the churchyard, Dominique Vandamme now sent forward the eight battalions of General Berthezène's fresh division. Two regiments, the 12th and 86th, stormed Saint-Amand, while the 56th opposed the Prussians who were advancing from Saint-Amand-la-Haye. The French regiments drove back the musketeers of the Prussian 12th and 24th Regiments and retook the village. Steinmetz threw in his Westphalian Landwehr, but they fled after losing their leaders. The Prussians regrouped behind the gun line on the slope above the village and Steinmetz launched a second attack, but it got no further than the church. He had already lost some 2300 men in the fighting, more than a quarter of his total strength, and the 24th remained exposed to heavy fire from the French artillery; their commander, Major von Laurens, was blown into the air with his horse by the explosion of a shell and badly bruised.[1]

French light infantry now pressed forward from Saint-Amand

towards the castle at the south of Saint-Amand-la-Haye. They drove
back the first line of Prussian defenders and captured their target – a
farm with a medieval tower and chapel – but a second line halted
them there. Meanwhile, Jean-Baptiste Girard's division was advancing in a pincer movement from the west with Tiburce Sébastiani's
11th Light infantry in the lead. They forced the Prussian right wing
back as far as the seventeenth-century Château de l'Escaille on the
Brye side of La Haye, before a counter-attack drove them back again
to the Château de la Haye, and eventually out of the village. Blücher
reacted to the setback at Saint-Amand just as Napoleon hoped he
would, by sending in fresh troops, ordering Otto von Pirch's brigade
to support General Steinmetz. Not all the troops were fighting, but
13,000 Frenchmen were now tying down 17,000 Prussians.

Blücher still hoped that about this time the Duke of Wellington
would march in from the west, but his next move was in accordance
with the original Prussian plan to use troops from Georg von Pirch's
II Corps to make a decisive flank attack on the western wing. This
would be Blücher's masterstroke: the idea was that while Otto von
Pirch pinned down Girard's division from the front, the Prussian
aristocrat Ernst von Tippelskirch would strike it from the side with
7000 fresh men and destroy it, thus turning the French army's left
flank.

It was Lieutenant Ludwig Nagel's turn to join the action. Over the
previous hour Tippelskirch's brigade had made a gruelling march,
first along the Roman road, then pushing through thick corn, from
their position in reserve north of Brye to Wagnelée on the army's
extreme right flank. They were very tired, Nagel's 25th infantry regiment having marched all day and all night to reach the battlefield.
About half their 2400 men came from the well-motivated and experienced Lützow Freikorps of black-garbed volunteers, but the other
half were blue-clad conscripts freshly drafted from the Rhineland and
barely integrated into the unit, 330 having arrived from Cleves three
days ago. Nevertheless, they were excited and enthusiastic: 'Double
time soon became a run,' recalled Nagel, 'which at the order of the
brigade commander, Major General von Tippelskirchen, grew faster
minute by minute.'[2]

Otto von Pirch advanced on Saint-Amand-la-Haye with his 28th Berg Regiment and Westphalian Landwehr in front and the dependable 6th West Prussians in the second line. Their assault was determined enough but the 28th could not conquer the Château de la Haye and lost their commander. The 6th Regiment stormed in after them but also failed to take the fortified farm. They did hit the enemy commander: General Girard was hit by several shots, one through his lung, while his horse was hit in the head and threw him to the ground. Shortly afterwards his successor was hit in the thigh and had to leave the field. Nevertheless, the French held off the Prussian assault, even if it seemed to occupy all their attention.

Meanwhile, Tippelskirch's brigade was jogging through and round the village of Wagnelée, part of which was on fire. They occupied the village without firing a shot and pushed ahead towards the higher ground beyond. However, they had become disordered by the broken terrain in the approach to the village, and their inexperienced troops became further confused by the ambitious wheeling manoeuvre required of them in order to pass it. The veteran fusilier battalions of the 25th and the 1st Pomeranians had been ahead as skirmishers and pathfinders but they ended up on the right. They drove away a few French skirmishers and captured Le Hameau, a farm complex west of La Haye, then left their sharpshooters to hold it while they pressed forward. But the fusiliers, who should have led the way, had been overtaken by two disordered battalions of Westphalian Landwehr who had cut the corner and found themselves in the lead, while the musketeer battalions of the 25th followed, all pushing blindly through head-high rye without skirmishers ahead to shield them. They could hear fighting to their left, but they could see practically nothing, although they were under fire from French artillery on distant heights.

In Saint-Amand-la-Haye Prince Blücher personally led Otto von Pirch's men into another assault, shouting, 'Children, keep up the struggle! Never let the "Great Nation" lord it over you again! Forward! Forward, in God's name!'[3] Enthused by their commander in chief, the second battalion of the 28th Berg retook the castle farm; their comrades fought fiercely for every house and finally drove Girard's severely depleted division out of the village.

At this point Tippelskirch's whole brigade ran into a French trap. Hidden in the tall corn, several French battalions were waiting in ambush with muskets levelled. A battalion of Westphalian conscripts from Paderborn, wheeling to correct their alignment, turned straight into a murderous volley of canister and musketry and carried away the other battalion in their flight. The first the two musketeer battalions of the 25th saw of the French was the flashes when they fired. Shaken Prussians deployed into line, only to find that their columns had been too close and one battalion masked the other. As they attempted to manoeuvre, fleeing Westphalians burst through their ranks and, Ludwig Nagel recalled, 'at this terrible moment an enemy battalion came from the left at full charge and hurled itself upon us and swept everything before it in the wildest flight.' They fled towards Wagnelée. 'Now I no longer wished to live and thought of nothing but death which roared behind us like a storm,' wrote Nagel in his 'Tagebuch' with a passion characteristic of the time. 'We stabbed and hacked at the fleeing troops. "Blacks form on me! Retrieve our honour or die! Volunteers to us!" That way most officers gathered a little group of men, nearly all Blacks; the Ersatzlings mostly ran for it.'

It was an officer's duty to attempt to halt the flight of his men and reassemble them as soon as they were out of immediate danger, sometimes seizing a flag as a rallying point. It was a difficult task to turn fleeing men round: the officers were sick at heart at having failed and the same feeling might make the men desperate and violent. Military rules allowed officers to strike at troops who were running away, and Nagel said he did so. The attempt to rally men was a great test not only of an officer's courage but of the moral authority he had gained during training, so it is hardly surprising that the men Nagel rallied were the volunteers he had campaigned with for years and that the Rhineland 'Ersatzlings' who had joined a few days ago fled.[4] Nagel and his knots of black-clad volunteers then fought alongside the Pomeranians.

The fusilier battalions were also surprised by the enemy at short range and the three senior officers of the 25th were shot. A lieutenant led a bayonet charge which drove off one French battalion, but others forced the fusiliers to retreat to Le Hameau and then drove them back from there to rally on the Pomeranian reserve.

The outflanking move that Blücher had hoped would bring victory had been crushed ignominiously and he was furious. He summoned 1000 lancers and hussars from the left wing to cover his extreme right flank and to send patrols westwards to look out for troops coming from that direction, possibly still hoping for intervention from Wellington. Around 5.15, what was left of Steinmetz's brigade pulled out of Saint-Amand, having exhausted their ammunition.[5] Blücher threw the remaining battalions of Karl August von Krafft's brigade – the 26th Regiment and the fusiliers of the Colberg Regiment – into the battle to support Otto von Pirch's men. The two fusilier battalions stormed into Saint-Amand-la-Haye and moved south down the main street, but they met with fierce French resistance and were eventually forced out. By this stage the artillery barrage had lost much of its intensity, for many batteries were running out of ammunition. Prussian horse batteries that were still mobile retired to the artillery park behind Sombreffe for more, but some batteries on the Prussian side were more or less knocked out.

The day remained oppressively hot, and over the battlefield thunder clouds were gathering. Napoleon had failed to make a crushing breakthrough, but – thanks to the French troops' training and experience – he was still achieving his objective of sucking in and pinning down superior forces. Around Saint-Amand 27,000 Frenchmen now held 41,000 Prussians, and although the timing of reinforcements may sometimes have altered the balance there were generally about a third more Prussians than Frenchmen in Ligny at any one time. On the French right wing, meanwhile, about 10,000 men opposed about 21,000 Prussians.

At some point during the afternoon, moreover, Blücher learned that Wellington was unlikely to help him; according to Baron Müffling 'the first intelligence I sent the Prince, after our return from the windmill, could leave no doubt of the Duke's inability to come to his assistance'.[6] Müffling had sent a series of verbal and written messages to Blücher warning that Wellington was unable to lead troops to help them, but that he was successfully containing a French corps so that there should be no threat to Blücher's right wing.[7] Then one of Blücher's patrols from the 8th Uhlans captured a French staff officer who told them that the 20,000 men of d'Erlon's French corps were approaching to attack their flank.[8] Wellington, it seemed, had failed him totally. Soon after, Jacquinot's brigade of 1500 French light cavalry appeared to the south of the distant Bois Delhutte, with Prussian cavalry retreating slowly in front of them. Blücher sent his aide-de-camp Count Nostitz to identify the approaching column, worried that Wellington had been defeated.

By Napoleon's calculations Marshal Ney himself, or a force sent by him, should appear above Brye at about 6 p.m., coming along the *chaussée* to the north of the Bois Delhutte. Earlier, at about four, he had ordered General Hulot's division, which had been left to guard the main road, to mount a decoy offensive in a new direction, between Sombreffe and Tongrenelle, to pin down the Prussians on that flank and clear the way for a breakthrough by the Guard near Ligny. Hulot's light infantry led, with three line regiments following, and Prussian outposts fell back before them until a battalion of the 8th Regiment was fighting to prevent them reaching the churchyard and presbytery of Sombreffe on the *chaussée* at the southern fringe of the village.

Kurmark Landwehr was defending the main road from Fleurus at the bridge over the river, with a 12-pounder battery on the Fleurus road halfway up the slope to Point du Jour. French skirmishers stormed Tongrenelle, then lost it to a counter-attack. The fighting sucked in yet more Prussian troops from III Corps, including most of the Kurmark Landwehr, who took heavy casualties from the efficient French artillery. The threat to Sombreffe even drew in Prussian reserves from behind Ligny. Steinmetz and Henckel, whose battered battalions had reloaded, rested and reorganised, were summoned to deal with the emergency and had marched over before it was realised that the threat was minor and their help was not needed. Eventually, a counter-attack by two Kurmark fusilier battalions drove the French back over the Ligne in front of Sombreffe. Each side continued to skirmish, the Prussians seeking to hold a line on the Ligne stream but unwilling to advance far into French territory in case they were ambushed. But Hulot had done his job splendidly by drawing reserves northward and away from Ligny.

Napoleon had sent the 3rd and 4th Grenadiers of the Guard with the brigade's battery of guns forward to replace Hulot as a reserve for Gérard's corps, and in readiness to spearhead an attack. Now, with half an hour to go to Ney's expected time of arrival, it was time for the Emperor to commit his reserve. He sent Guillaume Duhesme with the Young Guard division to reinforce the left wing, supported by Claude Michel's Chasseur division of the Old Guard, Jacques Subervie's division of light cavalry from the right wing and a Guard light artillery battery. In the centre he formed the rest of the Old Guard in two columns with the 2nd and 1st Grenadiers on the right and the 1st Chasseurs, sappers and seamen on the left, and led them forward in person. Behind them rode the Horse Grenadiers and the Empress's Dragoons on the right and Jacques Delort's division of cuirassiers on the left. They marched forward until they were just within range of the Prussian guns, when suddenly the columns halted.[9]

Just at the very moment Napoleon was going to unleash his Guard, a mass of troops appeared on the horizon to the south of the Bois Delhutte, instilling panic among Vandamme's weary infantry. When an officer sent to identify them returned with the alarming but totally inaccurate news that the column consisted of enemy troops Vandamme reported to Napoleon that hostile troops had appeared behind their left flank and that he would have to pull back.[10] Vandamme should have been warned by the staff to expect French troops to appear on his flank but it seems that the staff had failed to anticipate this issue. Napoleon had been expecting Ney to arrive from a different direction, the other side of the Bois Delhutte, and although this new body might have been the corps that he had demanded, it might also have been a hostile body that had broken through Ney's position at Frasnes. He may already have known that Ney considered himself outnumbered. Could it be that Ney had been defeated by the English? Could Vandamme be right? The recent capture of the French staff officer by the patrol of the Prussian 8th

Uhlans which alerted Blücher to the danger on his flank had probably contributed to French confusion, since the prisoner had presumably been on his way to Napoleon with news of d'Erlon's impending arrival.

The Emperor needed to find out what was really happening on the left wing. He sent General de la Bédoyère to direct affairs on the spot and help rally Vandamme's shaken men while another officer rode off to identify the distant force. For the moment the attack by the Old Guard on Ligny was halted and postponed.

30

D'Erlon's March

Between Frasnes and Brye, 4–9 p.m.

It is arguable that the campaign of 1815 turned on the actions of d'Erlon's corps on the afternoon of 16 June.

The orders with which he was issued that morning had not envisaged serious fighting and Napoleon's staff spent the day reacting to unexpected contingencies. Jean-Baptiste Drouet, comte d'Erlon, was forty-nine years old – a loyal Bonapartist with good revolutionary credentials. He had served as a corporal in the army of the *ancien régime*, but was catapulted to captain by election in 1793. He commanded a division that played a key role at Austerlitz, then commanded a corps in Spain and had defeated General Hill at Extremadura. Imprisoned by Soult for leading a premature Bonapartist rising of the soldiers in the north of France, he had recently alerted the government to suspected treachery within munitions factories that were issuing bad cartridges. He might have been cautious but he was not disloyal.

After strenuous early morning marches for the regiments that had camped up to thirteen miles behind the front, his corps was united in and behind the town of Gosselies by midday. Their orders were to march four miles north to Ney's headquarters at Frasnes, but to detach a division each of infantry and cavalry to Marbais, halfway between Sombreffe and Quatre Bras.[1] Kellermann meanwhile positioned his divisions in accordance with Ney's instructions of the late morning, with one at Frasnes, immediately behind the battlefield, and another near Liberchies, further back near the junction of the *chaussée* with the Roman road. These detached divisions were to be available for Napoleon's use against the Prussians, but with the possible exception of Kellermann's cavalry, they were not mentioned in later orders and one might suppose the staff had forgotten about their existence.

After cooking and eating, d'Erlon's column began to move forward from Gosselies around two o'clock, and Pierre Durutte's division, at the head of it, reached the Cabaret de l'Empereur, an alehouse south of Frasnes, before four. General d'Erlon later wrote that he himself had ridden ahead of the column to Frasnes, accompanied by his staff, where he found the generals commanding the Guard light cavalry. While they were briefing him on what had been happening on the battlefield towards Quatre Bras, a messenger arrived with the pencil note from the Emperor that was sent just after the second order to Ney.[2] D'Erlon later claimed that the note that he saw was addressed to Ney. General Dessales, who as commander of d'Erlon's artillery belonged to his staff and generally accompanied him, claimed to have seen the letter. In Dessales' recollection, the letter that he saw was addressed to d'Erlon but written in very similar terms to Soult's second order to Ney, ordering him to march at once to attack the flank of the Prussians at Saint-Amand and Brye because Napoleon had caught Blücher with his trousers down, and this letter was also on its way to Ney at that time.[3] He remembered it as saying:

Monsieur Count d'Erlon, the enemy is running blindly into the trap I have set for him. Head immediately with your four divisions of infantry, your division of cavalry, all your artillery, and the two divisions of heavy cavalry which I place at your disposal and take yourself with these forces to the height of Ligny and fall on Saint-Amand (or vice-versa, I can't remember which). Monsieur Count d'Erlon, you will save France and cover yourself with glory. Napoleon.[4]

It does not really matter whether there were two messages – one to d'Erlon, one to Ney – or, as some have argued, only one. D'Erlon wrote in 1829 that the staff officer who was carrying the message had already taken it upon himself to show the Emperor's order to General Durutte, leading d'Erlon's column, and redirect him towards Brye in accordance with the Emperor's wishes. The staff officer told d'Erlon where he would find his men and d'Erlon rode off to join them before sending back his chief of staff, General Victor-Joseph Delcambre, to tell Ney what he had done.

The key point is that, somehow or other, having delivered the message to d'Erlon, the messenger failed to deliver it to Ney.[5] If there were two messages and two messengers it might have been that the messenger with Ney's order got lost or failed to find him, while the general officer aide with the authority to redirect d'Erlon's divisions did so, told d'Erlon and then went back to the Roman road junction to find the heavy cavalry, since Dessales recalled that the heavy cavalry was also summoned by the Emperor and one of Kellermann's divisions certainly disappeared from the scene. By then, Kellermann himself, with at least a brigade, had already advanced to join Ney; his arrival was the cue for Ney to release the light cavalry of the Guard to go to Marbais in accordance with the instructions delivered by General Flahaut in the morning.[6] Ney was said to have led the attack on the Bois de Bossu in person, so he may well have proved difficult to find among the trees.

Thus, when chief of staff Delcambre arrived in order to explain d'Erlon's actions to Ney, the Marshal had not yet received any instruction from the Emperor regarding them and had already sent for d'Erlon to reinforce him in his battle, only to find that, inexplicably, his troops had marched away. Predictably, the hot-headed Ney had been furious to discover that his reserves had disappeared, apparently on their own initiative, at the moment that he needed them to deliver the killer punch. The blow had coincided with the revelation from British prisoners captured during the fighting that they belonged to a force 15,000 strong led by Wellington himself.[7] Now fearing he might be overwhelmed by Wellington's whole army, Ney sent Delcambre back with an angry, unequivocal order to d'Erlon to return immediately.

D'Erlon's corps had by now marched off to help the Emperor, at least two divisions taking the road that left the *chaussée* just south of the Cabaret de l'Empereur and skirted the Bois Delhutte, before crossing the Roman road on its way to Brye. It would have been logical for the rear divisions to take the Roman road itself. The vanguard had marched at least two miles when Delcambre returned with Ney's imperative order to turn back. This plunged d'Erlon into doubt, for he had to assume that Ney knew about the instructions that he had received from the Emperor. If this was the case and Ney was overriding the Emperor's order, then Ney presumably had a good reason for it, such as a new order that d'Erlon knew nothing about. Direct contradiction from his immediate superior made him hesitate and agonise over his proper course.

Delcambre must have returned to d'Erlon about half past five when the head of the column, less than three miles from Brye, became visible, causing consternation to Vandamme's corps which was struggling to hold Saint-Amand. There was then a period of debate and possibly even of marching first one way and then the other as messengers with conflicting instructions arrived from Fleurus and from Frasnes. General Durutte recalled:

While it was on the march, several commands from Marshal Ney arrived in a hurry to stop the I Corps and to make it march to Quatre Bras. The officers bringing these orders said that Marshal Ney had found superior forces at Quatre Bras and that he had been pushed back. This second order greatly troubled Count d'Erlon, for at the same time he received new entreaties from the right wing to march on Brye. Nevertheless, he made up his mind to return towards Marshal Ney. But, as he and General Durutte observed that an enemy column could emerge in the plain which lies between Brye and Delhutte Wood, which would have completely cut the Emperor's wing of the army off from that commanded by Marshal Ney, he decided to leave General Durutte in this plain. Under his orders, he left him, besides his own division, three regiments of cavalry commanded by General Jacquinot.

General Durutte, when leaving General d'Erlon, asked him clearly if he should march on Brye. D'Erlon replied to him that, in the circumstances, he could give him no orders and that he relied on his experience and caution.[8]

Ney had led d'Erlon to believe that his position was desperate, while d'Erlon later said that he obeyed Ney because he had never received a direct order from the Emperor and had only ever seen an order addressed to Ney.[9] Whether or not this was true, none of the 'entreaties from the right wing' carried sufficient authority to outweigh Ney's, and whatever emissaries Napoleon sent gave way in the face of Ney's desperation. Napoleon's aide General Drouot reported that between four and five o'clock the Emperor's staff had learned that Ney was facing a considerable English force and needed support, so it is possible that Napoleon conceded that Ney's need might be greater than his.[10]

During the entire period d'Erlon's corps behaved cautiously, and spent much time in square; not only was the news reaching them from Quatre Bras disquieting, but they could also hear fighting in the Bois Delhutte, which implied that Ney was not exaggerating his difficulties.

When General Carl von Alten's division had arrived at Quatre Bras Wellington had ordered him to take Piraumont and clear a path to open communication with Blücher. He had promised Blücher's latest messenger that he would make an attack with a view to helping the Prussians. Carl von Rettberg's battery was moved eastward to face what he took to be eighteen French guns, of which only five were in the open, the rest concealed or with just their barrels showing. Expecting trouble, he placed his own guns as far apart as possible with the minimum number of men serving them and sent the ammunition caissons into cover further back. But he was soon joined by the sixteen Brunswick guns, which for the first time in this sector gave Wellington's artillery a numerical advantage.[11] As the Hanoverian column approached along the cobbled road, the French abandoned the hamlet of Thyle and withdrew to the south of the cobbled road to Namur. The Lüneburg battalion used Thyle as a base for an assault on Piraumont, which the French also abandoned without much of a struggle.

The British riflemen then advanced with the Brunswick light battalion into the eastern part of the Bois Delhutte, in an attempt to clear it. John Kincaid was reappraising the Brunswickers, who this time 'joined us cordially and behaved exceedingly well. They had a very gallant young fellow at their head; and their conduct in the earlier part of the day can therefore only be ascribed to its being their first appearance on such a stage.'[12] All of these men except the black Brunswickers wore green uniforms which helped them distinguish friend from foe, since their French opponents were wearing blue. In the wood the fighting was fierce. Ned Costello was in the act of taking aim at a French skirmisher when his trigger finger was shot off and a second ball went through his mess tin. His lieutenant was hit in the leg and several riflemen were killed close to him. Costello made his way back to the rear for medical attention, and at Thyle he found the Belgian girl he had met earlier still looking after her house as her father had instructed her, though it now had six large holes through it. Major von Dachenhausen led the Lüneburg battalion to the 95th's support and the three battalions drove the French back across and right out of the Bois Delhutte. Among the trees, Britons, Brunswickers and Hanoverians intermingled and Carl Jacobi of the Lüneburg battalion shared his cognac with a Brunswick officer.[13]

However, the French then counter-attacked in force and drove them all pell-mell from the wood until they rallied on their reserve battalions in the fields outside Piraumont. With the Grubenhagen and York battalions in support, they attacked the woods again, but everybody was tired and progress was slow; casualties mounted until finally it grew dark and they could no longer see to shoot.

It is plausible that some of d'Erlon's troops intervened in this struggle, causing the reversal of fortune that drove the allies back out of the wood. Indeed, according to Brigadier Nicolas Schmitz, the artillery of his division took part in the action, and it is difficult to imagine how they did so if it was not in connection with the counter-attack on the Bois Delhutte.[14] Whether they were participants or not, fighting in the wood behind their flank would certainly have unnerved d'Erlon's troops and made them reluctant to advance towards Brye, and in this respect Wellington's attack helped to save the Prussians from annihilation.

When d'Erlon decided to turn back towards Quatre Bras he left Durutte's division of infantry and Jacquinot's cavalry behind, in accordance with Soult's original instructions to send a division of infantry and one of cavalry to cut the road and to be available to help the Emperor. D'Erlon warned Durutte to keep an eye on the Bois Delhutte, because if Ney retired he would have enemy troops behind his flank, but Durutte remained uncertain whether he should be cutting the road at Marbais or attacking Brye. Jacquinot's cavalry advanced to within cannon shot of the Namur–Nivelles road and exchanged artillery fire with the Prussians, while Durutte advanced to a position above Wagnelée. There an animated discussion took place between Durutte and Brigadier Jean-Louis Brue as to whether or not to attack, with Durutte reluctant because of the threat from the wood. Ultimately, the Prussians in front of Jacquinot fell back and Durutte's regiments captured Wagnelée around sunset, but it was far too late to be of any use in preventing a Prussian retreat.[15]

After sending back Delcambre with a flea in his ear, Ney should have received the duplicate 3.15 order, and should then have realised that he had done the wrong thing. But he had either not seen the note, not read it, or was too stupid, hot-headed or blinkered to grasp Napoleon's plan and the importance of instantly changing his mind. If he did learn what Napoleon's intention had been, he stuck to his guns and refused to change course. It was a selfish attitude, if understandable in the heat of a battle that he had thought he was on the verge of winning and now feared, given Wellington's presence with an ever-increasing force, that he might lose with dire consequences. Soult's aide Guillaume de Baudus claimed to have found Ney in the heat of the action, furious that his own plans had been ruined. Ney insisted that Baudus' order was the first official instruction that he had received. Baudus claimed that he argued forcibly that Napoleon's order should be carried out and thought he had prevailed until he left the battlefield with Ney at nightfall and found d'Erlon's men back in reserve at Frasnes.[16]

It is not surprising that over the distances across which communications had to travel, time was lost and understanding broke down. This was a normal condition of warfare: 'The very essence of the art of war in the age of Napoleon, and perhaps in any age, consists in the combination of careful planning with rapid improvisation, in a fog of partial, late and inaccurate information.'[17]

Faced with unexpected contingencies, the inexperienced staff failed to contact and mobilise the full resources of the French army. In addition to d'Erlon's corps one of Kellermann's divisions of heavy cavalry, the light cavalry of the Guard and the 1st Hussars took little part in the battles, and orders were issued too late to Georges Mouton, comte de Lobau for his corps to participate at Ligny. Attention focused on d'Erlon because his powerful force spent the afternoon ludicrously poised between one battlefield and the other, uncertain which way to turn, while messengers gave him conflicting orders. The subsequent allocation of blame, self-serving lies and mis-remembered anecdotes have obscured the circumstances to the extent that they are impossible to reconstruct with complete confidence.

The combination of circumstances had indeed been unfortunate. It was not the only time in Napoleon's career that a brilliant piece of improvisation failed to work out, but on this occasion it was to have disastrous consequences.

31

The Guard Enters the Battle

Saint-Amand and Ligny, 5.30–7 p.m.

On the eastern battlefield Dominique Vandamme's men were still fighting for Saint-Amand. Alarmed, on seeing d'Erlon's corps approach at 5.30, that they had been outflanked by hostile forces, and under severe Prussian pressure, Vandamme's men began to retreat in panic. In the eastern sector of Saint-Amand the 64th Regiment had just lost its colonel and General Lefol had to turn his guns towards these shaken troops to stop them running, while General Corsin, whose men still held the church, rallied other troops that had fled. Meanwhile, what was left of Girard's division, now commanded by one of the colonels, gradually began to fall back on Le Hameau.

Blücher had also seen the French troops on the western flank wavering and falling back and he took it to be the moment for an all-out assault, hoping that he might yet achieve the breakthrough on this flank that he had originally planned. The experienced and determined Karl August von Krafft ordered the fresh battalions of his brigade to make another attack on Saint-Amand. There was fierce fighting on the central road as the Prussians drove south-eastward towards the church, but there the Prussian commander was killed and the fighting reached deadlock.

Further west the Prussians had more success. With flanks covered

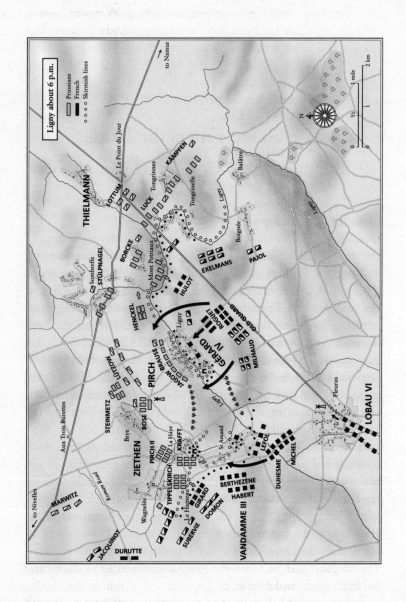

Ligny about 6 p.m.

Prussians ☐
French ☐
Skirmish lines ○ ○ ○ ○

to Namur

N

2 km
1 mile

THIELMANN

LOTTUM   Le Point du Jour
LUCK   Tongrinnes   KÄMPFEN
Tongrinelle   Balâtre

BORCKE   Mont Potriaux   Boignée
Sombreffe   EXELMANS   PAJOL
STÜLPNAGEL

HENCKEL   HULOT   MILHAUD   OLD GUARD
Ligny   ROGUET
GÉRARD
IV

LÜTZOW   PIRCH
BRAUSE
STEINMETZ   JAGOW
BOSÉ
ZIETHEN   PIRCH II   La Haye
KRAFFT   St Amand   LEFOL   LOBAU VI
Brye   DUHESME   Fleurus
MICHEL

Aux Trois-Burettes

to Nivelles   MARWITZ   Roman Road   Wagnelée   TIPPELSKIRCH
Le Hameau   BERTHEZÈNE
GIRARD   HABERT
SUBERVIE   DOMON
JACQUINOT   VANDAMME III
DURUTTE

by hussars and lancers, Tippelskirch launched a second attack with his Pomeranians and Freikorps volunteers from Wagnelée against Girard's troops in La Haye and Le Hameau. Ludwig Nagel had already collapsed with exhaustion and had been revived by a Pomeranian surgeon. '"Forward!" rang out the command, "all who are men of honour!", and we went forward, because we were all driven by despair.' Nagel shook hands with an old friend, August Schmidt, who was killed minutes later by a bullet to the heart that went straight through a silk patchwork wallet his sister had given him. They fought hand to hand in Saint-Amand-la-Haye; prisoners were taken at first but 'soon they gave no quarter, their bitter losses having enraged their people', until the remnant of Girard's division finally fled. 'That was a blessed moment when we saw their backs, now in hasty flight; the village was won, but dearly bought.'

The French now held only Saint-Amand and the castle farm of La Haye. As the remnant of Girard's division retreated from Le Hameau, the 4th Line panicked until General de la Bédoyère rallied them with 'Soldiers, do you not blush to retreat before men that you have defeated so many times, who threw their weapons at your feet and begged for mercy at Austerlitz, Jena and Friedland? Advance and you will see them flee once again and acknowledge you as their conquerors!'[1] Fresh French batteries threw a hail of fire at the Prussians and the commander of their cavalry was decapitated.

Inspired by La Bédoyère, the French assault columns reformed and charged back into Le Hameau and La Haye. Veteran friends of Nagel went down. His fellow Mecklenburger, Friedrich Schnelle, another academic, was shot in the leg as he led a weary knot of men in an attempt on a French flag. Their commander was carried away unconscious; Friedrich Stargardt got a bullet in the abdomen, the republican writer Friedrich Förster was shot in the knee. 'The sight almost tore me apart'; speechless, choked with pain, Nagel hoisted his bleeding friend Schnelle onto a horse and took him back to Wagnelée, where he smashed open a burning house to get him water. The surgeon said no bone was broken so Nagel left him, feeling hopeful. They broke into another house and found some milk, emerging to see a ball decapitate a Pomeranian officer. Le Hameau was won and lost repeatedly. Blücher himself led a charge by the fusiliers of the 2nd Pomeranians which took it by storm, and they held on to it despite a fierce French counter-attack.[2]

Then the Young Guard arrived, their drummers beating the *pas de charge* and their band, like that of Lefol's 28th Regiment, playing the *Chant du Départ*, the song from 1794 that had become Napoleon's anthem in this new war to save the Revolution: 'Tremble enemies of France, Kings drunk with blood and arrogance, the sovereign people advance!' Their appearance breathed new life into the exhausted and demoralised troops on the left wing. Their commander Guillaume Duhesme, the forty-nine-year-old author of the French light infantry manual *Essai historique de l'infanterie légère*, had a reputation for ruthlessness and daring. Highly intelligent and a brilliant leader, Duhesme's outspoken republicanism had impeded his career in the past, but now he was the ideal man to inspire the troops; Napoleon thought afterwards that he should have given Duhesme a corps.[3] Girard's men joined the *voltigeurs*, pushed back Tippelskirch and recaptured Le Hameau, while the *tirailleurs* finally seized the high ground over Saint-Amand. The Pomeranians and Freikorps held out at Wagnelée and the last reserve brigade advanced to steady the situation at La Haye. Frantic Prussian cavalry charges sought to stop the French.

At Ligny, the fighting was still raging. The Prussian commander was now Georg von Pirch, acting chief of II Corps since the sacking of its general over the Saxon mutiny. Georg, the elder brother of Otto, was a weak personality whose inexperience at this level made him reliant on subordinates, of whom the dominant personality was Colonel Heinrich von Zastrow, commander of the 9th Colberg Regiment. 'Zastrow's outstanding personal bravery had earned the respect of the entire army, but he assessed the probability of success according to the yardstick of his own courage; unfortunately, others were not always quite as brave, and to adopt his recommendations without close scrutiny could lead to mistakes.'[4] Zastrow held the northern and western part of the village, the French held the area round the church and the south-east.

For half an hour the French had brought down a murderous

artillery bombardment on western Ligny. The silver-embroidered blue and yellow colour of the 7th second battalion was shot through and its staff smashed by three cannonballs.[5] Then General Gérard led in his last reserves and again drove the Prussians back. He got two guns into the churchyard and with their help was finally able to capture the Ferme d'en Bas on the far bank. An attempt to recapture it by the Prussian 7th Regiment failed, while Westphalian sharpshooters, trying to reach the churchyard, were picked off on the narrow footbridge, or shot, clubbed or bayoneted at the wall. The Prussians fell back through a labyrinth of hedges on the north side of the village. Some Frenchmen had isolated the second battalion's tattered, broken colour and were wrestling with its bearer, Ensign Schulze, when two musketeers came to his rescue and killed his assailants, recapturing the flag. The Prussians were still holding out in the medieval castle, though the French bombardment was smashing the stonework and the troops there were isolated. An assault on the village by two battalions of the Prussian 23rd Regiment from their corps reserve failed to make any headway, but a second attack by the remaining battalion supported by Elbe Landwehr fared better and the Prussians recovered the western sector.

The French responded by firing incendiary shells at the western half of Ligny, from which they could not shift the obstinate defenders. At 6.30 the barn of the castle went up in flames, creating a blaze so hot that the Prussians were forced to evacuate the medieval stronghold. Much of Ligny was soon alight: the thatched roofs caught fire easily and burned fiercely hot. Prussians crawled out of cellars and leaped from attics, dragging with them what wounded they could. Smoke from the fire combined in the sky with an ever more intense blackness – the super-vivid purple grey of summer thundercloud. The stifling heat would soon explode in an electric storm.

Around the same time Napoleon finally learned that the mysterious force on the horizon was, in fact, d'Erlon's corps, but that it was obeying orders to return to Quatre Bras. Why his staff failed to communicate with General Durutte is not clear – Durutte's own staff had deserted in the morning – but 4000 infantry continued to stand idly

by in full view, no more than a mile from the Prussian-held village of
Wagnelée.

Napoleon decided to relaunch the attack of the Guard on Ligny in
an attempt to isolate the Prussian right wing. The crack regiments of
the Old Guard, the 1st Chasseurs and Grenadiers, were to attack to
the north-east of the village with the support of Claude-Etienne
Guyot's horse grenadiers and dragoons. François Roguet's grenadier
division – the 2nd, 3rd and 4th Grenadiers – was to seize Ligny, and
Jacques Delort's division of cuirassiers was to attack between Ligny
and Saint-Amand. The head of Lobau's column was just emerging
from Fleurus to form a fresh reserve. On the ridge between Saint-
Amand and Ligny the Prussian 12-pounders traversed to point at the
Guard and the ridge disappeared in billowing smoke, but they were
firing slowly now and there were fewer guns. When the smoke
cleared, Napoleon could see that the space behind the guns was relatively empty. 'They are lost: they have no reserve remaining!' he
remarked to Gérard.[6] The Guard advanced in solemn silence, drums
still, waiting for the signal to charge. 'Tell the Grenadiers that the
first man to bring me a prisoner will be shot,' yelled General Roguet.

The Old Guard was legendary, and it was well known that it
advanced into combat only in order to win battles by striking the
decisive blow. Its very appearance, therefore, struck fear into the heart
of the troops opposing it. Hippolyte de Mauduit painted a portrait of
the 1st Grenadiers, of which he was a sergeant: their average height
was five foot ten inches and their age thirty-five; many sergeants and
corporals in fact were over forty and had seen fifteen years of campaigning. A fifth of the privates had been NCOs in the line. They
were lean and sinewy, physically very fit, tanned and in many cases
showing grey in their hair. Obesity was unknown in the Guard.
Almost universally, they wore moustaches and gold earrings and they
were heavily tattooed. The British painter Benjamin Robert Haydon
said that 'they had the look of thoroughbred, veteran, disciplined
banditti.' The veterans wore their normal combat dress: blue over-
coats and wide trousers, white crossbelts and black bearskins and
gaiters, although the newly raised regiments did not even have the
proper kit and wore shakos instead of bearskins.[7]

Napoleon himself rode at the head of the pride of his army as far as the Tombe de Ligny, the ancient burial mound, from which he watched his men jog towards the smouldering ruins. Around the village the remnants of twenty-one Prussian battalions were still slugging it out with what was left of Gérard's corps.

Forty-eight fresh 12-pounders of the Guard artillery commenced a bombardment of the Prussian reserves around the Bussy windmill. The British liaison officer, Henry Hardinge, was hit in the hand and forced to leave the field. And as the heavy guns spoke, the storm finally broke. Rumbling, crashing thunder complemented the roar of artillery and warm rain fell in bucketloads. The guns stopped and through the sudden downpour rushed François Roguet's division of grenadiers, entering the smoking and steaming village in small sections.[8]

The Prussians pulled out, leaving their skirmishers and riflemen with orders to hold on for as long as they possibly could to give the main bodies time to reorganise a defence further back. Lieber's officer, Carl von Bagensky, was shot as they retreated, but his men returned for him, carrying him away to safety. Karl August von Krafft organised the tired Prussian survivors into squares behind the village, but they fell back before the Grenadiers of the Guard and their expert artillery. Westphalian Landwehr cavalry bought time for the retreat by charging the French infantry, taking the grenadiers by surprise. They completed their squares but could not get into the chequer formation, so the cavalry rode through the gaps between squares unscathed.[9]

Napoleon's personal bodyguard and the dragoons, horse grenadiers and *gendarmerie d'élite* had followed the grenadiers round Ligny. Now they chased off the Prussian cavalry and broke one of their infantry squares.[10] To avoid being trapped and captured, the Prussian front-line units at Wagnelée and La Haye had to retreat towards Brye and Les Trois Burettes. In yet one more battle Napoleon's Imperial Guard had made the decisive breakthrough for a glorious victory.

As the villages fell into French hands, Colonel Forbin-Janson of the staff found the Emperor and told him that Ney believed he was

facing the whole of Wellington's army. Napoleon said this was
nonsense: Ney was merely fighting a British vanguard. Giving
Forbin-Janson, who was feeling faint with heatstroke and hunger,
one of his own Arab horses, the Emperor told him to ride back and
tell Ney that he must take Quatre Bras.[11]

32

Kellermann's Charge

Quatre Bras, 6.30–7.30 p.m.

Seven miles away, Ney was seething with frustrated rage, more determined than ever to win his own battle. It is difficult to know what
was going through his head. If he had received and understood
Napoleon's 3.15 order, and especially if he had listened to the expla-
nations of the Emperor's envoys, he might have grasped what was in
Napoleon's mind: that Ney could now fight on the defensive while
detaching troops to the right. But he seems to have been consumed
by fury at being robbed of his own victory, blind to the possibility that
the Emperor might have a better opportunity to exploit than he had.
'The Emperor is in his chair. He can't see what's happening here. The
English are in front of me and I am going to beat them,' he shouted
at one of Napoleon's aides.[1] Behaving like a suicidal hero of *Sturm
und Drang*, he threw himself into the thick of the conflict, inspiring
his warriors, courting death, but never pausing for cool calculation.
To judge from contemporary writing this frenzied style of conduct
and expression was fashionable among officers of the period, especially on the continent. Finding himself without infantry reserves and
with only one division of the heavy cavalry corps that were supposed
to be supporting him, he raged, 'Oh how I wish these English cannonballs would all bury themselves in my chest!'

Since Napoleon's orders allowed him to use the cuirassiers if the

Emperor hadn't taken them himself, Ney must at some point have ordered Kellermann forward, although only his first brigade was at the front, the second being some distance to the rear in reserve. Ney still hoped to win the battle through a sudden aggressive stroke: when Kellermann objected that a single brigade could make little impact on 25,000 infantry, Ney insisted that he should charge, saying that he would support him with all the remaining cavalry. 'General, the salvation of France is at stake. A supreme effort is required. Take your cavalry, throw yourself into the middle of the English. Crush them! Trample them underfoot!'

The 8th and 11th cuirassiers formed south of Gémioncourt and Kellermann led them in a charge along the main road.[2] Dressed in blue, with shining steel breastplates – it was rumoured that these were bullet-proof – and helmets, long swords and trailing black horsehair plumes, the cuirassiers were the pride of the French cavalry. Although they did not belong to the Guard they were nevertheless regarded as elite, big men on big horses, battle-winning shock troops. The British had never faced cuirassiers in Spain, but their reputation had gone before them and they were a fearsome unknown quantity.

Towards 6 p.m. Colin Halkett's British brigade was another to find itself pushing through rye 'of an extraordinary height, some of it measuring seven feet'. Thomas Morris of the 73rd recalled that it 'prevented us from seeing much of the enemy; but, though we could not see them, they were observing us', for the French had a better view from the high ground near Frasnes and the rooftops of Gémioncourt. Morris remembered a Gordon Highlander whose arm had been shot off at the shoulder by a cannonball staggering by: 'On passing us, he exclaimed, "Go on, 73rd give them pepper! I've got my Chelsea commission!" Poor fellow! I should think from the nature of his wound, he would bleed to death in half an hour.'[3] They advanced in 'open column of companies', one company behind another, each in line, a formation from which it was easy to form square.

It happened that the grenadier company of the 33rd, reaching high ground, saw cuirassiers and shouted a warning in time for their battalion to adopt their defensive formation. The cuirassiers saw this in turn and changed their aim towards the 69th South Lincolnshire, who were in a dip and did not see the cavalry coming until they were fifty yards away. The 69th were raw troops, a few from the Lincolnshire area but over a third Irish, and one of the least experienced British units with an average age of twenty-one, a quarter of them being fifteen to nineteen. They broke and ran. Within a month officers were claiming that the Prince of Orange had ordered them from square to line, but one of their captains attributed the disaster to an order from Captain Lindsay to the grenadiers to halt and fire, rather than form square.[4] The 8th cuirassiers rode down the fleeing boys, of whom few were killed but very many were injured by cuts and stabs to their heads, shoulders, backs and arms, and after a fierce fight, two cuirassiers of the 8th captured the battalion's king's colour, their Union Jack. Captain George Barlow had heard that the best thing in these circumstances was to dive for the ground and play dead, and that was what he did – it really was what the manual recommended. After being ridden over, he made his way to the square of the 42nd Regiment, where he complained that what he had been told about horses avoiding prone bodies was simply not true.[5] By then the battalion was dispersed beyond recall.[6]

It seems that the 73rd were not charged, but some of them nevertheless ran for the trees. Their colonel afterwards insisted that they never retreated into the wood, but one lieutenant admitted that being in line, 'the 73rd to give effective fire threw back its left a little, not however in perfect order, for there was not time ... Some of the men might have unavoidably entered the wood.' Sergeant Morris was perhaps with that left wing, for he recalled, 'We continuing to advance, the glittering of the tops of our bayonets, guided towards us a large body of the enemy's cuirassiers, who, coming so unexpectedly upon us, threw us in the utmost confusion. Having no time to form a square, we were compelled to retire, or rather to run, to the wood through which we had advanced.'[7] If they did run, they soon recovered, because they and the 30th afterwards continued to advance towards Gémioncourt.

The 30th Cambridgeshire were Peninsular veterans, the only battle-hardened battalion in Halkett's brigade, and they also saw the cuirassiers early enough to form square and drive off their adversaries.

Sir Thomas Picton rode over to congratulate them.[8] The cuirassiers swept on, charging the Black Watch, who this time formed square successfully. The 33rd meanwhile had escaped the first wave of cuirassiers but its troubles were not over, for a second French regiment was poised behind the first. The French action was a fine example of how to combine artillery and cavalry. The cavalry obliged the enemy to form square, which made it an ideal target for artillery. If the square wavered at the casualties from the artillery, the cavalry finished it off. A private described their baptism of fire as they were targeted by the French 12-pounders:

Before we had been in the field half an hour we got it pretty hot. The officer of my company, I believe, was the first that was killed in the company. The enemy got a fair view of our regiment at that time, and they sent cannon shot as thick as hail stones. Immediately we got up on our ground and seen a large column of the French cavalry, named the French cuirassiers, advancing close upon us, we immediately tried to form square to receive the cavalry, but all in vain, the cannon shot from the enemy broke down our square faster than we could form it; killed nine and ten men every shot; the balls falling down amongst us just at the present and shells bursting in a hundred pieces. We could not be accountable for the number of men that we lost there; and had it not been for a wood on our right, about 300 yards, we should have every every [sic] man been cut in pieces with the cavalry, and trampled upon by their horses.

The 33rd were still on 'rising ground' where they were all too conspicuous, and the face of the square nearest the cannon began to crumple despite the sergeants using crossed halberds to push the rear men forward. Captain John Haigh stepped from his own company to the danger point, sword raised, shouting encouragement, but a cannonball hit him in the abdomen and almost cut him in half. His eyes strained and bulged, his lip quivered and his body convulsed as he fell on his back. His brother, standing nearby, burst into tears. Surgeon Finlayson wrote soon after that 'Captain Haigh was killed with a cannonball, as he was most coolly & gallantly encouraging his men & directing them how to act. His brother, Lieutenant Haigh was close by & saw him fall & his bowels all gush out. He exclaimed, "Oh kill me with him!" I endeavoured to console him and said it might soon be our own fate.' Immediately afterwards another ball cleanly removed the top of Arthur Gore's skull and, recalled his lieutenant, 'poor Arthur Gore's brains were scattered upon my shako and face.' Finlayson saw Gore, the man who had followed him from Nivelles, 'laying on his back with the upper part of his head shot away. The rest of his countenance was most pleasant, I never saw it more so, he seemed asleep.'[9]

As they hurriedly retreated from the exposed position a rumour spread that cavalry was behind their flank, and they panicked and ran. Some of those at the back were cut down and captured, and a cuirassier seized the battalion's colour and rode off with it. A corporal and a lieutenant were hiding in the rye when the corporal saw the horseman with the colour riding straight at him. He shot the Frenchman, tore the flag from the staff and gave it to the lieutenant, who ran for the wood. The corporal was quickly surrounded and taken prisoner.[10]

Scattered men gathered calmly beyond the trees. As a private recalled, 'we then went to the far end of the wood where we got out and formed up and numbered off, but we mustered very small.'[11] They did no further fighting.

The cuirassiers now swept into Quatre Bras. The Lüneburg Landwehr, who occupied the ditch formerly held by the 92nd, held their fire until the cavalry was within thirty yards and then shot off a volley, backed up by canister from two guns of Kuhlmann's horse battery that had raced ahead of the Guards division and unlimbered in front of the farmhouse on the Charleroi road just in time. To the right, the Brunswick line infantry remained steady in square. Their new commander, Colonel Johann Olfermann, was a trained oboist; having joined the British army as a music master, he was wounded and decorated at the battle of Alexandria, before becoming adjutant to Edward Pakenham in the Peninsula where he met and became an intimate friend of the Duke of Brunswick. He stood in the midst of the second battalion, encouraging them with shouts of 'Well done, men, bravo 2nd Line battalion!'[12]

In the face of this devastating close-range artillery and musket fire, the French charge was brought to an end and the cuirassiers fled back the way they had come, hopelessly routed. Kellermann had his horse shot; it fell on him and he only narrowly escaped, while his brigade lost 250 of its 791 men.[13] Those still on horseback galloped hell for leather from the field while, behind them, many unhorsed but unwounded cuirassiers attempted to scamper away, dodging bullets as they fled; among the escapees were Kellermann, General Guiton and Colonel Garavaque.

Kellerman reckoned that they would have had more success had the promised support from Piré's lancers actually materialised. In fact several British witnesses recalled lancers supporting the cuirassiers,[14] but whether or not this was so, nobody could blame Piré's cavalry, whose efforts during the day had already been extraordinary. So too had been Kellermann's charge; had Ney only had infantry in a position to make another major push, it might once again have turned the tide.

In the event, the charge had most effect in the opposite direction. The rout of the cuirassiers was spectacular. In the rear division of d'Erlon's corps, Louis Canler had been standing for hours within sight of the *chaussée* where their baggage wagons were stacked up south of Frasnes, barely moving while the head of the column dithered. Suddenly huge numbers of horsemen hurtled towards them. Canler's regiment formed square, but the baggage drivers panicked. Taking Guiton's cuirassiers for the enemy or expecting them to be closely pursued, the drivers streamed off in rout, telling everyone who would listen that British cavalry were on their heels. According to Jean-Baptiste Lemonnier-Delafosse, Foy's chief of staff, the remainder of the cuirassier division that had been waiting in reserve was carried away in the rout of Guiton's men – if this was so, it would explain their subsequent inactivity and the shock of other witnesses at the extent of the rout. So far did the cuirassiers flee, indeed, that they were said to have caused a disturbance in Charleroi.[15]

Ney could not have asked more of his men. But with the defeat of

Kellermann's cavalry and the arrival of yet more British reinforcements in the shape of the Guards division from Nivelles, he was now forced to stand on the defensive. Hope of victory had finally to be abandoned. In his post-campaign report of 26 June, Ney blamed the Emperor for depriving him of glory at Quatre Bras by taking away d'Erlon's corps without informing him, but, although to some degree his frustration was justified, he might have done better to obey orders.[16]

33

Blücher's Fall

Ligny, 7–10 p.m.

On the other battlefield, as the Imperial Guard pushed forward up the slope from the Ligne stream, it was the Prussians who were being forced into a fighting retreat.

Of the rifle bullets he had cast so recently, volunteer Jäger Franz Lieber had only one left, saved for an emergency. He first felt real uneasiness when his battalion was charged by horse grenadiers as the skirmishers of his Colberg Regiment fled from Ligny and they were ordered to 'hive' – to form clusters of men with bayonets pointing outwards – but they held off the cavalry and got away. During the retreat he met his brother, who had been wounded in the foot and was riding on an ammunition cart. Lieber's company had been reduced from eighty to thirty, but, to his satisfaction, they had earned the respect of the old regular soldiers of the regiment.[1]

To cover the retreat, the musketeers of the 21st Pomeranians formed line and tried to drive the French infantry back, but one battalion was mauled by General Delort's cuirassiers, who had got behind them without being seen by skirting the village to the west.[2] Skirmishers of the 29th Regiment fought fiercely to prevent the French seizing retreating artillery.

The storm that had broken over the battlefield was violent but short; as Blücher rode over from the right wing, the rain stopped and the sun shone through dispersing thundercloud. He now led Röder's cavalry in a bid to halt the French advance. Colonel von Lützow rode at the head of the 6th Uhlans, while General von Röder himself led the 1st West Prussian dragoons, with Landwehr following. Charging the square of the French 4th Grenadiers, under the impression that they were National Guard militia because they wore shabby uniforms with shakos instead of the Guards' usual bearskins, the Uhlan lancers had not seen that there was a ditch in their way. Just as they reached this obstacle the grenadiers fired a volley. They shot like Guards rather than militia, and thirteen officers and seventy men fell.[3] When some cuirassiers counter-attacked, the Uhlans fled and Lützow, the famous leader of the partisan brigade that had adopted his name was unhorsed and captured; he was a prisoner Napoleon had coveted for years.

As the 2nd Dragoons began to gain pace they were charged in the left flank by cuirassiers. At the same time the routed lancers galloped through their files and the regiment broke and fled. Other charges too failed, and in the confusion as they turned to flee, the white horse that the Prince Regent had given Prince Blücher was hit in the left flank by a bullet.[4] Blücher tried to ride on to escape the pursuing cuirassiers, but the horse quickly became weaker and he just had time to shout to his aide-de-camp, 'Nostitz, now I'm done for,' when his horse fell dead, trapping the old man underneath it. Nostitz, whose own horse was wounded in the neck, turned back, dismounted, and crouched low over Blücher's dead horse, pistol in hand.[5]

On the left, having discovered that the broad stream which protected them in defence proved to be an obstruction to an attack, the Prussians were finally advancing. Around 7.30 Johann von Thielmann made a general advance, pushing three cavalry regiments supported by a horse battery across the stream.[6] Finding themselves apparently faced by French artillery with no visible support, two squadrons of Prussian dragoons charged the guns. It was a trap. One brigade of French dragoons charged their front and another hit their flank. The Prussian dragoons carried away the rest of the cavalry in their flight, and the pursuing French captured the whole of horse battery no. 19, which they then turned against the Prussians. Kurmark Landwehr covered the debacle and when one squadron of French dragoons, disobeying orders, went in pursuit, they suffered 100 casualties in consequence.[7] This incident, however, quashed Prussian ambition to attack. Both Gneisenau and Röder felt that the cavalry had performed badly, blaming the untrained state of the new regiments and the dilution of the old, which had lost experienced squadrons and officers.

Meanwhile, French units poured into the breach in the Prussian centre. Delort's cuirassiers were now riding for the headquarters windmill on top of the hill, and Drouot's artillery was aiming at the Prussian reserves there. Gneisenau and his staff left the windmill and fell back. Nobody knew where Blücher was, but it seemed likely he was dead or captured. Behind the lines there was much disorder and some of the less experienced and motivated troops fled, dropping their guns and running east along the highway to Namur, although in the front line experienced units held out with determination.[8] The right wing pulled out in obstinate good order and at Brye Otto von Pirch's brigade, supported by sixteen guns and Westphalian Landwehr cavalry, acted as rearguard to receive and protect the retreating battalions. Krafft improvised a rearguard to cover the centre, getting the whole of his Elbe Regiment and the 9th Colberg in position to make a stand on the road from Brye to Sombreffe, a position they held until the early morning. To the east, Steinmetz's 24th Regiment, which had been decoyed towards Sombreffe, got into a three-sided square with its back to the Ligne stream to fight off French cavalry, before Steinmetz's other battalions advanced in squares to cover the retreat. The thunderstorm had made the fields muddy and sticky and the Prussians struggled to get their guns back, but infantry helped to haul the cannon and desperate cavalry charges bought time for the Prussians to save almost all of their artillery.

The 1st Grenadiers and Chasseurs marched eastward to support General Hulot's division which had taken the farm of Potriaux and was threatening to take Sombreffe, but Steinmetz was able to block their advance. Antoine Maurin, the commander of Gérard's cavalry division, was badly wounded in a charge on this rearguard at the close of the day.

It was the day's final action. The French camped on the battlefield; Vandamme had his headquarters at Saint-Amand, Gérard at Ligny. The 1st Chasseurs accompanied the Emperor back to Fleurus where he spent the night at the pretty Château de la Paix, on the northern fringe of the town, with his staff at the Château de Zualart, the home of the mayor.

Estimates of Prussian losses at Ligny have varied dramatically between the 6000 killed and wounded of the British historian James and the 24,856 of Sergeant Hippolyte de Mauduit, who had walked over the field the morning after. Since Blücher and Gneisenau admitted to losses of 12–15,000 in their report to the king written next day, James's figure can be dismissed.[9] Like some other British writers, he sought to minimise the apparent impact of a battle that might otherwise be seen to detract from the significance of the great British victory at Waterloo which was to follow two days later. The British horse artillery commander Sir Augustus Frazer heard the following day that the Prussians had lost 14,000 killed and wounded and sixteen guns; the final figure was probably twenty-two. It was also rumoured that the French had captured all the Prussian reserve ammunition.[10]

In fact the true figure for Prussian losses, at around 18,000, was probably higher than Gneisenau's top estimate,[11] Müffling gave total losses for 15 and 16 June in killed, taken prisoner or disabled by wounds as 20,900.[12] In addition, about 10,000 men, nearly all of them recently conscripted Westphalians and Rhinelanders, took the opportunity to run away during the night. At the close of the battle of Ligny Gneisenau had only 55,500 men remaining of the 83,500 who had begun the fight.

French casualties are equally difficult to compute since no official figures survive for most units. On the morning of 17 June Soult reported to Davout that his impression was that their losses had been light – no more than 3000. If he really thought so, he was soon disabused, for Gérard's official return next day gave his casualties alone as 3686, while Girard's division lost 1900 out of 3900.[13] Houssaye revised Napoleon's figure of 6950 upwards to 8500, but this is still too low. Sir Charles Oman derived a figure from known officer losses of 10–12,000.[14] Mauduit produced an estimate of French casualties of 13,860 and the most painstaking modern analysis has come up with 13,721.[15]

It had been a far more costly and a far less complete victory than Napoleon had envisaged, but it had at least been a victory and the Prussians had been very badly mauled. His inexperienced staff had proved incapable of coordinating the change of plan with Marshal Ney, who still had more or less no staff at all. Although ultimately futile to enquire what might have happened had d'Erlon's 20,000 fresh men stormed along the *chaussée* towards Quatre Bras in accordance with their original orders, or had they completed the Emperor's new plan by surging up the gentle slope to the north of Wagnelée to trap Blücher's Prussians, it is easy to imagine that in either case their contribution might have been decisive for that battle and possibly for the campaign. In the event, d'Erlon vacillated until it was too late, and because of the inaction of his corps Blücher's army was not surrounded and crushed; neither was a decisive breakthrough achieved against Wellington to clear the road to Brussels. The Emperor had missed a golden opportunity.

34

Wellington's Offensive

Quatre Bras, 7–9 p.m.

The arrival of the Guards division an hour or so after Alten's took Wellington's theoretical total force to 33,000 men and 70 guns. Although some battalions and some guns had been knocked out, this represented a third of his army.

The Guards had marched as quickly as they could from Nivelles, meeting among other wounded a staff officer who 'urged us to get on as the action was going badly'. They halted briefly at Houtain-le-Val to allow exhausted stragglers to catch up, and for the division's twelve guns to get to the front of the column, and while stationary they checked their flints and fixed their bayonets.[1] Ensign Edward Macready's light company of the 30th, which had been left behind the night before and was racing to catch up its regiment, overtook the Guards at Houtain. When Guardsmen taunted them about their hurry, the Cambridgeshire light bobs offered in return, 'Shall I carry your honour on my pack?' and 'It's a cruel shame to send gentlemen's sons on such business!'

Macready's men were dour veterans, but he was seventeen and had been in the army for only a year, son of a struggling theatrical manager and younger brother of an actor who was just establishing a reputation on the stage at Bath. The next troops Macready met were Nassauers as they approached the Bois de Bossu, 'over which was a heavy cloud of smoke, with birds in all directions flying and squealing about it'. A staff officer told the Cambridgeshires their regiment had only just entered the field and pointed where to find it, a round shot spattering them with dirt as they were talking. When they rounded the wood, the fury of the battle was revealed. Trotting forward, they met their colonel retiring wounded and he pointed the way the battalion had gone. Macready stumbled over the bodies of Gordon Highlanders as he passed La Bergerie in time to see the cuirassiers attack his regiment's square.[2] By then, he could hear firing in the wood as the light companies of the Guards advanced into it.

With deadlock in the centre, where French light troops were defending the line of Gémioncourt and its hedged stream with grim determination, Wellington now tried to make a breakthrough on the western flank. Peregrine Maitland's 1st Foot Guards went into the Bois de Bossu, while the Coldstreams and Sir John Byng's brigade remained behind it in reserve.

The light Guards companies went in first and others followed at intervals. In the wood, however, they quickly became confused. 'Our regiment marched into the wood without the slightest suspicion, when we were attacked on all sides by the enemy who had lain in the ditches on each side of the wood,' wrote one Guardsman, but in reality the Guards were shooting at each other and at any knots of troops who remained in the wood, few of which were French. There were still Brunswick Jägers there, lost and isolated Nassauers, and frightened fugitives of every nationality.

It was not until they reached the Gémioncourt stream that they met genuine opposition and the light companies, led by Alexander Fraser, Lord Saltoun, began pushing back French light infantry. As an officer wrote in his journal:

The men gave a cheer, and rushing in drove everything before them to the end of the wood, but the thickness of the underwood soon upset all order, and the French artillery made the place so hot that it was thought advisable to draw back to the stream, which was rather more out of range. A great many men were killed and wounded by the heads of the trees falling on them as cut off by cannon shot.[3]

A Guardsman recalled that the French 'opened a heavy fire from their guns which were posted on a hill about half a mile distant, which threw the whole of our men into confusion, some running one way and some another'.

While Maitland's brigade advanced through the wood, the light companies of Byng's brigade under James Macdonell, supported by Brunswickers, pushed up the eastern side of it. As he moved stealthily forward, driving back French skirmishers, the number of bodies near La Bergerie told Guardsman Matthew Clay that there had been a fierce struggle there. Curiously, he spotted Arthur Gore's body: 'I particularly noticed a young officer of the 33rd Regiment lying amongst the slain, his bright scarlet coat and silver lace had attracted my attention when marching over his headless body. Most of the dead were English, Brunswickers and Highlanders; the majority were the latter.' Further on, seeing French cavalry, the advancing British formed square, but were then pounded by the artillery. Clay provided a good description of the classic French use of cavalry and artillery in combination, and the simple British countermeasure of moving the square between volleys:

Being foiled by the timely movements of our square and ever obedient to the Commander, we escaped the destructive effects of the well-directed shells of the enemy, who, no doubt having observed our repeated escapes from the goring fire of their artillery, menaced us more daringly with their cavalry and prevented our taking fresh ground until their artillery had thrown their shells amongst us. By this means we had a more narrow escape than before, being compelled to remain longer in our position to resist the cavalry.

I, being one of the outward rank of the square, can testify as to the correct aim of the enemy, whose shells having fallen to the ground and exploded within a few paces of the rank in which I was kneeling.[4]

The Brunswickers advancing between Macdonell's men and Maitland's battalions 'formed square beautifully, and did their part most effectively'.[5]

When Maitland's battalions emerged from the wood, they threw out a skirmish line against French infantry whose main columns were defending a line from the farm of Grande Pierrepont, three-quarters of a mile south-east of Gémioncourt, to the high ground behind Gémioncourt and above Piraumont. The two battalions of Maitland's 1st Guards emerged from the trees into a cornfield. 'As all order had been lost in passing through the wood, the men formed up as they came out and extended the line into the standing corn. A great many men of other regiments who had been engaged before we arrived, very gallantly left the wood and fell in with our men.' A fierce firefight developed while French cavalry prowled. As a Brunswick battalion manoeuvred to form on the left of the Guards, the French cavalry saw an opportunity to charge the flank of the second battalion, who ran for the wood and took shelter in the hollow way. From there, their fire drove off the cavalry, but they left many dead on the slope between the field and the track. Lord Hay, winner of the sweepstake at Grammont three days previously, was shot dead by a French cavalryman as he urged his horse over a hedge. French infantry then followed up and 'their light troops advanced in such numbers as to oblige us to evacuate the wood at ten o'clock,' as a lieutenant wrote three days later.[6] Skirmishing continued until darkness, and in two hours of fighting the 1st Guards suffered over 500 casualties.

At the end of the day Wellington decided to take Gémioncourt, and Picton once again led the 28th and 32nd to the attack. The tough Welshman had been hit by a musket ball that had broken two of his ribs, but he was choosing to ignore the wound. The French abandoned the farm tamely, as it was now too far ahead of their front line, and the 30th took over the buildings. It was discovered that they had been used as a dressing station, and 140 wounded 'and some excellent beer' were found within.[7]

As the fighting died down, the 2834 men of General Kruse's 1st Nassau Regiment marched in: 'Some balls whistled over our heads, but not a single man was wounded.' They had set out at 9 a.m.

from the east gate of Brussels, and Heinrich von Gagern had found the gruelling twenty-five-mile ride in hot sun exciting but tiring. Gagern was nearly sixteen, the son of the prime minister of the Netherlands. He had studied at the military academy in Munich, but this was his first campaign. The regiment had marched round the city and then down the Charleroi road, stopping to rest in the forest shade and again at Mont Saint-Jean. From there they found the road forward blocked by an immense British baggage column which had followed Picton's 5th Division as far as Genappe, before turning back towards Brussels. The Nassauers had to walk through the fields beside the road until they had passed it and then found themselves marching between two files of wounded soldiers. Some were themselves Nassauers and their news was depressing: 'everything had been lost, their entire regiment dispersed, etc. The look of these wounded men was not encouraging, but, as one can imagine, their words made an even worse impression on our young soldiers.'[8] But all was not lost, after all, and Gagern, though tired, was exhilarated, for even camping under the stars was new. 'This was the first night I ever spent in the open air. I lay down at the rear of my battalion, next to a wall of the last house of Quatre Bras, and fell asleep, wrapped in my overcoat and hungry after all the exertions of the day.'[9]

As twilight gathered the British cavalry began to ride in. Some had ridden a very long way – the hussar brigade covered forty-five miles – but the whole of the British cavalry and its horse artillery had missed the battle. In the early morning, troops of horse artillery had got lost and had terrible problems dragging and pushing their guns along lanes that were deep in mud from weeks of rain. All the cavalry was delayed for hours at Enghien for lack of orders to move on, and one brigade stopped there for the night, twenty-five miles from the battlefield. Other regiments found their way forward obstructed by marching infantry or blocked by baggage trains; though the cavalry could ride round such obstacles, the artillery got stuck behind slow-moving wagons.[10]

Assistant surgeon John Haddy James, who had fallen behind when his horse lost a shoe, overtook a brigade of Hanoverian

Landwehr 'which had marched a weary way already that day, and were continually obliged to halt, and lie reclining on their mighty packs to procure some rest in the shade. Nevertheless they courageously pursued their march, singing as they went, a hymn-like music.' Ahead of him, as his regiment passed through Nivelles, they saw 'women seated at their cottage doors scraping old linen into lint, and this showed us that they expected many wounded soldiers to arrive'.[11]

There were a lot of wounded. Sir Edward Barnes told Sir Augustus Frazer that they totalled 5000, a higher figure than most historians have given; generally the allied killed and wounded together are set at about that figure. In addition there were about a thousand prisoners, most of them Netherlanders.[12] Netherlands casualties were relatively light except in the 27th Jägers and 5th Militia, which were more or less wiped out in terms of military value. Some of the best British units suffered very heavy casualties and although they obstinately fought again two days later, the 92nd, 79th and 42nd Highlanders were all reduced to little more than half strength, and the 1st Foot, 69th and Brunswick 2nd Line lost nearly a third of their men. The French artillery and snipers were responsible for most of the damage. French losses were around 4200 and the allies took about a hundred prisoners.[13]

As dusk set in, rifleman Ned Costello took shelter at Haute Cense, a farmhouse just north of the Bois des Censes. Here the 5th Division's wounded gathered, being brought in until the outhouses and barns were crammed. Straw and hay were strewn on all the floors for them to sleep on, but Costello lay awake, troubled by the 'anguish of my shattered hand and the groans of my fellow sufferers'. When he set out next morning his arm was in a sling but his wound had not been dressed, and it was not to be treated until some time after he reached Brussels.[14]

Indeed, at Quatre Bras the medical system could be said to have failed. Medical services were severely overstretched owing to the breakneck speed with which units had marched to battle. Just two days previously, on 14 June, the War Office had reappointed Sir James McGrigor, once a spectacularly efficient member of

Wellington's team in the Peninsula, as head of the medical service with a view to the invasion of France. He had no opportunity, therefore, to prepare his department for the unexpected battle on the 16th. The medical supplies, loaded on hospital wagons, had been left miles behind the marching battalions, and although some surgeons carried at least a small case of instruments with them, assistant surgeon James had to admit that 'I was unable to do anything for their wounds as I had no sort of medical supply with me'; it was generally the case, he implied, that 'the medical supplies had not been up the previous day.'[15]

In theory each battalion and cavalry regiment had a surgeon and two assistants – although there were rarely three surgeons in practice – and the British contingent also employed fifteen staff surgeons and a physician. This was a pathetically small group to deal with 5000 wounded at Quatre Bras, never mind what was to overtake them two days later. Usually, one surgeon provided first aid in the field, while the others were deployed at a dressing station established for a brigade or division in a suitable building a short distance behind the lines. The surgeons were helped by bandsmen, who stopped playing music when the fighting started, and they, or comrades, helped wounded men who could not walk from the rudimentary first aid post to surgeons equipped to saw off an arm in the dressing station.

The main dressing station at Quatre Bras had been established in the farm. Donald Finlayson, assistant surgeon to the 33rd Foot, said that he had been ordered to arrange for a field hospital at Nivelles where surgeons could operate in cleaner and less desperate circumstances than on the battlefield, but perhaps he was chiefly looking for help. In the evening some surgeons went out to locate and bring in wounded men, which proved a dangerous exercise. Not only was the Brunswickers' physician captured by the French, but sporadic shooting continued, as Finlayson noted:

The action ceased about 9 p.m., but solitary shots continued to be fired in various directions till the night was well advanced, which made it somewhat hazardous for the medical officers & the men with them to go in quest of the wounded. It is less pleasant to be killed by our own men or a random shot, & fall unheard of amidst a field of corn 5 or 6 feet high, than it is to die with the regiment in the execution of duty.[16]

About the same time Wellington left the battlefield and rode the two miles back to Genappe, where supper had been ordered at the Roi d'Espagne. The last messenger to reach him from Blücher had told him that when he left Brye the Prussians still held all the villages along the Ligne, but that they had taken heavy casualties and the best they could do was to hold their ground until nightfall. He had had no message since, and told his secretary Fitzroy Somerset that the Prussian was 'a damned fine old fellow'. He intended to propose to the Prince that they should jointly attack the French next morning. During dinner Captain Hardinge came in, looking for a surgeon for his brother the liaison officer, who wanted a British surgeon to amputate his wounded hand, and he confirmed that when he left Ligny the Prussians were still holding their ground.[17]

Wellington went to sleep while his staff wrote orders for the troops to concentrate at Quatre Bras, still believing, as Somerset wrote to his wife, that the Prussians had held off the French. There were, though, unsubstantiated darker reports. Another of Wellington's close aides, Felton Hervey, was to write in July that, although there had been no confirmation, rumours had reached them that the Prussians had been defeated with heavy loss and were retreating in confusion.[18]

The allied armies had narrowly avoided disaster. Sixty-two thousand of Wellington's 95,000 troops had failed to reach the battlefield, which meant that he had failed to come to Blücher's aid and so they had missed the opportunity to defeat Napoleon. Thirty thousand of Blücher's troops, moreover, had failed to turn up, as a result of which he had been defeated. On the other hand, 30,000 of Napoleon's troops had also failed to take part, which meant that he had missed the opportunity to destroy one of his two opponents.

Napoleon had lost the advantage of surprise, but he had succeeded in keeping his opponents apart from each other and one of them was badly wounded. What he did not know was that Wellington was ignorant of Blücher's fate and that his sleeping army, exposed by the retreat of the Prussians, with 40,000 Frenchmen in front of them and another 60,000 on their flank, was currently at the Emperor's mercy.

35

Council by Lamplight

Ligny and Mellery, 10 p.m. 16 June–2 p.m. 17 June

Around 10 p.m. the Prussian staff gathered in a moonlit huddle on the cobbled road north of Brye and spread out their maps. With Blücher missing presumed dead, Gneisenau took command of the Prussian army and reviewed the situation. The French had driven a wedge between Ziethen and Pirch, stationed around Brye, and Thielmann's corps beyond Sombreffe, but darkness had saved them from disaster and their rearguards still held Brye and Sombreffe itself. Many troops had already left the field, and were retreating in different directions. Broken units and deserting fugitives had fled eastward towards Namur, while Henckel's men had pulled out through Sombreffe towards Gembloux. Friedrich von Jagow had also taken five battalions and two cavalry regiments to Gembloux; the general, who had lost his horse, led his troops on foot, wrapped in a cuirassier's cloak, first to a lonely farm and then north-east up the Roman road.

Gneisenau was determined not to become separated from Wellington, but it was far from clear that the Prussians were in a position to join him to fight another battle next day, as they had all hoped, or indeed for some time to come. Gneisenau knew they had suffered serious losses and he was especially anxious about the fate of the artillery park, containing their reserve ammunition, which had disappeared. The regiments he still controlled could not simply march to join Wellington because there were French troops between them and Quatre Bras, and it would be impossible for Thielmann to follow. The army did at least have the solid support of Friedrich von Bülow's corps, which was approaching from Liège along the Roman road. About this time, in fact, its vanguard were stopping to camp just north of Gembloux, the remainder spread behind it along seven and a half miles of the road.

According to Ziethen's chief of staff, Ludwig von Reiche, Gneisenau recommended a retreat to the village of Tilly, about two miles north, towards which much of their right wing had already been forced. However, Reiche found that Tilly was not marked on his map, and suggested that many officers might fail to find the place for the same reason. As a rendezvous for their scattered troops they needed a town that was marked on all their maps, so they decided to spread the word for a retreat towards Wavre, fifteen miles away in the direction of Brussels.[1]

In fact Reiche's explanation of the retreat to Wavre was disingenuous. The Prussian army was in no state to withdraw to Tilly and renew the struggle next day, and they must really have decided that they had to try to buy time to rearm and regroup further back. Moreover, there was a perfectly good line of communication between Brussels and Germany through Wavre. The decision to maintain contact with Wellington by retreating north, rather than along their lines of communication to the east, was vitally important, although it is likely that they had already agreed to do this in case of defeat.

But if they were not to halt at Tilly, but instead to continue towards Wavre, then their retreat would leave Wellington's army exposed to a flank attack by Napoleon next morning. It was imperative, therefore, to warn Wellington so that he also retreated. Crucially, however, the final messenger sent by Gneisenau to Wellington with this grim news was shot and killed by the French, so Wellington was left in ignorance of both the outcome of the battle and the Prussian decision.[2]

At the crossroads at Les Trois Burettes behind Brye, a staff officer began directing troops up the Roman road towards Gembloux and another then instructed them to take a left turn up a track to Tilly on the road to Wavre. 'The detachments which had already taken the Roman road or the Namur road could not, of course, be recalled,' Reiche noted; 'in itself this was a bad thing, yet it had the advantage that the enemy would be deceived as to the line of our withdrawal.'[3] One virtue of Bülow's location was that troops that had missed the Tilly junction eventually walked up the Roman road into his camp. Around midnight the last regiments of Ziethen's and Pirch's corps began to move off towards Tilly, leaving rearguards on the battlefield. Ludwig Nagel was near Brye when 'shortly after midnight we decamped; it appeared the enemy was approaching. At the village of Tilly we encountered troops around invigorating fires, near which we also encamped. That did us good; soon I lay fast asleep.'[4]

Johann von Thielmann received orders to withdraw along a parallel course to the right wing if possible, or to go to Gembloux if not. He took the safer option, retreating to the town, four miles northeast along a clear road from Sombreffe. Regiments gathered in the darkness, an advance guard moved off at one in the morning, and the rearguard slipped away at four.

Some hours earlier, Blücher's faithful aide Ferdinand von Nostitz had led the bruised and semi-conscious field marshal off the battlefield, hoping he could keep the old man alive. They had been extremely lucky to escape: in the deepening twilight French cuirassiers had twice raced by the prone general and his aide without noticing them. A counter-charge had now driven the French back to their lines, and as the pursuing Prussian lancers approached the pair, Nostitz sprang to his feet and waved his arms for help. A group of Lützow's Black Lancers reined in and helped to pull Blücher's dead horse off the old man's body. He was still alive so a sergeant gave them his horse, a group of them hoisted the seventy-three-year-old general onto it, and Nostitz led him away from the battlefield, taking the dirt road to Tilly.

Nostitz trudged through the mud produced by the thunderstorm, surrounded by wounded men and fugitives. They passed through Tilly, but when they reached Mellery Blücher admitted that he could go no further and Nostitz began to search for a refuge. The village had been deserted by its inhabitants and Nostitz couldn't see a house with a light. Eventually, he spotted a glimmer behind a shutter and ushered Blücher into a farmhouse. There was nobody inside, so Nostitz stood guard at the door until some horsemen approached. Nostitz ordered them to guard the field marshal while he went for help.

Near Tilly he located General Steinmetz, told him where Blücher was and that he must be kept safe, and then returned to Mellery where he found the old man sitting on a stool, complaining of severe pain and a burning thirst. The farmhouse was now full of wounded men, moaning for help, but the owner returned, fetched a pot of milk, made a bed of straw on the floor, and Blücher slaked his thirst and slept. By chance Gneisenau had established his own headquarters elsewhere in the village, and he and the big, burly Grolmann joined them after midnight.[5]

By the dim light of an oil lamp, they held a council of war while the old general lay on his pile of straw, having his bruises massaged with garlic and schnapps. His surgeon had forbidden him to drink the schnapps, but had allowed him a magnum of champagne.[6] The situation looked desperate. Sitting on a barrel of sauerkraut, Gneisenau laid out the difficulties and the argument in favour of a retreat to the east: this was not something he wanted, but as things stood the army was not fit to continue fighting. 'Our ammunition was expended and our reserve munitions were nowhere to be found,' he was to write six days later to the Prussian Prime Minister. 'It was a dreadful situation and we were almost unable to come to help the Duke of Wellington. You can imagine my feelings.'[7] They had little idea where much of the army was, while there was a fair chance that their ammunition was already in French hands; men with no ammunition were little use. Nevertheless, Blücher insisted that they must fight on: 'We have taken a few knocks and shall have to hammer out the dents!' he said. By 2 a.m. they had worked out how to gather the army at Wavre, and Grolmann sent instructions to Ziethen and Georg von Pirch to march on immediately.

While some 10,000 of the less enthusiastic conscripts had taken the opportunity to run away during the night, the hard core of the Prussian troops were just about as resolute as their commander. 'Towards daybreak everything was again in movement and after covering several miles, all the troops bivouacked near the town of Wavre, where Blücher had his main headquarters,' wrote Ludwig Nagel of the Freikorps. 'We were defeated, we knew that; but far from looking upon ourselves as beaten, all of us were filled with a steadfast spirit, full of unshaken confidence in ourselves and the coming day, and we spoke a good deal with each other.'[8] Blücher reached Wavre before the rain started and spent the afternoon resting on a couch at his headquarters in an inn in the marketplace. On the way he had ridden with his men on the horse he had borrowed from the lancer, asking them, 'Are you tired yet?' When they answered 'No!' he responded 'Will you fight the French tomorrow?' To which the men roared 'Yes! Hurrah!'[9] Ziethen's corps had taken particularly terrible losses – more than a third of them dead, wounded or missing, and some of the Rhineland militia had melted away – but the men that remained were obstinately determined.[10]

Two regiments of hussars and a battery of horse artillery acted as rearguard, taking position about three miles north of the battlefield, to the east of the village of Mellery, and sending out patrols in all directions. A trustworthy member of the general staff remained with them equipped with a telescope to send back frequent reports on French movements for, to his surprise, they had not been pursued.[11]

In the morning General Thielmann received orders from Gneisenau to take his corps to a village just beyond Wavre, and Thielmann was able to give reassurances that he at least had his artillery park and ammunition with him and that his corps was still in fighting trim. Thielmann concerted his movement with Bülow so that he left Gembloux around ten and moved slightly north-east to a better defensive position, north of the river Orneau and just south of Bülow's camp on the Roman road. He left there at 1 p.m., following Bülow north and then taking a different route. III Corps thereby overtook IV Corps, which became the rearguard. The Prussians had thus achieved a managed withdrawal which would enable them to re-enter the struggle.

Nevertheless, the disappearance of the artillery park was a serious issue. Each brigade had a column which carried spare ammunition not only for the artillery, but also for the infantry and cavalry, in twenty to thirty wagons. In each infantry brigade column at full strength there would be six caissons of 6-pounder ammunition, six of 7-pounder howitzer shells, twelve small arms ammunition wagons, two supply wagons and one containing tools and spare parts. Thus, there were huge numbers of these wagons – about 200 for each corps – and they were commanded by inexperienced junior officers, who might well have panicked. During the battle the wagon train had been grouped in a large park north of Sombreffe and Mazy, but they had moved off early and nobody knew where they had gone. If all of it had been captured, two of their four corps would be unable to fight.

36

No Time to Lose

Napoleon and Ney's wing, 17 June, 8 a.m.–1 p.m.

As darkness fell, Ney wrote a brief report to Napoleon. It told the Emperor that the departure of d'Erlon's corps had robbed Ney of victory, although it revealed remarkably little about how many enemy troops he had been fighting and what the current situation was. Then he settled down to supper. Charles de Forbin-Janson of Soult's staff was invited to join Ney, Prince Jérôme and his aide, who were seated around a table consisting of planks resting on empty barrels, lit by candles stuck in the necks of bottles, feasting on black bread and *saucisson*.[1]

Ney's men were also hungry, as their provision wagons had fled in the panic caused by the flight of Kellermann's cuirassiers and rations arrived very late. So the soldiers went off marauding and some, like Lieutenant Jacques Martin, did well. The 45th bivouacked near a village and his grenadiers brought in sheep, pigs, calves and even bullocks 'until in the end it was more like a fair-ground than a camp; we made them drive most of them back'. Corporal Louis Canler, a future chief of police, was less fortunate, and his squad found that every house or barn to which they went had already been ransacked.[2] The French army then slept, occupying the houses and barns of Frasnes and the wood of Delhutte, while the fresh troops of d'Erlon's corps provided outposts and sentries.

*

Napoleon later complained that he had known little about what happened at Quatre Bras until Count Flahaut reported to him in the early morning, but he was probably lying. It was certainly the case that neither Ney's report nor Reille's, which Ney sent on, said anything about the strength and disposition of Wellington's army, which was careless, but it seems that Soult was not kept entirely in ignorance of Ney's predicament: Forbin-Janson claimed to have reported at 3 a.m. that Ney faced Wellington's entire army and that it would attack him in the morning and, what is more, the terms in which Soult wrote to Ney at 8 a.m. confirm that he had indeed considered such a report. He did not act on it instantly because neither he nor Napoleon believed it.

Napoleon still thought that Ney was exaggerating the threat he faced at Quatre Bras, and that if Wellington really had been there he would have retreated during the night after hearing of Blücher's defeat. He never dreamed that Wellington's own communications might have failed and that the Prussian retreat might have left the other allied army exposed.

Ney in his turn was also to complain that he had not been told what had happened at Ligny. At 8 a.m., which was already far too late in the day, Soult wrote to Ney claiming that he believed he had already told him that the Emperor had defeated the Prussians. Soult announced that the English could not possibly act against Ney since the Emperor was on the Namur–Quatre Bras road. If there really was an English army in front of him he was to tell Napoleon immediately and Napoleon would attack them from the east while Ney attacked from in front. If he merely faced an English rearguard he was to attack it and take position at Quatre Bras. If there was nobody there to attack, he was to occupy the crossroads and replenish ammunition, reorganise his troops and rest his men.[3]

Napoleon has received much criticism for wasting time on the morning of 17 June and his staff certainly took far too long to establish what was going on. However, most of his troops were in no condition to fight instantly. Like the Prussians, they had expended their ammunition, and the artillery train had been at Charleroi the previous day. Vandamme and Gérard's infantry and artillery could do little without more ammunition, and the same was true of Reille's corps whose baggage drivers had fled.

While waiting for information to come in and ammunition wagons to arrive, Napoleon rode off to inspect the battlefield, leaving Soult at headquarters. The battlefield at Ligny was shocking. Among the smouldering ruins of the villages bodies were piled high, with wounded men trapped among them, some burned, some trampled or mangled by artillery wheels. Napoleon had to wait a quarter of an hour for enough corpses to be shifted to clear a path into Saint-Amand, and he was deeply moved by the carnage he saw in the villages; Forbin-Janson, who accompanied him, wrote that in the narrow lanes their horses had to trample over the bodies. Napoleon was an emotional man and genuinely pitied those broken in pursuit of glory. It was something for which he liked to be noted – his compassion on the battlefield was the subject of a famous painting by Antoine Gros, showing the Emperor in the aftermath of the bloody battle of Eylau fought in the snow in 1807 – and he felt it important to make a great show of his appreciation of the sacrifice made by his brave troops.

Hippolyte Mauduit of the Old Guard had explored the battlefield in the early morning as sunshine broke through the mist. In Ligny clusters of troops, their faces still black with powder, were camped among the dead; fearful villagers, who had hidden in their cellars, began to creep out. Four thousand bodies were heaped up in an area barely bigger than the familiar gardens of Napoleon's Tuileries palace. The castle and the houses round it were smoking ruins, while every intact house was full of wounded from both sides. The scene at Saint-Amand and La Haye was no better, the cemetery choked with dead bodies, the 82nd Regiment practically wiped out. Mauduit noticed the priest from one of the villages helping carry the wounded to the ambulances, the *vivandières* giving drinks to the desperately thirsty.[4]

The French medical services were better organised than those of other armies, but they were not equipped for this. Hector Daure, the *Intendant Général*, chief of administration and procurement, reported to War Minister Davout that the walking wounded were marching over the border to hospitals in France, but the existing facilities were insufficient, given that more fighting was imminent. If the wet weather continued there would be fever cases, and they needed the hospitals of the nearest military districts expanded immediately and many more surgeons brought in. At headquarters there were only fifteen surgeons, and consequently many of the wounded were not yet bandaged. He wanted 100 surgeons as soon as possible and more hospital staff. He told Soult that he did not yet know the number of wounded, but 1600 had been treated at headquarters and 800 sent on to Charleroi which was now clear and ready for more patients. Seven to eight hundred were waiting for treatment at headquarters, but more were arriving all the time and the carriages were in the field sorting the living from the dead.[5]

Some of these 'carriages' were surgeon Dominique Larrey's famous 'flying ambulances', practical, light covered wagons with a detachable floor that could be used as a stretcher. The word 'ambulance' until now had normally signified a field hospital. It was Larrey who revolutionised its meaning to turn the ambulance into the modern fast-moving vehicle equipped to give first aid in the field and then to evacuate victims. Larrey recognised the medical importance of rapid treatment, especially in cases requiring amputation: 'When a limb is carried away by a ball, by the burst of a grenade, or a bomb, the most prompt amputation is necessary. The least delay endangers the life of the wounded.' His flying ambulances facilitated rapid treatment, and Larrey tried to introduce a standard whereby amputation took place within twenty-four hours.[6]

Napoleon had spotted Larrey's talent and demanded his services for his own army in 1797. In 1801 he appointed him Surgeon General of his Guard, which soon became the Imperial Guard, and he had been with the Emperor ever since. In 1812 he had been in charge of the whole army but when in 1815 Napoleon gave that job to Pierre-François Percy, another remarkable doctor, Larrey felt slighted. 'I must have Larrey for the Guard and the General Headquarters,' the Emperor exclaimed. 'He sulks because he has been replaced by Percy. Go and tell him that he is indispensable and that I count on him.'[7] Larrey's legions of medics and flying ambulances belonged to the

Guard, but Percy, surgeon-in-chief, did his best for the rest of the army until at Ligny he fell ill with heart disease. There were ambulances at corps and division level and each regiment had an ambulance caisson with medical supplies. Five field hospitals were established around Fleurus and they were all working furiously.

Meanwhile, the Provost General, Etienne Radet, a policeman who in 1809 had arrested the Pope, had been up all night trying to prevent marauding. He reported persistent pillaging, chiefly by soldiers of the Imperial Guard, who were a law unto themselves. Doors and windows had been broken and things stolen from those caring for the wounded and freely giving food and help to French troops, as well as from locked, isolated houses from which the owners had fled. Radet's overstretched gendarmerie had been out all night and had arrested numerous Guardsmen, who were all then sprung from prison by force. Radet's gendarmes had been insulted, threatened and beaten and two of their horses had been stolen. Nevertheless, six patrols of gendarmes were now in the field pursuing another of their duties, rounding up wounded men, prisoners and discarded arms and burying the dead.[8]

The Prussians were nowhere to be seen when the morning mist cleared and, while medics and gendarmes began to clear the battlefield, the French staff pondered their next move. Receiving a report from General Pajol, who was following a force of Prussians eastward and had captured a battery of enemy guns, Napoleon got the impression that, as he had hoped, the Prussians were in retreat towards Namur.[9] Then another message from Ney arrived, having crossed in transit Soult's order to him:

> The enemy presents several columns of infantry and cavalry which seem to be disposed to take the offensive. I shall hold out with the infantry of Count d'Erlon and the cavalry of General Roussel to the last extremity and I hope even to be able to hold the enemy off until his majesty tells me what he intends to do. I shall place Count Reille in a position between us.[10]

Wellington really was still at Quatre Bras and his army could be crushed! There was no time to lose.

The message had been sent to headquarters at Fleurus, so more time had already been lost before it reached Napoleon as he prowled the field. As soon as he received it, however, the Emperor prepared to attack Wellington. Kicking himself for not having acted earlier, he ordered Grouchy to release Vandamme's cavalry division under Domon and one of Pajol's divisions, Subervie's, to join VI Corps and to send General Milhaud's corps of cuirassiers to Marbais. He ordered these troops, Lobau's two fresh infantry divisions and the Imperial Guard to march immediately towards Quatre Bras.

After receiving reports of Prussians around Gembloux as well as on the Namur road, Napoleon gave Marshal Grouchy his marching orders. Leaving behind what little remained of the mortally wounded General Girard's division to help the hospital staff and the gendarmerie to clear the battlefield, he was to take all of the 30,000 remaining men commanded by Vandamme, Gérard, Exelmans and Pajol to Gembloux. From there he was to scout east towards Namur and north-east towards Maastricht, but to pursue the enemy in order to discover the direction Blücher was really taking, so that the Emperor could work out what the Prussians intended to do. Napoleon emphasised that he wanted to know whether the Prussians were separating from the British, or whether they were trying to reunite with them to fight another battle. He told Grouchy to keep his infantry united and to send cavalry detachments in Napoleon's direction so as to keep communication easy and open.[11]

According to Charles de Flahaut, Napoleon's final words to Grouchy were etched in his memory: 'Now then, Grouchy, follow up those Prussians, give them a touch of cold steel in their hinder parts, but be sure to keep in communication with me by your left flank.' Another witness, Prince Jérôme, said that Grouchy objected to his mission until Napoleon concluded angrily, 'That's enough! Obey me by being my shield against the Prussians and don't worry yourself about the English.'[12]

By taking away much of Grouchy's cavalry Napoleon had reduced his marshal's ability to locate, pursue and harass the Prussian army.

Presumably, he was gambling on destroying Wellington's army before the Prussians recovered sufficiently to help him, and Grouchy's force, composed chiefly of infantry, was designed merely to protect him from the Prussians while he did so. The orders were essentially in accordance with Napoleon's original plan to place a blocking force at Gembloux and Sombreffe, but with the huge flaw that in reality the direction of the Prussian retreat was not east but north. It should be noted that Napoleon had taken into his calculations the strong possibility that the Prussians might be trying to reunite with Wellington's army. He was not single-mindedly fixed on the over-optimistic delusion that the Prussians were in full retreat, but he hoped that was the case, and certainly did not expect them to be capable of fighting again in the near future.

As Napoleon waited impatiently for the sound of cannon from Quatre Bras, the heat built up to thirty degrees Celsius and the day became oppressively humid, still and sultry. By noon Napoleon's vanguard was three miles from Quatre Bras. Soult reiterated his order to Ney to attack Wellington's army, telling him that Napoleon was ready to support him with an infantry corps and the Guard:

> Monsieur le maréchal, the emperor has just placed a corps of infantry and the Imperial Guard your side of Marbais; His Majesty charges me to tell you that it is his intention that you should attack the enemy at Quatre Bras, to shift them from their position, and that the body at Marbais will support your operations. His Majesty is on his way to Marbais and awaits your reports with impatience.[13]

The Emperor sent Forbin-Janson off with the message, cracking the joke that the colonel must by now be familiar with the route. When Forbin-Janson reached Frasnes, only about four miles away, he was mobbed by people who wanted to hear about the Emperor's great victory. He recalled that Ney's officers suddenly became elated, thinking the conquest of Belgium assured. But Ney still did not launch an attack. His guns remained silent. Lieutenant Jacques Martin of the 45th Regiment wrote that they spent the entire morning in full view of Wellington's troops, who didn't fire a single cannon at them; only the skirmishers occasionally exchanged shots. Martin was in constant expectation of the order to advance, but nothing happened.[14]

Around Marbais, Napoleon's patrols skirmished with both British and Prussian outposts, and there had been an unfortunate incident in which the Red Lancers of the Guard and d'Erlon's 7th Hussars mistook each other for the enemy.[15] An hour later, a distinctly angry Napoleon, waiting very impatiently to hear some sign of activity from Ney before he launched his own attack, wrote again: 'I am surprised at your great delay in executing my orders. There is no more time to lose; attack with the greatest impetuosity everything that stands before you. The fate of the *patrie* is in your hands.' Without waiting any longer for Ney, the Emperor rode for Quatre Bras at the head of 10,000 horsemen with infantry marching behind.

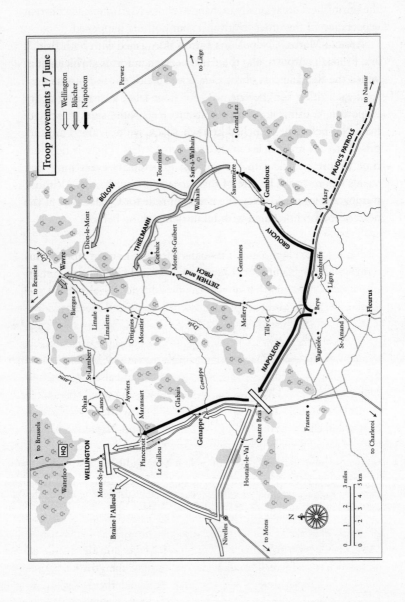

Troop movements 17 June

— Wellington
— Blücher
— Napoleon

to Liège

to Namur

PAJOL'S PATROLS

Perwez

Grand Lez

Tourinnes

BÜLOW

Sart-à-Walhain

Sauvenière

Gembloux

Mazy

THIELMANN

Walhain

GROUCHY

Dion-le-Mont

Corbaix

Mont-St-Guibert

Sombreffe

to Brussels

Wavre

Gentinnes

Ligny

Fleurus

Bierges

ZIETHEN and
PIRCH

Brye

Dyle

St-Amand

Limale

Ortignies

Mellery

Wagnelée

Limalette

Moustier

Tilly

St-Lambert

NAPOLEON

Lasne

Ohain

Aywiers

Glabais

Frasnes

to Charleroi

Lasne

Maransart

Genappe

to Brussels

HQ

Plancenoit

Le Caillou

Genappe

Quatre Bras

WELLINGTON

Mont-St-Jean

Houtain-le-Val

Waterloo

Braine l'Alleud

Nivelles

to Mons

N

0   1   2   3 miles
0 1 2 3 4 5 km

37

Losing the Scent

Grouchy's wing, 17 June, 3 a.m.–10 p.m.

Not long after Thielmann's Prussians left their lines in front of his outposts east of Sombreffe, Lieutenant-General Claude Pajol set off in pursuit. It appears that he was the only French cavalryman to be awake, alert and conscious of what needed doing at three that morning. To the west, the Prussians commanded by Ziethen and Pirch escaped undetected from Vandamme's sector of the battlefield. He should have followed their rearguard with his cavalry, but he showed no initiative, nor did Gérard, whose cavalry should also have been in motion, and nor did Marshal Grouchy, who was in overall charge. He later claimed that the Emperor left the field without giving him orders and that when he went to Fleurus to find Napoleon he was told he would receive instructions in the morning.[1]

According to several witnesses, Napoleon had been taken ill that night, although this was not one of the many excuses for the day's disappointments that he later gave to Gourgaud at Saint Helena. Possibly, he was simply exhausted by a long, tense day, not being as fit as he had once been.[2] That indeed was something he did later admit: 'If I had not been so worn out, I should have been in the saddle all night! What seem very small events often have the greatest consequences,' he lamented.[3] He may have expected the Prussians to remain on the battlefield in order to join Wellington next day and not anticipated that they would retreat, but he had become more reliant on others: Grouchy was supposed to be a gifted cavalry general and should have appreciated the importance of shadowing the Prussians, whether he had orders or not.

Hippolyte de Mauduit of the Guard later attributed Vandamme's inertia to jealousy of Grouchy, and there is evidence of mutual ill-feeling and distrust, but much of the confusion may have resulted from uncertainty about the command structure.[4] It is possible that Grouchy was not sure whether he was still in charge of a wing and still had direct authority over Vandamme and Gérard, since the Emperor had effectively superseded him the previous day. He did not know his officers, was not sure what troops he had, and did not have sufficient staff to help him exert control and communicate with headquarters.

He should have discovered and compensated for the fact that the two French light cavalry divisions concerned – those of Vandamme and Gérard – were both temporarily leaderless: Antoine Maurin of Gérard's division had been shot in the chest and seriously wounded at the end of the day, and Jean-Siméon Domon of Vandamme's had also been wounded. Either of these men might have followed Pajol's example had they been fit; as it was, their incapacity at this crucial moment contributed to an uncharacteristic lethargy in the French cavalry arm that night which was to prove disastrous.[5]

Whatever the reasons, the only initiative came from Pajol, who had just two regiments of cavalry, for Subervie's division had been taken from him, and the 1st Hussars, detached on 15 June, had still not returned from Frasnes. Pajol turned east towards Namur. It is not clear whether he had been ordered to go in that direction – according to his aide-de-camp Hubert-François Biot he had tried and failed to obtain orders – or whether he followed troops retreating that way, or rode towards Namur simply because everyone hoped and expected the enemy would retreat eastward. But the fact that he sent an aide to tell Grouchy what he had done implies that he had acted on his own.

The 5th Hussars led the way, accompanied by Biot, and Pajol followed with the 4th Hussars.[6] Towards Mazy they caught up with a

Prussian horse battery which had become stuck in a traffic jam of fugitives. A squadron of Prussian lancers that tried to defend the guns was brushed aside; killing or driving off the gunners the French captured all eight guns, as well as a large quantity of provisions in a column of baggage wagons from which the horses had already been stolen by fugitives.

Having sent back a report, Pajol rode eastward for seven miles, becoming increasingly uneasy about the apparent absence of large Prussian formations, before he stopped and threw out patrols to scout. Napoleon sent an infantry division from Lobau's corps to support him, but at midday Pajol reported to Grouchy that the Prussians were moving supplies from Namur north-west towards Louvain and that enemy units were cutting north towards Gembloux, both indications that the Prussians were retreating not east, but north.[7] Pajol intended that night to ride northward to cut the road from Namur to Louvain, but requested orders.

Hubert Biot with the 5th Hussars had already ridden north and run into Prussian outposts in a wood just south of Gembloux. Beyond the trees, Biot said, his French scouts saw a huge enemy artillery park stretched out on the plain. It was enormously tempting to attack, but they felt it unwise to cross the forest without infantry support, and so Biot went back to fetch the infantry at Mazy.[8] He returned too late, for the wagons soon moved off. This was another huge missed opportunity, indicating what might have been achieved had the French mounted the vigorous pursuit that Gneisenau feared. In the afternoon Pajol lost confidence; receiving no instructions and knowing that the enemy at Gembloux was behind him, he returned to Mazy, although Grouchy assumed that he was astride the road from Namur to Louvain, where he had said he would be. It was yet one more fatal misunderstanding.

Before daybreak on 17 June Grouchy tardily ordered some of his divisions to send out scouts. Patrols of his dragoons also discovered the presence of enemy troops around Gembloux, approaching the town about nine o'clock, in time to see masses of Prussian troops to the north. Joining his patrols, General Exelmans wrote to Grouchy that the enemy army was at Gembloux.[9] But Grouchy still did not order Vandamme to send out patrols, while Vandamme did nothing on his own initiative. Falsely assuming that they were with the rest, the French appear in fact to have had no idea where the Pussians on the western half of the battlefield had gone. This was a serious mistake, one that caused Napoleon to miss completely the existence of the column led by Gneisenau and Blücher, and so to mistake the direction of the Prussian retreat when he gave Grouchy his orders to follow the Prussians and shield him from them.

Once Napoleon had sent him to Gembloux, Grouchy should have realised that with Domon and Subervie's divisions both removed he was short of light cavalry to carry out his tracking mission and should have ordered Pajol to join him at Gembloux; it was evening, however, before he discovered that Pajol was not in front of him to the northeast but behind him at Mazy. Rémy Exelmans was already moaning that his dragoons were exhausted and ill suited to a light cavalry task.[10] The only other light cavalry at Grouchy's disposal were the two light regiments in Maurin's division, but they were covering the army's right flank, when in fact most Prussians were not to their east but to their west. But Grouchy failed to deploy any cavalry to scout in that direction or to establish the westward chain of communication with Napoleon's army that the Emperor had demanded.

Meanwhile it took some time for Vandamme to get moving. Probably this was because he had to wait for ammunition, but by starting off late the French had to march through the worst of the weather. Gérard, whose camp at Ligny was nearer, could have gone ahead, but followed because Vandamme was senior. Vandamme marched from Saint-Amand through Brye and Sombreffe to the crossroads at Point du Jour, just over four miles south-west of Gembloux, reaching there at about three in the afternoon. By that time it was pouring with rain. The road to Gembloux was bad and in boggy areas the heavily laden men were soon thigh-deep in cloying mud. Vandamme reached the town at about 5.30, while Gérard did not get there until ten at night because of the atrocious weather and the increasingly muddy roads.

In the early evening Grouchy wrote from Gembloux to Exelmans – who was at Sauvenières, where Thielmann had spent the

late morning – instructing him to send patrols north to Sart-à-
Walhain in the direction of Wavre and Brussels, and north-east to
Perwez in the direction of Maastricht. But when reporting to
Napoleon that night, he remained uncertain about what was going
on:

> It appears from all reports, that at Sauvenières the Prussians split
> into two columns: one took the route for Wavre passing through
> Sart-à-Walhain, the other column seems to be heading for
> Perwez.
>
> One might perhaps infer that a portion is going to join
> Wellington and that the rest, which is Blücher's army, is falling
> back on Liège, another column, with some of the artillery, having
> retreated via Namur.
>
> General Exelmans has been ordered to push six squadrons this
> evening towards Sart-à-Walhain and three towards Perwez. When
> I get his reports, if the main mass of Prussians is retiring on Wavre,
> I will follow them in that direction so that they can't reach Brussels
> and to cut them off from Wellington.

He reported that Thielmann and Bülow had left Gembloux about 10
a.m. (with a lead, therefore, of some twelve hours). The inhabitants
told him that the Prussians had admitted to losing about 20,000
men the previous day and Prussian officers had asked them (cun-
ningly intending to mislead pursuers, since the places were all in
different directions) the distances to Wavre, Perwez and Hannut.

It is not clear, however, why he thought a Prussian column had
gone north-east: perhaps he had misread Pajol's earlier report, perhaps civilians had deceived him. But it was this phantom column
that he chased with his cavalry, ordering both Maurin's division and
Pajol's to take that direction next day.[11] He sent these orders at the
same time as he sent the report to Napoleon. On the other hand he
ordered his slower troops, the main body of artillery and infantry, led
by the dragoons, to march to Sart-à-Walhain on the track of the
more westerly Prussians. Having promised Exelmans earlier in the
evening that he would have Vandamme on the march at the 'petit

point du jour', the first hint of light, in fact Grouchy ordered Vandamme to march at a leisurely 6 a.m. and Gérard two hours later.

It was dawning on Grouchy that the Prussians were not going east, as the Emperor had hoped, but north-west. Yet he was slow to grasp the implications. He followed instructions in looking east, but he failed to look west, where he would soon have heard rumours of far more Prussians.

Grouchy's chief of staff claimed that they had no orders to block Prussian interference with Napoleon's operations, but Grouchy's own report of 10 p.m. demonstrated his awareness that he was supposed to prevent the Prussians from joining Wellington.[12] As soon as it became clear that Prussians were heading for Wavre, common sense dictated that he should get some cavalry into the space between Wavre and the Emperor's location. It should also have been clear that in order to do this he had to get a move on. The quality of 'zeal', characteristic of the British Royal Navy of the day, was singularly lacking in Grouchy.

Looking back on the campaign with hindsight, Napoleon regretted his appointments, and he was right to do so.[13] Had he made Gérard a marshal in April instead of Grouchy, or had he, as he afterwards thought he should have done, given the job to Marshal Suchet, things might have developed differently:

When one looks at results one can commonly perceive what one ought to have done . . . I ought not to have employed Vandamme. I ought to have given Suchet the command I gave to Grouchy. More vigour and promptness were needed than Grouchy had as a general; he was only good at a splendid charge of cavalry; while Suchet had more fire and knew better my way of making war.

Ultimately, for the French this campaign was to turn on the drive and initiative shown by key subordinates, and in choosing such men the Emperor's judgement of personality had let him down.

38

Morning at Quatre Bras

17 June, dawn–2 p.m.

Wellington's army had slept close to its final positions on the battle-field, while new arrivals encamped by regiment beside the roads along which they had approached, all prepared to renew the combat next day. It was a night punctuated by disturbances. Private Clay and a fellow Guardsman, on outpost duty, were surrounded by wounded men crying out for water; being desperately thirsty themselves, Clay's comrade suggested that he keep watch while Clay went to look for water:

> I groped my way about among the sufferers and placed them in as easy a position as I could. Many had fallen in very uneasy postures, and the fact that they were altogether helpless increased their suf-ferings. Some had fallen with their legs doubled underneath them, others lay with the weight of the dead upon them. Having afforded them all the ease that lay in my power, and as all was quiet around us, I took a camp kettle from off the knapsack of a dead man, wended my way a short distance to the rear of our posts where I had observed the appearance of water when advancing after the enemy on the previous afternoon, and I found a narrow channel of water in a ditch which I traced into the wood. It was from here that our brave comrades of the 1st Guards had driven

the enemy in the evening. There was a pond from which I filled my kettle and drank freely from its contents, enjoying it much, whilst in the dark I found my way back to my post where my comrade and the poor sufferers from wounds gladly partook of the contents of the same.

Soon afterwards some movement provoked an outbreak of musketry among the pickets and one of Clay's company was killed. Just before dawn, when all was quiet, he went off again for water:

On arriving at the pond the light of day just enabled me to see that in and around lay the bodies of those who had fallen in the combat of the evening previous, and the liquid we had partaken of was dyed with their blood. I do not remember whether I returned with a further supply, although I am quite aware that I lost all relish for any more of it.[1]

About 3 a.m. Wellington rode back from the Roi d'Espagne in Genappe to Quatre Bras. He still had no news of how things stood with Blücher at Ligny. Sir Hussey Vivian, whose hussars had been on outpost duty, had seen no sign of Prussians, so Wellington sent off his aide Sir Alexander Gordon with a further escort of hussars, to find out where they were. Meanwhile, some Gordon Highlanders made Wellington a fire in a hut and after giving orders to make a probing attack on the enemy outposts, he took a short nap.[2] Gordon spotted French lookouts on the height above Marbais, which suggested that the road to Sombreffe was held by the enemy, but a peasant directed his patrol along a road he said the Prussians had taken and near Mellery they were challenged by an outpost of the Prussian cavalry rearguard.[3]

At daybreak fighting broke out between rival pickets around Piraumont. In a fierce skirmish between German light troops and British riflemen and the veteran captain André Ravard's 13th Light, backed by the 17th Regiment, the French lost 5 killed and 120 wounded, while the allies lost at least 11 killed, 117 wounded and 23 captured. This confirmed to Wellington that the French were still present and moreover determined to hold their ground, but he waited for Gordon to return with news of Blücher's situation.[4]

Costello, in the farmhouse of Haute Cense with the wounded, found that 'the balls kept patting through the doors and windows as we lay there. Such as were able to walk soon started for Brussels; but several of the severely wounded were obliged to be left behind for want of conveyances.' Those who could carried on walking towards the Brussels road, partly shielded from fire from the skirmish by a hedge, until one of them 'heard the cries of a child on the other side; on looking over he espied a fine boy, about two or three years of age, by the side of its dead mother, who was still bleeding copiously from a wound in the head, occasioned, most likely, by a random shot from the enemy.' They took turns to carry the child to Genappe 'where we found a number of women of our division, one of whom recognised the little fellow, I think she said, as belonging to a soldier of the First Royals.'

Indeed, several accounts indicate that many women followed the army to Quatre Bras. One rifleman married a woman who was badly burned there in the explosion of an ammunition caisson. Meanwhile, although the Guards had supposedly parted from their women near Nivelles, that morning Matthew Clay admired 'the heroism of the wife of a soldier of the Coldstream Light Company who fearlessly passed over the bodies of the dead, bringing a supply of provisions for her husband and companions in defence of the wood', and when the baggage train of the 69th was captured later in the day, their women were plundered by the French before being freed.[5]

Once it was light, search parties began to try to find the dead, beginning with the officers. The early morning 'was occupied in burying the officers who had been killed and the men made the best use of their time in fitting themselves out with a good kit' by looting the dead.[6] No doubt some of the women were engaged on a similar mission, making the best of the time before the more timid Belgian peasants moved in.

The battlefield had a distinctive, sweet smell, 'sickening to a degree which can scarcely be imagined. It is a combined effluvium arising from the bodies and from the crushed grass.' And the sight of it was equally stomach-turning: 'Many of the slain were shockingly mangled, some of their innards torn out and scattered all over the ground, others with their heads severed from their bodies, the heads lying, a shapeless mass, covered with blood and brains.' Near Quatre Bras the dead were lying in piles, and cartloads of wounded were setting off for Brussels and Nivelles. A Dutch militiaman watched one such load completed by a Brunswicker who had lost both legs and lay there singing 'Unser alter Stadtverwalter'. Walking back to his bivouac, he slipped over on another dead Brunswicker's bowels, which had oozed out of a bullet wound in his stomach.[7]

Some of the British wounded were lucky enough to be transported from Quatre Bras to Brussels in one of the forty-eight spring carriages of the Royal Waggon Train, directed by a colossus of a man known in the army as 'Magna Carta'. However, the spring wagons only had capacity for four hundred, so most were piled in carts which frequently broke down through overloading. A unit of the Royal Dragoons, among other cavalry squadrons, was 'ordered to the inn of Quatre Bras to assist in conveying as many of the wounded men to the rear as were able to bear the motion of a horse, and a considerable number were removed in this manner to the rear of the position at Waterloo, although several that were severely wounded were necessarily left behind.' The treatment of wounded prisoners was usually generous and humane, at least between the British and the French; both sides recognised that seriously wounded men stood a better chance of surviving treatment by an enemy surgeon than of surviving twenty miles in a cart.[8]

Sir Alexander Gordon returned to Quatre Bras a little before nine o'clock with the information that the Prussians were retreating to Wavre. Everybody in Wellington's entourage assumed that Wavre was a little village just behind Ligny until they spoke to liaison officer Müffling, who exclaimed, 'My God, that's a long way!' Looking at a map, they realised the extent of the Prussian retreat: Wavre was fifteen miles north of Brye.[9]

This was an emergency. If Blücher had retreated that far, Wellington with something like 45,000 men at Quatre Bras and 20,000 near Nivelles was exposed to attack by Napoleon's whole army of 100,000. He had to retreat and retreat fast. He gave immediate orders to fall back to Mont Saint-Jean.

In the spring he had selected the best place in which to fight a defensive battle on each of the approach roads to Brussels and had ordered his engineers to make large-scale maps of these 'positions'. Fortunately, the previous morning, the chief engineer, Colonel Carmichael Smyth, had thought it prudent to send to Brussels for the survey that his department had made of the ridge above Mont Saint-Jean, the battlefield selected in case of an attack from the direction of Charleroi. Wellington's neat copy not yet being ready, the engineers had dispatched the original plan, in the custody of a lieutenant who arrived with the map tucked into his saddle.

At that very moment, Wellington's staff was scattered by French chasseurs. In the mêlée the lieutenant was knocked off his horse and ridden over, and when he came to, his horse was nowhere to be seen. He had lost Wellington's map! After a few minutes of sickening anxiety, however, he found his horse grazing in a garden and retrieved the map, taking it at once to Carmichael Smyth. So, when Wellington called Smyth and asked him for the survey of Mont Saint-Jean, to Smyth's great satisfaction he was able to hand it straight to him.[10]

Wellington then retired to the hut with Quartermaster-General Sir William Delancey and they lay down on the ground over the survey to work out how best to place their troops, with the contours, features and buildings on the battlefield in front of them.[11] It was a unique advantage to know the battlefield so minutely in advance of the battle, but typical of Wellington's thorough preparation. He had also had the Staff Corps make surveys of all the routes his troops were likely to use, identifying bottlenecks and potential defensive positions and describing them with maps and profile drawings: the one that Basil Jackson had prepared of the river Dyle and the route from Gembloux to Wavre was being used by the Prussian staff as they made their retreat.[12] With the deployment sketched out in advance, Delancey's staff could guide the troops into approximately the right positions as soon as they arrived.

*

Marching orders for the infantry were issued as quickly as possible, but an inevitable gloom descended over the army as the rumour spread that they were to retreat because the Prussians had been defeated. Things looked bleak, given that the invincible Napoleon would be snapping at their heels, and the British officers were well aware of the challenge that they faced, since a retreating army was always liable to grow ever more demoralised, and bad troops might disband altogether. 'He sent the worst troops off first,' recalled Fitzroy Somerset, these being in his view the two Netherlands divisions. Wellington allowed the troops that were not moving off immediately to cook, Müffling having offered his opinion that in Germany Napoleon had always allowed his troops to cook in the morning if they had bivouacked late, so they would probably not press ahead immediately.

To reduce overcrowding, the Netherlands cavalry were sent via Nivelles, where they ran into the British divisions that were just arriving from Braine-le-Comte. Thomas Jeremiah and the Welch Fuzileers had just overtaken the 52nd, who – having marched thirty miles to Braine-le-Comte the previous day and having been soaked by a thunder shower during the night before marching on at dawn – were serving spirits. The Fuzileers had had no rations since they started marching the previous morning. 'We marched by them in gloomy silence cursing our Quartermaster for not having provided us with the same dose,' recalled Jeremiah.

At Nivelles the 51st waited for David Chassé's infantry and the Netherlands heavy cavalry to march by. For Sergeant Wheeler, the 'fine looking' Belgian horsemen yielded an unexpected windfall: 'One of the pitiful scoundrels in urging his horse through the gate way, by some means upset the horse and in the fall the fellow lost his purse. It was picked up by one of my section. In this section there is a few old campaigners, we had agreed to stick by each other come what would and all plunder was to be equally divided. This was not a bad Godsend to begin with.'[13]

About 9 a.m. a messenger arrived from Gneisenau's headquarters to find Müffling sitting on the ground with Wellington; speaking in French, he described the situation of the Prussian army, explaining

Gneisenau's anxiety that the reserve ammunition might have been lost and that consequently only one corps was definitely equipped to fight. Wellington 'put some questions' and 'received sensible and satisfactory replies', and then told them that 'he would accept a battle in the position of Mont St. Jean, if the Field-Marshal were inclined to come to his assistance even with one corps only.' Müffling wrote to Blücher to that effect.[14]

Staff Corps officers now rode off to Mont Saint-Jean to direct the troops arriving there to their battle stations, but on the way they found Genappe in chaos. As he walked towards Brussels, the wounded rifleman Ned Costello had also found the area behind the battlefield full of confusion and uproar. Soldiers' wives and other camp followers crowded 'in great numbers, making inquiries after their husbands, friends, &c, for whom they generally are prepared with liquors and other refreshments . . . The crowds of carts, horses, &c, which thickly thronged the roadway, were greeted on all sides by anxious faces and earnest inquiries.' The side of the road near Quatre Bras was littered with 'overturned ammunition carts, demolished guns or guns jammed into each other; and on the road were ambulances carrying the wounded and an endless wagon train with the camp followers of the Scottish troops'. In the narrow street of Genappe this northward-bound column had collided with artillery wagons and food transports from Brussels that were heading for Quatre Bras.[15]

Sir William Delancey found Basil Jackson there, trying to direct traffic, and ordered the grenadier company of the 5th German Legion to 'clear the high road of all carts and carriages as far as Brussels and to suffer nothing but artillery to come up'. Their captain ordered Lieutenant Edmund Wheatley with thirteen grenadiers to clear Genappe, while he went on towards Brussels with the rest. Wheatley, who disliked his captain intensely, anticipated that he would use this excuse to spend the next day in Brussels, which he duly did. He solved his traffic jam by emptying the beef and gin from the commissary carts into the ditch, filling them instead with wounded, and sending them back towards Brussels.[16] Meanwhile, the Netherlands infantry marched round the town through the fields, 'slogging their way through some terrible mud'. At one point some of the soldiers refused to wade through hip-deep water and General Kruse called in a troop of Scots Greys to force them to carry on.[17]

The two light companies of the 1st Nassau who had earlier been sent on picket duty into the Bois de Bossu were however forgotten and left behind, young Heinrich Gagern among them. When the Brunswick Avant-Garde was ordered to retire, they realised that everybody else appeared to have gone: 'Things were becoming scary: the French were already in possession of Quatre Bras, and we had to pass by them at a distance of a rifle shot. Fortunately, they appeared to be too busy plundering the place to be paying any attention to what was going on around them.' The Nassauers hurried off, taking two French stragglers prisoner.[18]

With the last of the infantry gone from Quatre Bras, the British cavalry was left alone waiting in three lines. It was very sultry. As on the previous day, black clouds were closing in, and distant rolls of thunder could be heard. Then, at about 2 p.m., Light Dragoon William Hay watched as 'At a great distance in the wood, on each side of those roads, clouds of dust began to spread over the trees. That dust approached thicker and thicker, and dead silence pervaded our ranks, I thought even the horses were more still than usual, no champing of bits, no clattering of swords. Every eye was directed anxiously to what was passing in the front.'[19] It was an ominous indication that something was about to happen.

39

The Road to Mont Saint-Jean

17 June, 2–10 p.m.

Finally, Napoleon had pounced, but it was too late. Wellington's infantry and artillery were now a minimum of three miles to the north, beyond Genappe, and all that was left facing the French was the cavalry rearguard. Nevertheless, although he had arrived too late to force Wellington to fight at Quatre Bras, Napoleon might still do considerable damage through an energetic pursuit.

Frederick Ponsonby, commander of the 12th Light Dragoons, accompanied cavalry staff and the Duke of Wellington, 'observing the preparations and movements of the immense mass of troops before us. He was occupied in reading the newspapers, looking through his glass when anything was observed, and then making observations and laughing at the fashionable news from London.'[1] When some French howitzers began to lob shells over, 'The Duke told Lord Uxbridge that it was of no purpose to wait: the sooner he got away the better: that no time was to be lost in getting off.'[2] The Duke then trotted off with his staff to Mont Saint-Jean.

The Earl of Uxbridge was reluctant to leave, hoping to get a crack at the French cavalry, and the 9000 British horsemen in three lines behind him were spoiling for a fight. But as more and more of the 10,000 French cavalry that Napoleon had gathered to envelop Wellington's army emerged from one side of the woods, and 6000 of

Ney's cavalry from the other, even the most daring hussars began to think that a retreat was prudent. Uxbridge gave the word and the British cavalry began to pull out at speed: 'a few minutes before, our three lines, with sabers [*sic*] drawn, were watching with breathless interest the approach of the French Cavalry, all, excepting superior officers, having no doubt they were going to be in personal conflict, and now we were retiring literally at a gallop in three separate columns by different roads.'[3]

To protect troops during an orderly retreat, one line of cavalry would delay the enemy by skirmishing with them until the last moment and then fall back onto another line of cavalry, which took over its duty – and so on. Uxbridge's withdrawal in three columns went smoothly until, close to the river Dyle, the French closed in on the rearguard of hussars covering Wellington's eastern column. Sir Hussey Vivian expected John Ormsby Vandeleur's brigade of light dragoons behind him to wait for his horsemen to pass through their line in the approved manner; Vandeleur was twelve years older than Vivian and thus his senior officer. But Vandeleur was generally regarded as stupid and incompetent in charge of cavalry, and instead his brigade cantered off as Vivian approached. A dragon said that 'there was not time for the Hussars to pass through our brigade, the enemy were so close upon them, and had we not got off with the least possible delay the Hussars and our brigade would have been in one confused heap.'[4]

Vandeleur's premature retreat could have been disastrous for Vivian's men had not the weather intervened dramatically:

> The enemy's lines began to close with ours, and when within a short distance, as if a sluicegate had been opened, down came such torrents of rain as quite obliterated from our view even our own advance, this continued with such violence in our teeth, that our position seemed untenable; our horses with spurs stuck in their flanks would not keep their heads to the storm.[5]

In teeming rain Vivian crossed the river a mile east of Genappe, protected against pursuit by some rifle-armed skirmishers of the 10th

Hussars who dismounted and took cover on the far bank. One squadron was cut off and had to cross the river lower down, but they almost all escaped, although they then found themselves retreating along 'a narrow cross-country road, full of holes and of broad, deep ruts full of water from the recent rains. Along this road was most horrid riding, on account of the nature of the soil, which was a stiff slippery clay; consequently, the crowding from the rear pushed many men and their horses into the deep ditches by the road side.'[6]

Napoleon was extremely unlucky with the weather. The torrential rain and howling gales with which the day ended certainly did him far more harm than it did the allies, who had a good head start before it rained. With all the cavalry Napoleon had gathered, many allied troops might otherwise have been cut off and captured. Indeed, as Assistant Surgeon James of the Life Guards acknowledged, had it rained like this the day before, Wellington's artillery might never have reached the army: 'the greater part of the cavalry and artillery were at the distance of nearly 56 miles from the infantry in front and the roads that led to it would have been very difficult if not nearly impassable in some places if the rain which had fallen on the 17th had fallen on the 16th when we were called upon to march.'[7]

The Emperor was nevertheless hugely disappointed and seemed depressed when he greeted d'Erlon mournfully, 'We have lost France. Never mind, my dear general, put yourself at the head of that cavalry and press the English rearguard as hard as you can.' Napoleon accepted that, since he had not believed Ney's assertion that he faced an army, this latest lost opportunity was largely his own fault. Through a failure of communication and the strained relations between Ney and Napoleon resulting from their misunderstanding the previous afternoon, the opportunity to force Wellington to fight in isolation had been lost.

Bonaparte summoned Jacques Subervie's two regiments of lancers to follow Wellington's central column through the town of Genappe. The British army might have been trapped in this difficult bottleneck had the French attacked sooner, or had the torrential rain not made it difficult to outflank the troops behind the town. To cover the lancers Napoleon personally established a twenty-four-gun battery on the river bank and began to pound the British positions behind the village. He had brought a Guard horse artillery battery with his duty squadrons and he shouted to the young officers, with an unmistakable note of hatred, 'Fire! Fire! They are English!'[8]

Wellington's rearguard of infantry, the 95th and the 2nd Light infantry of the Legion, formed square and trudged back through the fields, leaving several lines of cavalry facing the French.[9] On the hill to the north of Genappe the 1st Life Guards formed up across the main road, their bedraggled black horses steaming and snorting in the pouring rain. Surgeon James recalled that 'Captain Kelly, who commanded the rear troop, rode up to ask me if I had any gin in my case. Of this he took a sup and then said: "I should not be surprised if we had a bit of a fight just here. I believe the Duke is surprised that we have not been more pressed by the French before this."'

Below them, nearer Genappe, Uxbridge commanded two lines consisting of the 23rd Light Dragoons and 7th Hussars. The 7th was Uxbridge's own regiment and had the honour of bringing up the rear. And here, at Genappe, they and the Life Guards fought what went down in history as a glorious rearguard action, although not everybody had seen it that way. Soon afterwards, Uxbridge felt obliged to suppress 'reports as false as they were invidious, having been propagated by some enemy of the 7th hussars'. And on 28 June, in case anybody was in any doubt about what had really happened, he wrote to the officers, giving the 'plain honest truth' that became history.[10] According to Uxbridge the gallant charges of the 7th against serried ranks of lances, though repelled, had prepared the way for a decisive charge by the 1st Life Guards that had broken the French.

James's friend Captain Kelly described the action to another cavalry officer in rather less glorious terms:

a body of lancers debouched from the town & Lord Uxbridge ordered the 7th H to charge them; it was unsuccessful, the commanding officer & some few others penetrated, were taken & killed, the rest retired in some disorder. The rear of the 1st Life Guards was fronted in support, but on the enemy pursuing, they

also went about by order. Lord Uxbridge called out to them 'would
they also dessert [*sic*] him'. He had previously rallied the 7th, but
they would not stand or face the pursuing lancers, when Kelly, who
did not belong to the rear squadron of the Life Guards brought
them round & charged with half a squadron & fortunately broke,
pursued & killed many of them. He retired when he found himself
under fire of their supports. They rallied & he again charged them
with equal success ... from other sources, I believe all this.[11]

According to Kelly, not only was the leading squadron of hussars
routed, but the nearest squadron of Life Guards fled before the
French onslaught and the remainder of the 7th also made off, refusing Uxbridge's order to stand and face the French.

James gave a similar account. He was rejoining his regiment after
chatting to a friend in the Horse Guards, when 'from each side of the
houses on the top of the hill, down poured the 7th Hussars and part
of the 23rd Light Dragoons followed by the greater part of the French
cavalry, all in the utmost confusion. So utterly were they routed that
men and horses tumbled into the ditches on either side of the road,
such was their hurry. The French pushed them so hotly that some of
their dragoons were mixed up with our soldiers, and one of them was
killed by my side.'[12]

At this point Kelly turned a half squadron of Guards around and
charged. It was, as James realised, a crucial intervention. 'Had the
Life Guards joined the retreat of the other regiments, it is difficult to
say where the thing would have stopped, and this was an event not at
all unlikely to happen if young troops unused to action were to see
two of the elite British regiments running away at full speed.' Kelly
struck down a colonel and dismounted to cut off his epaulettes as a
trophy and capture his fine horse. In so doing he was attacked by several Frenchmen and, as he later admitted to his wife, would have been
killed had a corporal not joined him and fought by his side until they
had disabled or driven off their enemies.[13] It is possible that he
fought the great French hero Jean-Baptiste Sourd, colonel of the
2nd Lancers, who fell with six sabre cuts and afterwards had his arm
amputated by Larrey.[14] Without Kelly's intervention the British

retreat to Mont Saint-Jean might have turned into a glorious rout. Thanks to Kelly, order was restored.

The fighting continued with a number of confused charges and counter-charges. On the wet cobbles horses slithered and slid into the water-filled ditches either side of the *chaussée*, but only the British 7th Hussars and the French 2nd Lancers suffered significant casualties.[15] Of the squadron of 7th Hussars that charged first, admitted Uxbridge's future son-in-law, only about nineteen got back, he being one. A French staff officer claimed that his brother escorted eleven captured officers to Imperial headquarters and that the booty included sixty umbrellas, discarded by cavalry officers when they fled.[16] Napoleon interrogated one of them, employing the English-speaking Flahaut to interpret, before instructing Larrey to treat the hussar's wounds.[17]

The cannonade at Genappe was audible to Prussian cavalry out-posts about five miles away, and General Treskow, who had taken command of Lützow's Black Lancers after their leader's capture at Ligny, sent a lieutenant to investigate. The Prussians were reassured to discover that Wellington's army had not been trapped by Bonaparte, nor had it retreated in another direction to save itself, but was falling back alongside theirs so that the two armies could still combine:

> I took three picked men of our lancers, with a French guide, and rode in a dreadful storm in the direction of the thunder of the cannon. I fortunately hit the desired point. After inquiry of an English officer, at a picket, how the battle went, he informed me that the English army was obliged to retreat. This was good news for us. After several hours I arrived safe at our bivouac and made my report to the old general, who was also glad to hear this news.[18]

Having been sent ahead to prepare to treat the wounded, Surgeon James was waiting anxiously for the Life Guards to come up the road. 'I soon saw the regiment coming, so covered with black mud that their faces were hardly distinguishable, and the colour of their scarlet uniforms invisible. The ground was a quagmire and if any man took a fall he rose with a coat of mud from head to foot. The horses were in no better case.' As soon as his servant appeared with his surgical instruments, he treated the deep lance wound in a captain's back.[19] The splendidly colourful uniforms of the French were in no better state, for the regular carriage of coal along the road meant that it was 'covered in a black mud mixed like ink, which made our cavalry unrecognisable. Their clothing, men, and horses were painted from head to foot in such a way as to present a black and muddy mass.'[20]

Wellington was worried that Napoleon would manoeuvre round his defensive position at Mont Saint-Jean by marching to the west of it in order to force him to move away from the Prussians. However, Bonaparte did not then know that the Prussians had marched north, nor did he realise that Wellington had preselected a location in which to fight. He was merely driving on for Brussels, pushing the British before him. Napoleon later claimed that, during his advance, he had sent 2000 cavalry towards Hal, the small town ten miles south-west of Brussels at the junction of the main roads from Mons and Lille, threatening to turn Wellington's right and causing him to divert troops there. Given reports of skirmishing, Bonaparte may have sent cavalry in that direction, but Wellington did not divert troops in response to his feints, for he had already deliberately placed 16,500 men with 30 guns at Hal. The town had always been Wellington's preferred defensive position in the event of an attack on Brussels; indeed, if there were to be any such attack, he had expected it from that direction. The troops were there in case more French troops invaded from Lille or Maubeuge, as Wellington had always expected, or, as he later argued, because he expected Napoleon to turn his western flank.[21] It is conceivable that the force at Hal dissuaded Napoleon from an outflanking manoeuvre but, given the difficulty of shifting artillery across country in the prevailing weather, it is unlikely that he ever seriously considered one, as he didn't expect Wellington to halt and give battle. The troops at Hal were not of the highest quality and Wellington might even have felt that his field army was better off without them.[22]

North of Genappe, skirmishing continued as first the Horse Guards and then the Union Brigade protected the last three miles or so of the withdrawal. Napoleon had ordered Victor Albert Dessales, commander of d'Erlon's artillery, to press the British with two horse batteries and, chivvied by the Emperor, he did so.[23] The rain was unbelievable. It fell in buckets on ground that was already saturated by earlier downpours, and ditches filled with water and overflowed. With horses sinking to the knee at each pace, rapid progress off the cobbled road was hopeless. Visibility was very limited and morale sank in Wellington's retreating army. There were clashes between patrols of cavalry and the French captured several baggage trains, herds of cattle and numerous stragglers.[24] In the early evening the troops retreating from Nivelles reached Braine l'Alleud, where there was a stand-off when French troops appeared: they could not fight because neither side's weapons would fire.[25]

At around 7 p.m. Surgeon James climbed the hill just to the south of the straggling village of Mont Saint-Jean and looked around:

> From the top of the ridge of Mont St. Jean the view was of the most tremendous description, commanding the field of Waterloo and an immense tract of country, dark with woods and coloured with columns of troops, both French and English. The storm was breaking up, leaving patches of light and grey isolated showers in different parts of the landscape. At intervals wraiths of vapour were gathering.
>
> The straight chaussee which descended towards the village of Mont Saint-Jean was covered and encumbered with a triple column of retiring cavalry, infantry and artillery, while on each side the country was open for a great space, and would have allowed the enemy every facility in bringing up his forces to attack our flank. Had the ground been drier he might well have done so.

It was undoubtedly the case that had the weather been fine, Wellington's retreat, achieved more or less without loss, would have been altogether more difficult. As it was, however, James had looked round from the ridge that was to become Wellington's front line. To defend it, infantry and artillery were already in position, and north of that point his retreating troops were relatively safe. From the highest part of that ridge Captain Carl Jacobi of the Hanoverian Lüneberg Regiment studied what was going on around him through his field glass. For a while, the rain had stopped. As the cavalry gradually withdrew behind the infantry, with small detachments still skirmishing, he watched more and more troops deploying either side of him and realised that Wellington intended to make a stand here.

From an alehouse called La Belle Alliance, three-quarters of a mile south of Wellington's front line, Napoleon and d'Erlon were also studying the withdrawal. Thinking the enemy was still in retreat, Napoleon ordered d'Erlon, 'Continue to follow them.' But when one of Dessales' horse batteries opened fire, fifteen of Wellington's cannon responded with fearsome accuracy, a shot coming so close that Dessales' horse bolted.[26]

Deciding that a British rearguard must be making a stand to cover the passage of the great Forest of Soignes that barred the way to Brussels, Napoleon deployed Milhaud's cuirassiers and Subervie's lancers east of the Brussels road and placed more batteries on the high ground near La Belle Alliance. With these he feigned an attack. Much of Wellington's artillery responded to the French bombardment and Napoleon began to believe that perhaps the whole enemy army had halted in front of the forest.[27] Nevertheless, the French staff concluded that Wellington's army had only taken up this position to gain time for its artillery train and baggage to get through the bottleneck caused by the trees, before following it towards Brussels in the morning.[28] Napoleon wanted to press the attack, but his generals insisted that it was too late, too dark and too wet, and that the troops needed food and rest.

Gradually the firing died out. British artillery and cavalry moved to the rear, the cavalry leaving a weak line of pickets in front of the allied position. Wellington had reached his chosen battlefield, but at the headquarters that he had established in an inn at Waterloo, just over two miles behind the front line, the staff remained anxious. They were ready to fight the next day, but to have much chance of success they needed Prussian help and they still had no news of Blücher's whereabouts. Had he managed to pull his army back safely, had he found his ammunition, and would he be able to come to their aid?

Lord Uxbridge, later to be created Marquess of Anglesey, had another anxiety. If there was to be a great battle next day he was Wellington's second-in-command and was acutely conscious that if anything happened to the Duke he had to take over, but he had no idea of Wellington's intentions. He plucked up courage to explain his concern to the Duke, who heard him out patiently and then

> said calmly, 'Who will attack the first tomorrow, I or Bonaparte?' 'Bonaparte,' replied Lord Anglesey. 'Well,' continued the Duke in the same tone 'Bonaparte has not given me any idea of his projects; and as mine will depend on his, how can you expect me to tell you what mine are?' Lord Anglesey bowed: and made no reply.
>
> The Duke then said, rising; and at the same time touching him in a friendly way on the shoulder, 'There is one thing certain, Uxbridge, that is, that, whatever happens, you and I will do our duty.'
>
> He then shook him warmly by the hand: and Lord Anglesey bowing, retired.[29]

D'Erlon's divisions camped on and behind a ridge facing Wellington's line, between the château of Monplaisir, on the Nivelles road less than a mile from Hougoumont – an old château with an adjacent farm and walled garden that made a large strongpoint and was held by Wellington – and Plancenoit, a substantial village two miles away to the east, just beyond the Charleroi highway. General Jacquinot placed cavalry outposts in front and on the flanks. Some of Donzelot's men found shelter in houses and barns at Plancenoit, while others cut down boughs of trees in the nearby woods to make substantial huts.[30] The cavalry camped further back, while the corps of Reille, Lobau and Kellermann remained around Genappe where some, again, found shelter in buildings. General Bachelu worked late with his chief of staff Colonel Trefcon in a barn near Genappe, taking the reports of the colonels and generals and learning the effective strengths of their regiments after Quatre Bras. Then they lay down and slept on some straw.[31]

General Foy supped with Prince Jérôme and his experienced assistant General Guilleminot at the Roi d'Espagne at Genappe. Before he went to bed, Foy noted wryly in his journal that he had slept in the same inn during the campaign in the Low Countries twenty-two years ago. During the meal, 'a very competent waiter, who served at table, said that Lord Wellington had eaten at the hotel the night before, and that one of his aides de camp had announced at the table that the English army would wait for the French at the entrance to the Forest of Soignes and that they would be joined there by the Prussian army, which was heading for Wavre.'

This charming story of hotel espionage is vulnerable to the objection that Wellington had not known when he supped there on the night of 16 June that Blücher had been defeated. However, rumours to that effect had reached Wellington's staff and he certainly had the Mont Saint-Jean position in mind. Moreover, it is possible that these atrociously indiscreet remarks were made not on the night of 16 June, but during the day on the 17th, when it is pretty likely that Wellington or some of his staff might have eaten at the Roi d'Espagne. On the whole, it seems more likely than not that these generals really had learned the allied plan from the waiter at the Roi d'Espagne. Although the French feared that Wellington would still try to escape their clutches, and Wellington was still waiting for confirmation of Prussian participation before he would commit himself, in reality the scene was set for a battle next day.[32]

40

Panic Behind the Lines

Waterloo and Brussels, night of 17–18 June

At Brussels people waited anxiously for news. On 16 June the politician Thomas Creevey had dined with an acquaintance in the park and heard gunfire while walking home. Crowds of people were listening on the ramparts and scanning the horizon with telescopes. When, late that same night, his stepdaughter's boyfriend Major Andrew Hamilton, an aide to General Barnes, had ridden in to fetch fresh horses, 'his face black with smoke and gunpowder', he brought the news not only that on Wellington's arrival less than half the army and no cavalry were there, but that the French were already attacking them; 'many English regiments, particularly the Scotch were *nearly cut to pieces.*' Hamilton was full of praise for the British troops but also for Bonaparte's daring attempt to get between the British and Prussian armies. Creevey nevertheless spent 17 June 'free from much alarm' until a Belgian aristocrat told him 'your army is in retreat upon Brussels and the French in pursuit.'[1] The story was confirmed by the arrival of baggage wagons and an influx of wounded men.

At this, a great number of people decided to leave the city. Horses rapidly became scarce and expensive, and many set out on foot or by canal barge. Major Hamilton returned that night to Thomas Creevey's house, saying that Bonaparte's movements had been masterly and that when he left, Wellington did not know where the

Prussians were and had therefore been obliged to retreat to a position twelve miles from the city. He added that the French were 'in tremendous force' but if people did their duty he had no doubt that the French would get 'a very pretty licking'. 'This was by no means a comfortable account,' noted Elizabeth Ord, sister of Hamilton's girl-friend Ann.[2] Sir George Scovell too had ridden back to Brussels on the night of 16 June to change horses, for his black stallion was 'dreadfully knocked up'. He had ordered his brown mare to be ready for 2 a.m. and the stallion for the next day and had eaten a hearty supper. When he returned to Brussels to switch horses again, he told his grooms that Wellington was going to fight in his favourite posi-tion, made arrangements for the luggage in case they had to retreat and wrote final instructions which he locked in his desk, giving orders to break it open if he were killed. He then 'mounted his horse and took leave of us in a very kind manner, expecting never to see us again'.[3]

Magdalene Delancey had been sent to Antwerp on 15 June by her husband, the acting Quartermaster-General. On the day of the retreat from Quatre Bras her servant Maria, 'urged by curiosity, stood in the street, listening to terrible stories, seeing wounded men brought in, carriages full of women and children flying from Brussels, till she was completely frightened. She came and told me that all the ladies were hastening to England by sea, for the French had taken Brussels.' Magdalene got a letter from Delancey late that night: 'He said he was safe, and in great spirits; they had given the French a tremendous beating.'[4]

Meanwhile, north of Waterloo the allied baggage train was stacked up on the road through the forest to Brussels. There, in the late evening of 17 June, Napoleon's feigned attack and the ensuing artillery duel had sparked utter terror, and in this least military part of Wellington's army he finally achieved what he had been trying to induce in the whole army since the retreat began – an uncontrolled rout:

A dreadful panic had seized the men left in charge of the baggage, in the rear of the army, and they ran away with a rapidity that could not have been surpassed even by the French themselves. The road between Waterloo and Brussels, which lays through the Forest of Soigné, is completely confined on either side by trees; it was soon choked up; those behind attempted to get past those before – officers servants were struggling to secure their masters' baggage – panic-struck people forcing their way over every obstacle, with the desperation of fear – and a complete scuffle ensued which might really be called a battle burlesqued, in which numbers of horses were killed, and some lives lost, not mentioning broken heads and black bruises conferred on the occasion.

The road was covered with broken and overturned waggons – heaps of abandoned baggage – dead horses, and terrified people. In some places horses, waggons, and all, were driven over high banks by the road side, in order to clear a passage.[5]

The officers and men deputed to guard a unit's baggage were usually young and inexperienced, or known to be unreliable under fire. Those whose nerve had gone and who had sometimes declared themselves unwell, were given the job – one that most young soldiers did not want – by charitable senior officers. Behind the lines were also very large numbers of men deputed to be officers' servants, responsible for their possessions and spare horses. Nor were the drivers of the artillery train generally noted for their courage; to be fair, they were somewhat vulnerable if overtaken by the enemy, while many of those in charge of vehicles behind the lines were civilian contractors who had no wish to run extraordinary risks. Napoleon almost certainly did have strong cavalry patrols out, since he was trying to discover whether or not Wellington was retreating through the forest, but when the rumour spread that merciless French cavalry were hot on their heels, the result was absolute chaos.

Tupper Carey, Assistant Commissary-General to the 2nd Division, was in the middle of the column trying to get supplies for his battalions:

The servants got rid of their baggage, let it drop on the ground, then, jumping on their animals, galloped off to the rear. Others dispersed in various directions in the wood. The peasantry, carrying provisions in the country waggons, cut the traces of the harness and ran away with the horses, abandoning the waggons. As the tumult progressed down the road with approaching darkness, the apprehension of danger became so general, with the followers of the army as well as with officers and detachments of troops on the way to join their regiments, that the whole went towards Brussels like a sudden rush of water increasing as it went.

Carey was carried to Brussels with the mob. There he slept for a while, and was then told by the Commissary General that all supplies were on the road but nobody knew where, and he had better return to his division, albeit empty-handed.[6]

The outstanding loss in this panic was the Netherlands artillery park. General Carl van Gunckel, commander of the Netherlands artillery, who had been ill at Nivelles during the battle of Quatre Bras, sent one of his staff, Captain Jean-Baptiste Osten, to arrange their accommodation at Waterloo on 17 June. While he was there, a column of reserve ammunition wagons appeared and, not knowing where the artillery park was to be located, Osten sought Gunckel to discover his plans. Osten's account then became somewhat reticent, but he admitted that on 18 June the entire Netherlands artillery staff was at Brussels. Presumably Gunckel had again fallen ill.

In the evening of 18 June, Gunckel sent Osten to find the artillery park, which Gunckel said was then at Vilvoorde, a few miles north of the city. Osten discovered fifty-six deserted ammunition wagons between Vilvoorde and Mechelen and was told that their personnel had panicked and fled. The rest of the train, including two complete 12-pounder batteries, had fled twenty-five miles north to Antwerp during the night before the battle.[7] Another officer found reserve ammunition wagons destined for Adriaan Bijleveld's battery abandoned on the road to Brussels without horses or officers.[8] Apart from the loss of the two 12-pounder batteries, which could have proved invaluable in the battle, this debacle left the entire Netherlands army with no ammunition beyond what they were already carrying.

It seems that at least a part of the Hanoverian reserve ammunition also disappeared, since an officer sent from Captain Rettberg's battery was unable to find it, and Hanoverian batteries ended up borrowing British ammunition.[9] Surgeon James of the Life Guards wrote that:

> Some of the guns in the most important part of the position were almost without ammunition and at times entirely without, and it was from the first so scarce that the Duke had given the most positive orders that they should not fire upon the enemy's cannon, but only on his advancing columns. This arose from a great deal having been sent to Ghent under a mistake, and from the road to Brussels being blocked up by the retreat of an immense number of Belgians and other cavalry, artillery and their waggons.[10]

Much British baggage certainly also fled and some ammunition was probably lost with it.

An artillery park was eventually established behind Mont Saint-Jean; however, when James suggested there was an initial shortage he was probably correct: several batteries were forced to replenish their stock from the stores of those that had not yet been engaged. It is likely that he was also correct to identify this shortage of ammunition as the cause of Wellington's order next morning not to indulge in counter-battery fire but only to fire on attacking troops.

Before long, the road and the tracks behind the allied army were completely blocked by abandoned vehicles, which made obtaining food and ammunition during the night very difficult. The spring wagons used to convey the wounded were unable to get from Brussels to Mont Saint-Jean until 19 June. The situation was exacerbated because – with the exception of Lieutenant Wheatley's detachment, which rejoined the battalion at first light – the entire grenadier company of the 5th German Legion line, which had been sent to police the highway, also fled to Brussels.[11] Elizabeth Ord noticed that 'during the whole of the night between Saturday & Sunday the baggage ... was pouring down the Namur street & the whole of this part of the town was almost impassable from the crowd of wagons, horses & men.' Although she was persuaded that this was normal – and it was true that part of the baggage should have been moving to the rear – such a breakneck panic flight was not standard procedure.[12]

Nor did the flight stop at Brussels. Thomas Creevey received a letter from a friend saying 'he was leaving Brussels as things looked very bad, that in the retreat the 7th Hussars had been entirely cut up & that Lord Uxbridge was certainly killed'.[13] There were other witnesses to the chaos: an officer of the 32nd was brought into Brussels 'when my leg was so swelled for want of proper dressing that they could not tell whether the ball was in or not', having been wounded by a ball on the kneecap at Quatre Bras:

> I was just settled in bed after taking 30 drops of laudanum when a report was spread of our army having been beaten, and were retreating fast, and we expected the French would be in Brussels next day.
>
> I was so stupid from laudanum I knew not what I was doing, till next morning I found myself, with my servant and some wounded men, in a boat, proceeding for this place. The great road from Brussels to Antwerp is by the canal, and never did I witness so much confusion as was to be seen among the people on that day – the road covered with carriages, principally English, and the baggage of the army.[14]

As foreigners and wealthy occupants left, wounded men and fugitives from both Quatre Bras and Ligny crowded into Brussels. No hospitals had been prepared in the city, and the battles had happened so suddenly that the municipality had not even had time to arrange temporary accommodation, so the wounded sat in the street, unless charitable individuals offered them shelter. But there were many warm tributes to the immediate generosity and compassion of the people of Brussels in caring for the strangers discovered on their doorsteps.[15] Now, as after the battle, the city's inhabitants rose to the occasion.

41

The Heavens Open their Sluices

Mont Saint-Jean, 9 p.m.–2 a.m.

'Of all the terrible days and nights of rain I ever saw, that was worse than any of them,' wrote a sergeant of the Scots Greys to his wife.[1]

The break in the storm in the early evening of 17 June did not last, and on the front line Hanoverian Captain Carl Jacobi of the Lüneberg battalion was soon enduring 'the most terrible night of my life'. Their campsite had already been turned to sludge with trampled corn stalks when, after dark, it began to rain heavily again. They had no wood to light a fire and no food had been delivered to them for three days. Nobody could find any water. 'Lost in dull stolidity, the exhausted men threw themselves down on the watery ground, wrapped in their woollen blankets. The incessant rains streaming down on them had made them insensitive to the dampness of their place of rest.' Jacobi had left his horses, coat and provisions with his orderly, but the man was nowhere to be found. It later transpired that his servant, along with many others, had fled into the forest after the first cannonade and then, swept away in a panic behind the army, had ridden to Antwerp.

Wearing only his uniform with its short jacket, Jacobi was saturated. A few men stood over a fire made from wet straw but it gave no heat. His feet had swollen so he couldn't get his boots off. Another officer gave him the blanket belonging to his servant, and Jacobi collapsed on the ground. 'I was reduced to a complete indifference to being alive or not; my limbs collapsed from exhaustion and chill; my soul no longer seemed to dwell in my body. My total exhaustion eventually overcame everything and, notwithstanding my stiffness, I fell asleep.'[2]

Most soldiers were suffering similar misery. A few hundred yards away the Gordon Highlander, Sergeant David Robertson, who had lost nearly half his comrades in the traumatic experience at Quatre Bras, did his best to improvise some comfort:

> We could get no fuel here to make fires, as every thing was soaked with the rain. There was a field of green clover in our rear, of which we cut large quantities, and with some branches out of the hedges made a kind of bed on the ground to keep us from the clay. The place on which we lay was like a marsh, and, for the season of the year, the rain was very cold.[3]

In the same exposed area of the field, a mess of five officers of the 95th Rifles 'were looking at each other with the most deplorable faces imaginable', when 'one of the men brought us a fowl he had plundered, and a handful of biscuits, which, though but little, added to some tea we had boiled in a camp kettle, made us rather more comfortable; and we huddled up together, covered ourselves with straw, and were soon as soundly asleep as though reposing on beds of down.' The rifleman 'awoke long before daylight, and found myself in a very bad state altogether, being completely wet through in addition to all other ills. Fortunately I soon after this found my way to a shed, of which Sir And. Barnard (our commandant) had taken possession, where there was a fire, and in which with three or four other officers I remained until the rain abated.'[4]

The Hanoverian light infantry of the Legion, who had served with the 95th as rearguard during the day, did rather better. They found themselves at the farm of La Haye Sainte, where there was something of a party. Their commander, Major Georg Bäring, had the livestock slaughtered and pieces of meat shared out, although many of the men were too tired, gloomy and apathetic to try to light a fire in the pouring rain. Rifleman Friedrich Lindau, the former apprentice shoemaker who had run away to join the Legion in 1809, left his post in the kitchen garden to try to find some straw to sit on. Lindau, blond, blue-eyed, five foot nine inches tall and strong, was now a veteran of five years campaigning with the light infantry, something of a rogue but a very tough fighter. He met his younger brother Christian fetching straw for his nearby gun battery just as a barrel of wine was discovered in the cellar. Lindau went to fill his canteen, which was soon emptied by some men from the 1st Light battalion whom he met at the door. A second canteen went to a friend in a patrol from the Bremen battalion, but they went back and filled two more canteens. Lindau then made several more trips to the cellar to bring wine to his mates on picket duty in the garden. At midnight the trusty veteran took his post as sentry at the end of the garden facing the enemy, whose outposts were half a mile away, sat on his pack and fell asleep.[5]

The two Nassau companies forgotten earlier in the Bois de Bossu at Quatre Bras had reached the ridge above La Haye Sainte in the early evening, relieved to be back with their regiment and not prisoners of the French. It was the first time that the pampered young subaltern Heinrich von Gagern, who normally rode a little black horse, had ever walked a full day's march. He had eaten nothing but dry bread for two days, had suffered a sudden bout of nausea in the morning, and had then been roasted and subsequently soaked. When his coat became too heavy with water to carry, a soldier had taken it for him, and they had trudged on through the mud. Gagern piled some straw on the ground and fell asleep in the rain, but slept for only three hours. He now stood by the fire, trying to get warm. His portmanteau was with the baggage, but the baggage wagons had disappeared so he could not change his clothes.[6]

Seventeen-year-old ensign Jack Barnett was in an even worse plight. His Highland Light Infantry only reached their camping ground at 10 p.m., 'fatigued to death, & too late to build huts or light fires. I was sent out with a party for wood & water, before I could find which, it was 12 o'clock. I came into the Regt. & threw myself down on the ground at the first place I came to, without even a greatcoat & raining very hard, I fell asleep directly.'[7]

Even the elite of the cavalry were miserable. Surgeon James's Life Guards camped in the forest just beyond Waterloo. 'It was quite dark but the soldiers lighted some fires amidst the trees; as I found myself cold, chilly and wet to the skin, and I had given almost my last drop of gin to Kelly which I now regretted, I thought my only chance to avoid being utterly benumbed was to slip off all my clothes and put on a flannel jacket and a pair of worsted stockings that I had in my valise.'[8] Surgeon William Gibney of the 15th Hussars recalled:

> Officers, men and horses were completely done up with the long march of the day before and the continuous moving on this day, having very little to eat during the whole time. We were up to our knees in mud and stinking water, but not a drop of drinking water or a particle of food was to be found in the villages. We were half famished. We had marched and starved from our quarters in the village to Quatre Bras, and now had added a little fighting to starving and marching.

They found some straw and boughs of trees 'to make a rough shelter against the torrents of rain which fell all night; wrapping our cloaks round us, and huddling close together, we lay in the mud . . . notwithstanding the pouring rain, mud, and water, cold, and the proximity of the enemy, most of us managed to sleep.'[9]

In the villages at the edge of the battlefield there was widespread disorder. In pouring rain in Braine l'Alleud, nearly two miles west of La Haye Sainte, Dutch troops fought their own looters and there were summary executions. One captain obtained food for his men by forcing the bakers to bake and then guarding the building to prevent British soldiers breaking in.[10]

The British divisions that followed the Netherlanders from Nivelles paused at Braine l'Alleud before setting up encampments near Merbe Braine.[11] Thomas Jeremiah's Welch Fuzileers had begun to feel the wolf biting, for hard marching and little sleeping is none so pleasant without nourishment. By the evening of the 17th we were greatly fatigued from the extreme inclemency of the day's weather and from marching nearly 8 French leagues since 6 o'clock in the morning in the greatest rain that ever I saw, the heavens seemed to have opened their sluices and the celestial floodgates bursted open ... all we had about us was completely soaked ... our blankets which was on the back of our knapsacks were completely drenched.

Moving into the fields 'up to our knees in mud', while 'it continued to rain with the utmost fury', they 'pitched our blankets up to shelter us from the rain' and sent a party to obtain provisions from Braine l'Alleud, but the town was already full of soldiers 'all busy employed in getting rations not by a regular distribution out but by marauding. It was utterly impossible to get anything for love or money.'

At some point Jeremiah looted the château of Mon Plaisir on the Nivelles road. To his 'great mortification the house had undergone a complete ransacking and plundered of every portable article' and what couldn't be carried off had been smashed. He admired the statues, obelisks, fountains and cascades, like a tourist, and then thought of the wine cellar; having made the descent, he found two Germans there who had apparently drunk themselves to death. Undeterred, Jeremiah and his mates filled their canteens with wine and brandy and then began to look for money. Discovering 130 silver dollars in the guard dog's cage, they then made off and returned to their unit, where the spirits made some men quite drunk because of their empty stomachs.[12]

William Wheeler and the West Riding light infantry were luckier. They found that 'one man in the village was selling brandy and hollands [gin], the money picked up a few hours before procured us plenty of both'. It also enabled them to obtain bread and cheese, which 'was very acceptable as most of us had in the hurry of packing up neglected to provide ourselves with food. This neglect was natural enough in the young soldier but unpardonable to we old campaigners.' Wheeler got drunk enough to be 'wet and comfortable', and they sat on their knapsacks until daylight 'without fires, there was no shelter against the weather: the water ran in streams from the cuffs of our Jackets, in short we were as wet as if we had been plunged over head in a river. We had one consolation, we knew the enemy were in the same plight.'[13]

Indeed, many of the French infantry were still marching after dark. They struggled knee-deep in mud, unable to see each other in the pitch black, while the rain fell once again in torrents. Battalions got mixed up, men made their way as best they could. Lieutenant Jacques Martin's division turned into a shapeless mob. They set up camp near La Belle Alliance; the houses they had passed were quickly commandeered by generals, their servants, their horses, their aides and their secretaries, not to mention the commissariat, none of whom liked camping when they could avoid it. To get rid of unwanted visitors they shouted, 'This is the lodging of general or marshal so and so.' Deprived of shelter, Martin's regiment manoeuvred in the mud until they found their allotted position and sat down in the ice-cold rain and bitter east wind, on ground churned to sludge by the movement of thousands of men and in which the artillery had made deep ruts that had filled with water.

Believing that Wellington still needed time to gather his army together, they were not expecting to fight another battle for several days. There was no straw, no wood, no food and no prospect of getting any, and they found themselves on cultivated ground so saturated that the body sank comfortably into it. They still lacked rations because of the rout of the baggage train at Quatre Bras, for reserves of bread, rice and brandy had been pillaged and spoiled in the disorder. They moaned a lot, cursed those who had sent them there, then slept. Corporal Louis Canler, whose 28th Regiment camped close to Martin's 45th, was not so easily dissuaded from marauding, though this time he found only some wood and a small sheep. They decided to keep the sheep for next day, but made a fire with the wood and slept by it in the rain.[14]

The Imperial Guard was little better off. They had turned off the road after passing through the town of Genappe in order to leave the cobbled *chaussée* clear for the artillery, but found the paths almost impassable, and lost all order trying to pick a way through the fields. The shortest standing crops they pushed through were three or four feet high and they were all covered with water. Hippolyte Mauduit's grenadiers struggled on for two miles or so and camped in an orchard by a farm not far from Imperial headquarters. Many of them had lost their shoes and those of the rest had about 3 lb of clay attached to them. Two or three complete regiments of the Guard reached the village of Glabais, a mile north of Genappe, around midnight. The rest had lost all cohesion and were dispersed around the countryside marauding.[15]

Napoleon rode back about two miles from La Belle Alliance along the cobbled road to a smart building called Le Caillou that had been chosen by Pierre Baillon, the *Fourrier du Palais*, and Frédéric de Guerchy, *maréchal des logis*, to be his palace for the night. It was a substantial farm on the *chaussée*, abandoned by its inhabitants after being vandalised and pillaged by Brunswickers. All was bustle there, but his room was not yet ready so he lay down on a bundle of straw by a bivouac fire and ordered supper. The Imperial *vaguemestre*, Captain Coignet, was supervising the parking of the coaches and wagons belonging to headquarters. Chief surgeon Larrey had claimed one of the barns for his hospital should it be needed next day, his doctors checking their instruments while Imperial grooms scoured the outhouses for fodder for their horses. The first battalion of the 1st Chasseurs of the Guard marched in to guard the palace and camped in the orchard. The cook started work in the kitchen, unhappy that the wagon with the Emperor's tableware was missing in the darkness. The Emperor's room was cleared and his own campaign furniture replaced what had been there. They set up his folding bed, a silver washbowl and his folding leather armchair, with portfolios in reach and maps on the table.[16]

Once his room was ready, Napoleon's valets removed his saturated coat and pulled off his wet boots, and in dry clothes the Emperor sat by the fire in his leather folding chair. There he worked out a deployment and plan of battle for the following morning, hoping that Wellington would still be there to fight one. The plan envisaged the troops closing up as soon as possible in the morning, in order to attack at the earliest opportunity. His duty aides, Juvénal Corbineau, Charles de la Bédoyère and Charles de Flahaut, rode off to the various army corps to distribute deployment instructions and to establish the true situation of Napoleon's own forces.[17]

Meanwhile, General Milhaud sent in the intelligence that his cavalry patrols had reported significant numbers of Prussians retreating north towards the town of Wavre through the valley of the river Dyle.[18] In his memoirs Napoleon claimed that this led him to order Grouchy to send 7000 men to Saint-Lambert, a village situated on high ground just to the east of Wellington's position, but this was fantasy, since there was no mention of Saint-Lambert in Soult's letter to Grouchy the following morning.

Napoleon was confident that the Prussians could not yet fight another battle. If his *Mémoires* have a grain of truth in them, he expected them to head for Brussels and he feared that Wellington would slip away through the forest that night to join up with them. In that case, his problem would be dealing with the united armies, but the battle would not be tomorrow.

His valet Mameluk Ali recalled that as soon as he had succeeded in removing Napoleon's saturated boots, the Emperor dined and then slept, while Ali lay down in his usual station on the floor outside Bonaparte's door. Napoleon's pages and aides shared the ground floor with him, while senior officers such as Soult slept on straw on the floor above and junior staff occupied the stables and sheds. Napoleon's principal valet, Louis Marchand, had been delayed when his coach overturned in the rain and only turned up at Le Caillou an hour after the Emperor went to bed. He had been there two hours when the Emperor called him to ask what the weather was doing, to be told it was still raining hard.[19]

Napoleon woke again about two o'clock, probably as a result of the arrival of Grouchy's evening report, saying he thought that some Prussians were retreating north-east but that others were heading north-west to join Wellington, and assuring Napoleon that if he discovered the main mass was heading for Wavre he would make sure that he cut them off from Wellington. In fact, Grouchy had wasted too much time working out which direction he should take. The more energetic and determined Prussians were already several hours and miles ahead of him.

Napoleon spent some time with the secretaries of his cabinet dictating correspondence relating to political problems that were emerging at Paris. At three he sent first orderly officer Gaspard Gourgaud to ascertain the state of the ground and investigate whether the artillery could manoeuvre. 'You could tell that he was impatient to be able to attack,' recalled Marchand. The Emperor gave orders to his duty equerry to have his horse ready by seven.[20]

At about the same time that Napoleon received Grouchy's opinion that some Prussians might be heading for Wavre, Wellington received a firm commitment from Blücher that Bülow's corps would march at daybreak, followed by the rest of his army, to join him. Blücher's promise confirmed Wellington's resolution to stand and fight. In the small hours he wrote the duc de Berri an accurate report of the situation, warning that Napoleon might sidestep his defensive position by marching through Hal and overwhelming the troops he had left there. Should that happen he asked Berri to take his French royalist army further north to the fortified port of Antwerp and to persuade King Louis to go there. He also wrote to the Governor of Antwerp, and to his dancing partner and close friend Lady Frances Webster, warning her to be ready to move to Antwerp at a moment's notice.[21] Should he be defeated, he evidently intended to retreat to Antwerp himself.

Wellington's staff and senior officers passed the night in houses close to the Duke's headquarters at Waterloo, each man with his name chalked on the door of his quarters. In Thomas Picton's cottage the general slept fitfully in severe pain, thanks to the musket ball which had broken two of his ribs at Quatre Bras. Determined to continue to command his division, he had not shown the wound to a surgeon who might have forced him into a hospital, but had got an old servant to bind it up and it was now blackened and swollen.[22]

The three veteran battalions of Major-General Sir John Lambert's brigade reached Waterloo during the night and 'crept into any hole we could find'. This brigade had just returned from New Orleans, had only been together in Belgium for a week, and had just made a forced march of more than forty miles from Ghent. They were luckier than the troops in the field, for they found 'cowsheds, cart-houses, and all kinds of farmstead buildings for shelter'. Twenty-four-year-old grenadier Sergeant William Lawrence was the illiterate son of a small farmer from Bryant's Piddle in Dorset. In the hard times his father had lost his land and become a labourer and Lawrence, having run away from apprenticeship to a cruel builder, had joined the army and been shipped first to South America, then to Portugal, then to North America, twice achieving promotion to reach his present rank. Yet even in Lawrence's long experience this was exceptional misery: 'I never remember a worse night in all the Peninsular War, for the rain descended in torrents, mixed with fearful thunder and lightning.'[23]

Lawrence's commander, Arthur Heyland, distinguished in Spain and wounded at the siege of Badajoz in 1811 and the battle of Roncesvalles in 1813, was also in the village, and was writing a last letter to his wife, to be delivered only if he was killed:

My Mary, let the recollection console you that the happiest days of my life have been from your love and affection, and that I die loving only you, and with a fervent hope that our souls may be reunited hereafter and part no more.

What dear children, my Mary I leave you. My Marianna, gentlest girl, may God bless you. My Anne, my John, may Heaven protect you. My children may you all be happy and may the reflection that your father never in his life swerved from the truth and always acted from the dictates of his conscience, preserve you, virtuous and happy, for without virtue there can be no happiness.

My darling Mary I must tell you again how tranquilly I shall die, should it be my fate to fall, we cannot, my own love, die together – one or other must witness the loss of what we love most. Let my children console you, my love, my Mary.[24]

As was the custom before a battle many similar letters were written that night, but perhaps none was quite so beautiful and touching as this.

42

The Prussian March

Wavre to Saint-Lambert, 17 June, 5 p.m.–18 June, 11 a.m.

Thanks to early starts and good fortune with dry weather, the Prussians were a minimum of ten miles ahead of Grouchy and late in the afternoon of 17 June one of the two corps that he had failed to detect at all crossed the river Dyle and camped to the west of the town.

At two in the afternoon of 17 June Gneisenau had reported from Wavre to the king of Prussia on the previous day's defeat, expressing disappointment that because of the slow speed of concentration of Wellington's army the Duke had been unable to make a positive contribution to their joint struggle. He reported that Wellington now wanted to fight next day if they could reinforce him with one or two corps. They would do so willingly, Gneisenau wrote, if they had ammunition, but the ammunition for two of his corps was missing.[1]

Given the condition of their army, Gneisenau had reservations about the wisdom of Blücher's brave determination to support Wellington, for it was highly risky to fight on with two corps protecting a further forty thousand defenceless men. Although well aware that the misunderstanding with Bülow had been disastrous for the Prussians, he was upset at the Duke's failure to help them: after all, Wellington had assured them the day before that his army could be concentrated within twenty-two hours of the first cannon shot, and there had been, as far as he then knew, only a tiny French detachment to deal with at Quatre Bras. Indeed, he was to express his frustration a few days later to Prime Minister Hardenberg: 'The Duke of Wellington had promised to strike the enemy in the rear; he didn't come either, because his army, heaven knows why, couldn't concentrate in time.'[2] Undoubtedly this had increased his distrust in Wellington, whom he saw as arrogant and selfish; but he was nevertheless totally committed to the cause and determined to support Wellington if it was safe to do so.

Late in the afternoon of 17 June, to Gneisenau's intense relief, he got news that most of his ammunition had not only escaped the French, but was approaching Wavre. Georg von Pirch's artillery commander had located the column on the Namur road before the French got to it and had turned the wagons to the north and led them to safety. There was now enough ammunition, Gneisenau grudgingly admitted, to fight, even if with only two-thirds effectiveness; as he wrote a few days later, 'the fate of Europe was at stake and so we risked the battle'.[3] He pronounced himself satisfied that they were well enough equipped to march to join Wellington and fight the next day as Blücher wished.

'Gneisenau has given way! We are going to join the Duke,' announced Blücher triumphantly to the wounded liaison officer Henry Hardinge and embraced the Englishman, who recoiled at the smell of the noxious garlic-based ointment applied to Blücher's bruises. 'Ich stinke etwas!' apologised the field marshal.

Early in the evening the ammunition wagons of I and II Corps finally began to trundle over the Dyle bridge into the town, and, three hours later, Thielmann's vanguard followed. Before the downpour, marching had been easy, but the going had got slower and slower, muddier and muddier, and it was late at night before Bülow's tired men made camp just south-east of Dion-le-Mont, a village three miles east of Wavre.

Before midnight Blücher received a dispatch from Müffling, the Prussian liaison officer, confirming that Wellington's army had reached Mont Saint-Jean and was prepared to give battle next day if the Prussians could support them with one of their corps. Von Grolmann replied that Blücher was on the way with his whole army and would have Bülow's corps on the march from Dion-le-Mont at daybreak, followed immediately by Pirch's, with Ziethen's and Thielmann's ready to follow, apologising that because the troops were exhausted and some had not yet arrived, he could not set out to join Wellington earlier.

Soon afterwards Blücher sent orders to his generals to do what he had just promised, and to clear the roads of baggage,[4] while during the night and the early morning the infantry and artillery of I and II Corps received fresh supplies of ammunition. It was decided to send Bülow's corps first because it was fully equipped, having not yet fought, although unfortunately the weather had slowed it down so that it was still three miles from Wavre. There had been no choice but to employ Bülow to cover the retreat because only his troops could fight back if attacked.

At two in the morning Bülow sent out marching orders, warning his troops (in order to forestall marauding) to carry as much food as possible since the neighbouring villages offered little in the way of plunder, and around sunrise his vanguard crossed the river Dyle into Wavre. Before seven o'clock Prussian patrols took a look at Grouchy's camp at Sauvenière, ten miles south of Bülow's, and satisfied themselves that Grouchy's infantry had not yet marched off. The Prussian staff calculated that a single corps would be sufficient to hold the line of the Dyle against Grouchy, and Thielmann was given the job.

Wellington's German 1st Hussars had been selected to 'transmit communications to the Prussian generals and obtain information on their approaching columns', and their patrols had made contact with Prussians during the night; in the morning two of their officers brought Wellington the first news of Bülow's approach.[5] Between 8 and 9 a.m. a Prussian cavalry patrol reached the village of Ohain, a mile and a half north-east of Smohain at the eastern end of Wellington's defensive line, and was directed to Major Taylor of the 10th Hussars, the regiment known as 'the Prince's Dolls' from the way that their royal colonel the Regent liked to tinker with their pampered appearance. Taylor was in charge of a chain of lookouts (known as vedettes) protecting Wellington's eastern flank. While touring his lines, he had already seen two bodies of French cavalry uncomfortably nearby, and had watched a French cavalry patrol heading eastward. The Prussian patrol delivered the message that Bülow and 25,000 men were three-quarters of a league away.[6]

Müffling spent the early morning devising contingency instructions for the Prussians in case of various attacks by Napoleon. He recommended that should the Emperor attack Wellington's right, the Prussians should march the eight miles from Wavre to Ohain by the quickest route and provide Wellington with a reserve. Should he attack Wellington's centre or left, one Prussian corps should march seven miles to Saint-Lambert and Lasne to attack the French right flank, while another should march via Ohain to reinforce Wellington. Should the enemy march on Saint-Lambert in order to separate the two armies, the Prussians should make a stand there, while Wellington attacked the French in their flank and rear.[7] He put his suggestions to Wellington, who said, 'I quite agree.' Just then, a hussar officer delivered the news that Bülow's vanguard was approaching. Although nobody could locate on a map the place the Prussians were supposed to have reached, Müffling told his aide to show his proposal to Bülow if he passed him on his way to Wavre.

However, the Prussian approach was not going as smoothly as Blücher and Wellington would have wished. Soon after Bülow's vanguard had left Wavre, a major fire had spread from a bakery to neighbouring houses, causing panic because there were ammunition wagons nearby. The infantry marched round it by clambering through neighbouring gardens, but the cavalry and artillery had to wait while pioneers put the fire out. As a result most of Bülow's corps was delayed by two hours, while both Pirch's behind it and Ziethen's, which was waiting for it to pass, were also held up.[8] The roads, which in good weather were no more than sandy tracks, proved appalling after heavy rain, especially for artillery, which frequently bogged down to the axle and had to be hauled free with ropes. Bülow's vanguard of hussars and fusiliers reached Saint-Lambert, two and a half miles east of Wellington's left flank at Smohain, around 10.30 a.m. but the rest of General Michael von Losthin's leading 15th Brigade did not close up until noon, and the other brigades only trudged in during the afternoon.[9]

Having received Müffling's recommendations, Bülow issued him with a warning. There were problems – he had only two brigades with him and did not expect the rest for some hours:

> If it turns out that Wellington's centre or left wing is attacked, General Bülow is willing to cross the Lasne at Lasne with his corps and form up on the plateau between La Haye and Aywiers, thus attacking the enemy in his right flank and rear.
>
> My advice is that then another Prussian corps should go via Ohain, so that, according to circumstances, it can support the most threatened point of the English position. A third Prussian corps can go via Maransart and Sauvagemont to cover IV Corps' left flank and rear. The remaining fourth corps would form a reserve at Couture.[10]

As soon as Bülow reached Saint-Lambert he sent out scouts. Major Andreas von Witowski, leading a strong detachment of Silesian Hussars, explored the roads to the village of Maransart; this lay three and a half miles further up the Lasne valley, less than a mile east of Plancenoit, the village around which much of the French army had camped. Witowski did not see a Frenchman until he approached Maransart itself.

Simultaneously, Bülow sent Major von Falkenhausen with a hundred Silesian horsemen south-eastward to establish a chain of outposts connecting Bülow to a reconnaissance force he had posted the previous day at Mont Saint-Guibert, a village on the far side of the Dyle valley eight miles to the east. This was an area where they might expect to encounter Grouchy's patrols and ambush messengers travelling between Grouchy and Napoleon, and indeed, after three miles Falkenhausen ran into a French cavalry detachment and became involved in a sharp skirmish; prisoners taken by the Prussians claimed to have been sent by Grouchy to make contact with Napoleon's army. Meanwhile, patrols from Mont Saint-Guibert clashed with Exelmans' dragoons, who were inspecting the bridges over the Dyle.

While Prussian cavalry outposts intensified what was already proving to be a successful effort to inhibit communication between Napoleon and Grouchy, Bülow's chief of staff, Generalmajor von Valentini, set off to explore the terrain to the west of Saint-Lambert. Taking a local farmer as their guide, his party first identified another problem: their path westward was blocked by a deep, flooded valley, across which there were only three practical routes. On the other side, however, there was a wood, apparently unoccupied as yet, that would serve for a bridgehead.

Riding on through the wood they emerged in sight of Fichermont, a château and hamlet which was Wellington's eastern-most infantry outpost. They could see French patrols, but their own approach appeared to have gone totally undetected by the enemy.[11] The French, it seemed, had no idea that their right flank might soon be in danger from a Prussian attack.

43

Finding Breakfast

Mont Saint-Jean, 18 June, 4–10 a.m.

'The first hours of this 18th of June were bleak and cold, with a damp, chilly wind,' wrote Surgeon James; the 'change from intense heat to great cold' concerned the medic, especially as the 1st Life Guards had 'neither food to eat nor spirits to drink'. The rain had stopped before dawn, but everything in their bivouac under the trees at the edge of the forest was soaking wet, 'everyone was covered with mud, and it was with the greatest difficulty that the men managed to get fires lit, some breakfast cooked, and their arms cleaned and their ammunition dried.'[1]

Staff officer George Scovell, ordered to clear the road near the village of Waterloo of abandoned wagons, found General Lambert's newly arrived infantry division there, hoping to cook breakfast before marching to the battlefield. He made a bargain with the officers that they could use the wagons as firewood if they would guarantee to clear the road; this they did, though it took several hours. Meanwhile Lambert sent his veteran brigade major, rifleman Harry Smith, to find Wellington and get orders. When Smith located the general at the *château-ferme* of Hougoumont, Wellington told him to draw up the new brigade at the junction of the Nivelles and Brussels roads and then reconnoitre the quickest route to join General Best's Hanoverian brigade, also part of General Lambert's command, which

was situated to the east of Picton's division. Wellington was glad of
the opportunity this gave him to strengthen his weak left wing.[2]

In the fields behind the village of Mont Saint-Jean the 15th
Hussars were preparing for action. 'This we did in darkness, wet, and
discomfort,' recalled their surgeon, 'but a night spent in pouring rain,
sitting up to the hips in muddy water, with bits of straw hanging
about him, does make a man feel and look queer on first rising.
Indeed, it was almost ludicrous to observe the various countenances
of us officers, as, smoking cigars and occasionally shivering, we stood
round a watch fire giving out more smoke than heat.' They waited for
orders, impatient to move, 'for both horses and men were shaking
with cold'. Told to form up on the higher ground above
Hougoumont, a mile south-west, they went to its farmyard to look
for forage for their horses and, after a long dispute with the sentries
of the Guards who had orders to refuse all admittance, they succeeded in extracting some corn and drinking water.

Guards light infantryman Matthew Clay had reached the hill
above Hougoumont the previous afternoon and made a 'Portuguese
tent' out of two blankets and five muskets against the rain. He had no
opportunity to take advantage of it, however: during the artillery
duel when Bonaparte feigned an attack in the late evening, his company had been called to arms and in the course of their advance he
had fallen, after which he spent the night soaked through on sentry
duty in a ditch on the French side of the château's orchard. Nor was
there any respite: in the morning Clay's company fetched fuel to
light fires and straw to sit on from a barn in Hougoumont, and
shared some bread and a piece of a slaughtered pig. Clay changed his
underclothes, putting on homemade linen he had taken from the
pack of a dead German at Quatre Bras, and then started cutting
away inconvenient branches and making holes to shoot through the
orchard hedge. After much effort preparing the orchard for defence,
they were promptly marched off through the topiary garden and the
southern courtyard of the château to the kitchen garden that bordered the buildings to the west.

Others had endured the conditions in equal discomfort, but
managed to find some consolation. Young Jack Barnett 'never woke

till the Assembly blew, & woke with my side in a puddle of water'. His Highland light infantry were also in the open fields near Merbe Braine, the hamlet three-quarters of a mile behind Hougoumont. 'I got up with my teeth chattering, but I begged a smoke from a man in my compy. out of an old dirty pipe, who had a little tobacco, this warmed me, & made me once more fit for a march.' General Hill took a few of them to escort him while he made a reconnaissance. The French were only half a mile away, with d'Erlon's corps camped all over the high ground just across a narrow valley. Those who remained behind were given half an allowance of gin, which, one wrote, 'was the most welcome thing I ever received'.[3] A rifle officer from the same brigade had been out skirmishing in the evening, and then spent the night on outpost duty, unable to evacuate casualties:

> Our wounded were in a desperate situation, and those who were not wounded were like so many half drowned and half starved rats. At about seven o'clock however to our great satisfaction the skirmishers were called in, and as a reward for our nocturnal labours, we had leave from General Adam who commanded our (Light) Brigade to plunder three farm houses which were near us! The idea of a fire was a most consoling one! Chairs, tables, sofas, cradles, churns, barrels, and all manner of combustibles were soon cracking in the flames, our fellows then proceeded to the slaughter of all the living stock the yard contained, and in less than an hour we had as delicious a breakfast of beef, pork, veal, duck, chicken, potatoes and other delicacies as I ever made an attack upon.[4]

This licensed plundering seems to have been general near Merbe Braine. Thomas Jeremiah and a friend set out through the drizzle, armed with cudgels and haversacks, to find food. Just beneath the Welch Fuzileers' camp they saw 'a pig and calf closely pursued by 4 or 5 German soldiers, some with knives and others with their bayonets', and would have demanded a share had they not feared the Brunswickers would kill them. At Merbe Braine they scuffled with more Brunswickers to get some flour and took a large milk pan from a farmhouse. Sergeant William Wheeler wrote home:

> The morning of the 18th. June broke upon us and found us drenched with rain, benumbed and shaking with the cold. We stood to our arms and moved to a fresh spot to get out of the mud. You often blamed me for smoking when I was at home last year but I must tell you if I had not had a good stock of tobacco this night I must have given up the Ghost. Near the place we moved to were some houses, these we soon gutted and what by the help of doors, windows, shutters and furniture, we soon made some good fires.[5]

Two miles away from Merbe Braine, on the extreme eastern flank of Wellington's army, the Orange-Nassau Regiment had their sleep interrupted by an outbreak of shooting, and with it the rumour that 'the French had managed to break through at our right wing and were upon us in full force.' The rumour soon proved unfounded but, wrote Sergeant Johann Döring, a tanner from Herborn, south of Dillenburg in Hesse, 'only someone who has been through all this, on a pitch dark night with constant rain and even a thunderstorm, can have an idea of what that did to our spirits.' His friend, Sergeant Achenbach, a veteran of the Spanish campaigns and a huge man, found that he had burrowed so deep in the mud that he couldn't get up, and 'broke out into a series of the most violent curses'. Later they went raiding for food:

> the farms, mills, etc. located between the lines were plundered, both by our troops and the French, for cattle, pigs, geese, ducks, chicken, potatoes and other edibles. Some of the buildings were burned down. To lose no time, all of this, half boiled or half grilled, was devoured with the greatest haste and appetite; no wonder after several days of fasting ... During all this plundering, our soldiers and the enemy's were the best of friends, and nobody gave a thought to the prospect that in a few hours they would meet in a fight for life and death.[6]

A mile to the west, Sergeant Robertson of the Gordon Highlanders was roused at daylight and ordered to stand to arms: 'I never felt colder in my life; every one of us was shaking like an aspen leaf. An allowance of gin was then served out to each of us, which had the effect of infusing warmth into our almost inanimate frames, as before we got it, we seemed as if under a fit of ague.' Another half-mile west, on the other side of La Haye Sainte, Carl Jacobi woke up to find that he was lying in a pool of water, puddles having spread over any slight depression. The grey figures around the smoking fires 'looked like monuments made of rock, numbly staring down, unreceptive to the outside world . . . no cheerful word was heard from the merriest among the men'. In the dull light they stirred. 'They rose one by one from their wet bedding', unrefreshed, with 'tired, pale faces and the sound of stifled groans'.[7]

After standing guard until six, Robertson's Highlanders were 'ordered to clean ourselves, dry our muskets, try to get forward, and commence cooking'.[8] Some of those who had been wounded at Quatre Bras but had refused to leave the ranks were now persuaded to go to Brussels, and most of the fit officers took the opportunity to scribble on a scrap of paper a last will and testament, or a last letter home, and hand it to one of those who was walking to safety. 'Kempt's and Pack's brigades had got such a mauling on the 16th, that they thought it as well to have all straight. The wounded officers shook hands and departed for Brussels.'[9] At one point they were joined by the Duke of Richmond and his son William Pitt-Lennox, who had broken his arm in a horse race. Richmond cheered the officers – since his wife was a Gordon, the Highlanders were a favourite regiment – by telling them the news he had learned from Wellington: the Prussians were on their way.[10]

A few rays of fitful sunshine broke through as the wind began to blow away the rainclouds. At dawn Major-General Count Kielmansegge, commanding the Hanoverians half a mile to the Highlanders' right, had sent Captain Carl Jacobi's brother to find the ship's biscuit in the baggage wagons, but he had found the Brussels highway completely blocked by abandoned vehicles and had returned empty-handed. Despairing of breakfast, the officers had begun to supervise the removal of wet cartridges from the men's muskets when, miraculously, the battalion's sutler drove up with a wagon full of foodstuffs. This enterprising Jew had stayed with them since 1813 and the officers flocked to him; having gasped at the prices he was charging, they then bought everything he had, suffering some pangs of remorse as there was insufficient food to give any to their men. With the sun now shining more strongly on and off, Jacobi found a patch of dry ground and went to sleep again.[11]

Close by, Tom Morris sat with his friend Sergeant Burton, sharing the unwanted gin rations of those of their men who had been killed in the previous evening's cannonade. Burton told Morris to save some for after the battle and Morris replied that he thought 'very few of us would live to see the close of that day: when he said, "Tom, I'll tell you what it is: there is no shot made yet for either you or me."'[12]

The Netherlands chief of staff Jean-Victor Constant and the Prince of Orange, mounted on his horse Waxy, were visiting General Bijlandt's brigade, which at that time was in front of the Highlanders on the southern slope of the ridge to the east of the Brussels highway. To their right was a sand quarry above the farm of La Haye Sainte. Bijlandt's battalions were short of ammunition, having used most of what they carried with them at Quatre Bras, and nobody could locate the artillery park with the reserve ammunition. While Constant sent thirty cavalry to clear the road and try to find some ammunition wagons, the Prince of Orange promised the men food and water, and he contrived to find some, remaining with them for breakfast. 'He sat on the same ground as us to eat, he was hungry just as us,' recalled a star-struck militiaman.[13]

Staff officers began to scurry about on horseback, ensuring troops were in the right position. The old Peninsular veterans meanwhile found innumerable little jobs to fill the time, learned over years, in order to maximise their comfort during the fighting and their chances of survival; above Bijlandt's Netherlanders, a Scottish ensign reported what he saw looking northward from the ridge at the bulk of the allied army:

A moving mass of human beings – soldiers cleaning their arms and examining the locks, multitudes carrying wood, water and straw from the village and farm of Mont St Jean; others making large fires to dry their clothes, or roasting little pieces of meat upon the end of a stick or ramrod, thrust upon the embers. A few bundles of straw had been procured, upon which our officers were seated. Though nearly ankle-deep in the mud, they were generally gay, and apparently thinking of everything but the approaching combat ...[14]

Looking forward, south, from the ridge, the Scottish ensign then observed the allied cavalry vedettes on watch for enemy activity, far away in front, prancing about. 'Presently we could see, by the trampling of their horses, that they had become uneasy; one, then another, fired his carbine, retreated, loaded, advanced, and fired again.' The allied lookouts disappeared from view and then he saw enemy skirmishers in extended order, advancing and firing and, finally, enemy columns.[15]

About six hundred yards away to the west, Lieutenant Edmund Wheatley was also looking forward from where Alten's division of the King's German Legion stood above La Haye Sainte. Detached the previous day to clear the road at Genappe, he had slept in the Forest of Soignes but, determined not to miss the battle, had rejoined his battalion with his thirteen grenadiers. Like many others, he was fascinated by the spectacle of the approaching enemy army:

on the opposite heights we could perceive large dark moving masses of something impossible to distinguish individually. Where the edge of the ground bound the horizon, shoals of these gloomy bodies glided down, disjointing then contracting, like fields of animated clods sweeping over the plains, like melted lava from a Volcano, boding ruin and destruction to whatever dared impede its course. It had a fairy look and border'd on the supernatural in appearance. While gazing with all my utmost stretch of vision on the scene, little Gerson [the surgeon] struck me on the shoulder saying, 'That's a battle, my boy! That's something like a preparation! You'd better have stopped with Notting [the captain of his grenadiers] at Brussels. I must be off to the Hospital and I hope to see you there.'

They shook hands and Assistant Surgeon Gerson left for the field hospital which was being established at Mont Saint-Jean. Wheatley, disconcerted by his friend's black humour,

> walked up and down for some time and felt very uneasy that I had left no letter of remembrance behind me.
>
> I fancied the occupation of all at home. It was about six o'clock. Just then (a cloudy drizzly morning) my brother, I thought, was unconcernedly packing up orders or reading calmly some new publication. I concluded you, my Dearest Eliza, you, whom I always regretted, I was certain was asleep innocent and placid. The pillow that supported you was unconscious of its lovely bur-then.[16]

Wheatley had seen hard fighting in the Pyrenees and France, but unlike the surgeon he had never been involved in a really big pitched battle and their conversation had suddenly brought home to him the strong possibility that he might never see home or his beloved Eliza again.

44

Tyrans, Tremblez!

Napoleon's line, 18 June, 4–10 a.m.

The previous evening Napoleon had ordered his men to march forward at first light to attack as early as possible. Now, as he learned how scattered his army was, how many were out marauding, and how the minor roads were unusable with mud, reluctantly he postponed his assault. He ordered his generals, however, to make sure that their troops prepared their arms and cooked and then marched to the positions that he had designated in last night's order, so as to be absolutely ready to fight at nine o'clock.[1]

He rested in bed, then got up, shaved, and cut his nails, while thinking about the battle to come and looking frequently out of the window at the weather. Having dressed, he dictated to General Gourgaud, pacing up and down and still concentrating on the weather outside: as the drizzle stopped and the wind got up, his excitement grew.[2]

The Emperor was desperately anxious to start the battle, but even his more relaxed timetable was proving difficult to meet. Reille's men, starting from around Genappe, stood to arms at first light and marched off at five, but were then ordered to stop to cook and prepare their weapons. As a result of this halt they were not to reach the Emperor's headquarters at Le Caillou until about nine in the morning, by which time Napoleon – having been told by Reille of his delay and by Drouot that it was taking an age to get the Guard together – had postponed the attack again.

Moreover, Drouot gave his opinion that it would be some hours before the ground was dry enough for the artillery to manoeuvre. Alongside Napoleon, he was the army's leading artillery expert and Napoleon respected his judgement. Because their number and quality was the greatest asset of the French army, the performance of the cannon was crucial. And although the French artillery had always been better than that of other nations, in this campaign their numerical strength in guns was more marked than usual.

D'Erlon's corps meanwhile had time to kill: they dried, oiled and prepared their weapons and then cooked. Corporal Canler's company made a stew of the sheep acquired the previous evening with some of the flour he had found near Frasnes, but their cook, lacking salt, added saltpetre instead, which turned out to ruin the flavour. Lieutenant Martin's men cooked the veal they had obtained the day before, drinking a lot of eau de vie while waiting for orders.[3]

The Emperor ate his breakfast with his brother Jérôme, General Reille, *Grand Maréchal* Bertrand, *Major-Général* Soult, his principal secretary Hugues-Bernard Maret, duc de Bassano, the trusty General Drouot and Marshal Ney. Ney urged an early attack in order to prevent Wellington from escaping, but Napoleon objected that Wellington now had no choice but to fight. Jérôme warned his brother about the conversation with the waiter at the Roi d'Espagne, and the British expectation of Prussian intervention. The Emperor replied that after the sort of defeat the Prussians had suffered and with a substantial body of troops in pursuit, Blücher could not possibly link up with Wellington within two days.[4]

Soult was warier of Prussian intervention than the others and regretted the absence of Grouchy's troops; he knew the ground of old, for twenty-one years ago when chief of staff to General Lefèbvre in 1794, he had driven an Orangist-Austrian army off the plateau of Mont Saint-Jean. He also spoke of the obstinate defensive qualities of the English infantry, but Napoleon swept his doubts aside.[5]

When Napoleon asked for Reille's opinion of the English, Reille

emphasised the firepower and tenacity of British troops and recommended outmanoeuvring them, in preference to a direct
assault. Napoleon said they were lucky that the English were standing to fight and that this would be a famous battle that would save
France. He would make full use of his abundant artillery, he would
charge the allied line with his cavalry to make them show themselves, and when he was sure of where the English troops were
positioned, he would march straight at them with his Old Guard.[6]
Like everything Napoleon said that morning, this semi-jocular
speech was calculated to raise morale. He exuded optimism, especially when his generals pointed out difficulties, and concluded by
saying that if his orders were executed well, they would sleep that
night at Brussels.

The weather had begun to brighten up around seven o'clock: the
clouds had risen, there was fitful sunshine and a driving wind promised to dry the ground quite quickly, since this rich agricultural clay
soil was well drained. About half past nine Napoleon decided to
inspect the enemy positions, taking with him Jean-Baptiste Decoster,
who had been persuaded to leave his alehouse on the *chaussée* in
order to act as a guide. The Emperor wished to mount the horse that
had been waiting for him since seven but the duty equerry had gone
for breakfast, so his page, César Gudin – whose father, a school
friend of Napoleon from the artillery academy at Brienne, had been
killed during the Russian campaign of 1812 – helped him into the
saddle, giving him such an energetic hoist that Napoleon almost
rolled over the other side. '*Petit imbécile!*' exclaimed Napoleon, '*va-t-
en à tous les diables*,' and he rode off, leaving the discomfited Gudin to
mount and ride lamely after. After a few hundred yards the staff
parted and the boy saw the Emperor returning. '*Mon enfant*,' he said
kindly, 'when you help a man of my size to mount, it needs to be done
gently.'

Bonaparte sent his chief engineer, General Haxo, to ride close along
the enemy line to check that there were no defensive entrenchments.[7]

Marshal Soult remained at Le Caillou to write an order to
Marshal Grouchy, timed at 10 a.m., informing him of the sizeable
Prussian column Milhaud had identified the previous day heading

through Gentinnes to Wavre, since Grouchy seemed to be unaware of it, and telling him that the Emperor was about to fight Wellington at Waterloo:

> ... Therefore, His Majesty desires that you should direct your movements towards Wavre, in order to close up with us, to be in touch with our operations and link communications with us, pushing before you the Prussian army corps that have taken that direction and which may have halted at Wavre, where you should arrive as early as possible. You will follow the enemy columns that may be to your right with a few light units, in order to observe their movements and bring in their stragglers.
>
> Inform me immediately about your locations and your march as well as your news of the enemy and do not on any account neglect to link your communications with ours. The Emperor wants to hear your news very frequently.[8]

Soult issued no order to march to the battlefield, and there is no hint that Napoleon might have done so during the night, as he later insisted; Soult did rebuke Grouchy for his failure thus far to establish between them the communication chain of light cavalry outposts that the Emperor had ordered. There is evidence that Grouchy had finally made efforts to link his cavalry patrols with Napoleon's, but he had started too late and the Prussians were already disrupting progress.

In order to facilitate a meeting between his cavalry patrols and Grouchy's, Soult strengthened his own outposts on the eastern flank. He sent an order to a redoubtable veteran light cavalryman, Colonel Marbot, to take a battalion of light infantry and his 7th Hussars to the extreme right of the French line behind the château of Fichermont, a mile and a half to the east, placing 200 infantry half a mile further on in the Bois de Paris, the wood east of Fichermont, and a squadron of hussars at Lasne, the village a mile beyond the wood on the stream just below Saint-Lambert; he was to keep watch on the bridges over the Dyle at Moustier and Ottignies two miles further east. Each detachment was to establish a chain of posts so that news could be passed at the gallop to the battlefield. The object was to establish contact with Grouchy's troops and Marbot was to transmit all reports directly to the Emperor. Although Napoleon did not tell Marbot so, his troops would also serve to provide an early warning of any Prussian incursion.[9]

While the generals surveyed the enemy, the French troops made a show of marching into line. As Napoleon described it, the French advanced in eleven columns. The light cavalry of Reille's II Corps deployed in three lines astride the Nivelles *chaussée*. II Corps formed two lines, covering one and a quarter miles between the Nivelles and Charleroi roads, with Jérôme's division on the left, Foy's in the centre and Bachelu's on the right. D'Erlon's I Corps marched into a position with its left near La Belle Alliance and its right opposite La Haye, mostly out of allied sight behind a ridge onto which the artillery began to haul its wagons and cannon. Jacquinot's cavalry formed three lines opposite Smohain and Fichermont. Kellermann's heavy cavalry formed behind Reille, with his batteries on each flank. Lobau's VI Corps and the light cavalry divisions of Domon and Subervie remained in column either side of the Charleroi road. Milhaud's cuirassiers formed up behind d'Erlon's infantry. The Guard cavalry marched into line, with Guyot's heavy cavalry behind Kellermann and Lefèbvre-Desnouëtte's light cavalry behind Milhaud. Between them marched in the infantry of the Guard, which halted in six lines either side of the Charleroi road ahead of Rossomme. The reserve of Guard artillery remained behind, with the paved road clear ahead of it, so that it could deploy rapidly.

The reality was far less choreographically exact: in fact the Guard only set off from Glabais at ten, so that the battle was already under way by the time they reached their position at Le Caillou, while other bedraggled columns were still marching in.[10] Nevertheless, the precise manoeuvres of the front-line troops were watched by the opposing army with admiration, if not trepidation. Tricolour flags, cavalry guidons, the little pennons of the lancers, rippled in the fresh breeze. Drums beat, trumpets sounded, and the military bands played the old revolutionary song, '*Veillons au salut de l'Empire*', that had become an Imperial anthem, calling all the peoples of Europe to join the French in overthrowing tyranny. With its rising crescendos of

> *Liberté! Liberté! que tout mortel te rend homage.*
> *Tyrans, tremblez, vous allez expier vos forfaits.*
> *Plutôt la mort que l'esclavage!*
> *(Liberty! Liberty! Let every mortal pay you homage.*
> *Tremble, tyrants! You will pay for your infamy.*
> *Better to die than to be enslaved!)*

it was a call aimed chiefly at erstwhile friends in the other army, the formerly liberated Belgians and the Germans who had once again fallen under the yoke of kings.

At that moment Napoleon rode by to review his troops. He loved his army and his army loved him. They were old comrades who had shared many trials and triumphs and they were now fighting a necessary war for liberty and the revolution against tyranny, invasion and oppression. 'Never was "Vive l'Empereur!" shouted with more enthusiasm, never was more absolute devotion visible in the faces, gestures and voices of his soldiers. They were delirious.' Helmets and shakos were raised aloft on sabres and bayonets as the soldiers cheered the Emperor.[11] The troops were not sparkling with gold braid, for this was largely a scene of drab grey and blue greatcoats and cloaks, most of them coated in mud, but the commitment and the professionalism were impressive for all that.

Napoleon rode half a mile back from La Belle Alliance past his faithful aide Georges Mouton's columns, marching forward with the infantry to the left and the borrowed cavalry of Generals Domon and Subervie to the right of the main road. Then the Emperor dismounted and climbed up a hillock near the farmhouse of Rossomme, from which his staff had borrowed a table for his maps and a chair. It was the highest point on the battlefield. He pored over the map, wearing his signature grey greatcoat and black hat. Excluding staff and support services, he had about 74,500 men – 53,000 infantry,

15,000 cavalry and 6500 artillery – and 254 guns. Napoleon thought Wellington's army stronger, but he had 74,300 men and far fewer guns – only 156.[12] The Emperor considered matters for a quarter of an hour, and then dictated his orders.

45

The Position

Wellington's line, 18 June, 10–11 a.m.

Wellington's front line extended roughly a mile either side of the Charleroi road. About 10 a.m., the Duke rode along the line with his staff, 'looking entirely unconcerned and as smart as if they were riding for pleasure'. He was dressed in his usual blue coat under a 'grey great-coat with a cape, white cravat, leather pantaloons, Hessian boots, and a large cocked hat *à la Russe*.'[1] He was riding his dark chestnut charger, Copenhagen, a former racehorse and a grandson of the legendary racehorse Eclipse.

Wellington's tail of staff was usually at least forty strong, although his personal staff consisted only of his military secretary, Fitzroy Somerset, and about eight aides-de-camp, nearly all sons of dukes. The Adjutant and Quartermaster-General each had his own suite of half a dozen officers, and there were the commanding officers of artillery, horse artillery, engineers and their assistants. Sometimes Uxbridge, who was wearing his dashing blue, red and gold hussar uniform, was present with his cavalry staff, while Prussian liaison officer Müffling and his orderly officers were usually to be found close to Wellington. Finally there were the representatives of allied powers: Miguel de Alava representing Spain, Napoleon's inveterate Corsican enemy, Carlo Pozzo di Borgo, representing Russia, Charles, Baron Vincent, representing Austria, and others, all attended by their own aides. On this tour Wellington was also accompanied by the Prince of Orange and his substantial staff.

The command structure beneath Wellington was eccentric and pliable. Lieutenant-General Sir Rowland Hill nominally commanded II Corps but on the battlefield he actually commanded the troops on the right wing, including the 3rd Netherlands Division. Henry Paget, Earl of Uxbridge commanded all the cavalry, including the Netherlands cavalry, while Wellington generally left the artillery commanders to control their own arm. Sir Thomas Picton commanded the left wing, including the 2nd Netherlands Division. The young Prince of Orange, nominally in command of I Corps, controlled the centre of the position between the two cobbled roads with advice from Constant and Carl von Alten, 'despite the fact', Constant pointed out, 'that the Duke gave his orders directly to the troops on the right, being the Guards Division and the Brunswick troops'. The Prince of Orange chose for his principal station the highest point on the plateau in the centre of the 3rd Division.[2] Wellington took up position ahead of the centre of the Guards division and gave orders to particular units as he saw fit.

Wellington's army of 74,300 men was of very uneven quality and he placed little faith in large parts of it. Just over 26,000 were British, and of these some were inexperienced, but there was a hard core of reliable, veteran infantry. Thirty-one thousand were German: 5100 constituted the King's German Legion, all highly trained and experienced, including the most reliable cavalry; 12,100 men from King George III's kingdom of Hanover were of unknown quality, some being young militiamen with rudimentary training; the surviving 5450 Brunswickers were inexperienced, but had proved their commitment and determination at Quatre Bras, while Wellington was less sure of the 7200 Nassauers from the Rhineland. He and his staff expected little from his 15,200 Dutch and Belgian soldiers. Altogether he had nearly 56,000 infantry, 13,000 cavalry and 5000 artillerymen.[3] The figure of 74,000 was however a paper total; most units had far fewer men in the field since many were serving as servants and baggage guards, and most of these had run away to Brussels during the night.

The troops on Wellington's extreme right occupied Braine l'Alleud, although the post there was detached, three-quarters of a mile from the continuous line of troops further east. General David Chassé's 3rd Netherlands division, 6700 strong, bivouacked in and around the town with their sixteen guns. The place should have been fortified, and the only company of sappers and miners in the army had been summoned from Hal for that purpose, but they got lost during the night, arriving at Waterloo at 9 a.m. on the 18th to find that it had been barricaded by the Netherlanders. The division at Braine was the first link in a chain of outposts intended to obstruct the manoeuvre round the army's western flank that Wellington antic-ipated. Detached eight miles away further west still were two brigades of about 6000 men under Sir Charles Colville at Tubize on the Mons–Brussels road, and Prince Frederick's Netherlands division, about 10,500 strong, nearer Brussels at Hal, placed there in case Napoleon marched that way to draw Wellington further away from the Prussians or additional French forces advanced on Brussels from that direction.[4]

Wellington's front line roughly followed that of a lane running five miles along a ridge from Ohain to Braine l'Alleud; above Hougoumont, however, where the lane continued to Braine l'Alleud, his troops occupied the ridge that it had followed previously as this bent sharply to the north above a fairly steep-sided valley to Merbe Braine. The heights above the valley made a strong defensive posi-tion, should Napoleon try to turn Wellington's western flank, and were densely occupied: Hugh Mitchell's brigade stood four hundred yards behind Hougoumont. Behind them, the three brigades of Sir Harry Clinton's division of nearly 7000 men stood in reserve to the west of the Nivelles road on the triangular plateau between Hougoumont and Merbe Braine. Carl du Plat's German Legionaries were in front, with Frederick Adam's Light Brigade behind them and Hugh Halkett's Hanoverian militia furthest back, close to Merbe Braine. Hugh Halkett was the younger brother of Sir Colin, 'a bright, active cheery man speaking German very badly' in the words of one of his colleagues. He had started as a captain in his brother's 2nd Light infantry of the Legion and commanded that fine battalion before being given a brigade of raw Hanoverians. The divisional artillery, Major Augustus Sympher's German troop, and Captain Samuel Bolton's foot battery, each of five 9-pounders and a howitzer, accompanied them. Also in reserve on the right, between Halkett's men and the Nivelles road, stood the Brunswick Corps, reduced to 5450 men and sixteen guns.

The château farm of Hougoumont stood three hundred yards south of the front line and formed a sort of forward bastion, a break-water against French attacks on Wellington's right wing. The ridge described above, on which Wellington's army stood, turned to the north at the point that the dirt lane from Ohain met the Brussels–Nivelles cobbled *chaussée*. This then ran on south-west towards the French lines through a cutting, beyond which it passed over another sunken lane to Braine l'Alleud on an arched bridge and continued through another cutting. At the bridge the *chaussée* was blocked with felled trees and a troop of the 15th Hussars stood guard. From the bridge an avenue lined with trees led three hundred yards south-east to Hougoumont.

The previous evening the Duke's staff had made it clear that Hougoumont was 'to be defended to the utmost'. A supply of spare ammunition was placed in the buildings, and the pioneers of the 2nd German Legion from La Haye Sainte were sent there to help the light companies of the Guards make loopholes in the walls and build shooting platforms.[5] In the morning Lord Saltoun's two light companies rejoined the 1st Guards on the ridge behind the farm, to be replaced by the 800 men of his first battalion of the 2nd Nassau light infantry under Captain Moritz Büsgen, led by an aide across from the far left wing. They found the farm deserted but already prepared for defence. Private Johann Peter Leonhard took one look around, decided the place was a death trap, and said a quick farewell to the world.[6]

South of the buildings and walled garden was a wood, three hundred yards long and about the same wide. This had been occupied a little earlier by 330 Hanoverian riflemen, comprising companies of the elite volunteer Jägers and one each of the Lüneburg and Grubenhagen battalions.[7] Büsgen reinforced the riflemen in the wood with his *voltigeurs* and a reserve company. He placed his grenadiers in the buildings, two companies in the walled garden, and one company lining the hedge of an orchard that ran on eastward from the walled garden for another two hundred and fifty yards. James Macdonell's Guards light troops remained in a kitchen garden on the west of the buildings, so the estate had an initial garrison of 1330 specialist light infantry.

On the high ground north of Hougoumont stood the Foot Guards, still over 3000 strong, with Sir John Byng's brigade behind the château and Peregine Maitland's further east. In front of Maitland were Major Kühlmann's troop of Hanoverian artillery and Captain Sandham's battery, each of five 9-pounder guns and a how-itzer. The front-line infantry were supported by Colquhoun Grant and Wilhelm von Dörnberg's light cavalry brigades of 2400 sabres.

To the east of the Guards in the front line stood Carl van Alten's division, reinforced by the 1st Nassau Regiment. The men under Alten's command consisted, moving east, of Colin Halkett's 1780 British survivors of their baptism of fire at Quatre Bras, Friedrich von Kielmansegge's 3000 Hanoverian regulars and Christian von Ompteda's brigade of the Legion, 1530 strong. As positioned by Assistant Quartermaster-General James Shaw, Alten's men were in line, but could form a chequerboard of oblongs at any threat of cav-alry. Shaw was only twenty-seven but highly experienced. After distinguishing himself with the rearguard during the retreat to Corunna in 1808 he joined the staff of the Light Brigade, serving with bravery and sense in the Peninsula, and winning Alten's trust.

Around Alten's battalions the plateau broadened out, so that they were not able so easily to hide behind the crest; nor, unless they advanced close to La Haye Sainte, did they have the same height advantage over any assailants that the Guards enjoyed. Anticipating trouble from cavalry, Shaw instructed them to form oblongs with a frontage of four companies front and back and just one at each side, this being quicker to evolve than a square.[8] In front of them were Andreas Cleeves's and Major William Lloyd's batteries of guns, Lloyd's being hidden in rye over head-high.[9] On his early morning inspection Sir Augustus Frazer, commander of the horse artillery, found that the Prince of Orange had moved Lloyd's battery away to the crossroads. He had it restored to its original position and deployed Sir Hew Ross's battery of 9-pounders from the artillery reserve where the Prince wanted guns, with two on the *chaussée* and four in front of the sunken lane on the ridge above.

Behind these troops was the Household Brigade of heavy cavalry, theoretically 1226 sabres, although their officers reckoned subsequently that there were far fewer of them in the field; to their right were the excellent 3rd German Hussars, 622 strong on paper. The latter were commanded by fifty-nine-year-old Frederick von Arentsschildt, 'the Duke of Wellington's favourite old hussar', who had taken part in all the Duke's principal victories and was the author of the manual on light cavalry outpost duty.[10] Further back were the three brigades of Netherlands cavalry, a total of 3500 horsemen; to their east, across the *chaussée*, was Mont Saint-Jean farm, about five hundred yards north of the crossroads of the Charleroi *chaussée* with the Ohain lane.

About two hundred yards south of this crossroads was a second outpost at the farm of La Haye Sainte, occupied by the 2nd Light infantry of the King's German Legion. They had camped there the previous evening, but their commander Georg Bäring had been ordered to send his pioneer detachment to fortify Hougoumont and naturally assumed that he was not supposed to defend the farm they marched away from. Every battalion stationed nearby raided La Haye Sainte for straw, firewood and food and the big, west-facing barn door on the south side of the farm was broken up and burned, leaving a huge gap. Assistant Quartermaster James Shaw complained that 'nothing whatever was done during the night towards its defence; in place of which, the works of scaffolding, loopholing, building up gates and doors, partial unroofing, throwing out the hay and securing a supply of ammunition, should have been in progress all the night', but in the morning his proposals for strengthening the farm and placing a British battalion there were turned down by headquarters staff.[11]

In fact, the German battalion stationed there was one of the best in the army, but unfortunately there were fewer than 400 men in it, whereas Shaw argued that the garrison should have been 1000 strong. Partners in crime of the 95th Rifles, Bäring's green-coated riflemen had undertaken the majority of the least appealing tasks doled out during the Peninsular campaign and, as aide to Alten, their commander had been with them from the start. When a job cropped up from which the chances of survival were virtually nil, it was usually assigned to the light infantry of the Legion, so to be told to defend La Haye Sainte to the last man came as no surprise. 'As the day broke on 18 June, we sought out every possible means of putting the place in a state of defence, but the burned gate of the barn presented the greatest difficulty. Unfortunately, the mule that carried the entrenching tools had been lost during the day.' Friedrich Lindau helped build a barricade across the road at the top of the orchard out of carts and farm implements. With great difficulty they knocked three gaping holes that passed for loopholes out of the wall so that they could fire onto the road, but no reserve supply of rifle ammunition was placed in the building.

Whose fault was the poor state of defence of La Haye Sainte? James Shaw, who might have been to blame, was vociferous in his attack on Wellington's staff, and it does seem to have been the case that they were myopically concerned with Hougoumont to the exclusion of other priorities. Shaw absolved his friend Bäring, but it should have been apparent to Bäring long before the battle started that he had insufficient ammunition, and it ought to have been possible to find supplies from somewhere, even though there were acute logistical problems on the morning of the battle and there are signs that the Hanoverian reserve ammunition, like that of the Netherlanders, had disappeared.

If La Haye Sainte itself was inadequately prepared and garrisoned, it was very well supported from behind. Both the rifle-armed first battalion of the 95th, the best skirmishers in the British army, and the excellent riflemen of the 1st German light, were positioned close behind the farm to pick off assailants. Hew Ross's battery was also one of the best in the army, though its position on and next to the cobbled road was too conspicuous.

To the east of the Charleroi road, Wellington and Delancey placed the troops that had suffered most at Quatre Bras. Picton's 5th Division had been the best infantry in Wellington's army but it was reduced to half strength. Lining the hedge behind the sunken road to Ohain were two companies of the 95th Rifles, with three companies stationed 120 yards further forward in good cover behind a small knoll and in the sand quarry situated beneath it.[12] To the east of the 95th were Major Thomas Rogers's battery and Adriaan Bijleveld's six-gun horse artillery battery. Beyond them were the battalions of Bijlandt's Netherlands brigade who had also suffered heavy losses at Quatre Bras, with their *voltigeurs* and *tirailleurs* out ahead skirmishing. Bijlandt's strength was probably about 2400 men.

Behind the guns and the Belgians, in a full second line, were the veteran British battalions of Sir James Kempt's brigade (reduced to fewer than 2000). The 32nd Cornish were nearest the road, with the 79th Camerons to their left and the 28th Gloucesters to the left of the Camerons. An officer estimated that the 32nd only had about three hundred men in the field, and if this was so it reinforces the suggestion that the paper strengths of many battalions were much higher than numbers on the ground, a point on which officers present are unanimous.[13] The Union Brigade of heavy cavalry, which had never yet fought a battle, stood behind Kempt's men. Its commander Sir William Ponsonby, whose late father had kept 'the best hunting establishment in Ireland', was the nephew of the leader of the Whig opposition in Parliament, a man who greatly admired Napoleon. Sir William had more experience of fighting than his men and with his cousin Frederick had distinguished himself in a Peninsular cavalry action at Llerena in 1812.

At this point the Brussels road was cut deep into the hillside, so that the right flank of the 32nd was secured by a steep embankment. Sir Denis Pack's severely depleted brigade was to their left and even weaker, with only about 1700 survivors of Quatre Bras. The Royal Scots, the 42nd Black Watch, the 44th Essex and the 92nd Gordon Highlanders had only twelve officers to command about 330 men. Not only was Picton, the division's redoubtable commander, still concealing his musket wound, but three out of four of Pack's regiments were commanded by majors, two colonels having been killed.

Although the field in front of the hedge lined by Bijlandt's brigade was fallow, that on which this division stood had been recently ploughed, as had one to the west of La Haye Sainte, below the German infantry. After the troops had marched across it, the ploughed land took on 'the consistency of mortar' as Sergeant Robertson of the Gordons put it. Many of the men had slept submerged in mud, and now they stood in mud up to their knees.

Major Carl von Rettberg's battery stood just east of Bijlandt's men in an excellent position above the sunken lane to Ohain, protected by a high bank and partly concealed by a hedge, in which they cut gaps. From this point Rettberg could send enfilading fire across the slope below the British line to the west. However, he had used more than half his ammunition at Quatre Bras and had been unable to get more. Behind his guns and stretching east were Charles Best's Hanoverian Landwehr, who had emerged with credit from Quatre Bras, and Ernst von Vinke's 2366 untried Hanoverian militiamen, with Prince Bernhard's brigade largely in front of them. The 2nd Orange-Nassau battalion still had precious little ammunition for their French muskets and remained in reserve. Bernhard's light troops were disposed to skirmish from the farms of Papelotte and La Haye, in a marshy valley nearly a mile east of La Haye Sainte, and from the village of Smohain and the château of Fichermont further east on the south side of the stream. With them was a half-battery of three guns. Sir John Ormsby Vandeleur's brigade, with 1012 sabres, provided support.

Five troops of horse artillery were attached to the cavalry under Uxbridge's command, in central reserve, and there was a reserve of artillery, consisting of three batteries.

As far as possible, the British infantry was on the reverse slope of the ridge out of sight of the enemy and, once firing started, lying down. Few of them were exposed to view. Only the front-line artillery was clearly visible on the front face of the ridge and even then, some guns were partly concealed and protected by the banks of the Ohain lane or hidden in rye. The skirmishers were also exposed, and visible if they had not been able to conceal themselves in the tall crops, but in extended order they were not worth a cannonball.

Sir Hussey Vivian's brigade of 1240 hussars, still accompanied by Gardiner's 6-pounder battery, covered the left flank. The ground to the east of the position was open and without natural protection, but Wellington assumed his eastern flank would be covered by the Prussians and that they would soon join him and greatly reinforce the weaker eastern part of his line. An artillery officer with Gardiner's troop watched Vivian being given his orders:

Sir William de Lancey pointed to a direction to our left by which the Prussians would come, and, that Sir Hussey Vivian was on no account to move his Brigade from the position assigned to it until he had put himself in communication with the Prussians, and they, the Prussians, had joined or reached his left. Sir William de Lancey showed a dark spot on a hill by a plantation, and said if they were troops, it was certainly a Prussian picquet. I made the remark that they certainly were troops.[14]

Edmund Wheatley, whose watch was evidently slow, recalled: 'A Ball whizzed in the air. Up we started simultaneously. I looked at my watch. It was just eleven o'clock, Sunday (Eliza just in Church at Wallingford or at Abingdon) morning. In five minutes a stunning noise took place and a shocking havock commenced.'[15] They were the first moments of action. The battle of Waterloo had begun.

PART III

The Battle of Waterloo

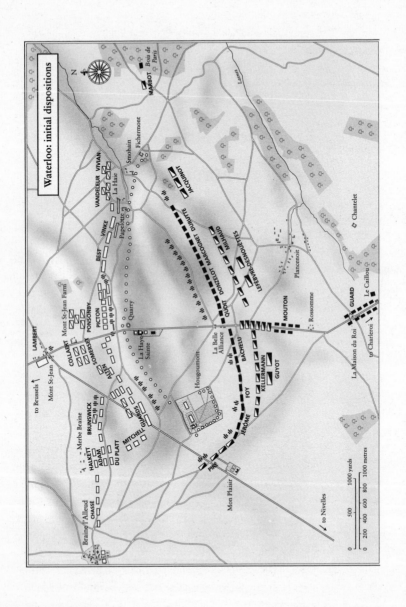

Waterloo: initial dispositions

46

The French Plan

Rossomme, 18 June, 11 a.m.

'A battle is a dramatic action that has its commencement, its middle and its end. The order of battle taken by the two armies, and the first movements to come to action, constitute the prelude. The contre movements of the attacked army forms the plot. This causes new dispositions, brings on the crisis, from whence springs the result.' So begins Napoleon's description of the battle of Waterloo.

For a battle that has been discussed so thoroughly, a remarkable amount remains unknown or contentious about how this dramatic action unfolded. The first uncertainty concerns the French plan, of which two sources, both claiming to derive from statements by Napoleon, gave two very different versions.

According to Napoleon's chief orderly officer Gaspard Gourgaud, writing on his return from Saint Helena in 1817, the deployment of the French army indicated that Napoleon's plan was to break straight through the allied centre, driving it back along the *chaussée* to the forest and cutting off the retreat of the left and right wings. On the other hand, the memoir 'dictated' to Napoleon's other companions on Saint Helena stated that Napoleon's intention was to break through on his right, while refusing his left. Two of d'Erlon's divisions, supported by two of Lobau's, were to attack La Haye Sainte; two more of d'Erlon's divisions, supported by the cavalry of both corps, were to attack further east and break through the line there so that 'the whole left of the enemy would be turned'. Meanwhile Wellington's strong right wing, pinned down by Reille, would be cut off from Brussels. Napoleon chose to turn the left in order to separate Wellington from the Prussians at Wavre, because Wellington's left wing appeared to be much weaker, and because if Grouchy appeared, it would be on the eastern flank and the Emperor did not want to be cut off from him.[1]

Napoleon's accounts of his own actions are notoriously unreliable: the question of whether what he gave posterity was what he did or what he ought to have done has to be taken into account. But on this occasion there is no particular reason to disbelieve his account and credit Gourgaud's. As Gourgaud argued, the deployment betrayed the intention, but it was not the stacking up of reserves along the *chaussée* that reveals Napoleon's thought but rather the placing of all the reserve artillery from the three front-line corps in a line that had its left resting on the cobbled road beyond La Belle Alliance, thus supporting Napoleon's right wing more than his centre. The deployment of the Grand Battery above and to the east of La Haye Sainte against Colonel Ompteda's brigade and Sir Thomas Picton's division proves that it was Napoleon's design to exert maximum force against that part of Wellington's line, since powerful artillery support was the keynote of the attack. Napoleon instructed General Dessales, who commanded d'Erlon's artillery, to construct a gun line from the twenty-four 12-pounders of the combined corps reserves and all thirty-two guns belonging to the four divisions of I Corps' infantry, and not to open fire until all could do so simultaneously in order to shock and intimidate the enemy.[2] Napoleon later claimed that this battery consisted of eighty guns and, although Dessales pointed out that he commanded only fifty-four, it is possible that Napoleon had deployed additional Guard artillery under separate command from the outset as some authorities have argued.[3]

It was a time-consuming business dragging the heavy guns through the thick mud and into position, and lining up behind them the ammunition caissons and supply wagons, so the attack had to wait until the artillery was in place; in the meantime the Guard and other troops were still marching up from the rear.

Execution of the attack was delegated to Marshal Ney, who now had more staff. Pierre Heymès had been joined on the evening of 16 June by a second aide and on 17 June at Quatre Bras by a third, Octave Levavasseur, who brought with him the marshal's own horses and military equipment. Soult then gave Ney at least one officer from his own staff: Colonel Jean-Louis Crabbé, an experienced Belgian cavalryman, who had been Ney's aide in the early years of the *Grande Armée*. Thus, by the morning of Waterloo Ney had a small but experienced team to help him direct his troops.[4] However, Napoleon retained a huge reserve under his own control in order to exploit the opportunities revealed by Wellington's reaction.

As a formality, at eleven o'clock Napoleon gave Ney a written order, stating simply that the objective of his first attack was the village of Mont Saint-Jean where the cobbled roads met and that the attack was to be supported by the massed heavy artillery of the three corps, firing over the ridge at the troops hidden from view on the far side:

> Once the army is deployed for battle, at about 1 o'clock, at the moment when the Emperor gives the order to Marshal Ney, the attack will commence with the objective of seizing Mont Saint Jean, where the roads meet. To this effect, the 12-pounder batteries of II Corps and VI Corps will be joined to that of I Corps. These 24 guns will fire on the troops at Mont Saint Jean, and Count d'Erlon will begin the attack by leading forward his left division and supporting it, as circumstances dictate, with the divisions of I Corps.
>
> II Corps will advance sufficiently to maintain alignment with Count d'Erlon. The sappers attached to I Corps will be ready to barricade themselves within Mont Saint Jean instantly.

To the copy of this order that he wrote for d'Erlon, Ney added a cryptic note: 'Count d'Erlon will understand that it is from the left that the attack will begin, rather than the right. Communicate this new arrangement to Lieutenant General Reille.'[5]

It might be thought that study of such orders would permit us better to understand Napoleon's intentions for the course of the battle. However, the order itself is extremely vague, while from Ney's postscript it is clear that Napoleon had already explained his intentions in detail to Ney, d'Erlon and Reille, presumably by word of mouth. In one respect the plan had changed, but just how it had changed is unclear: 'it is from the left that the attack will begin' has little meaning unless you already know what aspect of 'the attack' it refers to. It might mean that a diversionary attack on the far right had been abandoned in favour of one on Hougoumont on the left. Or it might mean that d'Erlon's left-hand division was to attack first rather than his right-hand division. Reille would need to know this so that his right-hand division was ready to advance sooner than originally expected in order to support it. Both of these changes would have the potential effect of sucking enemy reserves westward, in preparation for the delivery of a decisive blow from Napoleon's right.

Understanding of the order is further complicated by the consideration that d'Erlon's 'left' division might mean not geographical left, but his junior division, the fourth: that is, Durutte's. The French, like the British, often marched 'left in front' with the junior element leading the way. Given all these conflicting possibilities, it is pointless to use Ney's order and its postscript to speculate about the detail of the attack, because without knowledge of the verbal instructions that had been delivered previously the order is ambiguous.

It is apparent however that the role of Reille's corps was to be defensive: his officers understood that they were to seize and hold Hougoumont wood and to prevent any allied breakthrough on the French left. Their task was to contain Wellington's strong right wing, maintaining their position at all costs, while the rest of the French army pivoted on them to deliver a right hook.[6] They were only to advance as far as would allow them to support d'Erlon's attack on La Haye Sainte and, in the event that d'Erlon was successful in seizing Mont Saint-Jean, to form a diagonal line of echelons linking his left to the wood.

To divert enemy attention while the Grand Battery moved into position on the heights opposite the British right and d'Erlon prepared his attack, the French began to launch probing attacks to assess the strength of the enemy response in various parts of the battlefield. Although it did not take much scouting to discover that the bulk of Wellington's troops were on his right, most of his troops were out of sight.

The very first action of the day came with a demonstration by French cavalry and infantry skirmishers on the eastern flank. Major Taylor's lookouts fired off their carbines to issue the alarm and Taylor saw that three squadrons of French cavalry were approaching. His own squadron of hussars mounted and deployed to the west of Ohain; from here they could see French *tirailleurs* skirmishing with Nassauers from the cover of the hedges and ditches of the valley around the scattered farmsteads, before French horse artillery opened up, killing with one of their first, lucky shots the commander of the 3rd Nassau battalion. The other nine squadrons of Vivian's hussar brigade rode forward from their bivouac to support Taylor and formed a line on the higher ground above the hamlet of Smohain, after which the skirmish in front of them gradually petered out. Meanwhile, though, they began from their position to hear, further right, the noise of a much more formidable attack.

47

The First Assault on Hougoumont

Hougoumont, 11.30 a.m.–1 p.m.

One of the weaknesses of the new-fangled topographical map was that where several features coincided there was liable to be a confusion of symbols. Hence, Hougoumont was marked on Napoleon's map with the symbols for a chapel, a farm and a château, all of which were in fact combined in one complex of imposing buildings, hidden from French view by the tall trees of its park. The surveyors even got its name wrong: the sixteenth-century building was correctly the Château du Goumont.[1] The country seat of the eighty-six-year-old Chevalier de Louville, the grand house had seen better days; the geometric *bosquet* to the right of the elm wood had been cut down and reduced to a field of grass, for the chevalier had rented his estate to a farmer, although he still employed a gardener to maintain his cherished topiary parterres. The wood to the west of the former *bosquet* remained ornamental and, with little undergrowth, was easily crossed. Two carriage drives approached from the south and south-east, converging at the corner of the projecting garden wall; here the visitor might enter through the south gate, or continue round the corner of the farm to the west of the stables, to a junction with a sunken lane running along the north side of the farm and an avenue of poplars linking the house to the Nivelles highway and a lane to Braine l'Alleud.

The southern entrance to the château, set into an imposing gate-house where the gardener lived, was flanked by the garden wall. The windows above it had been bricked up but loopholes provided opportunities for defenders to shoot down on attackers. In the morning the gardener and his five-year-old daughter were still in their house, where the troops fed the little girl with biscuits, but after the fighting began a sergeant led her off the battlefield. The south gate led into a courtyard at the end of which stood the château itself, a tall brick building with a projecting chapel and a tower at the right, mounted by a spiral staircase. On the west side a narrow door in a short stretch of wall led across the carriage drive to the kitchen garden occupied by Matthew Clay's light company of the 3rd Guards. This was enclosed by a hedge beyond which were fields of tall crops. Also on the west side of the southern courtyard was a store shed, while the east side was bounded by a tall wall with a gate into the formal garden.

The farmhouse was a small building attached to the east side of the château; in the yard a disused central well was capped by a dovecote. On the west side was the great barn and a smaller shed, and to the east was a long, L-shaped stable. A north gate gave onto the junction of the formal avenue leading towards Braine l'Alleud with the sunken lane that ran along the northern boundary of the orchard, and beyond this path the rising ground was covered with trees. To the east of the buildings was the owner's pride and joy, an enormous garden of formal vegetable planting and topiary parterres which stretched for two hundred yards. 'A berceau or covered walk ran round it, shaded with creeping plants, amongst which honey suckles and jessamines were intermingled, en treillage.'[2] The garden was walled on the south and east and to the north it was separated from a narrow orchard by a hedge. Beyond the garden to the east a large orchard stretched for a further two hundred yards, bordered to the south by the thick hedge.

The target for the French was the wood to the south of the château. Their orders merely required them to take and hold that. French infantry columns began to march over undulating ground towards Hougoumont with skirmishers covering their front while, from the ridge to the north, allied batteries opened fire on them. At this late stage, Lord Uxbridge handed control of the horse artillery to Sir Augustus Frazer, who immediately sent for Robert Bull's battery of heavy howitzers from the artillery reserve. For ten minutes two allied batteries fired without reply; the 9-pounder guns were an unpleasant novelty, being more powerful than the 6-pounders previously standard to British artillery, and the very first shot wounded three light infantrymen.[3] Soon they were showering the French columns with shrapnel.

The attack on Hougoumont was led by Napoleon's brother, Prince Jérôme, with the help of the experienced General Armand Guilleminot, while the first assault on the wood was made by *voltigeurs* from the 1st Light Regiment in Pierre Bauduin's brigade. After 'a heavy cannonade with shell and case shot', Bauduin's light infantry swarmed into the elms to the south of the buildings and garden while the French artillery switched its aim onto the British guns on the ridge above.[4] Among the trees 600 or so French *voltigeurs* duelled with nearly as many Germans – 130 of Alten's Jägers, crack-shot foresters armed with rifles, and 200 Hanoverian riflemen, supported by a company of Nassau *voltigeurs*. For some time the Germans contested the wood with success against the elite French troops: a rifleman shot dead General Bauduin, leaving Colonel Cubières of the 1st Light to command the brigade.

To the west of the château French troops also advanced. Some of Count Piré's lancers rode westward along a sunken lane towards Braine l'Alleud, creeping round the British right flank, while a half battery of their artillery found a good position to fire north-east up the Nivelles road. Skilfully enfilading the British artillery above Hougoumont, they disrupted the gunners while covering French skirmishers who were moving stealthily through the crops to the west of the wood south of Hougoumont.

On this side of the château's park, two of the Guards' specialist light companies were defending the outer hedge of the kitchen garden, and their commander, James Macdonell, had just caught Matthew Clay and his comrades wandering about picking cherries. 'You scoundrels,' he roared, 'if I survive this day I will punish you all!'[5] Soon, however, Clay and his mates had more pressing anxieties as

French skirmishers advancing through the neighbouring cornfield began to shoot at them, completely hidden by the crops. Kneeling behind the hedge, Clay felt his pack and heels occasionally hit by spent crossfire from the wood. Eventually, pressure from the more numerous French skirmishers became too great and the Guards made a dash for the sunken lane to the north of the farm.

To help relieve the pressure on them General Hill sent the three light companies of Mitchell's battalions forward through tall corn against the French skirmishers. Coming upon the French suddenly in undulating ground and catching them by surprise, they fired, cheered, charged and pursued the *tirailleurs* southward past Hougoumont, while Macdonell's light troops made a counter-attack, chasing their opponents beyond the southern end of the vegetable patch, where Clay took cover behind a circular haystack. To drive back the allied skirmishers French lancers moved in and the light troops were ordered to make a rapid retreat to avoid capture. They were protected by British hussars, while Hill sent four more companies of the 51st, including Sergeant Wheeler's, to help extricate them.[6] Artillery peppering them with canister, they took shelter in the sunken lane linking Braine l'Alleud with Hougoumont.

Behind the French skirmish line Amadée-Louis Cubières led forward more powerful columns of elite French light troops. The colonel was the illegitimate son of the Marquis Louis-Philippe de Cubières, author of the *Histoire des coquillages de mer*. As an infant he had played Cupid at a party given by his parents for Marie Antoinette at the Hermitage at Versailles, and at the age of six he had been imprisoned when the people stormed the palace. He was brought up by the state as an *enfant de liberté*. Joining the army as a private in 1803, he had fought in all the *Grande Armée*'s great battles, winning the cross of the *Légion d'honneur* at Eylau in 1807, a bloody battle in the snow where he was bayoneted in the stomach. In 1813, the year he married the novelist Aglaé Buffaut, he was promoted to colonel, and in April 1815, he alone among Napoleon's colonels had the nerve to vote against the Emperor's new constitution because although it was more liberal, most republicans did not think it liberal enough.

As Cubières rode forward, his head was bandaged from sabre cuts received at Quatre Bras and his arm was in a sling because he had already been shot in the shoulder. He led his columns round the wood to the west, outflanking the Germans who were fighting among the tress and threatening to cut off their retreat. This finally unnerved the Hanoverian riflemen who made a sharp exit after a tough firefight lasting an hour, during which the French *voltigeurs* had been reinforced by more and more companies from the 1st Light. The riflemen sped northward past the buildings, some to the west into the kitchen garden and some through the gate into the orchard, where they were covered by the Nassau company at the hedge.

The French pursuit was brought to an abrupt halt by fierce fire from unseen assailants: the smoke was so thick that some said they mistook the red brick garden wall for a line of red-coated British infantry.[7] The ordinary French soldiers had not known that there were buildings hidden by the trees, but Captain Büsgen's Nassau grenadiers were shooting from the south gatehouse, two more companies of Nassauers were at the loopholes in the garden wall and one was lining the hedge of the orchard, where Matthew Clay and his company had earlier made holes to fire through.[8] Many of the 800 Nassauers were, like their leader, veterans of five years in the French army in Spain and Büsgen himself had been wounded in victories over the Spanish at Medellin and Ocaña. Being light troops, they were better trained for the task of defending buildings than the British Guards on the ridge behind them.

Private Johann Peter Leonhard, at a loophole in the garden wall, whooped with delight at the way the shower of lead toppled startled Frenchmen; those opposite him made a swift retreat. Further east, though, the defensive line failed: under pressure from larger numbers of pursuers, Leonhard's comrades abandoned the orchard hedge and fled back across the orchard.

Up above, from his station in front of the Guards on the ridge, Wellington watched their flight with disgust. 'Do you see those fellows run?' he remarked to the foreign attachés close to him. 'Well, it is with these that I must win the battle.'[9] Robert Bull's howitzer battery and a Netherlands horse battery arrived at the British front line above the château at this moment, taking the gun line there to twenty-six pieces. Frazer placed Bull's howitzers to command Hougoumont wood, assuring Wellington that he had perfect confidence in their accuracy, before explaining carefully to the bearded Bull and his officers that part of the park below them was held by the enemy and part by the allies. Frazer then rode further right and placed a horse battery so as to be able to fire down the Nivelles *chaussée* towards Piré's artillery, before summoning Norman Ramsay and Cavalié Mercer's troops to cover the right of Mitchell's brigade, where Piré's lancers threatened an outflanking movement.[10] Napoleon had thus succeeded in drawing five reserve batteries – thirty-two guns – to the Hougoumont area to meet his diversionary attack. This was going just as he had hoped.

Napoleon had ordered General Kellermann's horse artillery to reinforce Reille's, so that the French had forty-two guns firing on the British troops behind the ridge above Hougoumont. Here seventeen-year-old Ensign Thomas Wedgwood of the 3rd Guards, grandson of the potter and cousin of Charles Darwin, was fretting about whether or not he would prove to be brave. At Quatre Bras he had been 'rather nervous at first', but on that occasion his battalion had remained in reserve. Now, as he lowered his expensive uniform into five inches of wet mud, he felt better prepared, trusting that God would spare him. Nevertheless, the experience was trying. He hadn't eaten for two days, his boots were stuck to his swollen feet and later on he found that his face had contracted on one side so that his mouth went left when he smiled and he could no longer shut one eye without the other; having no mirror, he hadn't yet noticed this partial paralysis brought on by exposure. Like many others, he was finding waiting while under fire particularly stressful: 'The most disagreeable part was when we were on the top of our position, lying down doing nothing, with the shells and shot coming over like hailstones, and every now and then seeing 1 or 2 men killed.'[11] Only two officers were hit, however, and he was not one of them.

Further back and to the west a lively debate was taking place among the 14th Buckinghamshire Regiment, nicknamed 'the Bucks' at home but known to Flanders veterans as 'the peasants'. Here Mrs Ross, the Quartermaster's wife, was refusing to leave the field. Unlike most of the 'peasants', who had until recently been rustic militia, she was an old hand on a battlefield and had been wounded at Buenos Aires when her husband had been a sergeant with the 95th Rifles. Now she was insisting that

> 'accidents might arise . . . that would render her services useful.' At last it was suggested to her that what was right and proper in a sergeant's wife, was not so becoming in an officer's lady. Upon this hint she withdrew and passed the rest of the Sunday in a neighbouring church, not in the aisle in attendance upon divine service, but in the belfry, where she enjoyed a better view of the battle than could have been obtained by the commander of either army.[12]

A few hundred yards away another seventeen-year-old 'felt a very curious sensation before I went into the heat of the battle and all I could do would not hinder me from bobbing though the balls flew 100 yards over my head but that was only for a little while as I soon got accustomed to them,' as he wrote to his father two days later. 'Bobbing' was ducking down as cannonballs passed; strictly banned for those who had to set an example, it was instinctive when ricocheting, moaning cannonballs produced the optical illusion that they were heading straight for your face.[13]

Below these battalions, at Hougoumont, fierce fighting continued. In the hollow way (or sunken lane) north of the orchard, the Hanoverians and Nassauers fleeing to the east of the walled garden rallied on Lord Saltoun's light companies of the 1st Guards, who had been ordered down the slope as reinforcements. Their combined forces drove the French pursuers out of the orchard and into the wood, until French reinforcements made another attack, forcing Saltoun's light troops to fall back from tree to tree through the orchard to the sunken lane. The French dragged a howitzer up to the hedge, but four more companies of Coldstream Guards arrived to reinforce Saltoun and together they all again drove the French back to the southern hedge, where Saltoun tried but failed to capture the French gun.

While the fighting in the orchard to the east of the château and its garden see-sawed, to the west Colonel Cubières drove back the light companies of Mitchell's brigade who had been defending the 200 yards of the Hougoumont avenue and the sunken track leading westward to Braine l'Alleud. Wheeler and the Yorkshire light infantry fell back to their start line, while Macdonell's Guardsmen fled into the farmyard through the north door. Hidden behind his haystack and concentrating on the enemy, Clay did not see them go and he and a comrade were left behind, cut off outside. He thought he might get a better sight of the French from the bank close to the farm wall, but discovered first that this had merely made him more conspicuous and second that firing in the damp did not always work. On average a gun misfired one time in nine, but in wet weather this rose to one in five or six, and damp powder was not the only problem; Clay knew that 'from the effects of the wet, the springs of the locks became wood bound and would not act correctly, and when in action the clumsy flints became useless.' It was at this moment, with French bullets rattling against the wall behind him, that Clay's musket failed him; fortunately, he knew too that 'The quickest way of amending these failures which were very disheartening was to make an exchange from those that were lying about amongst the slain.' He made a dash southwards to a clover stack and found a better musket, still warm from use, lying on the ground.[14]

Three hundred yards north-west, French marksmen crept close enough to pick off the gunners of the British battery shooting down the Nivelles road and force it to retire.[15] Wellington responded by ordering the Brunswick battalions and a brigade of Hanoverians to advance to the high ground over the Nivelles highway, sending Brunswick light troops further forward to reinforce Mitchell's skirmishers.

Covered by a skirmish line that had pushed well north of Hougoumont and its park, Cubières launched an assault on the north gate to the château. He sent forward an assault squad led by the enormous Sous-Lieutenant Legros, known to the soldiers as *l'enfonceur* and armed with a huge axe. A former sergeant engineer, Legros had retired in 1814, but on Napoleon's return he had asked Cubières if he could rejoin his old regiment.[16] Now they ran forward under fire from the British Guards defending the farmyard. Cubières' horse was shot and he found himself trapped under the dead animal in full view of the British. He could not believe that none of the defenders chose to finish him off and concluded that the officers had ordered their men not to fire at him. His own troops rushed onward but Macdonell and his men slammed the north gate shut and barred it with logs. Clay's captain was shot while carrying a log to the gate and fell with his arm broken, before his men carried him into the farmhouse. Despite the logs, *l'enfonceur* smashed in the gate and burst into the yard, where he was shot dead during a fierce scuffle. The guards forced the gates shut again and killed every Frenchman trapped inside.[17]

In the meantime, three companies of Coldstream Guards tried to cut a way through to the château from the north. 'I was wounded in the act,' recalled their commander, and 'also had a beautiful grey horse shot. However, I did the best that lay in my power and succeeded in repulsing them till relieved by the remainder of the battalion. The whole were then obliged to fortify ourselves in the farmyard which we were ordered to defend.'[18] It took the intervention of the 1200 men of the Brunswick Avant-Garde, Guard and 1st Light battalions to stabilise the situation to the west of Hougoumont and finally drive back Cubières' men.[19] After the French fell back, four hundred of Byng's Coldstream Guards reinforced what was left of Macdonell's light troops in the farmyard; two companies of Coldstreams remained behind the ridge with the battalion's colours. The Brunswick Guard and Light battalions retired to the space Byng's brigade had occupied, leaving their Avant-Garde defending the avenue. Cubières himself walked back to the wood, amazed he was still alive.

Matthew Clay and his companion took the opportunity to rush after the reinforcing Coldstreams as they surged into the farmyard. Clay noticed that

> the gates, were riddled with shot holes, and it was also very wet and dirty. In its entrance lay many dead bodies of the enemy. One

which I particularly noticed appeared to be a French Officer, but they were scarcely distinguishable, being to all appearance as though they had been very much trodden upon and covered with mud. On getting inside the farm I saw Lieutenant-Colonel Macdonell carrying a large piece of wood or the trunk of a tree in his arms. One of his cheeks was marked with blood and his charger lay bleeding a short distance away. With this timber he was hurrying to bar the gates against the renewed attack of the enemy.[20]

The fierce battle within a battle in the park of Hougoumont was sucking in ever more troops. After Waterloo, British legend was to speak of the Guards holding out alone in Hougoumont against the whole of Reille's corps, while Wellington once announced that 'the success of the battle of Waterloo depended on the closing of the gates of Hougoumont'. Certainly, the Guards and their German comrades who played an equal part in the defence had ranged against them Jérôme Bonaparte's division, which after suffering considerable casualties at Quatre Bras was about 5900 strong, while eventually some of Foy's battalions played a supporting role. Contrary to Reille's orders – for his troops were only supposed to hold their ground in the wood – a succession of furious attacks were made on Hougoumont.

It is not true however that, while the French threw in more and more troops, Wellington never reinforced the initial garrison, which had been largely German. Nearly all the 1000 British Guards were themselves reinforcements, thrown in to support the 800 Nassauers and 330 Hanoverians, less casualties, defending Hougoumont, while another 2000 Brunswickers and British light troops were protecting the line of the avenue of trees and the sunken lane further west. Had the British lost the château, for Wellington it would have been a major blow, and he defended it strongly, as indeed he should have done.[21]

48

The Prussians Detected

Rossomme, 12.30–2 p.m.

While the attack on Hougoumont was in progress, Soult wrote a
second order for Marshal Grouchy. He had recently received a report
written by Grouchy at 6 a.m., in which Grouchy had said that the
Prussians were aiming for Brussels to unite with Wellington, and his
response was as follows:

> Monsieur le maréchal, you wrote to the Emperor this morning
> at 6 a.m. that you would march on Sart à Walhain. Thus your
> plan was to move to Corbaix and Wavre. This movement con-
> forms with the wishes of his Majesty which have been
> communicated to you. However, the Emperor commands me to
> tell you that you must continue to manoeuvre in our direction
> and seek to close in on the army, so that you will be able to join
> us before any force can get between us. I do not indicate your
> route, since it is up to you to work out where we are and how
> best to direct troops in order to link our communications and to
> be constantly in a position to fall on any enemy troops that
> might seek to trouble our right, and crush them. At present
> battle is engaged on the line of Waterloo. The 18th at 1 p.m.,
> Maréchal Duc de Dalmatie.

In fact, Grouchy had lied about how far the Prussians were ahead of him and about when he set out to pursue them, so Napoleon was genuinely misled in his future calculations.[1] Finally, however, the French staff had become worried about Prussian intervention.

Soult reassured Grouchy that his march on Wavre had conformed to the Emperor's instructions, but emphasised strongly that Grouchy must now manoeuvre to join Napoleon before any Prussian force came between them. He added an urgent line making their location quite explicit: 'in front of the Forest of Soignes, the enemy centre is at Mont Saint Jean, so manoeuvre to join our right.' This dramatic change in tone was explained by a postscript: 'A letter which has just been intercepted states that General Bülow will attack our right flank. We believe we can make out this corps on the heights of St. Lambert so do not lose a second in getting over here and crushing Bülow who you will catch *in flagrante delicto*.'[2]

The light cavalry from the right flank had just brought in a Prussian staff officer taken prisoner while carrying a message from Bülow to Wellington. It must have come as a sickening shock to Napoleon to discover that up to 25,000 Prussians were so close at hand, deploying to attack his right flank. If he had previously thought that fortune was not favouring him as she used to, this was clear confirmation. How could they possibly have moved so swiftly and boldly? And how had they evaded Grouchy? Napoleon's staff turned their field glasses to scour the eastern horizon. The village of Chapelle-Saint-Lambert was over four miles away and through the mist and drizzle it is doubtful that they could make much out, but they thought they could see troops.

Napoleon sent his aide and chief geographical engineer Simon Bernard to find out what was going on. The army's expert on the lie of the land, there was nobody better equipped than Bernard to understand the implications of what he observed. He rode two miles or more eastward to the Bois de Paris on the extreme right, where the officers of Marbot's *tirailleurs* told him that they could make out approaching columns preceded by skirmishers.[3]

Not only had Grouchy let the Prussians give him the slip, he had committed a much greater blunder: he had allowed the Prussians to do just what Napoleon's latest letter indicated that the Emperor had already begun to fear they might be doing – get between Grouchy and Napoleon. It was suddenly essential to locate Grouchy and get him onto the battlefield. If Grouchy attacked the Prussians at Wavre as he had been ordered, it would now have the effect of driving them onto Napoleon's right, so Grouchy must instead cut across towards Napoleon south of Wavre and head for the village of Plancenoit.

About fourteen miles away, meanwhile, Marshal Grouchy was still working to the leisurely timetable that had been perfectly acceptable twenty-four hours earlier. During the night he had received a report from Exelmans saying that his patrols had detected Prussians who had left the village of Tourinnes on the road to Wavre at 8.30 p.m. The officer sent north-east to Perwez had found no Prussians, but he also reported that the enemy were heading for Wavre. Moreover, a report from Walhain stated that three Prussian columns had passed through and soldiers had said that they were massing to give battle close to Brussels.[4] As a result of this belated revelation, at 6 a.m. he had written the letter of which the receipt by Soult was described above, stating his new conviction that the Prussians were heading north-west for Wavre in the direction of Brussels.

It does not appear to have crossed Grouchy's mind that the Prussians might be marching from Wavre towards Wellington's present position rather than towards Brussels and that if that were the case he would do better to take a more westerly line of march. He did not even change the deployment of his light cavalry, reiterating their order to ride to the east of his army when it should have become clear that they were better deployed to the west. It might now have been plainly obvious that he needed to move fast, but his infantry had been out marauding and their rations arrived late, so they marched off an hour and a half later even than their planned, leisurely, 6 a.m. start. A brigade of dragoons arrived at Walhain at seven o'clock but Grouchy did not get there until eleven.[5] He established that the three Prussian corps that fought at Ligny were marching towards Brussels and had been joined by a fourth, but a retired army officer had given him the incorrect information that the Prussians were concentrating to the north-east of Wavre, reassuring news that removed any immediate pressure. He reported to Soult: 'It would seem that their intention is to mass there, either to fight the troops pursuing them, or to reunite with Wellington, the project announced by their officers, who, with their usual boasting, pretend they only left the field of battle of the 16th so as to bring about their reunion with the English army near Brussels.'[6]

Having thus correctly divined Prussian intentions but not their speed of implementation, Grouchy sat down for his *déjeuner*. He was eating strawberries when Maurice Gérard's chief of staff came in to say that he could hear cannon fire from the garden. Outside, the staff were all listening intently, some with their ear to the ground to determine the direction from which the noise was coming. Locals estimated that the bombardment was taking place at the edge of the Forest of Soignes. General Gérard demanded that they should march towards the sound of the guns, for their local guides claimed they could be there in four or five hours. Offended that his subordinate should be giving his opinion so publicly and vociferously, Grouchy insisted that he already knew the Emperor intended to attack Wellington and that had Napoleon wanted them there, he would not have sent them away. Nevertheless, Gérard and other officers began to discuss the practicability of the cross-country roads for the artillery, given the appalling rain that had only recently slackened. Grouchy closed the animated debate by announcing that his duty was to obey the Emperor's instructions, which were to follow the Prussians.

At that moment one of Rémy Exelmans' aides arrived with the news that there was a strong Prussian rearguard in front of Wavre, and that all reports indicated that the Prussians had crossed the bridge during the night and the morning in order to link up with Wellington. Exelmans proposed crossing the Dyle at Ottignies, the nearest bridge to him, south of Wavre, in order to prevent a junction between the allied armies. Anticipating that Grouchy would fall in with his wishes, Exelmans had in fact already sent a brigade of dragoons to within a mile of Ottignies with that purpose in mind. From Ottignies to the crossing of the Lasne below Saint-Lambert was less than five miles, and had Exelmans crossed the Dyle there he would have been poised to interfere with Prussian progress at a point of great difficulty for them. But Grouchy was offended by the liberties taken by his generals: he said that he would give orders to Exelmans personally and asked for his horses. When Gérard begged to be allowed to take his own infantry and a brigade of cavalry towards the gunfire, Grouchy refused. He had, after all, promised Napoleon to keep his infantry together.[7]

The army hastened its march towards Wavre and at two o'clock Exelmans and Vandamme contacted a Prussian rearguard, which turned out to be that of Georg von Pirch's corps. Grouchy felt he had achieved his goal – he had caught up with the Prussians he had been chasing. So he urged on his troops towards the town in order to fight what would be known as the battle of Wavre.

49

The Grand Battery

The ridge east of La Belle Alliance, 12–1.30 p.m.

For Napoleon, getting into action had suddenly become most urgent. Captain Jonathan Leach and Lieutenant John Kincaid, commanding the British riflemen concealed about the sand quarry north of La Haye Sainte, were listening to the fighting at Hougoumont nearly a mile to their right when a random cannonball decapitated a rifleman. They looked at the space opposite them, trying to work out where the ball had come from, but there was no telltale puff of smoke. 'It had hitherto been looking suspiciously innocent, with scarcely a human being upon it,' recalled Kincaid; 'but innumerable black specks were now seen taking post at regular distances in its front, and recognising them as so many pieces of artillery, I knew, from experience, although nothing else was yet visible, that they were unerring symptoms of our not being destined to be idle spectators.' Captain Leach counted at least fifty guns facing the divisions of Alten and Picton.[1]

Napoleon loved artillery. He called his 12-pounders his '*belles filles*' and loved to employ them *en masse* to concentrate overwhelming fire on the point at which he intended to make his decisive attack. When defeating the Prussians at Jena in 1806 he had massed twenty-five guns, next year against the Russians at Friedland thirty-six, at Wagram in 1809 against the Austrians more than one hundred, at

Lützen in 1813 fifty-eight, at Leipzig eighty, at Hanau fifty-six, and at Craonne in 1814 in beating Blücher seventy-two. It was a fearsome trademark. The rapid advance of a mass of horse artillery to fire canister at the Russian line won the battle of Friedland, while at Lützen the artillery of the Imperial Guard was said to have fired fifty shots per gun per hour for two hours – 5800 rounds – to smash a hole in the enemy line. It was not just the casualties caused by such batteries that mattered: the effects were psychological as well. The morale of the men targeted was worn down by the constant barrage and the realisation that their own artillery could not reply in kind. A battery of eighty guns could throw 2000 shots per hour into the enemy opposite them and still increase its rate of fire during the minutes before an attack went in.[2] 'Columns do not break through lines, unless they are supported by a superior artillery fire,' he had castigated his brother Joseph after a defeat by the British in Spain.[3] Artillery was the one arm in which Napoleon had a clear advantage – 254 against 156 – and it was with this arm that he intended to blow the allied army away.

As it became evident that a mass of artillery was forming opposite the allied left centre, General Müffling wrote to Blücher and Gneisenau to tell them that the second of his three contingencies – an attack on Wellington's centre – was in fact occurring.[4]

Initially, Dessales formed his fifty-six guns on the ridge to the east of La Belle Alliance, the alehouse on the *chaussée*, behind or parallel to a lane leading to the farm of Papelotte.[5] The ridge was on a diagonal, projecting forwards to the east, making it roughly parallel to Wellington's front line. The guns were about half a mile from the allied guns and skirmishers and rather further from the infantry behind the ridge, but even the cavalry behind them were within long range, the range being measured by where the balls first bounced. General Ruty, commander in chief of the artillery, ordered Dessales to select a forward position to which the artillery could advance once d'Erlon's infantry had driven back Wellington's front line. There was a slightly lower ridge 500 yards further forward, in a much more commanding position some 250 yards behind La Haye Sainte and about 600 yards from the allied ridge – ideal effective range for artillery – and Ruty ordered the batteries to move forward to this position as soon as possible.[6] The movement would take place after d'Erlon's infantry closed on the allied line, during the period when the guns would have to cease fire to avoid killing their own troops.

An eight-gun battery would form on a frontage of about 100 yards, so, allowing for gaps between batteries, Dessales' line was spread across about 800 or 900 yards from a point to the east of La Belle Alliance, pointing over La Haye Sainte at Alten and Picton's divisions and beyond them at Mont Saint-Jean. If Napoleon had already added guns from the Imperial Guard, as he certainly did later, then the line was so much longer. Some 630 men served Dessales' guns. About thirty yards back were the limbers, drawn by six horses for the 6-pounders and eight for the 12-pounders with a rider controlling each pair of horses. Further back still were the first caissons containing ammunition, drawn by teams of four horses. Each 6-pounder had two caissons and each 12-pounder three. The ridge was thus covered with at least 1400 men, over 1000 horses and a minimum of 136 ammunition caissons.

When the Grand Battery opened fire, the artillery on the crest in front of Alten's infantry 'suffered heavily' and several ammunition caissons blew up.[7] The batteries of Lloyd, Cleeves and Ross took the brunt, being most exposed, and Cavalié Mercer recalled meeting Lloyd, who had ridden back to search for help, begging him, 'for God's sake, come and assist me, or I shall be ruined. My brigade is cut to pieces, ammunition expended, and, unless reinforced, we shall be destroyed.'[8] Not far to the east, three of Ross's guns were disabled in the opening barrage. 'Every man that never seed a bullet would a thought that the world was at an end,' wrote one of his gunners.[9]

Most of the British troops remained hidden on the reverse of the ridge, lying down in the mud in line, having piled their arms to try to stop them getting wetter. Behind the infantry, the cavalry were also lying down, holding their horses. They placed lookouts on the top of the ridge to see what was going on, but little could be made out. The weather had closed in again, dull and wet, and smoke lingered over any area where firing took place. Occasionally when the wind freshened people got a view, but most of the time it was murky, so that targets were difficult to make out at any distance.

The art of firing cannonballs was to get them to bounce on a low trajectory, like skimming stones on the sea, for this offered the maximum chance of killing people through their full flight. In this battle the soft ground deadened the impact of gunnery, but the ground was not so soft that cannonballs simply stopped on first impact with a huge squelch. Shots continued to bounce through the mud and most shells still exploded on wet ground, even if they had not already exploded in the air, as they were supposed to; as a result, for both sides artillery remained easily the most efficient and prolific killer.

Fifty-six guns firing at average speed threw 1400 balls and shells an hour at Wellington's line (and this was a minimum since Napoleon may have deployed more guns). When the gunners increased speed to maximum just before an attack or in order to strike fear into the opposition, they might for a short space of time throw the same number of rounds each minute.[10]

Because the ridge broadened out where they stood, so they could not hide behind it as effectively as other brigades, Kielmansegge's Hanoverians and the Nassauers near them were exposed to the direct fire of the Grand Battery. Captain Carl Jacobi of Kielmansegge's Lüneberg battalion was among those who felt the shock and awe that Napoleon had intended the bombardment to inspire, although it did not make his heart quail:

> A marvellous sublime feeling gripped all of us; we had courageously fought many a battle, but never before had we been part of as great a body of troops as this one; never before had we taken part in a battle which was to decide the fate of countries near and far. As the cannonade became ever more violent, as we beheld the enemies attack columns descending into the plain, as the foremost French battalions began to deploy ... all the misery of the night and morning were forgotten.

Lieutenant Edmund Wheatley of the 5th German Legion 'could almost feel the undulation of the air from the multitude of cannon shot. The first man who fell was five files on my left. With the utmost distortion of feature he lay on his side and shrivelling up every muscle of the body he twirled his elbow round and round in acute agony, then dropped lifeless, dying as it's called a death of glory, heaving his last breath on the field of fame. *Dieu m'en garde!'*

Although Alten's men suffered some casualties, most of the shot whistled over their heads and ricocheted into the spaces occupied by reserves, such as the Nassauers who reported some eighty casualties from this phase. Behind them, Major General von Arentsschild's hussars lost several men and twenty horses, despite shifting position to avoid the line of fire, and the colonel of the 3rd Hussars had one of his legs smashed by a cannonball, dying later in Brussels. The Life Guards, lying down behind the brow of the hill, were surprised that the Cumberland Hussars behind them had not followed their example; instead, their colonel rode forward to Ompteda to ask permission to withdraw to avoid the artillery fire. Many of the wounded, walking northward down the slope, were hit when they had passed the cavalry, because that was where many balls were landing. Private Thomas Hasker of the King's Dragoon Guards had been a stocking weaver or framework knitter before he joined up, though by his own admission he was 'a scoundrel from my youth up: and though I tried my hand at many things, I stayed at nothing long'. Nevertheless he had a strong religious streak and reflected, ironically, as 'the balls came whistling over the hills, occasionally striking one or other of our men or horses', that this was Sunday morning and at home 'many thousands of my countrymen are at this moment assembling to worship God!' As the onslaught continued, Lord Uxbridge rode forward to the brow of the hill so that he could see as much as possible of what was going on.[11]

At about the time the Grand Battery opened up, the Emperor gave the signal for the first serious assault on Mont Saint-Jean to start. D'Erlon's 20,000 infantry marched from a position some 3000 paces from the allied ridge. It is usually said that they all picked a way through the French gun line, but this would have involved separating into narrow files to pass the successive waves of vehicles and ammunition tenders, causing the guns to cease fire for a long time as the infantry passed them and inflicting considerable disorder on the infantry. Carl von Rettberg, who commanded the allied artillery battery that was best placed to view the movement, afterwards made a sketch map indicating that most French infantry marched not through the guns, but round their eastern flank, concealed from sight for most of their approach march by the high ground on which the guns stood. The map published in 1815 with *An Account of the Battle of Waterloo ... by a British Officer on the Staff* also showed French infantry moving round rather than over the ridges on which the guns stood. One of the *Générals-de-brigade* wrote that 'at midday, Count d'Erlon's corps, from the extreme right moved against the enemy left, towards La Haye Sainte.' Likewise, Müffling, the Prussian liaison officer, implied a starting position well to the east: 'about two o'clock there suddenly appeared four large masses of infantry, which having formed behind the heights of La Belle-Alliance towards Papelotte, advanced upon the position, marching *en echellon* from the left, its left being directed upon La Haye Sainte.' An artillery officer on the extreme left of the British line remarked on how the French marched past their flank without paying the slightest attention to the British cavalry in their rear.[12] Joachim Quiot, who had lost his arm during Napoleon's victory at Rivoli in 1797, was a much-decorated soldier with a remarkable fighting record; it is likely that his division marched to the west of the Grand Battery, with one brigade crossing the *chaussée* to head west of La Haye Sainte and the other turning east into the valley.[13]

Corporal Louis Canler, of General Charles-François Bourgeois' brigade, recalled that while they were at the bottom of the valley they were sheltered from the fire of the allied batteries: the shot and shells of both sides whistled over their heads. Having deployed, they stayed in their place for half an hour before advancing.[14] There would have been no reason for such a pause had they made a continuous advance through the artillery, but they might have had to wait for the other divisions, which had further to march. The skirmishers of the Cameron light company withdrew from the valley at the sight of an enemy column coming into sight ahead of them and another seen 'advancing along the valley to our left'.[15] To advance to deploy in this way had the advantage that the French guns could continue firing until the infantry left the valley for their final climb up towards the allied guns.

On the right General Durutte had sent a line of skirmishers to mask the farms of Papelotte and La Haye, and for a while French *voltigeurs* contested possession of Papelotte, but there cannot have been very many of them since a single Nassau company sufficed to drive them back. Durutte detached the small 85th Regiment to guard twelve guns on the left of his division, before halting his other three regiments opposite Papelotte and La Haye, while Marcognet and Donzelot's divisions turned left to continue their march westward along the valley bottom.[16] When they reached their assault positions they deployed.

There is considerable disagreement about the formation adopted by the French infantry. The normal French attack formation was a battalion column on a two-company frontage, a width of about forty-eight men and a depth of nine, with the *voltigeur* company skirmishing ahead. The battalion would approach the enemy in this compact column, one that was easy to manoeuvre past obstacles, then expand its frontage to form a line three deep, before closing with the enemy. However, the British habit of standing in line two deep, reserving their fire until the French were in the process of deploying, delivering one devastating volley from close range and then charging, had defeated this formation many times.

Jean-Baptiste Drouet d'Erlon was one of many French generals at Waterloo who had substantial experience of the difficulty of beating British infantry in the Peninsula. He recognised that the wild fervour of his men to get at the enemy was difficult to restrain and the prospect of deploying them at the last moment in an orderly manner was not good. Consequently, it is said, he adopted a crude formation that had been used successfully by the revolutionary armies in the early days of their success in the 1790s. This was a battalion frontage with battalions packed closely one behind the other, instead of 150 paces behind each other. In this formation, the masses would have formed so that each battalion had a front line of about 140 men and a depth of three, meaning that they were already in line. Baron

Bourgeois' brigade, on the left, comprised four battalions, giving it a depth of twelve men with only a few yards separating the battalions. D'Erlon hoped to use the impact and enthusiasm of this mass, invigorated with renewed revolutionary fervour, to punch through the thin British lines.

But there were disadvantages to forming in this way: lines were more easily disordered than columns by rough terrain and there was insufficient space between battalions to change formation or direction with any ease, although a crude square could be improvised easily enough in emergency by turning the platoons at the end of each line to face outwards. The closed column might do this if attacked in the flank by cavalry, but the last thing that d'Erlon had any reason to expect was an attack by British cavalry. In Spain British cavalry had rarely been seen on the battlefield.

The story of this unwieldy formation adopted by complete divisions emerged from Hippolyte de Mauduit's Bonapartist circle in the 1840s. The official government newspaper, the *Moniteur*, referred to brigades rather than divisions in its account of d'Erlon's attack and none of the senior commanders, Napolon included, commented on d'Erlon's formation in their reports. Lieutenant Martin, in Marcognet's division, wrote in August 1815 that when the troops formed up in the valley they deployed 'by brigade *en masse*' and 'in column by battalions and en masse'. Nicolas Schmitz, commanding one of Donzelot's brigades, wrote in June 1815 that his division formed 'in columns by battalion in echelon behind the 3rd [Marcognet's] Division'. These early accounts indicate that a massed formation was adopted, but Martin, like the *Moniteur*, spoke of brigades rather than whole divisions.[17]

After d'Erlon's troops had made their approach march, Jacques Subervie's eleven squadrons of lancers and chasseurs and the two divisions of infantry commanded by Count Lobau marched to their right into the valley previously occupied by d'Erlon's men, in preparation to come to their support or to exploit their success, while the Guard moved forward from Rossomme to fill the space on the left of the main road that Lobau had vacated. As they marched forward in closed columns of divisions, a *cantinière* who had followed her lover from Elba was walking behind him at the rear of the column when she was hit by a cannonball, her blood splashing all over his pack and bearskin. They buried her by the side of the road, marked her grave with a cross made from two branches cut from a hedge, and pinned an epitaph to it: 'Here lies Maria, *cantinière* to the 1st Regiment of foot grenadiers of the Old Imperial Guard, killed on the field of honour, 18 June 1815, at two o'clock.'[18] She was their first casualty of the battle.

50

D'Erlon's Assault

Wellington's left wing, 18 June, 1.30–2 p.m.

After the skirmishing, the diversionary attacks and the bombardment, the real assault was about to be launched. To experienced men on Wellington's side of the valley this may have been obvious from the way that the French gunners accelerated their rate of fire to two or three rounds a minute, the whirring balls and explosions no longer occasional but constant. But, even so, it was difficult to know where the main attack would come. The wall of smoke rising from the French Grand Battery to the left of the position of Wellington's staff on the ridge near the Guards was matched by smoke from an almost equally large number of French guns to their right.

Before d'Erlon made his attack, Marshal Ney ordered a second diversionary assault on Hougoumont to distract attention. Jérôme's elite line regiments from Reille's II Corps, still about 3000 strong after hard fighting at Quatre Bras, attacked the buildings, garden and orchard, where Major Jean-Louis Baux led two charges by the 1st Line. After a fierce fight in which many officers were picked off by the accurate fire of the German riflemen – to whom he later paid tribute in his report – they were repelled, and so, sending the remnant of the first two battalions round the flanks, he led in the third battalion. This time he himself was hit, his arm broken by a ball.[1]

From the upper floor of the château Captain Büsgen of the

Nassauers saw the French coming on in a great rush. They tried to climb the garden walls and they set fire to the haystack and straw-stack in the kitchen garden, hoping it would spread to the buildings. One French battalion commander later wrote that as he understood his orders, there was no need to attack the château, but the men kept hurling themselves at the walls and then running away, and he had to keep bringing them back into the wood, knowing that it was essen-tial for him to hold the wood because it was the point on which the army would pivot. Once, he was leaning against a bank at the edge of the wood when he heard something moving behind him, and turned to see a shell rolling down the slope to his right. He threw himself to the ground and it exploded without hurting him.[2]

The French 2nd Line launched its own attack on the orchard, within which Lord Saltoun's Guards, Nassauers and Hanoverians were also coming under fire from light troops in the wood and large numbers of *tirailleurs* lying down in the high corn in the field to their left. French assault columns drove Saltoun's men back through the fruit trees, but they rallied on two companies of Germans in the sunken lane to the north. Reinforced by Scots Guards, the Germans counter-attacked and the battle in the orchard swayed to and fro several times. To meet the next French attack, the remaining compa-nies of the Scots Guards marched down into the orchard. The Coldstreams defended the enormous walled garden, reinforcing the Nassauers at the loopholes in the southern wall but also manning the eastern wall facing the orchard. Apart from the two companies guarding the Coldstreams' colours, Byng's whole brigade was now in Hougoumont, taking the garrison within the enclosure, including casualties, to about 3000.[3]

Guards light infantryman Matthew Clay had been 'posted in an upper room of the chateau' overlooking all the other buildings and from his window he was well placed to 'annoy' the enemy skirmish-ers.[4] Meanwhile Jérôme's men renewed their attack to the west of the farm, advancing in a strong skirmish line through the tall crops against the Brunswick and Yorkshire light infantry lining the avenue and the sunken lane to Braine l'Alleud. With Piré's French lancers threatening to turn the flank of these light infantry, Lord Uxbridge had ordered General Grant's cavalry to the extreme right to oppose them; Dörnberg's horsemen rode west to replace Grant's as support to the Guards, thus weakening the centre.

Opposite them, Baron Gilbert Bachelu's division advanced to hold a line just south of Hougoumont and La Haye Sainte in order to support the assault on the farm by Joachim Quiot's men. From his hillock near Rossomme Napoleon looked on: 'When thoughtful,' recalled his coachman, 'he also took an immense quantity of snuff; the remains of which he shook from his fingers with great impetuosity, upon any sudden impulse. During the battle of Waterloo, at each movement of the army he evinced this habit in so remarkable a manner as to attract attention.'[5]

Although it had barely been prepared for defence, the white-washed brick farmyard of La Haye Sainte was naturally strong; it was situated two hundred yards below the junction of the cobbled road to Brussels with the lane to Ohain, both of which at this point were in deep cuttings. A farmhouse, white with grey tiles, and an adjacent L-shaped stable with copious provision for pigeons, enclosed the northern and western sides of the cobbled farmyard. On the south side was a large barn and a high wall which also shut off the eastern side of the farmyard, linking the house to the barn, although the only platform for shooting over it was a lean-to shed that they called 'the piggery'. The buildings occupied a site about sixty yards square with a pond in the south-eastern corner. To the south of the farmyard an orchard, eighty yards wide and two hundred long, enclosed by a hedge, bordered the road, and to the north was a very muddy kitchen garden, seventy yards wide and forty long, walled to the road and hedged elsewhere.

The buildings lacked outward-facing windows from which to fire, but five doors led into the farmyard in addition to the large principal gate from the road into the yard, and the gate into the west side of the barn. Since the barn doors had been used for firewood the previous evening, this unfortunately was now a gaping hole. Major Bäring posted three of his six companies in the orchard, two in the buildings and one in the garden; Bäring himself rode to the orchard. In addition, 170 riflemen from the 1st German light battalion were sent forward to skirmish near the garden; with 140 British riflemen in the quarry only fifty yards north of the farm, the initial total of defenders in and close to La Haye Sainte was about 700 green-coated riflemen.

In the orchard, the men lay on the wet grass behind the hedge in the hollow where the farm stood, until suddenly French skirmishers appeared over the rise ahead of them and crouched in the corn. The riflemen had orders to hold their fire until the main column was close, but the French *voltigeurs* began their work of picking off the officers. Bäring reckoned the very first French shot broke his horse's bridle, for as a mounted officer he was conspicuous, and the next shot killed the horse ridden by his second-in-command, Major Böseweil. After the skirmishers came formed infantry, moving very fast, their drummers beating the *pas de charge*. Only now did the riflemen fire; their first volley killed a number of the closely packed French, who nevertheless came on. Rifleman Lindau's friend was shot dead lying next to him and Lindau's brother carried their dying captain to the farm as the French stormed towards the hedge, while a second French battalion column headed past the orchard for the buildings, threatening to cut off the 200 riflemen among the fruit trees. They ran back to the wide open barn and as they ran Major Bösewiel was hit; he stood up but then fell dead on his face in the mud. Bäring's horse collapsed with a broken leg. The riflemen pushed past the French at the barn entrance in a fierce scuffle and then made a stand at the far end there; thanks to men in the yard passing forward loaded Baker rifles to those in the barn, they were able to produce such unbroken fire that the French didn't dare to come in.[6]

Lieutenant George Graeme's section fired from behind the barricade on the road until the French got close, when they ran into the farm and climbed on top of the 'piggery' to shoot down at the French on the road. Higher up the *chaussée* the riflemen in the sand quarry were ideally placed to snipe at the French officers attacking the farm entrance and kitchen garden.

Meanwhile, just to the east, half an hour after Baron Bourgeois' brigade reached its starting position near the Brussels road, Ney gave the order to attack. Three brigade columns, each of about 2000 men, were directed against Sir Thomas Picton's command; they were led by Bourgeois, Noguès and Grenier, with the two stronger brigades of Donzelot's division following in reserve. They moved in echelon, leading from the left, so that the 28th Regiment led the attack. To Corporal Canler their experienced *adjutant-majeur*, organising their tightly packed battalion columns, looked pale and preoccupied: the 28th had fought the British from Talavera in 1809 to Vitoria in 1813 and Captain Hubeau knew what to expect from British soldiers defending a ridge.

When the columns were formed the comte d'Erlon addressed them, telling them that this was the day when they must conquer or die. The signal to advance was greeted with deafening shouts of '*Vive l'empereur!*' The drums beat the *pas de charge* and the unwieldy columns began the ascent towards the riflemen and the twelve cannon. The allied guns turned their fire onto the columns as soon as they became visible. 'Whole ranks disappeared thanks to canister,' wrote Jacques Martin, 'but nothing could stop our march. It continued with the same order, the same precision.' Once more, the officers were picked off by riflemen: 'We had hardly gone a hundred paces before the commander of our second battalion M. Marans was mortally wounded,' remembered Canler.

> The captain of my company, M. d'Uzer, was hit by two balls; Adjutant Hubeau and the porte-drapeau Gosse were killed. And in the middle of all that, the calm, serious voices of our officers saw to the execution of just one command, 'Close up the ranks!' At the second discharge of the English battery, the grenadier drummer Lecointre had his arm taken off by a shell shard, but this brave man continued to march in front, beating the charge with his left hand until he fainted from loss of blood.

The third discharge shattered the front line, and the terrible shout of 'Serrez les rangs!' rang out again, but instead of filling them with horror their losses only hardened the men's will to win and avenge their brothers in arms.

One grizzled veteran who was an aide to Bourgeois reckoned the enthusiasm of the men was dangerous; they were tiring themselves by trying to move too fast through the cloying mud, so thick and heavy that it was ripping off their shoes, and as they came under fire there was disorder in the ranks. Some distance behind, at the front of Marcognet's column, Lieutenant Jacques Martin reckoned that the distance they had to cover would normally only have taken five or six minutes, but the soft wet clay soil and the tall rye through which they were marching slowed their progress so much that the enemy artillery had all the time it needed to complete its work of destruction.[7]

Fortunately for the French, however, they faced little of that artillery. Most of Wellington's guns were now deployed around Hougoumont, and to stop this massive assault there was only Thomas Rogers's and Adriaan Bijleveld's twelve guns in front and Rettberg's six to the flank. In the front line with the artillery were about 250 riflemen and the 2400 or so survivors of Quatre Bras in Bijlandt's brigade; behind them were the survivors of Picton's British division, about 3000 strong.

Both Rogers and Bijleveld had taken a battering at Quatre Bras, and they were soon taking another: Rogers used no shells at Waterloo, so his howitzer, which had fired during the retreat the previous day, was presumably destroyed early on, and his guns fired only 259 rounds during the whole day. Rettberg was particularly well placed to deliver enfilading fire against the French and had been doing so through much of their advance and deployment as well as during the attack. Unfortunately, he had used up a lot of ammunition on 16 June and had been unable to find more. He had practically no ammunition left after d'Erlon's attack, so the 477 rounds – 80 per gun – that his battery expended at Waterloo must nearly all have been fired during this first assault.[8]

'We were going to win the prize for our bravery,' wrote Martin: 'already the English were beginning to slip away; already their guns were retiring at a gallop.' As the French approached close, Bijleveld limbered up his 6-pounders and pulled out, determined to lose no more cannon. The senior captain of the Dutch 7th Militia was impressed with the way the French came on through the hail of fire:

'Their countenance was perfect,' he wrote to his sister in July. 'None of these masses disintegrated. Soon they were seen crossing the ground at attack pace, and the height where our brigade was deployed was in the first line. It was impossible for us to withstand this first shock. We received the order to fall back behind the British troops which were in the second line. By this time we had received heavy casualties.' General Perponcher had already lost two horses and his chief of staff had been wounded before his men fell back. Some of them rallied behind the British second line.[9]

French *tirailleurs* approached the sandpit, dropped to their knees in the rye and duelled with the riflemen, while the main column marched on, drums beating, still shouting. They had to manoeuvre to their right to avoid the quarry, causing delay and disorder, which meant that the brigade to their right almost caught them up. Meanwhile, battalions were moving past La Haye Sainte, outflanking the riflemen in the quarry on the other side. When the French threatened to cut them off, the riflemen legged it, seeking the protection of their support companies in the sunken lane to Ohain, and some rifle officers had to disengage swiftly from duels with their French counterparts. Kincaid rode his horse through the hedge and, finding the supports also beginning to fall back, rallied the men into a new line some yards behind it.

After what seemed an age, Canler reached the lane and climbed the high bank on the far side, from behind which the enemy guns had been firing. Scrambling through the hedge, he found that the guns that could be moved had gone, and watched as the British sergeant commanding a gun immobilised with a damaged carriage, drove a metal spike into the touch hole in order to prevent it being used by the French.[10]

While scrambling up the muddy bank, Canler had slipped on the wet clay; the strap on his gaiter broke and his heel came out of his shoe. As he bent down to put the shoe back on, something knocked his shako back: a ball had turned the number 28 on his plaque into a o and had shaved his head on its way through. He had had a lucky escape.

51

Crabbé's Charge

The centre, 18 June, 1.50 p.m.

It was evident to the Prince of Orange and his advisers in the centre of the allied position that a serious French assault was aimed at their area, and that it was essential above all to hold La Haye Sainte. To reinforce the farm against the masses of *tirailleurs* assaulting it, General von Alten therefore ordered forward the green-coated Lüneberg light battalion with the remainder of the 1st Light. The French fell back and the Hanoverians were able to recapture the orchard to the south of the farm. Some of Bäring's riflemen now sallied out from the yard and together they spread out in a strong skirmish line to oppose the French *tirailleurs*. Captain Jacobi's company took post in the orchard, defending the hedge.

Major Bäring was in the orchard with them when an officer rode over to tell him that the French had surrounded the kitchen garden behind them, and his men couldn't hold it. Bäring told him to abandon the garden and get the men into the farm. Just as Bäring realised that the French had outflanked him to the east, a French column charged forward again in front. Jacobi's men fled from the orchard, but even as they ran, they heard shouts of 'Cuirassiers! Cuirassiers!' Bäring tried to call his men around him to fall back to the farm but they were mixed up with the Lünebergers:

The number of the battalion which had come to our assistance,
exceeded, by many degrees, that of my men, and as, at the same
time, the enemy's infantry gained the garden – the skirmishers
having been driven out by a column attack – the former, seeing the
cuirassiers in the open field, imagined that their only chance of
safety lay in gaining the main position of the army. My voice,
unknown to them, and also not sufficiently penetrating, was,
notwithstanding all my exertions, unequal to halt and collect my
men together; already overtaken by the cavalry, we fell in with the
enemy's infantry, who had surrounded the garden, and to whose
fire the men were exposed in retiring to the main position. In this
effort a part succeeded.[1]

The cuirassiers are said to have belonged to a special, improvised
unit that Ney had created by asking his colonels to give him a
squadron each. If this was true, it was a sizeable and balanced force of
cavalry. From it, Ney sent out some squadrons of cuirassiers to cover
his infantry attack and gave command of them to his old aide Jean-
Louis de Crabbé, the Belgian veteran who had been returned to him
by the headquarters staff in view of his need for help. As one colonel
recalled, their objective was the twenty-four allied British guns above
La Haye Sainte.[2]

Some of Crabbé's cuirassiers charged through the Lüneburgers,
who could put up no resistance in their extended skirmish order,
and light infantry scattered for their lives in all directions. Their
colonel was wounded, their major was captured and one of their
colours was taken.[3] Such were the casualties of the battalion in
killed, wounded, prisoners and fugitives that it virtually ceased to
exist and as a unit took no further part in the battle, although those
who escaped sought shelter between the hedges and banks of the
sunken lane or within the squares on the slope. Carl Jacobi made it
back to a square, behind which he found his wounded colonel without a horse. 'Nobody among us knew how he had escaped the
horses' hooves or the horsemen's swords,' Jacobi wrote. 'There were
moments when the senses of hearing and sight had in fact shut
down.' Someone lent him a mount to get the colonel to Brussels,

and Jacobi with most of the other survivors followed him there.[4]

Colonel Michel Ordener claimed that it was his squadron that dispersed the skirmishers, before riding on against the gunners and finally taking on a square of infantry; at this point Ordener's horse was killed and he was hit in the neck. He may have led the force that mounted the ridge and charged Kielmansegge's Hanoverian brigade. Crucially, however, the two Hanoverian squares held, forming up in time and holding their fire until the French were forty paces away. The Germans captured a staff officer and a colonel whose horses had been killed, while the cuirassiers veered away to reform near the abandoned allied guns.[5]

Further east the cuirassiers found another promising target, for Christian von Ompteda had been ordered to send the 8th Line of the Legion to oppose French infantry that was advancing north from the kitchen garden of La Haye Sainte. Ompteda's division, though numerically weak, comprised four very good, experienced units and Ompteda was one of the Legion's outstanding officers, highly respected for personal bravery as well as good sense. Edmund Wheatley, who was not slow to criticise his officers, had the highest regard for him, first won during an afternoon spent sitting watching fighting in Spain with Ompteda and his nephews, Christian and Louis. The pair, now aged seventeen and fifteen, were with him again today.

The 8th Line charged the French battalion and had seen it turn around, when they were surprised and overwhelmed by cuirassiers who charged their own right flank and cut them to pieces. The ensign carrying their king's colour fell to the ground with three sabre wounds; a sergeant picked up the standard but a cuirassier hacked off his hand, seized the flag and rode off with it. Their commander was mortally wounded and the legionaries fled for the crest, where their major rallied the remnant into a small square.[6]

Ompteda's fifth battalion had advanced to support the 8th. Though seasoned troops, they had never faced cuirassiers in Spain and were naturally apprehensive of Napoleon's armoured elite. Lieutenant Wheatley now watched 'a black consolidated body' approaching with flashes of sunlight on steel breastplates, accompanied by the thunder of hoof beats that announced the famous heavy cavalry. He and his men formed square just in time:

> shouts of 'Stand firm!' 'Stand fast!' were heard from the little squares around and very quickly these gigantic fellows were upon us. No words can convey the sensation we felt on seeing these heavy-armed bodies advancing at full gallop against us, flourishing their sabres in the air, striking their armour with the handles, the sun, gleaming on the steel. The long horse hair, dishevelled by the wind, bore an appearance confounding the senses to an astonishing disorder.

But the 5th stood firm and the armoured horsemen whirled past them.[7]

Just in front of the sunken Ohain lane stood four 9-pounders of Sir Hew Ross's battery, with two more on the *chaussée* below. They got off a round of case shot, forcing the cuirassiers charging them to swerve off the road, and the gunners tried to limber up, 'but before we could move one yard the French was all round us'.[8] The cuirassiers cut up men and stabbed horses as they fled, slashing at the leather traces. From the other side of the cutting through which the highway ran, Adjutant Kincaid looked down to his right and realised with horror that the field that side was full of cuirassiers; further back, the irruption of French cavalry onto the plateau had caused all of the British infantry in the second and third lines to form square.[9]

The artillerymen of Cleeves's battery saw French cavalry sweeping over the field behind their left flank and pulled out. One of Cleeves's drivers brought up his limber in time to pull his gun down the hill to a new position right in front of the 1st Nassauers. The commander of the howitzer on the far right of the battery was concentrating on a target and didn't see the cavalry coming at all. His driver rode up with the limber, shouting to the officer that the enemy had reached the left of the battery. 'Because of the soft muddy ground, the gun could not be limbered up quickly enough; several gunners sprang on to the limbers with the rammer and hurried to the square.' The officer 'fired off the loaded round and then threw himself under the gun'. After the French cavalry retreated, the driver brought back his limber and they took this howitzer to join the other gun in front of the Nassau square.[10]

Seeing cavalry and infantry triumphing, the commander of the 12-pounders on the left of the French Grand Battery ordered his guns to limber up and advance to the forward position that General Dessales, the commander of I Corps' artillery, had previously selected. Dessales watched them with anxiety, for he had not intended to advance so soon, but soon saw them reach the new position, unlimber and open fire.[11] Encouraged, he ordered his own batteries to follow them. The French attack had started well.

52

The Charge of the Household Brigade

The centre, 18 June, 2.10 p.m.

What General Dessales could not see was that hidden from him beyond the plateau on which Carl von Alten's division stood in squares, and onto which Colonel Crabbé's cuirassiers had surged, the British Household Brigade of around a thousand heavy dragoons was waiting. Lying or standing by their large horses – those of the Life Guards and Horse Guards being uniformly black – they were impatient for action, watching their officers for a sign that their moment might have come. As Yorkshireman Thomas Playford recalled:

> After a time I saw the Earl of Uxbridge, who had been in front watching the progress of events, gallop towards us, when a slight murmur of gladness passed along the ranks. The word 'Mount' was given, and the trumpet sounded 'Draw Swords': and the command followed 'Form line on the leading squadron of the 2nd Life Guards'. This done the word 'Advance' was given, and the trumpet sounded 'Walk'. But we saw no enemy; yet there was a strange medley of shouts, musket shots, and the roar of cannon, beyond the rising ground in front of us.

The cavalry received its instructions via coded trumpet calls; now they waited for the call to accelerate from walk to trot. Playford recalled that the huge, blond hero of his regiment, John Shaw, who was said to have defeated the boxing heavyweight and former slave, Tom Molyneux, in a prize fight, rode three files to his left. These heavy cavalry were big men on big horses, taught to ride and fight in two lines in close order, like the French cuirassiers themselves.[1]

Lord Uxbridge was one of many senior officers who had been drawn to the right, like moths to a flame, to see whether the cavalry were deployed properly to defend the priority stronghold of Hougoumont. As he returned eastward from the right wing, he suddenly realised the seriousness of the deteriorating situation around La Haye Sainte. He galloped to Lord Edward Somerset, commander of the Household Brigade, and ordered him to form line, then joined Sir William Ponsonby who was watching the developing attack from the high ground further east, instructing him to wheel his Union Brigade into line when the Household Brigade did. Finally he returned to the 2nd Life Guards in order to lead them forward in person.[2]

The Household Brigade walked forward with the 2nd Life Guards to the east nearest the main road to Charleroi, the King's Dragoon Guards in the centre and the 1st Life Guards on the right. The Horse Guards were to remain behind as a reserve, which they did: if they charged at all, they did not advance far and Sir Robert Hill kept his men in hand.

A cavalry charge normally gathered pace from walk, to trot, to canter but in this case a number of obstacles impeded progress. The right wing met the enemy first, encountering the cuirassiers who had unsuccessfully charged the squares of the Hanoverian brigade 'on the ridge of the hill', thus on the allied side of the lane to Ohain, which at this point presented no serious obstacle.[3] According to Captain Edward Kelly the two opposing lines accelerated into something resembling a charge, and the French yielded when they met, but Kelly had a gift for exaggeration and it is fairly likely that the French were already retreating. The Life Guards pursued them to the west of the orchard of La Haye Sainte and any fighting took place where the *chaussée* ran through cuttings as it climbed towards La Belle Alliance, causing difficulties for the horses and bottlenecks on the road south of the farm. Kelly himself had his leg broken by a musket shot and had to leave the field.

Of the King's Dragoon Guards in the centre of the British line, the right-hand squadron led by their major and Colonel Fuller met little opposition at first and cantered away towards the French lines. The left-hand squadron had much more difficulty crossing the lane to Ohain, which itself entered an increasingly deep cutting as it approached the *chaussée*. Near it they met cuirassiers and trapped some in the corner of a field. Lord Uxbridge was fighting there, while Lord Edward Somerset leaped over the bank of the road and charged on, followed by those whose horses could cope with the slippery conditions.[4]

Here the French were definitely already pulling out. They had achieved their objective by silencing the allied guns, and had waited on the plateau for support, but they knew that they could not hold their ground against fresh cavalry. Some trotted eastward down the Ohain lane and were pursued by British dragoons onto the *chaussée*; some were said to have plunged to their death over the precipice of at least twenty feet above this main cobbled road.[5] The two bodies then raced southward for the cuttings through which the road ran above La Haye Sainte and below La Belle Alliance. There the retreating French collided with their own reinforcements, and in this bottleneck the pursuing British dragoons caught up with the trapped Frenchmen. The British slaughtered as many helpless cuirassiers as they could in a fierce, crowded mêlée, until General Colbert led the reinforcements' rear squadrons round the defile to charge the British pursuers in flank and rear. The tables were now turned; the British found themselves surrounded and outnumbered.[6]

When fighting cuirassiers, the British found it difficult to get close enough to use their curved sabres, being kept at a distance by the long, straight swords used by the French, but their own horses were bigger and better than the French ones, often giving them an advantage in height.[7] The British and French heavy cavalry adopted two different styles of horsemanship: the French adhered to the old style of 'manèged' training in slow-moving discipline, manoeuvre and obedience, whereas British horses were bred for the hunting field and the racecourse and valued for speed and endurance. The British advantage derived from the erosion of French breeding stock by the demands of war and the relative abundance of good, big, strong horses in Britain. Most foreigners were envious of the fine steeds that the British could still lay their hands on.

Dragoon Thomas Hasker came over the ridge to see cuirassiers cutting down infantry. As the Dragoon Guards charged, however, the cuirassiers turned and made off; the dragoons pursued, hacking at those they caught up with. A sergeant major reckoned that 'we lost but few men by their swords; it was the grapeshot and the musketry that cut us down before we got amongst them. We had to charge to meet them so far over heavy ground that many of our horses were stuck in deep mud. The men were obliged to jump off, leave them and seek their safety away from the cannon fire.'

In Hasker's recollection, 'many of them on our right flank got behind us, and thus we were at once pursuing and pursued', and while this may refer to the bottleneck on the cobbled road there were probably many knots of dragoons who were counter-attacked by French reserves. Hasker swung left of La Haye Sainte and found himself duelling with a cuirassier; they made 'several ineffectual passes at each other' before the Frenchman brandished his sword and muttered something Hasker didn't understand. 'I – thinking I must say something in reply – muttered in my turn, "The sword of the Lord and Gideon!"' At this the Frenchman 'very wisely turned his horse's head on one side, and rode off; and I as wisely turned my horse's head on the other side and rode off'.[8]

On the left the 2nd Life Guards had been delayed by fleeing troops, as Playford described: 'Presently we met a number of English foot soldiers running for their lives: they passed between our horses, or through squadron intervals, formed behind us and followed us. They were succeeded by a confused mixture of artillery and rifle men, hastening to get out of our way and form behind us.' The German Legionaries, dressed in British uniforms, looked English to Playford, while the fugitive Lünebergers and the 1st and 2nd Light looked like riflemen. One private trooper afterwards told his wife that 'the English infantry was broke and squandered, canon shot, grape and canister shot was flying like hail, our infantry making the best of their way to the rear and falling every moment from enemy fire, through all this & even over our own straggling infantry we were obliged to charge.' Charge is something of a misnomer, for having walked through the fugitives the 2nd had to find a way across the lane to Ohain on the ridge, which for four hundred yards was steeply banked as it descended to meet the Brussels *chaussée*.[9] For the first hundred it was ten to fifteen feet deep and the single path into the hollow from the field behind La Haye Sainte was wide enough for only two horses, very slippery and at an angle of around forty-five degrees, with a similar opening up into the field on the north side of the road.[10] Most of the squadron probably crowded into the cutting through which the *chaussée* from Brussels to Charleroi ran where it crossed the ridge north of La Haye Sainte

South of the crossroads where the *chaussée* met the Ohain lane the charge sounded, and 'at that moment a line of French horsemen in bright armour appeared in front of us; they were shouting, waving their swords, and sabring the English infantry and artillerymen who had not got out of our way. Our shouts had arrested their attention, and looking up they saw fearful ranks of red horsemen galloping forward, shouting and brandishing their swords.' What followed was a blur as the Life Guards spurred their horses into a hail of shot. Playford recalled seeing Corporal Shaw hit and then seeing his riderless horse. John Shaw had joined the Guards with his Nottinghamshire village friend Richard Waplington and the two were known as the 'Cossal giants'. When Shaw didn't return from the charge, legends grew overnight about how many cuirassiers he had dispatched before they got him and how Waplington had last been seen holding a French eagle. Playford allowed that Shaw might have survived the wound and the fall that he witnessed and might have found another horse, but he suspected that the truth about Shaw's death was more prosaic than the legends.[11]

Life Guards recalled passing through a line of cuirassiers, crossing the road and then running into a disorderly mob of French infantry who threw themselves to the ground, getting up and firing at them after they passed. A mass of Life Guards and Dragoon Guards wheeled to the east of La Haye Sainte, drove back any cuirassiers, and then cut and hacked at the infantry in their path. Skirmishers from the battalions attacking the farm were swept away in the general rout. By then squadrons were intermingled and, either side of the farm, were suffering from the fire of disciplined infantry in steady squares.[12]

Uxbridge sounded the rally in an attempt to stop his men from pursuing, 'but neither trumpet nor voice prevailed'. The British cavalry were enjoying the thrill of the chase. Nobody heard him, nobody stopped; so he went back 'to seek the support of the 2nd line, which unhappily had not followed the movements of the heavy cavalry'. He was already regretting the self-indulgence of leading the charge, conscious that he should really have been organising a reserve, for the light cavalry in the area had never received any clear orders to support the heavy cavalry; he had merely told their commanders to use their initiative.

By then, however, the effect of the charge of Uxbridge's other heavy brigade had become visible, and French infantry were streaming down the hill towards their own lines in utter rout. As Uxbridge later wrote, on his way back he met Wellington with his staff and diplomatic entourage, and 'never saw so joyous a group as was this *troupe dorée*. They thought the battle was over.'[13]

53

The Charge of the Union Brigade

The left centre of Wellington's line, 18 June, 2.15 p.m.

Wellington and his staff meanwhile had been watching the ridge to the east of the cobbled road. Here, the French sharpshooters, pushing ahead, had reached the crest of the position, driving before them the skirmishing riflemen and the broken Netherlanders. And as the French marksmen reached the hedge a new gallery of British officers became targets. The hero of Quatre Bras, the redoubtable Sir Thomas Picton, was shouting to Horace Seymour, one of Uxbridge's aides, to rally the men who were fleeing, when he was shot in the temple and fell from his horse. A second later Seymour's horse was shot and he too tumbled to the ground; as he scrambled back up to his feet he saw a grenadier looting Picton's spectacles and purse from his trousers. He ran over to the general and chased away the grenadier just as one of Picton's aides arrived, but Picton – 'a person in whom the troops had the greatest confidence, and of such experience and knowledge in his profession as to be of the greatest loss to the army' – was dead.[1]

Sir James Kempt, the senior brigadier, immediately took over, leading the three battalions of his brigade against the massed Frenchmen. They formed line and charged, checking the attack of Bourgeois' brigade. A French officer seized a colour belonging to the 32nd Cornwall, but he was instantly run through the body by the colour sergeant's pike and the ensign's sword. When the ensign fell wounded, a lieutenant took the flag and defended it stoutly.[2] British infantry witnesses claimed that they routed the French, although others stated that the British began to give ground.[3]

Soon after Canler's 28th at the head of Bourgeois' column reached the Ohain lane, the second assault column made their attack, having almost caught up when Bourgeois' men had to manoeuvre round the quarry. Lieutenant Jacques Martin was at the front with his 45th Line: 'A sunken lane with hedges both sides was the only thing separating us from them now,' he wrote to his mother in Geneva soon afterwards. 'Our soldiers didn't wait for the order to cross it. They threw themselves at it, jumping over the hedges and leaving their ranks disordered in their eagerness to run at their enemies.' Denis Pack's Highland Brigade, still in columns as Bijlandt's Netherlanders streamed through the gaps between the battalions, gave ground, shaken by the rout of the Dutch and the confident onset of the French, who were reforming on the crest of the ridge.[4]

Behind the two British brigades, however, about 900 heavy dragoons of the Union Brigade were walking up the slope.[5] Sir William Ponsonby, their commander, had ridden forward to the ridge with his aide, having told his senior colonel that if he wanted the brigade to charge he would wave his hat as a signal. At the crucial moment Ponsonby's hat blew out of his hand and while he dismounted to recover it, his aide waved his, whereupon a bugler signalled the cavalry to mount and advance. The contours hid them from the French infantry until they were at most ninety yards away, at which point the dragoons spurred their horses on. On the right of their line were the English Royal Dragoons, who rode through the units of Kempt's brigade that were opposing Bourgeois' column. The French front ranks fired and brought down about twenty men, before two squadrons of Royal Dragoons hit them, and at almost the same moment the rear of Bourgeois' column disintegrated as Life Guards swept by and into it, pursuing cuirassiers and hacking at the nearest French foot soldiers.

The Royals continued to press the French down the hill. As they did so, Captain Alexander Clark, commanding the centre squadron, according to his own account, spotted an eagle and ordered his men to 'attack the colour'. Just as British colours were sought after by the French, for the British army to seize an eagle was the greatest honour an individual or a regiment could aspire to – especially since, as the British were quick to point out, whereas each of their battalions carried two flags, there was only one eagle for the three or four battalions in a French regiment. Clark explained how he overtook the *porte-aigle* and ran his sword into his right side, but the eagle fell just out of Clark's reach onto the neck of the horse behind, to be caught by Corporal Francis Styles who was guarding Clark's back. Clark yelled, 'Secure the colour, secure the colour, it belongs to me,' so Styles gave it to him. Clark was trying to break the golden eagle off the top of the pole when Styles complained, 'Pray, sir, do not break it'; Clark ordered, 'Very well, carry it to the rear as fast as you can, it belongs to me,' and Styles with a few companions rode off with it. In his own account, Styles himself seized the eagle on the order of a junior lieutenant; this version, though less colourful, is probably more truthful.[6]

The Royals rode far enough forward to suffer from the fire of Donzelot's men who, following up as the reserve division, had by then formed a vast rectangle to defend themselves against the cavalry; some dragoons now turned back, Clark included, and began to herd as many French prisoners as they could back up the slope.

From Corporal Canler's point of view the French infantry had hardly got onto the plateau before they were assailed by dragoons shouting savagely. There was no time to form a square: the dragoons penetrated their ranks and from then on it was carnage, each man for himself, sabres and bayonets slicing and stabbing flesh, pressed against each other, with no space to get a shot off. To General Dessales, watching with Marshal Ney from the centre of the French artillery, it looked as if Bourgeois' brigade was charged in the rear by Life Guards coming from the west and that it disintegrated from the back. In fact it may well have been hit more or less simultaneously from both sides. Suddenly, Ney shouted to Dessales, 'You are being charged!' Life Guards and Dragoon Guards were spreading out in all directions from La Haye Sainte. Some were assailing squares of French infantry in the valley, others heading for the guns which were being towed forward from the Belle Alliance ridge to their new advanced position above La Haye Sainte. Some guns had reached the forward position and were unlimbering, but most were not firing for fear of mowing down the fleeing French troops running towards them.[7]

Further east, Lieutenant Martin was trying to stop his men pursuing the retreating allied infantry and get them back in formation:

> I had just succeeded in pushing one back into his place in the line when I saw him tumble to the ground at my feet from a sabre blow; I turned round sharply. There were English cavalry charging into our formation from all directions and cutting us to pieces. I just had time to throw myself into the crowd to avoid the same fate. The noise, the smoke, the confusion, inevitable at such times, had stopped us noticing that on our right several squadrons of English dragoons had come out of a sort of hollow, formed up in our rear and charged us in the back.

The 45th was hit in front by Irish Inniskilling dragoons; those that Martin said charged their right flank and rear were probably Scots Greys. Cavalry could slaughter disordered infantry with impunity, however brave the infantry. Soldiers would stretch to try to bayonet the horsemen towering above them, but they nearly always failed and any shots fired in the confused crowd were just as likely to wound one's own men as they were the enemy. Martin now found himself caught up and swept away in the current of a confused and turbulent mob. The French artillery fired into the mêlée, while the British, in an orgy of bloodlust,

> sabred everyone pitilessly right down to the children who served us as fifers and drummer boys in the regiment and who begged for mercy, but in vain. It was there that I saw death from closest to: my best friends were falling at my side, and there was no avoiding the logic that the same fate lay in store for me; but I no longer had clear thoughts; I just fought mechanically as if waiting for the fatal blow.[8]

Some of the Royal Dragoons and Inniskillings had nothing before them and charged on down the hill until they reached the valley, where Donzelot's division had been advancing in reserve. Donzelot's men had time to improvise one huge rectangle by folding back each battalion's wing platoons in order to fill the narrow gap between battalions – a dense formation filled with men, but one that sufficed for the present emergency. The dragoons failed to break in, suffering some casualties from musketry before careering on towards the French guns, some of which they caught limbered up and moving. Though the British horsemen were unable to spike the guns or to drag them away, they killed horses, cut traces and drove away riders so that the guns were immobilised. It is not clear just how much damage was done, but the French certainly lost the use of some guns for a considerable time, perhaps permanently. Sir William Ponsonby was in this central area and he with his staff tried desperately to halt the charge, 'but the helplessness of the enemy offered too great a temptation to the dragoons'.[9]

The Scots Greys had no business charging, for their orders were to support the other two regiments, but their colonel had no intention of missing out on this glorious party. So he charged in support, close behind and to the left. The Greys passed through the 92nd, 'who appeared to be giving way' or were 'retiring somewhat confusedly'.[10] The Gordons extended beyond the line of Martin's 45th Regiment and greeted their compatriots who were riding distinctive grey horses and wearing bearskins with shouts of 'Scotland for ever!' Some of the Greys hit the leading French brigade in the flank. Sergeant Charles Ewart, aged forty-six but a towering giant of six foot four in a bedraggled bearskin, cut his way to the eagle of the 45th and seized it, parrying a thrust at his groin from the *porte-aigle*, then slicing through his skull. He was set upon by several Frenchmen, but cut them down with the help of rough-rider James Armour, a relative of the poet Robbie Burns's wife, Jean. Ewart was ordered to leave the field and ride with the eagle to Brussels to ensure for the sake of regimental honour that the invaluable trophy remained captured.[11]

The Greys were followed by the Gordons, who turned, ran after them and attacked the flank of the French column, taking prisoners desperate to escape the chopping sabres of the Greys. Many of those initially rounded up escaped in the ensuing confusion, but hundreds were escorted from the field by dragoons or Dutch infantry.[12]

Most of the Greys charged on. Gathering pace down the slope, they actually had the impetus of a proper cavalry charge when after three or four hundred yards they hit and swept round the flanks of another column, probably that of Noguès' brigade. For the French, seeing the dragoons come suddenly into view over the brow, there was no time to form square, although the 21st Regiment tried. Hit in the flanks and rear, the column disintegrated. In the recommended manner some soldiers tried to form rings, the British 'hives', facing outwards, bayonets bristling; some tried to defend themselves, holding their muskets above their heads to parry the sabre blows. Others threw themselves to the ground, feigning dead until the cavalry passed. Antoine Noguès himself was shot in the hand but rallied some of his men in their starting position.

By what from a British point of view was a very happy accident, the timing of Ponsonby's charge had been perfect. It hit the French infantry just as they reached the crest of the ridge, so that they were totally surprised by the sudden appearance of cavalry. Captain Clark later wrote that 'had the charge been delayed two or three minutes, I feel satisfied it would probably have failed', and that since 'there were no infantry in reserve behind that part of the position' the French infantry would then have taken Mont Saint-Jean.[13]

Clark may have been right: had Ponsonby's charge failed, French infantry might have broken through decisively. If Picton's weak battalions had failed to hold them it is questionable whether the morale of the Hanoverian militia would have held up and the whole wing might easily have collapsed. But one way or another, the battered veteran infantry and the novice cavalry undertaking their first real charge had prevailed, and for a moment it seemed as if they might have won the day.

54

The French Counter-attack

18 June, 2.30 p.m.

When General Charles-Claude Jacquinot, commander of d'Erlon's cavalry, saw that the Grand Battery was in danger he unleashed a brigade of lancers. Simultaneously, to the west, a brigade of cuirassiers and a further substantial force of lancers moved in to bring off Crabbé's cuirassiers and drive away the British heavy dragoons who rode in scattered knots, their horses blown, out of breath and labouring in the heavy ground.

Lord Edward Somerset, 'having heard that the greater part of the KDG were broke & gone away without order into the enemy's lines, ordered [a captain] to rally & halt as many as possible, which was done, but too late, as no one seemed to know what was become of the right hand squadron and other broken troops & the ground in the plain where they had so far advanced was covered with immense columns of the enemy.' As a lieutenant of the King's Dragoon Guards admitted:

> Our brigade, never having been on service before, hardly knew how to act. They knew they were to charge, but never thought about stopping at a proper time ... the consequence was that they got among the French infantry and artillery, and were miserably cut up. They saw their mistake too late, and a few (that is about

half the regiment) turned and rode back again; no sooner had they got about five hundred yards from the French infantry than they were met by an immense body of Lancers.

Suddenly, the Guards realised the seriousness of their predicament. The French lancers, dressed in green with brass helmets, and with conspicuous red and white pennants towards the end of their nine-foot lances, were riding fresh mounts and could move faster. Led by their commander, Colonel William Fuller, the Guards

> resolved either to get out of the scrape or die rather than be taken prisoners, so they attacked them, and three troops cut their way through them; about a troop were killed or taken prisoners. In this affair poor Fuller lost his life; his horse was killed by a lance, and the last time he was seen he was unhurt but dismounted. Of course the Lancers overtook him and killed him, for our men were on the full retreat; he made a sad mistake in pursuing the Cuirassiers so far.

Fuller was killed somewhere south of La Haye Sainte; the major commanding the right-hand squadron also died, run through the side by a lance or sword, on the slope of the French position. Practically nobody from his squadron returned: almost all were killed, wounded or captured.[1]

After his duel with the cuirassier, Private Hasker realised that he had been left behind by the main body of the regiment. He tried to catch them up, 'but in crossing a bad, hollow piece of ground' his horse fell, and he had hardly got to his feet when another cuirassier rode over. The Frenchman

> began to cut at my head, knocked off my helmet, and inflicted several wounds on my head and face. Looking up at him, I saw him in the act of striking another blow at my head, and instantly held up my right hand to protect it, when he cut off my little finger and half way through the rest. I then threw myself on the ground, with my face downward. One of the lancers rode by, and stabbed

me in the back with his lance. I then turned, and lay with my face upward, and a foot soldier stabbed me with his sword as he walked by. Immediately after, another, with his firelock and bayonet, gave me a terrible plunge, and while doing it with all his might, exclaimed 'Sacré nom de Dieu!' No doubt that would have been the finishing stroke, had not the point of the bayonet caught one of the brass eyes of my coat – the coat being fastened with hooks and eyes – and prevented its entrance. There I lay, as comfortably as circumstances would allow – the balls of the British army falling around me, one of which dropped at my feet, and covered me with dirt; so that, what with blood, dirt, and one thing and another, I passed very well for a dead man.[2]

Life Guard Thomas Playford succeeded in getting back without having even crossed swords with the enemy; he had the opportunity to despatch a fallen cuirassier but didn't have the heart and pulled out of the blow, although he did save a comrade whose horse had been killed and who was running along, trying to catch a French one. What was left of his squadron found their way home blocked by French infantry, but Arentsschildt's German hussars 'menaced them into squares' and Playford made his escape by riding between the French squares without being hit by their fire.

Of those who charged in the front line of the Household Brigade, few returned to the battle. Only about thirty of the King's Dragoon Guards under a captain rejoined the brigade: the rest were lost and scattered even if they had survived.

Once the French infantry had surrendered, most of the dragoons had ridden on and only a few had remained to lead away the prisoners. Jacques Martin had just been bundled over by the horse of a dragoon who came past him at high speed, and he found himself lying among others, some dead, some wounded, some merely knocked over. The British marched off the men who were standing without bothering about those who were on the ground. Once they had gone, he was able to make his escape, walking unsteadily back across the valley through the smoke, feet catching in the downtrodden wheat, across mud that was strewn with bodies. Around him were groups of mounted dragoons, but they were intent on reaching the French guns, and for Martin the greater danger came from the French artillery. When the dragoons chased the gunners away, he slipped past the line of guns and found shelter.[3]

The French counter-attack enabled many more French prisoners to escape, among them Corporal Louis Canler of the 28th who had been captured by dragoons and disarmed. Suddenly he heard the familiar order, 'Au trot!' French lancers and cuirassiers were charging his captors and he found himself abandoned as the dragoons attempted to repel them. He threw himself into a nearby field of wheat, from where he watched the furious onset of the French horsemen and a fierce mêlée that ended with the flight of the dragoons. Canler began to creep through the wheat towards his own lines, but first he visited the body of a dragoon officer he had just seen felled. A sword blow had split the man's skull open and his brains were oozing out, but from his fob hung a superb gold chain. Canler swooped on that and also pocketed the gold watch attached to it. A little further on he found a shoulder bag with a copper plaque on the cover, on which was engraved '*Labigne, sous-lieutenant au 55e de ligne*'. In the bag was a writing case and some linen, valuable since Canler now possessed only what he was wearing. Walking south he discovered his colonel with a few officers, desperately trying to gather together soldiers from his regiment; when a wounded man from the 105th appealed to Canler to help him to the field hospital, though, Canler carried him back to the French ambulances.[4]

A little further east, Ponsonby and his staff of the Union Brigade also recognised their danger and sought to escape. Many, staying on the low ground or on the nearest ridge, tried to ride eastward back to British lines and, in so doing, encountered advancing French artillery which they were able to cut up and disperse. They were riding across the ridge to which Dessales' artillery had been advancing when they saw French lancers. Ponsonby tried to ride round to the east and was isolated and killed. According to a story current soon afterwards, he was on his spare horse, a small bay hack. Exhausted by the charge, the horse floundered and got stuck in a ploughed field. Ponsonby could see lancers approaching and gave his watch and a miniature of his wife to his aide-de-camp, but the lancers killed both of them. His body was found next day, beside his horse, pierced with seven lance wounds. A French account has it that a lancer, *Maréchal-des-logis* Urban, killed Ponsonby reluctantly to prevent his recapture when some British dragoons attempted a rescue.[5]

Wellington's moment of wild optimism had now been dampened by the virtual destruction of his strike cavalry. 'What with men lost and others gone to the rear in care of the wounded, and many absent from not knowing where to assemble, and other causes, there did not remain efficient above a squadron,' wrote a cavalry officer about the Union Brigade, and although the Horse Guards were still in good order, the rest of the Household Brigade was in similar plight. 'The fact was that the men did not know where to assemble after the charge, and this being the first action they had ever been in they, I suppose, fancied that nothing remained for them to attend to after this one attack, and many went in consequence to the rear.' The problem began with their training:

> We never teach our men to disperse and form again, which of all things, before an enemy, is the most essential ... they should be taught to disperse as if in pursuit of a broken enemy, with as much confusion as possible, but to form instantly on hearing the bugle, or rather retreat at that sound, and for fear anything should happen to the trumpeter, to return by word.[6]

If these men, most of whom were fighting their first action, had never been taught to form up after dispersing, it is hardly surprising that they failed to do so. It was a lesson that only hardened campaigners had learned, usually from their better-trained German colleagues.

Instead, some of those who escaped the lancers with their lives joined the increasing throng of fugitives who were running or riding up the road to Brussels spreading alarm and despondency behind the lines. Casualties had been heavy. Of the Greys' twenty-four officers, eight were killed and eight wounded. 'There was one squadron of the 1st Dragoon Guards in which not above one or two returned,' noted a cavalry officer shocked at the disappearance of about 120 men. 'They rode completely into the enemy's reserve and were killed.'[7] Wellington had accused his cavalry of 'galloping at everything' in the Peninsula, and once again they had shown more enthusiasm than discipline.

Nevertheless, the Duke had won the first round. Napoleon's first attack, intended to be decisive, had been resoundingly defeated. It was a serious setback for the Emperor.

55

The Charge of Sir John Vandeleur's Brigade

Wellington's left wing, 18 June, 3 p.m.

While skirmishing and cannonading continued around Hougoumont, the scene from La Haye Sainte to the east was chaotic. Of Quiot's division, the first to assault the farm and the slope above it, some battalions remained intact in square while others were in flight or rallying to their officers on the high ground near La Belle Alliance. Donzelot's supporting division was in a huge square in the valley, surrounded by fleeing British dragoons and pursuing cuirassiers and lancers. To the east Marcognet's whole division was running away or rallying somewhere near its start line, while wounded men and others streamed south along the *chaussée*. On the British side of the valley, what since the death of Picton had become Kempt's men were returning to their lines to reform to the right of a huge square of Hanoverian Landwehr, while wounded men and prisoners streamed towards the cobbled road leading to the British rear. Further east, skirmishing continued between Durutte's men and Nassauers around the farms in the marshy valley.

Sir John Vandeleur's brigade of light dragoons was riding westward from the left flank to reinforce Kempt's area, with permission to charge at discretion. Before them, the battalions of Durutte's division were still intact, while the surviving remnants of the Union Brigade were coming back in groups of twenty or thirty on blown horses, harried by merciless French lancers. Many of the dragoons were trying to reach the lower ground on the left of the British line, and Vandeleur's cavalry might save them.

In front of Vandeleur was Pégot's brigade of French infantry, uncertain whether to continue its attack on the huge square formed by the combined Hanoverian Landwehr of Best and von Vincke. Though these inexperienced young Germans were determined enough to fight, they had been looking shaky as the French attack went in 250 yards to their right, and they were still looking uncertain as a brigade of Jacquinot's light cavalry, riding in support of the French infantry, threatened to charge them.[1]

Holding back the 11th Light Dragoons in reserve, Vandeleur ordered the 12th and 16th to charge. Each regiment had three squadrons of about 140 men, making some 800 horsemen in total. Frederick Ponsonby, colonel of the 12th and second cousin of the late commander of the Union Brigade, fixed on a body of French infantry that he estimated at fifty men wide and twenty deep, so probably a regiment, and had his trumpeter sound the charge.

The blue-coated light dragoons of the 12th, who wore French-style bell-top shakos, surged forward, to find themselves fired on from behind; this 'friendly fire', they said afterwards, caused them more casualties than the French. Already badly shaken at the sight of what was happening to the infantry to their left, the French fired a loose volley at long range and then turned their backs. Ponsonby's men charged the regiment in the flank and were soon cutting and hacking at the retreating infantry. The light dragoons did 'much execution', but as they emerged on the other side of the infantry they were charged in their turn by a regiment of chasseurs, with dire consequences for their leader:

> Nothing could equal the confusion of this melee, as we had succeeded in destroying and putting to flight the infantry. I was anxious to withdraw my regt, but almost at the same moment I was wounded in both arms, my horse sprung forward and carried

me to the rising ground on the right of the French position, where
I was knocked off my horse by a blow on the head.[2]

Meanwhile Ponsonby's supports, the 16th Light Dragoons, had
been delayed in crossing the Ohain road, and they were further
delayed when their commander was shot in the back by 'friendly'
infantry and seriously wounded. By the time they charged the French
chasseurs, the men of the 12th were either fleeing for their lives or
galloping forward behind their runaway, disabled colonel towards
the French guns and reserves. Of the 12th Light Dragoons only about
a hundred men rallied from their first charge.[3]

André Masson's 85th Line, recruited in coastal towns in
Normandy in 1814, chiefly comprised former prisoners of war
returned from England after capture in the Peninsula. They were
experienced, determined and animated by hatred of the English. A
mere 631 men strong, they had been left to guard twelve guns on the
right flank of the Grand Battery. Masson had formed the regiment
into a small square in two ranks long before he was attacked by
Ponsonby's dragoons and by marauding heavy dragoons riding along
the French gun line from the west. His men met them with sharp
volleys; the light dragoons circled round them, and were then charged
by French lancers.

Masson, a forty-five-year-old Burgundian of enormous experience, had been a captain in the Grenadiers of the Guard in the great
days of the *Grande Armée*, and held his regiment together when under
a lesser man it might have melted away. The regiment held its fire
with perfect discipline as the cavalry mêlée took place around them,
and eventually Durutte's battalions rallied behind their square.[4]

Meanwhile, as the British dragoons sought to escape the merciless
lancers pursuing them towards their own line, Frederick Ponsonby
recovered from a brief loss of consciousness to find that only his
arms were wounded. Seeing a part of his own regiment at the foot of
the hill, he staggered to his feet, but a French lancer spotted him,
rode over and, snarling '*Coquin, tu n'es pas mort?*' plunged his lance
into Ponsonby's back. The colonel's mouth filled with blood and he
fell on his face, breathing with difficulty, for the lance had pierced his

lungs. But he remained conscious. Soon afterwards the French *tirailleurs* reoccupied their station on the crest of the rising ground where Ponsonby lay. The first to discover him plundered him, although later an officer gave him some brandy. Ponsonby begged to be sent to the rear but the Frenchman merely put a knapsack under his head and told him he would be taken care of after the battle. He assured him he would not have to wait long, since the Duke of Wellington had been killed and several British battalions on the right had surrendered. All the time the skirmishers fired away and a young *tirailleur*, who was using Ponsonby's body for cover, kept up a running commentary, 'always observing that he had killed a man every shot he fired'.[5]

On the other side of the valley and further west, the Prince of Orange's chief of staff Constant had ridden his black mare over to the left in order to rally the fleeing Netherlands infantry, leading Baron Charles-Etienne de Ghigny's Netherlands light cavalry, a thousand sabres strong, to block their path off the field. A sufficient number of well-motivated cavalry could force infantry to rally simply by pre-senting an imposing, steady and near-impenetrable 'friendly' obstacle and shaming the retreating foot soldiers into turning round. After rallying a part of Bijlandt's brigade, Constant saw Vandeleur's light cavalry in motion just to the east, charging the retreating French infantry, while in front efforts to break the huge square formed by Donzelot's division continued. Ghigny's Dutch light dragoons charged in support of Vandeleur and completed the rout of the French infantry that Ponsonby had charged, while his Belgian hus-sars turned their attention to Donzelot's men. The Netherlands heavy cavalry also launched a charge against French cuirassiers in order to cover the retreat of the Household Cavalry.

Meanwhile, Augustus Frazer, commanding the British horse artillery, had played his joker. When the heavy cavalry advanced, Captain Whinyates's rocket battery also rode forward.

Rockets were transported in a special cart attached to a normal limber; this 'rocket car' carried two gunners and sixty rockets in boxes. Looking very like the familiar firework, with a stick to steady them and a paper fuse, they could be fired from a triangular iron frame, adjustable to fire at any angle from parallel with the ground to forty-five degrees, or could be placed on anything that would hold them steady, such as a bush. The projectiles might be round shot, shell, canister or incendiary 'carcass', but the few rockets that were fired at Waterloo carried explosive shells. Whinyates placed his guns in the area vacated by the Dutch guns, about 200 yards east of the Charleroi *chaussée*, and then a colonel from the artillery staff ordered him to fire his rockets at Donzelot's unbroken division.[6]

A lieutenant sent by Whinyates with two crews to the barricade built by the riflemen above La Haye Sainte was wounded before they got there, but his men sited rockets in the bushes from which the barricade had been made and fired them off down the cobbled road. The other four crews fired their rockets out of the crops from further to the left. Leaving the two limber gunners behind to guard each gun, his horsemen then rode down the slope for a hundred yards, each carrying four rocket sticks in a bucket by their side, and more rockets in their holsters. Every third rider carried the frames in which the rockets were laid before firing. The group dismounted in tall rye to fire a series of ground rockets, aiming them flat so that they hugged the ground, sometimes ricocheting off it. They couldn't see their target, but Donzelot's dense square was massed ahead of them. When General de Ghigny saw this happening he sent his Belgian 8th Hussars forward into the valley opposite Donzelot's square, in which for a while the rockets created considerable surprise, alarm and disorder. In fact Whinyates fired only fifty-two rockets during the day, probably all at this time, but Ney's aide Heymès spoke of 300, and they usually feature in pictures of the fighting.

The hussars, though, failed to charge. They were not the most enthusiastic cavalry regiment in the army: indeed, during the day thirty-three of them took the opportunity to change sides and join the French. *Maréchal-de-camp* Nicolas Schmitz spotted that the rockets were coming from behind a hillock – he assumed there were machines concealed behind it – and sent two companies of *voltigeurs* from the 13th Light to dislodge them. It was possibly in directing this attack to drive away the rocketeers that the redoubtable old campaigner Captain André Ravard, wounded three times in Russia, was hit by an allied sharpshooter, probably a rifleman. 'I was wounded by a ball in the right arm. It made three holes in my arm, passed under the scapula and stopped between my shoulder blades against my spine.' It took him five hours to get back to Le Caillou, where a surgeon of the guard extracted the ball after much difficulty and much pain.[7] However, the *voltigeurs* succeeded in driving off the rocketeers, and the hussars pulled back with them. Then, for a while, there was a lull in the fighting.

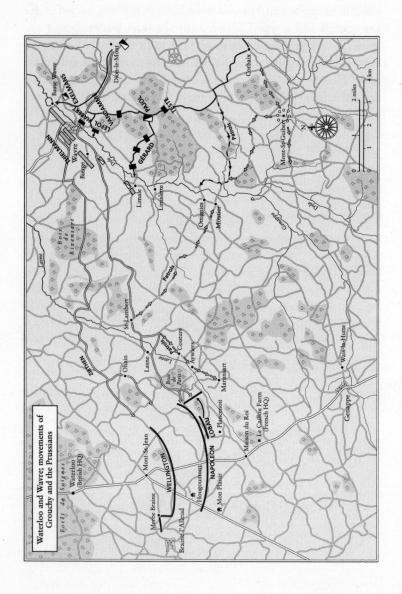

Waterloo and Wavre; movements of Grouchy and the Prussians

56

Where are the Prussians?

Wavre to Saint-Lambert, 18 June, 2–4.15 p.m.

Wellington was becoming anxious. His troops had defeated a massive French attack, but they had done so at great cost: Picton's division was further weakened, their commander was dead and the best of the heavy cavalry was played out. He had accepted battle at Waterloo in the certainty that the Prussians would reinforce him, and for that reason his left wing – the one that the French had attacked – was weakly manned by fellow Germans to leave space for Prussian troops. But the Prussians were late. He had hoped to see evidence of their presence on the battlefield by two o'clock, but there was still no sign of them. He sent Captain William Staveley of the Royal Staff Corps to try to find Blücher and to persuade him that the British army needed his help now.

Meanwhile the Prussians were stuck in the mud:

The ground was completely saturated with the rain which had fallen without interruption for sixteen hours. The rivulets had become torrents; every hollow was filled with water; some of the forest roads actually resembled watercourses through which the men had to wade for hundreds of yards together; deep pools of water that constantly forced the troops to break their files, had been formed in every direction.[1]

In these conditions, Prussian columns had become strung out over most of the eight miles between Wavre and Lasne. The going was in any case rough and hilly on the tracks through the woods, but the last stretch from Saint-Lambert to Lasne was really difficult. First there was a steep drop from the hill village to a tributary stream and a climb to a hill over the river. Then the track entered a narrow defile between high banks, dropping steeply into the river valley, crossing a narrow bridge and climbing steeply again into the village of Lasne. It was fine for infantry, but for a gun or a cart it was almost impossible.

James Shaw, assistant quartermaster to Wellington's 3rd Division, appreciated the Prussians' difficulties in reaching the battlefield. The previous day his own division had crossed the river Dyle at a small bridge with orders to proceed by minor roads parallel to the *chaussée*, but after losing part of their baggage to the mud they had returned against orders to the cobbled road as it was the only way to make progress. He found it perfectly easy to understand how General von Bülow took eight hours to march eight miles.[2]

Having sent out patrols and discovered that there were no Frenchmen in the Lasne valley, Bülow decided to secure the flooded river crossing by occupying the high ground on the other side. Just after midday he sent the Silesian Hussars and two battalions of fusiliers forward as a vanguard, and behind this screen the two brigades and his cavalry picked their way down the steep, muddy slope and waded across the valley.

With the swollen stream two to three feet deep and racing after the heavy rain and the valley deep in mud, it took far longer than anybody had anticipated and it was almost a miracle that they got the guns through at all. These had to be lowered down one side of the steep valley, using horses as a brake behind them on the slippery mud. Then the teams had to be hitched in front of the guns to pull, while the men pushed and strained with their shoulders against the wheels. It was exhausting work. Bülow's men had been on the march since first light – they had hardly stopped marching for days – and had not eaten since the previous evening. Blücher rode back to encourage the columns and it took all of his cajoling to keep them going: 'You do not want to make me break my word,' he appealed to his tired, hungry gunners as they struggled with cannon sunk up to their axles in cloying, sticky wet clay.[3]

Having eaten and received fresh ammunition, Ziethen's men left the village of Bierges, just south of Wavre, in the early afternoon. They followed a more northerly track through the woods than the other corps, one which led to Ohain, a mile and a half north-east of the eastern end of Wellington's front line. Karl von Steinmetz's brigade with two batteries of guns and Friedrich von Röder's cavalry formed Ziethen's vanguard, followed by the other three brigades and the reserve artillery. A major from the staff acted as guide, with light cavalry scouting ahead and maintaining contact with the corps to the south.

With the first of Vandamme's French troops appearing near Bierges before the last Prussian brigade set out, General Ziethen sent back the 19th Regiment and some cavalry to act as a rearguard.[4] Now, while the vanguard of the Prussian army struggled through the mud, that rearguard skirmished with Grouchy's vanguard. Meanwhile Friedrich von Jagow harangued the men of his brigade towards the rear of Ziethen's advancing column: 'Get going, lads! Be as brave today as you were the day before yesterday! Remember Kulm and Leipzig!' and as they tramped off the band played the traditional song 'Long live the old Prussian house'. Whenever they passed patrols they asked with eager anxiety, 'Comrades, how is it going further forward?'[5]

Ziethen's march led along 'sunken lanes cut through deep ravines'. The forest either side of the road was very thick 'so there was no question of avoiding the road, and progress was very slow, all the more so because in many places men and horses could get through only one at a time'. Troops at the head of columns were continually required to stop and wait for those further back to catch up.[6]

Georg von Pirch's II Corps had camped just east of Wavre, having trudged in after dark in pouring rain. They were ready to march at dawn, but the fire near the market place prevented them from crossing the bridge into the town until midday. Instead, they reorganised. Rifleman Franz Lieber of the Colberg Regiment recalled: 'Early in the morning of the 18th we found part of our regiment from which we had been separated. It was a touching scene to see the soldiers rushing to each other, to find comrades whom we had believed to be dead or missing.' Leaving two of his brigades behind around Wavre as a rearguard, Pirch marched off with the 5th and 6th Brigades. Franz Lieber remembered:

As we passed the Marshal, wrapped up in a cloak and leaning against a hill, our soldiers began to hurrah, for it was always a delight to them to see the 'old one' as he was called. 'Be quiet, my lads,' said he; 'hold your tongues; time enough after the victory is gained.' He issued this morning his famous order, which ended by assuring our army that he would prove the possibility of beating, two days after a retreat, and with inferior numbers, and which concluded with the words 'we shall conquer because we must con-quer.'[7]

Around 2 p.m. Pirch's rearguard had a first brush with Grouchy's troops two miles south of Wavre. The detachment that had been left to keep an eye out for the French at Mont Saint-Guibert was very nearly cut off by Exelmans' dragoons, but managed to join up with Pirch's rearguard, leaving the various patrols they had sent out to make their escape as best they could. Half an hour later the rearguard crossed the Dyle at Bierges and broke the wooden bridge, pressing on to the main body and leaving only a regiment of hussars and two battalions of infantry to delay any French pursuit.[8]

Johann von Thielmann's orders were to defend Wavre if he was attacked and to follow the Prussian army if he was not. By 3.30 the other Prussian corps had moved off and although French patrols had been seen, no large body of troops had been identified. Accordingly Thielmann gave orders to his four brigades to follow the rest of the army. Just before these orders were received by Karl von Borcke's brigade, which was acting as Thielmann's rearguard on the French side of the Dyle, the head of Vandamme's column made contact with his outposts. Borcke hurried back to Wavre to find that both the stone bridges in the town had already been barricaded and blocked against the French by two fusilier battalions from his own brigade.

He made a very rapid march downstream to Basse Wavre, crossed the river by the wooden bridge, destroyed it behind him and lined the banks with picked marksmen. Then, having detached another battalion and some cavalry to help the fusiliers defend the bridge at Wavre, he continued his march towards Waterloo. Thielmann, meanwhile, had decided to turn back and defend Wavre.

The Dyle, ordinarily an unimpressive river, was in flood from the heavy rain and presented a serious obstacle to any French advance. In the town were two stone bridges, one carrying the main road to Brussels. Three-quarters of a mile upstream, the mill of Bierges stood by a narrow wooden bridge carrying a country lane; the Prussians had already begun to dismantle this bridge. Two and a quarter miles upstream from Wavre, at Limale and at Limalette a little further away, were further wooden bridges. Thielmann placed one brigade at Bierges, another behind Wavre, and a third in reserve to its right at La Bavette. Borcke's brigade had taken a short cut from Basse Wavre to the Brussels road and he marched off with six battalions without receiving orders to turn back. The troops that Ziethen had left behind were posted to guard Limale.

When Vandamme reached Wavre at about four, Exelmans with around 3000 dragoons was at Dion-le-Mont. Gérard with his corps was about four miles away, and Pajol's cavalry were some miles further back, with Teste's division of infantry desperately trying to catch up. Without waiting for Grouchy, Vandamme immediately ordered General Habert's division to storm the bridges at Wavre. Habert's troops were met by intense fire from Prussian marksmen inside loopholed buildings and Prussian artillery placed on the high ground over the river, and their repeated assaults failed.

It was at about this moment that Staff Corps Captain William Staveley, sent by Wellington to find the Prussians, spoke to Blücher.[9] Staveley had passed Bülow's infantry and cavalry, who had been gathering to the east of the Bois de Paris for the last hour while their rearguard was still wading across the valley between Saint-Lambert and Lasne. From what Staveley told him and what Blücher's own scouts were reporting, the field marshal concluded that Wellington was in urgent need of help. He decided to attack immediately with just the two brigades and cavalry that were to hand, on the grounds that any diversion would be useful. Nevertheless, he stuck to the plan that he had agreed with his generals and with Müffling: he would not march to reinforce Wellington's vulnerable left flank, but would commence an outflanking drive directed at the village of Plancenoit, about two miles away to the south-west, in order to cut off the French line of retreat.

The battle had now become a race against time in three different locations. Could Napoleon break Wellington's army before Blücher intervened? Could Blücher get enough troops onto the battlefield to deliver a decisive attack against Napoleon's flank before Wellington's line gave way? And could Thielmann hold off Grouchy, or would the French cross the river and roll up the Prussians as they marched?

57

The Grand Battery Rebuilt

Mont Saint-Jean, 3–3.45 p.m.

Captain Staveley had set off in search of Blücher during the lull in the fighting that occurred after the British cavalry charge. The cannonade rumbled on at lower intensity, as did the skirmishing, especially around Hougoumont and La Haye Sainte; nevertheless, as Assistant Quartermaster James Shaw, attached to Alten's division, wrote, 'The interval between this attack and the next was very considerable, and no one in the Anglo-allied line could imagine what the next move would be.'[1]

Soldiers of the division that had been Picton's took the opportunity to locate and evacuate men who had been hurt, to preserve or loot the possessions of the dead and wounded, and to reorganise. An ensign of the Royal Scots watched 'a greater number of our soldiers busy in rifling the pockets of the dead, and perhaps the wounded, than I could have wished to have seen'. Then his brigade was ordered back behind the brow of the hill and the ensign lay on the ground to avoid the cannonballs, reading letters taken from prisoners. After the charge downhill in pursuit of the French, Sergeant David Robertson had missed his 'particular and well-beloved comrade', the sergeant-major, and went to look for his body. 'As I knew he had a valuable watch upon him, I went out between the fires of the two lines and took it, and some other things, off him, for the behoof of his widow.' Robertson also discovered that his captain was 'wounded, and amissing' and as all the subalterns had been wounded or killed on the 16th, he was now in command of what was left of two companies of Gordon Highlanders.[2]

Behind the front line, the ground was littered with displaced persons. Twenty-two-year-old Charles O'Neil from Dundalk was a fine example of Wellington's 'scum'. He had entered adult life as a bounty-jumper – someone who took the King's bounty of up to eighteen guineas for joining the army and then immediately deserted, before repeating the trick with a different regiment. This lucrative career was cut short after four bounties when he was suddenly shipped to Portugal before he could desert. He had never been wounded until Waterloo, but soon after Picton was shot a bullet hit his right arm and he started to walk back towards the field hospital. Faint with loss of blood, he was making slow progress when a second ball hit his thigh. He is probably a most unreliable witness, but he told of a woman carrying a child, prowling nearby. She had just bent to take a watch from a dead officer when a shell exploded, knocking her to the ground and cutting her child in half. She looked at it for a moment, and then continued her work of looting. Despite the cold-hearted callousness of this front-line looter, she helped the wounded Irishman to shelter from the hail of shot in the lee of a small hillock.[3]

It was perfectly permissible to leave the ranks with a wound and seek help behind the lines, although to leave with a very minor injury was likely to invite contempt from colleagues. Captain Edward Kelly of the Life Guards, the hero of Genappe the previous day, left the field with a broken leg, and subsequently wrote to his wife in confidence, 'There are some officers, who were absent from some idle excuse or other, who are envious of my praises. One you mentioned in your last letter might have been in the Field on Sunday but he reported himself wounded from a scratch and when he heard Ferrior was killed, he posted off to take command of the Regt. immediately. This to yourself.'[4]

It was also generally permissible to help a wounded man from the field. Bandsmen and other supernumeraries were supposed to help the wounded, but there were only a few bandsmen so they were quickly expended. Ney allowed two men to help a comrade with a fracture and one to assist a man with any other wound, while Napoleon sought to reduce the consequent wastage of manpower by providing ambulances to fetch the wounded from the front line. But the ambulance service at Waterloo was inadequate. An aide to Prince Jérôme wrote that soldiers returned from taking wounded men back complaining that the ambulance drivers had fled, abandoning the vehicles; this was hardly surprising, he continued, since the ambulances were being driven by postillions from the civilian post coach service who had been forced into the army and had never before been under fire.[5]

Having helped their wounded colleagues to the nearest advanced dressing station, soldiers were supposed to return, but many got lost or took the opportunity to linger out of harm's way. An experienced captain of the British light dragoons was proud that at the end of the battle his troop had 'less than one man away assisting each wounded': even so, this nearly doubled his effective casualties. This practice had serious implications for battlefield attrition, and explains how, in many cases, so few men remained with the colours after several hours of fighting. Captain Mercer of the horse artillery claimed with typical post-war British disdain for their Belgian allies that he saw Belgian wounded with 'six, eight, ten and even more attendants', but it wasn't only Belgian officers who required such care. A Scots Grey recalled early in the battle watching a wounded Highland officer being carried down the hill 'in a blanket by five or six of his regiment, when a shell came and fell near them and destroyed nearly the whole'. Where five or six men left a battalion each time an officer was wounded its strength was quickly eroded.[6]

Once rallied and reorganised, the infantry of d'Erlon's corps formed squares in the valley, and companies took turns to go forward to duel with the reduced forces of the British 5th Division in what became a prolonged skirmishing match. Lieutenant Martin's foot had been stood on by a horse and he had a slight bayonet wound above his knee, but he continued to lead a remnant of the 45th.

Although the failure of d'Erlon's attack had been a serious setback, the assault had resulted in a net gain in territory. When the gun line of the Grand Battery was rebuilt it was situated on the forward position, 250 yards from La Haye Sainte and 600 yards from the crest of the ridge, with the French squares on the slope beneath it and their skirmish line sometimes lining the hedge of the Ohain road.[7] The charge of the British heavy cavalry had caused Napoleon to mount his horse and gallop forward over the battlefield, surrounded by his staff. To repair the Grand Battery he called up Guard artillery, including 12-pounders, to replace what had been damaged or abandoned, and their rapid deployment and accurate fire put a stop to further allied cavalry attacks. Napoleon was discussing the situation with General Jean-Jacques Desvaux, commander of the Guard Artillery, when Desvaux was killed by a cannonball; this caused Napoleon to split the Imperial staff into less conspicuous groups.[8]

Meanwhile, Wellington's aides called forward reinforcements from the allied reserves. A brigade of German Legionaries and two battalions of Hanoverian Landwehr formed square and advanced to make a second line in the area behind Hougoumont. Two more Landwehr battalions marched off to the right to support the squares of Mitchell's brigade against Piré's light cavalry between Hougoumont and Braine l'Alleud.[9] Further west, Vinke's brigade of Hanoverian Landwehr took an hour to disentangle their battalions from Best's before marching to a position in central reserve close to the Charleroi road. Here they were replacing the Nassauers, who advanced into the front line to occupy the space left empty by the destruction of two German battalions. With these very inexperienced troops plugging gaps it was invaluable to have Sir John Lambert's fresh brigade of veteran British infantry marching in to replace Kempt's battalions in the front line east of the Charleroi road.

Their ordeal began during their march forward to Mont Saint-Jean, for this coincided with a renewed intensification of fire from the Grand Battery. The French cannonade became violent in the extreme, 'probably as much so as has been witnessed in any open field of battle'. Carl von Alten said that even the oldest soldiers (and he was one of them) had never seen anything like it.[10] Sergeant William Lawrence recalled:

> a shell from the enemy cut our deputy-sergeant-major in two, and having passed on to take the head off one of my company of grenadiers named William Hooper, exploded in the rear not more than one yard from me, hurling me at least two yards into the air, but fortunately doing me little injury beyond the shaking and carrying a small piece of skin off the side of my face.

The shell burned off the tail of his red sergeant's sash and blackened the handle of his sword.

A young lad named Bartram, who had never before been in action, came to Lawrence and told him he had to fall out of line because he had been taken ill. Despite encouraging words, 'Bartram fell down and wouldn't move another inch.' Lawrence felt he should have been shot for cowardice, but left him lying there.[11]

No soldier from the ranks of the British army had been tried or shot for such an offence during the whole of the Peninsular War: a good few were shot for desertion, but none for cowardice in the face of the enemy. The only punishment for cowardice in someone who was not an officer was personal shame and the contempt, silent or otherwise, of comrades, which could, as a Highlander of the Black Watch implied, make his future army life fairly unpleasant: 'a man may drop behind in the field but this is a dreadful risk to his reputation ... woe to the man that does it, whether through fatigue, sudden sickness or fear.' Tom Morris later prevented one of his men from receiving a Waterloo medal because during the conflict, 'he ran away to Brussels, and placing his arm in a sling, reported himself wounded.'[12]

Officers, however, faced dismissal, though the honour of the regiment tended to ensure this was kept private; if all the evidence survives, only two British officers faced a court martial for cowardice on 18 June, and that was because of the enmity of their ambitious and not very popular accuser. A more common penalty was to be forced out by one's colleagues. The Earl of Portarlington, commander of the 23rd Light Dragoons, was an example: accused by Uxbridge of refusing to charge at Genappe, he was 'taken dangerously ill with spasms and a violent bowel attack' and carried to Brussels that evening 'in a dangerous state'. He was forced to retire from the regiment in September 1815 and, despite the efforts of his friend the Prince Regent to uphold his honour – and despite, too, a story that he fought at Waterloo with another regiment – he 'took to dissipation, lost a large fortune, and died at a humble lodging in an obscure London slum'. A number of Hanoverian officers went sick between 16 and 18 June; the weather and the unusual exertion demanded of men on those days could genuinely have caused some to fall ill, but colleagues were inclined to be suspicious.[13]

British records tend not to document such things and they only emerge from private letters. Lieutenant John Gordon of the 18th Hussars was thought to have been killed at Waterloo but returned to the unit, his horse having been shot before he rode another to Brussels. Before his departure, 'Major Grant had found him so anxious during the business that he had relieved him of the command of his half squadron and put MacDuffy in his place.' Gordon left the army in 1816.[14]

Of the two officers who were court-martialled, the thorough investigation, which took place soon after the battle, revealed, better than any other evidence we have, how little people under oath remembered of just what had happened at any given moment on the day of Waterloo. Both officers were accused of sheltering behind a bank after their men had gone forward, but witnesses gave conflicting versions of when and where. The court's judgment reflected the existing reputation of the officers as much as what anybody could recall. Both were acquitted, although only one, Henry Ross-Lewin, was completely exonerated.[15]

Such detailed investigations as those trials often throw up enlightening details about battlefield behaviour. For instance, from the evidence given to the court it emerged that when that regiment – the 32nd – was ordered to lie down it was usual for the officers to lie down with the men. Whenever the artillery fire intensified and there was no threat

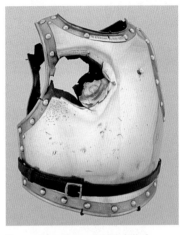

Breastplate of a carabinier killed
by a roundshot recovered from the
battlefield of Waterloo

Prussian cavalrymen of 1815: a
Silesian uhlan wearing the iron
cross, a cuirassier and a trumpeter
of dragoons

'Et moi aussi je viens de l'Isle d'Elbe!',
one of Napoleons braves, symbol of
French military might

North gate of Hougoumont from the north with the dovecote and burned-out château

South gate of Hougoumont from the south with the garden wall right, sketched on 20 June

Ruins of Hougoumont from the west with the sunken lane left and the wood right.
Matthew Clay was initially stationed on this side of the farm. The château itself has
been destroyed

La Haye Sainte looking north towards Wellington's position by Thomas Stoney, 21 June.
Note that the banks either side of the cutting are taller than the wagon passing through it

View looking south-east from the valley with La Haye Sainte left and La Belle Alliance
centre. The sketch gives an idea of the height of the wheat

Life Guards defeating cuirassiers

Cuirassiers charging British infantry squares

Fighting between the Prussians and the French Old Guard in Plancenoit

The arrival of Ziethen's corps with the French army in rout

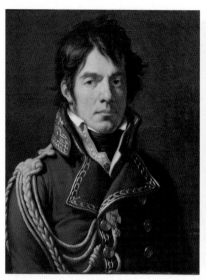

Dominique Larrey, chief surgeon to the Imperial Guard: Napoleon said he was 'the most virtuous man that I have known'
© Fine Art Images/Heritage Images/Topfoto

John Haddy James, assistant surgeon to the 1st Life Guards © Wellcome Library, London

The field of Waterloo covered with dead and wounded: the density of killing was greater than at the Somme in 1916

Drawings by the surgeon Charles Bell of wounded men in the hospitals at Brussels:

Voltz of the German Legion, an amputee who survived tetanus

Dominique Modere of the 1st Line lay for three days in a field near Hougoumont with a bullet in his brain but survived

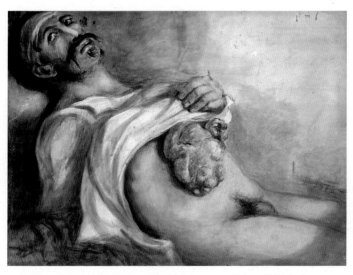

Peltier of the 3rd Lancers, stabbed in the stomach by a British dragoon

The Nec plus ultra of cannibalism; this caricature, published in August 1815, is a hostile French view of Napoleon after his defeat: 'In the name of liberty I hold them in chains,' proclaims his banner, and behind him is a view of the battle of Waterloo along with towns burned to ashes

The Present State of France Exemplified shows Louis XVIII with Talleyrand and Fouché, supported by bayonets; in the background his supporters take vengeance on Bonapartists, while Prussians, sitting on large bags of gold, pay the starving people to shout, 'Vive les Bourbons!'

from enemy cavalry the British troops lay down. The re-establishment of the French Grand Battery was one such moment and the British infantry in front lay down. The Prince of Orange, Charles Alten and their staff watched anxiously for developments from a commanding position on the ridge midway between the two main roads (today occupied by the Lion Mound, a monument built by the Belgians in order to commemorate the battle on the spot where the Prince had stood).

As the French barrage increased in intensity their own artillery suffered serious damage and 'several powder wagons blew up in front of, and close to, the brigade.'[16] Major Lloyd, who had earlier appealed to Mercer for help, had his leg shot off – a wound that also proved fatal. Captain Friedrich Weiz of the 1st Nassau Regiment vividly remembered the moment when 'three guns of a recently arrived battery were smashed before having fired a single shot' and one of the battery's caissons blew up just as it was passing in front of Weiz's own battalion. Then 'with the caisson all ablaze, its horses panicked and drove it straight towards the large artillery park, from where they had come. A major disaster was averted when some dragoons rode up in a hurry and, while racing along, stabbed and brought down the horses.'[17] Cleeves's battery, immediately in front of the Nassauers, was reduced to two guns without horses, although the crews of these guns remained with them, firing until the last second when threatened, and then taking shelter in the ranks of the Nassau battalion. The rest of the battery had gone. The French guns fired canister at the skirmishers out in front: the three senior officers with Edward Macready all fell within two minutes before he retreated with a surviving third of the men.

Experienced troops were constantly changing formation according to the threat, line for artillery, square for cavalry: Edmund Wheatley recalled that 'In order to destroy our squares, the enemy filled the air with shells, howitzers and bombs, so that every five or six minutes, the whole Battalion lay on its face then sprang up again when [the danger] was over. The Prince of Orange gallop'd by, screaming out like a new born infant, "Form into line! Form into line!"'

Lying down offered further opportunities for the risk averse. One of Lieutenant Wheatley's duties as he prowled the square of the 5th German Line was 'inspecting the fallen to detect deception or subterfuge', in order to determine whether his men were really dead or wounded or just pretending to be. Sticking a sword point in them usually worked.[18] Wheatley tried to walk about and appear calm, 'chatting and joking with the young officers who had not then smelt powder', but even he had really seen nothing like the carnage around him:

> An ammunition cart blew up near us, smashing men and horses. I took a calm survey of the field around and felt shocked at the sight of broken armour, lifeless bodies, murdered horses, shattered wheels, caps, helmets, swords, muskets, pistols, still and silent. Here and there a frightened horse would rush across the plain trampling on the dying and the dead. Three or four poor wounded animals standing on three legs, the other dangling before. We killed several of these unfortunate beasts and it would have been an equal Charity to have perform'd the same operation on the wriggling, feverish, mortally lacerated soldiers as they rolled on the ground.[19]

Wheatley was finding the renewed bombardment very difficult to endure: 'We still stood in line. The carnage was frightful. The balls which missed us mowed down the Dutch behind us, and swept away many of the closely embattled Cavalry behind them. I saw a cannon ball take away a Colonel of the Nassau Regiment so cleanly that the horse never moved from under him.' And it was altogether too much for the Duke of Cumberland's Hussars, who 'at first fell into some agitated movements and then took off in the wildest of flights'. Though pursued by Uxbridge's burly aide Horace Seymour, they refused to return to the battlefield and continued on to Brussels and beyond.[20]

At about this time and in this area Quartermaster-General Sir William Delancey was on the ridge talking to Wellington when a ricocheting cannonball, or possibly just its wind, hit him and, 'striking him on his back, sent him many yards over the head of his horse. He fell on his face and bounded upwards and fell again.' The staff ran to Delancey, who told Wellington to let him die in peace. But his cousin, one of his assistants, had him carried to the rear and eventually to Waterloo, where he was placed in a bed in a cottage.[21]

Casualties were mounting and the cumulative stress imposed on the troops in its path by the French Grand Battery was beginning to have an effect on their morale. How long could the French keep up the pressure and how long could the troops in Wellington's line take the punishment that the French artillery was handing out?

58

Sauve Qui Peut!

Waterloo to Brussels, 4–6 p.m.

Behind the allied lines at Waterloo, many of the villagers had gone outside or upstairs to watch the battle. 'We could see the flashes of the guns and heard quite distinctly the sound of firing, but smoke prevented us from making out the actual fighting. Mama was very frightened,' recalled the sixteen-year-old son of the schoolmaster. At about three o'clock wounded men began to trudge up the path from Mont Saint-Jean, the cobbled part of the road being choked with wagons full of ammunition and ambulance wagons and ration carts. The wounded came to the boy's house asking for water and his father stationed him outside with a barrel of watered beer. After a while they heard shouts of '*Sauve qui peut!*'

Tupper Carey, the twenty-two-year-old who was responsible for supplies for the British 2nd Division, had stayed with his headquarters until his general, Sir Harry Clinton, told him to go to the rear and 'to endeavour to find them out when the action was over and if possible bring up supplies'. He lingered until the troops were ordered forward from Merbe Braine, and then rode back half a mile and joined some fellow commissaries who were watching the battle.

Very soon, 'the whole position became enveloped in a dense smoke, and nothing could be perceived'. Carey took two of his officers to Waterloo to look for provisions, but they had only just reached the village 'when another panic, worse than the last, seized the followers of the army and renewed the scenes of the previous evening, which put an end to any transaction of business'. Belgian troops, he said, were 'deserting their standards, spreading reports as they came along that the enemy was at their heels'. Carey was swept away with the crowd but after a while he decided to go back and looped round Waterloo to see what was really going on.

The road was thronged with Belgian fugitives in whole companies, both horse and foot, intermingled with numerous wounded officers and soldiers giving sad and desponding accounts of the progress of the action, together with numerous prisoners of all ranks and sorts, forming a melancholy exhibition of the usual occurrences in the rear of a general action.

However, these first gloomy impressions were dispelled when

Shouts were heard at a distance, and immediately after a group was seen approaching and producing a singular and exulting contrast to the scene around us. It consisted of a detachment of Scots Greys and Inniskilling Dragoons bringing in two eagles just captured from the enemy. Every man was wounded or disabled. One eagle was still on the pole of the standard, and was held up high in the air; the other had been broken off the pole in the scuffle, and was in the possession of two other men, who equally did their utmost to show their trophies to the best advantage. The appearance of the men was not less striking. Some had lost their helmets in the fray, and had handkerchiefs bound round the heads, from which the blood was still trickling; others had their arms in slings, while others had their clothes tattered, as if they had been in personal conflict hand to hand, and been dragged in the mire. The horses appeared to have equally suffered by sabre cuts and other wounds in various parts of the body. In particular, I perceived one as it passed me had had a large portion of flesh torn off his rump by the splinter of a shell.[1]

These wounded but exultant men mingled with lost, confused and sometimes despondent troops of all nationalities. Men from badly damaged units like Carl Jacobi's Lüneberg battalion and the brigades of heavy cavalry were heading for Brussels along with members of units with less excuse, like the Duke of Cumberland's Hussars. In addition, some of those who accompanied the wounded had decided to leave the battlefield; others, such as Tom Morris's rear-rank man or Lieutenant Gordon of the 18th Hussars, simply ran away.

The surgeons of the Hanoverian militia divisions had set up their hospital in some buildings near the windmill at Mont Saint-Jean, but having seen nothing like this devastation before, the junior surgeons and musicians deserted their posts and joined the rout. Only Best's senior surgeon and one junior remained to tend to the wounded, while all of Best's quartermasters and many NCOs and privates retreated with the baggage to Brussels and even Antwerp. The same was doubtless true of other divisions. Later in the afternoon the British evacuated the advanced dressing station that had been established in Mont Saint-Jean farm when it came under heavy fire and its capture by the French seemed imminent, and the walking wounded set off for Brussels.[2]

In the meantime, Tupper Carey and his assistants

got into the Forest of Soignies; and no wonder that an alarm could at such a moment be easily propagated, for the reverberations or echo of the cannonade of the action (in which from three to four hundred guns were at work) was astounding, and enough to frighten those not under military discipline. The fugitives were not in such considerable numbers as the evening before, but they looked as frightened, and as the enemy were not far off, it was easy to apprehend that some detachments of theirs might have found their way to the rear of our army. The road, too, as well as the forest, swarmed with Belgian deserters, horse and foot, dressed much like Frenchmen, and in espying some of these fellows emerging from different points, it was not difficult to conjure them into the shape of enemies. This kept up the impetus of running away, and as this time the right and left of the road was encumbered by the debris of the former panic, the scene altogether was most disheartening. On each side of the Chaussee there was a ditch, in which lay the country waggons upset, with their loads of sacks of corn and biscuit burst out and soaked with wet. In other places remnants of baggage, among which there lay the carriage of the Duke of Richmond upset and set aside as everything else, to enable the ammunition waggons to come up from the rear.

Not everybody on the road was panicking, however; Carey paid special tribute to one 'detachment of artillery with ammunition' which was 'deliberately going up to the front against the stream of fugitives pursuing their way in the opposite direction'.

Returning to Waterloo, he found some fellow commissaries there. 'These were most anxious moments for us all, especially as the reports brought in from the front by the wounded were most discouraging. In this state of things no one dared to get off their horses, much less leave them for a moment, for in the confusion they might have been unceremoniously laid hold of by those who had none, and who were hurrying to the rear.'

About 5 p.m. he rode back towards the village of Mont Saint-Jean seeking information. 'Wounded officers and men continued to come down, and now and then a cannon ball was seen bounding along, but nothing could be heard or seen except clouds of smoke over the hills, and an incessant clatter of great guns and musketry.'

Ten miles further back at Brussels, the politician Thomas Creevey was 'most anxious'. About 3 p.m. he walked 'two miles out of town towards the army, and a most curious, busy scene it was, with every kind of thing upon the road, the Sunday population of Brussels being all out in the suburbs out of the Porte Namur, sitting about tables drinking beer and smoking and making merry, as if races or other sports were going on, instead of the great pitched battle which was then fighting.'[3]

Within the city, however, 'on Sunday the terror and confusion reached its highest point. News arrived of the French having gained a complete victory, and it was universally believed.'[4] Creevey's step-daughter Elizabeth Ord thought that this was 'the most miserable day I ever spent in my life'; during the morning there was no news, but about four she 'came running in' to Creevey 'to announce that the French were in the town'. Then reports of the charge of the Heavy Brigade circulated, followed, about an hour later, by prisoners and the captured eagles.[5] George Scovell's groom witnessed the arrival in Brussels of the same British dragoons that Tupper Carey had seen passing earlier near Waterloo with the eagles, 'so completely plastered in mud that the red of their coats could only be seen in patches'.[6] Some carried the bad news of their subsequent defeat by French cavalry.

Creevey went out and met another politician who had been 'look-ing at the battle, or very near it', and he 'thought everything looked as bad as possible'. It was not a rare opinion. On the steps of the Hotel Bellevue a Life Guard told him, 'Why Sir, I don't like the appearance of things at all. The French are getting on in such a manner that I don't see what's to stop them.'[7]

59

Napoleon Prepares a Second Assault

Hougoumont and La Haye Sainte, 3.15–4 p.m.

At about three o'clock Napoleon had received the message sent by Grouchy from Walhain late that morning, after being misinformed that the Prussians were gathering north-east of Wavre. It told him little, except that at that time Grouchy had not been marching in his direction, but after the three Prussian corps that he thought to be near Wavre. If Grouchy was right in his supposition that this was where these corps had gone, then the Emperor might only have to deal with the one missing, fresh, corps of Bülow, which might not be all that strong and not yet be more than a vanguard. Grouchy should be in contact with any other Prussians. In the meanwhile, Napoleon hoped that a repeat of his earlier attack with cavalry in the centre followed by infantry on the right would succeed before any Prussians interfered.

He now had General Lobau's 6000 fresh infantry in d'Erlon's original starting position east of La Belle Alliance, ready to march round the right flank of the artillery and attack the British left-centre. In his own later narrative, Napoleon claimed that he sent Lobau to delay the Prussians, but sources close to Lobau told a different story: Lobau marched to the French right in order to support d'Erlon's attack in accordance with Napoleon's original plan and he was advancing to renew the assault on the British line.[1]

The second French assault now began. And, like the first, it commenced with attacks on the farms of Papelotte and La Haye, the hamlet of Smohain and the château farm of Fichermont, the strongpoints at the east of the allied line, defended by Nassauers. Skirmishers of the 3rd Nassau battalion were lining a hedge and occupying small buildings at the edge of the marshy valley south of Papelotte when a strong French skirmish line approached, followed by a support column belonging to Durutte's division. The Nassauers pulled back to Papelotte, where four more companies helped to hold the farm with its strong buildings surrounded by hollow roads and thick hedges. The Nassauers, supported by the inexperienced skirmishers of the Verden Landwehr, drove back the French, but in pursuing they ran into an enemy battery firing case shot from 500 paces. The Germans fell back in their turn and the two forces continued to skirmish, the Hanoverians wasting bullets at too long a range.[2]

Papelotte was the only strongpoint they were able to hold against this more determined attack. Further east, at Fichermont, the first battalion of the Orange-Nassau Regiment had been exchanging musketry for hours with French light troops but they were now forced into rapid retreat by intense fire from much larger formations. Durutte's men also seized Smohain and La Haye.[3]

Meanwhile, three miles to the west at the opposite extremity of the French line, Piré's light cavalry had deployed in line, looking as if they were about to threaten Wellington's right flank. The 15th Hussars rode westward to face up to ten squadrons of French cavalry on the other side of the valley and the 13th Light Dragoons lined up behind them in support. General Dörnberg was told to detach his 2nd German Light Dragoons to the extreme right and they formed up in front of Mercer's guns, before being ordered to ride to Braine l'Alleud along a hollow way in which they were concealed from the enemy in order to take up a position from which to charge Piré's left flank. While in the town they seized the opportunity to buy some bottles of wine.

The French front line now ran more or less through Hougoumont and they established artillery batteries to the west of the *château-ferme*. Seeking to set the buildings on fire, they loaded their howitzers with incendiary 'carcasses' – canvas bags reinforced with iron hoops and cord, containing a mixture of turpentine, resin, tallow, sulphur, saltpetre and antimony, which burned for up to twelve minutes and were very difficult to extinguish.[4] While the howitzers set the buildings ablaze, the French guns blasted down the side door into the southern courtyard and grenadiers forced their way in, fighting hand to hand with the Nassau grenadiers defending the compound. The French took seven Nassauers prisoner but were eventually forced out again by shots from the windows and a counter-attack by British Guards from the northern courtyard. Private Matthew Clay was alarmed when the château caught fire, but his officer 'placed himself at the entrance of the room and would not allow anyone to leave his post until our positions became hopeless and too perilous to remain'. Eventually they ran for it; several were injured in leaving the burning building. Clay claimed to have carried a wounded French drummer boy into one of the outhouses, where 'the wounded of both armies were arranged side by side' since they had 'no means of carrying them to a place of greater safety'.

Clay took post under the archway of the southern gates, until another hit from a round shot burst them open and 'wood which was meant for kindling and which was lying inside the farm was quickly scattered in all directions'. This time they stopped the French assault outside the gate, Clay being sent upstairs to defend a breach in the wall of the gardener's house above the gateway, where 'the shattered fragments of the wall were mixed up with the bodies of our dead countrymen who were cut down whilst defending their post'. He found himself under his own company captain and opposite his sergeant.[5]

Private Johann Peter Leonhard from Nassau, one of those defending the garden, was petrified by the French artillery:

> The hornbeam trees of the garden alley, underneath which we stood, were razed by the immense cannonade as if chopped down, and so were the beautiful tall trees along the outside of the farm.

Walls were collapsing ... The skies seemed to have been changed
into an ocean of fire; all of the farm's buildings were aflame. The
soil beneath my feet began to shake and tremble.[6]

From his position on the rising ground above, next to Major-General
Maitland's brigade of Guards, Wellington was micro-managing the
defence. He sent Macdonell, still in command of the farm's British
defenders, a pencil note:

> I see that the fire has communicated from the haystack to the
> roof of the Chateau. You must, however, still keep your men in
> those parts to which the fire does not reach. Take care that no men
> are lost by the falling in of the roof or floors. After they will have
> fallen in occupy the ruined walls inside of the garden, particularly
> if it should be possible for the enemy to pass through the embers
> in the inside of the house.[7]

Within Hougoumont, meanwhile, the Guards' stock of ammunition was getting low. Uxbridge's aide Horace Seymour claimed that
some officers shouted to him from the farm 'to use my best endeav-
ours to send them musket ammunition'. Soon afterwards, Seymour
found 'a private of the Waggon Train in charge of a tumbril on the
crest of the position. I merely pointed out to him where he was
wanted, when he gallantly started his horses and drove straight down
to the farm, to the gate of which I saw him arrive. He must have lost
his horses, as there was a severe fire kept on him.'[8]

The Scots Guards defending the orchard were under sustained
pressure and running short of officers. One lieutenant had been 'shot
through the miniature of the lady he was to have married', a parting
gift from his Belgian sweetheart on 15 June. An ensign was shot
through the head above the right temple and, on recovering consciousness, found himself

> in the arms of kind Colonel West (commanding No. 8 Company),
> who was bandaging my head with a pocket handkerchief. He said
> that he would order a couple of men to take me off the field, but

this I objected to, fancying that I could stand my ground somewhat longer, but this I unfortunately could not, having
immediately fainted from loss of blood. Poor Sir David Baird
(when I fell) took up my sword to try and save it for me, and
sheathed his own; but he had not had it in long when a musket
ball struck him immediately above the chin and lodged in his
throat.

Command of the company passed to a sergeant. The defenders
were driven back across the orchard to the hollow road, but the crossfire from the Coldstream Guards behind the garden wall to their left
was punishing for the French and they were pinned down among the
trees.[9]

A new assault on La Haye Sainte then began. Pierre Aulard's brigade
formed columns to attack the farm.[10] Strong skirmishing lines from
d'Erlon's corps moved up again to the hedge lining the Ohain road,
although they were eventually driven from their position by a second
charge by Kempt's men. Soldiers from Quiot's division skirmished
ahead of the troops assaulting the farm and the artillery discouraged
reinforcements from reaching the hard-pressed German garrison.

Bäring had already been reinforced by two companies from the 1st
Light battalion. He had placed them in the garden, north of the
farm, with the rest of his men in the farm buildings, leaving the
orchard to the south unoccupied. Other Hanoverian riflemen joined
the British rifles around the sandpit, 'where for quite some time they
forcefully resisted the attacking columns'.[11] When two French
columns attacked the farm from either side, the dense formations
presented an easy target for the riflemen and Bäring brought as much
fire to bear on them as he could. Men passed loaded rifles to his best
shots, although without firing platforms or loopholes – only the
crude holes in the brickwork that the men themselves had bashed –
few could fire. They targeted the officers and General Aulard was
shot and killed. Of his two colonels, Jean-Aimable Trupel of the
19th received his sixth wound fighting for France when he was shot
in the chest, while Baron Rignon of the 51st, the son of an alpine

peasant who in 1800 had helped guide Bonaparte's army over his mountains to Italy, and had fought in the Old Guard in all the campaigns of the *Grande Armée*, was finally killed leading his regiment against La Haye Sainte.

Eventually the Frenchmen reached the buildings, whereupon they threw themselves against the walls and tried to pull the rifles out of the hands of the defenders through the holes in the brickwork. Doors and gates were heaped with bodies: at the open barn door 'seventeen Frenchmen already lay dead, and their bodies served as a protection to those who pressed after them to the same spot.' Bäring was proud of his men: 'These are the moments when we learn how to feel what one soldier is to another – what the word "comrade" really means – feelings which must penetrate the coarsest mind, but which he only can fully understand, who has been witness to such moments!' When finally the French gave up and fell back, they were 'accompanied by our shouts, and derision'.[12]

It was around this time that the Emperor's topographical expert, General Simon Bernard, returned from the Bois de Paris on the extreme eastern flank, having accomplished his mission to identify the troops that had been seen approaching from the east. Having crept through the trees close enough to the Lasne to identify through his telescope the crosses on the caps of a line of Prussian skirmishers coming towards him, he rode back to the line of Colonel Marbot's French *tirailleurs*, who had pointed him towards the Prussians, and warned them of what they had to expect. Then he cantered back to Napoleon, who was on his mound near the farm of Rossomme pacing up and down with his hands behind his back.

The Emperor asked in a low voice, 'What tidings, general?'

'Bad ones, Sire.'

'That they are Prussians?'

'Yes, Sire, I recognised them.'

'I thought so. Good, messieurs,' he said while turning towards his suite, 'It goes well, there is Grouchy who arrives.'

Nevertheless, he called another aide-de-camp to whom he told the truth, and who he despatched to Comte de Lobau with the order to change front with his army corps towards the right wing so as to oppose the enemy troops who were about to arrive.[13]

This report by General Bernard is the key to Napoleon's next enforced change of plan. If more Prussians were to appear behind these he would need to break the British line quickly. Obliged to redeploy Lobau's infantry in order to stall the Prussian advance from the Bois de Paris, he no longer had fresh troops to carry the left centre. Instead he ordered Bernard to go and reconnoitre the cutting through which the cobbled road to Brussels passed above La Haye Sainte and to tell him if the cavalry could pass through it with the front of half a squadron. He hoped now to carry the centre through a massed attack by cuirassiers.

To take shelter from the hail of shot thrown by the artillery barrage, the British infantry had retreated to the relative protection of the other side of the ridge, while many of the allied guns had recoiled down the hill and no longer stood on the crest. Ney's next move therefore was to send one brigade of cuirassiers to repeat the attack above La Haye Sainte that had preceded d'Erlon's assault, with the goal of capturing the line of guns on the ridge and breaking any troops that might prove to be demoralised The charge, however, was to develop into something on an altogether grander scale.

60

Milhaud's Charge

Responsibility for the mass attack of French cavalry at Mont Saint-Jean is a matter of dispute. According to the official Bulletin of the French Army published by the *Moniteur* on 21 June, the cavalry saw the British infantry retreat to the shelter of the far slope and attacked spontaneously, without orders, one division supporting another. Although 'To lie like a Bulletin' had become proverbial in France, some later writers have supported this assertion.[1]

It has, however, been more common to attribute the decision to launch mass cavalry attacks to Marshal Ney, mistakenly encouraged by the sight of fugitives, prisoners and wounded men leaving the field. But it seems unlikely that Ney could have seen what was happening on the other side of the hill, although he might have misread the withdrawal of British infantry pulling back to shelter behind the crest of the ridge from the artillery as a retreat. This was what Napoleon's aide Charles de Flahaut believed: 'Seeing the enemy's position apparently denuded, Ney imagined that the Duke of Wellington had commenced a retirement; for he forgot that the English never man the heights, but always use them as a curtain behind which to conceal their troops.'

On the other hand, Ney's aide Pierre Heymès admitted that Ney wanted to occupy the abandoned part of the plateau with cavalry, although he denied that Ney intended to commit more than a brigade, serving to test the resolve of the infantry on the plateau and the strength of the remaining allied cavalry. General Delort, commander of the 14th Division, gave yet another version, recounting that when he saw a brigade of his cuirassiers moving forward without his orders and attempted to call them back, Ney rode over in person, bristling with impatience, to tell Delort that he had instructed the brigade to advance. Delort wanted orders from Count Milhaud, his immediate superior, but in the course of an animated discussion, Ney's demand escalated and finally, in the name of the Emperor, he required both of Milhaud's divisions to charge.

Flahaut claimed, however, that it was Napoleon who caused the escalation in the scope of the mounted assault from Ney's brigade to two divisions. Bonaparte may have thought Ney had thrown in cavalry too early, before the artillery had completed its job, as he later claimed, and it was typical of the Emperor to blame Ney in advance for a risky attack that might well fail, but he knew that he was running out of time. He was gambling that his massed cavalry might achieve a sudden and decisive breakthrough. If this didn't succeed, the cavalry would at least force the enemy into square, making them better targets for the artillery. It may be that Napoleon's light-hearted encouragement of his cautious generals that morning contained the essence of his real design: he would pound them with his numerous artillery; he would charge with his cavalry to force Wellington to reveal his hand; then he would hit them with his Old Guard.

So, without explaining the danger from the Prussians to the east, or the urgent reason for such an attack, he called on Flahaut, his most loyal and intelligent aide, to send in all the cavalry:

I was close to the Emperor on a knoll, where he remained for the greater part of the day, and when he saw Ney beginning the movement by sending a corps of cavalry across the ravine, he exclaimed, 'There is Ney hazarding the battle which was almost won' (these words also are fixed in my memory), 'but he must be supported now, for that is our only chance.' Turning then to me, he bade me order all the cavalry I could find to assist the troops which Ney had thrown at the enemy across the ravine.[2]

Huge cavalry charges against unbroken infantry had succeeded gloriously in the past: at the bloody battle of Eylau, eight years earlier, such a charge had turned the tide of adversity.[3] Napoleon knew that his previous cavalry attack had punched a hole in Wellington's centre, destroying two infantry battalions; he knew that the capacity of the enemy's cavalry to counter-attack was very much reduced, and he may well have hoped that another imposing attack by armoured cavalry on a larger scale would finish the job. Moreover, he had to do something dramatic to obtain a quick result: his hand had been forced by the emergency on the right flank caused by Blücher's decision to show himself.

With the assault on La Haye Sainte still in progress, therefore, Milhaud's cuirassiers – of whom a good 2500 or more remained – followed by 1500 or more lancers and chasseurs of the Guard, now formed up for an attack aimed at Alten's division in the centre of Wellington's line between Hougoumont and La Haye Sainte. There was only room to pack a few hundred of them in line at once into the thousand yards between the two farms, so they formed in columns. The time was around 4 p.m. – 4.15 at the latest.

The leader of the cuirassiers, Jean-Baptiste Milhaud, had proved himself an extremely gifted commander over long years in the army. Now forty-eight years old, had been a political hothead in his youth, at the cutting edge of the Jacobin party. He had taken part in the storming of the Bastille, was a regicide, having voted for the execution of Louis XIV without consulting his electorate, and had been a Representative of the People. He was just the sort of figurehead Napoleon needed: if revolutionary fervour was to inspire his troops to superhuman feats, Milhaud was a leader they could believe in.

To make the attack the regiments had to cross the Brussels high road, having started to the east of it (a manoeuvre that makes any suggestion that the charge was spontaneous somewhat implausible), and they went forward in columns of squadrons rather than in a simple continuous line. The wheeling advance led to a charge with the right wing to the fore, so that the first squadrons to make contact were on the right of the French line and they swept across the plateau from east to west, avoiding the deep cutting of the lane, close to the *chaussée*. 'This was effected in beautiful order and the formation and advance of that magnificent and highly disciplined cavalry had, as a spectacle, a very grand effect,' recalled James Shaw. To the enemy the sight, accompanied by the noise of so many horses, was awe-inspiring: 'You perceived at a distance what appeared to be an overwhelming, long moving line, which, ever advancing, glittered like a stormy wave of the sea when it catches the sunlight. On came the moving host until they got near enough, whilst the very earth seemed to vibrate beneath their thundering tramp.'[4]

The first battalion to be attacked was the 5th of the German Legion, who were taken by surprise when the cavalry emerged from the smoke before they could complete their square. Lieutenant Edmund Wheatley was 'busy in keeping the men firm in their ranks, closing up the vacuities as the balls swept off the men' when 'a regiment of Cuirassiers darted like a thunderbolt among us', and the lieutenant-colonel admitted that 'although the enemy Cuirassiers received the fire of the 5th and of the Grubenhagen Battalion, they managed to break into the square.' Wheatley 'made for the Colors to defend them', and Christian von Ompteda, colonel of the battalion, rushed over to help close the ranks. They were saved by a squadron of cavalry who charged and drove off the cuirassiers, while Ompteda and his officers 'succeeded with infinite difficulty in rallying the men again'. Disaster had only just been averted: Wheatley 'parried with great good fortune a back stroke from a horseman as he flew by me and Captain Sander had a deep slice from the same fellow on the head the instant after'.[5]

Some seven hundred cuirassiers attacked the square formed by the Bremen and Verden battalions, but they mistimed their charge through what may have been ploughed land and came to a premature halt, horses blowing, seventy or eighty paces away from their target. As the cuirassiers wheeled away to their left the Hanoverians fired at them; the captain remembered the French leader lying flat on his horse to avoid the shooting and getting away unscathed.[6]

From behind this Hanoverian square, Belgian carabiniers launched a counter-charge. They were supposed to attack the French flanks but, over-eager, went straight in and suffered at the hands of the more experienced armoured horsemen. Two more squadrons of carabiniers followed up in support, but a mass of more skilful French Guard chasseurs then charged them in the flank and, as the leader of the cuirassiers recalled, 'the Dutch brigade that he sent against us was broken: its debris fled in terror.' Two squadrons of Arentsschildt's 3rd German Hussars charged and drove off the cavalry pursuing the Belgians, but as they galloped off the fleeing horses spooked and almost carried away the horses of the remaining squadrons of hussars.[7]

As soon as the routed Belgians had passed, Lord Uxbridge ordered the remaining two squadrons of hussars to charge two squadrons of advancing cuirassiers. Old Colonel Arentsschildt led his hussars through the line of armoured horsemen but they then found themselves facing an even larger number of French lancers and chasseurs, who so enveloped their flanks that few escaped. After these two charges this large and experienced regiment, which had been holding the centre ground almost single-handed, was reduced to about 120 men.[8]

Just to the right, at the sight of the French cuirassiers coming over the crest and taking possession of the guns of Lloyd's battery that were lined up on the ridge, the two columns of General Sir Colin Halkett's British brigade had also rapidly formed square. The 73rd Highlanders and 30th Cambridgeshires reserved their fire until the cuirassiers were close and then made them veer away with a determined volley. Luckily, the cuirassiers did not at first charge the 1st Nassau, whose commander – judging them incapable of forming square – left his very inexperienced men in column. The Nassauers were inspired and emboldened by the skilled and disciplined way in which the British square 'fired its first volley when the riders were at a distance of 60 to 80 paces' and scattered the attacking French. Fortunately, smoke prevented them from seeing the next square along, which did not fare so well. Sergeant Tom Morris of the 73rd watched the neighbouring square of the 69th and 33rd broken, to be saved from destruction only by the intervention of the Household

Cavalry. An officer of the French cuirassiers fired his pistol at Halkett, hitting his neck and causing severe pain but no lasting damage.[9]

Lord Uxbridge now sent his aide Major William Thornhill to order the Horse Guards to charge. Samuel Ferrior, commander of the 1st Life Guards, was shot dead at the outset, but the Guards drove off the cuirassiers pursuing the British infantry and checked their supports after a severe and bloody conflict in which Major Packe of the Horse Guards was killed while leading a squadron, run through by the officer leading a French squadron. Thornhill, said to be the strongest man in the British army and afterwards credited with having 'slain more men at Waterloo than any other single individual', accepted Sir Robert Hill's courteous invitation to join the charge, but was stunned in the fall when his horse was shot. Hill afterwards told Thornhill how amused he had been at the 'uncommon ugly face' Thornhill had made at a cuirassier who was fighting him.[10]

A reserve squadron of French cuirassiers then hit the 1st Nassau column and the Bremen and Verden square simultaneously, but both units withstood the charge. The survival of the combined square of the 73rd and 30th and that of the 5th German Legion was crucial, as these were the last two experienced units holding up the centre. Lieutenant Wheatley of the 5th had 'fired a slain soldier's musket until my shoulder was nearly jellied and my mouth was begrimed with gunpowder to such a degree that I champed the gritty composition unknowingly'. The 5th was charged again and again, with cuirassiers reforming out of sight and leaving an officer on the ridge to direct their charges. Ompteda urged his men to take down the officer, but nobody could hit him until a rifleman from the first battalion, lying within the square with a broken leg, volunteered to be carried into a sniping position and brought him down with his first shot.[11]

A few hundred yards further west an officer of the 2nd Line of the Legion, in the second line, half a mile behind the first, was watching what was happening ahead:

we observed the Regiments of the first Line form Squares to repel Cavalry – this movement was scarcely executed when the French Cavalry made a dashing charge. they were received with a severe and galling Fire, that did much execution. they did not however retire immediately, but finding they could make no impression on the 52nd which received their charge they galloped down the Line of Squares, perhaps in the idea of finding some Corps in Confusion. but they were at every point repulsed with the greatest Steadiness. they finally came in Confusion and our Cavalry observing the opportunity cut in amongst them and completed the Havock previously made by the Infantry. those that escaped were immediately supported by numerous Forces, and our Cavalry were obliged to retire in their turn.

Some French squadrons now engaged with one of their objectives, the allied artillery on the ridge, which had been left exposed some distance in front of the infantry as they took shelter from the French artillery bombardment. The same officer observed:

At this charge the French had passed within our Artillery and many of the Men were cut down at the Guns, others escaped by creeping under and the moment the French had repassed, jumped up and fired with the greatest coolness and gallantry. It was also at this charge the Duke of Wellington and his Staff were exposed to considerable hazard of being taken Prisoners. He had been riding on the summit of the Hill (where some Batteries of Artillery were placed) the whole Morning. the best Spot where a general view could be had of the Battle. but certainly the most dangerous Post in the Field – The French Cavalry came on so rapid that the Duke had scarcely time to get within the protection of the Squares. His personal danger, great exertions, and Gallantry were conspicuous to the whole Army throughout the Day.[12]

When the cavalry swept round behind the left flank of the guns above and to the east of Hougoumont, for the most part the gunners limbered up and rode away. Some were saving guns that were already damaged. Some, who had fought at Quatre Bras and had been unable to obtain more ammunition, or whose ammunition had blown up, needed in any case to get more. However, Wellington was furious:

> The French cavalry charged, and were formed on the same ground with our artillery, in general within a few yards of our guns. We could not expect the artillery men to remain at their guns in such a case. But I had a right to expect that the officers and men of the artillery would do as I did, and as all the staff did, that is to take shelter in the Squares of the infantry till the French cavalry should be driven off the ground, either by our cavalry or infantry. But they did no such thing; they ran off the field entirely, taking with them limbers, ammunition, and everything; and when in a few minutes we had driven off the French cavalry, and could have made use of our artillery, we had no artillerymen to fire them; and, in point of fact, I should have had NO artillery during the whole of the latter part of the action, if I had not kept a reserve in the commencement.[13]

Accounts by artillerymen tend to confirm Wellington's allegation, though with many extenuating excuses. They had taken serious damage from the French artillery and some were genuinely short of ammunition after caissons blew up. They were also an alarmingly long distance in front of the squares, although each time the guns recoiled they moved further down the reverse slope and in the heavy soil the gunners couldn't drag their guns back up: 'their best exertions were unable to move the guns again to the crest without horses; to employ horses was to ensure the loss of the animals.'[14] Moreover, with the guns on the downslope, firing up the hill, the French were sheltered from their fire behind the ridge. Cleeves claimed to have pulled his guns back to a position between the squares until he ran out of ammunition, but other evidence indicates that only two of them were repositioned there, possibly the only two still capable of firing. There was not much left of Lloyd's battery. Kühlmann and Sandham pulled out, as did Sinclair, Ramsay and Bull.[15]

The sight of the artillery haring backwards certainly animated the French. Piré's lancers had a good view from their high ground; just as the British 15th Hussars were trying to work out how best to cross the valley to attack them, 'the lancers began cheering, and on looking towards the position we had quitted, the cause of cheering was discovered to be an impetuous attack by the French cavalry upon our infantry and guns, the limbers of which were going rapidly towards the Nivelles road.'[16]

61

Lobau and the Prussians

Eastern flank, 4.30–5.30 p.m.

While the cavalry charged, 7000 fresh infantry commanded by George Mouton, comte de Lobau, were advancing to deliver the knockout blow east of La Haye Sainte. The ninth child of a baker from Lorraine, Mouton had volunteered to fight for the Revolution in 1792 and was elected captain later in the year. His bravery in Italy attracted the attention of Bonaparte, who made him an aide-de-camp from 1805. Tall and robust with black hair and grey eyes, he was frank and direct, a great organiser. He distinguished himself in 1809, winning his title and causing the Emperor to remark, '*Mon mouton est un lion*'. At Napoleon's invitation, he married one of Josephine's ladies and it proved an enduring love match. In 1813 he briefly commanded I Corps, and in 1815 he was again appointed an aide and then put in charge of VI Corps. He was one of Napoleon's most faithful and dependable servants.

Aiming to drive home the French advantage in the area d'Erlon had attacked earlier, Lobau's columns had just reached the crest of the ravine that separated the two armies when his chief of staff, who had gone on ahead to reconnoitre, came back wounded and announced that there was a line of enemy skirmishers on their right flank. Alarmed, Lobau, his aide Janin and General Jacquinot rode over to investigate. There they were, sure enough, and after a while the generals perceived two columns that they estimated at roughly 10,000 men emerge from the trees. Lobau thought it reckless to launch an attack while a force of enemy infantry of equal size to his own was in a position to attack his flank and rear. After an exchange of messages with the Emperor, he redeployed his forces to face the new threat.[1]

At half past four the Prussians had left the cover of the Bois de Paris with slightly more troops than Lobau's staff had guessed: 12,000 infantry, 3000 cavalry and 64 guns. Finding themselves under fire from the small detachment of French infantry posted at the edge of the woods by Colonel Marbot, sharpshooters from the fusilier battalion of the 15th Regiment fired the first Prussian shots of the day. Marbot's men retreated rapidly, covered by a detachment of cavalry.[2] Riding ahead of the Prussian infantry, Silesian Hussars and lancers pushed back the main French skirmish line, while Johann von Hiller's 16th Brigade set off towards Plancenoit with two fusilier battalions under Major von Keller detached to guard the left flank, covered by Falkenhausen's Silesian cavalry.[3]

In front of the Prussians an open and relatively level plateau about half a mile wide stretched almost all the way to Napoleon's tactical headquarters at Rossomme farm, although the ground was more hilly and broken over the last stretch between the village of Plancenoit and Rossomme itself. To their right was the lightly wooded and marshy valley of the Ohain stream with straggling buildings leading to the hamlet of Smohain; to the south of Smohain, the chateau of Fichermont overlooked the valley with woods to the south of it. To their left was the wooded valley of the Lasne stream with the Bois du Ranson and another wood at the edge of the higher ground north of the valley. Both streams were running unusually high, with their valleys flooded or boggy.

The fusilier battalions of the 18th Regiment led off Michael von Losthin's 15th Brigade towards Fichermont. Lancers and horse artillery covered their right flank.[4] Prince Blücher watched them set out, shouting, 'Keep it lively, kids! Keep going forwards! Over fences, hedges and ditches. There is no obstacle too big for us, there must be none. Keep going forwards!' After some exchanges of fire with men who, wearing blue with red facings and bell-top shakos, looked almost exactly like Frenchmen, delegates from the 'enemy' persuaded the fusiliers that the defenders of the farms they were attacking were actually on their side – men from the Orange-Nassau Regiment. Having resolved this misunderstanding, the Prussians probed further west, where they found Fichermont in the hands of genuine enemies and staunchly defended.[5]

The commander of a squadron of Colonel Marbot's 7th Hussars, standing guard on the extreme right wing, had just spoken to General Jean-Siméon Domon, whose chasseurs were deploying to support Lobau's attack on Wellington's left flank. Domon had commented that the fire of the British guns had just about ceased, and that he reckoned the battle was won and the enemy army was already retreating. Reminding the squadron chief that his hussars were there to link up with Grouchy, Domon had ridden off, cheerfully predicting that they would be in Brussels that evening. A few minutes later, rather than meeting Grouchy's patrols as they expected, Marbot's men were charged by the Silesian Hussars of the Prussian vanguard. 'We pushed them back vigorously and gave chase,' the squadron chief recalled, 'but we were forced to retreat by canister fire from six guns.' Prussian horse artillery turned the French hussars around and then Silesian lancers chased them off. Colonel Marbot was speared in the side.[6]

The comte de Lobau's two divisions of infantry took position facing eastward across the lane from Lasne to Plancenoit on the high ground above the track leading from Fichermont southward to the Bois de Ranson. The fighting was done by strong lines of skirmishers supported by cavalry. Lobau had nearly 7000 infantry, 2000 cavalry and 28 guns, and his divisions included some fine regiments. He was able to take the offensive, driving back the Prussians towards the woods.

There was a bitter struggle on the bush-covered high ground near Fichermont, where the Prussians fought to hold a line. When the rest of the corps reserve cavalry arrived, Bülow used most of it to hold a central position, filling the gap between the two brigades, although it was exposed there to fire from Lobau's artillery and both cavalry brigade commanders were killed.

Blücher's decision to send in the two available brigades, made after Stavely had alerted him to Wellington's precarious situation, had been a crucial intervention, one that prevented Lobau, Domon and Subervie from attacking Wellington's left flank. By this stage Wellington had few remaining reserves, especially of any quality. The fresh troops of Lambert's brigade would have put up a fight and Picton's men were tough, but it is unlikely that his weak left flank could have held out against another assault by fresh forces if they had not been diverted elsewhere.[7] Although Blücher's troops were unable to drive back Mouton's men, their intervention at this time was vital to the survival of Wellington's army.

62

The Great Cavalry Charges

Mont Saint-Jean plateau, 5–6 p.m.

When Milhaud's cavalry fell back, the French artillery opened up again. Nearly all of Wellington's reserves had been committed and it is possible that if Napoleon had ordered the Old Guard to attack his centre at this moment he might have prevailed. But he did not yet know the strength of the Prussians, and time was pressing. There was no alternative but to repeat the cavalry attack, so the same forty squadrons – still more than 4000 cavalry – surged uphill again.

Wellington called in some of his remaining reserves of artillery. Having advanced to the crest of the ridge above Hougoumont where they deployed, the Brunswick foot battery were almost immediately attacked by a regiment of cuirassiers advancing at the trot. In response, General Dörnberg ordered his 23rd Light Dragoons to attack the left flank of the cuirassiers and his 1st German Light Dragoons to attack their right. He gave strict instructions that if they were successful only the first squadron was to pursue, but the reserves joined in instead of waiting and were then beaten by the enemy reserve which lapped round their flanks. Some of the 23rd, with an ill-discipline sadly typical of British cavalry, went charging across the valley and up the other side; there, some were captured while those who could escape fled, sweeping away the Brunswick artillery in their rout. The Brunswickers took one gun with them and abandoned the other seven, the gunners riding for their lives until the cuirassiers veered away from the fire of the 1st Brunswick line regiment, behind whose square the gunners took refuge.[1]

Dörnberg gathered the remains of his brigade behind the squares. When another cuirassier regiment attacked, his dragoons charged again but head-on could make no impact on the armoured cavalry. Dörnberg was stabbed through the left lung; unable to speak clearly, with blood filling his throat, he rode to find a surgeon.

Grant's brigade of light cavalry now abandoned its planned attack on the French lancers threatening the right wing and returned to its original position behind Hougoumont. From there they countercharged the enemy cavalry, the 13th Light Dragoons leading with the 15th in support. They drove the cuirassiers back a short distance, but the French supports enveloped the line of light cavalry and forced them to ride back and seek shelter behind the squares.

Both lines of infantry on the right wing were now formed in squares to receive cavalry, and with little firing taking place, the impressive spectacle could actually be appreciated. Jack Barnett, the young Highland Light Infantryman, told his mother that 'It was a beautiful sight to see 10 or 12 fine regiments formed in hollow squares, the French cavalry galloping all round us, not able to penetrate,' and a lieutenant of the 2nd Line of the Legion was similarly impressed: 'I believe at this moment was displayed the grandest Sight and most heroic Courage and firmness ever witnessed on both sides – in my view there were at least 20,000 Infantry Occupying a Space of half an English Mile each Regiment formed into Squares four deep, the two Front Ranks kneeling.'[2]

Sometimes French cavalry swept across the plateau. Captain Mercer watched light cavalry squadrons charging at each other as if there would be a huge clash, but actually passing through one another with only one or two men falling. The inexperienced 14th Buckinghamshire 'peasants' had moved from a sheltered situation in a gully onto the plateau, where they were exposed to shot and shell. A bugler of the 51st, mistaking their square for his own, had just said, 'Here I am again safe enough!' when a round shot shattered his head and splattered the colour party with his brains, causing an aristocratic ensign who was a notorious dandy to drawl, 'How extremely disgusting!' A second shot removed six bayonets in a row. Another broke a sergeant's breastbone and his screams unnerved the young soldiers who lay down in the mud to minimise casualties. Sixteen-year-old ensign the Hon. George Keppel sat on a drum with his arm round the colonel's mare, until a shell exploded, knocking over the drum. A shard struck the horse on the nose and killed it.[3] The regiment moved again, taking cover behind a slight rise in the ground, not far from Captain Mercer's troop of horse artillery. Behind them ammunition wagons exploded and a loose horse had the whole of the lower part of its head blown away.

Mercer was talking to the local artillery commander 'when suddenly a dark mass of cavalry appeared for an instant on the main ridge, and then came sweeping down the slope in swarms'. The artillery officers watched as

the hollow space became in a twinkling covered with horsemen, crossing, turning, and riding about in all directions, apparently without any object. Sometimes they came pretty near us, then would retire a little. There were lancers amongst them, hussars, and dragoons – it was a complete melee. On the main ridge no squares were to be seen; the only objects were a few guns standing in a confused manner, with muzzles in the air, and not one artilleryman. After caracoling about for a few minutes, the crowd began to separate and draw together in small bodies, which continually increased; and now we really apprehended being overwhelmed, as the first line had apparently been. For a moment an awful silence pervaded that part of the position to which we anxiously turned our eyes. 'I fear all is over,' said Colonel Gould [*sic*: Charles Gold, commander of the artillery of Clinton's division], who still remained by me. The thing seemed but too likely, and this time I could not withhold my assent to his remark, for it did indeed appear so.

Nearby, Thomas Jeremiah of the 23rd Welch Fuzileers watched the 23rd Light Dragoons in flight and then faced up to French cavalry, who 'passed us after failing to break into our square and was very near annihilating one of our regiments who was all composed of inexperienced soldiers'.[4] He meant the 14th, 'fresh from the plough' but stiffened by the transfer of a few battle-hardened officers, such as Captain Loraine White, who had fought all the major battles of the Peninsular campaign with the Cambridgeshires. Momentarily confused, the regiment just scampered into square in time as French cavalry swept past the 23rd and then passed them.

Aiming to escape along the Nivelles road, the cavalrymen had to veer away from the barricade on the bridge over the lane where Sergeant William Wheeler was stationed. Wheeler had just stalked and killed a French hussar officer who was 'sneaking down to get a peep at our position':

> One of my men was what we term a dead shot, when he was within point blank distance. I asked him if he could make sure of him. His reply was 'To be sure I can, but let him come nearer if he will, at all events his death warrant is signed and in my hands, if he should turn back.' By this time he had without perceiving us come up near to us. When Chipping fired, down he fell and in a minute we had his body with the horse in our possession behind the rock.

His section's syndicate took the opportunity to add to its fortune: 'We had a rich booty, forty double Napoleons and had just time to strip the lace of the clothing of the dead Huzzar when we were called in.' It was then that the French cavalry, returning from the plateau to their own lines by the Nivelles road, were ambushed:

> Not choosing to return by the way they came they took a circuitous rout and came down the road on our left. There were nearly one hundred of them, all Cuirassieurs. Down they rode full gallop, the trees thrown across the bridge on our left stopped them. We saw them coming and was prepared, we opened our fire, the work was done in an instant. By the time we had loaded and the smoke had cleared away, one and only one, solitary individual was seen running over the brow in our front. One other was saved

by Capt. Jno. Ross from being put to death by some of the Brunswickers.[5]

Jean-Baptiste Lemonnier-Delafosse, acting chief of staff to General Maximilien Foy, saw some survivors return – 'fifteen to eighteen cuirassiers' under a sous-lieutenant, 'covered in blood, black with mud', their horses soaked in sweat and steaming, eighty-four of the squadron having failed to get back. Foy watched the enormous cavalry mêlées with astonishment, remarking that he had never seen anything like them in his life; he said that several squadrons went straight through the centre of the English army and formed up again behind his own division, having circled all round the Hougoumont wood.[6]

Around the same time the troops on the British right suffered another alarm, as 'loud and repeated shouts (not English hurrahs) drew our attention to the other side. There we saw two dense columns of infantry pushing forward at a quick pace towards us, crossing the fields, as if they had come from Merbe Braine.' Pat Brennan, an experienced Irish officer of the 14th, loudly identified them as French. '"Hold your tongue, Pat," thundered Colonel Tidy, "What do you mean by frightening my boys?" but the expression of his countenance showed that he shared Pat's apprehension.' The fear was that French infantry had taken Braine l'Alleud and had got round their right flank, just as French cavalry appeared to be over-running their left. Captain Mercer turned his guns to face this new threat. Everyone thought they were French, but still Mercer held his fire.

Shouting, yelling, and singing, on they came, right for us; and being now not above 800 or 1000 yards distant, it seemed folly allowing them to come nearer unmolested. The commanding offi-cer of the 14th, to end our doubts, rode forward and endeavoured to ascertain who they were, but soon returned, assuring us they were French. The order was already given to fire, when, luckily, Colonel Gould [sic] recognised them as Belgians.[7]

It was General Chassé's 3rd Netherlands division, advancing to support the British right flank; it formed up against the Nivelles–Brussels road.

Then, towards 5 p.m., Sir Augustus Frazer galloped up and shouted to Mercer, 'Left limber up, and as fast as you can.' Frazer was calling in his last reserves of horse artillery to face a new attack. Having suffered heavy casualties, including more than half its officers, Milhaud's cavalry was being pulled out and replaced by Kellermann's, supported by the Dragoons and Horse Grenadiers of the Guard. The troop limbered up, formed in pairs, three guns deep, and trotted off. Mercer rode with Frazer, 'whose face was as black as a chimney-sweep's from the smoke, and the jacket-sleeve of his right arm torn open by a musket-ball or case-shot, which had merely grazed his flesh'. Frazer explained that the enemy 'had assembled an enormous mass of heavy cavalry in front of the point to which he was leading us . . . and that in all probability we should immediately be charged on gaining our position.'

As they ascended the reverse slope of the main position, the atmosphere changed dramatically:

> the air was suffocatingly hot, resembling that issuing from an oven. We were enveloped in thick smoke, and, *malgré* [despite] the incessant roar of cannon and musketry, could distinctly hear around us a mysterious humming noise, like that which one hears of a summer's evening proceeding from myriads of black beetles; cannon-shot, too, ploughed the ground in all directions, and so thick was the hail of balls and bullets that it seemed dangerous to extend the arm lest it should be torn off.

The unfamiliar hum was that of cannonballs and bullets whizzing through the air.

The troop's kind-hearted surgeon, who had not been in a battle before, 'began staring round in the wildest and most comic manner imaginable, twisting himself from side to side, exclaiming, "My God, Mercer, what is that? What is all this noise? How curious! – how very curious!" And then when a cannon-shot rushed hissing past,

"There! – there! What is it all?"' With difficulty, Mercer persuaded him that it was important to them that their surgeon should not be killed and it was time for him to withdraw. Frazer indicated where he wanted Mercer's guns, between two squares of Brunswick infantry, and left them with a reminder to economise their ammunition and withdraw into the squares when cavalry charged.[8]

The British staff was anxious about these inexperienced Brunswick battalions above Hougoumont. The first cavalry attack on them had been foiled by their foot artillery, which unlimbered rapidly and hit the cavalry with canister, but since then the Brunswick foot battery had been badly cut up and Frazer had brought in his reserves to reassure the infantry.

Mercer, though, did not like the look of the squares behind him. 'The Brunswickers were falling fast – the shot every moment making great gaps in their squares, which the officers and sergeants were actively employed in filling up by pushing their men together, and sometimes thumping them ere they could make them move.' The young Brunswickers seemed to be in shock, standing 'like so many logs'. Their officers and sergeants were doing a good job, 'not only keeping them together, but managing to keep their squares closed in spite of the carnage made amongst them', but Mercer felt that if his gunners ran away towards them, they were quite likely to cause the Brunswickers to run too.[9]

Another battery came up from reserve into a position to the right of Mercer, with Ramsay and Bull on their right.[10] The first charges took heavy punishment from the fresh artillery. The Horse Grenadiers and Dragoons of the Guard, each about 800 strong, attacked in this area, although Napoleon later claimed that he had given no orders for this ultimate reserve of cavalry to join in.[11] Their commander, General Claude-Etienne Guyot, was the son of a farm labourer and had risen to be a captain in Napoleon's horse chasseurs of the Consular Guard by 1802. From 1807 to 1814 he had been responsible for the Emperor's personal safety on campaign and while travelling, and he was a devoted supporter, intelligent and capable. In the second charge Guyot had his horse shot under him and as he walked down the hill was knocked over, trampled and sabred by pursuing cavalry, but before they could capture him he was rescued by a fresh French attack. Someone gave him horse, but an instant later he was shot in the chest and hit in the arm by a shell splinter. He went to have his wounds dressed – after treatment, he eventually rejoined his troops – handing over command to a colleague who was killed in the next charge.[12]

On the western side of Wellington's line where the Guards and Brunswickers stood, this pattern repeated itself several times: after an aborted charge the British and German cavalry would drive the French back into the valley, but this allowed the French artillery to fire into the allied squares. Then the French cavalry walked up the hill to see if any squares had weakened. To the east, it is not so clear that the French were ever driven from the high ground, though they presumably allowed their artillery to play their part. The remaining British cavalry here was soon more or less exhausted and there was no fresh artillery. Something of a stand-off now developed: the cavalry became tired and unwilling to charge home, given the prospect of a volley fired from very close range, while the infantry knew that they were vulnerable if they wasted their volley at long range. They were ordered to hold their fire both for this reason and because most units were now short of ammunition.

The commander of a squadron of Kellermann's 7th Dragoons described the conundrum from the French point of view:

> The squares resolutely awaited the cavalry and held their fire until point blank range. The powerful impact of infantry fire on morale, being greater than its physical effect on cavalry, was never better illustrated. The steadiness of the English infantry was more remarkable still by the absence of the volley that we awaited and to our great surprise we did not receive. This disconcerted our troops. Realising that they would be exposed to a fire that would be much more murderous from being at point blank range, fright seized them, and probably to escape such a fire, the first squadron wheeled to the right and caused a similar movement by all the following squadrons. The charge failed . . .[13]

Even the fire-eating Colonel Michel Ordener, in his frustration, paid tribute to the resilience of the enemy infantry: 'We were almost masters of the plateau. But the English seemed to be rooted to the soil; although they were three quarters annihilated, you had to keep killing them until the last soldier fell.'[14] The British infantry were less troubled by the cavalry than by the artillery that played on them when the cavalry withdrew: 'Though we constantly thrashed our steel-clad opponents,' wrote Edward Macready of the 30th Foot, 'we found more troublesome customers in the round shot and grape which all this time played on us with terrible effect, and fully avenged the Cuirassiers. Often as the volleys created openings in our square would the cavalry dash on, but they were uniformly unsuccessful.'[15] The infantry refused to present gaps to tempt the cavalry to charge and the cavalry refused to charge the unbroken infantry. On the other hand, the infantry caused very few casualties when the cavalry came close enough to make them fire, 'to the surprise of those officers present who allowed themselves to see with their own eyes', as one officer commented. 'Indeed, the ill-directed charges, of which we have been speaking, could not have continued so long and been so frequently renewed, had not the destroying power of the infantry been exceedingly small.' An engineer officer could not believe 'how few fell: only one officer and two men, though no doubt many were wounded. Many squares fired at the distance of thirty yards, with no better effect.'[16]

Gradually, the charges petered out into stalemate. Kellermann was at a loss, desperate for relief:

> It was not possible to force the cavalry, excellent as it was, into new charges: it found itself in the cruellest of positions, without infantry or artillery support.
>
> The enemy squares reserved their fire, but were covered by a cloud of skirmishers whose each shot counted. It was in this awful position that our cavalry remained several hours.[17]

In some cases the allied skirmishers were thin on the ground or non-existent and it was French mounted skirmishers who rode close to the allied squares and fired into them, hoping to provoke a reaction. But both sides accepted the casualties and obstinately remained where they were. Having formed square, the men of Picton and Lambert's divisions to the east of the Charleroi highway were rarely threatened by the cavalry, though Robertson recalled one charge on the Gordons by lancers, but they suffered terribly from uninterrupted artillery fire that mowed them down where they stood.

Old soldiers realised that now 'the battle was not a trial of skill or soldiership but a trial of who should hold out longest', while even young Edward Macready understood that 'it was now to be seen which side had most bottom, and would stand killing longest.' In the centre of the position, Lieutenant Wheatley stood within the little square of the 5th German infantry, took a pinch of snuff, and 'thought of the old ballad' – actually Robert Southey's anti-war poem 'The Battle of Blenheim' – that he had heard when young. Although mis-quoting the detail, he remembered the spirit of 'the aged Nurse who describes the glorious battles of Marlborough to the child' who asked:

> 'Ten thousand slain you say and more,
> What did they kill each other for?'
> 'Indeed I cannot tell', said she,
> 'But 'twas a famous victory'.[18]

63

The Fall of La Haye Sainte

Brussels road, 5–5.45 p.m.

At La Haye Sainte, Major Georg Bäring's men were running out of ammunition. He sent first one, then another officer back; they 'requested ammunition, which was promised', but instead he was sent the skirmishers of Ompteda's 5th line battalion. He had wanted ammunition, not more men. After half an hour more of uninterrupted fighting, Bäring sent off a third officer who applied first to the Somerset Regiment and then to the Nassauers. Major von Nauendorf sent down two hundred light infantry from the 1st Nassau, but still without more ammunition.

The source of the problem was the failure to stockpile ammunition in the farm in the morning, but there should nevertheless have been ammunition nearby – both the nearest units, the 1st German light and the neighbouring 95th, were armed, like Bäring's men, with British Baker rifles – but it is possible that local supplies had been destroyed by French artillery.[1]

Young Heinrich von Gagern of the inexperienced 1st Nassau Regiment had been standing under fire for the last few hours. The first ball to hit his battalion killed the man in front of him and either the ball or a piece of the man's smashed musket knocked him sideways several files. Later, when a canister ball smashed the fitting that attached his scabbard to his belt, he stuck his sword in the ground by his side. Then a shell exploded close by, killing three men. It broke his sword, tore apart his trousers and burned his foot, but although the foot hurt so much that he had to hop on one leg, it didn't seem to be seriously damaged. He picked up a dead man's musket as a weapon and rejoined the square, which had shifted forward forty paces in an attempt to avoid more shells.

Gagern's light company was one of the two chosen to go to La Haye Sainte, but Major von Nauendorf refused to let him join his comrades, pointing out to him that he was wounded. Nauendorf was a friend of Gagern's parents and his real reason, no doubt, was that he did not think the young second lieutenant would come back from La Haye Sainte alive. In the event, the detachment commander was wounded by a cannonball before he reached the farm and killed by a second as his men tried to evacuate him; within half an hour the other company commander was also wounded.[2]

More than ever, the French needed La Haye Sainte, the key to the centre of the battlefield. Marshal Ney now ordered *Maréchal-de-camp* Nicolas Schmitz to take the farm with his brigade, and Schmitz marched the 17th Line to the west of the farm to cover a series of assaults by the 13th light. It was the first time specialist light troops had been given the job.

Private Friedrich Lindau stood with others at the loopholes by the gate, from where they shot at the French wherever they were most tightly packed. The Frenchmen pressed against the walls, poking their guns through the loopholes from outside and firing in. Men wounded while they fired over the wall were falling off the piggery above Lindau's head.

Lindau himself had his eye on a French officer who was positioning troops. Eventually he got him lined up, fired, and saw the French officer's horse leap, rear up and crash down with its rider. A little later the riflemen made a sortie and Lindau found himself close to the officer he had shot:

> I hurried towards him and grabbed his golden watch chain. But I hardly had it in my hand when he reached for his sabre, shouting abuse at me. I then hit his head with the butt of the rifle that made

him fall back and stretch out and I then noticed a golden ring on his finger. But I first cut a small portmanteau off his horse, and was about to pull off the officer's ring when my comrades shouted: 'Better get going; the cavalry is upon us!' I saw some thirty horsemen charge towards us, and with my booty I ran as fast as I could to rejoin my comrades who, with a volley, forced the enemy to retire.[3]

There was a new attack and Lindau was ordered to stay at the gate. He found that he was running out of cartridges, and was searching the pouch of a dead comrade when he was shot through the back of the head. Lieutenant Graeme, who was standing above him on the piggery, told him to go to the rear but Lindau refused, saying, 'No, as long as I can stand upright I will stay at my post.' He took off his neckerchief, wetted it with rum and asked a comrade to pour rum on his wound and tie the neckerchief round his head. Graeme was leaning over the wall hacking at the French with his sword, and Lindau warned him that he too would be shot. 'Let the dogs shoot!' came the reply. There was shouting from the barn so Lindau ran across the cobbled yard to help. While he was firing at the open end, choking smoke spread from under the beams: failing to break in, the French had set the barn on fire. Fortunately the young Nassau reinforcements were carrying large kettles for cooking; a fire party filled kettles from the pond and succeeded in putting the fire out, though several were shot in the process. While they were concentrating on the barn, the French gained domination of the loopholes and fired at them from behind. There was a struggle during which a Frenchman grabbed Lindau's rifle before a comrade shot him. Another grabbed at it and was stabbed in the face by the man on Lindau's right.

As Lindau tugged his rifle free, shots came through the loophole and rattled against the wall behind. One ball hit his shoulder roll, another smashed his rifle. He went to the pond, where he had seen a sergeant who had a good rifle shot down. The sergeant was dying, but when Lindau reached for his weapon the sergeant made a face at him, so Lindau took a different gun. But he was spending more and more time searching for cartridges and less and less time firing.

Bäring told him to go and get his wound treated, but again Lindau refused.

Bäring was feeling the weight of responsibility – 'never greater than when an officer is thus left to himself, and suddenly obliged to make a decision upon which perhaps, his own as well as the life and honour of those under him – nay even more important results – may depend. In battles, as is well known, trifles, apparently of little importance, have often incalculable influence.' With two enemy columns approaching again, he knew that this time the defenders' chances were slim:

On my exhortations to courage and economy of the ammunition, I received one unanimous reply: 'No man will desert you, we will fight and die with you!' No pen, not even that of one who has experienced such moments, can describe the feeling which this excited in me; nothing can be compared with it! Never had I felt myself so elevated; but never also placed in so painful a position, where honour contended with a feeling for the safety of the men who had given me such an unbounded proof of their confidence.

The French attacked again and set the barn on fire a second time. Again men carried pond water in kettles and put the fire out. Bäring sent back a message 'with the positive statement that I must and would leave the place if no ammunition was sent me'. The fire from the defenders gradually diminished, and they became increasingly uneasy as they called for ammunition. The officers began to tell Bäring that it was impossible to defend the post under the circumstances.

Sensing the defence was growing weak, the French began looking for ways to smash their way in. Nicolas Schmitz demanded artillery, but in the meantime another huge engineer officer, who had attached himself to the company of sappers leading the assault on the farm, broke through a door. He had to pass on his axe after he was shot through the wrist, but continued to direct the attack until he was shot through the shoulder.[4] Since the few Frenchmen who could come through this breach at a time were instantly bayoneted, others hesitated to follow, but while attention was focused on the doors Frenchmen swarmed onto the roof and walls, from where they could shoot down on the defenders. Cannon fire eventually smashed the main entrance and Frenchmen pressed in through the open barn.

Deciding he must save his men, Bäring gave the order to retreat through the house into the garden. Those who made it down the narrow passage to the garden with their commander gathered outside the farm. Bäring quickly decided that there was no point attempting to defend the enclosures and sent off the men, running singly, to their own lines.

Hearing shouts of 'Defend yourselves! Defend yourselves! They are coming in everywhere!' Lindau saw that the riflemen had abandoned the piggery roof and Frenchmen were clambering over the wall. 'One of them jumped down off the scaffold. I drove my sword bayonet into his chest. He fell down on me and I flung him to the side; but my sword bayonet had been bent and I had to throw it away.' Lieutenant Graeme and Ensign Frank were fighting hand to hand to hold off the French at the entrance to the passage through the house, trying to help as many riflemen as possible to escape. Lindau glimpsed a Frenchman trying to shoot Graeme, but Frank stabbed him and punched another in the face. Lindau tried to reach them but was surrounded as he laid about him with his rifle butt. The French were shouting 'Couillons Hanovriens and Couillons anglais!' Lindau was grabbed and dragged into the barn by several men and forced to surrender, before he and his companions were driven out onto the road and pillaged. Lindau lost two silver watches, a gold one and his bag of gold coins, before bandaged cuirassiers escorted them to the rear.

Elsewhere in the farm, Ensign Frank and Lieutenant Graeme were trying to escape. Frank shouted to Graeme, 'Take care!' A Frenchman standing five yards away levelled his musket at Graeme, but before he could pull the trigger Frank stabbed him in the mouth, his sword exiting through the man's neck. Frank pulled his sword out, flailed wildly and ran into the house. He was hit twice, but ran into a room and hid under a bed. Two men who followed him were caught by the French who, shouting 'No pardon for you bastard greens!' shot them dead. Frank was lucky, remaining undiscovered under the bed until the farm was recaptured, but Graeme was trapped. An officer grabbed him, saying *'C'est ce coquin.'* Two men dashed to bayonet him, but Graeme turned the muskets aside with his sword and, seeing that the three looked jittery, made a dash for it through the lobby and out into the garden. They fired after him but missed, and Graeme ran back up the slope to the hollow way. Major Bäring sent the surviving Nassauers back to their unit, while the remnant of men from his own brigade joined a group of riflemen who were sniping from the shelter of the hollow road above the farm.[5]

The Duke and his party had ridden east to the elm tree over the crossroads, the furthest east they ever went. They watched from the ridge above until the fall of La Haye Sainte became inevitable and then urged their horses through the gate and down the steep slope to the hollow way and up the other side. George Cathcart, the quarter-master-general of the cavalry, waiting his turn, stayed to watch longer. His horse was shot dead and he followed them on foot,[6] the fighting rising in intensity as Frenchmen from Schmitz's brigade pressed forward.

The loss of La Haye Sainte was the source of a genuine crisis for Wellington's army. With the farm in their hands, the French could push infantry and artillery forward to support their cavalry. According to a British officer,

The French immediately set about making the most of their conquest. Vast swarms collecting behind, and under the protection of the buildings rushed *en tirailleur* against the front of the third and fifth divisions. No collected onset was made, but whole clouds of these skirmishers poured a most destructive fire on the constantly diminishing line of the allies. It was in following up success of this kind, and in the manner here described, that the real strength of the French Imperial and Republican armies consisted during the war. In these tirailleur onsets and advances from post to post, the natural gallantry and intelligence of the soldiers, the skill of the inferior commanders, as well as the spirit of enterprize which distinguished the whole, were always eminently conspicuous.[7]

The riflemen lining the hollow way now found themselves pinned down in a fierce firefight with these French *tirailleurs*. Two of the surviving captains were wounded and Lieutenant Graeme, swinging his cap in the air to cheer on the men, had his right hand shot. Bäring was riding a dragoon horse he had found, in front of whose saddle were large pistol holsters and a cloak, and four balls lodged in the holsters and another in the saddle. Bäring dismounted to pick up his hat, which had been knocked off by a sixth ball.

Slightly further west, French skirmishers reached the hedges above the hollow way and from this cover they poured fire into the remaining squares of Hanoverians. Ordered by the Prince of Orange to advance and clear the hedge, Christian von Ompteda found that the 200 or so remaining men of the 5th Line, his own old regiment, were all that remained to undertake the task. Having lost the 8th and almost the 5th in similar attacks earlier in the day, he realised at once that the order was suicidal, and protested that there was cavalry in the valley behind the hedge and he would need support to have any chance of getting back. The Prince had galloped off, but his aide, Lord John Somerset, returned to repeat the order. Knowing he was sending the men that he had commanded for years to their death, Ompteda bravely led the battalion on. 'Try and save my two nephews,' he said to Lieutenant-Colonel von Linsingen, and then he gave the order to form line and walk forward.

'When within sixty yards he cried "Charge",' wrote Edmund Wheatley, and 'we ran forward huzzaing.' The trumpet sounded and as they reached the hollow way at a jog, the French *tirailleurs* fled back towards the hedges of La Haye Sainte to reform. Wheatley remembered what happened next:

I ran by Colonel Ompteda who cried out, 'That's right, Wheatley!' I found myself in contact with a French officer but ere we could decide, he fell by an unknown hand. I then ran at a drummer, but he leaped over a ditch through a hedge in which he stuck fast. I heard a cry of, 'The Cavalry! The Cavalry!' But so eager was I that I did not mind it at the moment, and when on the eve of dragging the Frenchman back (his iron-bound hat having saved him from a cut) I recollect no more.

The cuirassiers hit the right flank and rear of Ompteda's battalion. They were ridden down and the cuirassiers captured both of the battalion's colours. Linsingen's horse was shot and when he had extricated himself from under it he saw his battalion was annihilated, but the 120 remaining horsemen of Arentsschildt's 3rd Hussars had charged the left flank of the cuirassiers to help the survivors escape. Linsingen spotted Ompteda's nephews, Christian and Louis, grabbed them, and hauled them back into the hollow way. Just a handful of men joined them there; most had been cut down or captured.

Looking to break through the line, the cuirassiers now took sharp fire from the riflemen near the crossroads. The hussars and cuirassiers fought a short but bloody mêlée 200 paces from Bäring, who watched a duel between a corporal of the hussars and a cuirassier, each of whom was trying to rejoin his comrades after riding through the other line. 'I feared for the hussar as I saw him bleeding; however, all his training showed above the strength of his opponent, and managed to get on his left side, gave a mighty blow to his face which laid him on the ground and he then rode calmly back to his side while his comrades were cheering and congratulating him.'[8]

Wheatley remained below in the ditch enclosing the kitchen garden of La Haye Sainte: 'On recovering my senses, I look'd up and found myself, bareheaded, in a clay ditch with a violent head-ache. Close by me lay Colonel Ompteda on his back, his head stretched back with his mouth open, and a hole in his throat. A Frenchman's arm lay across my leg.' Wheatley was utterly dazed. 'So confused was I that I did not remember I was on the field of Battle at the moment.' But when he peered over the edge of the ditch and saw the backs of a French battalion, it all came flooding back. He heard a voice say, '*En voici! En voici!*', and lay back pretending to be dead, holding his breath. '*Voici un autre bougre!*' A hand tugged at his epaulette. Realising the Frenchman would turn him to rifle his pockets,

Wheatley jumped up, but his head swam and he hit the mud before the Frenchman grabbed him, growling '*Où vas tu, chien?*' and dragged him into the farmhouse.

La Haye Sainte was badly damaged and burned. 'The floor, covered with mortar bricks and straw, was strewed with bodies of the German infantry and French tirailleurs. A Major in green lay by the door. The carnage had been very great in this place.'

After questioning, Wheatley was led back along the main road, but the British artillery fire down it was so intense that his guard took shelter in the ditch. From there, Wheatley surveyed the British lines, where little red squares held out proudly. But the area where his own battalion had been standing was now alarmingly bare.

64

Guns and Horses

The centre, 5.45–6.45 p.m.

Exactly when La Haye Sainte fell is difficult to pinpoint. The times given by witnesses ranged from 2 p.m. to 6.30 p.m., but a time around 5.30 is most likely. In trying to save the farm, Ompteda's brigade had effectively ceased to exist, while the centre of Wellington's army was becoming very weak. Meanwhile, French witnesses emphasised the difficulty of the conquest and the number of attempts they made, but there was still time left in the day for them to exert great pressure on the allied line after its fall.[1]

Napoleon now ordered the two batteries belonging to the Guard light cavalry to go forward as far as they could and open fire. Once over the crest of the hill the French unlimbered two of their twelve 6-pounders opposite each allied square, and began hitting them with murderous case shot from close enough to hear the allied officers giving frantic orders to close up their ranks.[2] Practically all of the Allied artillery in this area had gone by now, and a strong French infantry battalion was advancing against the Bremen and Verden square, while the Nassauers were being menaced by cuirassiers.

The French gunners soon found their aim, and the third volley of canister hit the first Nassau battalion. Major von Weyhers had formed it in a column with a frontage of two companies, nine ranks deep, which made it exceptionally vulnerable to artillery. The

Hanoverian and British battalions either side had constantly changed formation from line (under artillery fire) to square (when threatened by cavalry), which kept the men busy and minimised casualties, but Weyhers made no attempt to follow their example. He ordered Friedrich Weiz to take command of the first company, which stood in the front rank along with the grenadier company; its three officers had all just been wounded and its sergeant was dead. The cuirassiers had edged closer and were now barely a hundred yards away on their right flank. Each time the gunners got ready 'the circular movement of the portfires to the fireholes could clearly be seen, even at a distance, and each time that this occurred, a certain uneasiness or painful sensation could be noticed in our soldiers' eyes.' At every shot groups of men were cut down and it was ever harder to get the ranks cleared and closed up.[3]

Two or three hundred yards to the right, Sergeant Tom Morris surveyed the guns opposite their square apprehensively. His 73rd Regiment had been combined with the 30th Cambridgeshires, and they had spent the afternoon deploying into line to minimise casualties, then forming square to defy two charges from French cuirassiers. Now the guns were up with the horsemen. Ensign Edward Macready of the 30th recognised the gunners as Guard artillery, and 'had scarcely mentioned this to a brother officer, when two guns unlimbering at a cruelly short distance, down went the portfires and slap came the grape into the square'. The first shots hit true on the Cambridgeshires' side of the square and the cuirassiers rode for the gaps the guns had torn, but the Cambridgeshires closed them and the horsemen turned aside. It had begun to drizzle again. Through the smoke Morris could just make out the light that the French gunner applied to the touchhole, and this time the balls hit his side 'thick as hail'. Morris turned and 'saw my left hand man falling backwards, the blood gushing from his left eye'. His comrade to his right was screaming: a ball had gone through his right thigh and Morris dragged him inside the square where all their wounded lay groaning. The other was dead: they threw him out for cover, an addition to the barrier of bodies against the French horsemen.[4]

A howitzer shell came plummeting out of the sky and stuck in the mud a few feet in front. 'While the fuse was burning out, we were wondering how many of us it would destroy.' Seventeen of them were killed or wounded, Morris with 'a piece of rough cast-iron, about the size of a horse-bean, which took up its lodging in my left cheek; the blood ran copiously down inside my clothes, and made me feel rather uncomfortable.' The company captain was sixty, and before Quatre Bras had been in the army for thirty years without seeing a fight. He was 'horribly frightened' and kept going to Morris for 'a drop of something to keep his spirits up'. The battalion sergeant-major, on the other hand, had fought his way from Portugal to France in the famous Light Brigade, but even he was appalled by this carnage. His face grew deadly pale and he turned to Colonel Harris saying, 'We had nothing like this in Spain, Sir.'

The cuirassiers advanced again. It was hardly a charge: they trotted slowly through the deep mud and over piles of bodies into the faltering fire of the haggard huddle that was all that remained of Colin Halkett's brigade. They walked their horses right up to the bayonets, and one of them leaned over his horse and made a thrust at Morris. Since Morris was wedged in and couldn't avoid the sword he instinctively closed his eyes, but when he opened them again the Frenchman was lying in front of him, sword arm outstretched. A man standing behind Morris had shot him in the groin. His face twisted in agony, the cuirassier tried to raise himself to fall on his sword but it was too long. He couldn't lift himself high enough. Reaching out he grabbed a bayonet, wedged its end in the mud, inserted the point under his breastplate and killed himself.[5]

With his Nassauers on the point of disintegration, Major von Weyhers decided to rush the guns. They had advanced forty paces before the next volley of case shot hit and Weyhers went down severely wounded, along with many others. The charge faltered and then stopped as they tried to fill the gaps. One of Wellington's aides rode up to order them to move back and an experienced Nassau staff officer took command to direct the retreat, but the leading companies, firing at the approaching cavalry, never heard the order.

In no time the two companies – 140 men at most, led by Weiz and the veteran grenadier officers – were surrounded by cuirassiers. Their line disintegrated immediately. Some ran until they were sabred by pursuers, slashing down on their shoulders from above. Little knots of older grenadiers fought like tigers, 'hiving' back to back. A sergeant bayoneted two cuirassiers from their horses though his right eye was stabbed from its socket and hung down over his face, his head lacerated by sabre cuts. In the end the horses trampled and pushed their way among them. Weiz was trapped between two horses and forced to surrender. Passed to the care of a trooper as the French pulled back, he saw his chance to make a run for it and reached the nearest English square, rolling underneath the bayonets that bristled from it.

Colonel Michel Ordener of the 1st Cuirassiers had suggested he might have to kill every single allied infantryman to capture the plateau. Major Georg Bäring of the Legion, now alone somewhere near Mont Saint-Jean farm, was reaching the same conclusion; he remarked that 'nothing seemed likely to terminate the slaughter but the entire destruction of one army or the other'. His third horse, formerly the property of an English dragoon, had been shot in the head and had fallen dead, trapping Bäring's right leg beneath it. His men, sheltering with others from the 1st battalion between the banks of the Ohain lane behind him, had thought him dead, and he lay there for some time before one of them crawled up to pull him free. Bäring's leg was not broken but he couldn't move it. Nobody would find him a horse, so he limped and crawled to a cottage called La Valette in the direction of Mont Saint-Jean, where an Englishman finally helped him onto a stray mount. In the meantime, the 1st battalion's adjutant recalled, 'the attacks of the enemy cavalry and infantry became so severe and followed each other so very quickly that our losses were very large and the battalion melted away.' Some had occupied La Valette, some fell back to the houses of Mont Saint-Jean, some fled.[6]

The French cavalry attacks still could not break the allied infantry. Groups of horsemen trotted from square to square testing their resilience and the infantry brought down a man or two. But despite their obstinate resistance to the cavalry, the squares were gradually being destroyed by artillery fire and the sniping of *tirailleurs*:

On one or two points, squares became, at times, exposed to the fire of musketry; and the 27th regiment was almost entirely destroyed in such a situation, the soldiers in the most dauntless manner stepping into the place where a comrade had stood the instant that he fell. Fortunately, however, the enemy did not possess the skill of combining cavalry and infantry attacks or it is impossible to say how destructive the result might have proved.

Standing in square somewhere in front of Mont Saint-Jean farm, the 27th Inniskilling Fusiliers took terrible casualties: of its 750 men, 478 were killed or wounded. In the centre of their square the pregnant Elizabeth McMullen tended the wounded until she herself was hit in the leg. Her husband Peter lost both arms, but the two of them survived and 'Frederica McMullen of Waterloo' was born later in the year in Chelsea.[7]

The veteran rifleman John Kincaid had fallen back with what was left of his men to the cottage of La Valette north of the Ohain lane:

> I felt weary and worn out, less from fatigue than anxiety. Our division, which had stood upwards of five thousand men at the commencement of the battle, had gradually dwindled down into a solitary line of skirmishers. The twenty-seventh regiment were lying literally dead, in square, a few yards behind us ... The smoke still hung so thick about us that we could see nothing. I walked a little way to each flank, to endeavour to get a glimpse of what was going on; but nothing met my eye except the mangled remains of men and horses, and I was obliged to return to my post as wise as I went.
>
> I had never yet heard of a battle in which every body was killed; but this seemed likely to be an exception, as all were going by turns.[8]

On the allied right, things were going much better. This, though, was hardly apparent to the participants; a sergeant of the 1st Guards wrote that 'the fight, at one time, was so desperate with our battalion, that files upon files were carried out to the rear from the carnage, and the line was held up by the sergeants' pikes placed against the rear –

not for want of courage on the men's parts (for they were desperate), only for the moment our loss so unsteadied the line.'[9] The seven-foot pikes carried by sergeants in the British army were often wielded horizontally to push men back into an even line, but here they were preventing the line from disintegrating under fire.

Wellington now tried to clear the plateau of French cavalry and *tirailleurs* by ordering three battalions of Brunswickers, the 2nd and 3rd Light and the 3rd Line, to cross the ridge onto the forward slope to the right of Maitland's Guards, where Byng's brigade had stood. But they suffered severely from artillery fire and fell back over the ridge, where they formed square against cavalry supported by horse artillery. Trying to advance over the ridge again, they were again forced back.

Wellington tried again, finally bringing forward the best of his reserves. The four small, veteran battalions of the 1st Brigade of the German Legion were lined up on the reverse side of the slope, and Wellington ordered the crack light infantry battalions of Frederick Adam's British brigade to join them to their left. Adam's men had spent the first three hours of the battle lying down in front of Merbe Braine; then, during the cavalry charges, they had advanced and formed square behind the junction of the track to Merbe Braine with the Nivelles *chaussée*, remaining there under artillery fire for another two hours. Now, at last, they were ordered forward.

Passing between the squares of the Brunswickers, they came over the brow of the hill above Hougoumont and into a hail of lead. The Highland Light Infantry could see little but smoke as they approached the brow 'but all around the wounded and slain lay very thick. We then moved on in column for a considerable way and formed line, gave three cheers, fired a few volleys, charged the enemy and drove them back.'[10]

The battalions of the Legion approached Hougoumont with their riflemen skirmishing ahead. They attacked a strong line of *tirailleurs* and drove it into the Hougoumont orchard, but forming square to defend themselves against cuirassiers, found themselves under heavy fire from the boundary hedge and ditch and from artillery to their left. Brigadier Carl du Plat was mortally wounded as his squares advanced. The third battalion of the 95th Rifles shifted from square to skirmish formation and took the *tirailleurs* on, while to their right the combined German rifle companies stormed the Hougoumont hedges. They were reinforced in the orchard by the second battalion of the German Legion, temporarily driving the French out.[11]

Just to the east, the second battalion of the 95th Rifles advanced well beyond the Hougoumont boundary. Private John Lewis was to describe this advance to his family in Axminster on 8 July:

> My front rank man was wounded by a part of a shell through the foot & he dropt as we was advancing. I covered the next man I saw and had not walked twenty steps before a musket shot came side-ways and took his nose clean off, & then I covered another man which was the third; just after that the man that stood next to me on my left hand had his left arm shot off by a nine pound shot just above his elbow & he turned round and caught hold of me with his right hand & the blood ran all over my trousers, we was advancing so he dropt directly.[12]

During the advance the battalion's five most senior officers were wounded by snipers or artillery, and it was a junior captain who ordered them into extended order as skirmishers at the very front, with the artillery of both sides firing over their heads. The main lines were only 450 yards apart – much closer than infantry usually fought – and Lewis was 150 yards in front of the British front line, between 250 and sometimes only 100 yards from the French. Then they were charged by cavalry and succeeded in 'hiving' only just in time to present a porcupine of bayonets to their opponents. The French rode up and fired at them with their carbines. At that moment, Lewis wrote, 'the man on my right hand was shot through the body & the blood run out of his belly & back like a pig stuck in the throat, he drop on his side, I spoke to him, he just said "Lewis I am done" & died directly.' As Lewis was loading his rifle, a ball hit it just above his hand and bent it. When, as they redeployed into skir-mish order, their sergeant was cut in two by a cannonball nearby Lewis went and grabbed his rifle.

The Highland Light Infantry were also charged by French cavalry and hardly had time to form up ready to receive them: 'The square was only complete in front when they were upon the points of our bayonets. Many of our men were out of place. There was a good deal of jostling, for a minute or two, and a good deal of laughing. Our quartermaster lost his bonnet in riding into the square; got it up, put it on, back foremost, and wore it thus all day.' Jack Barnett reckoned that the 71st gave a good account of themselves even so, for 'our men never fired a single shot, till they were nearly touching our bayonets, front rank kneeling, they then gave a volley you heard a scream, & saw them fall like leaves, horses with legs shot off limping about, the few who were not killed, faced about, & our dragoons who were in rear of us, past by us, & cut them down in all directions.'

While the dragoons pursued, the Scots discovered an unexpected bonus in their accidental choice of position: 'A French General lay dead in the square; he had a number of ornaments upon his breast. Our men fell to plucking them off, pushing each other as they passed, and snatching at them.' The 13th Light Dragoons chased the French dragoons down the hill and then returned to their lines.[13]

For the moment the British right was secure, but the last, strong British reserve was now in the front line. The centre of the position was under very great strain, with the best regiments destroyed and the line held by young and inexperienced troops from Hanover and Nassau. Further east there was less pressure, but the best units had suffered very heavy casualties. Things were looking grim, as an engineer officer explained:

Our loss had been severe, perhaps not less than 10,000 killed and wounded. Our ranks were further thinned by the numbers of men who carried off the wounded, part of whom never returned to the field; the number of Belgian and Hanoverian troops, many of whom were young levies, that crowded to the rear, was very considerable, besides the number of our own dismounted dragoons, together with a proportion of our infantry, some of whom, as will always be found in the best armies, were glad to escape from the field. These thronged the road leading to Brussels in a manner that none but an eye-witness could have believed, so that, perhaps, the actual force under the Duke of Wellington at this time (half past six), did not amount to more than 34,000 men.

Baron Müffling estimated only 30,000 remaining combatants. And still, as far as the beleaguered British infantry could see, there was no sign of Prussian help.[14]

65

The Prussian Advance

The eastern flank, 5.30–6.30 p.m.

In fact, Prussian reinforcements were finally arriving. But they were making their presence felt a mile south of the British left wing and most of Wellington's men could not tell that they were there. Indeed, the first Prussian assault from the Bois de Paris, made by the first two of General von Bülow's brigades, had stalled against a fierce counter-attack by the two divisions commanded by Georges Mouton, comte de Lobau. For an hour Lobau's men held off the Prussians with ease, driving them back, although their presence had crucially served to prevent the attack which Lobau was to have made against Wellington's left centre – an attack that would have been difficult to resist.

Then, around half past five, the 13th Brigade marched onto the battlefield, taking the ground between the two that Blücher had first led out of the Bois de Paris, Michael von Losthin's brigade to the north and Johann von Hiller's to the south. This enabled the cavalry nominally commanded by the eighteen-year-old Prince Wilhelm of Prussia, second son of the King, which had been holding this central area, to ride to the left flank, and thus increase the threat to Lobau's line of retreat. Blücher now had a clear numerical advantage and could begin to advance. He could contain Lobau's men with Losthin's brigade while driving for their objective, Plancenoit, the large village three-quarters of a mile to the east of Napoleon's tactical headquarters at the farm of Rossomme; Hiller's brigade, always edging southward to his left, could meanwhile manoeuvre round Lobau's open right flank. Towards six o'clock Gustav von Ryssel's 14th Brigade appeared and marched to support Hiller in his thrust towards Plancenoit.[1] By six, Blücher had 29,000 men and 64 guns deployed against Lobau's 9000 on Napoleon's right wing.

At this moment he received a message from General Thielmann, the commander of the Prussian rearguard at Wavre, saying that he would not be able to hold the bridges over the Dyle without reinforcements. Having received Napoleon's letter of 10 a.m., instructing him to attack the Prussians at Wavre, Grouchy had done so energetically. Arriving in person, he had ordered Exelmans downstream to Basse Wavre and General Lefol upstream to attack the mill at Bierges with his division. Meanwhile, Vandamme launched more assaults on the bridges in the town with the 2nd Swiss Regiment repeatedly attacking the stone Pont du Christ, so named after the statue of Christ at its centre, but whenever troops stormed across the bridges the Prussians drove them back.

Thielmann felt that he could not hold out long against these fierce attacks since more French troops were marching in. But Blücher sent back an uncompromising order to contest every step of his retreat: there could be no reinforcements. Everything had to be committed against Napoleon at Mont Saint-Jean and Plancenoit. It did not matter if Thielmann was crushed at Wavre so long as Blücher was victorious.[2]

At about this time, the vanguard of Hans von Ziethen's corps – comprising the reserve cavalry, two batteries of guns and the dynamic Karl von Steinmetz's infantry brigade – reached Ohain, the village on the extreme eastern flank, a mile and a half north-east of Smohain. Although the rest of the corps was well behind, strung out and still slithering along the muddy tracks, the first troops were now on their way to reinforce Wellington. Ziethen's chief of staff, Ludwig von Reiche, had ridden ahead of the column and when he emerged from the woods at about half past five he found the battle in full swing. He rode forward to make contact with the Nassauers and they directed him to General Müffling, who had long been stationed on that flank, waiting anxiously for the Prussians to appear. Müffling told Reiche that the Duke was at his last gasp and that if the Prussians didn't soon make their presence felt on his left flank, Wellington would be forced to retreat. He had already been forced to take troops from the left wing in order to shore up the centre and it was urgently essential that Ziethen should reinforce that wing.

Reiche rode back with these instructions. Deciding not to waste time looking for Ziethen, he gave directions to the advance guard and then hurried back to the battlefield. Already, things were looking much worse and the Nassauers on the extreme left were retreating. He implored them to hold on, assuring them that Prussian help would arrive at any minute. Riding back to find Ziethen, he instead met one of Blücher's staff, who shouted that Ziethen's corps must turn left and push on immediately south-west to Blücher, because things were beginning to go badly in that sector. Reiche explained Wellington's need for help, but the staff officer would not listen and told Reiche that he would hold him responsible for the consequences if Blücher's order was not carried out. 'Never in my life have I found myself in such a difficult situation. On the one hand Blücher's order ... and the thought that our troops were perhaps in danger there and could not hold out any longer. On the other hand the certainty that Wellington was counting on our arrival.'

At that moment the advance guard arrived, but without Ziethen, and demanded instructions on where to go next. Despairing, Reiche made up his mind to seek death on the battlefield if his decision caused a mishap, but he was still in torment over what to do. General Steinmetz rode up, furious that his troops had halted, 'stormed at me in his usual violent manner, and insisted upon an advance', refusing to listen as Reiche sought to explain the problem. Steinmetz led the vanguard on beyond the junction and Reiche had to stop him and make him go back, pleading that he ought to wait until the column had closed up before advancing.

Fortunately, at this moment General Ziethen finally appeared. Reiche hurried over and made his report, whereupon Ziethen issued orders for the march to continue immediately in the direction of the English army, whose left wing was nearly a mile away.[3]

Napoleon watched the arrival of Bülow's Prussians with increasing resignation: this was further proof that luck had not been running for him. However, there was still a chance that things could be turned around: Grouchy should be following right behind the Prussians, while Wellington's line was under severe pressure and beginning to give ground. Napoleon could probably still have disengaged to fight again another day, but either he didn't think that there was any political future in that course or he, like many of his officers, still believed they were in the ascendant. The question for the Emperor was how to deploy his reserves.

The infantry of the Old Guard was drawn up in squares either side of the main road north of Napoleon's tactical headquarters at the farm of Rossomme, a mile south of La Haye Sainte along the *chaussée* and just over half a mile west of the village of Plancenoit, the largest settlement in the area. The farms and cottages of Plancenoit were loosely spaced around a central church, set in a churchyard surrounded by a stone wall, in an open grassy space on a commanding rise above the little river Lasne. The river ran to the south through a grassy valley between fairly steep and wooded banks. Other houses lined the lanes running to the south and west of the churchyard and along a valley through which a stream ran down to the river. To the north and north-east Plancenoit commanded the open, undulating fields, but the ground was rougher and higher towards the *chaussée* where the Old Guard waited.

Only the junior regiments, furthest forward on the crest of the ridge, had a view of the battlefield and those further back were impatient to know what was happening. Hippolyte de Mauduit and some comrades from the 1st Grenadiers got permission to go to see friends in the 2nd Regiment further forward and, once there, climbed trees in an orchard to get a view. From there they watched the cavalry charges and the movements of the *tirailleurs*. Once a cannonball felled an apple tree and eight grenadiers tumbled to the ground. Trees to their right, however, masked the Prussian advance from view and it was only after they had returned to their square that some batteries they had assumed to be French opened up on them from the far side of Plancenoit. Cuirassiers and *chasseurs-à-cheval* formed up on the right of the 2nd Chasseurs.

For an hour the squares of the Old Guard served as a target for Prussian guns, while shots also fell among Napoleon's staff as the Emperor paced up and down, taking frequent pinches of snuff: 'many persons were killed around him; one of the staff ventured to expostulate with him on the imprudence of remaining in so perilous a position; he smiled and said, "The balls that will injure me, are not made yet."' Jean Pelet, commander of the 2nd Chasseurs, walked around their square, laughing and joking with his soldiers and getting them to sing patriotic songs, while Napoleon walked over and stood by the second battalion.[4] Mauduit's battalion of the 1st Grenadiers took some fifty casualties without reply, for their guns had been loaned to Lobau. Eventually a battery of 12-pounders deployed on the slope above them and the incoming fire slackened noticeably.[5]

The French artillery did serious damage to the approaching Prussian columns and Ryssel's 14th Brigade soon came under fire. Wilhelm von Rahden was a twenty-year-old veteran of the war of liberation. The stepson of a Silesian Prussian officer, he had joined the regiment at fifteen, and had fought at Lutzen, Bautzen, Kulm, Dresden and Leipzig. A shell that burst in the midst of his company of the 11th Silesians wounded twenty-one men and tore off the arm of his captain, leaving Lieutenant von Schätzel in charge of the company. They were walking past the artillery when Rahden's brother Fritz recognised the regiment by their yellow collars and cuffs and came over to share a bottle of wine with him. They parted with 'Good luck, and good hunting!' and 'God protect you, brother William,' and Fritz galloped off. Meanwhile the Silesians got into attack formation, sending skirmishers forward.

Lobau had already decided that he had to fall back. It had become clear that the Prussians were aiming to capture Plancenoit, which threatened to leave him surrounded and unable to retreat. His line had gradually wheeled as his southern, right flank fell back, but so many Prussians were slipping around this flank that the cavalry supporting him could no longer hold them off. So, at about six o'clock, he formed his brigades into four large squares and withdrew, sending one square off in advance to occupy Plancenoit, from where they could cover the retreat of the others. Lobau held the village strongly with five battalions. Two more took position in the orchards on its northern fringe, and his remaining eight battalions were strung out thinly, defending the line of the lane that led north from Plancenoit to Smohain and provided good cover where it had high banks.[6]

When Lobau withdrew, the Prussians captured Fichermont and pressed forward, although Durutte's *tirailleurs*, with whom they skirmished fiercely, were difficult to shift from strong positions in the cottages of Smohain and the strongly built farm of La Haye, and from the orchards, hedges and ditches to the south of Papelotte.[7] The vast majority of Wellington's troops, however, were still quite unaware that the Prussians were making such progress. This new front line was still well over a mile from Wellington's own position and quite invisible to him, while any noise made by advancing Prussian guns came from behind the French gun line and so was easily confused with the noise that the French guns were making.

It must have been not long after six that Napoleon received news of Lobau's decision to retreat. His equerry recalled that

> an Aide-de-Camp came from the right wing to tell him they were
> repulsed and that the artillery was insufficient. Napoleon immedi-
> ately called General Drouot in order to direct him to hasten to
> reinforce this army corps which was suffering so heavily, but one
> saw on Napoleon's face a look of disquietude instead of the joy
> which it had shown on the great day of Fleurus.[8]

Drouot sent the eight battalions of the Young Guard, about 3800 strong, which were furthest east, nearest Plancenoit, to reinforce Lobau's troops in and around the village. Despite determined French opposition, the Prussian pressure was drawing in more and more of the reserves on whom Napoleon had counted in order to crush Wellington's army.

To Wellington's troops their presence remained imperceptible.

Blinded by smoke and suffering constantly from artillery, their resistance depended on grit, determination, discipline and courage. Slowly but surely, however, their will to win and belief in victory were seeping away.

66

Slowly but Surely

Wellington's centre, 6.45–8 p.m.

After the fall of La Haye Sainte and the advance of French horse artillery onto the crest of the ridge above the farm, what Ney needed was fresh infantry in order to hold the territory that had been gained and to capture the village of Mont Saint-Jean. New battalions could exploit the gaps that were being punched into the allied centre and breathe new life into d'Erlon's tired men. He had been expecting Lobau's divisions – but no infantry support had arrived, so he sent his principal aide Pierre Heymès to the Emperor to request reinforcements. At that moment, however, Napoleon was preoccupied with the threat to Plancenoit; the only fresh troops he had were the Guard and he was unwilling to release them given the extent of the threat to his right. '*Des troupes!*' he exclaimed. 'Where do you want me to take them from? Would you like me to make some?'[1]

Left to his own resources, Ney recalled that the divisions of Foy and Bachelu, around 8000 strong, were still waiting, unused, behind Hougoumont wood. They were in the wrong area: what Ney needed was an attack launched with fresh men from La Haye Sainte. But he had no better option.

So General Foy began by clearing the orchard once again. He pinned down the German Legionaries with a frontal attack from *tirailleurs* and then sent more round their flanks, forcing most to the ditch and a few into the garden. Outflanked and attacked in front, the Light Brigade and the German battalions fell back, taking heavy casualties as they climbed back up the slope. The ensign carrying the colour of the 52nd was shot through the heart by grapeshot and killed along with the colour sergeants, but their flag remained on the ground all night without anybody noticing it.

Once Foy's left flank was secure, the infantry moved forward in echelon, with Bachelu's two divisions leading the way. These four brigades had taken significant casualties at Quatre Bras and were short of officers. Foy advanced with his left flank secured by the Hougoumont hedge and his front covered by a battalion in skirmish order. As they rode up the hill, he clapped his chief of staff Jean-Baptiste Lemonnier-Delafosse on the shoulder, predicting cheerily, 'Tomorrow you'll be at Brussels and made colonel by the Emperor!'

Uxbridge ordered the 15th Hussars to charge the advancing squares of French infantry, and the French sharpshooters as usual aimed at the officers. With the hussars' colonel having already lost his leg to a cannonball that had also killed both his horse and his brigadier's, their intelligent major, who had commanded a squadron all through the Peninsular War, was experienced enough to recognise the danger of the enterprise before he spurred his horse forward. Nevertheless, he was hit by five musket balls, one of which was instantly fatal. A lieutenant was shot through the stomach and liver and died next day, and a captain had his left arm shattered between the elbow and the shoulder, after which the hussars veered away and reformed behind the infantry.

In this attack one squadron of the 13th Light Dragoons lost all its officers, and the colonel of the 7th Hussars had a horse shot under him. Meanwhile the British cavalry charges had taken some impetus out of the French attack and bought time for the artillery and infantry to prepare, but no more.[2]

Once over the crest of the ridge and close to the allied line, the French columns began receiving canister from the batteries of Ramsay, Bolton and Mercer; the cones of musket balls spreading so thick that Foy called it 'a hail of death'. General Bachelu was hit and unhorsed and a brigadier was wounded; Bachelu's other brigade commander had been seriously wounded at Quatre Bras, so chief of staff Toussaint Trefcon took command of the division. And when Bachelu's regiments reached the allied line, they found it reinforced and resolute. The allied squares had their front rank kneeling, presenting a hedge of bayonets, while their musketry was devastating, and in consequence the French squares broke. Trefcon's horse was hit by canister shot and he fell, badly bruised on his chest although sheltered from the musketry by his dead horse. Dragoons who followed the retreating infantry rode straight past Trefcon, and he then limped down the hill to where his routed infantry was rallying. Trefcon was hurt badly enough to leave the field and walked back to find the hospital with a wounded squadron commander from the cuirassiers.[3]

After seeing Trefcon's men take flight, Foy's also broke up. Foy himself was wounded by a ball that ran the length of his upper right arm without touching the bone, although he thought it was only a bruise and stayed on the field, rallying the debris of his division in the hollow road north of the Hougoumont orchard.[4] Foy was not pursued: 'Our cavalry stayed on the plateau. The enemy's didn't dare move.' His chief of staff Lemonnier-Delafosse meanwhile, going to look for another horse, glimpsed half a loaf of bread in the knapsack of a dead soldier; then, even better, found butter in a pouch. He devoured it, having had nothing but beer all day.

After the French infantry had fallen back from the plateau the Brunswick 1st light and the German Legion 2nd Line made a new attack on the orchard; fighting tree by tree and step by step, they very gradually drove back the French. The Salzgitter Landwehr battalion from Hugh Halkett's brigade was brought forward into the front line in their place. Halkett himself accompanied the Osnabrück battalion, which joined the squares on the ridge in line with the Brunswickers.

With the French in retreat, the artillery that had stopped their attack counted the cost of their resistance. Samuel Bolton's battery, five guns strong after the loss of its howitzer, had been deployed to the right of Maitland's guards, at a slight angle, enabling the guns to fire across the front of the infantry, but Bolton was killed by a ball that ricocheted from the ground into his left breast and his lieutenant was badly wounded when a shrapnel shell burst in the barrel of a gun. Captain Norman Ramsay, an extremely good officer who was one of Sir Alexander Frazer's oldest and dearest comrades, was also killed, his head 'carried away by a round shot'. Frazer described how:

> In a momentary lull of the fire I buried my friend Ramsay, from whose body I took the portrait of his wife, which he always carried next to his heart. Not a man assisted at the funeral who did not shed tears. Hardly had I cut from his head the hair which I enclose, and laid his yet warm body in the grave, when our convulsive sobs were stifled by the necessity of renewing the struggle.[5]

Meanwhile, assistant surgeon William Gibney, who had spent the day either with his 15th Hussars or in a makeshift dressing station in Mont Saint-Jean, or riding between the two, had been ordered once again to rejoin the regiment. He had come to hate the ride along the Nivelles *chaussée* because the cobbles splintered when cannon balls hit them, making progress especially hazardous, but this time as he rode towards their position north of Hougoumont he became resigned to impending defeat:

> The contest seemed to me to be nothing diminished, but more general and desperate. The thunder of cannon and the rain of bullets were considerably augmented, men and horses every moment falling. To me, coming fresh on this part of the field, it seemed as if the French were getting the best of it slowly but surely, and I was not singular in this view, for a goodly number of experienced officers thought the same, and that the battle would terminate in the enemy's favour.[6]

The pressure from French artillery that was now close enough to fire canister and from French *tirailleurs* was finally causing a crisis in the area of the battlefield that was controlled by the young Prince of Orange. While the right was still secure, the centre of Wellington's line was on the point of collapse. Had Napoleon been able to throw in his Old Guard against Wellington's centre soon after the fall of La Haye Sainte he might well have broken through and won the battle. But Napoleon's piercing eyes were focused on his own crisis further south, where the Prussians were advancing on Plancenoit, so that he failed to see the opportunity arise.

Not that it was possible to see anything on the plateau of Mont Saint-Jean: 'by now the smoke lay thick and dark over the field, restricting the visibility to a few yards. The noise was tremendous with the roar of guns and rockets, the rattle of small arms, the ever-recurring beat of drums calling for yet another charge, and the wild cries and shouts of the horsemen.'[7] Lord Uxbridge ordered Lord Edward Somerset to lead what was left of the Household Brigade against the columns of Donzelot's division that, with cuirassiers in support, were pressing forward in the centre. When the heavy cavalry attacked, however, the French infantry stood firm and received them with steady fire, and the Dragoon Guards returned reduced to a mere handful.[8]

To the remnant of Colin Halkett's brigade, meanwhile, the French seemed to be advancing in overwhelming numbers and they found themselves under devastating fire. They formed in four-deep line but 'were forced to retire'. General Halkett had already been bruised in the neck and shot in the thigh but he had remained with his men. Now he was shot through the cheek, the ball smashing teeth in both upper jaws as well as his palette before it lodged in the skin of his other cheek. Sir Colin fell from his horse and, dazed and deaf with tinnitus, was carried to the rear. His men fell back with him.

As they retreated down the slope, Sergeant Tom Morris reported, 'the fire from the French infantry was so tremendous that our brigade divided, and sought shelter behind some banks.'[9] According to Ensign Edward Macready, 'the fire thickened tremendously, and the cries from men struck down, as well as from the numerous wounded on all sides of us, who thought themselves abandoned, was terrible.' Men and officers were cut down in rapid succession:

Prendergast of ours was shattered to pieces by a shell; McNab killed by grape shot, and James and Bullen lost all their legs by

round shot during this retreat, or in the cannonade preceding it.
As I recovered my feet from a tumble, a friend knocked up against
me, seized me by the stock, and almost choked me, screaming,
(half maddened by his five wounds and the sad scene, going on), 'Is
it deep, Mac, Is it deep?'

The four battalions had disintegrated and become mixed up; 'all
order was lost, and the column (now a mere mob,) passed the hedge
at an accelerated pace.' Officers who tried to turn men around and
stop them found themselves physically swept away in the press of
bodies. Then, 'At this infernal crisis someone hurra'd – we all joined,
and every creature halted, and retraced his steps to the hedge.'

This hedge was somewhere in the vicinity of the village of Mont
Saint-Jean, and there they crouched under cover. The one remaining
captain of the 73rd tried to lead an advance but he was shot after a
few paces and the survivors fell back behind the hedge again.[10]

To their left, the remnant of the first Nassau battalion also
retreated in disorder, but rallied on the second battalion in the second
line of troops before the Prince of Orange and General von Kruse led
both battalions in a bayonet charge to halt the French attack. By
now all the allied artillery in the area was destroyed or out of ammunition, so there was no supporting fire, while the Prince was shot in
the chest and fell wounded from his horse. The French line wavered,
but at that moment the Nassauers panicked and ran. Kruse brought
some of them back to join the 3rd Nassau battalion which huddled
close to the Brussels road, falling back closer and closer to Mont
Saint-Jean. They remained extremely uneasy, unable to see anything
through the smoke, but 'sounds of firing from the left flank made it
appear as if the extreme left flank of the army had been considerably
pushed back'. Before the charge in which the Prince was wounded,
Kruse reported three days later, the French had taken 'possession of
the plateau from which our men withdrew but only for 100 paces';
after it the French were only opposed 'by small bodies of brave men'.

Count Kielmansegge's Hanoverians also broke, although when
case shot turned the square of the Bremen and Verden battalions into
a triangle, blowing away the whole front face, Kielmansegge managed

to rally them sufficiently to repel a cavalry attack. They finally disintegrated in rout, running back through the village, despite the count's
efforts to stop them. Carl von Alten had tried to rally the other
square of the Duke of York and Grubenhagen battalions but the
close-range artillery fire was too much for them. After the square's
commander had been killed and Alten had been badly wounded in
the thigh by a shell splinter, forcing him to leave the field, these battalions too broke. The little square of Ompteda's eighth battalion
fled with them.[11]

Two of General von Vincke's Landwehr battalions, Gifhorn and
Hameln, brought in as reinforcements from the left wing, were still in
line with the Nassauers, but equally shaky, in the area of Mont Saint-
Jean farm. The other two were marching back towards Waterloo, in
the belief that they had been given orders to retire and none as to
where to stop. The nearest steady units were the 27th Inniskillings,
32nd Cornwall and 40th Somersets, still obstinately in square south
of the farm, though cut to pieces by artillery and sharpshooters.

Meanwhile French *tirailleurs* from d'Erlon's divisions spread out
on the plateau. The few heavy cavalrymen remaining with the Union
Brigade now moved up in line behind the infantry to try to keep the
wavering Nassauers and Hanoverians – still 'suffering severely from
grape and musketry' – from running away. The hundred or so men of
the Household Brigade joined them, but their commander was also
soon wounded. Colonel von Arentsschildt took over what was left
and tried to plug the gap to the right of La Haye Sainte, which was
'void of British infantry' and threatened by a strong force of the
enemy. The broken British and Hanoverian troops rallied on this
line of cavalry, short of the forest to the north of the village of Mont
Saint-Jean, as General Alten's report, written next day, confirmed.[12]

A Dutch cavalry staff officer spotted the Prince of Orange in the
smoke, staggering through the mud alone, on foot and obviously
wounded. He rushed over to him and at once several of the Prince's
aides arrived and helped him off the field to have his wound treated.
General von Alten himself had left the field wounded, as had the
Hereditary Prince of Nassau and General Halkett, while Colonel
Ompteda was dead and Baron Kielmansegge had disappeared with

his troops. Assistant Quartermaster-General James Shaw no longer knew who was in charge. Sensing that it might be him, he galloped to Wellington for advice.

The Duke was on the right of the Nivelles road behind the left flank of Maitland's Guards brigade. Shaw told Wellington that the line was open as far as Kempt's brigade, a space of about half a mile to the Charleroi *chaussée*. 'This very startling information he received with a degree of coolness, and replied to in an instant with such precision and energy, as to prove the most complete self-possession.' Wellington told Shaw that he would order some Brunswickers to the spot and instructed Shaw to muster as many Germans from the division as he could and collect all the guns he could find. Fitzroy Somerset rode over to assess the extent of the problem, but had his arm broken by a musket ball; after reporting to Wellington, he rode back to the Duke's quarters at Waterloo.[13]

All observers admired Wellington's magnificent calm and reassuring confidence. One of Hill's aides wrote, 'Lord Wellington was exposed as much as any soldier in the field, & his escape as well as that of my dear general's is a miracle, I was with them the whole day, I never saw either of them in action before, & it is impossible to say which is the coolest.' However much, to outward scrutiny, Wellington maintained the prototype stiff upper lip, though, intimates detected anxiety. In 1826 Adjutant-General Barnes's aide, Major Andrew Hamilton, described to Jean-Baptiste Lemonnier-Delafosse the state of despair Wellington was in at the time Hamilton left the field. With his aides dead or very busy, he was leaning against a tree, almost all alone, with tears forming in his eyes as his army fled around him.[14]

The *troupe dorée* had suffered severely. Wellington's Peninsular aide Colonel Canning had been hit in the stomach by grapeshot and died an hour or two later on the battlefield. Everyone assumed that Quartermaster-General Delancey was dead too. Sir John Elley was stabbed in the stomach in the last charge of the Horse Guards. He recovered, but with a hernia that obliged him to wear a band round his belly for the rest of his life. Adjutant-General Sir Edward Barnes was about to lead a charge on foot when Andrew Hamilton insisted that Barnes should take his horse. 'Just as Major H touched the ground a French soldier stepped from the ranks, levelled his musket & the ball struck the general with such force as to turn him round.' Barnes was badly wounded through the shoulder, although he recovered; Hamilton got him on the horse and walked him to Brussels. About 10.30 p.m. Major Hamilton arrived at Creevey's house, himself slightly wounded in the head and the foot. He said 'that never had there been such a battle fought before or such things done by both officers and men, that the French might be beat by such determined skill & courage, but that the loss was so immense & their superiority in numbers ... He doubted whether Lord W would be able to keep the field, he therefore begged us to consider what we ought to do.'[15]

Barnes's assistant Colonel Currie was shot through the head with grape and killed. As he rallied one of the wavering Brunswick squares, Alexander Gordon was shot in the thigh by a bullet that smashed his femur and lodged in the knee; some guardsmen found a door and carried him on it to the headquarters in the inn at Waterloo, where surgeon John Hume cut the leg off.[16]

Sir George Scovell had just halted the two retreating battalions of Vincke's brigade, countermanding the order to withdraw that they believed they had been given by a British officer who spoke no German and bad French. He was at the headquarters inn when the Prince of Orange and Fitzroy Somerset were brought in wounded, and he supported Somerset while his arm was cut off. He then persuaded the unwilling driver of the Duke of Wellington's carriage to take Somerset and the Prince to Brussels, accompanied by General Alava and Dr John Gunning, the senior surgeon with the army, who had performed the operation on Somerset and looked after the Prince.[17]

At the time that Hamilton left for Brussels with the wounded adjutant-general the sense of imminent doom was widespread. The badly bruised Major Bäring had persuaded an Englishman to catch a stray horse, place a saddle upon him, and help him onto it. His account describes the despair of an officer deserted by his men and facing defeat, as well as giving a strange sense of how sparsely populated his part of the smoke-filled plateau now was:

I then rode again forward, when I learned that General Alten had been severely wounded. I saw that the part of the position, which our division had held, was only weakly and irregularly occupied. Scarce sensible, from the pain which I suffered, I rode straight to the hollow road, where I had left the rest of the men; but they also, had been obliged to retire to the village in consequence of the total want of ammunition, hoping there to find some cartridges. A French dragoon finally drove me from the spot, and riding back, in the most bitter grief, I met [Ompteda's aide] ... I directed him to bring my men forward, if there were only two of them together, as I had hopes of getting some ammunition.[18]

Sergeant William Lawrence had been surprised at the endurance of the soldiers of his 40th Regiment, which formed one of the crucial remaining squares in front of Mont Saint-Jean: 'The men in their tired state were beginning to despair, but the officers cheered them on continually throughout the day with the cry of "Keep your ground, my men!" It is a mystery to me how it was accomplished, for at last so few were left that there were scarcely enough to form square.'[19] Then Lawrence was ordered to the colours:

There had been before me that day fourteen sergeants already killed and wounded while in charge of those colours, with officers in proportion, and the staff and colours were almost cut to pieces. This job will never be blotted from my memory: although I am now an old man, I remember it as if it had been yesterday. I had not been there more than a quarter of an hour when a cannon-shot came and took the captain's head clean off. This was again close to me, for my left side was touching the poor captain's right, and I was spattered all over with his blood.

There was still room for gallows humour. On the other side of Captain Fisher from Lawrence, talking to him, was Lieutenant Hugh Wray, who found himself splattered all over with Fisher's brains. Seeing Fisher's head smashed to smithereens a private remarked wryly, 'Hullo, there goes my best friend.' Taking command, Wray answered gallantly, 'Never mind, I'll be as good.' However, as Lawrence was well aware and Wray was not, Fisher had repeatedly flogged the private for slovenliness and as a consequence was loathed by him – hence the private's reply, 'I hope not sir.'[20] But it was about this time, too, that Major Arthur Heyland, who had survived so many hard battles in the Peninsula, was killed by a ball in the neck. That last tender letter of his, written the night before, had to be delivered to his beloved wife.

Even further east, Sergeant Robertson of the Gordons had been admiring the steadiness of the squares of the 27th and 40th near Mont Saint-Jean farm, south of the village. Increasingly, however, things looked bleak, and the experienced sergeant was weighed down with the responsibility of commanding two companies, everybody senior to him having been killed or wounded. 'I now began to reflect on what should be done in case of a retreat becoming inevitable, over a long plain, in front of cavalry. I was aware it would be difficult for me to keep the men together, as they had never retreated before under similar circumstances. In fact, any word of command misunderstood in the smallest degree would be sure to produce disorder.'[21]

The troops were close to the edge of their capacity to take punishment. One private of the 28th Foot, the 'Old Slashers', claimed to have overheard Sir James Kempt admit to Wellington, 'My Lord if I am charged again by the enemy, I am not able to stand for my division is cut up to a skeleton.' Wellington answered, 'You must stand while there is a man, and so must I. The Lord send night or Blücher!'[22]

67

Ziethen Attacks

Northern sector of the eastern wing, 6.30–7.30 p.m.

Wellington's prayer was answered almost instantly. Suddenly, he heard the sound of fresh artillery on his left wing as, towards 7 p.m. General Ziethen's vanguard under Karl von Steinmetz – around 5000 infantry, 2500 cavalry and two batteries of guns – threw themselves eagerly into the attack. The skirmishers and fusiliers of the 12th and 24th Regiments led, their guns thundering in support. Unfortunately, it was Wellington's left wing that they attacked: for the second time that day, Prussians had taken the men of the Orange-Nassau Regiment for Frenchmen.

Prince Bernhard rode over to remonstrate with Ziethen, who told the junior officer somewhat brusquely that he couldn't help it if Bernhard's men looked exactly like Frenchmen. The misunderstanding was resolved only after Ziethen's chief of staff Ludwig von Reiche explained diplomatically to him that the colonel he was talking to was a prince, and Ziethen adapted his tone more appropriately to Bernhard's social status.

Sergeant Johann Döring of the 1st Orange-Nassau recalled fighting the Prussians until 'some Prussian officers waved at us with white cloths', after which the fellow Germans advanced together into what for Döring was, though exhilarating, the hottest fighting of the day. He recalled a Prussian Landwehr NCO running by, shouting 'We

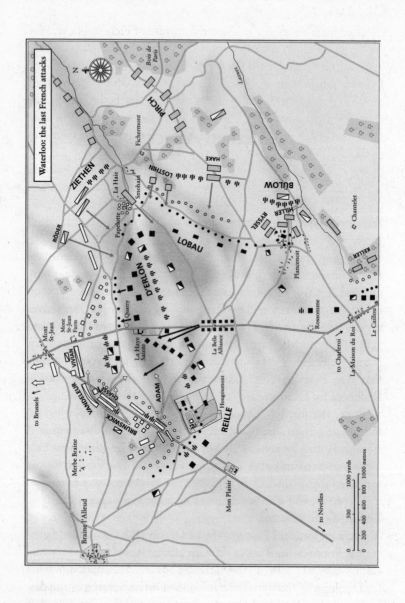

Waterloo: the last French attacks

N

Bois de Paris

PIRCH

ZIETHEN

RODER

La Haie

Papelotte

Smohain

Fichermont

LOSTHIN

HAKE

BÜLOW

HILLER

RYSSEL

KELLER

Chantelet

Plancenoit

LOBAU

D'ERLON

Quarry

Mont St-Jean

Mont St-Jean Farm

VIVIAN

VANDELEUR

CHASSÉ

BRUNSWICK

ADAM

La Haye Sainte

La Belle Alliance

Rossomme

Le Caillou

La Maison du Roi

to Brussels

REILLE

Hougoumont

Merbe Braine

Braine l'Alleud

Mon Plaisir

to Nivelles

to Charleroi

0   500   1000 yards
0 200 400 600 800 1000 metres

will yet make them smoke some Prussian tobacco!' before he fell wounded.[1]

The united forces quickly took the château of Fichermont and the hamlet of Smohain as the French pulled back, the Prussians turning Fichermont into their field hospital. Meanwhile Reiche established his two batteries on a height behind Smohain which commanded most of the battlefield. The artillerymen were reluctant to fire in case they hit their own side; Ziethen insisted that the noise that announced their presence was important – they must fire, whatever they hit.[2]

There was more confusion. Nassauers defending Papelotte, puzzled by the sudden, inexplicable disappearance of French skirmishers, advanced to La Haye, but found upon being driven back to the road between it and Papelotte that there were skirmishers behind them, and in repelling these realised that they were Prussians. Only after an officer scampered across in the cover of a sunken lane to tell the Prussians they were on the same side did the Nassauers join the Prussian skirmishers. Together they advanced towards La Belle Alliance.[3]

Ziethen's appearance at last released Sir Hussey Vivian's hussar brigade, ordered to remain on the wing until the Prussians arrived to relieve him, to take part in the battle. He and his men had been itching to get involved. Vivian's men were among the few Britons who were aware that the Prussians had already been engaged with the French for some hours further south, as one of them reported:

> We could ... perceive that the right of the French was engaged in, and opposed by, a heavy cannonade on their right rear, which could only be another body of Prussians, although from the distance, and dusk, which at this time was commencing, we could discern nothing with the eye but the flashes and smoke of their cannon, and the sound even extended beyond where we could see, and it was evident that the French were engaged in rear of the heights on which they showed their front to us.[4]

Napoleon too was straining his ears to work out what was happening out of sight. As Wellington's troops fell back, he and his staff had moved forward more than half a mile to La Belle Alliance. He knew all too well about the fire from Bülow's artillery that Vivian's men could hear but not see against Plancenoit behind his eastern flank, where the Prussian assault on the village was under way, but the new gunnery opening up to the north-east was a mystery. Being an optimist by instinct, he hoped it was Marshal Grouchy arriving behind the Prussians, for it appeared that the buildings around Smohain were being shelled and attacked from the rear.

General Drouot, who was by Napoleon's side, reported in Paris soon afterwards that 'towards seven o'clock we perceived in the distance towards our right, a fire of artillery and musketry. It was not doubted but that Marshal Grouchy had followed the movement of the Prussians, and was come to take part in the victory. Cries of joy were heard along our whole line.'[5] While Napoleon's retelling of a battle was notoriously untrustworthy, Drouot was regarded as a model of probity, so there is every reason to suppose that when the French staff saw the fire of Ziethen's column, which was initially directed against the Nassauers on the allied flank, they genuinely entertained hopes that this was Grouchy attacking the Prussians in the rear.

It was this belief that decided Napoleon around seven o'clock to launch the remaining battalions of the Guard in a final attack to break through Wellington's line. Drouot reported that the Emperor saw this as the decisive moment: to shore up the morale of the exhausted French troops that he required to make a final attack, moreover, he ordered his aides to spread the word that Grouchy had arrived and the battle was won. Lieutenant Martin of the 45th, whose depleted regiment had been skirmishing with men from Picton's division, reported that the news of Grouchy's arrival reinvigorated everybody and their enthusiasm burned anew with the certainty of imminent victory.

In doing this Napoleon has often been accused of callous hypocrisy, but he was not lying – he hoped and wanted to believe that Grouchy had come. The French were very close to breaking through above La Haye Sainte and that part of the line would collapse once the British realised they had French troops behind their flank. What was needed now was a last crushing effort in the area where Bachelu and Foy had been repelled.

With this in mind, Napoleon initiated the last part of his plan: the attack of the Guard. Unfortunately after Prussian intervention he barely had half of them left. He led forward the ten remaining battalions straight at Wellington's own position.[6] The breakthrough had to be achieved quickly, for the news from the right was not good. Several aides rode in saying that the Prussians were 'penetrating the right wing of the French army'. Napoleon dismissed them with much ill-humour: '"Be off," said he to one of them, "you are frightened!"'[7] D'Erlon's battered corps advanced again and shouts of '*Vive l'Empereur!*' rang out from the right where he was, to the left at Hougoumont, while in the centre the Guard marched forward to attack.

68

Plancenoit

The southern sector of the eastern flank, 6.30–8 p.m.

Friedrich von Bülow had deployed forty-eight guns in front of his
16th Brigade to bombard Plancenoit before making an assault on
the village, where five battalions from Lobau's corps had made their
stand. Launched from the east, the attack was led by Johann von
Hiller, who formed six battalions into three assault columns. On the
right were the musketeers of the 15th Regiment; in the centre those of
the 1st Silesian Landwehr; and on the left the two fusilier battalions
led by Major von Keller, which made an outflanking march to the
south through the woods on the far side of the flooded Lasne stream.
Hiller's cavalry was stationed behind the village with orders to turn
back any troops who were absconding.

Preceded by skirmishers, the Prussian columns attacked at assault
pace into a hail of canister and musketry. The 15th pushed along a
hollow lane leading to the church and Hiller captured the churchyard
as well as a howitzer, two cannon, ammunition wagons and several
hundred men. Further south, the Silesians reached the western fringe
of the village but there met reinforcements from the Young Guard,
sent in by General Drouot.

The fighting around the church was intense, for the French were
dug in behind hedges and walls and packed into the houses and
farms on the far side of the open space where the church and its

walled graveyard stood. As Hiller tried to fortify the churchyard, using pews from the church as firing platforms, shots were exchanged at a range of fifteen to thirty paces, a range at which even muskets were deadly accurate. A bullet drilled through one lieutenant's head in the instant he looked over the tall churchyard wall. Men were using ramrods as weapons and trying to pull the muskets out of the hands of those who poked them over the wall. One of the French regiments engaged in the defence was the 5th Line, including the battalion that had refused to shoot Napoleon and had instead joined him when sent to intercept him in the Alps in March. During their defence of Plancenoit, twenty-two of their officers were killed or wounded, including the colonel and one battalion commander. Of the two battalion commanders of the 15th Regiment, one was shot dead and the other severely wounded by shrapnel.

Despite such losses, General Guillaume Duhesme's crack light infantry succeeded in forcing back the Silesians, who sent Hiller a message saying that their men couldn't hold on in the western side of the village. Hiller held the churchyard long enough to allow them to fall back, but when a Young Guard assault column reached the open space around the churchyard, Hiller himself pulled out. The Prussians were pursued out of the village and General Domon's chasseurs threatened to surround them and cut them off, but Prussian artillery drove off the French cavalry and a squadron of Silesian Hussars chased the pursuing French infantry back to the houses. The Prussian fusiliers had succeeded in turning the village, but fell back when the main body retreated.[1]

The Prussian infantry rallied and the 15th, reinforced by four battalions from the 11th Silesians and the 1st Pomeranian Landwehr, launched a second attack, the fusiliers again infiltrating the wooded Lasne valley to get round the French southern flank. The Prussians stormed in, splitting up among the houses, and Lieutenant von Schätzel led Wilhelm von Rahden's company up a side alley to the far side of the village. Stopping at the last cottages, they found themselves in sight of the Charleroi *chaussée* and cheered wildly, for they could see the road packed with French fugitives running from the fight with the English. Behind them the fighting continued fiercely, but after a long struggle, the Prussians took the whole of Plancenoit except the churchyard and a few houses round it and forced the Young Guard to retreat.

General Pelet of the Old Guard chasseurs could see Young Guard fugitives emerging from the village and sent a small detachment to rally them. When Drouot ordered him to retake Plancenoit and hold the place at all costs, he sent one company forward to make an initial attack, and followed with the remaining 450 men of the first battalion of the 2nd Chasseurs of the Old Guard. Seeing these men in bearskins coming down from their hill, Schätzel decided to pull back and he and Rahden took their men back to the centre of the village. Units were all mixed up there, Silesians like them with yellow collars, West Prussians with red, Pomeranians with white.

As the chasseurs entered the village Pelet met General Duhesme, who was being carried away on his horse, shot in the head. His *tirailleurs* and *voltigeurs* had scattered in small groups and most were falling back. Pelet promised to stop the enemy, while the Young Guard officers promised in turn to rally their men behind him and support his attack.

As he approached the centre of Plancenoit, however, Pelet found his vanguard retreating towards him, pursued by Silesians storming up a street. The Silesians, Rahden among them, charged on confidently, but Pelet had a trick up his sleeve. Suddenly, to Rahden's astonishment, anguished cries of 'Fall back!' came from behind his leading group. Pelet had sent his 3rd Company to charge the Silesian column in the flank with their bayonets, and this incursion threatened to cut the Silesians off. Their commander was shot dead and a dozen French grenadiers went for the standard, but its bearer, Sergeant Schmidt, who had saved Rahden's life the year before, drove them off and pursued them down the lane. The rest of the Silesians scattered, desperate to save themselves. There was no way of rallying them within the village and the choice for Rahden and Schätzel lay between capture and running for it. They ran, Schätzel a few paces ahead, yelling 'Quick! Quick, dear Rahden!' As they passed the church Rahden was shot in the hip, his boot filled with blood and he felt himself swaying. The enemy seemed to be everywhere, cutting off every route. Rahden threw himself into a house where he found men from his battalion with a wounded captain. They all left together and within five minutes they were out in the fields.

Once in the open, Rahden passed a lieutenant he knew with his arm in a sling, at the head of twenty of his *tirailleurs*, rallying men round him. Rahden was limping across a meadow when he suddenly sank up to his knees in boggy mud. He couldn't push himself out and nobody heard his shouts. Three or four *voltigeurs* spotted him, taking pot shots at him as they closed in. Bullets whizzed by before he saw a Prussian officer with some men and shouted. The very last of them paused, turned and ran over. He shot the nearest *voltigeur*, reloaded, and fired after the others, who were now running off. Hauling Rahden out of the mire, he hoisted him onto his back, carried him a hundred paces to the nearest bush and laid him down behind it. Then he got a bandage out of his knapsack and bound Rahden's wounds, before helping him to the casualty station where a sergeant was looking after the wounded. Rahden was carried to the field hospital that the Prussians had established in the château at Fichermont; there he found an old friend whose left foot had been smashed by grapeshot.[2]

General Pelet found that each company that he sent into the attack split up and started to skirmish, and following every charge his men dispersed in pursuit of the enemy. He ordered a captain to guard the church but he led his men too far forward, to the very edge of the village, opposite a wood where the Prussians were, and the Young Guard *voltigeurs* who followed went charging off into the fields. Pelet set up a base in the churchyard, but found himself pinned down there under effective fire from Prussian snipers still concealed in the surrounding houses no more than thirty yards away. Meanwhile the Prussian artillery laid down a barrage of shellfire which set some of these houses and barns alight.

As at Ligny, the fighting within the village was bloody and merciless, animated by mutual hatred. Having found, it was rumoured, some Frenchmen who had been hanged by Prussians, the French were cutting the throats of any Prussians that they caught alive. Pelet tried to stop the murder but saw one Prussian dispatched as he approached. An officer pleaded for his life, speaking of his French friends. Pelet took him into his personal protection, along with a few others, keeping them behind his mare, Isabelle, and then handing them over to his sappers, who were to answer for them to him.

At first General von Bülow believed that he had been attacked by the whole of the Old Guard, but it did not take him long to form a more correct estimate of the enemy's numerical weakness. Moreover, he himself had further reinforcements on the way. Towards 7.30 p.m. the head of Pirch's II Corps marched onto the battlefield, cavalry in the lead, followed by Tippelskirch's 5th Brigade which was ordered to march to Plancenoit, easily identified in the dusk by the smoke and flames rising from it. To Ludwig Nagel's disappointment, the musketeer battalions of Lützow's Freikorps were told to stay at Saint-Lambert as a rearguard; this 'vexed us bitterly, for we were burning to fight; but many regiments met the same fate.' Franz Lieber's brigade followed Tippelskirch's but the Colberg Regiment did not get into the fight either, merely gaining a distant view of the battle. Excluding Ziethen's troops, Blücher now had some 44,000 men and 104 guns deployed against Napoleon's right wing.

Pelet meanwhile was taking off his greatcoat in order to display himself as a general officer, riding Isabelle here and there, trying to bluff that his strength was greater than it was. Then, at the moment when he felt most pressed, a company of Baron Golzio's battalion of the 2nd Grenadiers appeared from nowhere. Golzio with his 545 veteran grenadiers had been sent to support Pelet with orders from the Emperor himself, who had ridden into their square and instructed Golzio not to fire a shot but to go straight in with the bayonet. Having driven a Prussian battalion from the gardens around the village, Golzio had then sent one company to help Pelet, keeping the other three companies in reserve. Since the grenadiers were able to maintain better discipline than the chasseurs, Pelet now used them wherever a bayonet charge was needed. For the moment, he had Plancenoit under control: he was being bombarded with explosives, there were fires burning all around and he was surrounded by snipers, 'but it made no difference. I held on like a demon. I couldn't bring my men together but they were all under cover. They brought down murderous fire which kept the Prussians pinned down. They would have silenced the sharpshooters completely had there not been so very many of them.'[3]

Meanwhile Keller's battalions of Prussian fusiliers had manoeuvred round the village through the woods that bordered the Lasne and were ready to break out towards the main road. Napoleon ordered the 1st Grenadiers of the Old Guard under General Petit to form square, the first battalion near Rossomme, the second half a mile south on high ground dominating the lane from Plancenoit to the hamlet of Maison du Roi. Initially Petit's grenadiers had had a quiet time, waiting in reserve; then, after the attack on Plancenoit began, he sent a hundred grenadiers under the adjutant in skirmish order to contain the Prussian skirmishers lapping round the village. But there turned out to be far more Prussians than he had imagined: they ambushed the adjutant, shot his horse and peppered him with musket balls. Only one of these hit, but he was so badly wounded by it that the Prussians left him for dead in a ditch. He lay there for six days before somebody found him.

A few hundred yards further south, the farm of Le Caillou, where Napoleon had established his palace, was defended by 653 veterans of the first battalion of the 1st Chasseurs under a Dutchman, Johan Coenraad Duuring from Rotterdam, charged with guarding the Emperor's possessions. For most of the afternoon they had sat around idly, although between two and three o'clock Duuring was alerted to the existence of French fugitives and mounted up with the Gendarmerie d'Elite to stop them, round them up and return them to the battlefield. After an hour the stream of fugitives had dried up and everything became very quiet: a number of British cavalry officers were brought in as prisoners, and then French artillery ammunition wagons and even some guns came past, claiming they had run out of ammunition. Some ammunition wagons were empty, some were not and Duuring parked them either side of the road.

Napoleon's valet Louis Marchand was waiting at Le Caillou anxiously. When he left the front line, all had been looking good, but recently Mameluk Ali had ridden in to fetch something for the

Emperor and had told him hastily, 'It's going badly. We've just seen masses of troops in the distance. At first we thought it was Marshal Grouchy and there were shouts of joy, but it is Blücher's corps, and we have no news of Grouchy.' Duuring advised the Grand Equerry, Albert Fouler, to get the treasure loaded, harnessed up and ready to move. Marchand packed up Napoleon's bed and locked up the portable treasury which contained 100,000 francs in gold and 300,000 in banknotes.[4]

Towards seven o'clock Duuring was alerted by a lookout to the presence of two enemy columns in the wood behind Le Caillou. He guessed there might be 800 men in each but their strength was difficult to evaluate because of the trees. At around the same time more runaways appeared, while many more artillery batteries which had run out of ammunition were driving off along the *chaussée* towards Genappe. Duuring placed two companies to block the road, with orders to let only wounded men pass.

By eight it was evident that there were large numbers of Prussians in the woods near headquarters and that they were preparing to attack. Duuring improvised a battalion of about 200 runaways and placed it near his own, detached 200 men as *tirailleurs*, sending a hundred into the wood with another hundred in support, and stationed his chasseurs with their backs to the farm. He had placed a battery close to him in support but its gunners ran away. At this juncture Provost-General Radet appeared, having been sent by Soult to arm the unhorsed cavalry with muskets taken from the wounded at the Imperial Guard field hospital at Le Caillou. He was able to reinforce Duuring's duty battalion by uniting a lot of unhorsed cavalrymen with men who were helping the wounded to hospital, Corporal Canler being one of those who were thus rearmed. When Radet saw the enemy advancing towards them he sent some of the chasseurs forward and deployed others as skirmishers in the little wood behind Le Caillou. Meanwhile, one of Radet's aides continued to gather men together until eventually he had a force of 1200.

It was now imperative to get the Imperial baggage and treasure out before the Prussians cut the road. Grand Equerry Fouler had been waiting for an order from the Emperor, but now, belatedly, he decided to take the initiative on his own responsibility. In order to drive the Prussians away from the road while the precious column of carriages made its escape, Radet led his improvised force against the Prussian skirmishers and drove them into the wood, killing fourteen. Meanwhile, having strapped the Emperor's bed to a mule, Marchand climbed into his coach with the safe full of gold and notes, and they rolled off. Despite Radet's efforts, the coach of Napoleon's private secretary, the duc de Bassano, was brought to a halt by Prussian fire and he had to leap out and run to escape in that of the cabinet secretary, Fleury de Chaboulon; once they were clear of the Prussians, however, Marchand thought the convoy of seven coaches was safe, even though the road was encumbered with retreating vehicles and wounded men.[5]

Five of the eight senior battalions of the Old Guard, the best troops in the army and the ultimate reserve, had now had been drawn into a desperate struggle to hold the line of the Charleroi–Brussels road against the Prussians, and the Emperor's headquarters staff had fled. Radet and Duuring sent a message to tell Napoleon what was happening behind him; it seemed unlikely that they could hold out for long.[6]

69

The Last Reserves

The centre, 7–8 p.m.

The noise of artillery on the left, followed by the news that Ziethen, finally, was reinforcing his left flank, served to revive Wellington's flagging spirits. When he sent Uxbridge's aide Horace Seymour to ask for Prussian infantry to shore up his centre left, Seymour's horse was instantly killed, but John Fremantle went instead to meet Ziethen, who told him that his whole force was on its way.

Wellington summoned the cavalry brigades of Vandeleur and Vivian to plug the gap and give support to the wavering infantry in the centre, while Uxbridge sent his Quartermaster-General George Cathcart to guide them into position. Just as Cathcart returned from this mission, Uxbridge was hit in the right knee by a grapeshot that smashed the head of the tibia and filled the ligament with shards of bone. Looking down, he realised that there was little chance of saving his leg; his legendary exchange with Wellington, 'By God, Sir, I have lost my leg,' to which the Duke replied, 'By God, Sir, so you have,' may thus have some factual basis. Horace Seymour, rehorsed, rode to Waterloo to prepare a surgeon, while other aides hoisted Uxbridge into a gig.[1]

Above Hougoumont, the brigade major of Adam's light infantry brigade was talking to Sir Augustus Frazer when a French deserter rode in and announced that the Imperial Guard would attack within half an hour. Frazer rode off to tell Wellington. Although the French were short of ammunition now, having fired away so much earlier on, their artillery bombardment grew in intensity one last time.[2]

To plug the gap in the centre of his line the Duke ordered Maitland's Guards to move to their left and form line four-deep. Having been in the front line since the start of the battle, the Guards had taken heavy casualties and by this stage, allowing for those who had escorted wounded men away, they can have numbered barely five hundred men.[3] He ordered five Brunswick battalions across to the centre, pointing the way in person, before returning to the Guards. He sent an aide to summon three battalions from Colonel Hendrik Detmers's Netherlands brigade and these fresh soldiers marched to their left in attack columns, well down the hill for shelter, moved clear of Maitland's brigade and then wheeled into line.

The 3rd Netherlands Division, not having been attacked at Braine l'Alleud, had been summoned to the battlefield and had thus become Wellington's very last reserve. It was not a reserve that he trusted much, being led by a Belgian who had fought for Napoleon. They had been waiting under fire lining the Nivelles road, while their commander, David Chassé, grew increasingly anxious:

> When I saw that an English artillery battery positioned on the left and forward of my division had stopped firing, I went there to enquire the reason and learned there was no ammunition. At the same time I saw the Garde Impériale advancing, while the English troops were leaving the plateau en masse and moving in the direction of Waterloo; the battle seemed lost. I immediately ordered the battery of horse artillery under the command of Major van der Smissen to advance, to occupy the height and to direct an emphatic fire upon the enemy column.

At this stage of a battle Napoleon traditionally committed the Guard en masse to deliver a final crushing blow. In this combat, however, he had already been forced to commit them piecemeal in defensive measures against the Prussians behind his flank. The eight battalions of the Young Guard having been thrown in to support

Lobau, this left the Old Guard consisting of fifteen battalions, five of which were engaged or drawn up in support near Plancenoit. There remained therefore only ten battalions for a strike force, fewer than 6000 men. Napoleon nevertheless deployed them between La Haye Sainte and Hougoumont with the right in the lead to sweep westward across the plateau, mopping up the British right wing.

It was around half past seven. The first battalion of the 3rd Grenadiers, led by General Friant, took the lead with its right against the *chaussée*. To its left and behind, in echelon, were the 4th Grenadiers, the 4th Chasseurs, and two battalions of the 3rd Chasseurs – around 3500 men in what may have been six battalions. Between each pair of battalions was a pair of guns from the Horse Artillery of the Guard. The second battalion of the 3rd Grenadiers had already been detached to secure the left flank. Napoleon rode down from La Belle Alliance toward La Haye Sainte and watched from a position near the orchard by the road.[4]

Ney and Friant led the attack. What was left of the allied front line artillery caused some casualties, but not many; there was no more ammunition and the allied artillery was remarkable for its silence. The Guard passed over the crest of the ridge and to their astonishment found the plateau empty, except for the corpses with which it was littered. They could see no great distance ahead through the smoke, but passed a line of abandoned British guns as they moved on down the slope. On the right they contacted hostile troops but the enemy retired in disorder in the face of the fire from their *tirailleurs*, who formed a loose line ahead of the battalion squares.

Vincke's Hameln and Gifhorn Landwehr, about a thousand shaky young recruits, had formed a joint square near the Nassauers and rapidly blasted off some thirty cartridges each at the advancing French *tirailleurs* – no doubt too fast and at too long a range – before falling back. The Brunswick battalions, now led by Rudolph Heinemann for Olfermann's right hand had been smashed by a grapeshot, were shocked by the 'unexpected nearness' of the enemy skirmishers, and 'the all enveloping dense clouds of powder smoke, the men's exhaustion, the partial disorder of the still incomplete deployment, and, lastly, the powerful thrust of the attack caused several battalions to hesitate at first and fall back a little.' But the example of one battalion steadied the others. 'They gave way once bodily just as they reached the crashing line of fire,' noted Ensign Macready, 'but were rallied and afterwards stood well, throwing out light troops to the left of our skirmishers.'[5]

When the dashing, black-haired Sir Hussey Vivian led his hussar brigade across the *chaussée* and wheeled it into line the army's prospects still looked grim. As Vivian's artillery crossed the road, 'Sir Robert Gardiner and Captain Dyneley both expressed their distrust of present appearances; they did not like them.' Lieutenant Ingilby, recalling discussions overheard earlier, 'expressed a contrary opinion, that it was the Duke's turn and that he was now attacking their centre, his time for doing which evidently having depended upon the Prussians making their appearance in force on the right flank of the French'. However, on the far side of the main road, they found 'the ground was strewed with wounded, over whom it was hardly possible sometimes to avoid moving. Wounded or mutilated horses wandered or turned in circles. The noise was deafening, and the air of ruin and desolation that prevailed wherever the eye could reach gave no inspiration of victory.' Ahead of the cavalry several tiny squares were disintegrating in rout. They came across Lord Edward Somerset with 'the wretched remains of the two heavy brigades, not 200 men and horses'. 'Vivian asked, "Lord Edward, where is your brigade?" "Here," said Lord Edward.'[6]

The worn-out cavalry of the centre retired through the fresh troops from the left wing, who then 'remained for about half an hour exposed to the most dreadful fire of shot, shell, and musketry that it is possible to imagine. No words can give any idea of it (how a man escaped is to me a miracle), we every instant expecting through the smoke to see the enemy appearing under our noses, for the smoke was literally so thick that we could not see ten yards off.'[7] Sir John Ormsby Vandeleur's brigade formed up to the right of the hussar brigade behind Maitland's Guards.[8] They, similarly, at once encouraged the troops ahead of them and prevented them from leaving the field.

The appearance of the cavalry effectively steadied the Brunswickers first ordered across by Wellington. The Nassauers also rallied on the 18th Hussars, and this probably encouraged what was left of Colin Halkett's brigade to face about. There were few of Halkett's men remaining: the 30th mustered only 160 men at the end of the day, while the 73rd, who after Quatre Bras had a paper strength of 489 men remaining fit to fight, had suffered 289 casualties. When they mustered behind the hedge there were two officers and seventy men. The remaining 128 had either been servants or baggage guards, absent at the start, helped wounded men to the rear and not come back, run away towards Brussels, or become scattered and detached from their unit. Morris did not mention the cavalry as a steadying influence, but they probably were, nevertheless. A light dragoon noted in his journal that 'two columns (one of which, I think, were Hanoverians, the other Scots) were driven back, when some of our officers and cheers from the men succeeded in making the latter front.'[9] The three fresh Netherlands battalions, 1500 strong, led forward by Detmers, appeared to the right of the Cambridgeshires. The Netherlands report mentioned a triangle and a battalion of light infantry – the remains of Kielmannsegge's division – set back from the front line and wavering as they approached.[10] Once the remnant of Ensign Macready's Cambridgeshires had rallied and formed a four-deep line with the 73rd behind their hedge, they sent out skirmishers against the enemy, who were about three hundred yards away.

Macready wrote in his journal, 'A sort of lull now took place, close skirmishing with heavy columns in grey greatcoats formed to the left of our front, being all our work ... neither party advanced. All at once the fire of musketry thickened so as to tell on our skirmishers, (who were crouched behind dead horses) and to cause many casualties in the line.' The skirmishers of the French Guards had arrived on the scene.

70

La Garde Recule

The centre, 8–8.30 p.m.

The French Guard battalions and their accompanying horse artillery battery continued to advance down the reverse slope of the ridge above Hougoumont and La Haye Sainte towards the line of Guards, Netherlanders, Brunswickers and Nassauers that Wellington had improvised to oppose them. Both generals had now committed their last reserves, and as calm as he looked, Wellington must have been nervously aware that his were not of the quality of the Imperial Guard. On the other hand he knew that the Prussians were coming and that with luck he only had to hold the line for a short time longer. Near him a devout Methodist colour-sergeant of the Guards was praying 'Lord, stretch forth thine arm.'

Even Captain Mercer admitted that the British guns were losing the contest against the French Guard artillery. It was only the arrival of eight previously unused guns commanded by Chassé's artillery chief, Major van der Smissen, that stopped the Guard in their tracks:

The fire continued on both sides, mine becoming slacker and slacker, for we were reduced to the last extremity, and must have been annihilated but for the opportune arrival of a battery of Belgic artillery a little on our left, which, taking the others in flank nearly at point blank, soon silenced and drove them off. We were so reduced that all our strength was barely sufficient to load and fire three guns out of our six.[1]

The exchange of canister at short range was violent in the extreme. General Friant was shot and seriously wounded, General Michel, commander of the chasseurs, was killed, Ney's horse was shot and he was rolled on the ground. The attack wavered, but Paul Poret de Morvan led on his battalion and Ney joined him in front of the 3rd Grenadiers. At first this battalion faced seriously weakened troops who were falling back, but further to the west, as they approached the British line the French battalions suddenly faced disciplined musketry from bodies of infantry that did not appear to be on the verge of disintegrating.

The decisive intervention came with the confident onset of the six fresh Netherlands battalions of Detmers's brigade, General Chassé having marched up with the remaining three battalions, another 1500 men. Having united his brigade, they formed closed columns and attacked. As Ensign Macready recalled, 'A heavy column of Dutch infantry (the first we had seen) passed, drumming and shouting like mad, with their shakos on the top of their bayonets, near enough to our right for us to see and laugh at them, and after this the noise went rapidly away from us.'[2] According to a British hussar, they 'advanced at double quick, their drums rolling, and drove back the enemy. The Bruswick Oels faced about and advanced at the charge also', with Vivian and his extra aide 'cheering them on'.[3] Rudolph Heinemann, their new commander, was shot in the throat or the heart as he ordered this final advance and killed. His body was never found.

And at the same time that the Dutch and Brunswickers charged, the grenadiers were unnerved by the sight of troops fleeing to their right. Macready remembered 'a strange hurly-burly on all sides – firing and shouting, and movement, and it lasted several minutes. Our grey greatcoated opponents disappeared as if the ground had swallowed them.' The discovery that the newcomers from the east were not Grouchy's men but Prussians had brought despair to the hard-pressed French defenders. Those in the eastern front line already knew that they were fighting yet more Prussians, and when a battalion chief of the 95th Line was told by one of Napoleon's messengers that Marshal Grouchy was deploying on the right he pointed out that actually, on the contrary, it was Prussians that they had in front of them, and that they had already killed and wounded several of his men. At that moment the captain of his *voltigeurs* fell wounded by a ball in the thigh.

In the smoky desolation to the east of the Charleroi road the situation had looked desperate to the British. The regiments had suffered casualties so heavy that most of them had no more than one or two hundred men left: the officers of the 32nd agreed that they had no more than a hundred. The 27th can have had practically nobody left, having lost from 'the terrible play of artillery, and the fire of the light troops' nearly 500 casualties out of a paper strength of under 700 men – the few remaining had joined other units, so they must have looked to be lying dead in square. 'We had not a single company for support, and the men were so completely worn out, that it required the greatest exertion on the part of the officers to keep up their spirits,' wrote a rifleman. The subsequent court martial of Henry Ross-Lewin revealed that when ordered to attack, the men of the 32nd refused to form line; they would advance only when Ross-Lewin exhorted them with, 'Come on my Brave Boys, for God's sake men move on,' and then he had to walk behind the twelve remaining men of his company to keep them going forward. They left their colours behind them to secure them from capture.

By this stage they were mixed up with men from the 27th and the 95th. To a rifle officer,

Not a soldier thought of giving ground; but victory seemed hopeless, and they gave themselves up to death with perfect indifference. A last effort was our only chance. The remains of the regiments were formed as well as the circumstances allowed, and when the French came within 40 paces, we set up a death-howl, and dashed at them. They fled immediately, not in a regular manner as before, but in the greatest confusion.[4]

It was here, where the French troops had been inspired by the good news of Grouchy's arrival, that bewildering disappointment struck most acutely. Lieutenant Martin of the 45th was with the men of Marcognet's division, who had once again stormed onto the plateau. From the high ground at the end of the line where the smoke was thin, they could see the mass of fresh troops who were rushing onto the battlefield and they quickly realised that they were not French, but Prussian. Prussian cavalry and fusiliers were charging towards their flank. Everything suddenly gave way, men losing hope and giving up. Thinking they had been betrayed, they fled back down the slope into the valley, pursued by Ziethen's cavalry. There were no formed bodies to be seen and it was all a question of who could flee fastest and furthest. 'I did what the others did,' recalled Martin. 'The other regiments broke at the same time. The whole army panicked. It was just a confused mass of infantry, cavalry, and guns, pressing against each other and rushing across the plain in a raging torrent, away from the Prussian squadrons charging them and in front of the English battalions who descended from the plateau with shouts of victory.'[5]

On the plateau between La Haye Sainte and Mont Saint-Jean farm, Poret de Morvan's 3rd Grenadiers held together for some time in square, with Ney insisting to Poret that this was where they must die, but the sight of 3000 fresh troops charging towards them was too much for the 4th Grenadiers and the chasseurs who were in their path. The Netherlanders pursued them down the hill, although they lost cohesion as they advanced.

Just to the east, Maitland's Guardsmen had been lying down behind a bank, possibly that of the Nivelles *chaussée*, to take shelter from the artillery. The skirmishers of the chasseurs facing them advanced, shouting *'Vive L'empereur!'* As the skirmishers in front of Chassé's Netherlanders advanced on their left, Wellington ordered Maitland's Guards to charge, saying something resembling, 'Up Guards and at 'em!' They stood up and fired a fierce volley at fifty yards' range. The French skirmishers were surprised by their sudden appearance and, as they wavered, Lord Saltoun led the Guards in a bayonet charge.[6]

To the west of the Guards, Sir John Colborne, one of the outstanding officers of the Peninsular War, wheeled his veteran 52nd Oxfordshire Light Infantry to the right and advanced, with a company skirmishing ahead, towards the nearest French column. He had some companies of the 95th to his left, and was followed at a distance by the 71st Highland Light Infantry and behind them the remainder of Clinton's division. The flank attack caused the French column to pause and the nearest French battalion – probably one of the 3rd Chasseurs – turned to its left to face them. Colborne estimated that his battalion took 150 casualties as they advanced – they halted once to fire on the 23rd Light Dragoons, who had crossed their line and were wrongly assumed to be French. The 71st moved up on their right with the third battalion of the Rifles on their flank. It is reasonable to suppose that the intervention of the Light Brigade was crucial; they were good and relatively fresh troops, however brave and obstinate were Maitland's exhausted Guards. Three out of four battalion commanders of the 3rd and 4th Chasseurs were mortally wounded, as was the battalion chief of the 4th Grenadiers.

Major-General Hugh Halkett sent one battalion of Hanoverian militia to clear the Hougoumont orchard and advanced with the Osnabrück Landwehr, covering the right flank of Frederick Adam's brigade. The leading company and skirmishers rushed and captured a French battery. Casualties among the French chasseurs who were trapped by the Light Brigade, the Guards and the light cavalry were very high – it appears that more than half were killed or wounded.[7] As the British pursued up and over the ridge, they found more squares of Guards in the valley below.

On the western flank the second battalion of the 3rd Grenadiers was holding its position, and General Cambronne came to its support with the second battalion of the 1st Chasseurs. Halkett's sharpshooters shot the horse of a senior officer and then dashed forward, capturing the defenceless Frenchman who identified himself as Cambronne. A French newspaper had it that Cambronne, in the midst of a square of his Old Guard, was summoned to surrender and replied with '*La garde meurt et ne se rend pas!*' ('The Guard dies, it does not surrender!'); in the 1970 film *Waterloo*, the Old Guard was then mown down by artillery. The reality was less picturesque. Cambronne was caught out in the open, well outside the square, and if he said anything it was not that.[8]

The reserve, consisting of the second battalion of the 2nd Chasseurs and the first battalion of the 2nd Grenadiers, marched to a position near the orchard of La Haye Sainte, close to Napoleon and General Drouot, but by the time they arrived everything was in retreat. The Emperor watched the horse artillery of the Guard riding back down the hill for a moment, and then, dazed and tired, mounted and made off. His army to the east was in rout and the only possible explanation was that the new force that he had taken to be Grouchy had actually been yet more Prussians. A battle that they had seemed so close to winning was utterly lost. Meanwhile, on the other side of the ridge, Wellington rose high in the saddle and waved his hat over his head.

71

Right Ahead, To Be Sure

Belle Alliance, 8.30–10 p.m.

The firing stopped, which puzzled those who had not been fighting on the smoke-filled slope behind the ridge. A staff officer of the Netherlands light cavalry rode eastward to see what was going on. To his alarm, he saw lancers riding towards him through the smoke and assumed that since there were practically no lancers in Wellington's army, they must be French. He was about to gallop away for his life when, seeing their costumes more clearly, he realised that they were not French but Prussian.

Sergeant Robertson of the Gordon Highlanders had been 'ordered to pay particular attention to any signal or movement I might see in front, for which purpose I was furnished with a spy-glass'. He described what happened next:

> In a short time one of our skirmishers came running in, and called to me to look at the French lines, as something extraordinary was going on. On the enemy's right I perceived that a cross fire had been commenced, and that troops in the same dress had turned the extremity of their line, and were advancing rapidly. I immediately informed the adjutant, who said that perhaps it was a mutiny in the French army, and that we would better form our companies close, so as to be ready to march to any point. At this instant, an

aide-de-camp came galloping down our rear, and calling out, 'The day is our own – the Prussians have arrived.'[1]

Where Harry Smith, brigade major to General Lambert, stood, 'the field was so enveloped in smoke that nothing was discernible. The firing ceased on both sides, and we on the left knew that one party or the other was beaten.' He wrote afterwards that 'this was the most anxious moment of my life'. When the smoke cleared, they saw 'the red-coats in the centre, as stiff as rocks, and the French columns retiring rapidly, and there was such a British shout as rent the air'. The Duke and a single staff officer were riding his way and Smith went to meet him. '"Who commands here?" "Generals Kempt and Lambert, my lord." "Desire them to get into a column of companies of Battalions, and move on immediately." I said, "In which direction, my lord?" "Right ahead, to be sure." I never saw his Grace so animated.'

Behind the front line, tired little bands of muddy, powder-blackened British infantry prepared to advance, among them the seventy-two surviving members of the 73rd. Sergeant Burton gave Sergeant Morris 'a hearty slap on the back, and growled, "Out with the grog, Tom; did I not tell you there was no shot made for you or me?"'

'In less than half an hour,' reported General Kruse three days later, 'a brilliant victory had been won over an enemy who had believed they were the victors and that with good reason.'[2]

The fighting wasn't over, though. Sir Hussey Vivian got the order to attack; emerging from the smoke, he saw the French retreating up the road with two squares and two bodies of cavalry covering. He went for the nearest cavalry with his 10th Hussars in the lead, taking fire from the square and grapeshot from a battery. Lord Byron's cousin Major Howard led a squadron against the infantry and tumbled from his horse in front of the square, where a grenadier finished him with the butt of his musket. The 10th drove away the cavalry that side, so Vivian attacked the flank of the cuirassiers covering the square with his 18th Hussars, drove them off and cut down the gunners. They suffered no other artillery fire from then on as they pursued, harrying the infantry.[3] Vandeleur's 11th and 16th Light Dragoons charged a body of infantry and captured much of it, but attacked no cavalry. The indestructible Major Bäring, overjoyed at the sudden, joyous and unexpected turn of events, 'joined the 1st Hussars, and with them followed the enemy until dark, when I returned to the field of battle'.[4] An officer of the horse artillery with Vivian's horsemen said that 'we with the guns alternately unlimbered and advanced, bringing them to bear on every possible occasion, until it was too dark to fire without danger to our own Cavalry, which continued to press upon the rear of the French, and turned their retreat into a complete rout and confused flight.'[5]

A lieutenant of the 16th Light Dragoons described how they advanced a mile and a half before they reached the valley where La Haye Sainte was burning on their left. If his estimate of distance was remotely accurate, the cavalry had started from a position well to the north of Mont-Saint-Jean, an indication of how far back the British line had really been driven. One of the 11th Light Dragoons said that they charged various bodies of infantry, but 'Just as it was getting dark we came in sight of some of the Imperial Guards, who rapidly retreated behind a column of infantry, which we charged and received a volley from close to their muskets.' They received most of their fifty-five casualties during this last phase.

D'Erlon's artillery commander General Dessales was reluctant to withdraw his guns and gave the order too late. Although his 12-pounders had good teams, hauling them up the slope was a slow business and consequently the allied cavalry was onto them as they reached their original front line. Dessales managed to reach the safety of a square of Imperial Guards, but his guns were captured.

The British cavalry making their charge along the main road into the mass of fleeing troops now encountered the two Imperial Guard battalions that had been in reserve. Retreating in square, assailed by British skirmishers and hit by occasional artillery shots, the Guards held together until they reached Rossomme, where Petit had united the two battalions of the 1st Grenadiers as well as the sappers and seamen, holding their ground either side of the *chaussée* with the support of a battery of 12-pounder guns. They were obstinately beating the *grenadière* to rally Imperial Guard grenadiers and many joined the squares, but at about this point the square of the first battalion 2nd Grenadiers broke up in rout.[6] The Emperor took refuge in Petit's square with the 1st Grenadiers until Soult persuaded him to leave the field. He told Petit to hold the line behind him and rode on.

Napoleon's military coachman Jean Hornn had been abandoned near La Belle Alliance with his vehicle, which contained diamonds belonging to Joseph Bonaparte worth 800,000 francs, Princess Pauline's necklace, worth 300,000 francs, and a large amount of gold. Hornn too drove off, forcing his way through the confusion on the highway.

As the number of French fugitives swelled, Johan Duuring gathered his 1st Chasseurs of the Guard together so that they could either form square against cavalry or move off in retreat, swelling his numbers by accepting into his ranks fugitives from the Guard. At dusk they were attacked again by skirmishers, for by now the nearby woods were full of Prussian fusiliers. Then the Emperor appeared with his aides Antoine Drouot, Charles de Flahaut, other generals and an escort of *chasseurs-à-cheval*. Napoleon ordered Duuring to follow him and cover his retreat and rode on.

The remains of Reille's II Corps, on the French left, pulled out in reasonable order. Although under pressure and under fire, most of them marched off the battlefield, bypassed Genappe, and crossed the Sambre at Marchiennes-au-Pont. A British cavalry officer admired the hauteur with which what was left of the Horse Grenadiers of the Guard walked away, ignoring his 12th Light Dragoons, who considered themselves too weak to attack the heavy cavalry.[7] This good order was fragile – although Reille himself claimed that it lasted until Genappe and Quatre Bras, where units broke up in the darkness, some accounts indicate that regiments disintegrated in rout much earlier – but probably the French to the west retreated in relative calm. An officer of the French 2nd Dragoons claimed that 'The disorder ... has been exaggerated ... The enemy were so surprised by their success, that in their pursuit they only attacked the soldiers in disorder on the plain immediately to the left and right of the road ... the enemy kept away from those bodies who kept their order,' and most accounts by allied cavalry officers support this contention. Piré's cavalry division, too, retired in good order, covering the retreat of Reille's corps.[8]

Trapped between the British and the Prussians, the French right, which had broken first, suffered most. General Durutte marched the two regiments of Brue's brigade westward in good order, intending to act as a rearguard to shield the fugitives, but they reached a point where the lane they were following became a hollow way so narrow that they were unable to move along it in formation, and so he told his officers to wait while he looked for a better route forward. He had hardly left them when Marshal Ney appeared, exasperated, riding a horse spattered with mud and blood, brandishing a broken sword, and ordered the troops to follow him so that he could show them how a marshal of France died on the field of battle. Amazingly, they shouted '*Vive l'Empereur! Vive le maréchal Ney!*' and followed. After an advance of 200 paces, however, they could see the whole allied line surging towards them and a violent hail of canister, followed by a cavalry charge, cut down more than half their number. Those who were not hit by a bullet or a ball were sabred and trampled by horses. An English officer and a dragoon threw themselves against the eagle bearer of the 95th and seriously wounded him in an attempt to seize the eagle; a battalion chief just had time to tear it from his hands and plunge into the hollow way after Marshal Ney, who by some miracle was untouched. Brisk fire from a battalion of Imperial Guards halted the charge of the British cavalry in which they were engulfed and they both galloped towards its square.[9]

When General Durutte returned to look for his men he was surrounded by English cavalry who sabred him mercilessly, practically severing his wrist and cutting him hideously about his face. The English left him behind, covered in blood, but his horse, which he could no longer direct because he had practically lost consciousness, followed their charge and took him to the high road among the French fugitives. A cuirassier recognised him there and escorted him to Genappe, where his hand was amputated. Durutte's men were followed westward by the Prussians, with Bieberstein's fusilier battalion of the 18th Infantry in the lead. The regiment suffered the highest casualties in the Prussian army as they pressed at Durutte's division and the Young Guard, whose retreat eventually turned into a wild flight; nevertheless, after about an hour Bieberstein's men reached La Belle Alliance.

As they advanced through the smoke following the retreating Imperial Guard the Netherlands units began to lose cohesion. Captain Gerard Rochell of the 19th Militia saw Frenchmen firing from an orchard on his left – possibly La Valette – and he hurried there with his flankers. The 2nd Dutch line regiment was attacking La Haye Sainte, which was still held by the French 13th Light. Having driven the French out of the orchard, Rochell continued forward through a ploughed field where many of his men lost their shoes in the mud, then up a slope, where he met another captain of his battalion who only had two of his company with him. Finally, they ran into Prussian skirmishers who thought they were French until they waved their orange sashes in the air. 'They welcomed us with great joy and although we did not know each other we shook hands; everyone shouted: "The victory is ours!" Those who still had something to drink shared this with their comrades. Many Prussians offered me their bottle and my flankers as well, which enlivened us, as we had not had anything to drink.'[10]

The Prussians were storming through everywhere now. Fresh units from II Corps were thrown into the battle as spearheads of a third attack on the burning village of Plancenoit. The 2nd Regiment, 2900 strong, moved on the churchyard, which by now was piled with bodies – several thousand dead and dying men lay in and close to the village. The fusiliers captured the churchyard and the wounded General Barrois of the Young Guard. The 2400 men of the 5th Westphalian Landwehr attacked north of the village while the fusiliers of the 25th Regiment – Lützow's Freikorps, dressed in black – made their assault along the track that ran above the Lasne to the south.

The main attack was preceded by an assault by the 2nd Pomeranian Landwehr, who were driven out again. But, as the troops massed for the final attack, Pelet's officers told him that most of their men had gone and that they stood no chance. He gave the order to retreat, and, gathering together what was left of the chasseurs and grenadiers in a body containing, he reckoned, about half his men, fell back on Le Caillou. The commander of one of Lobau's brigades told a similar story: outflanked on both sides by cavalry, 'one sensed that our battalions were in danger of falling into disorder and the order was received to abandon Planchenoit in flames and retire towards the main road.' His square disintegrated between Plancenoit and the *chaussée*. He tried to rally his men near the Bois de Chantelet, but found it full of Prussians and had to run for the main road.[11]

The defenders had fought hard and the Young Guard was almost wiped out in the defence of Plancenoit. Having started the day with 3800 men, a week after the battle it was able to muster only 598: doubtless many had deserted, but casualties at Plancenoit were high.

The 1st Regiment of Grenadiers, together with the seamen and sappers, retired some distance in squares, covered by their *tirailleurs*. As they passed Le Caillou they were joined by the remnant of Pelet's troops from Plancenoit. They came under fire from a battery and from Major von Keller's Prussian fusiliers around the building, but once past this threat they were not closely pursued.

A part of the French army got away in good order, but by gambling everything in search of a victory the bulk of the army had been engulfed in catastrophe. The damage was greatest among Napoleon's artillery, much of which was lost on the battlefield. At this stage, few could assess the extent of the victory; the allies merely knew that they had won. After such a long and anxious struggle they celebrated accordingly, warmly congratulating each other, whatever they might have said soon afterwards when rivalry set in and embittered them.

As the Foot Guards and Adam's brigade marched past La Belle Alliance, the band of a regiment of Prussian cavalry played 'God Save the King'.[12] Wellington rode on with Felton Hervey and a small knot of other unwounded staff, including Basil Jackson, as far as Maison du Roi, the village at the southern end of which the farm of Le Caillou, Napoleon's burning headquarters, was situated, and then turned back. As they rode north, said Jackson, 'a group of horsemen were seen crossing the fields to our right; on seeing them the Duke left the road to meet them. They proved to be Marshal Blücher and his suite.' Wellington and Blücher shook hands and embraced, and Blücher said '*Mein lieber Kamerad! Quelle affaire!*'[13] They rode back together to La Belle Alliance, where Prussian cavalry greeted them with a fanfare of trumpets. Wellington handed over responsibility for the pursuit to Blücher and the two heroes parted, Wellington for Waterloo and Blücher to follow his pursuing cavalry along the road to Genappe.

'Darkness shrouded the spectacle of the dead and dying near La Haye Sainte,' continued Jackson, 'but the frequent snorting of our horses as they trod between them showed that the ground, so fiercely contested during the day, was very thickly strewed with bodies of the brave.'[14]

72

The Pursuit

Charleroi road, 9 p.m.–morning

There had already been sufficient casualties from 'friendly fire' for it to appear preferable for just one army to undertake the pursuit of the French. Blücher was eager: many of his men had been marching for hours – even days – with no chance to kill Frenchmen. They were better motivated than the remains of the battle-weary, if euphoric, allied cavalry, so after discussing the issue with Blücher, Wellington told his cavalry to stop and make camp. They pursued no further than the level of Plancenoit.

It had already become too dark to be sure who was friend and who was foe. Sir Hussey Vivian was at the head of the 1st Hussars of the German Legion when they almost fought the 11th Light Dragoons; they were in the process of charging each other when they recognised each other's cheers as being performed in British army style. By then Vivian's brigade had improved its bank balance by capturing nearly 200 horses.[1] Prussian cavalry scoured the country close to the road to Charleroi, sabreing and spearing those they caught up with, and many wounded men were killed in this way. Their object was to spread fear and harry the French retreat to prevent any rally.

The fusiliers of the Prussian 2nd Regiment meanwhile stormed Le Caillou and set it on fire, and if Larrey and other survivors can be believed, they and their cavalry did their best to massacre the surgeons in the hospital. And in the Bois de Chantelet below Le Caillou, General Gneisenau found Major von Keller with his fusiliers. Keller said that his men were still ready for anything, so Gneisenau led them along the *chaussée* after the retreating French with a drummer beating incessantly and horns blowing. At the very head of the column was a lieutenant of the 15th Regiment, with a hornist, two sergeants and twenty fusiliers; two hundred yards behind marched a vanguard of two or three hundred men and behind them came Gneisenau leading the main body.

The 1st Grenadiers of the Imperial Guard were well ahead of the Prussian fusiliers. Once they had passed Le Caillou they were not closely pursued, and so they formed column and marched to Genappe. Ney rode with them, along with a small remnant of the light cavalry of the Guard, including generals Lefèbvre-Desnouëttes and Lallemand, while General Guyot had retreated in good order with several hundred of his Horse Grenadiers and the Empress's Dragoons, together with both of his batteries of guns.

At Genappe, however, they found the way forward blocked. Panic had seized the artillery train and they had cut the traces and abandoned their guns, leaving them piled at the edge of the village and by the side of the road. There was utter chaos at this bottleneck: the wounded were crushed under the wheels of vehicles and people fought each other to force a way along the narrow road, blocked by abandoned vehicles, that wound towards the little stone bridge over the Dyle. There was no need for men on foot or horseback to cross here – the Dyle, swollen as it was, was still little more than a stream, and sensible people bypassed the town and crossed it elsewhere – but rumours of pursuit produced panic. More determined soldiers, perhaps inspired by some of the Old Guard generals, had barricaded the road and determined to defend the place. They held the barricades until they heard the loud music heralding Gneisenau's approach, when in the ensuing confusion they fled with the rest.[2]

When Pelet's men were fired on from a barricade at the edge of the village, the grenadiers left the *chaussée* and marched across the fields towards Charleroi. Guyot decided that he could take his guns no further and abandoned them, judging it impossible to carry them round the village. During the night, as they tried to make their way by narrow lanes, even the grenadiers broke up into groups of a hundred or so.

Most French troops had passed Genappe by this stage. Corporal Louis Canler had marched through with wagon loads of wounded from the hospital at Le Caillou, which had been evacuated before the Prussians burned it. Canler walked across the fields to Charleroi. Lieutenant Jacques Martin had limped round the town, helped and guided by a Belgian sergeant from his battalion who took him to the bridge at Ways la Hutte and then on to Quatre Bras; there, he believed, he glimpsed the Emperor warming himself by a campfire in the woods.

Stumbling along at the head of the retreating French column were British prisoners. Friedrich Lindau and the others who had been captured at La Haye Sainte were marched along the *chaussée* for three hours and then pushed into a dark barn. When Frenchmen burst in to rob them, Lindau escaped in the confusion. He came across a well and begged water from a French Guardsman, who turned out to be German and pointed him towards the Prussians. Lindau and a comrade overpowered and killed a lone Frenchman, then hid in a chicken shed and in the morning found their way to a patrol of Prussian lancers who took them to Genappe; from there they eventually found Major Bäring.

Edmund Wheatley had been captured too and was marched through Genappe with French wounded. The sights he saw left him with a lasting revulsion for war and ideas of honour:

Against the wall of a Garden I saw a foot soldier sitting with his head back and both his eyeballs hanging on his cheeks, a ball having entered the side of his head and passed out at the other. Nothing could equal the horror of his situation. His mouth was open, stiff and clotted, clear blood oozed out of his ears and the purulent matter from his empty sockets emitted a pale stream from the vital heat opposed to the evening cold.

After being briefly shut up with some wounded British Life Guards, he was marched on. The road became choked and the sense of disorder increased. Between Genappe and Quatre Bras he was robbed of his boots and epaulette and forced to walk barefoot on the road; at Quatre Bras, they walked over the naked corpses still lying on the field. Wheatley 'felt a temporary relief to my feet in treading on through soft jellied lumps of inanimate flesh. The French assured me they were all Prussians.' His only drink had been brandy and he felt feverish. Having marched all night he reached Charleroi at dawn:

> Here at the entrance, my two guards lay on the heaped up ruins of a delapidated [sic] house and fell asleep exhausted, while I sat shrivelled up with cold and misery, my feet black with dirt and bruises, viewing the passing troops, pale with fatigue and exertion, entering the town.
>
> A Grenadier of the Imperial Guard sat himself by me, struck with my unhappy appearance, and, asking me if I spoke French, pulled out a small memorandum book which he told me he took from an Hanoverian Officer whom he had killed and asked me its contents; but I found only the names of his Company. He then took out the pencil and begged of me to write some recommendation of him that it might be of use if ever he fell into our hands so, taking the pencil, I scrawled the following words: 'I Edmund Wheatley, Lieutenant in the German Legion, write this on a bundle of bricks, June 19th 1815 at the entrance of Charleroi in the middle of the retreating French Army. Cold, wounded, barefooted, bareheaded, like a dog in a fair, every one buffets me ad libitum. If the bearer, named Riviere, is in your power, prove to him how differently an Englishman can treat a poor unhappy victim of human instability. Signed, E Wheatley.[3]

Several days later Wheatley rejoined the army.

Back at Genappe, Napoleon's coachman Jean Hornn had found the road barricaded. He had tried to drive round the village but soon became stuck. Minutes afterwards Prussian lancers and fusiliers arrived. They bayoneted the postillion and lead horses, and Major von Keller himself cut down Hornn. Hornn was unarmed and thought they would take him prisoner, but instead 'they drove their lances into his back, shot him in the legs, and in the right arm; cut off two of his fingers, and having inflicted ten wounds upon him, he fell senseless and was left for dead.'[4]

Gneisenau's vanguard stormed the barricade at the edge of the town and the rest of their battalion followed. They captured some two thousand Frenchmen there, including many wounded, and eighty guns. Keller believed that Napoleon had escaped from his carriage just as he captured it, but in reality Bonaparte had not been in the carriage – he had ridden away across country; according to Flahaut, he was very tired and would have fallen from the saddle had Flahaut not been by his side.

The Emperor stopped at Quatre Bras, where four or five thousand naked corpses glowed palely in the moonlight. He had been hoping to find Girard's division, to whom Soult had earlier sent an order, but they were not there. They paused around a campfire in the woods and Soult wrote to Grouchy, who was still trying to break through the Prussian lines at Wavre, telling him of the defeat and ordering him to cross the lower Sambre; it took the officer Soult sent nine hours to find the marshal. With Gneisenau still pressing, they pushed on through Gosselies.[5] Johan Duuring with the 1st Chasseurs of the Imperial Guard took a route away from the *chaussée* in the direction which he thought the Emperor had taken. He got lost, but was led in the direction of Fleurus, reaching it at dawn.[6]

General Gneisenau halted his men beyond the bridge at Genappe and together they sang Luther's German *Te Deum*, '*Herr Gott dich loben wir!*' When Gneisenau asked them to go on, the men answered with joyous cries of '*Vorwärts! Vorwärts!*' At a point just beyond Quatre Bras the Prussians caught up with the headquarters baggage train, whose seven carriages, led by those of Napoleon's valet Louis Marchand and cabinet secretary Pierre Fleury de Chaboulon, had been held up by an abandoned howitzer and a queue of wagons near Frasnes. Prussian cavalry fell on the rear of the column, sabreing the drivers and ransacking the coaches. Marchand stuffed 300,000 francs in notes into the front of his uniform and abandoned the rest. He, Fleury de Chaboulon and Maret, duc de Bassano escaped 'by a miracle', running for it on foot. They were terrified, since 'the Prussians, in determined pursuit of us, treated the miserable creatures that they caught with unparalleled barbarity.'[7]

The pursuit ended at the alehouse called L'Empereur south of Frasnes, where Gneisenau spent the night, giving Napoleon's treasure to the men with him.[8] The booty in banknotes, gold, silver and diamonds was huge. Fusiliers stuffed their knapsacks and pockets with riches: an NCO of the 2nd Regiment made 1000 Reichsthalers from selling booty and another found 500 gold Napoleons.[9] At first the soldiers only went for the gold, rejecting the silver and assuming the diamonds were glass: initially, in the Prussian camp five diamonds were trading for a gold coin. One fusilier discovered a gold box full of jewels and wanted to throw them away but an experienced sergeant recognised that they were the real thing and bartered for them, making the biggest fortune of the night.

Other Prussian units had followed Gneisenau. Hans von Ziethen led his cavalry as far as Maison du Roi, then let Röder take them on and set up camp.[10] Blücher rode on as far as Genappe before stopping for the night at the Roi d'Espagne. There he found the mortally wounded General Guillaume Duhesme, who had been captured on the road, and had his own surgeon do all he could for the wounded Frenchman. The comte de Lobau, who had also been wounded and captured, visited Duhesme before he died at the inn the following night. He was buried at Ways church.[11]

In the Roi d'Espagne, Blücher wrote to his wife: 'Together with my friend Wellington, I have brought Napoleon's dance to an end. His army is completely routed and the entirety of his artillery, caissons, baggage and equipage is in my hands. I have just been brought the insignia of all the different decorations he had won, found in a box in his carriage.'[12] Here, where the staff had witnessed so much of the drama of the four-day campaign, it seemed a fitting place to note its conclusion.

73

Victory! Victory!

By 2 a.m. the Prince of Orange at Brussels had recovered sufficiently from his wound to write a triumphant letter to his mother and father: 'Victory! Victory! My very dear parents, we have had a magnificent affair against Napoleon today. It was my corps which principally gave battle and to which we owe the victory, but the affair was entirely decided by the attack which the Prussians made on the enemy's right. I am wounded by a ball in the left shoulder, but only slightly.'[1] It was a vainglorious letter, but the claim that his corps had borne the brunt of the battle was not without substance.

Wellington returned, exhausted, to his inn at Waterloo towards midnight. Dismounting from Copenhagen, he spotted his cook James Thornton in the shadowy entrance passage and said, 'Is that you? Get dinner.' Early that morning Thornton had been ordered to prepare a supper and had bought food from the market at Brussels; he had then packed it in baskets with wine, sent it to Waterloo and followed with Wellington's butler. While the battle raged, Thornton had cooked.

They dined upstairs because Wellington's aide Alexander Gordon was 'lying with his leg cut off in the dining room'. The table was laid for the entire staff with guests, but their numbers were very much thinned by casualties. The Spanish representative, Alava, said that each time the door opened the Duke looked up enquiringly.[2]

At about half past three Delancey's deputy quartermaster-general called, asking for movement orders for the troops. The war had not suddenly ended with this battle and daily military routine continued. Dr Hume woke Wellington, naked but still covered in grime, to tell him that Gordon had just died, before giving a resumé of other casualties. Wellington wept and said, 'Well, thank God, I don't know what it is like to lose a battle; but certainly nothing can be more painful than to gain one with the loss of so many of one's friends.' He told Fitzroy Somerset, 'I have never fought such a battle, and I trust I never shall fight such another.'[3] He was right: Waterloo was to prove his biggest, toughest and last fight.

The Duke wrote again to Lady Frances Webster to tell her that she was perfectly safe because he had won a great victory; just about all his staff had been wounded but the finger of Providence had preserved him. And he began, very tired, and knowing little of what had happened out of his own sight, to write a dispatch to the government. At dawn he took it to Brussels to finish and gave the honour of carrying it to London to Major Harry Percy.[4]

The first man in London to discover the outcome of the battle of Waterloo was Nathan Rothschild, the banker who had supplied the Duke with twenty-five million francs to pay for the campaign. But he didn't hear the news from Harry Percy. Rothschild's own agents had moved faster than Wellington's envoy. Rothschild had already sold on the stock exchange, apparently on the news of the retreat following Quatre Bras. The likelihood that his pessimism was well-informed caused others to follow his example, but then, when the price had fallen sufficiently low, he bought, making up to £7000.

Percy disembarked at Broadstairs on 21 June and took an express coach for the metropolis. Rumbling into town with an eagle sticking out of each window, he found nobody at the offices in Horse Guards Parade, but was directed to Grosvenor Square where Earl Bathurst, the war minister, was dining. From there, he, Bathurst and the Prime Minister, the Earl of Liverpool, went to the merchant Edmund Böhm's house in St James's Square where the Prince Regent was attending a ball. Percy laid his eagles at the Prince's feet, and the Prince promoted him to lieutenant-colonel, bursting into tears at his account of the casualties.

'After two Days Impatience for Accounts from Abroad, last Night Major Percy arriv'd from Ld. Wellington with an Account of a glorious but terrible & bloody Victory gain'd on Sunday June 18th,' wrote the well-connected Lady Lucas. 'My Servants heard it from Ld. Bathurst's Servants in the Morning.'[5] At ten o'clock on 22 June guns boomed out in Green Park and from the Tower to announce the victory. Wellington's dispatch was published in a *London Gazette Extraordinary* and in the newspapers the following day. It was a rushed piece of work, followed by corrections, and the press published every other shred of information they could lay their hands on.

On 23 June the town was illuminated in celebration, with ordinary people putting lights in their windows and others showing off. As the *Morning Post* reported, 'The town was last evening in a blaze. The crowds of people at the west end were greater, if possible, than on the first night of lighting up in honour of the Victory of Vitoria.' All along its façade, the Admiralty acclaimed with large capitals picked out in lights 'Unconquered Wellington'. The name 'Wellington' was displayed at Carlton House, the Earl of Liverpool's home, the Treasury, the Bank of England and the Horse Guards, while the Horse Guards, Earl Bathurst and the House of Commons correctly added 'Blucher'. The Ordnance Office was decorated with cannon, and private houses, clubs, theatres and significant shops were also lit up. The prize for originality went to the printseller Rudolph Ackermann, who displayed 'A most humorous Transparency, about fifteen feet long', surmounted by a circle of gas lights. In it 'Bonaparte flying frightened, and pursued by Wellington, is running direct into the arms of Blucher, who is preparing to meet him with an engine of destruction (an English blunderbuss) . . .'[6]

The human cost of the battle was soon known to have been high: 'this Victory has been purchas'd with a terrible Loss of brave Officers, & many who survive are desperately wounded,' wrote Lady Lucas on 22 June. The newspapers printed long lists of casualties but they were known to be incomplete. The painter John Constable had two cousins in the battle, and he and his family were desperately anxious about their fate:

We are full of anxiety about our relations who were in the late dreadfull battle – we can get no account of them whatsoever – beside what are made publick they have a list of 800, killed & wounded, at the War Office which they will not publish. My poor Aunt at Chelsea is almost shaken to peices, with anxiety, but she hopes for the best.

It turned out that the cousin closer to Constable, who used to advise him on fashion, was dead, killed instantly by a cannonball during a charge. The son of the aunt in Chelsea came through unharmed.

'The late dreadfull battle' was all the name the conflict had. General Gneisenau put in the first bid to name it in his official report; acclaiming the success of determined cooperation between two allies in which Wellington had held the French and Blücher had moved heaven and earth to come to his support, he explained how finally, by chance, Blücher and Wellington had met at the inn named La Belle Alliance, where they greeted each other as victors. 'In commemoration of the alliance which exists today between the English and Pussian nations, of the meeting of the two armies and of their confidence in each other, the Field Marshal has asked that the Battle should be known as la Belle Alliance.'[7]

The editor of the *Morning Post* had had the same happy thought, possibly independently, writing on 24 June that 'the splendid victory of the 18th appears to have been achieved at a place called *La Belle Alliance* – a happy omen of the success by which the Alliance against rebellion, perjury and perfidy will be crowned. The affair may therefore be correctly called the Battle of *La Belle Alliance*.'[8] He tried again on 27 June, asserting prematurely that Wellington and Blücher had agreed to 'call this famous battle by so auspicious a title, "the battle of La Belle Alliance"'.

By then it was clear that the French in their newspapers had already named it the battle of Mont Saint-Jean. And it soon became equally clear that as a name for what the papers still referred to as 'the tremendous battle', Londoners preferred the more easily anglicised 'Waterloo'. On 23 June in the Lords Earl Bathurst referred to the enemy attacking Wellington at Waterloo and that day Lady Lucas noted, 'Nothing almost can be talk'd of but this Battle (I believe it will be call'd the Battle of Waterloo) which is one of the most glorious, but also one of the most bloody in our Times'.[9] Without naming the battle, Wellington's dispatch had been dated from Waterloo and referred to the British line being formed in a position in front of Waterloo. Other letters were sent from 'Waterloo', chiefly because there happened to be a post office there.

Despite its editor's efforts, in the *Morning Post* of 27 June there was a notice headed 'Battle of Waterloo', inviting merchants and bankers to attend a meeting to 'consider the propriety of a public subscription for the relief of the sufferers in the late glorious battles'. A poem, 'Wellington's words after the Glorious Victory of Waterloo', was printed on the same page. It seems that the setting aside of Gneisenau's noble proposal was attributable chiefly to the adoption by the British public of the most obvious, if least accurate, name on offer.

74

Butcher's Bill

Most of those left in Brussels stayed up long into the night to find out what had really happened in the end. The Whig politician Thomas Creevey learned of the victory at 4 a.m. from his Belgian friend, into whose house the badly wounded General von Alten had been carried. After a few hours' rest he was eager for further information and at eleven on a hot summer morning Creevey walked to the Duke's house; seeing Wellington on the balcony, he was invited to come up. 'It has been a damned serious business,' said the Duke. 'Blücher and I have lost 30,000 men. It has been a damned nice thing – the nearest run thing you ever saw in your life.'[1]

Later that day Wellington wrote to his brother William:

It was the most desperate business I was ever in. I never took so much trouble about any Battle, & never was so near being beat.

Our loss is immense particularly in that best of all instruments British infantry. I never saw the Infantry behave so well.

The Anglo-German infantry in the centre were heartbroken that so many old comrades, veterans of scrape after scrape in Spain, had not made it to the end of the war. What was left of Alten's division camped on their positions in the front line, but Major Georg Bäring could round up only 42 of his 400 men:

Whoever I asked after, the answer was 'Killed', or 'Wounded!' I freely confess that tears came involuntarily into my eyes at this sad intelligence, and the many bitter feelings that seized upon me. I was awakened from these gloomy thoughts by my friend Major Shaw, Assistant Quartermaster General to our division. I felt myself exhausted to the greatest degree, and my leg was very painful. I lay down to sleep, with my friend, upon some straw which the men had collected together for us: on waking we found ourselves between a dead man and a dead horse![2]

In the morning Shaw and Bäring buried Colonel von Ompteda, one of the bravest and longest-serving opponents of Napoleon, along with many other old friends and comrades.

For the surgeons, the work went on long after the battle ended. Most of them, like John James of the Life Guards, 'being fully engaged with my colleagues in a house at the rear with the wounded, of which there were many', had not seen much of the battle after the beginning:

Our work behind the lines was grim in the extreme, and continued far into the night. It was all too horrible to commit to paper, but this I will say, that the silent heroism of the greater part of the sufferers was a thing I shall not forget. When one considers the hasty surgery performed on such an occasion, the awful sights the men are witness to, knowing that their turn on that blood-soaked operating table is next, seeing the agony of an amputation, however swiftly performed, and the longer torture of a probing, then one realizes fully of what our soldiers are made. Most of the wounded were sent back to hospitals in Brussels in carts or any sort of transport that could be found. One's mind shrinks at imagining the sufferings they must have endured on that long, jolting ride, or that weary tramp, and then only to face in so many cases the pain and disgust of a spreading gangrene.[3]

From an average battle British surgeons expected 10 per cent casualties: at Waterloo, casualty rates were around three times as high.

Figures are muddled – confused by multiple nationalities and several days of fighting – but the best available figures suggest that at Waterloo alone Wellington's army lost 3500 dead, 3300 missing and 10,200 wounded. About half of the missing subsequently proved to be dead and between one and two thousand of the wounded soon died. A return of 13 April 1816 stated that of 7687 British and King's German Legion wounded from all three days of fighting, 856 had died, 854 remained in hospital, 236 had survived amputation, 5068 had rejoined their units, 506 had been discharged and 167 transferred to garrison duties. The total dead was one and a half times the number originally reported.[4]

Where the Prussians were heavily engaged, casualty rates were if anything higher. They lost 1200 dead, 1400 missing and 4400 wounded at Waterloo, as well as another 2500 in the fierce fighting at Wavre.

French losses are impossible to calculate. About 30,000 mustered at Laon, when reviewed by Marshal Soult on 23 June, leaving 40,000-plus unaccounted for, but many of these had deserted. The French press estimated losses at Waterloo at 24–26,000, including 6–7000 prisoners, and these figures are not impossibly low although there may really have been more killed and wounded.[5] According to a recent analysis of records of officers killed, the French lost 207 dead and disappeared against the Allies' 279, which might reasonably suggest that casualties were actually lower in the French army than in the Allied armies.[6] It is usually argued that French casualties must have been higher since they spent the day attacking; in most battles the attacking army suffered higher casualties and in the fierce Prussian assaults on Plancenoit they seem to have lost considerably more men than the French. But attacks on Wellington's line were sporadic and against the cavalry the British infantry usually held its fire. Between attacks there were artillery bombardments and prolonged exchanges of fire between skirmishers, and given the substantial numerical superiority of the French artillery and skirmishers, it is possible that Wellington's army might have suffered more casualties.

Two hundred thousand men had fought over an area barely two and a half miles square. That night there might have been as many as

40,000 dead and seriously wounded bodies lying on the battlefield. There cannot have been fewer than 20,000, together with the best part of 10,000 dead and dying horses. Most were concentrated where the fighting had been heaviest, or where the artillery had mown them down, and in some places the dead lay in piles. The positions of allied squares remained marked by lines of red-coated bodies, and not far away lay heaps of horses and French cavalrymen. Behind La Haye Sainte could be seen areas where concentrations of cuirassiers and Life Guards had been cut down. Scavengers closed in on the dead and the living, taking first their valuables and then their clothes, to reduce them to the naked state of the corpses littering the ground, or washed by the heavy rain into the ditches at Quatre Bras.

The skies had cleared at sunset to produce a cold night of eerie moonlight, raucous with shrieks, shouts and groans. A sergeant of the Scots Greys wrote to his wife, 'believe me dear Mary, the cries of those poor creatures to God Almighty to take them out of this world frightened the horses.' Most front-line soldiers, like Tom Morris, were however spared this horror through deafness: 'the cries and shrieks of the poor creatures would have been dreadful in the night, if we could have heard them; but the continued discharges of the artillery, during the battle, had so affected the drums of the ears, that we could scarcely hear anything for two or three days afterwards, but the roaring of cannon.'[7]

On the French gun line, it was time for the French *tirailleur* who had sought cover behind the wounded Colonel Frederick Ponsonby to take his leave. 'Towards the evening the fire became much sharper, he told me our troops were moving on to attack and with his last shot he said: *Adieu mon ami nous allons nous retirer.*' Soon afterwards a squadron of Prussian cavalry rode over Ponsonby, inflicting several bruises: 'in general horses will avoid treading upon men', the cavalryman pointed out, 'but the field was so covered, that they had no spare space for their feet.' It grew dark, and Ponsonby now knew they had won the battle. Earlier, he had assumed that he would soon die, but now it seemed easier to breathe and he began to hope for a rescue. He was plundered by Prussians, but then, terribly thirsty, a condition exacerbated by loss of blood, persuaded a British soldier to stay with him.

In the morning the soldier found a dragoon from Ponsonby's brigade and the two of them tried to hoist Ponsonby onto a horse; failing in this, the dragoon rode to fetch help. They took Ponsonby to the inn at Waterloo where Dr Hume dressed his wounds and, after a week in the village, he was taken to Brussels.[8] His sister, Lady Caroline Lamb, came to look after him and his mother, Lady Bessborough, also travelled to Brussels from Italy to be by his side.

Thomas Hasker of the King's Dragoon Guards had fallen near La Haye Sainte. He was quickly plundered by French soldiers of his valuables, trousers and boots, and as night fell a dragoon regiment rode over him. Then he saw fires and tried to stand, but fell again:

The dead and dying lay thick about me. Hearing two men talking very near, I called to them as well as I could to come and help me. They said they could not for a while. Soon after this two foreigners passed by, to whom I made signs; they came, and raising me up between them, took me to one of the fires, and brought me a surgeon; they afterwards wrapped a cloak about me, and left me there for the night. The next day I was kindly treated by some English soldiers, come to reinforce the army, and was laid, with many more, on some straw near the road side. The following morning several of my comrades were dead, and I prevailed on some one to take the trousers off one of these, which I managed to put on. There was much crying out for water, and some was brought. I requested to be allowed to taste, but finding there was blood in it, I could not drink. In the course of the day I saw two or three wagons standing, and the wounded men getting upon them, I made an effort, and succeeded in mounting one of these, and we rode on towards Brussels. The stench from the bodies of men and horses was horrible. We stopped more than once, when some that had died from the shaking of the wagon were pulled off, and others who had travelled as far as they could on foot were taken up.

It was common for the British troops to blame the looting and stripping on their Belgian colleagues, who in the words of a fellow King's Dragoon Guard, 'were without exception the greatest set of cowards and rascals in the world'. In reality, the practice of instant plundering of the dead was widespread, and another officer noted that next day French watches were five francs apiece and horses also changed hands cheaply. One light dragoon admitted that the moment their pursuit ceased he and some comrades went looting corpses in the moonlight:

> It is one of the worst results of a life of violence that it renders such as follow it selfish and mercenary: at least, it would be ridiculous to conceal that when the bloody work of the day is over, the survivor's first wish is to secure, in the shape of plunder, some recompense for the risks which he has run and the exertions he has made. Neither does it enter into the mind of the plunderer to consider whether it is the dead body of a friend or of a foe from which he is seeking his booty.

Indeed, having searched a number of haversacks without worthwhile reward, the dragoon suggested riding off to find the body of a British officer who had been shot dead near some dunghills and whose gold watch and seals he had glimpsed in the twilight. He did locate the corpse but was disappointed to find that it had already been stripped naked. Having passed a pen containing animals, they were looting a farm where the dragoon had found some china and glass and was eating a ham, 'when a General Officer rode into the farm-yard, and instantly there was a cry from all quarters of "escape as you best can."' They fled just before the provost and his guards turned up and rode back to camp, where they told their comrades about the animals they had seen and 'party after party sallied out' until they had mutton for all.[9]

Anything the front-line troops overlooked was taken by a second army of camp followers or a third of local scavengers – the latter perhaps seizing some recompense for what had earlier been taken from them. It was common to strip bodies of everything but their shirts.

With such a high proportion of dead and wounded in this state or even naked by morning, when parties of Dragoon Guards went to identify their dead and search for their wounded they were hard to recognise:

> Our officers were only known by the name on the shirts; I daresay many died of cold in the night. Our brigade was so totally cut up that a party could not be mustered that night to go over the ground and consequently the wounded men and officers were left to shift for themselves. Such a scene of misery was never seen before; the action took place about eighteen miles from Brussels, and the road was strewed with dead men the whole way, who had been trying to crawl to the town from the field and had died on the road, some through cold, other through hunger and thirst. For the space of six miles (beginning from the field of battle and going over the road that the French had retreated) the way was literally so strewed with bodies of horses and men that no carriage or horse could pass unless they went considerably to the right or left.[10]

Crawling to the road was a risky business since several witnesses noticed both corpses and wounded men by the roadside who had been driven over by vehicles.[11]

Sergeant David Robertson of the Gordon Highlanders was another to be confronted by the ghastly aftermath of the battle. Walking out at first light, he was shocked to see 'the number of the dead was far greater than I had ever seen on any former battlefield. The bodies were not scattered over the ground, but were lying in heaps – men and horses mixed promiscuously together.' He 'turned away with disgust from this heart-melting spectacle, and had scarcely arrived at my quarters when every person that could be spared was sent out to carry the wounded to the road side, or any other convenient place where the waggons could be brought to convey them to hospital.'

Soon they were ordered to prepare to march and at 7 a.m. took the Nivelles road, sad and vexed to leave most of their dead unburied and their wounded on the field.

Being on the extreme left, we had to pass along between the two lines to the right. We moved on as silent as the dead that lay so thickly around us. No one could speak, so awestruck were we with the horrid spectacle. Here lay French and British in all the agonies of death, many of them calling on us to shoot them and put an end to their sufferings; while others were calling on us to come back, and not leave them exposed to the inclemency of the weather . . .[12]

Robertson wept bitterly, while the officer of the Rifles who had fought close to him marched to Nivelles with him, similarly drained and exhausted, and shocked by the situation. He recalled seeing

some thousands of wounded wretches who remained without assistance through a bitter cold night, succeeded by a day of most scorching heat; English and French were dying by the side of each other; and I have no doubt, hundreds who were not discovered when the dead were buried, and who were unable to crawl to any habitation, must have perished by famine. For my own part, when we halted for the night, I sunk down almost insensible from fatigue; my spirits and strength were completely exhausted. I was so weak, and the wound in my thigh so painful, from want of attention, and in consequence of severe exercise, that after I got to Nivelles, and secured quarters, I did not awake regularly for 36 hours.[13]

A Guards officer reckoned there were 2000 men lying around Hougoumont when he walked round it in the morning.[14] As another officer noted:

close to Hougoumont lay the corpse of an officer of our Guards, and across his breast the dead body of a French Grenadier; the officer had been shot through the head, a loaf of brown bread half out of the Frenchman's haversack was spattered with his brains; I had not tasted food since daylight of yesterday's morn, and ravenous with hunger, I scraped off the brains and feasted on the bread; at any other time I should have turned from it with disgust.[15]

Harry Smith, brigade major of Lambert's division, had walked over many battlefields, but only the scenes at Badajoz and New Orleans – both assaults on fortifications – bore any resemblance to what he saw here:

> the whole field from right to left was a mass of dead bodies. In one spot, to the right of La Haye Sainte the French Cuirassiers were literally piled on each other; many soldiers not wounded lying under their horses; others, fearfully wounded, occasionally with their horses struggling upon their wounded bodies. The sight was sickening, and I had no means or power to assist them . . . All over the field you saw officers, and as many soldiers as were permitted to leave the ranks, leaning and weeping over some dead or dying brother or comrade.[16]

As Smith gazed at the many dead, he murmured Sunday's psalm, 'A thousand shall fall beside thee and ten thousand at thy right hand, but it shall not come nigh thee.' Having thus been spared himself, he was anxious to let his wife know he was all right.

75

Wives

For anxious wives – even the most feisty – the hours after the battle were fraught with tortuous anxiety. Having left her husband at Waterloo on the morning of the battle, Juana Smith, Harry's Spanish bride, found herself in Antwerp.

Her husband had instructed her to ride back to Brussels and look after their baggage, which she found in the Place Royale. In the afternoon the baggage cleared out of the city, by order, and stopped by the canal on the road to Antwerp. Suddenly, at about five o'clock, an alarm had gone up that the enemy was upon them. Amid much noise and panic Juana's servant got her mounted, but just as he was passing her pug to her, her mare bolted and carried her away to Malines, when she suddenly stopped. Looking back Juana saw a knot of horsemen and, taking them for French dragoons, she decided to surrender. But the first turned out to be one of her servants, the others being a commissary, a Hanoverian rifle officer and a British hussar officer who swore that the French were in hot pursuit. They galloped on to Antwerp, where Mrs Smith was welcomed into the commandant's household.[1]

At Antwerp long rows of carriages lined the streets, filled with civilians who could find nowhere to stay. People of rank and fortune found themselves sharing what they considered 'miserable holes'. Although it poured with rain all day on Sunday, the market square was full of the curious and anxious under umbrellas waiting for news;

strangers found themselves conversing like friends. But most of the rumours were gloomy. Between nine and ten that evening some wounded officers rode in and announced that the battle was lost and Brussels was in the hands of the French. This dreadful news was corroborated by fugitives from Brussels who had seen the French in the town – one gentleman claimed to have been pursued halfway to Malines. Hearing this, many set off for Holland, while wounded men, stores and a fresh contingent for the army from one of the Hanse cities of north Germany surged in.

Then, during the afternoon of 19 June, news of victory arrived. A British refugee recalled the 'tumultuous joy' of wounded Highlanders who threw their bonnets in the air shouting 'Boney's beat! Boney's beat!' while old women questioned them in Flemish and were answered in incomprehensible Scots.[2]

When Magdalene Delancey was told that her husband was not on the list of killed and wounded, she too felt a wild elation – until, a few hours later, another officer's wife admitted that she had written the list and had left Sir William's name out, intending to spare Magdalene from the shock of seeing it. She conceded first that William was wounded, then desperately wounded and finally still alive but not expected to live. Magdalene, plunged from joy into grief, insisted on a carriage to Waterloo, but she only got halfway there, along a road jammed with vehicles, before she met William Hay who had ridden ahead for news. He told her that Delancey was dead and accompanied her back to Antwerp.[3]

Juana Smith meanwhile could get no word at all of Harry. She determined to ride back to Brussels, setting out at three in the morning and arriving at seven on 20 June. 'Seeing some of our Rifle soldiers, with an eagerness which may be imagined, I asked after my husband, when to my horror they told me that Brigade-Major Smith of the 95th was killed.' Galloping for the battlefield 'to seek my husband's corpse', she found the road packed with wounded men and horses and corpses being taken to Brussels for burial, so that every moment she expected 'to see that of my husband, knowing how he was beloved by officers and soldiers'.

She intended to complete her life by dying 'on the body of the only thing I had on earth to love, and which I loved with a faithfulness which few can or ever did feel, and none ever exceeded'. In an ever-increasing agony of grief, she said, she approached the battlefield, searching for Enrique, Brigade-Major Harry Smith.

> I saw signs of newly dug graves, and then I imagined to myself, 'O God, he has been buried, and I shall never again behold him!' How can I describe my suspense, the horror of my sensations, my growing despair, the scene of carnage around me? From a distance I saw a figure lying; I shrieked, 'Oh, there he is!' I galloped on. 'No, it is not he!' ... Educated in a convent, I was taught to appeal to God through Jesus Christ. In this my trouble I did so.

In response to her prayers she glimpsed an old friend, Charles Gore, ADC to Sir James Kempt.

> In my agony and hope, hope alone of finding the body, I exclaimed, 'Oh, where is he? Where is my Enrique?' 'Why, near Bavay by this time, as well as ever he was in his life; not wounded even, nor either of his brothers.' 'Oh, dear Charlie Gore, why thus deceive me? The soldiers tell me Brigade-Major Smith is killed. Oh, my Enrique!' 'Dearest Juana, believe me; it is poor Charles Smyth, Pack's Brigade-Major. I swear to you, on my honour, I left Harry riding Lochinvar in perfect health, but very anxious about you.' 'Oh, may I believe you, Charlie! my heart will burst.' 'Why should you doubt me?' 'Then God has heard my prayer!'[4]

The same night, Sir George Scovell sent a messenger to Magdalene Delancey with news of her husband. He had been discovered, by chance, lying in the cottage in which he had been placed during the battle. A Staff Corps officer had seen him on Monday morning; eight of his ribs had been detached and one had smashed to pieces in his lung, but he was still alive.

When she set out again on Tuesday, the road was less badly blocked, but it was still a long, slow journey. At Brussels William Hay was waiting for them with horses saddled, and he rode ahead with his sword drawn to clear a path for them. The day was very hot: at first the air smelled of gunpowder, but later it smelled so badly of rotting flesh that the horses began to scream. It took them three and a half hours to ride nine miles; when they approached Waterloo Hay rode forward to ascertain Delancey's condition.

Magdalene was taken in by Sir George Scovell to see her husband, and he was well enough to talk to her. 'He asked me if I was a good nurse. I told him that I had not been much tried. He said he was sure he would be a good patient, for he would do whatever I bade him until he was convalescent; and then he would grow very cross. I watched in vain for a cross word.' But the surgeons' initial hopes for his recovery were eventually to fade; she spent six days holding his hand before he died.[5]

76

What Misery War Causes

Nobody had anticipated a battle near Brussels until the campaign began so unexpectedly and so violently; hence, when the first wounded arrived from Quatre Bras, little had been done to receive them. Small army hospitals already existed in the city, as well as at Antwerp and Ostend, to care for those soldiers who had fallen ill in Belgium, but there was nothing like sufficient capacity to cope with the sudden influx of wounded men.

So, on 17 June the Mayor of Brussels issued an urgent appeal, inviting 'his fellow citizens to deposit at the Hôtel de Ville the largest possible amount of bedding, in particular mattresses or palliasses, bolsters, bed sheets and blankets'; confident that the well-to-do would respond, he warned that if they did not 'he will feel himself obliged to billet wounded or sick soldiers on them.' Later in the day he warned the public that 'the large general hospital of the allied army has today been established in this city' and requested anyone with old linen or lint to deposit it with the priests of their parish.

The hospital took some time to set up, most surgeons being with the army, but the public responded with generous humanity. By the morning of 19 June:

thousands of wounded French, Belgians, Prussians and English; carts, waggons, and every other attainable vehicle were continually arriving heaped with sufferers. The wounded were laid, friends and foes indiscriminately, on straw, with avenues between them, in every part of the city, and nearly destitute of surgical attendance. The humane and indefatigable exertions of the fair ladies of Brussels, however, greatly made up for this deficiency; numbers were busily employed – some strapping and bandaging wounds, others serving out tea, coffee, soups, and other soothing nourishments; while many occupied themselves stripping the sufferers of their gory and saturated garments, and dressing them in clean shirts and other habiliments; indeed, altogether careless of fashionable scruples, many of the fairest and wealthiest of the ladies of that city now ventured to assert their pre-eminence . . .[1]

That morning, when the 15th Hussars accompanied Wellington's army towards Nivelles in pursuit of the French, accompanied by their senior surgeon, the junior assistant went to Brussels. William Gibney was thus left at Waterloo to look after his colonel, Leighton Dalrymple, and other seriously wounded officers. 'The accommodation for the wounded in these villages was hideously bad: each house was packed to overflowing, each room was full as it could hold, and little relief given, often none. The cries of these wounded for help were heard in the street; but even this, bad as it was, was shelter.' At daybreak

I was horrified to see, lying about indiscriminately on each side of the road, wounded soldiers of every arm of the service in all stages of suffering; some imploring medical aid and others silent, only looking to death as an alleviation to their miseries. Of course aid could not be given to all. The numbers lying about were too considerable for even a fair proportion to receive relief, and doubtless not a few perished from want of immediate attendance; though this last is applicable chiefly to the French prisoners, as our own countrymen naturally claimed first attention.

As the British had been moved to Brussels, after three days at Waterloo Gibney was left almost exclusively with French wounded. The village was chaotic, violent arguments breaking out on the busy and crowded roads. 'Even now, at the end of three days, all the wounded had not been brought in, some of the French yet awaiting removal. There was a sad paucity of medical officers and assistants.'[2] He was impressed by the wounded men's fortitude; he and others noted how many of them devoted their dying breath to Bonaparte.

Like Gibney, Donald Finlayson, assistant surgeon of the 33rd Foot, remained at Waterloo, 'collecting as many, taking care of dressing & sending away the wounded', until on 23 June he was instructed to go to Brussels to 'assist at the hospitals'. He wanted to stay there to look after 'a school fellow of mine in the same regiment with a sad compressed fracture of the thigh' and told the senior doctor that his friend 'was very ill, that I was apprehensive for his life & that I should very much like to remain & take care of him,' but as soon as things were a little less frantic he was ordered to rejoin his regiment in France, told that 'other officers were in the same predicament, what misery war causes'.[3] Finlayson himself was to die before November of unknown causes.

Hospital assistant George Finlayson, Donald's brother, had arrived in Brussels from Britain on 21 June and went straight to work:

> For three successive days we were constantly occupied in getting our wounded under cover & getting their wounds dressed. During that time no medical officer shut an eye; at least I can say this much for myself. Hundreds of wagons, carts, &c., crowded the streets leading to the hospitals. We have had numerous operations, though many of the cases requiring it did not come into our hands [until] four or five days after they had been wounded. Those operated in the field are doing well ... It has been found impossible to bury the killed, they are thrown with horses on one heap & burnt. A hundred men from all the neighbouring parishes are employed for this purpose & the field of battle will be clean of the dead by today [26 June].[4]

In Brussels thousands of people were now volunteering to make lint, dress wounds and attend sick beds. Six military general hospitals were suddenly improvised in churches and barracks, together with

Belgian civilian hospitals. The best were the Jesuits' and the Annunciate in the higher part of town, followed by the Orpheline, the Notre Dame and the Elizabeth Caserne which, although it was low lying, was clean and well ventilated. The worst was the Gendarmerie, set in the swampy low town, which had been a particularly filthy police barracks before it became a hospital for the most seriously wounded Frenchmen. The Brunswick hospital, near their late Duke's former headquarters at Laeken, was also set on low-lying, swampy ground, and was far too small for their numerous wounded, who lay crowded together on the floor. Gangrene was rife and almost all amputations terminated fatally, not through gangrene but through a feverish disease that killed the patients within a day or two. Further back at Antwerp another five hospitals treated at least 2500 casualties: there was capacity for 1000 beds in the Corderie alone, this being the converted ropewalk attached to the naval base, a quarter of a mile long. Hospitals in other towns, such as Termonde, also cared for casualties.

On 23 June, when the flow had just commenced, Donald Finlayson estimated that there might be 6000 wounded French prisoners, writing that 'one of the Purveyor's department last night drew rations for 4,000 of them'. The diarist Fanny Burney, married to a French royalist officer, spent half her day tending to the British wounded while some of her aristocratic French friends devoted themselves to their countrymen. The vast strain on resources from sheer numbers of casualties meant that they suffered worst, as Burney explained:

> The immense quantity of English, Belgians, and Allies, who were first, of course, conveyed to the hospitals and prepared houses of Brussels, required so much time for carriage and placing, that although the carts, waggons, and every attainable or seizable vehicle were unremittingly in motion – now coming, now returning to the field of battle for more, – it was nearly a week, or at least five or six days, ere the unhappy wounded prisoners, who were necessarily last served, could be accommodated. And though I was assured that medical and surgical aid was administered to them

wherever it was possible, the blood that dried upon their skins and their garments, joined to the dreadful sores occasioned by this neglect, produced an effect so pestiferous, that, at every new entry, eau de Cologne, or vinegar, was resorted to by every inhabitant, even amongst the shopkeepers, even amongst the commonest persons, for averting the menaced contagion.[5]

Succour for the French was a lower priority, but their lives were saved if they were discovered in time. *Chef de bataillon* Joseph Lugnot of the 93rd Line had been with a unit that spent much of the day skirmishing from the high corn, which might be why he lay on the battlefield for five days before being found by the British and ultimately cured in England. Dominique Modere of the 1st Line had been involved in the fighting around Hougoumont, where he was shot in the head. He lay on the field for three days before being taken to a village and from there to a church in Brussels; he was admitted to the Gendarmerie hospital only on 30 June.[6]

As a distinguished Irish staff surgeon, John Hennen, noted:

Three hundred men were collected in this hospital, the majority desperately, not to say incurably, wounded. Among them were one hundred and forty compound fractures, viz. 86 of the thigh, 48 of the leg and 6 of the arm. They had been collected all over the country by the peasantry, and dragged from barn to barn, often without food or dressings, and did not arrive at Brussels until various periods from the 8th to the 13th day after they were wounded ...[7]

Some of the most badly wounded Frenchmen had been placed in the Gendarmerie, but the wounds they had suffered were fairly typical, as Donald Finlayson remarked to a senior doctor on the nature of the wounds suffered by all armies:

Of the total loss, one in 7 or 8 may be killed, the rest are wounded. A great number of the wounds are from cannon balls. Officers have compared the discharge from the cannon to discharges of musketry. Most wounds of the limbs are in the lower extremities. There are perhaps 15 or 16 legs taken off for one arm, there are not many bayonet wounds. There are sabre & lance wounds ...

And among those with sabre wounds, Finlayson told his correspondent, was one of their most esteemed medical colleagues, the man, ironically enough, who had insisted on the importance of rapid treatment: 'Poor Larrey the French surgeon is there, a prisoner & wounded, having two sabre cuts in his head.' Larrey had been at Le Caillou with other surgeons of the Imperial Guard tending to the wounded when a squadron of Prussian lancers appeared. Expecting no mercy, Larrey fired his pistols at them and fled. The Prussians fired carbines and wounded his horse. He fell and at this point received the two sabre cuts; they knocked him out and the Prussians left him for dead.

When he regained consciousness Larrey tried to walk to France, but at the Sambre he was taken prisoner by a Prussian cavalry patrol. They seized his arms, his ring, his watch and most of his clothes and took him to an officer who sentenced him to be shot. A quarter of an hour before this sentence was to be carried out, however, a Prussian surgeon recognised Larrey as the doctor whose lectures had so impressed him in Berlin and obtained a reprieve. Larrey was taken to Bülow and then to Blücher. It happened that when Blücher's son had fallen wounded into French hands during the Austrian campaign, Larrey had operated on him and saved his life. Blücher cancelled the sentence of death and gave him an escort to the hospital in Brussels. His wounds healed, Larrey then helped the British surgeons as he convalesced, suggesting measures to relieve the wounded of all nationalities brought in from the battlefield.[8]

The regimental and staff surgeons of the various armies worked tirelessly, helped by Belgian civilian surgeons, captured French surgeons and a number of men who came out from England, for 'amateur surgeons flocked over from London'. Charles Bell, famed anatomist, consultant to the Middlesex hospital and author in 1814 of *A Dissertation on Gun-shot wounds*, left London with his brother-in-law on 26 June. Asked for a passport, they flourished their surgical instruments; they reached Brussels three days later, entering a very dirty, crowded, low-lying part of town with a rag market, a fish market and a fair. 'The wounded everywhere conspicuous, dragging, pale; a great many wounded in the head. Those, of course, move about, and on the doors, 5 blessés, 3 blessés, 4 blessés . . .'

Bell's main motive in travelling had been medical research and he spent his first five days in the hospitals making sketches and studies of difficult cases on which he gave his advice; he sketched a considerable number of patients and later worked his sketches up to fine and shocking watercolours of subjects such as William Wanstell of the 10th Hussars, who had suffered terrible damage to the brain and died, confused, six days after Bell drew him, or Voultz of the German Legion who, to the astonishment of the medical staff, survived tetanus. He found arrangements for receiving the wounded were still not complete and new hospitals were being opened. 'The expression is continually heard, "We were not prepared for this",' he noted.

On 1 July Bell saw French wounded laid out in the hospital 100 in a row in low beds, and was impressed with the 'strong, thick-set, hardy veterans' who turned each others' moaning into tunes. But by 3 July he 'could not sleep for thinking of the state of the wounded French. "Pansez! pansez, [dress my wound] majeur docteur," or "coupez, coupez," sounded in my ears.' He got up at four o'clock and wrote to the chief surgeon, offering to perform the necessary operations on the Frenchmen.

At six o'clock I took my knife in my hand, and continued incessantly at work till seven in the evening; and so the second and third day. All the decencies of performing surgical operations were soon neglected; while I amputated one man's thigh there lay at one time thirteen all beseeching to be taken next; one full of entreaty; one calling upon me to remember my promise to take him, another execrating. It was a strange thing to feel my clothes stiff with blood, and my arms powerless with the exertion of using the knife.

It was Bell who operated on Dominique Modere, an intelligent man who thought surgery unnecessary since he suffered no more than a headache, but acknowledged that Bell had probably been right when he removed a musket ball from the left hemisphere of his brain. A month later Modere was still alive and saying that 'from his present sensations he could not know that he had been wounded'.[9]

Modere was fortunate: the mortality rate of amputations carried out by Bell ran at approximately 90 per cent. But this was almost inevitable with patients treated so long after being injured, as the French surgeon Larrey had established. 'Assuredly no body of men ever laboured harder in the cause of humanity than the British surgeons after the battle of Waterloo,' wrote Staff Surgeon John Hennen, with Bell in mind, but as another famous surgeon noted, 'nothing could recall ... the irretrievable mischief the insufficient medical care had occasioned in the first few days.'[10]

On 3 July another noted surgeon arrived from London. George Guthrie had turned down a job with the army but came to Brussels to give advice and learn from what he saw. He undertook three operations, one of them being to remove at the thigh the leg of a Frenchman of the 45th Line who had been hit in the right buttock by case shot as he retreated and had lain on his back on the field for five days able only to turn his head to lap at puddles. Guthrie successfully kept him alive and he recovered in the York Hospital in London. Another patient, offered the same operation, refused until he was too weak. 'I gently stated this to him, he thanked me, a tear for a moment glistened in his eye, he waved his hand once more over his head, and cried out "Vive l'Empereur". He died a few hours afterwards.'[11]

The Hardest Battle that Ever Was Fought

The campaign ended swiftly. Having failed to break through General Thielmann's defence at Wavre on 18 June though he had kept fighting until midnight, Marshal Grouchy renewed the struggle at two in the morning; until the messenger sent by Soult from Quatre Bras in the middle of the night arrived at half past ten, he was unaware that Napoleon had been defeated, while his Prussian opponents only found out half an hour earlier. It is remarkable that Grouchy's troops had failed to make contact with those on Napoleon's right flank – perhaps a tribute to the Prussian cavalry seeking to prevent it – but neither Grouchy's cavalry nor Napoleon's appears to have got a message through to their comrades at any point on 18 June. Grouchy pulled out skilfully, winning a defensive battle at Namur.

Napoleon rode south from Charleroi over the border to Philippeville in France, from where he wrote in fighting terms to his brother Joseph, and then travelled to Paris via Laon. News of the calamitous outcome of the battle spread through Paris on 21 June, the day that Napoleon returned to the capital. He spoke of creating a new army, but both the Senate and the Chamber of Deputies were openly opposed to him. Napoleon hesitated to dissolve them, refused to use force and abdicated in favour of his son on 23 June. Joseph Fouché took charge of the government but did nothing to prevent the advance of the allies, with whom he was already secretly in contact. On 26 June Grouchy took over the army at Laon and fought a number of skirmishes with the Prussians as he withdrew to Paris with 50,000 men, arriving three days later.

Blücher advanced fast, leaving troops behind him to mop up the fortresses that he had bypassed, and by 29 June he was close to Saint-Denis and Vincennes. In the words of Assistant Surgeon James Gibney, the Prussians 'were like a swarm of locusts, making all barren around them. Indeed, for miles round they seem to have wantonly destroyed all they could lay their hands on. If revenge for the French occupation of Berlin a short time previously was their object, they certainly obtained it.'[1]

As an officer of the King's Dragoon Guards wrote on 26 July to his father:

> The hatred that exists between the two nations is astonishing; the French shudder at the very name of the Prussian, who plunder and burn wherever they go, and spare nothing. This retaliation is perfectly just, for the French committed much more atrocious when they were in Prussia. You may imagine what comfortable work it was following their troops who were a day's march before us; nothing but the bare walls of houses, not a soul in the villages, and nothing but water to be had – not a bit of bread, if you were to give your life for it.[2]

Wellington followed at a more sedate pace, escorting the king of France, who was to be restored to his throne whether the French wanted him or not. He crossed the border near Malplaquet on 21 June, issuing a general order forbidding plundering the French. The town of Cambrai was stormed and the citadel surrendered to General Colville on 25 June. As Sergeant Wheeler of the 51st noted in a letter home:

> The 25th. we halted and His pottle belly Majesty, Louis 18th, marched into the loyal town of Cambray. His Majesty was met by a deputation of his beloved subjects who received their father and their king with tears of joy ... But the papers will not inform you that the 4th. Division and a brigade of Hanovarian Huzzars were

in readiness within half a mile of this faithful city, and if the loyal citizens had insulted their king, how it was very probable we should have bayoneted every Frenchman in the place. The people well knew this, and this will account for the sudden change in their loyalty or allegiance from their *Idol Napoleon* (properly named) *the Great*, to an old bloated poltroon, the Sir John Falstaff of France.[3]

Having detached forces to deal with the numerically powerful French garrisons in the north, Blücher had only 66,000 men when he approached Paris; Wellington, further back, was down to 52,000. Napoleon, now resident at his Château de Malmaison, just west of Paris, was eager to take them on again with the 120,000 troops around Paris, but the government refused. Blücher sent cavalry with orders to take Napoleon dead or alive but Marshal Davout had the Seine bridge nearest Malmaison blown up to prevent them.

Napoleon's British admirer, Sergeant Wheeler, watched the Prussians go past towards Paris, noting that 'they did not forget to destroy every thing they could as they moved on. Ney's country seat was none the better for their visit, everything they could lay their hands on was knocked to pieces. A small town about two miles from us which we marched through was completely sacked ...'[4]

On 2 July the Prussians advanced on Saint-Cloud and Versailles. When General Sohr raided Versailles, however, Rémy Exelmans attacked and defeated him at Issy, and after this reverse Blücher paused to allow Wellington to catch up. A convention was signed at Saint-Cloud by which the French army would evacuate Paris and retire south of the Loire. The government recognised Louis XVIII – he would return to the Tuileries on 8 July after 110 days' absence – and the Prussians entered Paris on 6 July in vengeful mood. Wellington was worried that Prussian retribution would cause the city to rise against them and quashed a plan by Blücher to blow up the Pont d'Iéna, which he had mined. 'It is now spared on Condition of paying four Million Livres – and altering its name. The Statues, Paintings &c. plundered from other Countries are immediately to be restored to their right owners, on Paris alone Marshal Blucher has laid contributions to the amount of five Million Sterling independent of which the Parisians are under the necessity to provide 150,000 Thousand [sic] Prussian troops with extravagant rations.'[5]

Tom Morris of the 73rd Foot found himself in a pleasant encampment in the Bois de Boulogne, making occasional visits to the city. While guarding the duc de Berri's apartments, he 'had an opportunity of witnessing the removal of the celebrated Group of Horses, of which Napoleon had despoiled the Venetians and which were now about to be restored'. They were lowered from the Arc de Triomphe du Carrousel, which served as a gate to the Tuileries Palace, into wagons guarded by British and Prussian soldiers, while the Parisians looked on in gloomy silence. William Nicolay, commander of the Staff Corps, wrote:

> Their pride has been also greatly humbled by the removal of so many monuments of the <u>gloire of la grande nation</u> – The 4 famous horses in bronze, brought from Venice, have been taken down from the triumphal arch for the emperor of Austria – this was performed by a party of the Staff Corps under Major Tod, the Austrians not understanding how to do it – he likewise attempted to remove another famous statue, but unfortunately failed by the tackle giving way – So many of the pictures & statues have been removed from the Louvre that the famous Gallery is now hardly worth looking at.[6]

The allies got on with this cultural work quickly: 3000 statues and 2000 paintings, surrendered to France through treaties imposed after victorious campaigns, were restored to their previous owners, leaving only a few that had been overlooked. Morris witnessed the dismantling of the 'celebrated gallery of pictures, selected by Bonaparte, at the various places he had conquered, and deposited in the palace of St Cloud'. He saw many of the famous pictures, but regretted that he was 'not connoisseur enough to describe them'.

Morris derived some pleasure from the idea that King Louis must have realised uneasily 'that he was only secure on the throne of his ancestors so long as he was supported by foreign bayonets'; it was ironic, he added, that he remained with the army of occupation, designed 'to prevent any further out-break against "Louis le Désiré", as the French King was most inappropriately styled'.[7] The Bonapartist Cockney sergeant was not alone in registering the distaste of Parisians for their new ruler. The aristocratic John Fremantle, aide to Wellington, was fairly shaken by it, writing to his uncle on 17 July, 'I never could have believed there had existed such a rooted aversion to the Bourbons as I now find reigns.'[8] There were parades and reviews throughout July as the Austrians and Russians arrived, and nobody left in a hurry: the last British regiment departed from Paris only on 23 November 1818.

The battle of Waterloo would be significant historically simply as the defeat that brought an end to the remarkable career of Napoleon Bonaparte. His final campaign had been brilliant in conception, but its execution required a degree of speed and precision that proved to be beyond his staff, his subordinates and possibly even the ageing Napoleon himself. He had tried to assemble an old and practised team but key components – most obviously Berthier and his people – were missing. He had plenty of leisure in which to identify his errors afterwards: he should have chosen better subordinates – Grouchy lacked initiative, Ney lacked calm intelligence, others should have been employed differently – his staff lacked experience; he should have slept near Fleurus on the night of the fifteenth and had he done so he would have destroyed the Prussians before they all marched in; he had been too tired to stay in the saddle all night; he detached too much of his infantry with Grouchy; the rain . . .

Though he did admire the discipline of the 'English' infantry, Napoleon gave little credit to the enemy. The fact was, however, that both allied armies were a different proposition to the forces over which Napoleon had won his early victories. Both were led by efficient and talented generals with experienced teams of staff and subordinates who for the most part trusted each other. Both armies had an experienced core and some of the British infantry and the German Legion were veterans of very high quality. Most of all, Napoleon underrated the determination of the leaders to help each other: he thought that Wellington would not try to support the

Prussians on 16 June and he was wrong. At Waterloo he thought the Prussians could not come to the aid of Wellington and he was wrong.

Napoleon lost at Waterloo because the Prussians intervened, but as Brigade Major Harry Smith sensibly pointed out, 'to those who say the ultimate success of the day was achieved by the arrival of the Prussians, I observe that the Prussians were part of the whole on which his Grace calculated.'[9] The whole point of the Waterloo campaign was that the armies of Wellington and the Prussians should fight united. Napoleon almost succeeded in preventing them from so doing, but in the end the determination of the allies prevailed. Wellington's claim – implied in his dispatch and reiterated in later years – that he had won the battle on his own before the Prussians intervened decisively, fails to stand up to close scrutiny: the Prussians diverted French reserves for much longer than Wellington's staff on the British right wing may have realised. Similarly, the idea that the French never seriously troubled the allied infantry belittles the astonishing bravery and discipline of the best of that infantry, who dropped dead in square rather than admit defeat. The weight of evidence now points to an allied line whose centre had fallen back a considerable distance and which was under severe strain. If the whole allied line had actually disintegrated under the hail of French shot and shell, and the constant threat of cavalry, Prussian intervention would have been futile, and Wellington deserves great credit for keeping it in being.

Towards the close of the battle the French still believed that they were winning. Had the battle not been so close that Napoleon gambled everything to win it, the allied victory would not have been so complete. Participants were struck by the extraordinary intensity and violence of the fighting. Frenchmen had known other bloody battles and although most, like Leipzig, were spread over many miles, some, like Borodino, had been similarly compact. Nevertheless, even for Frenchmen Waterloo had seemed extremely hard fought and sanguinary, while for Britons there was nothing to match it. 'Military men say it is the hardest battle that has been fought for many years & that in comparison Leipzig was nothing to it,' wrote the surgeon Donald Finlayson. 'We who escaped out of the bloody Battle of the

18th do bless ourselves most amazingly,' remarked an experienced cavalryman a week later. 'Never was such a severe one fought before – all we have ever before seen are a joke to one hour of this ... by the immense number of deaths one scarce dared ask for a friend.' Sergeant Billy Tennant of the 3rd Guards was not wrong when he wrote to his wife Ann the day after, 'This was the hardest battle that ever was fought, but it is a glorious victory. We have give them a complete drubbing and I think another month the war will be over and then my love I shall embrace you in my arms once more.' Only the last hope failed him; Tennant was to remain in France with the army of occupation until 1818.[10]

To the great majority who believed the doctrine of the British government 'that the existence of the French power, with Napoleon at the head, is incompatible with the safety of Europe' the final defeat of Bonaparte was a great achievement that closed more than twenty years of warfare. It sealed the triumph of counter-revolution in Europe and secured the restoration of the Bourbons in France and Spain and of the House of Orange in the new Kingdom of the Netherlands, leaving aristocracies and monarchies stronger in material terms than they had been prior to the French Revolution.

To the enduring fury of the Prussians, Wellington succeeded in claiming most of the credit. From a British perspective Waterloo and the negotiations that followed, premised on Britain's prime role in Napoleon's defeat, were brilliantly successful. Britain emerged as the world's leading naval, colonial, commercial, financial and industrial power, and retained its dominance for most of the next century. Waterloo had brought to a close 'the second Hundred Years War', a bitter commercial rivalry between France and Britain that began with the struggle against Louis XIV and ended with the defeat of Napoleon. In this context the Waterloo campaign confirmed the result of the battle of Trafalgar, for the harvest of the long war, in which Britain had refused to make peace, was reaped through mastery of the seas and global trade. The Congress of Vienna brought huge immediate dividends to Britain through the acquisition of many prize French, Spanish and Dutch colonies – Trinidad, Tobago, Saint Lucia, Demerara, Essequibo, the Cape, Mauritius and Ceylon, some with strategically valuable harbours – and Britain gained Mediterranean naval bases at Malta and Corfu. Britain retained the huge empire that Wellesley and his successors had conquered in India, while the peace produced a balance of power that made Hanover safe, removing the need for regular intervention in Continental affairs. After Waterloo, Britons had every reason to congratulate themselves on having scored an unusually decisive victory.

The tiny minority in Britain who, like Napoleon, blamed the endless wars on the acquisitive self-interest of the ruling British oligarchy, who were supporting a cause that was detrimental to the common good of Europeans, saw Waterloo in a different light. The news, combined with other blows, caused the leader of the opposition, Samuel Whitbread, to commit suicide. For some liberals, like the journalist William Hazlitt, who went about unwashed, unshaven and drunk for weeks afterwards, Napoleon's defeat represented 'the utter extinction of human liberty from the earth'.[11] There was much discontent in post-war Britain, far closer to revolution after 1815 than it had been when Bonaparte was a threat. Waterloo coincided with the passing of the corn laws, designed to protect the income of landowners. Demands for change culminated in a huge demonstration at St Peter's Field in Manchester in 1819, where policing cavalry panicked and charged. Ironically, the 15th Hussars next saw action after Waterloo in a bid to restrain the enthusiasm of the Manchester Yeomanry, who were sabreing demonstrators and bystanders at 'Peterloo'; one Waterloo veteran was among those killed by the cavalry.

For all that, Waterloo left the nation with enormous confidence throughout the nineteenth century and a pride in its army that had never previously existed in England, and British prestige was at an unprecedented height in Europe. On 20 July 1815 Willem I created Wellington Prince of Waterloo and gave him parcels of land between Nivelles and Quatre Bras to produce an income of 20,000 Dutch florins.[12] Meanwhile, Alexander Baring, who in 1803 had arranged finance for the Louisiana purchase, the proceeds of which funded Napoleon's attempted invasion of Britain, now chaired a committee to raise a subscription for relief of the wounded and the families of those killed. Within a fortnight the Waterloo subscription brought in

£40,000 to which Lloyds added £10,000 and the Bank of England £50,000. By the end of 1815 it had raised £350,000.

At the first opportunity civilians flocked to the battlefield and some drew what they saw. An Irishman named Thomas Stoney was one of the first, riding from Louvain to sketch in watercolours scenes at Waterloo, Mont Saint-Jean and Quatre Bras dated 20 and 21 June. At Quatre Bras pale corpses still littered the ground. James Rouse made sketches while the dead were still being buried or burned. A traveller who had arrived at Brussels on 15 June visited the battlefield a week later, riding past a line of vehicles carrying wounded men to the city. He found Waterloo church full of casualties and could not go in without lighting a cigar against the effluvia. Houses had the number of wounded they contained chalked on their doors. Swollen horses lay on their backs with their legs in the air. Newly discovered wounded were propped against La Haye Sainte, while bodies were heaped in the farmyard. Men were flaying horses.[13]

On 2 July, while Charles Bell was drawing amputees in Brussels, Lady Charlotte Paget, wife of Lord Uxbridge, visited the battlefield with Lord and Lady George Seymour and Lady Emily Somerset, wife of Fitzroy and Wellington's niece. Uxbridge's aide Thomas Wildman, who had himself suffered a slight wound to the foot, endeavoured to show the ladies the exact spot where Uxbridge had been hit in the leg, but was less certain where Fitzroy Somerset had lost his arm. They visited the cottages at Waterloo where their husbands' limbs had been amputated; there, Lady Charlotte wrote to Uxbridge's sister Caroline, a farmer's wife 'took me into the garden to show me where his poor *dear* leg was buried, & she has promised me to plant a tree over the spot'. She continued,

> The road all the way to the field of battle is dreadfully disgusting, the smell from the dead horses is so horrid, but the field itself is *perfectly sweet*. The whole ground there is *covered* with caps, helmets & different bits & scraps of all sorts but nothing worth picking up. It has been so completely searched that nothing remains, but what I stated. The whole of the field of battle is now

composed of heaps of earth thrown up where the poor dead bodies have been buried, they are as thick as *mole hills*, & in one part there is still a pile burning of dead bodies which were consuming by fire.

They visited Hougoumont and saw the ruins where 'all the poor wounded perished in the flames', lamented over the ruined, trampled flower garden and took away souvenirs. 'Lady Fitzroy and I have each got some grape shot picked up there, & one of mine is the exact size that wounded your beloved papa. It just fits the hole in his *col-packs* [trousers] which he wore that day.'[14]

Two weeks later, when the travel writer Charlotte Waldie visited the battlefield, 'the road between Waterloo and Brussels was one long uninterrupted charnel house: the smell, the whole way through the Forest, was extremely offensive, and in some places scarcely bearable. Deep stagnant pools of red putrid water, mingled with mortal remains, betrayed the spot where the bodies of men and horses had mingled together in death.'[15]

In the area where Picton's division had fought, she found 'a long line of tremendous graves, or rather pits, into which hundreds of dead had been thrown ... The effluvia which arose from them, even beneath the open canopy of heaven, was horrible; and the pure west wind of summer, as it passed us, seemed pestiferous, so deadly was the smell that in many places pervaded the field.'[16]

The field was still covered in relics that the peasants considered relatively worthless – she picked up a copy of *Candide* – and there were moments of gothic horror, when a skull peered from a shallow grave and when she found the bones of a human arm and hand sticking out of the ground and fled with a shudder of terror. She was moved by the beautiful remains of the garden at Hougoumont and again, leaving its wood, was 'struck with the sight of the scarlet poppy flaunting in full bloom upon some new-made graves, as if in mockery of the dead. In many parts of the field these flowers were growing in profusion: they had probably been protected from injury by the tall and thick corn amongst which they grew, and their slender roots had adhered to the clods of clay which had been carelessly thrown upon the graves.'[17]

Painters and poets were quickly onto a scene that promised both inspiration and profit. The painter Robert Hills visited the ground in late July to make drawings for *Sketches in Flanders and Holland; with some account of a tour through parts of those countries shortly after the battle of Waterloo*, published in 1816. Sir Walter Scott visited the battlefield in August 1815 and during his tour composed his poem 'The Field of Waterloo', written in aid of the Waterloo subscription to raise money for the wounded and bereft; he later wrote a life of Napoleon. According to the journalist John Scott, who visited during the summer, hundreds, perhaps even thousands, of British visitors made the pilgrimage to the field of Waterloo at the earliest opportunity.

Robert Southey followed on Scott's heels in October. When he first heard the news of Waterloo, he and William Wordsworth, who had once admired Napoleon as the saviour of the Revolution and the Liberator of Italy, had danced around a bonfire on Skiddaw, singing 'God Save the King' and feasting on 'roasted beef and boiled plumpuddings'.[18] Now, Southey wrote, feeling 'in some degree bound to celebrate the greatest victory in British history, I persuaded myself that if any person had a valid cause or pretext for visiting the field of Waterloo, it was the Poet Lauriate'. His *Poet's Pilgrimage to Waterloo* appeared in 1816.[19]

Whereas Southey had abandoned his youthful admiration for Napoleon and viewed his downfall with delight, Byron continued to hold Bonaparte in high esteem and was bitterly disappointed by his defeat. After the collapse of his marriage he went abroad, reaching Ostend on 25 April 1816 and then travelling in a replica of Napoleon's coach to Waterloo, visiting the battlefield on 4 May and buying a collection of 'spoils', before continuing his journey down the Rhine. He wrote the first lines of *Childe Harold's Pilgrimage*, canto III, best known for its description of the Duchess of Richmond's ball, more or less on the battlefield. In contrast to his fellow poets, Byron saw Waterloo as the defeat of enlightenment and rationalism and a victory for tyranny, a battle whose only positive result was to fertilise the fields with rotting matter:

How that red rain hath made the harvest grow!
And is this all the world hath gained by thee,
Thou first and last of fields! king-making victory?

Like Constable, Lord Byron had lost a cousin: Major Frederick Howard of the 10th Hussars had been killed leading a charge against the retreating squares of the Imperial Guard, and Byron's guide showed him the spot where he was killed and initially buried. After his visit he wrote to his friend John Cam Hobhouse, whose brother was killed at Waterloo, 'The plain at Waterloo is a fine one – but not much after Marathon and Troy – Cheronea – & Platea. – Perhaps there is something of prejudice in this – but I detest the cause and the victors – & the victory – including Blucher and the Bourbons.'[20] By the time he published his final lament for Napoleon, *The Age of Bronze*, in 1823, Byron saw the battle in an even more bitter light:

Oh, bloody and most bootless Waterloo!
Which proves how fools may have their fortune too,
Won half by blunder, half by treachery.

The painter J.M.W. Turner, who visited the battlefield on Saturday 16 August 1817, was struck most by the bloodiness of the conflict and was interested in the concentration of carnage. His sketches for *The Field of Waterloo*, which showed women searching for husbands among the dead and wounded, were annotated with '4000 killed here', '1500 killed here', 'Hollow where the great Carnage took place of the Cuirassiers by the Guards.'

Turner followed a newly devised itinerary for tourists that gave the field of Waterloo a prime place in a European tour. The second edition of *The Traveller's Complete Guide through Belgium and Holland* recommended a new route from Margate to Waterloo, across Belgium to Cologne and along the middle Rhine, and this route to Switzerland and Italy became increasingly popular. On the battlefield monuments to the fallen proliferated but all were dwarfed by the Lion Mound, ordered in 1820 to commemorate the spot where the Prince of Orange was wounded, and completed in 1826. A huge amount of earth was moved to create it, destroying the original appearance of the battlefield. The 'perpendicular height of forty feet above the Charleroi road' of which Captain Arthur Gore of the Cambridgeshires spoke in 1817 in his notes to accompany cartographer Benjamin Craan's survey, became a drop of a few feet as earth was removed from the ridge to make the mound. Gore presumably exaggerated its original height, which drawings suggest was about twenty feet, but it had been enough of a precipice to kill some unfortunate cuirassiers.[21] In 1831 the mound narrowly escaped destruction by the advancing French army, but changes to the topography continued as a century of improved farming levelled most other irregularities in the landscape.

A tax of 50 million francs was levied from France to provide prize money for the victorious armies. The share allocated to Wellington's army and paid in 1817 was split between all participants: the Duke of Wellington was awarded £61,000 (but gave £40,000 back), general officers £1,274 10s 10¾d, field officers £433 2s 4¼d, captains £90 7s 3¼d, subalterns £34 14s 9½d, sergeants £19 4s 4d and privates £2 11s 4d.

The Duke gave an annual banquet at Apsley House on the anniversary of Waterloo. Returning from France in 1818, Wellington went back into politics, taking office in successive Tory governments. He was Prime Minister from 1828–30 and briefly in 1834; he championed Catholic emancipation but fought hard to resist reform. His amours continued and his connection with the courtesan Harriette Wilson led to another famous *bon mot*, 'publish and be damned'. After leaving office in 1846 he was commander in chief of the army until his death in 1852.

Lord Uxbridge was made Marquess of Anglesey as a reward for his services. He supported the Regent against Queen Caroline, sister of the Duke of Brunswick, and served as Lord Lieutenant of Ireland in Wellington's government. Like Wellington, he supported Catholic emancipation. Rowland Hill was commander in chief of the army from 1828 to 1842, while Wellington was in office, and became an enthusiastic foxhunter. Fitzroy Somerset followed Wellington into Tory politics. He was promoted to lieutenant-general in 1838 and became Baron Raglan in 1852. He led the British expedition to the Crimea, where he died from dysentery and depression in 1855. Henry Hardinge also entered politics and was Secretary at War in Wellington's government. He was Governor-general of India in 1844, fought the first Sikh War and succeeded Wellington as commander in chief of the army in 1852. Harry Smith served in India and South Africa, where he had a troubled reign as governor of the Cape, and his wife Juana gave her name to Ladysmith. He was a standard bearer at Wellington's funeral. Magdelene Delancey wrote the story of her sad experiences, *A Week at Waterloo*, for private circulation. She remarried but died in 1822 giving birth to her third child. Her book was published in 1906.

George Keppel was the last Waterloo officer to die, in 1891, as a general and 6th Earl of Albemarle. The last rank and file survivor was Maurice Shea of the 73rd Foot who died in 1892.

The fate of the lesser officers and lower ranks is often obscure, but a few can be picked out. John Haddy James (1788–1869) was elected surgeon to the Devon and Exeter Hospital in 1816 and became a general practitioner in his home town of Exeter, of which he was mayor in 1828. He was an original member of the Provincial Medical and Surgical Association and an expert on inflammation. Being a 'Waterloo man' may have been the key to Edmund Wheatley finally obtaining her family's permission to marry his Eliza Brookes in 1820. They had four daughters.

Thomas Morris left the army in 1817 when his seven years were up, 'being disappointed in the nature of the service, and having no desire to wear away the best portion of my existence in a subordinate capacity, where the chances of promotion were so precarious, and the reward, at last, so trifling.' He soon 'attained a respectable position in civil society'. David Robertson also left the army in 1818 and retired to his native Perthshire where he lived off his pension.

Rifleman Ned Costello was invalided out aged thirty-one on sixpence a day and suffered great hardship until he became a Yeoman Warder of the Tower of London. Sergeant William Wheeler was discharged in 1828 aged forty-three, while Thomas Jeremiah left the Welch Fuzileers in 1837 to become chief of police in Brecon. After

Waterloo, Matthew Clay was promoted to corporal and then sergeant. He transferred from the regular army to the Bedford Militia in 1833 with the rank of sergeant-major and was finally discharged in 1852, aged fifty-seven, after thirty-nine years of service. Charles Ewart, the Scots Grey who captured the eagle, was given an ensigncy in a veteran regiment as a reward for his services at Waterloo, and earned money as a fencing master. After meeting Sir Walter Scott in 1816 at an anniversary dinner in Edinburgh, Ewart toured the country with him, making celebrity appearances at events. He died near Manchester but in 1938 was reinterred in Edinburgh Castle's Esplanade.

After a few months in Paris, Prince Blücher retired to his Silesian estate, where he died in 1819. August von Gneisenau, a liberal, resigned from the army for political reasons in 1816, but became a field marshal in 1825 and died of cholera serving on the Polish border six years later. Karl von Grolmann occupied posts in the Ministry of War and tried to reform the General Staff. He supervised the author Karl von Damitz's history of the Waterloo campaign (1837–8).

Ludwig Nagel of Lützow's Freikorps became a poet and author and was director of the Gymnasium at Cleves. The European liberals who had fought to overturn Bonaparte's tyranny were bitterly disappointed by the reactionary policies of the regimes that took power after Waterloo. The hopes of Freikorps intellectuals for German unity and a more liberal society were dashed by measures suppressing the freedom of the press and banning demonstrations. Their black, red and gold uniform was adopted for the flag of federal Germany but it was many years before their dreams were realised. On returning to Berlin, volunteer rifleman Franz Lieber joined a student union opposed to the Prussian monarchy and was refused admission to Berlin University. He studied at Jena until his identity was discovered, and then fought in the Greek war of independence, but on returning to Prussia was imprisoned. He fled to England and then to America where, after a spell in Carolina, he became a professor of history and political science at Columbia University. He was influential in formulating Republican Party ideology before the American Civil War and his Lieber Code of legal guidelines for the Union army formed the basis for the first laws of war.

Major Georg Bäring transferred from the Legion to the Hanoverian army, where he rose to the rank of lieutenant-general and was made a Freiherr by William IV, King of Britain and Hanover, on the seventeenth anniversary of the battle. Friedrich Lindau was awarded the Guelphic Medal for his courage at La Haye Sainte; this carried a pension and he got another for the wound he had suffered at Vitoria in 1813. He returned to Hamelin, his home town, married twice and had nine children. He resumed his career as a shoemaker but did not prosper and was struggling when his reminiscences were published in 1846.

The young Nassau officer, Heinrich von Gagern, studied law at Heidelberg, Göttingen and Jena, and began a legal career in Hesse, but as a liberal he opposed the unconstitutional nature of the state and was ejected from state service in 1833. He was propelled back into power by the revolution of 1848, when he was elected president of the German National Assembly, thus becoming the first *Reichspräsident*, though the Assembly's attempt to create a united Germany failed and Gagern resigned after a year in office.

The Prince of Orange married the youngest sister of the Emperor Alexander, got an heir in 1817, but was blackmailed over 'unnatural and shameful lusts' in 1819. When trouble brewed up in Belgium in 1830, the Prince, who, being affable and conciliatory, was relatively popular there, tried to broker an agreement but his deal was rejected by his father and his army was defeated in the campaign of 1831 that won Belgium independence. He succeeded his father as King William II in 1840 and produced a liberal constitution that staved off revolution in 1848.

In defiance of the terms of the capitulation negotiated by Marshal Davout, twenty Bonapartists were accused of treason and about forty others, including Queen Hortense, were ordered to leave France. Wellington argued that the terms agreed with the British and Prussian generals were not binding on the new royalist government, but this convenient interpretation does not bear close scrutiny. Charles de la Bédoyère, who on 23 June 1815 had pleaded for the succession of Napoleon's son, was one of those excepted from the amnesty. In advance of fleeing to Switzerland, he tried to visit his wife and child in Paris but was captured, arrested and shot on 19 August. His grave at Père Lachaise cemetery became a Bonapartist shrine. Behind the hedge of foreign bayonets the Bourbons sought revenge through the 'White Terror'. In Provence and elsewhere supporters of Napoleon were hunted down in a campaign initially supervised by Joseph Fouché, still Minister of Police.

Marshal Ney was arrested on 3 August. After what had happened to La Bédoyère he demanded a trial before his fellow peers, but they were no more sympathetic than a court martial. He was tried on 4 December, condemned for treason, and shot on 7 December. Count Lavalette, Napoleon's postmaster, was also condemned to death but escaped from prison in his wife's clothes, thanks to her bravery, and was spirited out of the country by three Britons who were then tried for treason.[22] General Antoine Drouot gave himself up in August but did not face trial until April 1816. His defence turned on his being a subject of Napoleon as ruler of Elba, not of the French king, having advised Bonaparte against leaving the island, and having persuaded the Guard to surrender peaceably, as well as a glowing character reference from Marshal Macdonald, one of Napoleon's soldiers who during the Hundred Days had stayed loyal to the king. Acquitted by the narrowest margin, he went into retirement. General Cambronne, who had been captured at Waterloo, was tried after Drouot and got off by a clear majority on the same grounds.

Many Bonapartists fled to the United States, where Simon Bernard designed a number of forts and waterways. Dominique Vandamme went to Philadelphia, returning in 1819, and Charles Lefèbvre-Desnouëttes set up a shrine to Bonaparte in his log cabin. Marshal Grouchy fled to the United States and spent the rest of his life defending his conduct. Rumours that he had been bribed abounded among Bonapartists in America, and there was, indeed, a tradition in the family of William Wood, confidential servant to the diplomat Sir Charles Stuart, that Wood had delivered the bribe, but this was probably a fabrication.[23] Grouchy returned to France in 1821 and was given back his marshal's baton in 1830. Georges Mouton was exiled to Belgium but allowed back in 1818, much honoured after

1830 and died in the Louvre in 1838. Maurice Gérard also went to the Netherlands, but returned to France in 1817 and commanded the French army that drove the Prince of Orange out of Belgium in 1831.

The adaptable soldier Jean-de-Dieu Soult returned from exile in 1819 and turned fervent royalist until 1830 when he became a Bonapartist again, and was Prime Minister 1832–4, 1839–40 and 1840–7. In 1848 he became a republican, but he died in 1851. The Bourbons dispensed with Joseph Fouché's services in 1816 and he died four years later in exile in Trieste.

The veteran Captain André Ravard, still splitting blood from his wound at Waterloo, escaped the pursuit and rejoined his family near Angoulême, married, had a son and farmed his five hectares, but died young in 1828. Lieutenant Jacques Martin did not rejoin the army but took refuge in Cambrai, eventually becoming a Protestant minister in his native Geneva. Corporal Louis Canler joined the Bourbon Restoration police force and rose to become head of the Sûreté, retiring without fortune after thirty years. He then wrote a colourful memoir packed with the vices and crimes of Parisian society, high and low, that went through seven editions before being suppressed by the French authorities and translated into English. Sergeant Hippolyte de Mauduit was promoted to captain in the 5th Regiment of the Royal Guard. He became a military historian and pamphleteer, dedicating himself to the wellbeing of soldiers, and author of *De l'Armée française en 1832*, *L'Ami du Soldat* in 1834 and founder and editor of the military journal *Sentinelle de l'Armée*. In 1847–8 he published a well-informed account of the campaigns of 1814 and 1815, *Derniers jours de la Grande Armée*.

Napoleon left Malmaison for the coast on 29 June 1815, having been allowed a frigate by Fouché in which to quit France.

Most Frenchmen were heartily sick of Bonaparte after Waterloo – an attitude expressed vividly in a print published in August, *Le nec plus ultra du cannibalisme* (The Ultimate in Cannibalism). In this parody of the coronation portrait by Ingres, Napoleon bears a flag with the motto 'In the name of liberty I hold them in chains'. He holds both a sabre of despotism and a revolutionary axe, while his eagle darts lightning and thunderbolts at anything that resists. His robe is embroidered with 'Cunning, bluster, charlatanism, exile, proscriptions and firing squads', together with allusions to various specific crimes. He is enthroned on the corpses of victims sacrificed in the campaigns in Spain and Russia and supported on the throne by a leopard (then known as a 'tiger'), symbolic of deceit and cruelty behind an appearance of beauty. He has his foot on religion. In the background to one side are towns reduced to ashes, on the other Mont Saint-Jean – the French name for the battle of Waterloo. In the foreground is a river of blood.[24]

Napoleon hoped to find refuge with his friends in the United States. On 8 July he embarked at Rochefort for America in the frigate *La Saale*, and reached the Isle of Aix, but with characteristic duplicity Fouché had alerted the British navy to his intended point of departure and HMS *Bellerophon*, a seventy-four-gun Trafalgar veteran, barred his way. On 13 July Napoleon decided that England would not be such a bad place to retire to and wrote to the Prince Regent:

> A victim to the factions which distract my country, and to the enmity of the greatest powers of Europe, I have terminated my political career, and I come, like Themistocles, to throw myself upon the hospitality of the British people. I put myself under the protection of their laws; which I claim from your Royal Highness, as the most powerful, the most constant, and the most generous of my enemies. Napoleon.

On 15 July Napoleon went on board *Bellerophon* and surrendered to her captain. Unfortunately for the former Emperor, neither the generosity of the Prince Regent, nor the hospitality of the British people proved equal to that of the Persian Empire. He was not allowed to land in England but kept on board *Bellerophon* in Plymouth Sound for eight days until the decision had been reached to send him to the island of Saint Helena, isolated in a vast space of ocean between Africa and South America. He sailed for Saint Helena from Torbay on 9 August with a small group of companions and passed five and a half miserable years of dull isolation on the barren island, where he died on 5 May 1821 of stomach cancer.

The only Frenchmen allowed to step ashore in England were the prisoners captured at Waterloo. Around the beginning of July they were shipped to Portsmouth and Plymouth and taken to inland towns for six months of captivity. Having heard much of the prison hulks, the French were dreading worse. Captain Heuillet of the 2nd Chasseurs of the Old Guard had been a hero of the fighting at Plancenoit, where in the evening he had been wounded in the leg and captured by the Prussians. He was sent to Brussels and there met colonels Jean Genty of the 105th and Jean-Nicolas Carré of the 21st Line, both wounded victims of the charge of the Union Brigade. As they were embarking on a barge for Ostend, Heuillet was greeted by General Pierre Cambronne. 'Hello Heuillet,' he said. 'You are a prisoner? I am very sorry; still, in our position, it is good to meet up with old friends.' They were shipped to Plymouth and then sent to Ashburton. One day they read the newspaper account of Cambronne's defiant words, 'The Guard dies. It does not surrender.' Since they ate their meals together, they were able to congratulate Cambronne on these glorious words which immortalised his memory and shed lustre on the whole Imperial Guard.

'I am very sorry,' he replied, 'but I did not say the words attributed to me; I replied with something else, and not with what is reported.'[25] After painstaking research into alternative theories, Henry Houssaye, the leading French historian at the time of the hundredth anniversary of Waterloo, concluded that Cambronne's true response to the summons to surrender was 'Merde!'[26]

ACKNOWLEDGEMENTS

I first refought the battle of Waterloo as a schoolboy aged about twelve and using Airfix soldiers on a huge table set up for exhibition on a school open day. I owe this latest opportunity to refight the battle chiefly to Phil Craig, my friend and collaborator, whose idea it was, but who took up a post as head of factual television with the Australian Broadcasting Corporation which prevented him from carrying the project through. Many a schoolboy military enthusiast dreams of the chance to write up Waterloo and I seized it with enthusiasm – too much enthusiasm, perhaps, since the project has taken much longer and is rather bulkier than either I or my publishers intended. The result is so different from what Phil originally envisaged that perhaps he still has the chance to write a book on the battle his way! I hope he will forgive me. I am grateful, therefore, for the indulgence and support of my publishers, especially Richard Beswick and Iain Hunt who have been very supportive. Jane Greenwood and David Andress read the manuscript at various stages and made many very helpful criticisms. Steve Gove did an excellent copy edit; John Gilkes showed great patience in producing fine maps; and Linda Silverman produced the original paintings behind my monochrome prints.

Anybody writing on the Waterloo campaign at present owes a great debt of gratitude to those who have been working hard over recent years to publish manuscript letters and journals and to bring rare published material into wider currency, namely Gareth Glover who is about to publish his own conclusions from the new material he has discovered in *Waterloo: Myth and Reality*, and John Franklin and their colleagues and collaborators. John Franklin is also making his own interpretation of the new material in a series of books with

Gary Embleton, *Waterloo 1815*. I am also grateful for the hard work of
Pierre de Wit in his painstaking and detailed moment-by-moment
reconstruction of the campaign in his website 'The Campaign of
1815: a Study' (http://www.waterloo-campaign.nl). This is especially
useful as a ready way of consulting the orders issued by all armies
which are there transcribed in their original language.

The web has made many things possible that were unimaginable
a few years ago. For the appearance of places one can get a long way
with a combination of Google Earth and the Ferraris survey
(http://www.ngi.be/FR/FR1-4-2-3.shtm) but the topography of the
Ligny battlefield is exceptionally well presented on the web, with
zoomable panoramas from the sites of the windmills used
by Napoleon (http://www.fleurus-tourisme.be/photographies/
panorama360.htm) and Blücher (http://www. fleurus-tourisme.be/
photographies/panorama360bussy.htm), as well as views of all areas
of the battlefield (http://napoleon-monuments.eu/Napoleon1er/1815
Ligny-Fleurus.htm) and a selection of useful documents (http:/
/www.fleurus-tourisme.be/napoleon/documents_ancients.htm).
Some of the other websites that I have found most useful are listed in
the bibliography, but there are a lot, and I would like to say a general
thank you to all concerned in publishing articles, documents, uniforms, discussions and pictures. One of the reasons why I have not
included detailed orders of battle for the armies in this book is that
they are so readily consultable on the web. Not all are perfect (some
details remain debatable!) but they all get the basics right.

For various favours and loans I would like to thank Neil Clayton;
Guillaume and Nicolas Cousin and the Poulle family collective; the
Marquess of Douro and Lady Jane Wellesley; Bill Drummond; Alan
Forrest; Robert Gildea; Loyd Grossman; JJ Heath-Caldwell (for kind
gifts and an introduction to his splendid family archive); David
Kenyon; Anne Lyles for help with Constable, encouragement and
hospitality; Peeps Macdonald, Kevin Rogers; Martin Stiles; Nigel
Talbot and the staff of Grosvenor Prints.

I must thank Alastair Massie of the National Army Museum for
permission to quote from manuscripts in their collection and the
staff there for their help; the staff of the British Library; Cambridge

University Library; Alexandra Franklin of the Bodleian Library, Oxford; Josephine Oxley at Apsley House; Professor Chris Woolgar, former Head of Special Collections at the University of Southampton, and the staff of the archive, especially for returning the lead of my laptop; Mark Philp and Katherine Astbury of Warwick University for a useful preliminary exchange of views in the run-up towards their Hundred Days exhibition.

My interest in the Napoleonic period was greatly stimulated and my awareness of its issues broadened through conferences and exhibitions organised by Wolfgang Cillessen, Philippe Kaenel, Alberto Milano and Rolf Reichardt (sorry, Rolf). For help with French affairs I would like to thank Pascal Dupuy for invaluable advice on journalism and caricature in England and France, Philippe de Carbonnières, whose book on the Grande Armée in caricature will appear in the near future, Stéphane Calvet and Martine Sadion.

As ever I owe a great deal to my agent, Julian Alexander, and to regular hosts and friends David and Barbara Bradshaw, Steve and Pauline Mobbs, Phil and Frances Craig, to my old wargaming opponent and now fellow author Robert Fabbri, and to my family who have put up with a lot. (My son is at last proving himself useful, though: I owe one footnote to his research).

I am especially grateful to Sheila O'Connell and her colleagues at the Print Room of the British Museum where I have been helping to prepare and curate the exhibition *Bonaparte and the British* which will run from February to August 2015. Inevitably, the two projects have collided and those at the British Museum have been very patient over my commitment to *Waterloo*. At the same time there has been a great deal of cross-fertilisation and it has been extremely useful to discuss ideas and canvass the opinion of the many highly talented specialists I have met there.

NOTES

AN Archives nationales, Paris
BL British Library, London
BM British Museum, London
BNP Bibliothèque nationale, Paris
ImofFr Image of France (website)
NAM National Army Museum, London
SHD Service historique de la Défense, Vincennes
TNA The National Archives, London
WD Wellington's Dispatches
WSD Wellington's Supplementary Dispatches

Prologue

1 Lean, *Napoleonists*, 261.
2 Gneisenau to Hardenberg, 22 June 1815, in Delbrück, *Leben*, 531.
3 Creevey, *Creevey Papers*, 236.
4 Pringle, 'Remarks', cxli.
5 Wellington to John Wilson Croker, 8 August 1815 in *WD*, XII, 590.
6 Wellington to Sir John Sinclair, 13 and 28 April 1816 in *WSD*, X, 507. Sinclair edited Müffling's *History of the Campaign* (1816).
7 Wellington to William Mudford, 8 June 1816 in *WSD*, X, 509.
8 Ellesmere, *Personal Reminiscences*, 192.
9 James in Glover, *Waterloo Archive*, I, 6.
10 Lord Uxbridge's letter giving the officers of his favourite 7th Hussars his authorised version of their 'complete rout' is an example: see pp. 263–4.
11 Gourgaud, *Campagne*, iii; defence of Ney begins with Gamot, *Réfutation*, Janin, *Campagne de Waterloo*.
12 Carey, 'Commissariat officer', 730.
13 Waymouth in Siborne, *Letters*, no. 25.
14 For instance, Erckman and Chatrian's fictional memoir, *Waterloo*, is quoted by Adkin, *Waterloo Companion*, 346, as if it were a genuine memoir; the authors claimed, however, that their work was a novel based on interviews with genuine veterans.

1 The Violet Season

1 See Woodberry, *Journal*, 271; *Violettes du 20 Mars* after Jean Canu, registered 27 March 1815 (BM 1868, 0808.8194). A print of violets was also published by Marchand in September 1814 (ImofFr. no. 4390).
2 Schom, *Hundred Days*, 13–15.
3 Mauduit, *Derniers jours*, I, 204–10, but see Waresquiel, *Cent Jours*, 86–92.
4 Foulkes, *Dancing into Battle*, 30.

5 Levavasseur, *Souvenirs Militaires*, 261–74.
6 Amabel Yorke, Lady Lucas, diary, 30, 67–8 – she noted that the Duchess of Wellington left Paris on 13 March; Ravard to his brother, 27 March 1815, in Calvet, *Destins de braves*, 43.
7 Edmund Walcot in Brett-James, *Hundred Days*, 11; see Waresquiel, *Cent Jours*, 47–53.
8 Postmaster Antoine-Marie Lavalette in Brett-James, *Hundred Days*, 14 ; Bourdon de Vatry in Grouchy, *Mémoires*, 98–9.
9 Chevalier, *Souvenirs*, 316; Martin, *Souvenirs*, 268; Canler, *Mémoires*, 14.
10 Houssaye, *1815: Waterloo*, 1.
11 *Je jure que ça sent la violette* (BM 1868, 0808.8242).

2 The Devil is Unchained

1 Pitt-Lennox, *Three Years*, 100–1. A dispatch from the Austrian consul at Livorno stating simply that Napoleon had disappeared from Elba caused Metternich to hold an immediate conference; the news was kept secret but rumours spread instantly (Muir, *Britain and the Defeat*, 344).
2 Hamilton-Williams, *Waterloo*, 44–8; Hofschröer, *German Allies*, 30–8.
3 Morris, *Memoirs*, 55.
4 Miller, *Duchess of Richmond's Ball*, 45; see Moore Smith, *Life of John Colborne*, 210–13.
5 Mackworth in Glover, *Waterloo Archive*, IV, 8.
6 *Capel Letters*, 97–8; Hope, *Military Memoirs*, 92; Miller, *Duchess of Richmond's Ball*, 46–7 and 28.
7 Wheatley, *Diary*, 57.

3 Glory, Liberty and Peace

1 Richard Whately, *Historic Doubts relative to Napoleon Buonaparte*, Oxford 1819, Third edition 1827, 2; Walter Scott, quoted in Simon Bainbridge, *Napoleon and English Romanticism*, Cambridge 1995, 9.
2 Couvreur, 'Des Belges à Waterloo', 24.
3 Gibney, *Recollections*, 146–7.
4 Waresquiel, *Cent Jours*, 217; James, *Campaign of 1815*, 13n.
5 Charras, *Campagne de 1815*, 6, 11–12.
6 Mathieu Molé, Director-General of Roads and Bridges, in Tulard, *Napoleon*, 333.
7 Waresquiel, *Cent Jours*, 86–7; Bertaud, 'Regard des Français', 112.
8 Martin, *Souvenirs*, 268.
9 The diary of the architect Pierre Fontaine in Tulard, *Napoleon*, 335.
10 Pion des Loches, *Mes Campagnes*, 465. Recent studies tend to stress the equivocal nature of the welcome for Bonaparte. See Forrest, 'Des droits de l'homme à Waterloo', 70–1; Calvet, *Destins de braves*, 195–6.
11 Ravard in Calvet, *Destins de Braves*, 43; Lemonnier-Delafosse, *Campagnes*, 348–50. Martin, *Souvenirs*, 167, received an eagle in 1813 and described the experience in very similar terms.

4 Old Hooky Takes Charge

1 *WD*, XII, 288. The King of Prussia had replaced Kleist with Prince Blücher. Gneisenau took over at Aachen on 2 April and Blücher arrived on 12 April.
2 *WD*, XII, 292.
3 Longford, *Years of the Sword*, 32–3.
4 Chandler, *Waterloo*, 43.

5 Longford, *Years of the Sword*, 114–22.
6 Charles Greville, *The Greville Memoirs: a Journal of the Reigns of King George IV, King William IV and Queen Victoria*, ed. Henry Reeve, 3 vols, London: Longmans, II, 83. At the time of Waterloo Greville was private secretary to Lord Bathurst.
7 Chandler, *Waterloo*, 41–7.
8 Bell, *Letters*, 230.
9 Tomkinson, *Diary*, 273.
10 Amabel Yorke, diary, 30, 68; Gibney, *Recollections*, 148–9.
11 Muir, *Britain and the Defeat*, 354.
12 Couvreur, 'Des Belges à Waterloo', 24 and 26.
13 On 10 April Wellington was expecting to get contingents from Saxony, Brunswick, Oldenburg, Nassau and the Hanse towns. Two days later he complained that apart from the Saxons he was only likely to get the Brunswick corps and was hoping for Portuguese troops (*WD*, XII, 296, 300 and 302).
14 Jacobi in Glover, *Waterloo Archive*, II, 121–3.
15 *WD*, XII, 319.
16 *WD*, XII, 358.

5 The Prussians

1 Lieber, *Letters*, 99.
2 Grolmann, 'The English and Prussian Armies', 291.
3 Schmidt, *Prussian Regular Infantryman*, 43.
4 Jackson, 'Recollections', part 3, 2.
5 Chandler, *Waterloo*, 51.
6 Hofschröer, *German Allies*, 100.
7 *WSD*, X, 62; Ollech, *Feldzuges von 1815*, 20–25.
8 *WD*, XII, 293–4.
9 *WSD*, X, 69–70; *WD*, XII, 311. Muir, *Britain and the Defeat*, 352 agrees that 'contrary to some accounts, [Gneisenau] showed a great inclination to cooperate closely with the British.'
10 *The Examiner*, IX, 308.
11 *WSD*, X, 204–5, 216.
12 *WD*, XII, 346.
13 Müffling, *Memoirs*, 231–2; Houssaye, *1815: Waterloo*, 116–17; Chesney, *Waterloo Lectures*, 119; Ollech, *Feldzuges von 1815*, 45. Müffling, 224, claimed that the demarcation line between Prussians and Britons was his idea, agreed with Lowe in March and afterwards approved by Wellington.
14 Ollech, *Feldzuges von 1815*, 45–6; *WSD*, X, 239.
15 Ollech, *Feldzuges von 1815*, 38–9; Nostitz, 'Tagebuch', 11. *WD*, XII, 345 and 349–50.
16 *WD*, XII, 350.

6 Honneur aux Braves

1 Charras, *Campagne de 1815*, 15.
2 Fouché, *Memoirs*, 283. France and Britain were at peace but if this is true it is typical of Britain's rapacious commercialism.
3 Morris, *Memoirs*, 50.
4 Calvet, *Destins de braves*, 123.
5 Calvet, *Destins de braves*, 58 and 134.
6 Calvet, *Destins de braves*, 134n from SHD, 22 Yc 107 (*registre matricule* of the 13th

Demi-brigade of Light Infantry).

7 'Rectification de quelques faits relatifs à la campagne de 1815 par un officier général ayant combattu à Waterloo' in *Souvenirs et correspondance*, 93.

8 Bowden, *Armies at Waterloo*, 18 and note.

9 Bonaparte, *Mémoires*, 161–2.

10 Neither Berthier's intentions nor his death has ever been explained. Gus Frazer, commander of the Royal Horse Artillery, who had heard about the 'suicide' by 9 June, assumed Berthier was hostile: 'being known to be entirely in Bonaparte's interest he has been under the surveillance of the police' (*Letters*, 531).

11 Guyot, *Carnets*, 288–9.

12 Soult's Order of the Day, 1 June 1815, in Mauduit, *Derniers jours*, I, 463–8.

13 Las Cases, *Mémorial*, 1823, VII, 179–82; misquoted by Houssaye, *1815: Waterloo*, 499–500, see Le Gallo, '"Waterloo" de Houssaye', 58–9.

7 The Scum of the Earth

1 Mainwaring, 'Four Years', 406.

2 Hope, *Military Memoirs*, 379.

3 James, *Journal*, 6; Gibney, *Eighty Years Ago*, 156.

4 Tomkinson, *Diary*, 273–4; Mercer, *Journal*, 7; Edward Heeley Journal, NAM 1984-09-98.

5 Frazer, *Letters*, 487; Wheeler, *Letters*, 160.

6 Haythornthwaite, *Waterloo Armies*, 41.

7 Haythornthwaite, *Armies of Wellington*, 54.

8 Hennen, *Military Surgery*, 159 and 172.

9 A British Officer, 'The Statements of the Pussian Generals Grollmann and Muffling refuted', *United Service Journal*, XCII (July 1836), 311. In June 1815 Parliament was debating military punishment and it was pointed out that in the 10th Hussars in one year sixty-two people had received a total of 14,100 lashes, and that 'no person would dare treat his own brute animal at Charing Cross as cruelly as those English soldiers were used' (*Morning Post*, 22 June 1815, 2). The system was not abolished until 1880, the Duke of Wellington being a strong advocate of strict discipline enforced by corporal punishment and chiefly responsible for its longevity.

10 Since 1782 infantry regiments had had some local affiliation but usually it was merely nominal. The Royal Scots were 18 per cent Scottish, 42 per cent Irish and 37 per cent English; the 73rd, originally a Highland regiment, was 20 per cent Scottish; the Royal Welch Fuzileers were 27 per cent Welsh. The exceptions to this rule were the 27th Inniskilling Fusileers, who when first recruited were 96 per cent Irish (half Protestant, half Catholic), and the three kilted Highland regiments: the Gordon Highlanders and Black Watch were 89 per cent Scottish and the Camerons 82 per cent. Among themselves these soldiers often conversed in Gaelic. TNA, WO 27/77; Haythornthwaite, *Waterloo Men*, 11.

11 Playford, *Lifeguardsman*, 9.

12 Morris, *Memoirs*, 51.

13 Lowe had been attaché to the army of Silesia in 1813–14, so he was able to brief Sir Henry Hardinge on the personalities of Gneisenau and the Prussian Quartermaster-General Karl von Grolmann when Hardinge joined the Prussian staff as liaison officer in April (Müffling, *Memoirs*, 215).

14 Frazer, *Letters*, 520; Gibney, *Eighty Years Ago*, 173.

15 Mackworth in Glover, *Waterloo Archive*, IV, 14.

16 Urban, *Rifles*, 261.
17 Woodberry, *Journal*, 292–3.
18 Woodberry, *Journal*, 302.
19 Mercer, *Journal*, 115.
20 Mercer, *Journal*, 92.
21 Mercer, *Journal*, 108–9.

8 Intelligence

1 Wellington to Lord Charles Stewart, 8 May 1815, *WD*, XII, 359.
2 Fouché, *Mémoires*, II, 341–3; De Bas and Wommerson, *Campagne de 1815*, I, 346; Mauduit, *Derniers jours*, I, 495; Hamilton-Williams, *Waterloo*, 108. Secret intelligence from Paris was a prized asset, guarded with discretion, as Müffling, *Memoirs*, 218 confirms: 'The Duke of Wellington communicated to me verbally all I wanted to know; and as this included all his secret intelligence from Paris, I considered these communications confidential, and observed strict silence on the subject of them with all the military envoys at head-quarters.' Creevey Papers, I, 227.
3 *WD*, XII, 336.
4 The idea that Grant was 'in advance of the British outposts' came from William Napier in 1857. Long ago, Pflugk-Harttung (*Vorgeschichte*, 220–2) convincingly discredited Napier, point by point. The unpublished order of battle (Wellington papers 1/466/42) attributed to Colquhoun Grant AQMG is headed 'Quartier Général à Bruxelles 7 juin 1815'. On Grant see Haswell, *Spy*, 220; Hamilton-Williams, *Waterloo*, 148; Fletcher, *Desperate Business*, 31–2; Uffindell, *Eagle's Last Triumph*, 59–60 and 81.
5 See *WD*, XII, 362, Wellington to Hardinge 8 May. Diarist Fanny Burney's husband Alexandre d'Arblay was one of those involved.
6 *WD*, XII, 323.
7 Dörnberg had fought the French until 1806, latterly under Blücher. After the French conquest of Germany he fled to England to organise resistance to French rule of his homeland, Kassel having become the capital of Napoleon's new Kingdom of Westphalia. With the *Tugendbund* ('League of Virtue'), a patriotic German underground movement that included Gneisenau, Grolmann and the Duke of Brunswick, Dörnberg plotted risings in Westphalia as part of a national insurgency in 1809. Dörnberg's part was dangerous, being planted in Kassel as a double agent, commanding the Jägers of King Jérôme's guard. In the event, Napoleon swiftly defeated the Austrians and the Prussian conspirators failed to persuade their king to declare war. The risings were crushed, including Dörnberg's attempt to seize Kassel with 5000 men. Dörnberg escaped in disguise with a price on his head, but joined the Black Brunswickers who fought their way to the mouth of the Elbe. He then fought with the British until 1812, when he was sent to north Germany to foment patriotic resistance to France. The *Tugendbund* was a Prussian secret society dedicated to the revival of national spirit after the Treaty of Tilsit. It was suppressed by the French after the risings of 1809. See Müffling, *Memoirs*, 226: 'Gneisenau, Boyen, Grolmann, were noted as the most active members of the *Tugendbund*, who were accused of very anti-royal tendencies.'
8 *WSD*, X, 217–18; 261–2.
9 *WD*, XII, 360, 8 May; 366–7, 9 May; *WSD*, X, 12/14 May; *WD*, XII, 372, 11 May. Müffling had been Quartermaster-General to the Prussian army, but was replaced by Gneisenau, and he replaced Röder as Prussian representative at British HQ shortly after the Tirlemont conference when Blücher moved his headquarters to Namur.

10 When he proposed Müffling to be Governor of Paris, *WD*, XII, 410.

11 *WD*, XII, 11 May. *WSD*, X, 275–6; Hervey, 'Letter', 431.

12 Hussey, 'At what time', 90–1.

13 *WSD* X, 423–4. Excited by what he heard, the comte de la Porterie took his agent to Dörnberg and offered him to Wellington for further interrogation. The report is that of the Dutch commander at Mons, General Behr, to the Prince of Orange.

14 Ilbert in Glover, *Waterloo Archive*, III, 189; *WSD*, X, 368.

15 Dörnberg-Hausen, *Dörnberg*, 176; Pflugk-Harttung, *Vorgeschichte*, 291–2.

16 Bonaparte, *Mémoires*, IX, 53.

17 *WD*, XII, 378; Mercer, *Journal*, 125: 'We afterwards learned that a number of officers had been sent the same evening into our cantonments to ascertain whether we remained quiet, etc. etc.'; Barral, *L'épopée de Waterloo*, 71–3; Pawly, *Imperial Headquarters*, 8.

9 Waiting for the Invasion of France

1 Private Charles Stanley http://www.militaryheritage.com/waterloo.htm; also in Glover, *Waterloo Archive*, III, 25, cp. Tomkinson, *Diary*, 276; prices from Woodberry, *Journal*, 294–5; Wheeler, *Letters*, 162.

2 Ompteda, *Memoir*, 26–7; Brandis in Glover, *Waterloo Archive*, V, 51–2.

3 Wheeler, *Letters*, 162; Morris, *Memoirs*, 64.

4 Robertson, *Journal*, 115, 126, 138.

5 Kinchant in Glover, *Waterloo Archive*, III, 30.

6 Frazer, *Letters*, 514; Staveley, NAM 1999.06.149; Thorpe, 'Two Diaries of Waterloo', 548.

7 Mackworth in Glover, *Waterloo Archive*, IV, 17.

8 Jackson, *Notes and Reminiscences*, 11; Capel, *Letters*, 102.

9 Jeremiah, *Life and Adventures*, 17. See also Frazer, *Letters*, 521–4; Mercer, *Journal*, 117–22; Glover, *Corunna to Waterloo*, 256–7.

10 Jeremiah, *Life and Adventures*, 18.

11 Jeremiah, *Life and Adventures*, 18; Glover, ed. *Corunna to Waterloo*, 257.

12 Staveley, NAM 1999.06.149.

13 Hofschröer, *German Allies*, 122.

14 Delbrück, *Leben*, 511–12; Lettow-Vorbeck, *Untergang*, 180–1; Hofschröer, *German Allies*, 120.

15 Woodberry, *Journal*, 299–300.

16 Wheeler, *Letters*, 164.

17 Heeley, 'Journal', 105.

18 Fouché, *Memoirs*, II, 291.

10 The French in Motion

1 Mauduit, *Derniers jours*, I, 496.

2 Heymès in Elchingen, *Documents inédits*, 2–3, *Waterloo : Récits de combattants*, 43; Levavasseur, *Souvenirs Militaires*, 287–8. It is curious that the accounts of Ney's aides are so much at variance. Levavasseur was staying at Ney's chateau, Les Coudreaux, near Evreux, and implied that Ney was there when he received the letter and left immediately, while Levavasseur went via his own home in Picardy. Gamot says the same. Heymès, who is unreliable, claims that Ney started from Paris, reached Laon the same day as the Emperor and dined with him at Avesnes. It is more likely that Ney only caught up with the Emperor at Charleroi.

3 Martin, *Souvenirs*, 269; 'Lettre', 495; Canler, *Mémoires*, 15.

4 Martin, *Souvenirs*, 272–3; 'Lettre', 495.

5 Grouchy, *Mémoires*, IV, 126.

6 Berthaut, *Ingénieurs* II, 407; Houssaye, *1815: Waterloo*, 318n. The original map, drawn
   on a scale of 1:11,520 on 275 hand-coloured sheets, each measuring 900 × 1400 mm,
   of which there were three copies, is available online.

7 *Journal général de la litterature étrangère*, Paris 1808, 170; 1814, 82; Reiche, *Memoiren*,
   II, 201n.

8 Drouet d'Erlon, *Vie Militaire*, 94.

9 Hornn, *Narrative*, 54.

10 Martin, 'Lettre', 496.

11 Order of the day in *WSD*, X, 465–7 and Mauduit, *Derniers Jours*, II, 7–8; for its recep-
   tion by the troops see also Canler, *Mémoires*, 14 and Robinaux, *Journal de Route*, 206.

12 Identified by Couvreur, 'Des Belges à Waterloo', 24–5. So too did Guilleminot and
   Lobau.

13 Biot, *Souvenirs anecdotiques*, 233.

14 Bowden's figure (*Armies at Waterloo*, 309), the most thoroughly researched, is 122,652,
   excluding staff and medics.

11 Sang-froid

1 *WSD*, X, 456.

2 Ollech, *Feldzuges von 1815*, 89–90.

3 *WSD*, X, 470; Vivian in Siborne, *Letters*, no. 70.

4 Müffling, *Memoirs*, 220.

5 Fouché, *Mémoires*, 341–3. This account was accepted by de Bas and Wommerson,
   Campagne de 1815, 346.

6 The story was elaborated by Grant's biographer Haswell, 220, without any apparent
   further evidence. It seems odd, if it reached Wellington, that the document is not in
   the Wellington papers.

7 Madelin, *Fouché*, II, 382. 'If I had been the conqueror at Waterloo, I would have had
   him summarily shot,' Napoleon told Gourgaud at Saint Helena (Latimer, *Talks of
   Napoleon*, 188).

8 Amabel Yorke, Lady Lucas diary, XXX, 158–9.

9 Keppel, *50 Years*, 136.

10 Maxwell, *Life of Wellington*, II, 10.

11 Houssaye, *1815: Waterloo*, 109; Gneisenau to Hardenberg in Delbrück, *Leben*, 518;
   WSD, X, 449–50; *WD*, XII, 462.

12 Reiche, *Memoiren*, II, 153–4.

13 Dörnberg-Hausen, *Dörnberg*, 176; Pflugk-Harttung, *Vorgeschichte*, 292.

14 Lettow-Vorbeck, *Untergang*, 196; Hussey, 'At what time', 92.

15 Ollech, *Feldzuges von 1815*, 88.

16 *WSD*, X, 476.

17 Uffindell, *Eagle's Last Triumph*, 65; Ollech, *Feldzuges von 1815*, 90–1; Lettow-Vorbeck,
   Untergang, 197–8; Hussey, 'At what time', 93.

12 The French Cross the Border

1 Barrington in Glover, *Waterloo Archive*, IV, 135. The diary kept by Captain Thackwell
   of the 15th Hussars confirms that the weather at the end of May and beginning of
   June was very unsettled, with rain falling nearly every day. Thackwell began each

day's entry with a brief weather report (Wylly, *Military Memoirs*, 69). Frazer (*Letters*, 530) wrote that he travelled to Ghent on 6 June through 'the heaviest rain I remember'. See Wheeler and Demarée, 'Weather of the Waterloo campaign'.

2 Mauduit, *Derniers Jours*, I, 500–6; *WSD*, X, 472–5; Bonaparte, *Mémoires*, 61, Bowden, *Waterloo Campaign, passim*, for troop totals.

3 Gourgaud, *Campagne*, 43, had claimed that Vandamme got lost; Janin, *Campagne de Waterloo*, 6–7, said that orders failed to reach him because the only messenger broke his leg; see also Mauduit, *Derniers Jours*, II, 9–10; Colson, *Rogniat*, 504–6. Berthezène (*Souvenirs Militaires*, II, 360), one of Vandamme's generals, claimed that because Imperial headquarters had demanded his quarters Vandamme had gone off in a sulk without telling anybody where he was spending the night, and that was why orders failed to reach him.

4 Pontécoulant, *Napoléon à Waterloo*, 194–5.

5 Sciatica is the usual explanation for Mortier's absence. Levavasseur, *Souvenirs militaires*, 288, said that Mortier had received a letter similar to Ney's and had ridden to Avesnes, but had then been disgraced and left behind.

13 The Prussian Outposts Attacked

1 Nostitz, 'Tagebuch', 50.

2 Nostitz, 'Tagebuch', 18; Ollech, *Feldzuges von 1815*, 64–7.

3 Ziethen's plan, given in full in Reiche, *Memoiren*, 407–9, envisaged a battle in 'the Fleurus position'.

4 It is sometimes stated, for instance by Adkin, *Waterloo Companion*, 60, that the 2nd Light was with Jérôme's division. Reille's report of 15 June (SHD C15, nr. 5, published by de Wit) proves that they led the advance in Bachelu's division. See also Dumas, *Histoire du 2e régiment*, 298. Maigrot had spent four years with the army of the Sambre and had been wounded at the battle of Fleurus in 1794, before becoming a grenadier of the Consular Guard in 1798 and an officer in the Old Guard in 1806. He rose to colonel in 1813. Leading the 16th Regiment at Leipzig he was wounded three times and captured on the field.

5 Reille report to Soult 15 June. The orders and reports in the Service historique de la Défense at Vincennes (C15, nr. 5) can be consulted along with most of the Prussian and Anglo-Netherlands documents on the excellent website constructed by Pierre de Wit, 'The Campaign of 1815: a Study' (http://www.waterloo-campaign.nl). Where no other source is given, documents cited in this book can be found there, transcribed in the original language.

6 Biot, *Souvenirs anecdotales*, 234–6. Domon had been ordered to leave his battery behind with the infantry, so Biot had to summon a gun from one of Pajol's two batteries. De Wit corrects Damitz and Ollech on the locations.

7 Guyot, *Carnets de Campagnes*, 290.

8 Reiche, *Memoiren*, II, 157, said that the first message to Blücher was sent at 5 a.m. and he then went to get the signal guns fired. He could not remember whether a message was sent to Wellington then, but pointed out that Merlen knew what was afoot.

9 Hofschröer, *German Allies*, 170–2.

10 On this vexed issue see Pedlow, Hussey and de Wit, who all agree that the account in Ziethen's so-called journal is unreliable and that Ziethen sent no message to Wellington before the one timed at 9 a.m. (which no longer exists). In any case, Wellington would have ignored a message that merely told him that there had been an alarm along the outpost line in the night.

11 Unless he took the long Gembloux–Wavre route, the messenger had also to ride
conservatively because there was no relay of horses for the use of couriers on either
of the other roads.

14 The Fall of Charleroi

1 Powell in Siborne, *Letters*, no. 108 quoted from his journal to the effect that at 'Two
o'clock p.m. Dragoon brought word that the French were crossing the frontier and
to hold the brigade in readiness to move. Eight o'clock – A second dragoon arrived
with intelligence that the Prussians had been forced across the Sambre.' This 'journal' was written after the event 'when the thing was strong in my recollection', so the
times may not be accurate.

2 Robinson, *Quatre Bras*, 46; Brandis in Glover, *Waterloo Archive*, V, 53; Morris,
Memoirs, 66.

3 Willem van Reede to Willem von Nagel in Franklin, *Netherlands Correspondence*,
27–8; *WD*, XII, 469–72; Godert van der Capellen to Willem von Nagel in Franklin,
Netherlands Correspondence, 26.

4 Hussey, 'At what time', 100–1.

5 Reiche, *Memoiren*, II, 196; the character portrait is based on Nostitz, 'Tagebuch',
50–1.

6 Panhuys in Franklin, *Netherlands Correspondence*, 28; Ollech, *Feldzuges von 1815*,
99–100; Hussey (his translation of the report to Müffling); Parkinson, *Hussar
General*, 217 in Uffindell, *Eagle's Last Triumph*, 52.

7 Pétiet, *Souvenirs Militaires*, 189–90.

8 Heymès in Elchingen, *Documents inédits*, 4 or *Waterloo: Récits de combattants*, 43–4;
Houssaye, *1815: Waterloo*, 122. Napoleon had requisitioned all the post-horses so Ney
had bought what he could from a peasant. They left the carriages at Beaumont,
Ney's secretary and financial manager having accompanied them at least that far.

9 Ney's arrival was timed at midday by Pajol (Houssaye, *1815: Waterloo*, 121) and 7 p.m.
by Heymès (in Elchingen, *Documents inédits*, 4, *Waterloo: Récits de combattants*, 44);
the truth lies between 2 p.m. and 3.30 p.m., and it is likely that the interview took
some time; see Houssaye, *1815: Waterloo*, 122–4.

15 The Skirmishes at Gilly, Gosselies and Frasnes

1 Mauduit, *Derniers Jours*, II, 13.

2 Ollech, *Feldzuges von 1815*, 101.

3 Reiche, *Memoiren*, II, 159.

4 Siborne, *Waterloo Campaign*, 35n. 'Einerlei was das Volk für ein Zeichen ansteckt!
Hundsfott bleibt Hundsfott.' *Hundsfott* is a strong German swearword signifying
cowardly, mean and despicable. Derived from a word for the vulva of a dog, it does
not translate easily.

5 Reiche, *Memoiren*, II, 165.

6 What happened at Gosselies is debated, since reports are difficult to reconcile.
Steinmetz claimed to have retaken the town but it seems unlikely Maigrot could
have got there first. See Houssaye, *1815: Waterloo*, 128–9; Reiche, *Memoiren*, II, 167;
Ollech, *Feldzuges von 1815*, 101; Damitz, *Feldzuge von 1815*, I, 68; Lettow-Vorbeck,
Untergang, 261.

7 Glover, *Waterloo Archive*, II, 152–4; Bijleveld in Franklin, Netherlands
Correspondence, 103; Mittelacher, 'Nassauers at Hougoumont'.

8 See Martinien, *Tableaux*, 789.

9   Döring in Glover, *Waterloo Archive*, II, 164.
10 Basslé in Franklin, *Netherlands Correspondence*, 30–1; Gagern in Franklin, *Netherlands Correspondence*, 60–1.
11 Bernhard in Glover, *Waterloo Archive*, II, 147–8; Sattler in Glover, *Waterloo Archive*, II, 152–3; Lefèbvre-Desnouëttes' report to Ney (James, *Campaign of 1815*, 74–5). It is curious that although both the Nassauers and the French mention the lighting of a beacon at Quatre Bras, it does not seem to have served to alarm anybody. Perhaps it was not part of a chain stretching to Brussels but was only intended to be visible to local troops.
12 Gourgaud, *Campagne*, 47. Berthezène, *Souvenirs Militaires*, II, 359 wrote that Soult told him he witnessed the conversation in which Ney was ordered to take Quatre Bras that evening. D'Erlon (*Vie militaire*, 94–5) emphatically denied that Ney was supposed to take Quatre Bras. Janin (*Campagne*, 12–17) pointed out that Quatre Bras played no part in the 1794 campaign but the junction with the Roman road was central: he speculated that Ney confused the two, but insisted that under the circumstances no sensible general should have pushed for Quatre Bras. For a good discussion of these issues and Ney's activities that evening see Laudy, 'Bourgogne du Maréchal Ney'.
13 James, *Campaign of 1815*, 74–5.

16 The French and Prussian Camps

1   Trefcon, *Carnet de campagne*, 83. Ney did not visit Napoleon at Charleroi, despite the claim of Heymès, Elchingen, *Documents inédits*, 5, *Waterloo: Récits de combattants*, 45. See Laudy, 'Bourgogne du Maréchal Ney', 331–2.
2   According to Gourgaud, *Campagne*, 47, Napoleon had already told Reille and d'Erlon that they were under Ney's orders and had ordered Ney to tell d'Erlon to call the troops who were guarding the Sambre bridges, but according to d'Erlon this was what the Emperor should have done, not what he did. Brouwet, 'Quatre documents', 360, instruction from Delcambre to Donzelot warning him that the bridges were to be cut dated 15 June. Quiot was acting commander of Allix's division. Allix, a loyal supporter, had been appointed by Napoleon to head a government commission at Lille and only returned to the army when it was defending Paris.
3   Brouwet, 'Quatre documents', 361–2.
4   Martin, *Souvenirs*, 275.
5   Grouchy, *Relation succincte*, first series, 12 and third series, 11 and 14.
6   Mauduit, *Derniers Jours*, II, 32.
7   Reiche, *Memoiren*, II, 169; Bowden, *Armies at Waterloo*, 323–4.
8   Ammon and Herold, *Leben . . . Nagel's*, 125.
9   Lieber, *Letters*, 101–2; Schmidt, *Prussian Regular Infantryman*, 13–14; Bagensky, *Geschichte des 9ten*, 233.
10 Hofschröer, *German Allies*, 218–19.
11 Reiche, *Memoiren*, II, 172.

17 The Duchess of Richmond's Ball

1   Ellesmere, *Personal Reminiscences*, 185: 'I was in the habit of dining at three o'clock punctually.'
2   Müffling (*Memoirs*, 214) gives the top speed of an ADC like the Earl of March as 14 miles per hour. Hussey ('At what time', 107) suggested 4.30–5 p.m.
3   In his *History*, 1, Müffling wrote that the news reached the Duke at 4.30. Hügel's

letter, timed at 6 p.m., was written after Müffling had listened to the Duke's first orders being issued. See Hussey, 'At what time', 110–12. Wellington said Orange's news arrived first and Müffling's not long after (Ellesmere, *Personal Reminiscences*, 185–6).

4 Müffling, *Memoirs*, 221–2.

5 Hervey, 'Letter', 431.

6 Hussey, 'At what time', 108 and 110; Jackson, *Notes and Reminiscences*, 12. Lady Delancey's timings are about two to three hours late.

7 Hussey, 'At what time', 109; Vivian in Siborne, *Letters*, no. 71; Thomas Wildman, one of Uxbridge's aides, learned of the fighting as he dressed for the ball, NAM 1981-12-53-557.

8 Mudie, 'Operations of the Fifth', 172.

9 Bridgeman, *Young Gentleman at War*, 176–7.

10 Mudie, 'Operations of the Fifth', 172; Cadell, *Narrative of the Campaigns*, 231–2.

11 *Flying Sketches*, 18; Scott, *Paris Revisited*, 92–3; Owen, *Waterloo Papers*, 7; Mudie, 'Operations of the Fifth', 172.

12 Chesney, *Waterloo Lectures*, 61; Ilbert in Glover, *Waterloo Archive*, III, 192 and 194.

13 Bernhard in Glover, *Waterloo Archive*, II, 148; Bergmann in 1815 Limited On-line Archive.

14 Van Nyevelt in Franklin, *Netherlands Correspondence*, 43. Robinson (*Quatre Bras*, 78) thinks the deserter was Durutte's chief of staff, Gordon, but he did not come over until the following morning. Van Nyevelt says he was a *capitaine adjoint* in peasant's clothing.

15 Swinton, *Lady de Ros*, 119.

16 Sophie von la Roche, *Geschichte des Fräuleins von Sternheim*, 1771; *The Times*, July 1816.

17 Robinson *Quatre Bras*, 108; Maxwell, *Life of Wellington*, II, 11.

18 Officer of 95th in Waldie, *Near Observer*, 51; Bridgeman, *Young Gentleman at War*, 177.

19 Maxwell, *Life of Wellington*, II, 13.

20 Glover, *Waterloo Archive*, I, 225.

21 Franklin, *Netherlands Correspondence*, 26–7.

22 Malmesbury, *Letters*, II, 445–6.

23 Maxwell, *Life of Wellington*, II, 13. Webster's account, which is embroidered and inaccurate, has him doing the twenty-one-mile journey in an hour and delivering the message as the company went upstairs from supper to the ballroom (Brett-James, *Hundred Days*, 42–3).

24 Miller, *Ball*, 140.

25 Glover, *Waterloo Archive*, I, 226.

26 Mudie, 'Operations of the Fifth', 173.

27 Maxwell, *Life of Wellington*, II, 13; Müffling, *Memoirs*, 230; Lady Caroline Lamb to Viscountess Melbourne in Mabell Airlie, *In Whig Society, 1775–1818* (London: Hodder and Stoughton, 1921), 171–3.

18 Marching Orders

1 Jackson, 'Recollections', 3.

2 Jackson, 'Recollections', 3–4; Müffling, *Memoirs*, 214–15.

3 Jackson, 'Recollections', 3–4. Müffling, *Memoirs*, 221.

4 Playford, *Lifeguardsman*, 45–6.

5 James, *Journal*, 12–14.

6 Ponsonby in Bessborough, *Lady Bessborough*, 240; Mercer, *Journal*, 127–9. None of Mercer's officer's or RHA colleagues were invited to the ball, though many cavalry officers were absent.

7 Glover, *Waterloo Archive*, II, 38.

8 Robertson, *Journal*, 143.

9 Costello, *Campaigns*, 149.

10 Waldie, *Residence in Belgium*, 42–3.

11 Waldie, *Near Observer*, 1815, 3.

12 Winchester and Ross of the 92nd (Siborne no. 169; Glover, *Letters*, 279) confirm that they formed in the park and not the Place Royale where the Hanoverians gathered.

13 Jackson, *Notes and Reminiscences*, 14–15.

14 Cappel and Langenstrassen in 1815 Limited On-line Archive; Herzberg in Glover, *Waterloo Archive*, V, 148 and Schutte in Glover, *Waterloo Archive*, II, 206–7.

15 Gronow, *Reminiscences*, 126–7.

16 George Hemingway in Glover, *Waterloo Archive*, I, 166; Scriba in Glover, *Waterloo Archive*, II, 99; Bülow in Glover, *Waterloo Archive*, V, 61; Morris, *Memoirs*, 67.

19 The Emperor's Orders

1 Latimer, *Talks of Napoleon*, 185–6.

2 Marshal Grouchy later published reports he had sent of Prussian columns approaching Brye from Namur at 5 a.m., but there were no Prussians doing so at that time. If the reports that he published are at all genuine they must have been sent later, towards 10 a.m. at the earliest. Grouchy, *Relation Succincte*, 2nd series, 2–3; de Wit, 'The French Right Wing', 2–3.

3 Pontécoulant, *Napoléon à Waterloo*, 193.

4 Grouchy's later recollection that he had been ordered to destroy the Prussian cavalry and push through to cut the road from Sombreffe to Namur, so as to prevent Prussian reinforcements arriving, refers to this plan (Grouchy, *Mémoires*, IV, 23; *Relation succincte*, first series, 16).

5 Gérard, *Quelques documens*, 48–9.

6 Nyevelt report of 25 October 1815 in Franklin, *Netherlands Correspondence*, 45; Robertson (*Journal*, 145) reported that inhabitants of Genappe told him a French patrol had been there that morning. These reports contest Houssaye's assertion that Ney made no effort to find out what he had in front of him.

7 Houssaye (*1815: Waterloo*, 142n) thinks Reille sent this report with reference to Girard's observations, but Houssaye was anxious to prove that Ney carried out no reconnaissance and it seems far more likely that it was Lefèbvre-Desnouëttes.

8 Forbin-Janson in BL Add Mss 30147A, account dated London December 1817.

20 The Prince of Orange at Quatre Bras

1 Marco Bijl, 'History and organisation of the Dutch 8th Militia', http://www.napoleon-series.org/military/organization/Dutch/8thMilitia/c_8thMilitia3.html

2 Costello, *Campaigns*, 149.

3 Nyevelt in Franklin, *Correspondence*, 45.

4 Dörnberg in Glover, *Waterloo Archive*, V, 11; Robinson, *Quatre Bras*, 155–6.

5 Morris, *Memoirs*, 67.

6 Fraser, 'First Guards', 19; Powell in Siborne, *Letters*, no. 108.

7 Franklin, *Netherlands Correspondence*, 81.

21 The View from Brye

1 Reiche, *Memoiren*, 183-4.

2 See Uffindell, *Eagle's Last Triumph*, 74.

3 Reiche, *Memoiren*, II, 174; Niemann in Thorpe, 'Two Diaries of Waterloo', 541.

4 See Reiche, *Memoiren*, II, 175.

5 Busse, *Geschichte*, 163; Ammon, *Leben ... Nagel's*, 125; Lieber, *Letters*, 102; Schmidt, *Prussian Regular Infantryman*, 24.

6 Schmidt, *Prussian Regular Infantryman*, 24; Lieber, *Letters*, 102.

7 Hofschröer, *German Allies*, 218-9.

8 This allows for the loss of 1200 men to which the Prussians admitted. They may have lost five guns, although Reiche says they didn't. Uffindell gives 83,000 men and 224 guns, following Wagner, and allowing for the failure to make the battlefield of two battalions of infantry and a regiment and four squadrons of cavalry.

9 Ollech, *Feldzuges von 1815*, 65-7; de Wit, 'Blucher's plan'.

10 Müffling wrote that he expected the army too be concentrated at Nivelles and Quatre Bras by four (*History*, 3); Fitzroy Somerset wrote that he expected Orange's corps and the cavalry by two (Owen, *Waterloo Papers*, 8-9).

11 Müffling, *History*, 4; Owen, *Waterloo Papers*, 9; Reiche, *Memoiren*, 184, wrote that the promised support, not knowing that he would himself face Ney. Damitz (*Geschichte des Feldzuges von 1815*, I, 118), whose account was based on the documents of Grolmann, another eye-witness, wrote that Wellington said he thought he would have enough troops in place by 2 p.m. to take the offensive and that Blücher decided to give battle in the expectation of this help in the afternoon. Gneisenau to Hardenberg, 22 June 1815, in Delbrück, *Leben*, IV, 530. See Uffindell, *Eagle's Last Triumph*, 74-6 and Hofschröer, *German Allies*, 233-42.

12 Dörnberg in Glover, *Waterloo Archive*, V, 12.

22 Napoleon Changes his Plan

1 Uffindell, *Eagle's Last Triumph*, 252, n.13.

2 Forbin-Janson in BL Add Mss 30147A.

3 De Wit, 'The morning of the 16th of June', 10.

4 Rumigny, *Souvenirs*, 99-100; Mauduit, *Derniers jours*, II, 51.

5 The original and a duplicate in AN, fonds Ney 137 AP18 (one sent via the Bois de Lombuc and one sent via Ransart); copies in Registre du major-général BNP, FR.Nouv.acq.4366 and in SHD C15, nr. 5 according to de Wit, 'Napoleon's plan at Ligny', note 4; Mauduit, *Derniers jours*, II, 54; Houssaye, *1815: Waterloo*, 162-3.

6 Petit, 'Waterloo Campaign', 323.

7 Bowden (*Waterloo Campaign*, 323) gives 65,731, de Wit 66,600. Mauduit, *Derniers jours*, II, 54 gives 65,241 for the force that took part. Uffindell, *Eagle's Last Triumph*, 79, 63,000 and 230 guns.

8 Mauduit, *Derniers jours*, II, 40.

9 Elting, *Swords around a Throne*, 338-40, 615-16.

23 Ney Attacks the Netherlanders

1 Dallas, 'the enemy posted in an immense wood' in Glover, *Waterloo Archive*, I, 178; Stephens, 'their position which was a very formidable one in a thick wood' in Glover, *Waterloo Archive*, III, 134.

2 According to Martinien, the lancers suffered two officers wounded during the day, so they were evidently engaged somewhere, though not heavily. There were no offi-

cer casualties among the chasseurs. Gustave de Pontécoulant did not list the batteries as having been left behind with the cavalry, and since he was an officer with one of these batteries he should have known (Pontécoulant, *Napoléon à Waterloo*, 120).

3 Girod de l'Ain, *Vie Militaire du Général Foy*, 271.

4 Glover, *Corunna to Waterloo*, 257; Ferrior in Glover, *Waterloo Archive*, III, 20; Surgeon James wrote of 'riding through fields of rye as tall as ourselves on horseback', *Journal*, 24; Ross-Lewin of the 32nd infantry recalled 'amazingly tall rye' at Quatre Bras, *Thirty-second*, 256; 'The rye in the fields was so high that to see anything beyond our own ranks was almost impossible', Colonel Llewellyn, 28th Foot, Siborne, *Letters*, no. 149.

5 Robinson, *Quatre Bras*, 167.

6 Nyevelt in Franklin, *Netherlands Correspondence*, 46.

7 Brunswick report in Glover, *Waterloo Archive*, V, 148; Robertson, *Journal*, 145; Cappel in 1815 Limited On-line Archive.

8 Clay, 'Narrative of Adventures', 139.

9 'Rectification de quelques faits' in *Souvenirs et correspondance*, 94–5; Nyevelt in Franklin, *Netherlands Correspondence*, 47.

10 Robinson, *Quatre Bras*, 181.

24 Probing Attacks on Saint-Amand and Ligny

1 Urban, *Rifles*, 34.

2 Haythornthwaite, *Waterloo Armies*, 18; Hanger, *To All Sportsmen*, 209–10.

3 Two men are said to have thrown shells out of squares at the battle of Waterloo (Haythornthwaite, *Waterloo Armies*, 65).

4 Martin, *Souvenirs*, 110.

5 Hofschröer, *German Allies*, 264–5.

6 Elting, *Swords around a Throne*, 477.

7 Report of Major von Hymmen in 1815 Limited On-line Archive.

8 Henckel, *Erinnerungen*, 353.

9 A revolutionary volunteer in 1791, Gérard fought with the *Grande Armée* except for a period in the Peninsula in 1810–11. His promotion had been slow, and he only got a division after Borodino in 1812. He commanded a corps at Leipzig where he was seriously wounded and had distinguished himself further in 1814.

10 Haythornthwaite, *Waterloo Men*, 47 and 64; Howard, *Napoleon's Doctors*, 77.

11 François, *Journal*, 734; Rumigny, *Souvenirs*, 100.

12 Henckel, *Erinnerungen*, 655.

13 Mauduit, *Derniers jours*, II, 65.

25 Don't Hesitate a Moment

1 Original in AN, fonds Ney 137 AP18, being a duplicate message sent 3.30; copy in Registre du major-général BNP, FR.Nouv.acq.4366 and SHD C15, nr. 5, de Wit, part 3, 4; Mauduit, *Derniers jours*, II, 57–8; Houssaye, *1815: Waterloo*, 165.

2 Original in SHD C15, nr. 5; de Wit, part 3, 4; Houssaye, *1815: Waterloo*, 165–6. As Houssaye points out, Janin's estimate of the enemy force at Frasnes was a gross over-estimate of what he can have seen there. Either he was misled by the Dutch attempt to make their line appear stronger than it was or he had heard reports from prisoners or patrols of imminent reinforcement.

3 Houssaye, *1815: Waterloo*, 166 and 205–9, who quotes most sources, assumes there were two messages but d'Erlon took the wrong route. Uffindell, *Eagle's Last*

Triumph, believes that Forbin-Janson carried both the message and the pencil note.

4 D'Erlon named La Bédoyère as the messenger in 1829, but possibly because he was dead and could not reply, having been executed by the royalists in 1815. The ingenious theory that La Bédoyère forged the order can be dismissed out of hand (see Uffindell, *Eagle's Last Triumph*, 153). The reasons for supposing that Napoleon might not have issued the order himself are that, as we shall see later, he was puzzled when d'Erlon's corps appeared and that when d'Erlon later received a conflicting order, he was not sure which to obey.

5 Soult to Ney in SHD C15, nr. 1–5; Soult to Davout in Grouchy, *Mémoires*, IV, 173–4.

6 Uffindell, *Eagle's Last Triumph*, 154.

7 Houssaye, *1815: Waterloo*, 166–7n. In Uffindell's view (*Eagle's Last Triumph*, 156), he sent Baudus to Ney after Forbin-Janson returned and admitted he had not seen Ney. This makes sense of Baudus' late arrival with Ney, though it seems unlikely that much could have been done to rectify matters by that stage.

8 Latimer, *Talks of Napoleon*, 186–9; Bonaparte, *Memoirs*, trans. O'Meara, 152. Some complaints relate to the non-arrival of mythical, invented orders that Napoleon claimed in his memoirs to have sent but which in reality were never dispatched. On the other hand, events on 16 June and on other days indicate a genuine problem.

9 Bonaparte, *Memoirs*, trans. O'Meara, 83.

26 Thin Red Line

1 Kincaid, *Adventures*, 323–4.

2 Costello, *Campaigns*, 151.

3 Gronow, *Reminiscences*, 126.

4 Robertson, *Journal*, 146

5 Rogers in Siborne, *Letters*, no. 101; Rogers fired 11 shells and 90 shot to Rettberg's 24 and 270 (BL Add Mss 19,590).

6 Cléty de Witterzee and van Doren in 1815 Limited On-line Archive.

7 The French chasseurs only lost one officer wounded during the day (Martinien, *Tableaux*, 587–8), so either the fire of the 92nd was relatively ineffective or it hit the Belgians.

8 Hope, *Military Memoirs*, 398–9.

9 Anton, *Retrospect*, 191–2; Burney in Glover, *Waterloo Archive*, III, 139.

10 Muir, *Tactics*, 205.

11 Crowe in Glover, *Letters*, 271; Mudie, *Operations of the Fifth*, 183.

12 Mauduit, *Derniers jours*, II, 149; Trefcon, *Carnets de Campagne*, 84.

13 Martin, *Souvenirs*, 169.

14 Stephens in Glover, *Waterloo Archive*, III, 134.

15 Vallance from Robinson, *Quatre Bras*, 245.

16 Calvert in Siborne, *Letters*, no. 153; Mauduit, *Derniers jours*, II, 149.

27 Clubbed Muskets and Bayonets

1 Waldie, *Near Observer*, 1817 edition, II, 109.

2 Marshal Macdonald, quoted in Haythornthwaite, *Waterloo Armies*, 103.

3 Henckel, *Erinnerungen*, 354.

4 Hofschröer, *German Allies*, 311.

5 René Bourgeois or François Thomas Delbarre, *The journal of the three days of the battle of Waterloo, by an eye-witness*, 28–9.

6 François, *Journal*, 735.

7 Lieber, *Letters*, 103. Bagensky, *Geschichte*, 237.

8 Lieber, *Letters*, 104–5.

28 Ney's Second Assault

1 Swiney, *Historical Records*, 116. Ross-Lewin, 261, remembered his death differently: 'A captain of my regiment, toward the close of the day, was remarking what a number of escapes he had had, and showing how his clothes had been shot through in several places, when a musket-ball entered his mouth and killed him on the spot.'

2 Tomkinson, *Diary*, 280.

3 Martin, 'Lettre', 503.

4 Llewellyn in Siborne, *Letters*, no. 149; Black in Glover, *Waterloo Archive*, I, 182; Patton in Glover, *Waterloo Archive*, I, 176–7.

5 The German dragoon comes from Anton, whose account is not all that reliable; McEween in Siborne *Letters*, no. 165.

6 Mauduit, *Derniers jours*, II, 152; O'Malley and Riddock in Siborne, *Letters*, nos 166–7.

7 Riddock in Siborne, *Letters*, no. 167; Fletcher, *Desperate Business*, 60–1.

8 Mauduit, *Derniers jours*, II, 151–2. Martinien adds sub-lieutenants to give three officers killed and eight wounded out of thirty-four. Robinson, *Quatre Bras*, 369. Elsewhere the initial figure is 561. The Adjutant-General's return for 17 June (prior to battle casualties) was 577 rank and file (*WSD*, X, 500).

9 Herzberg's report in Glover, *Waterloo Archive*, V, 150 (BL Add Mss 34706, f. 23).

10 Forbin-Janson in BL Add Mss 30147A. Uffindell believes Forbin-Janson carried the 3.15 message, but his account seems to make more sense if he carried the first one.

11 Bourdon de Vatry in Grouchy, *Mémoires*, IV, 101–2.

12 Langenstrassen in 1815 Limited On-line Archive.

13 Mauduit, *Derniers jours*, II, 153; Jolyet in *Souvenirs et correspondence*, 75; Büsgen in 1815 Limited On-line Archive.

14 Leonhard in 1815 Limited On-line archive.

15 Morris, *Memoirs*, 67.

16 Rudyard in Siborne, *Letters*, no. 98.

17 They were temporarily in possession of the enemy but were recovered and remounted next day (Frazer, *Letters*, 541 and 545).

18 According to Martinien they lost five officers killed and twenty-two wounded, casualties matched on the day only by the 4th Light who lost six killed and twenty-three wounded. Losses sustained by Bachelu's division were significantly lighter – 2nd: eleven wounded; 61st: three killed, eleven wounded; 72nd: two killed, three wounded; 108th: three killed, fourteen wounded.

19 See Laudy, 'Mort de Frederic Guillaume' and Herzberg in Glover, *Waterloo Archive*, V, 151–2.

20 Winchester in Siborne, *Letters*, no. 169. It has also been said that Cameron was shot by one of his own men, whom he had flogged a few days before (Muir, *Tactics*, 178 citing Richard Holmes, *Firing Line* (London, Cape, 1985), 330–1).

21 Macready in Glover, *Waterloo Archive*, I, 162 thought they were broken but he was not in a position to see it, and to judge from his own and other accounts most of the losses of the 92nd were suffered around La Bergerie. Köhler in 1815 Limited On-line Archive said they were broken attacking La Bergerie.

22 Angus McDonald to his father, Antwerp, 20 June 1815, private collection.

23 Finlayson in Glover, *Waterloo Archive*, III, 220.
24 Petty, *First Napoleon*, 116 and 119.
25 Forbin-Janson in BL Add Mss 30147A.

29 Saint-Amand

1 Damitz, *Geschichte des Feldzuge von 1815*, 136.
2 Ammon and Herold, *Leben ... Nagel's*, 122, 126; Stawitzky, *Geschichte*, 37–9.
3 De Wit, *Campaign of 1815*, 'Ligny part 3', 6.
4 Ammon and Herold, *Leben ... Nagels*, 127–8; see Muir, *Tactics*, 184–5.
5 Henckel, *Erinnerungen*, 354.
6 Müffling, *Memoirs*, 238.
7 Müffling, *History*, 5–6; *Memoirs*, 238; Ollech, *Feldzuges von 1815*, 139–40.
8 De Wit section 6 and Hofschröer, *German Allies*, 287, citing Hans von Förster, *Geschichte des königlich preussischen Ulanen-Regiments Graf zu Dohna nr.8* (Berlin: Mittler 1890), p. 66.
9 Mauduit, *Derniers jours*, II, 82–3; Duuring in d'Avout, 'Documents', 115.
10 Pétiet, 195, said that Vandamme identified the column as Prussian cavalry; Mauduit, *Derniers jours*, II, 83. According to Piérart, *Le Drame de Waterloo*, 134, an aide sent by Vandamme was too frightened to approach the column sufficiently closely and misidentified it as English.

30 D'Erlon's March

1 Ney's letter to Reille and report to Soult of 11 a.m. from de Wit.
2 The identity of the messenger is mysterious. In one version d'Erlon said it was La Bédoyère, possibly because La Bédoyère was conveniently dead. In his autobiography, d'Erlon said that the messenger was an *officier d'ordonnance* (*Vie Militaire*, 95). Pétiet (*Souvenirs Militaires*, 198) named Colonel Laurent. Colonel Baudus, who claimed to have taken the duplicate message, named Forbin-Janson. Uffindell, *Eagle's Last Triumph*, 157, blamed Forbin-Janson for the entire fiasco, calling him 'disastrously inexperienced, totally inefficient and monumentally incompetent'.
3 The letter is quoted in full, p. 169. It is interesting that there is only one copy of the message in Ney's archive, in contrast to the two copies of the 2 p.m. order, since this might suggest that he really did only receive the duplicate.
4 Dessales in *Souvenirs et correspondance*, 50; Houssaye, *1815: Waterloo*, 206n.
5 Uffindell's view is that in the excitement of persuading d'Erlon to march towards Brye, Soult's aide Forbin-Janson forgot to ride on to deliver the order to Ney. Forbin-Janson's own version of events is entirely different from Uffindell's reconstruction, but it is sufficiently evasive and confused as to make it credible that it was he who botched the mission (*Eagle's Last Triumph*, 156). Forbin-Janson's account is in BL Add Mss 30147A, ff. 17–18.
6 The following morning the Guard light cavalry seems to have been in the Marbais area and it may well be that they also rode off in response to the urgent demand for intervention against the Prussian right wing. Evidence for their activity is totally lacking. Chevalier's account (*Souvenirs*, 320–2) implies that he was with the Emperor, but this might be explained if his squadron of chasseurs of the Guard had been one of the duty squadrons.
7 Reille's report of 17 June.
8 *La Sentinelle de l'Armée*, 8 March 1838, reprinted in Chapuis, *Notice sur le 85e de ligne* and in Uffindell, *Eagle's Last Triumph*, 250.

9 D'Erlon, *Vie Militaire*, 95. This would be true if the order in question was Soult's missive of 3.15. If Napoleon ever sent a direct order to d'Erlon as some have claimed, then he should have obeyed it.

10 Drouot's report in Waldie, *Near Observer*, 1817, II, 109–10.

11 Rettburg in Glover, *Waterloo Archive*, II, 46 and Glover, *Letters*, 152.

12 Kincaid, *Adventures*, 329–30.

13 Costello, *Campaigns*, 151; Jacobi in Glover, *Waterloo Archive*, II, 126–8.

14 Canler, *Mémoires*, 15; Brouwet, *Quatre Documents*, 262–3.

15 Chapuis, *Notice sur le 85e de ligne*, 26 and 53; Rullière in Largeaud, *Napoléon et Waterloo*, 372–3; D'Erlon, *Vie Militaire*, 95; Durutte in Elchingen, *Documents inédits*, 71–4.

16 Baudus, *Etudes sur Napoléon*, I, 213.

17 Muir, *Britain and the Defeat*, 357.

31 The Guard Enters the Battle

1 Pétiet, *Souvenirs Militaires*, 198.

2 Ammon, *Leben ... Nagel's*, 129–32; Stawitzky, *Geschichte*, 64–5.

3 Latimer, *Talks of Napoleon*, 186.

4 Nostitz, 'Tagebuch', 51.

5 Salisch, *Geschichte*, 199; Reiche, *Memoiren*, 190–1.

6 Siborne, *Waterloo Campaign*, 139.

7 Tom Taylor, ed. *The Life of Benjamin Robert Haydon, Historical Painter, from his Autobiography and Journals*, London: Longman, 1853, I, 278-9; Mauduit, *Derniers jours*, I, 453–61 and II, 39–40.

8 Friant, *Vie militaire*, 384–5; Petit, 'Waterloo Campaign', 323. All the grenadier battalions suffered slight officer casualties, proving that they were all involved in some fighting as they drove out the exhausted Prussian defenders for the last time.

9 Christiani in d'Avout, *Documents*, 111; Bagensky, *Geschichte*, 239–40.

10 Petit, 'Waterloo Campaign', 323.

11 Forbin-Janson in BL Add Mss 30147A.

32 Kellermann's Charge

1 Pétiet, *Souvenirs militaires*, 198. One of Soult's senior staff, Pétiet claimed that this was how Colonel Laurent, a supernumerary aide to the Emperor, reported Ney's reaction to his delivery of Soult's 3.15 order.

2 Uffindell, *Eagle's Last Triumph*, 146.

3 Morris, *Memoirs*, 68–9.

4 Siborne, *Letters*, no. 143. Interestingly, Pigot referred to chasseurs rather than cuirassiers. The Prince of Orange was already being blamed in July 1815 when Captain Barlow wrote to his father (Owen, *Waterloo Papers*, 38). See Martin Aaron, '2nd Battalion 69th', in Napoleon Series.

5 Barlow in Owen, *Waterloo Papers*, 39–40.

6 Rudyard in Siborne, *Letters*, no. 98.

7 Lloyd in Glover, *Letters*, 224; Morris, *Memoirs*, 68. See Macready, 'Siborne's History', 393.

8 Macready, 'Journals', 345.

9 Hemingway in Glover, *Waterloo Archive*, I, 166–7; Pattison in Siborne, *Letters*, no. 142; Finlayson in Glover, *Waterloo Archive*, III, 220.

10 Robinson, *Quatre Bras*, 332.

11 Hemingway in Glover, *Waterloo Archive*, I, 167.

12 Lindwurm in 1815 Limited On-line Archive.

13 Figure in de Wit, without a source; the 8th lost thirteen out of thirty-two officers wounded, none killed; the 11th one killed and three wounded according to Martinien.

14 Macready, 'Siborne's History', 391.

15 Lemonnier-Delafosse, *Campagnes*, 362; Levavasseur, *Souvenirs*, 288, reported routed cuirassiers in Charleroi. Lemonnier is an inconsistent witness, but he could be well be correct here. Other witnesses were shocked by the extent of the rout of the cuirassiers.

16 Uffindell, *Eagle's Last Triumph*, 248.

33 Blücher's Fall

1 Lieber, *Letters*, 105–7.

2 The Prussian official account (*WSD*, X, 503) speaks of a division of infantry turning the village without being seen in the gloom and some regiments of cuirassiers doing the same the other side and taking in the rear the principal corps behind the village.

3 Ollech, *Feldzuges von 1815*, 155.

4 Houssaye, *1815: Waterloo*, 180.

5 Nostitz, 'Tagebuch', 29–30.

6 Johann von Thielmann, aged fifty, commanded the Saxon forces in the Low Countries in 1814. He had fought for the Prussians at Jena, but having been sent as Saxon ambassador to Napoleon became an ardent admirer of the French Emperor. He helped to bring about the Franco-Saxon alliance and fought at Friedland for the French, commanded a Freikorps opposing the Austrian attack on Saxony in 1809, commanded the Saxon heavy cavalry at Borodino and was taken into Napoleon's personal suite. He defected in 1813 and fought as a Russian general. Despite difficult relations between the Saxons and Prussians he was given command of III Corps. He was an intelligent and studious soldier with long experience and proved to be a willing and able subordinate. Carl von Clausewitz, later famous as a military theorist, was his chief of staff.

7 Mauduit, *Derniers Jours*, II, 204–6.

8 See Houssaye, *1815: Waterloo*, 186 and his sources.

9 Mauduit, *Derniers Jours*, II, 119–20, working from Damitz's incomplete figures; James, *Campaign of 1815*, 136; Ollech, *Feldzuges von 1815*, 163.

10 Frazer, *Letters*, 544. Lettow-Vorbeck, *Untergang* gave 12,000, as did Siborne; Bowden calculated losses at 18,772 and twenty-one guns (*Waterloo Armies*, 324); Uffindell calculated fourteen guns lost on the 16th and eight to Pajol the following morning, making twenty-two.

11 Henckel's 4th Brigade, which suffered the highest losses, recorded 4 officers and 638 men dead, 15 officers and 507 wounded, 5 officers and 1396 men captured or otherwise missing; nearly all the missing subsequently turned out to be dead or wounded (Henckel, *Erinnerungen*, 357). The rest of I Corps was also badly hit and the chief of staff wrote that by the end of 16 June his corps had lost in killed, wounded, missing and prisoners, 12,486 men and 225 officers, 1006 horses and 16 guns, from its original 30,831 (Reiche, *Memoiren*, II, 195).

12 Müffling, *History*, 10–11; 13,245 for I Corps, 5655 for II Corps and more than 2000 for III Corps.

13 Soult to Davout in Grouchy, *Mémoires*, IV, 173–4; Gérard, *Quelques documens*, 45;

Charras, *Campagne de 1815*, 180.

14 Houssaye, *1815: Waterloo*, 189. French 7–8000; Uffindell, *Eagle's Last Triumph*, 204 accepted Oman's figure.

15 Mauduit, *Derniers Jours*, II, 124; Scott Bowden gives 13,721 (*Waterloo Armies*, 323).

34 Wellington's Offensive

1 Powell in Siborne, *Letters*, no. 108.

2 Macready, 'Siborne's History', 389–90.

3 Powell in Siborne, *Letters*, no. 108; Saltoun in Siborne, *Letters*, no. 106.

4 Clay, 'Narrative of Adventures', 140.

5 Powell in Siborne, *Letters*, no. 108; Clay, 'Narrative of Adventures', 140–1.

6 Nixon in Glover, *Waterloo Archive*, I, 134.

7 Macready, 'Journals', 519.

8 Gagern in Glover, *Waterloo Archive*, II, 191.

9 Gagern in Glover, *Waterloo Archive*, II, 192.

10 Mercer, *Journal*, 126–41.

11 Playford in Glover, *Waterloo Archive*, IV, 35.

12 Frazer, *Letters*, 540. Mauduit, *Derniers Jours*, II, 168 claims 1390 Anglo-Hanoverians dead and 2388 wounded, 1500 Netherlanders and Brunswickers killed and wounded; 172 Anglo-Hanoverian prisoners; and 750 Dutch and Brunswicker prisoners, totalling 6170. Fletcher gives 2205 British casualties including 300 dead; 2600 allied.

13 In his report Ney estimated his casualties at 2000 killed and 4000 wounded. Reille's report contained no numbers, but insisted opposition losses were higher. Foy reckoned his division lost 800 hors de combat, and the other infantry divisions 11–1200. Estimating losses based on officer casualties yields a figure of about 3500, which might well be reduced to Foy's 2300 if walking wounded stayed with their units. Mauduit estimated French casualties at 4000, Lemonnier at 5000. Houssaye, *1815: Waterloo*, 218, assessed French casualties as 4300 and allied as 4700. Scott Bowden (*Waterloo Campaign*, 323) calculated 4100.

14 Costello, *Campaigns*, 152–3.

15 James, *Journal*, 21.

16 Cappel in 1815 Limited On-line Archive; Finlayson in Glover, *Waterloo Archive*, III, 216.

17 He returned to Prussian headquarters next morning with Assistant Surgeon Gough of the Life Guards (James, *Journal*, 21; Frazer, *Letters*, 541).

18 Fitzroy Somerset in Owen, *Waterloo Papers*, 10; Hervey, 'Letter', 432.

35 Council by Lamplight

1 Reiche, *Memoiren*, II, 201.

2 Müffling, *History*, 13.

3 Brett-James's translation of Reiche, *Memoiren*, II, 201–2.

4 Quoted in Muir, *Tactics*, 245.

5 Nostitz, 'Tagebuch', 30–2.

6 Brett-James, *Hundred Days*, 82–3 and 86; Delbrück, *Leben*, IV, 522. Twenty-five years later, Hardinge recalled rhubarb and brandy, but the schnapps and garlic identified by the fictional Captain Fritz and Barbero (*The Battle*, 19) seem more likely.

7 Uffindell, *Eagle's Last Triumph*, 118; Gneisenau to Hardenberg, 22 June 1815 in Delbrück, *Leben*, IV, 530.

8 Quoted in Muir, *Tactics*, 242 and 245.
9 Busse, *Geschichte*, 177.
10 Busse, *Geschichte*, 178–81.
11 Ollech, *Feldzuges von 1815*, 168–70.

36 No Time to Lose

1 Ney's report in Houssaye, *1815: Waterloo*, 224. Forbin-Janson in BL Add Mss 30147A; Bourdon de Vatry in Grouchy, *Mémoires*, IV, 103. Bourdon de Vatry got the impression that Forbin had just arrived, six hours late, with the order to attack the Prussians in the flank, but he was probably mistaken.
2 Martin, 'Lettre', 499; Canler, *Mémoires*, 46–7.
3 Copy in SHD C15, nr. 1–5 (de Wit).
4 Mauduit, *Derniers jours*, II, 100–8.
5 Daure from de Wit. This report is probably the origin of Soult's figure of 3000 wounded.
6 Ortiz, with quotations from Larrey, *Memoirs*, I, 80–1.
7 Howard, *Napoleon's Doctors*, 61.
8 Radet in de Wit.
9 Bonaparte's claim in *Mémoires*, 94, that Pajol followed Blücher in the direction of Tilly and Wavre is wishful thinking, part of a story designed to lay blame squarely on Grouchy. The correction of what *was* done to what *ought to have been* done was a clear indication that Bonaparte recognised that his crucial error was to suppose that the Prussians had fled towards Namur.
10 Lachouque without reference in de Wit.
11 Original in SHD; de Wit lists publications with slight variations.
12 Petty, *First Napoleon*, 117; Bourdon de Vatry in Grouchy, *Mémoires*, IV, 105.
13 SHD C15, nr. 1–5 (de Wit).
14 Martin, 'Lettre', 499.
15 Bonaparte, *Mémoires*, 96; Houssaye, *1815: Waterloo*, 264. This suggests that at this stage the Guard light cavalry was around Marbais.

37 Losing the Scent

1 Grouchy, *Mémoires*, IV, 23–4.
2 Chandler, 'Napoleon and Death', *Napoleonic Scholarship: The Journal of the International Napoleonic Society*, Volume 1, Number 1, April 1997 (online).
3 Latimer, *Talks of Napoleon*, 190.
4 Mauduit, *Derniers Jours*, II, 201. See, for instance, Sénéchal's report that Vandamme refused Grouchy's order to attack Gilly (Grouchy, *Mémoires*, IV, 127), Vandamme's report of 10 p.m. 15 June: 'Je pense que l'ennemi n'a que 12 à 15.000 hommes. Le maréchal Grouchy croit qu'il y a 30.000 hommes,' or Pajol to Grouchy 10 p.m. 15 June: 'J'aurais occupé ce village, si le général Vandamme eut voulu m'envoyer et me soutenir par quelque infanterie; mais il paraît que ce général a pris à tache de faire tout ce qui est contraire à la guerre.'
5 Martinien, *Tableaux*, 16.
6 Biot, *Souvenirs*, 244–5.
7 SHD C15 in de Wit. He complained that his only division was weak, still lacking Clary's 1st Hussars. They rejoined at some point before 20 June, when they suffered casualties at the battle of Namur (Martinien, *Tableaux*).
8 Biot, *Souvenirs*, 245.

9   Grouchy, *Mémoires*, IV, 127 and de Wit.

10 In his letter from Gembloux he reiterated the complaint made earlier that morning (SHD).

11 One might speculate that Gneisenau's missing ammunition train had taken a route through Grand-Leez and Perwez before turning towards Wavre.

12 Grouchy, *Mémoires*, IV, 128.

13 Latimer, *Talks of Napoleon*, 186. He had appointed Suchet to command a small army to oppose the Austrians.

38 Morning at Quatre Bras

1   Clay, 'Narrative of Adventures', 141.

2   Jackson, 'Recollections', 8; Fitzroy Somerset in Owen, *Waterloo Papers*, 10; Vivian in Siborne, *Letters*, no.71; Hope, *Military Memoirs*, 416–17.

3   Anthony Bacon of the escort in Glover, *Letters*, 102.

4   Brouwet, 'Quatre documents', 363; Bülow in Glover, *Waterloo Archive*, V, 62; Hanoverian staff report in Glover, *Waterloo Archive*, II, 10; the brigade report (Glover, *Waterloo Archive*, II, 94) gave ninety killed and wounded; Brunswick returns from Olfermann in 1815 Limited On-line Archive. An officer of the 95th in Waldie, *Near Observer*, 52.

5   Costello, *Campaigns*, 152; Clay, 'Narrative of Adventures', 139–40; Hemingway in Glover, *Waterloo Archive*, I, 168.

6   George Maule in Glover, *Waterloo Archive*, I, 130.

7   Robinson, *Quatre Bras*, 370, 366, 373. Reille's report mentions a flag having been taken by the 4th Light, but the man carrying it off having been killed.

8   Keppel, *Fifty Years*, 137; Howard, *Wellington's Doctors*, 73–4; Clark in Siborne, *Letters*, no. 34; Brunswick Hussars helped (Glover, *Waterloo Archive*, V, 154).

9   Jackson, 'Recollections', 11; Fitzroy Somerset in Owen, *Waterloo Papers*, 10; Müffling, *Memoirs*, 240.

10 Porter, *Royal Engineers*, I, 280; Delancey, *Week at Waterloo*, 112.

11 British Library, Add MSS 57, 635 ff. 3–4.

12 One set of surveys made by Brains, Dumaresq and Staveley in May 1815 is at NAM 6807/137. Jackson, *Notes and Reminiscences*, 5 and 97.

13 Owen, *Waterloo Papers*, 10; Jeremiah, *Life and Adventures*, 20; Wheeler, *Letters*, 169. By the time he wrote on 19 June he had been told (incorrectly) that the Belgians were 'running away, helter skelter, the Devil take the hindmost'.

14 Müffling, *Memoirs*, 241; Ollech, *Feldzuges von 1815*, 180; in Müffling, *History*, 16, the Duke asked for two corps. Houssaye's version (*1815: Waterloo*, 261, followed by Hamilton-Williams, *New Perspectives*, 240) exemplifies his free way with quotation: Müffling gave his own opinion that Wellington should retire beyond the Scheldt were Blücher unable to fight but did not say that this was what Wellington said. Frazer's knowledge of the worries over ammunition indicates that von Massow had revealed them.

15 Costello, *Campaigns*, 152; Döring in Glover, *Waterloo Archive*, II, 165.

16 Jackson, *Notes and Reminiscences*, 32–3; Wheatley, *Diary*, 60–1.

17 Döring in Glover, *Waterloo Archive*, II, 165; Nyevelt in Franklin, *Netherlands Correspondence*, 51.

18 Gagern in Glover, *Waterloo Anecdotes*, II, 193.

19 Hay, *Reminiscences*, 168, echoed by Ingilby, 'Waterloo Diary', 54.

39 The Road to Mont Saint-Jean

1 Bessborough, *Lady Bessborough*, 241.
2 Fitzroy Somerset in Owen, *Waterloo Papers*, 11.
3 Ingilby, 'Waterloo Diary', 55.
4 Tomkinson, *Diary*, 284.
5 Hay, *Reminiscences*, 170.
6 Hay, *Reminiscences*, 171; Ingilby, 'Waterloo Diary', 55.
7 James to his brother, 9 July 1815 in Glover, *Waterloo Archive*, I, 7.
8 Pontécoulant, *Napoléon à Waterloo*, 186. Pontécoulant was the officer thus addressed.
9 Kincaid, *Adventures*, 333; Baring in Glover, *Letters*, 241.
10 Cotton, *Voice from Waterloo*, 22; the main accounts are by Uxbridge (Siborne, *Letters*, no. 4) and O'Grady, who married Uxbridge's niece and became colonel of the 7th (*Letters*, no. 65 and Glover, *Waterloo Archive*, III, 77–9). Sir John Elley gave Siborne a brief verbal account via another officer, who wrote, 'he was averse to put it on paper himself for reasons which I would say – but cannot write' (Glover, *Letters*, 30).
11 Radclyffe in Glover, *Waterloo Archive*, I, 24–5.
12 James, *Journal*, 24–5; see also Schreiber in Siborne, *Letters*, no.56. Macready, 'Journals', 521; Houssaye, *1815: Waterloo*, 269–71; Pontécoulant, *Napoléon à Waterloo*, 186; Pétiet, *Souvenirs militaires*, 205–8.
13 Kelly, NAM 2002-01-254.
14 One way or another Kelly certainly obtained the epaulettes, but the identity of his victim is mysterious since no colonels appear to have been killed on 17 June. Sourd was an extremely brave man, many times wounded. He had risen through the ranks after volunteering in 1792 and undertook numerous dangerous missions and special tasks requiring bravery and initiative. According to Mauduit, *Derniers Jours*, II, 226–8, Sourd outflanked an infantry rearguard drawn up short of Genappe and drove off Hanoverian hussars that supported it, pursuing them with one squadron while the other three pushed back the enemy on the Brussels road. Ordered to Genappe to support the 1st Lancers, he pushed the English back onto their main body. Finding himself unsupported, he returned but found the road through Genappe blocked by English cavalry. He was summoned to surrender by a senior officer but ran him through and then fought bravely against a host of enemies who eventually overwhelmed him.
15 The 7th Hussars admitted to only six killed (all privates), twenty-one wounded (five sergeants and sixteen men), one trumpeter and fourteen men missing. Seventeen horses were killed and twenty wounded. However, this list does not include officers and Charles Radclyffe, for one, did not believe their return to the Adjutant-General. The return provides for heavy losses on 18 June where there is little evidence of heavy fighting to cause such losses. Hodge and Myers were killed, and O'Grady named five lieutenants taken prisoner. Simmons, *British Rifle Man*, 364, wrote: 'The 7th Hussars charged, but were sadly mauled. The Life Guards and Oxford Blues made some very fine charges, and literally preserved the 7th from being cut to pieces.' Maule wrote, 'two troops of the 7th Hussars were taken nearly complete'; while Captain Thackwell said of them at Waterloo, 'the 7th Hussars were very weak, having suffered most severely on the debouch of the French cavalry from Genappe the preceding afternoon'. Uxbridge's son Henry wrote on 24 June that 200 out of 400 in the regiment had been killed and all but one of the officers wounded (Glover, *Waterloo Archive*, III, 5). Radclyffe in Glover, *Waterloo Archive*, I,

23: 'The great loss of the 7th was in an unfortunate affair with a corps of lancers on the 17th.' Out of forty-one officers in the 2nd Lancers, fourteen were wounded on 17 June. There were no officer casualties in other French regiments except one wounded in the 1st Lancers. This suggests that the 2nd was the only regiment seriously engaged.

16 Pétiet, *Souvenirs Militaires*, 206. O'Grady named a captain and four lieutenants who were taken prisoner; Paget mentions another lieutenant (Glover, *Waterloo Archive*, III, 6 and 78).

17 Bonaparte, *Mémoires*, IX, 99; Saint-Denis, *Tuileries to Saint Helena*, 128–9.

18 Niemann in Thorpe, 'Two Diaries', 542.

19 James, *Journal*, 26.

20 Duthilt in Field, *French Perspective*, 36.

21 Bonaparte, *Mémoires*, IX, 101; Wellington's engineers had surveyed a potential battlefield at Hal, as they had at Mont Saint-Jean.

22 The less experienced part of 4 division and Prince Frederick's Netherlands division.

23 Gourgaud, *Campagne*, 79; Dessales in *Souvenirs et correspondance*, 50. Napoleon, who refers to twenty-four guns, was probably exaggerating but he may have led some Guard artillery himself.

24 Dupuy, *Souvenirs*, 289; Thackwell, *Military Memoirs*, 70; Byam in Glover, *Waterloo Archive*, I, 84; report of 2nd Light Dragoons KGL in Glover, *Waterloo* Archive, II, 33.

25 Johannes Koch in 1815 Limited On-line Archive.

26 D'Erlon, *Mémoires*, 96; Dessales in *Souvenirs et Correspondance*, 52.

27 Gourgaud, *Campagne*, 79–80; Bonaparte, *Mémoires*, 88–9.

28 Report to Chambre des Pairs, *Moniteur* 24 June in Waldie, *Near Observer*, 1817 edition, II, 111.

29 Fraser, *Words on Wellington*, 1–3. Fraser was an aide to Uxbridge.

30 Brouwet, 'Quatre Documents', 363.

31 Trefcon, *Carnet de Campagne*, 86.

32 Girod de l'Ain, *Vie Militaire du Général Foy*, 277–8.

40 Panic Behind the Lines

1 Glover, *Waterloo Archive*, I, 226; Creevey, *Creevey Papers*, I, 230–1.

2 Glover, *Waterloo Archive*, I, 227.

3 Heeley, 'Journal', 109–10.

4 Delancey, *Week at Waterloo*, 48–9.

5 Waldie, *Near Observer*, xiv–xv.

6 Carey in Brett-James, *Hundred Days*, 96–7.

7 Captain Jean-Baptiste Osten in Franklin, *Netherlands Correspondence*, 36–7.

8 Koopman in Franklin, *Netherlands Correspondence*, 111.

9 Rettberg in Glover, *Waterloo Archive*, II, 47.

10 James, *Journal*, 34–5.

11 Glover, *Waterloo Archive*, II, 89; Wheatley, *Diary*, 61–2.

12 Glover, *Waterloo Archive*, I, 227.

13 Glover, *Waterloo Archive*, I, 227–8; in fact, Uxbridge survived the rout of his hussars unscathed.

14 Swiney, *Historical Records*, 117.

15 Jackson, 'Recollections', 181.

41 The Heavens Open their Sluices

1 Glover, *Waterloo Archive*, I, 32.

2 Jacobi in Glover, *Waterloo Archive*, II, 131–2.

3 Robertson, *Journal*, 152–3.

4 Officer of 95th in Waldie, *Near Observer*, 52–3.

5 Lindau, *Waterloo Hero*, 161–2.

6 Gagern in Glover, *Waterloo Archive*, II, 193–4.

7 Barnett, NAM 1991-06-31.

8 James, *Journal*, 27–8.

9 Gibney, *Eighty Years Ago*, 183–4.

10 Gerard Rochell in Franklin, *Netherlands Correspondence*, 142–51.

11 Barnett, NAM 1991-06-31; *A Soldier of the Seventy-first*, 105–6. KGL reports in Glover, *Waterloo Archive*, II, 17–19.

12 Jeremiah, *Life and Adventures*, 20–1 and in Glover, *Waterloo Archive*, IV, 185–7. Jeremiah sets this story on the morning of 18 June, but if Glover is correct in identifying the chateau as Mon Plaisir – and there is no other obvious candidate – it seems unlikely that Jeremiah could have gone there in the morning without being captured by the French.

13 Wheeler, *Letters*, 170.

14 Canler, *Mémoires*, 48; Martin, 'Lettre', 501.

15 Houssaye, *1815: Waterloo*, 273–4.

16 Pawly, *Imperial Headquarters* (2), 52–4.

17 Houssaye, *1815: Waterloo*, 277; Macbride, *With Napoleon at Waterloo*, 183.

18 Gourgaud, *Campagne*, 83–4; Bonaparte, *Mémoires* 102–3. Houssaye, *1815: Waterloo*, 277. The source is Napoleon's memoirs, but Soult's letter to Grouchy of 10 a.m. confirms the receipt of such a report. Milhaud's men had contacted von Sohr's rearguard.

19 Marchand, *Mémoires*, 221.

20 Marchand, *Mémoires*, 221; Keppel, *Fifty Years*, 143.

21 *WD*, XII, 476–8; *WSD* X, 501.

22 Robinson, *Memoirs of Picton*, II, 386–9.

23 Lawrence, *Autobiography*, 204.

24 Heyland in Glover, *Waterloo Archive*, III, 140.

42 The Prussian March

1 Ollech, *Feldzuges von 1815*, 164.

2 Gneisenau to Hardenberg, 22 June 1815, in Delbrück, *Leben*, IV, 530–1.

3 Uffindell, *Eagle's Last Triumph*, 168; Gneisenau to Hardenberg, 22 June 1815, Delbrück, *Leben*, IV, 530–1.

4 Ollech, *Feldzuges von 1815*, 187–8 and 191. Ziethen's baggage had fled from Gembloux to Wavre and was sent north to Louvain, as was Bülow's.

5 George von der Decken in Glover, *Waterloo Archive*, II, 36.

6 Taylor in Siborne, *Letters*, no. 75; Bülow's report in Ollech, *Feldzuges von 1815*, 192.

7 Müffling, *Memoirs*, 242; *History*, 17; Ollech, *Feldzuges von 1815*, 214–15, noting that it survived in the Kriegsarchiv; Frazer, *Letters*, 553. As Houssaye pointed out, it is clear from Prussian orders that they had already made their plan to attack Napoleon's flank with the bulk of their force and reinforce Wellington with the rest. As it happened, this more or less coincided with what Müffling proposed.

8 Rahden, *Wanderungen*, 365.

9 Wedell, *Geschichte*, 164, Dörk, *15tes Infanterie*, 128. Ollech, *Feldzuges von 1815*, 192 is Bülow's account.

10 De Wit Copy in former KA, VI.C.55.I.11; it bears the title: 'Disposition des gener- als Bülow von Dennewitz, vor der Schlacht am 18. an den Lord Wellington geschickt'; Ollech, *Feldzuges von 1815*, 216. Cf. Pflugk-Harttung, *Von Wavre bis Belle Alliance*, 620–1; Lettow-Vorbeck, *Untergang*, III, 401.

11 De Wit; Hofschröer, *German Victory*, 93–6.

43 Finding Breakfast

1 James, *Journal*, 31.

2 Glover, *Waterloo Archive*, III, 2. Frazer, *Letters*, 545–6.

3 Barnett, NAM 1991-06-31; *A Soldier of the Seventy-first*, 105–6.

4 Eyre in Glover, *Waterloo Archive*, III, 115.

5 Wheeler, *Letters*, 170; Jeremiah in Glover, *Waterloo Archive*, IV, 185–7. British soldiers tended to call all the German troops in their army Brunswickers.

6 Döring in Glover, *Waterloo Archive*, II, 166–7.

7 Robertson, *Journal*, 153; Jacobi in Glover, *Waterloo Archive*, II, 132–3.

8 Robertson, *Journal*, 153.

9 Mudie, 'Operations of the Fifth', 175.

10 Pitt-Lennox in Siborne, *Letters*, no. 17; Hope, *Military Memoirs*, 425.

11 Glover, *Waterloo Archive*, II, 132–4.

12 Morris, *Memoirs*, 77.

13 Jan Rem in 1815 Limited On-line Archive.

14 Mudie, 'Operations of the Fifth', 176.

15 Mudie, 'Operations of the Fifth', 176–7.

16 Wheatley, *Diary*, 62. Gerson was the senior assistant surgeon attached to the bat- talion.

44 Tyrans, Tremblez!

1 Order from Soult, Houssaye, *1815: Waterloo*, 286. The order confirms that Napoleon had intended to attack earlier and that orders for deployment had already been issued.

2 Marchand, *Mémoires*, 221.

3 Canler, *Mémoires*, 18; Martin, *Souvenirs*, 283.

4 Girod de l'Ain, *Vie militaire*, 278.

5 Houssaye, *1815: Waterloo*, 319, citing mss notes by Baudus for this conversation.

6 Girod de l'Ain, *Vie militaire*, 279.

7 Mauduit, *Derniers jours*, II, 242, felt the staff failed to master the topography of the battlefield, and more and better guides would have revealed that the vulnerable part of Wellington's position was his left, but in my view the staff had identified this weakness and intended to attack the left.

8 Register of the major general, Houssaye, *1815: Waterloo*, 324–5.

9 Marbot, III, 403 and 405; Houssaye, *1815: Waterloo*, 325. Houssaye correctly observes that the deployment of hussars was intended to facilitate communication with Grouchy, not to give early news of Grouchy's approach, as Marbot believed.

10 Petit, 'Waterloo Campaign', 324.

11 Martin, *Souvenirs*, 284; Canler, *Mémoires*, 18–19. Interestingly, this passage is not in Martin's letter of 1 August.

12 Bowden's figures (*Waterloo Campaign*, 271–2 and 337); Houssaye's figure (*1815:*

Waterloo, 330–1) for the French is similar but his figure of 68,000 for the allies is based on Siborne's numbers. Bowden demonstrated (*Waterloo Campaign*, 227) that Siborne's figures, though traditionally accepted, did not include NCOs or officers, and have to be revised upwards. Muir (*Britain and the Defeat of Napoleon*, 361) concurs, agreeing with Bowden that Wellington had about 74,000 men. Adkin (*Waterloo Companion*, 37) obtained a slightly lower figure by allowing fewer wounded to return to the ranks. The figures for French guns vary considerably but the most likely are 246 (Adkin) or 254 (Bowden), depending on whether the Guard had three or four 12-pounder batteries. The figures are parade-ground strengths and there were markedly fewer men actually on the field because many were detached as baggage guards and servants in rear of the armies.

45 The Position

1 James, *Journal*, 31–2; Gronow, *Reminiscences*, 129.
2 Constant in Franklin, *Netherlands Correspondence*, 17.
3 These figures are based on those of Bowden and Adkin (see note 12 in the previous chapter). The artillery figure (157/156) turns on how many Dutch guns survived Quatre Bras.
4 Ellesmere, *Personal Reminiscences*, 183.
5 Shaw Kennedy, *Notes*, 72.
6 Glover, *Waterloo Archive*, II, 156–8
7 The Hanoverian army staff report (Glover, *Waterloo Archive*, II, 12, 17) states fifty from each battalion, but the more detailed brigade report (Glover, *Waterloo Archive*, II, 95) is quite specific that 100 from each battalion marched to Hougoumont.
8 Shaw Kennedy, *Notes*, 99–102.
9 Frazer, *Letters*, 554–5; Rudyard in Siborne, *Letters*, no. 99.
10 Mercer, 120; *Instructions for officers and non-commissioned officers of cavalry on outpost duty* (1810), as refined by Frederick Ponsonby, was still in use by the Confederate Army in the American Civil War.
11 Shaw Kennedy, *Notes*, 71.
12 Kincaid, *Adventures*, 340.
13 Belcher in NA, WO 71/242 161. If this was so, Haythornthwaite's figure of 503 is too high by some margin.
14 Ingilby, 'Waterloo Diary', 55.
15 Wheatley, *Diary*, 63.

46 The French Plan

1 Gourgaud, *Campagne*, 88. Bonaparte, *Memoirs*, 115–18; Bonaparte, *Mémoires*, 118–19. I agree with Barbero (*The Battle*, 96–8) against Houssaye (*1815: Waterloo*, 333), that Napoleon expected a breakthrough on the right.
2 Dessales in *Souvenirs et correspondance*, 52; Dessales somehow made the total 54 guns when the three reserve batteries plus those of d'Erlon's infantry divisions made 56; perhaps two guns were deployed elsewhere. Houssaye added three Guard batteries to make a total of eighty, but Dessales, 54, said that these were deployed after the British cavalry charge in order to replace damaged and unmoveable guns.
3 Bowden (*Waterloo Campaign*, 321) makes eighty by adding the 12-pounders of the Old Guard reserve foot artillery to six foot batteries, while Adkin (*Waterloo Companion*, 298) includes additional Imperial Guard 6-pounder batteries.
4 Heymès in Elchingen, *Documents inédits*, 15, *Waterloo: Récits de combattants*, 48 and

50. Levavasseur, *Souvenirs Militaires*, 291–4; the third aide was named Devaux.

5 Elchingen, *Documents inédits*, 53–4. The phrase 'at the intersection of the main roads' shows that Napoleon knew where Mont Saint-Jean was on the map, although some of his subordinates seem to have confused Mont Saint-Jean with La Haye Sainte, there being a road junction just behind the farm and two nearby cottages.

6 Reille in Elchingen, *Documents Inédits*, 62; Robinaux, *Journal de route*, 208; Girod de l'Ain, *Vie militaire*, 281; Jolyet in *Souvenirs et correspondance*, 77; see also Combes-Brassard in *Souvenirs et correspondance*, 16: 'In the initial plan, the French army was to attack on the right and in the centre, refusing the left.'

47 The First Assault on Hougoumont

1 The name Hougoumont first occurred on the Ferraris map, the surveyors having written down 'du Goumont' as 'd'Hougoumont'; the manuscript survey shows the earlier, grander layout of the park.

2 Waldie, *Residence in Belgium*, 289.

3 'Ten minutes': Glover, *Waterloo Archive*, II, 104; Colborne in Siborne, *Letters*, no. 123.

4 Jolyet in *Souvenirs et Correspondance*, 77; Büsgen in Glover, *Waterloo Archive*, II, 157; elms according to a Hanoverian report in Glover, *Waterloo Archive*, II, 10; Bull in Siborne, *Letters*, no. 78.

5 Fletcher, *Desperate Business*, 106–7.

6 Mainwaring, 'Four Years', 409; Wheeler, *Letters*, 171; Siborne, *Letters*, no. 63.

7 Elting, *Swords around a Throne*, 475.

8 Büsgen in Glover, *Waterloo Archive*, II, 117.

9 For the development of this favourite anecdote of Wellington's, see Mittelacher, 'Nassauers at Hougoumont'; the earliest version reported by Pozzo di Borgo dates from 24 July 1815 (J. Malcolm, *The Life and Correspondence of Major-General Sir John Malcolm*, ed. J. W. Kaye, 2 vols, London, 1856, II, 102).

10 Hervey, 'Letter', 433 says twenty-six guns; Frazer, *Letters*, 556–7.

11 Glover, *Waterloo Archive*, I, 148–9.

12 Keppel, *Fifty Years*, 145.

13 Hart, NAM 1981-11-84; see Martin, *Souvenirs*, 110, quoted above.

14 Clay, 'Adventures at Hougoumont', 220:

15 Walcott in Siborne, *Letters*, no. 80.

16 Pétiet, *Souvenirs militaires*, 215; Mauduit, *Derniers jours*, II, 321n. Pétiet names the leader as Bonnet, but there is no Bonnet in Martinien's list of casualties, whereas Legros is listed. It is possible that Pétiet's hero of Tarragona was Legros.

17 Jolyet in *Souvenirs et correspondance*, 73. I am not convinced by Sergeant Frazer's claim to have unhorsed the colonel with his halberd and then ridden the stolen horse into the farmyard (Fletcher, *Desperate Business*, 109). Glover, *Waterloo Archive*, III, 111.

18 Fletcher, *Desperate Business*, 113.

19 Wachholtz in 1815 Limited On-line Archive. There are many witnesses to the presence in the front line of the Avant-Garde battalion. These Brunswick units had been significantly depleted at Quatre Bras but had proved themselves trustworthy to the Duke.

20 Clay, 'Adventures at Hougoumont', 28.

21 Longford, *Years of the Sword*, 459. Figures from Mauduit and the returns before the campaign started and allowing only 500 casualties for Quatre Bras. Adkin's figure for this division is way too high, partly because he incorrectly included the very strong 2nd Light within it, instead of the 3rd Line which had 1200 men fewer.

48 The Prussians Detected

1 See Houssaye, *1815: Waterloo*, 293–4.

2 Houssaye, *1815: Waterloo*, 343–4.

3 Gourgaud, *Campagne*, 89 has all these troops sent to oppose the Prussians in case Grouchy failed to appear in accordance with the Emperor's (mythical) overnight message. *Mémoires*, 120–1, have him spotting what might be troops in the distance on the right and sending Domon and Subervie to reconnoitre. In the *Mémoires* Bonaparte timed these events at 11 a.m., but set them after the attack on Hougoumont and immediately before Ney unleashed d'Erlon's corps (see Mauduit, *Derniers jours*, II, 287–9; Houssaye, *1815: Waterloo*, 340–1 and 346). For Bernard see Charras, *Campagne de 1815*, 260 and Bernhard of Saxe-Weimar in Franklin, *Netherlands Correspondence*, 97–8.

4 Houssaye, *1815: Waterloo*, 292.

5 Houssaye, *1815: Waterloo*, 295.

6 James, *Campaign of 1815*, 196–7; *Mémoires du Maréchal Grouchy*, iv, 71.

7 Houssaye, *1815: Waterloo*, 300–5.

49 The Grand Battery

1 Kincaid, *Adventures*, 341; Leach, *Rough Sketches*, 386.

2 Muir, *Tactics*, 34.

3 Girod de l'Ain, cited by Field, *French Perspective*, 71.

4 Müffling, *History*, 17–18; *Memoirs*, 242.

5 Napoleon claimed there were eighty guns in the battery. Pontécoulant, *Napoléon à Waterloo*, 263–4, said sixty pieces including two foot batteries of the Guard. Mauduit, *Derniers jours*, said ten batteries, including several of the Guard, took part. However, Pontécoulant states that his own Guard light horse batteries only joined in later to replace losses.

6 Some authors believe the Grand Battery started on the forward line, but at this stage it would have been desperately exposed and vulnerable, far in front of the French infantry and outflanked by Papelotte and La Haye. Shaw Kennedy (*Notes*, 86–7) confirms that the Grand Battery moved to the forward ridge but does not say when.

7 Glover, *Waterloo Archive*, II, 17.

8 Mercer, *Journal*, 161.

9 Ross in Siborne, *Letters*, no.91; the third was probably Beane's, which Frazer says was placed close to Ross's. Gunner John Edwards, Glover, *Waterloo Archive*, I, 102.

10 Muir, *Tactics*, 34.

11 Glover, *Waterloo Archive*, II, 39; Brandis in Glover, V, 56; Playford, *Lifeguardsman*, 48–9.

12 Rettberg in Glover, *Letters*, 156. Noguès, *Mémoires*, 274; Müffling, *History*, 21; Ingilby, 'Waterloo Diary', 55.

13 The order in which the divisions advanced has been interpreted very differently by different historians, owing to the lack of evidence. Batty said that Donzelot attacked La Haye Sainte, Quiot and Marcognet attacked Picton with the half of Durutte's division that was not at Papelotte. Shaw Kennedy has Quiot attack La Haye Sainte, while Donzelot, Marcognet and Durutte attack Picton. Siborne, *Waterloo Campaign* 247–8, Roberts and Barbero follow Batty. Charras, Houssaye, James, Weller, Chandler and Hamilton-Williams follow Shaw Kennedy. Mauduit, *Derniers jours*, II, 293–7 gives the version I follow. Janin, 53, says little, but has three attacking columns rather than four.

14 Canler, *Mémoires*, 19.
15 Siborne, *Letters*, no. 157.
16 Chapuis, 'Notice sur le 85e de ligne', 45.
17 Canler, *Mémoires*, 20; Noguès, *Mémoires*, 274; Martin, 'Lettre d'un officier Genèvois du 45e', 502; Schmitz in Brouwet, 'Quatre documents', 363; Rullière in Largeaud, *Napoléon et Waterloo*, 375–6.
18 Mauduit, *Derniers jours*, II, 291.

50 D'Erlon's Assault

1 Field, *French Perspective*, 70: a report to Soult on the advantages of rifles.
2 Büsgen in Glover, *Waterloo Archive*, II, 157; Jolyet in *Souvenirs et correspondance*, 77.
3 Mackinnon, *Coldstream Guards*, 217–8; Hepburn in Siborne, *Letters*, no. 117.
4 Clay, 'Adventures at Hougoumont', 222.
5 Hornn, *Narrative*, 59.
6 Lindau, *Waterloo Hero*, 167–8 and 187.
7 Canler, *Mémoires*, 19–20; Duthilt in Field, *French Perspective*, 99; Martin, *Souvenirs*, 287.
8 D'Huvelé in 1815 Limited On-line Archive; Rettberg in Glover, *Waterloo Archive*, II, 48; expenditure of ammunition in BL Add Mss 19,590. It is not clear, however, whether the expenditure includes ammunition lost when caissons exploded.
9 Martin, 'Lettre', 503; Koopman in Franklin, *Netherlands Correspondence*, 109; von Bronkhorst in 1815 Limited On-line Archive; Nyevelt in Franklin, *Netherlands Correspondence*, 55.
10 Kincaid, *Adventures*, 343–4; Canler, *Mémoires*, 21; Rogers and Maule in Siborne, *Letters*, nos. 102–3.

51 Crabbé's Charge

1 Brigade report in Glover, *Waterloo Archive*, II, 95; Jacobi in Glover, *Waterloo Archive*, II, 135; Bäring in Lindau, *Waterloo Hero*, 187–8; Biedermann in Glover, *Waterloo Archive*, V, 42.
2 Levavasseur, *Souvenirs Militaires*, 298. He may not have taken a squadron from every regiment (see Field, *French Perspective*, 85–6), but there seem to have been lancers operating in this area of the field. Lot, *Ordener*, 91. Macready, 'Journals', 523. Müffling, *History*, 22, confirms that a cavalry attack in the centre preceded d'Erlon's assault: 'No sooner had the artillery opened upon this fresh corps [d'Erlon's], than a body of cavalry advanced to the right and left of the high road.'
3 Charras, *Campagne de 1815*, 275; Lot, *Ordener*, p. 91; Houssaye, *1815: Waterloo*, 383; Field, *French Perspective*, 94; Barbero, *The Battle*, 160, who says it was recovered after the battle. The Hanoverian sources are silent.
4 Jacobi in Glover, *Waterloo Archive*, II, 135–6.
5 Brigade report in Glover, *Waterloo Archive*, II, 95–6. Ordener (Lot, *Ordener*, 91) spoke of twenty-four guns, which would match the combined total of Ross, Beane, Kühlmann and Lloyd.
6 Beamish, *King's German Legion*, 355–6; Glover, *Waterloo Archive*, II, 91.
7 Wheatley, *Diary*, 64.
8 Edwards in Glover, *Waterloo Archive*, I, 102–3.
9 See, for instance, von Dreves in Glover, *Waterloo Archive*, II, 68.
10 D.D. Vigors, 'Voices from the Napoleonic Wars', *Journal of the Royal Artillery*, CXI (September 1984), 138–9.

11 Dessales in *Souvenirs et correspondance*, 53–4. Simmons, *British Rifle Man*, 365, wrote that the guns moved forward before d'Erlon's attack went in.

52 The Charge of the Household Brigade

1 Playford in Glover, *Waterloo Archive*, IV, 38.
2 Uxbridge in *Siborne*, Letters, no. 5.
3 Somerset in *Siborne*, Letters, no. 18.
4 Elton in Glover, *Waterloo Archive*, IV, 49–50.
5 Gore, *Historical Account*, 89. Gore made the precipice forty feet but he was prone to exaggeration. The incident was a celebrated feature of Victor Hugo's account of Waterloo.
6 Levavasseur, *Souvenirs*, 294.
7 See Dörnberg in Glover, *Waterloo Archive*, II, 30.
8 Hasker in Glover, *Waterloo Archive*, I, 20; Page in Glover, *Waterloo Archive*, III, 23.
9 Playford, in Glover, *Waterloo Archive*, IV, 40; Lord in Glover, *Waterloo Archive*, I, 14; Houssaye, *1815: Waterloo*, 354.
10 Cathcart in Siborne, *Letters*, no. 15.
11 All of the four men who rode to Playford's immediate left were killed. Published tales of Shaw begin modestly with Kelly, *Waterloo*, 94, and less modestly with Waldie, *Near Observer* (1817 edition), 30, where he died fighting six Imperial Guardsmen, of whom he killed four, after earlier cutting a cuirassier's head in two. They culminate in W. Knollys, *Shaw the Lifeguardsman* (London, 1885), 62–3.
12 Marten in Siborne, *Letters*, nos 26–7; Waymouth in Siborne, *Letters*, no. 20.
13 Uxbridge in Siborne, *Letters*, no. 5.

53 The Charge of the Union Brigade

1 Seymour in Siborne, *Letters*, nos 9–10; Tomkinson, *Diary*, 302.
2 Two versions of this in Swiney, *Historical Records*, 121 and Belcher in Siborne, *Letters*, no. 154, who says he had taken the colours from the wounded ensign when a French officer seized them.
3 Batty, *Campaign of 1815*, 94–5; Müffling, *Memoirs*, 244, wrote, 'I arrived on the left wing at the same moment that General Picton (who fell on this occasion) was repulsed in his attack on the enemy's 1st corps.' Kempt's report (*WSD*, X, 535) admitted that the French reached the crest of the position, but claimed that the infantry defeated the French before cavalry arrived on the scene. It is possible that this was true of Bourgeois' brigade, which may have crumbled from the rear as the Household Brigade arrived behind its flank. Captain Cadell of the 28th (Glover, *Letters*, 268) spoke plausibly of 'checking with the bayonet and musketry, a heavy French column that was charged shortly after by the heavy cavalry'. Ingilby (Siborne, *Letters*, no. 82), recalled that 'our troops recoiled and some Highlanders were in confusion'.
4 Martin, 'Lettre d'un officier Genevois', 503, written 1 August 1815. His later account is entirely different. In this, the French are surprised at close range with shots from the hollow road. Having dislodged this (presumably Dutch) infantry at bayonet point, they are themselves charged by new (Scottish) adversaries after they cross the hedge and in the middle of a mêlée he is reorganising the ranks when the cavalry charge. My view is that the earlier letter is more likely to be accurate.
5 Clark in Siborne, *Letters*, nos 35 and 38 got the impression that the French to his left had reached the crest of the ridge and that Kempt's British infantry in front of him

had crossed the hedges in confusion, moving towards him. He allowed that they might be doing so in reforming after a successful charge. De Lacy Evans, Siborne, *Letters*, no. 32 said that 'As to Colonel Gurwood's account of 1,123 sabres, I dare say it is all very right as a return, but the 1,123 sabres were not on the field according to my humble recollection and belief.' Clark (Siborne, *Letters*, no. 39) reckoned their strength at 950–1000 at the highest.

6 Clark in Siborne, *Letters*, no. 37; Styles in Summerville, *Who was Who*, 77 and 368–70.

7 Dessales in *Souvenirs et correspondence*, 53–4.

8 Martin, 'Lettre', 504.

9 Schmitz in Brouwet, 'Quatre Documents', 363; Shelton, in Siborne, *Letters*, no. 150, stated that some Royal Dragoons went round the left of the 28th Foot and and 'passed on to engage a large reserve column which was coming on' still lower down the hill. Ensign Mountsteven in Siborne, *Letters*, no. 151, recalled 'the intense anxiety we felt when we saw some of the gallant, but over-rash fellows, without stopping to form again, ride on headlong at what appeared to me an immensely strong corps of support in perfect order, but which I do not see marked down on the plan. On this column they, of course, made no impression, but suffered some loss, although as far as I could see, a fire was opened upon them by only a small portion of it'; de Lacy Evans in Siborne, *Letters*, nos. 31–3.

10 Wyndham in Siborne, *Letters*, no. 41; Crawford in Glover, *Letters*, 60.

11 Ewart in Glover, *Waterloo Archive*, III, 32–4.

12 There were probably fewer prisoners than the 2000 or more that have been claimed. Vivian spoke to Wellington around 4 a.m. on 19 June, at which point the Duke was under the impression that 1200 Frenchmen had been taken to the rear (Siborne, *Letters*, no. 71).

13 Clark in Siborne, *Letters*, no. 36.

54 The French Counter-attack

1 Elton in Glover, *Waterloo Archive*, IV, 50–1; Hibbert in www.qdg.org.uk/diaries, CARDG: 1985.1199. According to Waymouth, Fuller was killed 'down the slope of our position to the right of La Haye Sainte' (Siborne, *Letters*, no. 21). The presence of lancers in the centre is explained if Ney really had created a central strike force under his own command. Levavasseur thought that they were commanded by General Colbert, of whom there were two, so they may have belonged to the Guard or to Subervie's division.

2 Hasker in Glover, *Waterloo Archive*, I, 20–1.

3 Martin, 'Lettre', 504–5.

4 Canler, *Mémoires*, 21–2. Surprisingly, a sous-lieutenant of the 55th named Labigne really was a victim of Waterloo and Martinien, 246, records him as '*disparu*'. This suggests that Labigne met his end skirmishing in the tall crops, or at the hands of the dragoons, and that Canler kept his bag.

5 Waldie, *Near Observer*, Second edition 1815, xxvi. This sets Ponsonby's death at Hougoumont in the course of a charge against Polish lancers, but the core of the story may still be true; the account by Sergeant Dickson of the Greys, who claimed to have experienced every picturesque incident in the charge, is untrustworthy. Urban in Mauduit, *Derniers jours*, II, 300–1, though Urban's claims look as ambitious as Dickson's.

6 Tomkinson, *Diary*, 136n; Muir, *Tactics*, 117–18.

7 Tomkinson, *Diary*, 301 and 304.

55 The Charge of Sir John Vandeleur's Brigade

1 Berckefeldt in Glover, *Waterloo Archive*, V, 88.
2 Ponsonby account of 10 August 1815 in BL Add Mss 19,590; Bessborough, *Lady Bessborough*, 242.
3 Hay, *Reminiscences*, 184.
4 Mauduit, *Derniers Jours*, II, 307–9.
5 Bessborough, *Lady Bessborough*, 242–3.
6 Frazer, *Letters*, 560.
7 Hope, *Military Memoirs*, 431–2 recalled the rocketeers spending half an hour trying unsuccessfully to break d'Erlon's solid column of support. Schmitz recalled more than 200 rockets being fired at their division, Brouwet, ('Quatre Documents', 363), Heymès (Elchingen, *Documents inédits*, 15, *Waterloo: Récits*, 50) and Mauduit (*Derniers Jours*, II, 299) 300, but the account of expenditure of ammunition recorded fifty-two (BL Add Mss 19,590); Couvreur, 'Des Belges à Waterloo', 26. Ravard in Calvet, *Destins de braves*, 37.

56 Where are the Prussians?

1 'Campaign of Waterloo', 467.
2 Shaw Kennedy, *Notes*, 133. By the same token Shaw found it incredible that Grouchy might have achieved the twenty-mile march from Gembloux to Mont Saint Jean on 18 June.
3 Cotton, *Voice From Waterloo*, 85.
4 Henckel, *Erinnerungen*, 642 (Diary of 19th Regiment). He had at least one squadron of 6th Uhlans under Count Leutrum.
5 Salisch, *Geschichte*, 203.
6 Reiche, as translated in Brett-James, *Hundred Days*, 148.
7 Lieber, *Letters*, 107–8.
8 Ollech, *Feldzuges von 1815*, 207–8.
9 Batty, *Campaign of 1815*, 105, based on information given him by Staveley himself, as Batty says in Glover, *Letters*, 165–6.

57 The Grand Battery Rebuilt

1 Shaw Kennedy, *Notes*, 114.
2 Mudie, 'Operations of the Fifth', 180 and 183; Robertson, *Journal*, 155.
3 O'Neil, *Military Adventures*, 246–51.
4 Kelly, NAM 2002-01-254.
5 Bourdon de Vatry in Grouchy, *Mémoires*, 106.
6 Muir, *Tactics*, 203–4. Tomkinson, *Diary*, 289; Mercer, *Journal*, 138; Wyndham in *Siborne*, Letters, no. 40.
7 See Dessales in *Souvenirs et Correspondence*, 55: 'I had not moved from the forward position in which I received that charge.'
8 Pétiet, *Souvenirs Militaires*, 218; Mauduit, *Derniers Jours*, II, 326; Houssaye, *1815: Waterloo*, 364–5.
9 Glover, *Waterloo Archive*, II, 71.
10 Shaw Kennedy, *Notes*, 113; Alten letter of 20 June cited by Houssaye, *1815: Waterloo*, 364.
11 Lawrence, *Autobiography*, 206–7.
12 Muir, *Tactics*, 201–2; Morris, *Memoir*, 105.
13 Dalton, *Roll Call*, 94; the Lüneberg battalion journal recorded on 16 June that

'Lieutenant Duwe, who became ill during the march, could not take part in the encounter' and on 17 June that 'Lieutenant Stegmann, who felt unwell, went to the hospital in Antwerp' (1815 Limited On-line Archive). Best in Glover, *Waterloo Archive*, II, 120–11, reported that Captains Siegner and Ostvald of the Verden battalion, Lieutenant Kuhlmann of the Munden battalion, Captains Jormin and Schneider of the Lüneberg battalion and Captain von Rauschenplatt of the Osterode battalion, went sick on or after 16 June and retired to Antwerp.

14 Woodberry, *Journal*, 317.
15 WO 71/242 161 and 164. Charles Hames found less support than Henry Ross-Lewin.
16 Reports of Hanoverian army and Bremen battalion in Glover, *Waterloo Archive*, II, 17 and 105.
17 Weiz in Glover, *Waterloo Archive*, II, 184. This was probably Sinclair's battery.
18 Wheatley *Diary*, 65.
19 Macready, 'Journals', 524; Wheatley, *Diary*, 65.
20 They may have fled earlier; see Meier in Glover, *Waterloo Archive*, V, 15–16; Seymour in Siborne, *Letters*, no. 9. Colonel von Hake faced a court martial in Hanover in 1816 and was cashiered, his second-in-command severely reprimanded.
21 Wellington to Samuel Rogers in Delancey, *Week at Waterloo*, 14 and note on p. 109.

58 Sauve Qui Peut!

1 Carey, 'Commissariat officer', 730–1.
2 Glover, *Waterloo Archive*, II, 120–1; the evacuation of Mont Saint-Jean farm by the British is vividly described in Simmons, *British Rifle Man*, 367 and 375.
3 Creevey, *Creevey Papers*, I, 232.
4 Waldie, *Near Observer*, 1815 edition, xiv.
5 Elizabeth Ord in Glover, *Waterloo Archive*, I 228.
6 Heeley, 'Journal', 114.
7 Creevey, *Creevey Papers*, I, 233–4.

59 Napoleon Prepares a Second Assault

1 Bourdon de Vatry in Grouchy, *Mémoires*, 108 : 'Le comte de Lobau, commandant la droite à Waterloo, fit dire à l'Empéreur qu'il était attaqué par les Prussiens. Napoléon ne voulut pas admettre d'abord que la chose fût possible'; Combes-Brassard in *Souvenirs et correspondance*, 19–20: 'Le 6e corps, formant la réserve ... marcha pour soutenir l'attaque de la droite'; Janin, *Campagne de Waterloo*, 35; cp. Barbero, *The Battle*, 144–5.
2 Best in Glover, *Waterloo Archive*, II, 120.
3 Glover, *Waterloo Archive*, II, 161, 167–8.
4 Adkin, *Waterloo Companion*, 264.
5 Clay, 'Adventures at Hougoumont', 222.
6 Leonhard in Glover, *Waterloo Archive*, II, 159.
7 Adair, 'Coldstream Guards', 30–1.
8 Seymour in Siborne, *Letters*, no. 9.
9 Gow, '3rd Guards', 42. Miller, *Ball*, 42. A friend afterwards followed Forbes's instruction to return what was left of the miniature.
10 Brouwet, 'Quatre documens', 363.
11 Alten's report, *WSD*, X, 534; Brinckmann in 1815 Limited On-line Archive.
12 Lindau, *Waterloo Hero*, 189–90.

13 Simon Bernard as reported by Prince Bernhard in Franklin, *Netherlands Correspondance*, 97–8; Ollech, *Feldzug von 1815*, 226.

60 Milhaud's Charge

1 *Bulletin de l'Armée* printed in *Moniteur* 21 June 1815, reprinted in *Morning Post*, 27 June 1815, 'Important French Papers'. See Houssaye, *1815: Waterloo*, 366. Captain Fortuné de Brack of the Guard lancers claimed that it was his fault that the Guard charged after the cuirassiers (*Waterloo: récits de combattants*, 14–15), a story given by Mauduit (*Derniers jours*, II, 346-8) and repeated most recently by Andrew Roberts (*Waterloo: Napoleon's Last Gamble*, 76).

2 Petty, *First Napoleon*, 126.

3 Field, *French Perspective*, 138.

4 Shaw Kennedy, *Notes*, 114–16; Gronow, *Reminiscences*, 129.

5 Wheatley, *Diary*, 62–6; Linsingen in Glover, *Letters*, 254–5.

6 Scriba in Glover, *Waterloo Archive*, II, 105–7.

7 Lot, *Ordener*, 94. Arentschildt in Glover, *Waterloo Archive*, II, 39.

8 Göben in Glover, *Letters*, 126, and 1815 Limited On-line Archive; reports Glover, *Waterloo Archive*, II, 24 and 39. This may well be the episode described by Chevalier, *Souvenirs*, 323.

9 Weiz in Glover, *Waterloo Archive*, II, 184–5; Morris, *Memoir*, 78; Crumplin, *Guthrie's War*, 150.

10 Dalton, *Roll Call*, 17–18; Somerset in Siborne, *Letters*, no. 18; Thornhill in Siborne, *Letters*, no. 8.

11 Wheatley, *Diary*, 67; Beamish, *King's German Legion*, 359. Rifleman John Milius was awarded the Guelphic Medal.

12 Hamilton, NAM 2002-02-1352.

13 Wellington to Mulgrave, 21 December 1815 in *WSD*, XIV, 618–20, cited Muir, *Tactics*, 44–5.

14 Frazer, *Letters*, 558–9.

15 Bull in Siborne, *Letters*, no. 78.

16 Captain Thackwell in Siborne, *Letters*, no. 62; see also Wylly, *Thackwell*, 71.

61 Lobau and the Prussians

1 Janin, *Campagne de Waterloo*, 35.

2 Dörk, *15tes Infanterie*, 129, whose account conflicts with Houssaye's assertion that the wood was clear of Frenchmen. It would appear that there were a few, right at the edge. Marbot claimed to have been told to place 200 infantry at the edge of the wood and the cavalry was probably his (Marbot, *Mémoires*, II, 405).

3 Damitz, *Geschichte des Feldzuges von 1815*, 290.

4 Ollech, *Feldzug von 1815*, 242–3.

5 Wedell, *18.Infanterie-Regiments*, 165.

6 Dupuy, *Souvenirs*, 290.

7 Ollech, *Feldzug von 1815*, 242, citing Chesney on Wellington's reliance on Blücher's support.

62 The Great Cavalry Charges

1 Dörnberg in Glover, *Waterloo Archive*, II, 29; Hellemann in 1815 Limited On-line Archive.

2 Barnett, NAM 1991-06-31; Hamilton, NAM 2002-02-1352.

3 Keppel, *Fifty Years*, 149–50.
4 Jeremiah in Glover, *Waterloo Archive*, IV, 189.
5 Wheeler, *Letters*, 172–3.
6 Lemonnier-Delafosse, *Campagnes*, 395–6; Foy, *Vie militaire*, 281.
7 Mercer, *Journal*, 168–9. Keppel, *Fifty Years*, 151.
8 Mercer, *Journal*, 169–70.
9 Mercer, *Journal*, 170.
10 Walcott in Siborne, *Letters*, no. 80.
11 Latimer, *Talks of Napoleon*, 186–7.
12 Guyot, *Carnets de Campagnes*, 396.
13 Létang in Field, *French Perspective*, 148.
14 Lot, *Ordener*, 94.
15 Macready, 'Journals', 526.
16 Pringle, 'Remarks', cxxviii n.
17 Field, *French Perspective*, 149.
18 'Campaign of Waterloo', 468; Macready, 'Journals', 527; Wheatley, *Diary*, 67.

63 The Fall of La Haye Sainte

1 Shaw Kennedy, *Notes*, 122–3, commented, 'This matter had certainly been grossly mismanaged. The arrangement for the brigades getting their spare ammunition was, that each brigade should communicate with the guard over the ammunition, and order forward what was wanted. How the brigade failed to do this has not been explained, as so many of its superior officers fell in action. Baring could not account for it, which I know from our having slept together on the ground close to the Wellington Tree on the night of the action … The spare ammunition should have been sent for early in the morning. What were 60 rounds per man for the defence of such a post?' Other Hanoverian units also suffered shortages.
2 Glover, *Waterloo Archive*, II, 175 and 195; Ross-Lewin, *With the thirty-second*, 274–5.
3 Glover, *Waterloo Archive*, II, 81–2.
4 Mauduit, *Derniers Jours*, II, 334; Houssaye, *1815: Waterloo*, 390, who also cites dossier of *chef de bataillon* Borel-Vivier of 1er régiment du génie.
5 Lindau, *Waterloo Hero*, 168–75; Bäring in Glover, *Waterloo Letters*, 244–8; Graeme in Siborne, *Letters*, nos. 179–80.
6 Cathcart in Siborne, *Letters*, no. 15.
7 'Campaign of Waterloo', 465.
8 Linsingen in Glover, *Letters*, 253–4; 5th Line report in Glover, *Waterloo Archive*, II, 89–90; von Ompteda, *Memoirs*, 311–13; Wheatley, *Diary*, 69–70.

64 Guns and Horses

1 Wellington's dispatch gave no time for the fall of La Haye Sainte. In a letter of 17 August 1815 he said that the farm fell at 'about two o'clock' through the 'neglect of the officer commanding on the spot' (*WD*, XII, 610). Gourgaud (*Campagne*, 93) timed its fall before 4.30. Most accounts place the time of the fall between 5.30 and 6.30.
2 Pontécoulant, *Napoléon à Waterloo*, 315–6.
3 Weiz in Glover, *Waterloo Archive*, II, 186–9.
4 Macready, 'Siborne's History', 395; Morris, *Memoirs*, 78.
5 Morris, *Memoirs*, 78; Macready, 'Journals', 526.
6 Bäring in Glover, *Letters*, 247; Buhse in Glover, *Letters*, 239.

7 'Campaign of Waterloo', 469; Haythornthwaite, *Waterloo Men*, 87–8.
8 Kincaid, *Adventures*, 351–2.
9 Sergeant Charles Wood letter of July 1815 in *United Service Journal*, 1834 part 2, 555–6.
10 *A Soldier of the Seventy-first*, 108.
11 Dehnel in Glover, *Waterloo Archive*, V, 32–3.
12 Lewis in Glover, *Waterloo Archive*, I, 159.
13 *Soldier of the Seventy-first*, 108; Barnett, NAM 1991-06-31.
14 Pringle, 'Remarks', cxxxi; Müffling, *History*, 32.

65 The Prussian Advance

1 There is a good description by Major Taylor of the 10th Hussars of the shape of the Prussian advance in Siborne, *Letters*, no. 75.
2 Wüssow in von Ollech, *Feldzuges von 1815*, 195; Houssaye, *1815: Waterloo*, 381.
3 Reiche, *Memoiren*, 210–13, translation from Brett-James, *Hundred Days*, 148–50; Von Ollech, *Feldzuges von 1815*, 243–4.
4 Hornn, *Narrative*, 55–6; Pelet in d'Avout, 'Infanterie', 38–9.
5 Mauduit, *Derniers jours*, II, 390.
6 Rahden, *Wanderungen*, 365–6; Tromelin in Field, *French Perspective*, 164.
7 Damitz, *Geschichte des Feldzuges von 1815*, 296.
8 Macbride, *With Napoleon at Waterloo*, 184.

66 Slowly but Surely

1 Heymès in *Documents inédits*, 18, and *Waterloo: Récits de combattants*, 52; Houssaye, *1815: Waterloo*, 393.
2 Thackwell in Siborne, *Letters*, 68. From Thackwell's own account it looks as though he fell in the same desperate charge as Major Griffith, and not, as his biographer has it, charging the Guard; Siborne, *Letters*, no. 67, nos 62 and 63.
3 Girod de l'Ain, *Vie militaire*, 282; Lemonnier-Delafosse, *Campagnes*, 384; Trefcon, *Carnet de campagne*, 90–1.
4 Major Göben, commanding the 1st KGL line, confirmed to Siborne on a plan that this was the sheltered ground Foy meant.
5 Tomkinson, *Diary*, 306; Frazer, *Letters*, 548.
6 Gibney, *Eighty Years Ago*, 197–8.
7 James, *Journal*, 35.
8 Somerset in Siborne, *Letters*, no. 18; in this charge Joseph Lord's brother John was killed (Glover, *Waterloo Archive*, I, 17).
9 Morris, *Memoirs*, 80.
10 Macready, 'Siborne's History', 400–1; Morris, *Memoirs*, 80.
11 Glover, *Waterloo Archive*, II, 96–7, 112, 114, 115–18 and V, 63 and 137. See also Scovell in Glover, *Waterloo Archive*, III, 3.
12 Alten's report: 'The squares by this time had been so much reduced by the continued fire of cannon, musketry, and ultimately grape shot of the enemy, that they had hardly men enough left to remain in squares, and therefore were withdrawn from the position by Count Kielmansegge; and the remains of the Legion and Hanoverian brigades and part of the British brigade reformed on the high road in rear of the village of Mont St. Jean.' WSD, X, 534.
13 Shaw Kennedy, *Notes*, 127–8. In reality Halkett's brigade had also vacated its ground and Shaw doubtless told Wellington that too. Owen, *Waterloo Papers*, 13.
14 Bridgeman, *Young Gentleman at War*, 179; Lemonnier-Delafosse, *Campagnes*, 373.

15 Ord in Glover, *Waterloo Archive*, I, 228.
16 Tomkinson, *Diary*, 315; Hume in Glover, *Waterloo Archive*, I, 216–7; Wellington's 19 June letter to Aberdeen in Pitt-Lennox, 121; he died about 3 a.m. next day.
17 Glover, *Waterloo Archive*, III, 3 and II, 115.
18 Bäring in Glover, *Letters*, 247.
19 Lawrence, *Autobiography*, 210.
20 Lawrence, *Autobiography*, 210–11; Wray in Keegan, *Face of Battle*, 160–1 and 1815 Limited On-line Archive.
21 Robertson, *Journal*, 157.
22 Patton in Glover, *Waterloo Archive*, I, 177.

67 Ziethen Attacks

1 Glover, *Waterloo Archive*, II, 168.
2 Reiche, *Memoiren*, 214–15.
3 Reichenau and Rettberg in Glover, *Waterloo Archive*, II, 159–62.
4 Ingilby, *Waterloo Diary*, 57–8.
5 Drouot's report to the Chamber of Deputies, translated in Waldie, *Near Observer* 1817, II, 112–13.
6 Gourgaud (*Campagne*, 99) later wrote that 'At half past seven we could at last hear the cannonade of Marshal Grouchy; it was judged to be six miles distant to our right'; it is most unlikely that anybody on the battlefield of Waterloo could have heard a cannonade six miles away, but the noise of which Drouot spoke was evidently closer: the noise of Grouchy six miles away would hardly have caused Napoleon to unleash the Guard in the belief that the battle was won.
7 Hornn, *Narrative*, 56.

68 Plancenoit

1 Von Hiller's account in Ollech, *Feldzuges von 1815*, 248–9; Dörk, *15tes Infanterie*, 129–30; Damitz, *Geschichte des Feldzuges von 1815*, 298; Houssaye, *1815: Waterloo*, 380–2. Authorities differ on when and where the Young Guard was committed but it is unlikely that the first Prussian attack could have had any success if the Young Guard was already present at Plancenoit in force.
2 Rahden, *Wanderungen*, 367–73.
3 Pelet in d'Avout, 'Infanterie', 43.
4 Marchand, *Mémoires*, 222–3.
5 Marchand, *Mémoires*, 223–4; Combier, *General Radet*, 342–3; Fleury de Chaboulon, *Mémoires*, 190–1.
6 Duuring in d'Avout, 'Documents', 116–19; Canler, *Mémoires*, 28; Combier, *General Radet*, 342–3.

69 The Last Reserves

1 Greenock in Siborne, *Letters*, no. 7; *Capel Letters*, 116; Seymour in Siborne, *Letters*, no. 9; Hume in Glover, *Waterloo Archive*, I, 213–14; Glover, *Waterloo Archive*, III, 5.
2 Blair and Colborne in Siborne, *Letters*, nos 122–3; Frazer, *Letters*, 552; Girod de l'Ain, *Vie militaire*, 281.
3 Nixon in Glover, *Waterloo Archive*, I, 135 said that the following day the second battalion mustered 340 men.
4 The account of the Guard's deployment is based on Petit in d'Avout, 'Documents', 107–10. His account is followed by Houssaye, *1815: Waterloo*, 409–10; Friant, *Vie*

militaire, 388–90; Mauduit, II, 397–8. The only variation concerns the 4th Chasseurs, who some give two battalions and others one and who Petit places in the centre, but others on the left. The highest officer casualties were suffered by the 3rd Chasseurs, so they may have borne the brunt of Colborne's flank attack, although it is also possible that the Netherlands artillery caused most casualties.

5   Herzberg's 'detailed report' on the Brunswick contingent in Glover, *Waterloo Archive*, V, 160; Scovell in Glover, *Waterloo Archive*, III, 2–3; Macready, 'Siborne's History', 401.

6   Ingilby, 'Waterloo diary', 58; Murray in Siborne, *Letters*, no. 76.

7   Vivian in Siborne, *Letters*, no. 70.

8   Sleigh in Siborne, *Letters*, no. 53, Barton in Siborne, *Letters*, no. 58.

9   Bullock, 'Journal', 550. See also Taylor in Siborne, *Letters*, no. 75, 'they rather fell back upon us'; and George Luard, 18th Hussars: 'We were brought from the left of the line to support our infantry on the right who at that moment were excessively pressed and rather losing ground. Our appearance rallied them . . .' Glover, *Waterloo Archive*, I, 93.

10 Glover, *Waterloo Archive*, II, 97, 109–10 ; van Delen in Franklin, *Netherlands Correspondence*, 125.

70 La Garde Recule

1   Mercer, *Journal*, 180.

2   Macready, 'Siborne's History', 401. Elsewhere, Macready insists that their main opponents to their front wore blue greatcoats and belonged to the Guard, though he also gives them bearskins which the Middle Guard did not wear. The timing of this part of the action is very uncertain, but it would seem that if Halkett's brigade did face Imperial Guardsmen they ran away from them. Billarderie, ADC to Napoleon says infantry fought in grey greatcoats, Guard in blue, and reckons they fought in trousers of same colour.

3   Taylor in Siborne, *Letters*, no. 75.

4   Courts martial of Charles Hames and Henry Ross Lewin, NA WO 71/242 161 and 164; Officer of the 95th in Waldie, *Near Observer*, 54–5.

5   Martin, *Souvenirs*, 296–7.

6   Swinburne in Glover, *Letters*, 165, who says there was a call for skirmishers and he went out; Maitland, Saltoun, Powell, Dirom in Siborne, *Letters*, nos. 105, 106, 109, 111. Nixon in Glover, *Waterloo Archive*, I, 135 mentions a Dutch brigade that charged with the Guards.

7   D'Avout, 'Infanterie de la Garde', says that from 16 to 18 June the 3rd and 4th Chasseurs lost 1141 out of 2168 in killed, wounded and prisoners, according to figures after the other 'missing' had rejoined.

8   Houssaye, *1815: Waterloo*, 418n.

71 Right Ahead, To Be Sure

1   Robertson, *Journal*, 158–9.

2   Smith; *Autobiography*, 272; Morris, *Memoirs*, 80; Kruse in Glover, *Waterloo Archive*, V, 137.

3   Vivian in Siborne, *Letters*, no. 70; Taylor in Siborne, *Letters*, no. 75; George Luard in Glover, *Waterloo Archive*, I, 93.

4   Bäring in Lindau, *Waterloo Hero*, 197.

5   Ingilby, 'Waterloo Diary', 58.

6 Pelet, Guillemin and Christiani in d'Avout, 'Documents', 109–10, 113, 114.

7 Captain Barton in Siborne, *Letters*, no. 58.

8 Rigau in Field, *French Perspective*, 222.

9 Rullière, in Largeaud, *Napoléon et Waterloo*, 377–8. Much of Rullière's account is open to doubt but his part in saving the eagle of the 95th is supported by a tribute in his army record, SHD Dossier Rullière, G.D. 2e Série 1135. Chapuis, *Waterloo*, 50.

10 Franklin, *Netherlands Correspondence*, 148–9.

11 Pelet in d'Avout, 'Infanterie de la Garde', 51–2; Tromelin in Field, *French Perspective*, 212 and 223.

12 Maitland and Reed in Siborne, *Letters*, nos. 105 and 126.

13 Wellington later said cattily and incorrectly that this was almost all the French Blücher knew. Gneisenau's official report stated that Blücher met Wellington by chance at La Belle Alliance and used it as a reason to name the battle after the ale-house farm. For this reason, in 1816 the Duke denied emphatically that any meeting had taken place there and said that he visited Blücher's headquarters at Genappe after 10 p.m. (*WSD*, X, 509 in a letter to William Mudford of 8 June 1816). This was not true: his aide Felton Hervey wrote on 3 July that he and the Duke went no fur-ther south along the Charleroi road than the village of Maison du Roi, before turning back for Waterloo which they reached between 11 p.m. and midnight. Wellington later told his biographer that he and Blücher met at Maison du Roi, and another aide said that Wellington rode back with Blücher as far as La Belle Alliance, confirming Jackson's story (Williams-Wynne, *Diaries of a Lady of Quality*, 293). Müffling, who rode with the Prussian pursuit as far as Genappe, reported to Wellington at Waterloo on his return after midnight. Both the Russian representa-tive Pozzo di Borgo and the Austrian Baron Vincent stated in their reports that Wellington and Blücher met at La Belle Alliance (Waldie, *Near Observer*, 1817, 208 and 214). *WSD*, X, 506. The scene forms a big set-piece in von Ollech, *Feldzuges von 1815*, 252 where Grolmann leads Ziethen's men via Papelotte to La Belle Alliance, Gneisenau and Blücher ride there from Plancenoit, Röder's cavalry appears and they all sing Luther's hymn. Von Reiche stated that the meeting took place there although he implies that Ziethen, Röder and Gneisenau were elsewhere.

14 Gronow, *Reminiscences*, 138; Jackson, *Notes and Reminiscences*, 57–8.

72 The Pursuit

1 John Luard in Siborne, *Letters*, no. 61; Vivian in Siborne, *Letters*, no. 72.

2 Christiani in d'Avout, 'Documents', 111–13.

3 Canler, *Mémoires*, 298; Martin, *Souvenirs*, 298–301; Lindau, *Waterloo Hero*, 174–9; Wheatley, *Diary*, 74–7.

4 Hornn recovered. The entrepreneur William Bullock brought him to England, along with Napoleon's coach and he was a fixture at Bullock's Museum and wrote his memoirs.

5 Hornn, *Narrative*, 57–8; Houssaye, *1815: Waterloo*, 440–1.

6 Duuring in d'Avout, 'Documents', 116–9.

7 Marchand, *Mémoires*, 224; Fleury de Chaboulon, *Mémoires*, 192. Dörk (142) and von Keller ('Description of the … Carriage', 13) variously site the capture of the head-quarters convoy at Quatre Bras, Villers and Mellet. The quotations are from Fleury de Chaboulon.

8 It sounds ironic, but the inn had this name long before the advent of Napoleon.

9 Mach, *Geschichte*, 342.

10 Reiche, *Memoiren*, 216–17.
11 Houssaye, *1815: Waterloo*, 434; *Spectateur Militaire*, III, 1827, 666–7; Nostitz, 'Tagebuch', 44.
12 Brett-James, *Hundred Days*, 184.

73 Victory! Victory!

1 Longford, *Years of the Sword*, 485.
2 Thornton, *Cook*, 49; Longford, *Years of the Sword*, 485. At least Felton Hervey, Percy, Arthur Hill (another aide), Pozzo di Bogo and Vincent had shared the night ride.
3 Delancey, *Week at Waterloo*, 116; Pitt-Lennox, *Three Years*, 217–18; Frazer, *Letters*, 560.
4 *WSD*, X, 531.
5 Amabel Yorke, Lady Lucas, diaries, XXX, 132–3.
6 *Morning Post*, 24 June 1815.
7 *WSD*, X, 506.
8 *Morning Post*, 24 June 1815.
9 Amabel Yorke, Lady Lucas, diaries, XXX, 135.

74 Butcher's Bill

1 Creevey, *Creevey Papers*, 236.
2 Brett-James, *Hundred Days*, 183; Bäring in Lindau, *Waterloo Hero*, 198.
3 James, *Journal*, 35–6.
4 Barbero, *The Battle*, 419; Adkin, *Waterloo Companion*, 73. See *WD*, XII, 485; Muir, *Tactics*, 263.
5 Barbero, *The Battle*, 420. Wellington reported having 5000 prisoners with 2000 more coming and the Admiralty was asked to provide ships for 7000 prisoners.
6 Barbero, *The Battle*, 420–1.
7 Identity unknown in Glover, *Waterloo Archive*, I, 31; Morris, *Memoirs*, 82.
8 Bessborough, *Lady Bessborough*, 242–3.
9 Hasker, in Glover, *Waterloo Archive*, I, 19; Hibbert in www.qdg.org.uk/diaries CARDG:1988.1764; Farmer, in *United Service Magazine*, 1842, part 1, 529–36 and part 2, 550–3.
10 Hibbert in www.qdg.org.uk/diaries CARDG:1988.1764.
11 Hasker in Glover, *Waterloo Archive*, I, 19; Ingilby, 'Waterloo Diary', 58.
12 Robertson, *Journal*, 160–2.
13 Officer of rifles in Waldie, *Near Observer*, 55
14 Gronow, *Reminiscences*, 132.
15 Mainwaring, 'Four Years', 410.
16 Smith, *Autobiography*, 275–6.

75 Wives

1 Smith, *Autobiography*, 281–4.
2 Waldie, *Narrative*, 124ff.
3 Delancey, *Week at Waterloo*, 62.
4 Smith, *Autobiography*, 286–7.
5 Delancey, *Week at Waterloo*, 63–99.

76 What Misery War Causes

1 Brett-James, *Hundred Days*, 196; Costello, *Campaigns*, 154.

2 Gibney, *Eighty Years Ago*, 206–7 and 209.

3 Glover, *Waterloo Archive*, III, 217.

4 Glover, *Waterloo Archive*, III, 222.

5 Burney, *Diary and Letters*, VI, 240.

6 Blackadder in Glover, *Waterloo Archive*, IV, 239.

7 Hennen, *Principles of Military Surgery*, 236n.

8 Larrey, *Memoir*, 229–32.

9 Bell, *Letters*, 227; Blackadder in Glover, *Waterloo Archive*, IV, 239–40. The case is also described in Hennen, *Principles of Military Surgery*, 289–92.

10 Hennen, *Principles of Military Surgery*, 236–7 n.

11 Crumplin, *Guthrie's War*. Cp Gibney, *Eighty Years Ago*, 209.

Epilogue: The Hardest Battle that Ever Was Fought

1 Gibney, *Eighty Years Ago*, 223–4.

2 Hibbert, letter of 26 July to his father in www.qdg.org.uk/diaries, CARDG:1985.1199.

3 Wheeler, *Letters*, 176–7.

4 Wheeler, *Letters*, 177.

5 James Hamilton in NAM 2002-02-1352.

6 William Nicolay in NAM 1989-03-48.

7 Morris, *Memoir*, 93–4, 97.

8 Fremantle, *Wellington's Voice*, 215.

9 Smith, *Autobiography*, 276.

10 Finlayson in Glover, *Waterloo Archive*, III, 216; Arthur Shakespeare, letter of 23 June 1815 in NAM 1977-06-17; Tennant in Glover, *Waterloo Archive*, III, 94.

11 Lean, *Napoleonists*, 106–11; Duncan Wu, *William Hazlitt, the first modern man*, Oxford: OUP, 2008, 180; cp. Ian Bruce, *Lavallette Bruce*, London: Hamish Hamilton, 1953, 117–19 and 124–5.

12 Logie, *Waterloo*, 186.

13 Newman Smith, *Flying Sketches*, 34–6.

14 Glover, *Waterloo Archive*, III, 15–16.

15 Waldie, *Residence in Belgium*, 256. This was 15 July.

16 Waldie, *Residence in Belgium*, 270–1.

17 Waldie, *Residence in Belgium*, 296–7.

18 Simon Bainbridge, *Napoleon and English Romanticism*, Cambridge: CUP, 1995, 153.

19 *Journal of a Tour to the Netherlands*, quoted in Bainbridge, *Napoleon and English Romanticism*, 156; Scott, *Paris Revisited*, 39–40.

20 *Byron's Letters and Journals*, V, 76.

21 Gore, *Historical Account*, 89. This is a different Arthur Gore from the lieutenant of the 33rd, killed at Quatre Bras.

22 See Ian Bruce, *Lavallette Bruce*, London: Hamish Hamilton, 1953, 144–245. Bruce obtained the aid of Sir Robert Wilson and Captain John Hely-Hutchinson and they got Lavallette out of Paris disguised as an English officer.

23 Wood family documents, East Sussex Record Office AMS 6297. Wood, a fluent French speaker, made a fortune in the service of Sir Charles Stuart, but it is more likely that his wealth derived from smuggling items across the Channel in the diplomatic bag, for which he became notorious, than delivering a bribe to Grouchy.

24 BM 1989,1104.38 by Louis Charon, announced in the *Bibliographie de France* on 2 September 1815.
25 Heuillet in d'Avout, 'Documents', 121–2.
26 Houssaye, *1815: Waterloo*, 418.

BIBLIOGRAPHY

Unpublished sources
Leeds, West Yorkshire Archive Service
Diary of Amabel Yorke of Studley Royal (in 1815 Lady Lucas)

London, British Library
Add Mss 34703-08, Siborne correspondence
Add Mss 30147A, Colonel Forbin-Janson's account of the campaign, dated
    London December 1817
Add Mss 19590, Papers relating to the battle of Waterloo including details of
    the expenditure of ammunition by the various artillery batteries, a letter
    from Wellington to William Mudford and accounts by John Hume the
    surgeon and Frederick Ponsonby.
Add Mss 57635, ff. 3–4, survey of the battlefield by Lt Col James Carmichael-
    Smyth
Add Mss 63585, A-C Carte de Belgique used by Soult

London, National Army Museum
6807/137 surveys made by Brains, Dumaresq and Staveley in May 1815
1991-06-31 Jack Barnett
1995-01-118 Samuel Boulter
1992-12-138 James Gubbins
2002-02-1352 James Hamilton
1981-11-84 John Hart
1984-09-98 Edward Heeley
2002-01-254 Edward Kelly
1989-03-48 William Nicolay
1977-06-17 Arthur Shakespeare
1999-06-149 William Staveley
1981-12-53-557 Thomas Wildman

London, The National Archives
WO 71241-5 Courts Martial 1815–16

University of Southampton, Hartley Library
Wellington papers

Private collection

Angus McDonald to his father, Antwerp, 20 June 1815,

Books and articles

Aaron, Martin, '2nd Battalion 69th (South Lincolnshire) Foot during the Waterloo Campaign', Napoleon Series

Abbott, P.E., 'A Waterloo letter: the Royal Artillery and its casualties', *Journal of the Society for Army Historical Research*, 42 (1964), pp. 113–20

Adair, P.R., 'The Coldstream Guards at Waterloo', *The Household Brigade Magazine* (1965), pp. 24–31

Adkin, Mark, *The Waterloo Companion*, London: Aurum, 2001

Aerts, Winand, *Waterloo; opérations de l'armée prussienne du Bas Rhin pendant la campagne de Belgique en 1815 depuis la bataille de Ligny jusqu'à l'entrée en France des troupes prussiennes*, Bruxelles: Lib. Militaire Spineux et Cie, 1908

Ammon, Friedrich von and Theodor Herold, *Das Leben Dr Christian Samuel Gottlieb Ludwig Nagel's*, Cleve: F. Char, 1829

Anglesey, Marquess of and Hodge, F.R., 'Correspondence concerning the death of major Hodge 7th hussars, at Genappe 17 june 1815'. in *Journal of the Society for Army Historical Research*, 43 (1965), pp. 80–92

Anton, James, *Retrospect of a Military Life*, Edinburgh, 1841

Avout, Vicomte A. d', 'La cavalerie de la garde à Waterloo', *Carnet de la sabre-tache* (1901), pp. 360–73

Avout, Vicomte A. d', 'L'infanterie de la garde à Waterloo', *Carnet de la sabre-tache* (1905), pp. 33–54 and 107–28

Bagensky, Carl von, *Geschichte des 9ten Infanterie-Regiments genannt Colbergsches*, Colberg: Post, 1842

Baldet, Marcel, *La Vie Quotidienne dans les Armées de Napoléon*, Paris: Hachette, 1964

Barbero, Alessandro, *The Battle: a New History of Waterloo*, trans. John Cullen, London: Atlantic, 2005

Barral, Georges, *L'épopée de Waterloo: narration nouvelle des cent jours et de la campagne en Belgique de 1815*, Paris: Flammarion, 1895

Barral, Georges, *Itinéraire illustré de l'épopée de Waterloo*, Paris: Flammarion, 1896

De Bas, F., and Augustin de Wommersen, *La Campagne de 1815 aux Bays Bas d'après les rapports officials néerlandais*, 3 vols, Brussels, 1908

Batty, Robert, *An Historical Sketch of the Campaign of 1815*, Second edition, London: Rodwell & Martin, 1820

Baudus, Marie Elie Guillaume, *Etudes sur Napoléon*, Paris: Debécourt, 1841

Beamish, North Ludlow, *History of the King's German Legion*, 2 vols, London: Thomas and William Boone, 1837

Beauchamp, Alphonse de, *An Authentic Narrative of the Campaign of 1815, comprising a circumstantial detail of the Battle of Waterloo*, London: Henry Colburn, 1815

Becke, Archibald Frank, *Napoleon and Waterloo: The emperor's campaign with the*

Armée du nord 1815. A strategical and tactical study, London: Routledge Kegan Paul Ltd, 1914

Bell, Charles, *Letters of Sir Charles Bell*, London: John Murray, 1870

Bertaud, Jean-Paul, 'Le regard des Français sur les Anglais, des Révolutionnaires de l'An II au « Jacobin Botté »', in Bertaud, Alan Forrest and Annie Jourdan, *Napoléon, le Monde et les Anglais: Guerre de mots et des images*, Paris: Éditions Autrement, 2004

Bertaud, Jean-Paul, *Quand les Enfants parlaient de Gloire: l'Armée au Coeur de la France de Napoléon*, Paris: Flammarion, 2006

Berthaut, Henri Marie Auguste, *Les ingénieurs géographes militaires, 1624–1831*, 2 vols, Paris : Imprimerie du Service géographique, 1902

Berthezène, Pierre, *Souvenirs Militaires de la République et de l'Empire*, II, Paris: J. Dumaine, 1855

Berton, Jean-Baptiste, *Précis historique, militaire et critique des batailles de Fleurus et Waterloo en 1815*, Paris, 1818

Bessborough, Vere Brabazon Ponsonby, 9th Earl of (ed.), *Lady Bessborough and her Family Circle*, London: John Murray, 1940

Bickert, Hans Günther, 'Der Aufstands-Dörnberg: zu seiner Rolle im Widerstand gegen Jérôme Bonaparte vor 200 Jahren', *Zeitschrift des Vereins für hessische Geschichte*, 114 (2009), pp. 177–98

Biot, Hubert-François, *Souvenirs anecdotiques et militaires du colonel Biot, aide de camp du général Pajol campagnes et garnisons*, Paris: H. Vivien, 1901

Bonaparte, Jérôme, *Mémoires et correspondence du roi Jérôme et de la reine Catherine*, VII, Paris: E. Dentu, 1866

Bonaparte, Napoleon, *Historical Memoirs of Napoleon, translated from the original Manuscript by B. E. O'Meara*, Philadelphia: Almon Ticknor, 1820

Bonaparte, Napoleon, *Mémoires pour servir à l'histoire de France sous la règne de Napoléon*, Second edition, vol. IX, Paris: Bossange père and Dufour et Cie, 1830

Bourgeois, René [or François Thomas Delbarre], *Relation fidèle et détaillée de la dernière campagne de Buonaparte*, Paris: Dentu, 1815

Bowden, Scott, *Armies at Waterloo*, Arlington: Empire Games, 1983

Brett-James, Antony, *The Hundred Days: Napoleon's Last Campaign from Eyewitness Accounts*, London, 1964

Bridgeman, Orlando, *A Young Gentleman at War*, ed. Gareth Glover, Godmanchester: Ken Trotman, 2008

Bro, Louis, *Mémoires, 1796–1844*, Paris: Plon, 1914

Brouwet, Emile, 'Quatre documents inédits sur la campagne de 1815', *Revue des études Napoleoniennes* (1932), pp. 360–5

Busse, Max Rudolph von, *Geschichte des königlichen Preussischen dreiundzwanzigsten Infanterie-Regiments*, Görlitz: Remer, 1859

Cadell, Charles, *Narrative of the Campaigns of the Twenty-eight Regiment Since their Return from Egypt in 1802*, London: Whittaker, 1835

Calvet, Stéphane, *Destins de braves: les officiers charentais de Napoléon au XIXe siècle*, Avignon: Université d'Avignon, 2010

'The Campaign of Waterloo Strategically examined', *United Service Journal*, 69 (August 1834), pp. 444–78

Canler, Louis, *Mémoires de Canler*, Paris: F. Roy, 1882

Capel, Caroline Paget Lady, *The Capel Letters: being the correspondence of Lady Caroline Capel and her daughters with the Dowager Countess of Uxbridge from Brussels and Switzerland, 1814–1817*, London: Jonathan Cape, 1955

Carey, Tupper, 'Reminiscences of a commissariat officer', *The Cornhill Magazine*, New series 6 (1899), pp. 724–38

Chandler, David, *Waterloo: the Hundred Days*, London: Osprey, 1980

Chapuis, François Claude, *Waterloo: Notice sur le 85e de ligne pendant la campagne de 1815*, Paris, 1863

Charras, Jean-Baptiste, *Histoire de la Campagne de 1815: Waterloo*, Brussels: Meline, Cans & Co, 1857

Chesney, Charles Cornwallis, *Waterloo Lectures*, London: Longmans, 1868

Chevalier, Jean-Michel, *Souvenirs des guerres napoleoniennes*, Paris, 1970

Clausewitz, Carl von, *Der Feldzug von 1815 in Frankreich*, Berlin, 1835

Clausewitz, Carl von and Arthur Wellesley, 1st Duke of Wellington, *On Waterloo: Clausewitz, Wellington, and the Campaign of 1815*, ed. and trans. Christopher Bassford, Daniel Moran and Gregory W. Pedlow, Clausewitz.com, 2010

Clay, Matthew, 'Adventures at Hougoumont', *Household Brigade Magazine* (1958), pp. 219–24

Clay, Matthew, 'A narrative of adventures at the battle of Quatre Bras, 1815 by private M. Clay, light company 2nd bataillon 3rd guards', *Household Brigade Magazine* (1958), pp. 139–42

Cluny, Claude Michel, *Waterloo: une bataille pour l'Europe*, Paris: La Différence, 2012

Coignet, Jean-Roche, *The Notebooks of Captain Coignet: Soldier of the Empire*, London: P. Davies, 1928

Colson, Bruno, *Le Général Rogniat Ingénieur et critique de Napoléon*, Paris: Economica, 2006

Combier, Amédée, *Mémoires du Général Radet, d'après ses papiers personnels et les archives de l'état*, Saint-Cloud: Blin frères, 1892

Conrady, Emil von, *Geschichte des königlich Preussischen sechsten Infanterie-Regiments*, Glogau: Flemming, 1857

Costello, Edward, *The Peninsular and Waterloo Campaigns*, ed. A. Brett-James, London: Longmans, 1967

Cotton, Edward, *A Voice from Waterloo*, Mont Saint-Jean: the author, 1854

Couvreur, Pierre, 'Des Belges à Waterloo?', in *Waterloo: lieu de Mémoire Européenne*, ed. M. Watelet and P. Couvreur, Louvain, [2000]

Creevey, Thomas, *The Creevey Papers: a Selection from the Correspondence & Diaries of the late Thomas Creevey M.P*, ed. Sir Herbert Maxwell, 2 vols, London: John Murray, 1904

Crumplin, Michael, *Guthrie's War: a Surgeon of the Peninsula and Waterloo*, Barnsley: Pen & Sword, 2010

Crumplin, Michael and Pete Starling, *A Surgical Artist at War: the Paintings and*

Sketches of Sir Charles Bell 1809–1815, Edinburgh: Royal College of Surgeons, 2005

Dalton, Charles, *The Waterloo Roll Call, with Biographical Notes and Anecdotes*, Second revised and enlarged edition, London: Eyre and Spottiswood, 1904

Damitz, Karl von, *Geschichte des Feldzuges von 1815 in den Niederlanden und Frankreich*, Berlin: Ernst Siegfried Mittler, 1837–8

Delancey, Magdalene, *A Week at Waterloo in 1815*, ed. B. Ward, London: John Murray, 1906

Delbrück, Hans, *Das Leben des Feldmarschalls Grafen Neithardt von Gneisenau*, IV 1814–15, Berlin: G. Reimer, 1880

Demiau, Lt, *Historique du 5e Régiment d'Infanterie de Ligne*, Caen: Brulfert, 1890

A Description of the Costly and Curious Military Carriage of the late Emperor of France taken on the evening of the Battle of Waterloo, London: William Bullock, 1816

Dezaunay, Capt, *Histoire du premier régiment de cuirassiers*, Angers: Lachèse & Dolbeau, 1889

Dörk, E.M., *Das königlich Preussischer 15tes Infanterie Regiment Prinz Friedrich der Niederlande in den Kriegsjahren 1813, 1814 und 1815*, Eisleben: Reichardt, 1844

Dörnberg-Hausen, Hugo, *Wilhelm von Dörnberg: ein Kämpfer für Deutschlands Freiheit*, Marburg, 1936

Drouet, Jean-Baptiste, comte d'Erlon, *Vie Militaire*, Paris, 1844

Duhesme, Guillaume Philibert comte, *Essai sur l'infanterie légère ou traité des petites opérations de la guerre*, Paris: L.G. Michaud, 1814

[Dumas, Alexandre], Armée francaise. *Histoire du 2e régiment d'infanterie légère*, Paris, 1843

Dupuy, Victor, *Souvenirs militaires, 1794–1816*, Paris, 1892

Edmonds, James E., 'Wellington's staff at Waterloo', *Journal of the Society for Army Historical Research*, 12, (1933), pp. 239–47

Elchingen, Michel Louis Felix Ney duc de, *Documents Inédits sur la Campagne de 1815*, Paris: Anselin, 1840

Ellesmere, Francis 1st Earl of, *Personal Reminiscences of the Duke of Wellington*, London: John Murray, 1903

Elting, John R., *Swords around a Throne: Napoleon's Grande Armée*, New York: The Free Press, 1988

Erckmann, Emile and Alexandre Chatrian, *Waterloo: a Story of the Hundred Days*, London: Smith Elder & Co., 1865

Fairon, Emile and Henri Heuse, *Lettres de Grognards*, Liege: Bernard, 1936

Fforde, C.W. de L, (ed.), 'The Peninsula and Waterloo letters of captain Thomas Charles Fenton', in *Journal of the Society for Army Historical Research*, 53 (1975), pp. 227–31

Field, Andrew W., *Waterloo: the French Perspective*, Barnsley: Pen & Sword, 2012

Fletcher, Ian, *Wellington's Regiments*, Stroud: Spellmount, 1994

Fletcher, Ian, *Galloping at Everything: the British Cavalry in the Peninsular War and at Waterloo, 1808–15*, Staplehurst: Spellmount, 1999

Fletcher, Ian, *A Desperate Business: Wellington, The British Army and the Waterloo Campaign*, Staplehurst: Spellmount, 2001

Fleury de Chaboulon, *Mémoires pour servir à l'histoire de la vie privée, du retour et du regne de Napoléon en 1815*, 2 vols, London: John Murray, 1820

Forrest, Alan, 'Des droits de l'homme à Waterloo', in *Waterloo: lieu de Mémoire Européenne*, ed. M. Watelet and P. Couvreur, Louvain, [2000]

Forrest, Alan, *Napoleon's Men*, London: Hambledon and London, 2002

[Fouché, Joseph and Alphonse de Beauchamp], *The Memoirs of Joseph Fouché, Duke of Otranto, Minister of the General Police of France*, London: Charles Knight, 1825

Foulkes, Nick, *Dancing into Battle: a Social History of the Battle of Waterloo*, London: Weidenfeld & Nicolson, 2006

François, Charles, *Journal du Capitaine François*, ed. Jacques Jourquain, Paris: Tallandier, 2003

Franklin, John, ed., *Waterloo: Netherlands Correspondence*, Ulverston: 1815 Limited, 2010

Fraser, D.W., 'The first guards – 2nd and 3rd battalions 16th/18th June 1815', *The Household Brigade Magazine* (1965), pp. 18–23

Fraser, Sir William, *Words on Wellington*, London: Nimmo, 1889

Frazer, Augustus Simon, *Letters of Colonel Sir Augustus Simon Frazer, K.C.B., commanding the Royal Horse Artillery in the Army under the Duke of Wellington. Written during the Peninsular and Waterloo Campaigns*, ed. Edward Sabine, London: Longman, 1859

Fremantle, John, *Wellington's Voice: the Candid Letters of Lieutenant John Fremantle, Coldstream Guards, 1818–1837*, ed. Gareth Glover, London: Frontline, 2012

Friant, Jean-Franois, *Vie militaire du Lieutenent-Général Comte Friant*, Paris: Dentu, 1857

Gamot, Charles-Guillaume, *Réfutation en ce qui concerne le Maréchal Ney de l'ouvrage ayant pour titre Campagne de 1815 ... par le général Gourgaud ...*, Paris: Antoine Bailleul, 1818

Gérard, Maurice, *Quelques documens sur la bataille de Waterloo*, Paris: Verdière, Denain and Mesnier, 1829

Gibney, Thomas, *Eighty Years Ago, or the Recollections of an Old Army Doctor*, London: Bellairs, 1896

Girod de l'Ain, Maurice, *Vie militaire du général Foy*, Paris: Plon, 1900

Glover, Gareth, ed., *Letters from the Battle of Waterloo: the unpublished correspondence by Allied officers from the Siborne papers*, London: Greenhill, 2005

Glover, Gareth, ed., *From Corunna to Waterloo: the letters and journals of two Napoleonic Hussars, 1801–1816*, London: Greenhill, 2007

Glover, Gareth, ed., *The Waterloo Archive*, 5 vols, Barnsley: Frontline, 2010–13

Glover, Gareth, ed., *Diary of a Veteran: The Diary of Sergeant Peter Facey, 28th (North Gloucester) Regiment of Foot 1803–1819*, Godmanchester: Ken Trotman, 2007

Gore, Arthur, *An Historical Account of the Battle of Waterloo*, London: Samuel Leigh, 1817

Lagneau, Louis-Vivant, *Journal d'un Chirugien de la Grande Armée*, 1803–1815, Paris, 2000

Largeaud, Jean-Marc, *Napoléon et Waterloo: la défaite glorieuse de 1815 à nos jours*, Paris: Boutique de l'histoire, 2006

Larreguy de Civrieux, Sylvain, *Souvenirs d'un cadet 1812–1823*, Paris : Hachette, 1912

Larrey, Dominique Jean, *Memoir of Baron Larrey, Surgeon-in-Chief to the Grande Armée*, London: Henry Renshaw, 1861

Las Cases, Emmanuel comte de, *Mémorial de Sainte-Hélène*, VII, Paris: the author, 1823

Latimer, Elizabeth Wormeley, *Talks of Napoleon at Saint Helena with General Baron Gourgaud*, Chicago: A.C. McClurg & Co, 1903

Laudy, Lucien, 'Le Bourgogne du Maréchal Ney', *Revue des Études Napoléoniennes*, XXI (June 1932), pp. 321–39

Laudy, Lucien, 'Le Maison Dumont à Gosselies', *Revue des Études Napoléoniennes*, XXI (June 1932), pp. 340–8

Laudy, Lucien, 'La Mort de Frederic Guillaume, Duc de Brunswick-Lüneberg-Oels et Bernstadt au Quatre-Bras, 16 Juin 1815', *Revue des Études Napoléoniennes*, XXI (June 1932), pp. 349–59

Laudy, Lucien, 'Waterloo: à travers la « Morne Plaine »', *Revue des Études Napoléoniennes*, XXI (June 1932), pp. 366–76

Lawrence, William, *The Autobiography of Sergeant William Lawrence*, ed. G.N. Bankes, London: Sampson Law, Marston, Serle & Rivington, 1886

Leach, Jonathan, *Rough Sketches of the Life of an Old Soldier*, London: Longman, 1831

Lean, Tangy, *The Napoleonists: a Study in Political Disaffection 1760–1960*, London: Oxford University Press, 1970

Leeke, William, *The History of Lord Seaton's Regiment at the Battle of Waterloo*, London: Hatchard, 1866

Le Gallo, Émile, 'Le « Waterloo » de Henry Houssaye', *Revue des Études Napoléoniennes*, VII (1915), pp. 341–52 and (1916), pp. 58–71

Lemonnier-Delafosse, Jean-Baptiste, *Campagnes de 1810 à 1815. Souvenirs militaires*, Le Havre: Auray le Haure, 1850

Lettow-Vorbeck, Oscar von, *Napoleons Untergang 1815*, Berlin: Mittler und Sohn, 1904

Levavasseur, Octave, *Souvenirs militaires d'Octave Levavasseur, officier d'artillerie, aide de camp du marechal Ney, 1802–1815*, Paris, 1914

Lieber, Francis, *Letters to a Gentleman in Germany, written after a Trip from Philadelphia to Niagara*, Philadelphia: Carey, Lea & Blanchard, 1834

Lindau, Friedrich, *A Waterloo Hero: the Reminiscences of Friedrich Lindau*, ed. James Bogle and Andrew Uffindell, London: Frontline, 2009

Lippe-Weissenfeld, Ernst Graf zur, *Geschichte des Königliche Preussische 6. Husaren-Regiments (ehemaligen 2. Schlesischen)*, Berlin: Decker, 1860

Logie, Jacques, *Waterloo: the Campaign of 1815*, Staplehurst: Spellmount, 2006

Longford, Elizabeth, *Wellington: The Years of the Sword*, London: Weidenfeld and Nicolson, 1969

Lot, Henri, *Les Deux Généraux Ordener*, Paris: R. Roger et F. Chernoviz, 1910

Macbride, Mackenzie, ed. *With Napoleon at Waterloo and other unpublished Documents of the Waterloo and Peninsular Campaigns*, London: Francis Griffiths, 1911

Mach, Anton von, *Geschichte des königlich Preussischen zweiten Infanterie-Regiments genannt Königs-Regiments*, Berlin: Mittler, 1843

MacGrigor, Sir James, *Autobiography and Services of Sir James MacGrigor*, London: Longman, 1861

Macready, Edward Nevile, 'On a part of Captain Siborne's History of the Waterloo Campaign', *United Service Magazine*, 47 (1845), pp. 388–404 and 69 (1852), pp. 51–7

Macready, Edward Nevile, 'Extracts from the Journals of the late Major Edward Macready', *United Service Magazine*, 69 (1852 part 2) pp. 338–46 and 518–30

Madelin, Louis, *Fouché 1759–1820*, Paris: Plon, 1903

Mackinnon, Daniel, *Origin and Services of the Coldstream Guards*, London: R. Bentley, 1833

Mainwaring, Frederick, 'Four Years of a Soldier's Life', *United Service Magazine*, 46 (1844), pp. 403–16

Malmesbury, John Howard Harris 3rd Earl of, *A Series of Letters of the First Earl of Malmesbury his Family and Friends*, II, London: Richard Bentley, 1870

Marbot, Jean-Baptiste, *Mémoires du Général Baron de Marbot*, Paris: Librairie Plon, 1891

Marchand, Louis-Joseph-Narcisse, *Mémoires de Marchand: premier valet de chambre et exécuteur testamentaire de l'empéreur Napoleon*, ed. Jean Bourguignon and Henry Lachouque, Paris: Tallandier, 2003

Martin, Jacques, *Souvenirs de guerre du lieutenant Martin: 1812–1815*, Paris: Tallandier, 2007

[Martin, Jacques], 'Lettre d'un officier genevois du 45e', *Carnet de la sabretache*, 3, (1895), pp. 493–517

Martinien, Aristide, *Tableaux par corps et par batailles des officiers tués et blessés pendant les guerres de l'empire 1805–1815*, Paris: Charles-Lavauzelle, 1899

Martinien, Aristide, *Tableaux par corps et par batailles des officiers tués et blessés pendant les guerres de l'empire 1805–1815: Supplément*, Paris: L. Fournier, 1909

Maxwell, Herbert, *The Life of Wellington, the Restoration of the Martial Power of Great Britain*, 2 vols, London: Sampson Lowe, 1899

Mauduit, Hippolyte de, *Les derniers jours de la grande armée*, 2 vols, Paris: the author, 1847–8

Mercer, Cavalié, *Journal of the Waterloo Campaign* [1870], reprinted London: P. Davies, 1969

Miller, David, *The Duchess of Richmond's Ball*, Staplehurst: Spellmount, 2005

Mittelacher, Martin, 'Nassauers at Hougoumont', *Journal of the Society for Army Historical Research*, 81 (2003), pp. 228–42

Moore Smith, George Charles, 'General Petit's account of the Waterloo Campaign', *English Historical Review*, LXX (1903), pp. 321–6

Moore Smith, George Charles, *The Life of John Colborne, Field Marshal Lord Seaton*, London: John Murray, 1903

Morris, Thomas, *Military Memoirs: Thomas Morris, The Napoleonic Wars*, ed. John Selby, London: Longmans, 1967

[Mudie, Charles], 'Operations of the Fifth or Picton's Division in the Campaign of Waterloo', *United Service Magazine*, XIII (June 1841), pp. 170–203

Müffling, Friedrich Carl Ferdinand, *The Memoirs of Baron von Müffling*, ed. Peter Hofschröer, London: Greenhill Books, 1997

Müffling, Friedrich Carl Ferdinand, *History of the Campaign*, ed. Sir John Sinclair, London: T. Egerton, 1816 (facsimile: Wakefield: S.R. Publishers, 1970)

Muir, Rory, *Britain and the Defeat of Napoleon, 1807–1815*, New Haven and London: Yale University Press, 1996

Muir, Rory, *Tactics and Experience of Battle in the Age of Napoleon*, New Haven and London: Yale University Press, 1998

Noguès, Antoine, *Mémoires du Général Noguès*, Paris, 1922

Nostitz, Ferdinand Graf von, 'Das Tagebuch des Generals der Kavallerie Grafen von Nostitz', II Theil, *Kriegsgeschichtliche Einzelschriften*, Heft 6, Berlin, 1885

Ollech, R. von, *Geschichte des Feldzuges von 1815, nach archivalischen Quellen*, Berlin: Ernst Siegfried Mittler, 1876

Ompteda, Louis von, ed., *Memoirs of Baron Ompteda*, London: H. Grevel & Co., 1894

O'Neil, Charles, *The Military Adventures of Charles O'Neil*, Staplehurst: Spellmount, 1997

Ortiz, José, 'The Revolutionary Flying Ambulance of Napoleon's Surgeon', *U.S. Army Medical Department Journal* (October–December 1998), pp. 17–25

Owen, Edward, ed. *The Waterloo Papers 1815 and Beyond*, Tavistock: AQ and DJ Publications, 1997

Pajol, Charles Pierre Victor comte, *Pajol, géneral en chef*, III (1812–44), Paris: Firmin-Didot, 1874

Pawly, Ronald, *Napoleon's Imperial Headquarters (2): On Campaign*, Oxford: Osprey, 2004

Pedlow, Gregory W., 'Back to the Sources: General Zieten's Message to the Duke of Wellington on 15 June 1813', *First Empire*, 82 (2005), pp. 30–6

Pétiet, Auguste, *Souvenirs Militaires*, Paris: Dumaine, 1844

Petit, Jean-Martin, 'General Petit's account of the Waterloo Campaign', *English Historical Review*, XVIII (1903), pp. 321–6

Petty, Henry William Earl of Kerry (ed.), *The First Napoleon: some unpublished documents from the Bowood papers*, Boston and New York: Houghton Mifflin, 1925

Pflugk-Harttung, Julius von, *Vorgeschichte von der Schlacht bei Belle-Alliance*, Berlin: R. Schröder, 1903

Pflugk-Harttung, Julius von, 'Die Verhandlungen Wellington's und Blücher's an der Windmühle bei Brye', *Historisches Jahrbuch*, 23 (1902), pp. 80–97

Pflugk-Harttung, Julius von, 'Die Preussische Berichterstattung an Wellington vor der Schlacht bei Ligny', *Historisches Jahrbuch*, 24 (1903), pp. 41–61

Pflugk-Harttung, Julius von, *Belle Alliance (Verbundetes Heer). Berichte und Angaben uber die Beteiligung deutscher Truppen der Armee Wellington's an dem Gefechte bei Quatre Bras und der Schlacht bei Belle Alliance*, Berlin: Eisenschmidt, 1915

Piérart, Z. J., *Le Drame de Waterloo*, Paris: Bureau de la *Revue Spiritualiste*, 1868

Pigeard, Alain, *L'Armée de Napoléon 1800–1815, organisation et vie quotidienne*, Paris: Tallendier, 2000

Pigeard, Alain, *La Garde Impériale 1804–1815*, Paris: Tallendier, 2005

Pion des Loches, Antoine-Auguste-Flavien, *Mes Campagnes (1792–1815)*, Paris: Firmin-Didot, 1889

Pitt-Lennox, William, *Three Years with the Duke, or Wellington in Private Life*, Second edition, London: Saunders & Otley, 1853.

Playford, Thomas, *A Lifeguardsman in Spain, France and at Waterloo: the memoirs of Sergeant-Major Thomas Playford 2nd Lifeguards*, ed. G. Glover, Godmanchester: Ken Trotman, 2006

Plotho, Carl von, *Der Krieg der verbündeten Europas gegen Frankreich im Jahre 1815*, Berlin: Carl Friedrich Amelang, 1818

Pontécoulant, Philippe Gustave le Doulcet de, *Napoléon à Waterloo*, Paris: Dumaine, 1866

Porter, Whitworth, *History of the Corps of Royal Engineers*, vol. 1, London: Longmans, Green & Co, 1889

Pringle, John W., 'Remarks on the Campaign of 1815' in Sir Walter Scott, *The Life of Napoleon Bonaparte, Emperor of the French*, IX, Appendix VIII, xcv–cxli, London and Edinburgh: Longman and Cadell, 1827

Quinet, Edgar, *Histoire de la Campagne de 1815*, Paris: Michel Lévy Frères, 1862

Quintin, D. and B., *Dictionnaire des Colonels de Napoleon*, Paris: SPM, 1996

Rahden, Wilhelm von, *Wanderungen eines alten Soldaten*, I, Berlin: Alexander Duncker, 1846

Reiche, Ludwig von, *Memoiren des königlich Preussischen Generals der Infanterie Ludwig von Reiche*, ed. Louis von Weltzien, part 2, Leipzig: Brockhaus, 1857

Reynell, Thomas, 'Sir Thomas Reynell on the movements of the 71st during the crisis at Waterloo', *United Service Journal* (1833), Part II, pp. 542–3

Rigau, Dieudonné, *Souvenirs des guerres de l'Empire*, Paris: Librairie des Deux Empires, 2000

Rogniat, Joseph, *Considérations sur l'Art de la Guerre*, Second edition, Paris: Magimel, Anselin & Pochard, 1817

Ross-Lewin, Henry, *With the thirty-second in the Peninsula and other campaigns*, Dublin: Hodges, Figgis & Co., 1904

Roberts, Andrew, *Waterloo: Napoleon's last gamble*, London: HarperCollins, 2005

Robertson, David, *Journal of Sergeant D. Robertson, late 92nd Foot*, Perth, 1842; facsimile, London: Maggs, 1982

Robinaux, Pierre, *Journal de route (1803–1832)*, ed. Gustave Schlumberger, Paris: Plon, 1908

Robinson, Mike, *The Battle of Quatre Bras 1815*, Stroud: History Press, 2009

Roy, D.R.H., 'The memoirs of private J. Gunn 42nd Highlanders', *Journal of the Society for Army Historical Research*, 49 (1971), pp. 90–120

Rumigny, M.T.G., *Souvenirs du général comte de Rumigny*, Paris: Emile-Paul Frères, 1921

Saint-Denis, Louis Etienne, *Napoleon from the Tuileries to St. Helena: Personal Recollections of the Emperor's Second Mameluke and Valet, Louis Etienne St. Denis (Known as Ali)*, New York and London, Harper & Brothers, 1922

Salisch, Gustav von, *Geschichte des königlich Preussischen siebenten Infanterie-Regiments*, Glogau: Flemming, 1854

Schom, Alan, *One Hundred Days: Napoleon's Road to Waterloo*, London: Michael Joseph, 1993

Schmidt, Oliver, *Prussian Regular Infantryman 1808–15*, Oxford: Osprey, 2003

Scott, John, *Paris Revisited, in 1815, by way of Brussels, including a walk over the field of battle of Waterloo*, London: Longman, 1816

'The 2nd battalion of the Rifle Corps at Waterloo', *United Service Journal* (1833) Part III, pp. 255–6

Shaw Kennedy, James, *Notes on the Battle of Waterloo*, London: John Murray, 1865

Siborne, Herbert Taylor (ed.), *Waterloo Letters*, London: Cassell, 1891

Siborne, William, *History of the Waterloo Campaign*, London, Greenhill Books, 1990; facsimile of the third revised edition of *History of the War in France and Belgium in* 1815, London: Boone, 1848 (First edition 1844)

Smith, Harry, *The Autobiography of Sir Harry Smith 1781–1819*, London, 1902

[Smith, Newman], *Flying Sketches of the Battle of Waterloo by a young traveller*, London: privately printed, 1852

Swiney, George Clayton, *Historical records of the 32nd (Cornwall) light infantry*, London: Simkin, 1893

Simmons, George, *A British rifle man. The journals and correspondence of Major George Simmons, Rifle Brigade, during the Peninsular War and the campaign of Waterloo*, London: Black, 1899

Souvenirs et correspondence sur la bataille de Waterloo, Paris: Teissèdre, 2000

Stawitzky, E. H. Ludwig, *Geschichte des königlich Preussischen 25sten Infanterie-Regiments*, Koblenz: Bädeker, 1857

Summerville, Christopher, *Who was Who at Waterloo: a Biography of the Battle*, London: Routledge, 2007

Swinton, J. R., *A Sketch of the Life of Georgiana, Lady de Ros*, London: John Murray, 1893

Thorpe, Francis Newton, 'Two Diaries of Waterloo', *The English Historical Review*, 3, No. 11 (July 1888), pp. 539–52

Tomkinson, William, *The Diary of a Cavalry Officer in the Peninsular and Waterloo Campaigns*, ed. James Tomkinson, Second edition, London: Swan Sonnenschein & Co., 1895

Trefcon, Toussaint Jean, *Carnet de campagne de colonel Trefcon*, Paris: Dubois, 1914

Tulard, Jean, *Napoleon: the Myth of the Saviour*, London: Methuen, 1985

Uffindell, Andrew, *The Eagle's Last Triumph: Napoleon's Victory at Ligny June 1815*, London: Greenhill, 1994

Uffindell, Andrew, *Napoleon's Immortals: the Imperial Guard and its Battles, 1804–1815*, Stroud: Spellmount, 2007

Urban, Mark, *Rifles: six years with Wellington's legendary sharpshooters*, London: Faber and Faber, 2003

Verner, William, 'Reminiscences of William Verner (1782–1871) 7th hussars', *Journal of the Society for Army Historical Research*, 43 (1965), pp. 39–51

[Waldie, Charlotte], *The battle of Waterloo also of Ligny and Quatre Bras etc. by a near observer*, ed. Hannibal Lloyd, London: Booth, Second edition, 1815; Tenth enlarged edition, 2 vols, 1817

[Waldie, Charlotte], *Narrative of a residence in Belgium during the campaign of 1815; and of a visit to the field of Waterloo*, London, 1817

Waresquiel, Emmanuel de, *Cent Jours: la tentation de l'impossible mars-juillet 1815*, Paris: Fayard, 2008

Waterloo: Récits de combattants, Paris: Teissèdre, 1999

WD: Gurwood, John (ed.), *Despatches of Field Marshal the Duke of Wellington*, 13 vols, London: John Murray, 1834–9

Wedell, Rudolph von, *Geschichte des königlichen Preussischen 18.Infanterie-Regiments von 1813 bis 1847*, Posen: Scherk, 1848

Weller, Jac, *Wellington at Waterloo*, London: Longmans, 1967

Wenzlik, Detlef, *Waterloo*, 3 vols, Hamburg: Roger Zörb, 2008

Wheatley, Edmund, *The Wheatley Diary*, ed. C. Hibbert, London: Longmans, 1964

Wheeler, Dennis and Gaston Demarée, 'The weather of the Waterloo campaign 16 to 18 June 1815: did it change the course of history?', *Weather*, 60 no. 6 (June 2005), pp. 159–64

Wheeler, William, *The Letters of Private Wheeler*, ed. Liddell Hart, London: Michael Joseph, 1951

[Williams-Wynne, Frances], *Diaries of a Lady of Quality from 1797 to 1844*, ed. A. Hayward, Second edition, London: Longman, 1864

[Wood, Charles], *Some Particulars of the Battle of Waterloo in a Letter from a Sergeant in the Guards*, London, 1816

Woodberry, George, *Journal du lieutenant Woodberry; campagnes de Portugal et d'Espagne, de France, de Belgique et de France; 1813–1815*, Paris: Plon, 1906

WSD: *Supplementary Despatches, Correspondence and Memoranda of Field Marshal Arthur Duke of Wellington, K. G.*, 15 vols, London: John Murray, 1858–72.

Wylly, Harold Carmichael (ed.), *The Military Memoirs of Lieutenant General Sir Joseph Thackwell*, London: Murray, 1908

Zychlinski, Franz von, *Geschichte des königlichen Preussischen 24sten Infanterie-Regiments*, Berlin: Mittler, 1854

Websites and online resources

16 juin 1815 Bataille de Ligny http://napoleon-monuments.eu/Napoleon1er/1815Ligny-Fleurus.htm

1815 Limited On-line Archive http://www.battleofwaterloo.net/

The British Museum collection online http://www.britishmuseum.org/
research/collection_online/search.aspx

The Campaign of 1815: a study by Pierre de Wit http://www.waterloo-
campaign.nl/

Carte de Cabinet de Ferraris http://www.ngi.be/FR/FR1-4-2-3.shtm

Diary of Amabel, Lady Lucas http://library.hud.ac.uk/calmview/Record
.aspx?src=CalmView.Catalog&id=Yorke%2f30

Fondation Napoléon http://www.napoleon.org/

Hannoversche Militär Geschichte http://www.kgl.de/

Image of France http://artfl-project.uchicago.edu/content/image-france

Napoléon à Gilly en 1815 http://www.gilly.be/VVV/Napoleon_Gilly_1815.html

The Napoleon Series http://www.napoleon-series.org/

Panorama de l'entité de Fleurus http://www.fleurus-tourisme.be/
photographies/panorama360.htm

Les uniformes pendant la campagne des cent jours http://centjours.mont-
saint-jean.com/

INDEX